Navdeep Mutti

THE SIMON & SCHUSTER
GUIDE TO WRITING

Douglas Olson, *Detail, Door*

THE SIMON & SCHUSTER
GUIDE TO WRITING

Jeanette G. Harris

University of Southern Mississippi

Donald H. Cunningham

Auburn University

PRENTICE HALL, Englewood Cliffs, New Jersey 07632

Library of Congress Cataloging-in-Publication Data

Harris, Jeanette. (date)
  The Simon & Schuster guide to writing / Jeanette Harris, Donald H.
Cunningham.
      p.   cm.
  Includes index.
  ISBN 0–13–814617–9
  1. English language—Rhetoric.   2. English language—Grammar.
3. College readers.   I. Cunningham, Donald H.   II. Title.
III. Title: Simon and Schuster guide to writing.
PE1408.H3456   1994b
808'.042—dc20
                                                    93–35957
                                                    CIP

Acquisitions editor: Alison Reeves
Editorial production/supervision: F. Hubert
Development editor: Joyce Perkins
Production coordinator: Tricia Kenny
Design director: Paula K. Martin
Interior design: Maureen Eide
Cover design: Carbone Smolan Associates
Cover art: Eliot Porter, "Mist on Coast, Big Sur, California,
        September 25, 1975". The Metropolitan Museum
        of Art, Gift of Eliot Porter, 1985. (1985.1033.2)
        Copyright Amon Carter Museum, Eliot Porter Collection.
Credits begin on page 693, which constitutes
a continuation of the copyright page.

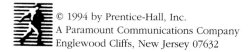

© 1994 by Prentice-Hall, Inc.
A Paramount Communications Company
Englewood Cliffs, New Jersey 07632

Printed in the United States of America
10 9 8 7 6 5 4 3 2 1

ISBN   0-13-814617-9

Prentice-Hall International (UK) Limited, *London*
Prentice-Hall of Australia Pty. Limited, *Sydney*
Prentice-Hall Canada Inc., *Toronto*
Prentice-Hall Hispanoamericana, S.A., *Mexico*
Prentice-Hall of India Private Limited, *New Delhi*
Prentice-Hall of Japan, Inc., *Tokyo*
Simon & Schuster Pte. Ltd., *Singapore*
Editora Prentice-Hall do Brasil, Ltda., *Rio de Janeiro*

In memory of Cowboy and B.B.

ABOUT THE AUTHORS

JEANETTE GREGORY HARRIS received her B.A., M.A., and Ed.D. from East Texas State University. She currently teaches composition and directs the composition program at the University of Southern Mississippi.

Her past administrative duties include Director of Composition and Director of the Writing Center at Texas Tech University and Supervisor of the Writing Center and Coordinator of Reading Instruction at East Texas State University.

Author of *Expressive Discourse* (Southern Methodist University, 1990) and co-author of *Contexts: Writing and Reading,* Third Edition (Houghton Mifflin, 1993) and *Interactions,* Second Edition (Houghton Mifflin, 1994), Harris also has recently co-edited a collection of case studies entitled *Writing Centers in Context* (National Council of Teachers of English, 1994).

DONALD H. CUNNINGHAM received his B.A., M.A., and Ph.D. in English at the University of Missouri. Cunningham currently teaches composition at Auburn University, where he is also Director of Technical and Professional Writing. Cunningham's previous responsibilities have included Director of Technical Communication at Texas Tech University, Acting Chair of the Department of Languages and Literature and Coordinator of Writing Courses, Morehead State University, and Coordinator of Written and Oral Communications at Southern Illinois University–Carbondale.

Author of many books and articles, Cunningham edited *The Teaching of Technical Writing* (National Council of Teachers of English, 1975) and co-authored *How to Write for the World of Work,* Fifth Edition (Harcourt, Brace, 1994) and *Fundamentals of Good Writing* (Macmillan, 1988).

CONTENTS

PREFACE

For the Instructor

We want this book to provide students with a variety of reading and writing experiences—experiences that will prepare them for the reading and writing they will do throughout their lives, not just as college students but as professionals, citizens, members of families and communities, and literate human beings who use language to enrich and enhance both their personal and public lives.

Several basic convictions guided us as we wrote this book:

❖ First, we believe it is important to integrate reading and writing instruction as fully as possible. Thus, each chapter includes reading selections, assignments, and instruction that reinforce the writing instruction and assignments. We also encourage and guide students in reading their own work in progress.

❖ Second, we believe students learn to read and write primarily by engaging in reading and writing. Thus, we provide students with a wide range of reading and writing assignments that are personal as well as public and pragmatic as well as aesthetic.

❖ Third, we believe that learning is incremental and requires reinforcement. Thus, instruction related to important concepts such as purpose and audience, modes of development, and thesis/support occur in each chapter.

❖ Finally, we believe that a college-level writing book should reflect the diverse nature of the typical college classroom. Thus, we balance the number of female and male authors and include authors with diverse ethnic backgrounds. In addition, the assignments are designed to accommodate students of different ages and backgrounds.

Scope and Organization of This Book

The organization of *The Simon & Schuster Guide to Writing* is simple, yet innovative. It is divided into four parts.

Part One, Concepts (Chapter 1), provides students with an overview of the important concepts of purpose and audience. This part also describes the reading/writing process and includes a student's text in various drafts to illustrate the overall progression from rough draft to final draft.

Part Two, Purposes (Chapters 2 through 8), is the main part of the book, the part students will use most often in class. Each chapter in this section focuses on a specific purpose and theme and guides students through a writing assignment based on that purpose and theme. Here is a summary:

Chapter	Purpose	Theme
2	Writing to Explore	On Exploring Writing
3	Writing to Reconstruct Experience	Holidays
4	Writing to Inform	On Change
5	Writing to Instruct and Advise	Advice for College
6	Writing to Solve Problems and Present Solutions	Human Relations
7	Writing to Persuade	Perception versus Reality
8	Arguing from Sources	The Environment

Each chapter in Part Two consists of the same five sections.

1. Introduction to the purpose

2. Instruction in reading for this purpose.

3. Reading selections that focus on the chapter's purpose and theme. Each of these reading selections is preceded by a brief introduction and followed by a series of questions that encourage students to respond thoughtfully to the selection and by three writing activities—individual, collaborative, and computer—that are less formal and extensive than the major writing assignment of the chapter.

4. Discussion of the rhetorical decisions and strategies involved in writing for the particular purpose.

5. A detailed writing assignment that guides students through the process of writing a text.

Part Three, Strategies, is a reference section designed primarily for students to use individually. It consists of entries that explain the terms and concepts we think a student in a writing course might need to know. The entries are arranged alphabetically so that both you and your students can locate a specific entry easily. In addition, these entries are clearly cross-referenced; that is, when a particular concept or strategy (such as coherence or thesis statement) is discussed or even mentioned in the text, students are referred to the corresponding entry in the Strategies section. Thus, if students encounter a term they do not understand or want to know more about, they can simply turn to the entry in Strategies and read about it.

This reference section gives both you and your students great flexibility. The entries can be used in a number of different ways. You may assign particular entries to the class as a whole or to individual students. You may use some of the entries as the basis for classroom instruction and discussion or may simply allow students to use this section on their own.

Part Four, the *Handbook,* consists of guidelines for diction, usage, punctuation, and mechanics. This part of the book, like Part Three, is intended primarily as a resource for students.

The Supplements

The Simon & Schuster Guide to Writing is supported by the following supplements:

❖ *The Annotated Instructor's Edition,* which is the student text enhanced with four types of teaching annotations in the margin. Most numerous are the Teaching Suggestions, which are further categorized as individual, collaborative, or computer. Second, the Connections annotations make specific linkages between the material where it occurs and related material elsewhere in the book. Third, the Resource annotations refer to one or more of the scholarly articles in the third part of *The Instructors' Manual.* Fourth, the annotations designated by the ABC News' logo refer to the ABC News Video Library, which is available as an additional supplement.

❖ *The Instructors' Manual,* which consists of three parts. The first part is devoted to information and suggestions that we hope will make *The Simon & Schuster Guide to Writing* a more effective, teachable textbook. The second part provides an overview of each chapter and suggested responses to the questions that follow each of the readings. The third part consists of articles by well-known composition theorists and teachers.

❖ *ABC News/PH Video Library for Composition,* which includes thematically arranged video segments from ABC News' award-winning news programs such as *20/20, Nightline, World News Tonight, American Agenda,* and *Prime Time Live.* Serving as springboards for critical thinking and writing, the segments range from 5 to more than 20 minutes, and the Library contains nine segments. The *ABC News/PH Video Guide for the Simon & Schuster Handbook for Writers* by William Costanzo provides complete teaching notes for using the videos with the chapters and rhetorical strategies in the text.

Video Library Contents

Nightline:
How the World Sees America, via Hollywood
What Are the Differences Between Men and Women?
Putting in Who and What U.S. History Has Excluded

Prime Time Live:
Virtual Reality
Joey's Best Friend

20/20:
Hidden Messages

World News Tonight/American Agenda:
Media Studies Would Help Kids Watch TV More Critically
AIDS Among Teenagers

❖ *The New York Times: A Contemporary View* provides a newspaper-sized collection of time-sensitive articles from one of the world's most distinguished newspapers, *The New York Times.* These articles demonstrate the ongoing connection between what is learned in the classroom and the type of writing that occurs in the world around us. These collections are updated twice yearly.

❖ *Supplementary Essays for Writers* is a collection of 31 additional essays by professional writers, grouped according to the major rhetorical categories. Each essay is accompanied by questions for discussion and writing, and each rhetorical section ends with several writing suggestions.

❖ *The Research Organizer* is a 64-page 8½ × 11 booklet providing guidance on the research process and ample room for students to record their research strategy, notes, citations, outlines, and drafts. This supplement allows students to organize and manage their research process by providing them with one convenient and structured tool for assembling all of their notes and drafts for one research paper.

❖ *Model Research Papers for Writers* is an 8½ × 11 collection of 11 actual student research papers. Including fields ranging from biology and political science to art history and English literature, this collection is intended to serve as models of documentation, stylistic conventions, and formal requirements for various disciplines.

❖ *Prentice Hall ESL Workbook* by Stacey Hagen and Bernice Ege-Zavala highlights grammar, usage, and writing problems of particular interest to nonnative speakers of English.

❖ *Prentice Hall/Simon & Schuster Transparencies for Writers* is a set of 100 two- and four-color transparencies containing exercises, examples, and suggestions for student writing. These transparencies focus on various aspects of the writing process, from generating ideas and shaping an outline to preparing a draft to revising and editing the final paper. They include coverage of usage, punctuation, and mechanics via overlays that show how sentence and paragraph errors can be most effectively corrected. Special attention is given to the effective use of research sources. Each section also contains a transparency of a work of fine art intended to serve as a springboard for student writing.

❖ *The Prentice Hall Critical Thinking Audio Study Cassette* is a 60-minute cassette that helps students develop their critical thinking skills. The first 50 minutes demonstrate how asking the right questions leads to better critical reading and thinking skills. The final 10 minutes consist of helpful tips on how to study, how to take effective notes, and how to become a more active learner.

❖ *Profiles of a Writer Video Offer* is a professionally produced video series that documents the lives and works of such respected authors as Nobel Laureate Toni Morrison and Norman Mailer. Average playing time for each tape is 55 minutes. This series provides a glimpse into the real lives of eight renowned authors. The videos are produced by organizations such as the BBC and by gifted contemporary filmmakers.

❖ *On-Line Handbook* is a computerized reference system that is compatible with most word processing packages. By using this reference system, students can access information from the handbook section of *The Simon & Schuster Guide to Writing* on usage, punctuation, and mechanics as they compose on the word processor. The *On-Line Handbook* also includes information on MLA and APA documentation formats and is available in both IBM and Macintosh versions.

❖ *Blue Pencil* is an interactive editing program that allows students to practice writing-related skills by making revisions in paragraph-length passages on the computer screen. The program is organized around skill categories that students encounter most often in their writing. A counter at the bottom of the screen keeps track of the corrections that remain to be made and feedback is made for each response that students enter. If students have trouble with a particular concept, they can solicit additional instruction from the program. Including a final review of all skill categories presented together, *Blue Pencil* is available for the IBM and Macintosh PCs.

❖ *Blue Pencil Authoring System* is a program that allows you to create your own exercises for the Blue Pencil program. This system includes two Blue Pencil exercise disks totaling 80 passages, 40 on each disk, representing many skill areas. The exercises on disk 2 are of a higher level of difficulty than those on disk 1. To this extensive bank of lessons you can easily add your own exercises to the skill areas provided or create entirely new skill areas. You can also customize the existing passages by adding or deleting errors to be corrected and/or modifying the feedback and hints available for your students. On-line directions and a manual are included.

❖ *Webster's New World Compact School and Office Dictionary Offer* combines *The Simon & Schuster Guide to Writing* and a comprehensive paperback dictionary available in a shrinkwrapped package. Featuring over 56,000 entries and assistance in pronunciation and spelling, this compact dictionary can serve students as a reference tool throughout their college careers.

❖ *Webster's New World Dictionary, Third College Edition Offer* combines the text with an authoritative hard-cover dictionary containing more than 11,000 American words and phrases and over 170,000 entries.

❖ *Bibliotech* is a computerized Bibliography Generator for MLA, APA, and CBE documentation styles. Available for both IBM and Macintosh.

For more information about these supplements or to see them, please contact your Prentice Hall sales representative.

Acknowledgments

This book has been a collaborative project in every sense of the word. As the two of us wrote the book, sometimes each took responsibility for drafting a major segment and then sent the draft to the other for review and revision. Less frequently, but more often than we had anticipated, we wound up sitting down together at a computer to draft or revise parts of the book.

However, the collaboration involved more than just our efforts. We are aware that a significant part of our collaboration was only possible because of the shared knowledge of the scholarly and pedagogical traditions in which we work. While we cannot make adequate acknowledgment of our debt to individual scholars, researchers, and theorists who have helped shape our thinking, readers familiar with recent composition and rhetorical theory will recognize our many obligations to those who have influenced us. We are grateful to them all.

We wish to single out for special thanks the following persons for their generous and helpful suggestions and support as we wrote this book:

❖ Those who took time out of their busy schedules during the late winter of 1992 to read parts of an early draft of this book and to participate in a focus group discussion during the Conference on College Composition and Communication in Cincinnati in March 1992. These persons became active collaborators at a crucial stage in the development of the book.

Irwin Weiser, Purdue University
Duane H. Roen, Syracuse University

David R. Russell, Iowa State University

Elizabeth Metzger, University of South Florida

Lady Falls Brown, Texas Tech University

Francis Hubbard, Marquette University

Jimmie Killingsworth, Texas A&M University

Christine Hult, Utah State University

❖ The group at Prentice Hall who helped guide and transform our manuscript into the book in your hands: Tracy A. Augustine, who provided encouragement at the very beginning; Phillip Miller, who made important suggestions while the manuscript was still in its infancy and whose great enthusiasm for the project fueled our own enthusiasm; Joyce Perkins, whose knowledge of writing has taught us much and whose unfailing help and patience make her as close to the ideal editor and collaborator as we could hope for; Alison Reeves, whose aesthetic sense and decisions about the book's design insured that it would be physically attractive as well as theoretically sound; Gina Sluss, who shared with us the marketing viewpoint; and Frank Hubert, who guided us expertly through the important final production stage of the book.

❖ Mary Rees, who worked diligently to help secure permissions to reprint copyright material for use in this book.

❖ Colleagues at the University of Southern Mississippi and Auburn University whose contributions and counsel benefitted us greatly: Evelyn Ashton-Jones of USM's Department of English; James Flanagan, Chair of USM's Department of Sociology; Orazio Ciccarelli, Chair of USM's Department of History; Gerald Johnson of AU's Department of Political Science; Larry J. Lutz of AU's Department of Agricultural Engineering.

❖ The reviewers who critiqued various drafts of the manuscript.

Beverly Ann Chin, University of Montana

Irwin Weiser, Purdue University

Duane H. Roen, Syracuse University

Tom Hawkins, Butler County Community College

David R. Russell, Iowa State University

Elizabeth Metzger, University of South Florida

Barbara Wiedemann, Auburn University–Montgomery

Richard Batteiger, Oklahoma State University

Mitchell E. Summerlin, Calhoun Community College

Patricia Harkin, University of Toledo

Carol S. O'Shea, Bowling Green State University

James Moody, South Suburban College

Lady Falls Brown, Texas Tech University

These people offered many helpful suggestions that we incorporated into this book. However, their participation does not imply that they endorse all the views expressed in this book.

Finally, we are especially delighted to state our indebtedness to past students in our writing courses. They have been a continuing source of insight and useful ideas. This book is yet another of our responses to their healthy curiosity and desire to improve as writers and readers. It is with great pleasure that we also acknowledge the students whose writing appear in this book: Tammy Adams, Frank Cedeño, Toni Gagnon, Morgan Hands, Diane Johnson, Rebecca Williams Skidmore, Warren Slay, Paige Snyder, Kerry Whittman, and Jim Whorton.

In dedicating this book to the memory of Albert F. McKee (Don's step-father) and Bernice B. Gregory (Jeanette's father), we attempt to express our love and admiration for two of the most influential persons in our lives.

Jeanette G. Harris
Donald H. Cunningham

PREFACE

For the Student

This book is pretty straightforward, but to make the best use of it, you need to know a few things about how we have designed it. *Part One, Concepts,* provides you with an overview of the reasons why purpose and audience are important concepts for readers and writers to know. This section also describes the reading/writing process.

Part Two, Purposes, is the part of the book you will use most often in class. Each chapter in this section explores a different purpose for writing and reading, and its reading selections all relate to that purpose and to a single theme. Each chapter ends with a writing assignment for you that deals with the same purpose and theme.

Part Three, Strategies, is designed primarily for your individual use. It includes explanations of terms and concepts that we think a student in a writing course might need to know. Some of the entries in this section you may never need to read or consult because you will already understand the term or concept being addressed; some you may need to refer to briefly in order to review the concept or to obtain specific information; others you may need to read carefully, perhaps more than once. This section is our attempt to make this book as useful as possible for you as an individual student. The information in it is easily accessible (entries are arranged alphabetically) and as clear and direct as we could make it. Throughout the book, boldface type is used for the terms included in the Strategies section, and in the page margin you will find the term and the page number for its entry. If you do not understand a term that is marked in this way, you can simply turn to Part Three and read about it.

The final section of the book, *Part Four, Handbook,* includes guidelines for diction, usage, punctuation, and mechanics. This part of the book, like Part Three, is intended as a resource for you, to provide you with information on these matters if you need it.

THE SIMON & SCHUSTER
GUIDE TO WRITING

▼

PART ONE

CONCEPTS

Frederick Evans, *The Sea of Steps*, 1903,
The Royal Photographic Society, Bath.

1

▼

HOW WRITERS AND READERS CONSTRUCT TEXTS

There is no royal path to good writing; and such paths as exist . . . lead through . . . the jungles of the self, the world, and of craft.

JESSAMYN WEST

We wrote this textbook because we want to share what we know about reading and writing. Of course, we have other reasons—some of them less altruistic and certainly more practical than the one we've just given. As a student, you also write for a variety of reasons—to fulfill assignments, to communicate, to remember, to learn, to prove that you know something, to share your feelings, to record your thoughts, to organize your life, and perhaps to change the minds of others. Obviously, people write (and read) for a great variety of reasons. However, some reasons for writing have become commonplace. That is, large numbers of people write for these same reasons.

This textbook focuses on some common purposes for writing: writing to explore, to reconstruct experience, to inform, to instruct and advise, to solve problems, and to persuade. We chose these from the multitude of reasons why people read and write because they represent the kind of writing that people routinely and typically do. This book can provide you with a variety of reading and writing experiences—experiences that will prepare you for the reading and writing you will do throughout your lives, not just as college students but as professionals, citizens, members of a family and community, and literate human beings who use language to enrich and enhance both your personal and public lives.

▶ PURPOSE — WHY A TEXT IS CONSTRUCTED

We focus on reasons for writing rather than on types of writing because *purpose* is the driving force behind all acts of reading and writing. People always read and write for specific purposes, and these purposes significantly shape the forms their texts take. To illustrate,

here are two accounts of an automobile accident: one a poem by Karl
Shapiro, the other a police officer's report.

Auto Wreck
Karl Shapiro

Its quick soft silver bell beating, beating,
And down the dark one ruby flare
Pulsing out red light like an artery,
The ambulance at top speed floating down
Past beacons and illuminated clocks
Wings in a heavy curve, dips down,
And brakes speed, entering the crowd.
The doors leap open, emptying light;
Stretchers are laid out, the mangled lifted
And stowed into the little hospital.
Then the bell, breaking the hush, tolls once,
And the ambulance with its terrible cargo
Rocking, slightly rocking, moves away,
As the doors, an afterthought, are closed.

We are deranged, walking among the cops
Who sweep glass and are large and composed.
One is still making notes under the light.
One with a bucket douches ponds of blood
Into the street and gutter.
One hangs lanterns on the wrecks that cling,
Empty husks of locusts, to iron poles.

Our throats were tight as tourniquets,
Our feet were bound with splints, but now,
Like convalescents intimate and gauche,
We speak through sickly smiles and warn
With the stubborn saw of common sense,
The grim joke and the banal resolution.
The traffic moves around with care,
But we remain, touching a wound
That opens to our richest horror.
Already old, the question Who shall die?
Becomes unspoken Who is innocent?

For death in war is done by hands;
Suicide has cause and stillbirth, logic;

And cancer, simple as a flower, blooms.
But this invites the occult mind,
Cancels our physics with a sneer,
And spatters all we knew of denouement
Across the expedient and wicked stones.

Shapiro describes the auto wreck in subjective and emotional terms, focusing ultimately not on the accident itself but on death, especially death by accident, and its effect on those who witness it. If Shapiro's purpose had been to explain exactly what happened—as a journalist's, police officer's, or insurance adjustor's purpose might have been—he would have constructed a very different text. Since his purpose was to construct a poem, a text seldom read primarily for information, he was free to construct a subjective, selective account of the accident.

Notice how the following traffic accident report, written in an exact and factual manner by the investigating officer, differs from Shapiro's poem in content, organization, and **style and voice.**

STYLE AND VOICE, PAGE 596

On March 3, 1993, at approximately 10:05 P.M., my partner, Cpl. Alex Kolwalski, and I were dispatched to the intersection of West Main Street and Airport Road, where a two-vehicle accident had just occurred. We arrived at the scene at 10:07, and our back-up unit with Cpl. Kimberly Arnold and Sgt. Frank Sydow arrived at 10:09.

Upon our arrival a witness, Terry Lee, 2816 Forsythe Avenue (phone number 621-6059), said that at approximately 9:55 P.M. she had witnessed a two-vehicle accident. A 1993 green Chevrolet pickup truck had just passed her at a relatively high speed, northbound on Airport Road, when the driver tried to turn right onto West Main Street and overshot the center line on Main Street and struck a white 1989 Ford van owned and driven by Mary Powell, who was stopped westbound on Main Street.

The driver and owner of the pickup truck (PA 134-682), Elmer Houghton (PA dl 821-76-9440), received a cut on his forehead and an apparent broken nose. The truck sustained extensive damages to the front bumper and left front fender and was undrivable.

The driver of the Ford van (NJ 288-496), Mary Powell (NJ dl 546-18-3826), 4480 Tyler Street, Elkhurst, New Jersey, was unconscious and bleeding from severe lacerations on her head and a compound fracture of the left leg just above the knee. A passenger in the van, Gerald Thompson, 4482 Tyler Street, Elkhurst, New Jersey, who was sitting in the right front seat, received injuries to his left arm and leg and deep lacerations on his left cheek and ear, apparently from broken glass. My partner and I administered pressure bandages to Powell's cuts, and then I called an ambulance to the scene. Upon arrival at 10:21 P.M., the ambulance paramedics placed a temporary splint on Powell's left leg and took Powell and Thompson to Northside Medical Center. Thompson stated that both he and Powell were wearing their seat belts when the accident occurred.

The Ford van sustained extensive damage to the driver's door and the mid-section of the left side. The driver's door was jammed and could not be opened.

Houghton was shaken, but he was able to answer my questions satisfactorily. He said that he was travelling at approximately 50 mph and slowed to approximately 25 mph as he began his right turn onto Main Street. He stated that he apparently misjudged the distance between his truck and the intersection. He stated that he applied his brakes but skidded into the left side of the van. The witness, Terry Lee, corroborated Houghton's account of the accident. There were two skid marks measuring 12 feet, 6 inches behind Houghton's truck. There were no other witnesses.

After being examined by paramedic Wu Chang, Houghton refused treatment and said that he would see his private physician. There being no evidence that Houghton was intoxicated, I issued him a citation for negligent driving and causing an accident and released him on his own recognizance to report to the City Magistrate's office at 8:45 A.M., March 4, 1993.

I called for tow trucks to remove both vehicles from the scene. Cpl. Kolwalski and I swept up the broken glass and retrieved a rearview mirror and short strip of metal that had been dislodged from the van. Cpl. Arnold and Sgt. Sydow directed traffic during our handling of the situation.

Note that the accident report is far less dramatic and much more factual than the poem. The report's style is straightforward and direct, its tone matter-of-fact, whereas the poem's style is metaphoric, imaginative, and indirect, its tone reflective. The report begins at the beginning, with the accident, and then relates each subsequent development in strict chronological order. The poem begins with the arrival of the ambulance and only suggests the accident, dwelling on the aftermath rather than the event itself. The report tells what happened to the people involved in the accident; the poem explores the feelings of those who witnessed the accident. The report depends primarily on factual information; the poem focuses on sensory images. All these differences are directly related to the writers' purposes: the police officer's need to reconstruct the accident as accurately as possible and the poet's desire to evoke in readers the imminent sense of death at the scene of the accident.

A writer often has multiple and complex purposes. A novelist may write a novel to share something with readers, to create a thing of beauty, to earn money, and to keep proving to himself and others that he can still write. A research scientist may write a grant proposal to gain funding for a project, to get a grant for her department, to establish her position in the scientific community, and to enjoy the power that a large grant confers.

Writers have purposes for writing that they do not think about but that help to shape what is written. The novelist's desire to create something of beauty is tempered by his awareness of the publisher's deadline; the scientist's desire for funding is counterbalanced by her need to present herself in her writing as a credible professional. Writing purposes, both conscious and unconscious, are the forces that nudge and stretch and squash a text into a certain shape.

When you have a writing assignment, you probably write primarily because the assignment is required, but you may also have other purposes—to communicate information, to express your ideas, to impress your teacher and perhaps your classmates, to demonstrate knowledge, and to improve your skills as a writer. These multiple purposes inform your writing process and shape the resulting text. You may think you are solely motivated by your instructor's assignment, but once you begin to write, other motivating forces probably invade the process.

The rhetorical purposes in this book are common and varied. You will write to explore, to reconstruct your own experiences, to inform, to instruct and advise, to solve problems, and to persuade. You will also have other reasons for writing each assignment, and they will influence the resulting text. Inevitably, the experience you gain with these rhetorical purposes and the awareness you develop about your own motivations will make you a better reader and writer.

A U D I E N C E — T O   W H O M   A   T E X T   I S   A D D R E S S E D

Like purpose, audience influences the form a text assumes. *Audience* consists of the people for whom a text is written—those the writer expects will read it. Experienced writers always consider their readers when they write. In fact, *consider* may be too weak a word. Good writers do more than acknowledge the existence of an audience. They write *for* their readers, analyzing their needs and purposes in order to produce an appropriate text. Think of the Shapiro poem: audience and purpose, much more than subject, determine the content and form of the text. The poet is writing for readers literate enough to appreciate the rich details, metaphoric language, rhythms, ambiguities, and nuances of meaning found in the poem and with enough leisure time to enjoy reading a poem.

In contrast, the police officer who describes a similar accident is writing primarily for readers who want to spend as little time as necessary with the text. The readers of accident reports—police officials, clerks, lawyers, judges, social workers, insurance people, litigants—want fast and unambiguous information. The police officer's account includes accurate, specific information ("On March 3, 1993, at approximately 10:05 p.m., my partner, Cpl. Alex Kolwalski, and I were dispatched to the intersection of West Main Street and Airport Road, where a two-vehicle accident had just occurred"). It focuses on what happened and why ("A 1993 green Chevrolet pickup truck had just passed her traveling at a high rate of speed, northbound on Airport Road, when the driver tried to turn right onto West Main Street and overshot the center line and struck a white 1989 Ford van . . . "). The reader of a police report is interested not in how the ambulance looked and sounded as it approached—Shapiro's "quick soft silver bell beating, beating / . . . the one dark ruby flare / Pulsing . . ."—but rather in whether an ambulance was summoned, by whom, and when it arrived: ". . . I called an ambulance to the scene. Upon arrival at the scene at 10:21 p.m., . . ." In this way readers' interests, needs, and expectations influence the text a writer constructs. Even the subject of a text ultimately shapes it less than do the writer's considerations about audience and purpose. You will read more about these concepts, which are the cornerstones of effective rhetoric, throughout this book.

▶ P R O C E S S — H O W   A   T E X T   I S   C O N S T R U C T E D

Although every writer constructs a text in a particular way and every reader comprehends a text in a particular way, all texts are written and read using roughly the same process. Here is a generalized version of how texts are constructed—how writers write and readers read.

Writing

Any piece of writing originates as an idea. The most informal note, like the most complex treatise, originates as an idea that both anticipates and shapes the completed text.

But writing is not as straightforward as this statement suggests. Writers do not simply come up with an idea and then transfer it directly onto paper. The written text that evolves from an idea is constructed by means of a *process*. In some instances, this process is brief and seemingly uncomplicated, as when you leave a note for a friend. In most instances, though, the process is more complicated, involving a series of forward and backward movements between the writer's ideas and the written text. This back and forth pattern characterizes the writing process. A freshman student, Kerry, went through the following process of planning, constructing, and editing as he wrote an essay about a trip he had made to Saltillo, Mexico.

PLANNING THE TEXT.   From several topics Kerry chose the following one because he had recently made a trip to Mexico:

> Write a travel narrative, describing what you learned (not what
> you saw or where you stayed) on a trip. Don't bore readers
> with a day-by-day itinerary of your travels; instead, provide a
> candid and thoughtful narrative of your mental adventures and
> explorations of different people, attitudes, and assumptions.
> One point—you don't have to travel to an exotic locale to tell
> an intriguing story.

> (Adapted from Elizabeth Cowan Neeld,
> *Writing*, 3rd ed., Scott, Foresman/
> Little, Brown, 1990: 112)

Kerry had just returned from Mexico and thought it would be easy to write an essay about the week he had spent there at a Catholic mission. He also chose this topic because the trip had been important to him. Of course it had been exciting to travel to a foreign country, but the trip had also given him a glimpse of a kind of life very different from his. Kerry spent little time planning what he was going to write about, confident that he had plenty to say and that the words would come once he began to write.

CONSTRUCTING THE TEXT.   The night before the first draft of his essay was due, Kerry sat down and quickly wrote six pages about his trip, describing the highlights of his visit to the Catholic mission. Here is the introductory paragraph of that early draft:

```
            During the summer of 1992 I joined a church group
    in a journey to a small mission in Saltillo, Mexico.
    This would be my second time to travel to Saltillo.
    Unfortunately I was much younger the last time, and
    most of the experiences once learned were now lost to
    time. I had planned to return every year after that
    first year, but I was forced to stay home because of
    pre-season football practice. With an opportunity to
    finally return I left with great expectation.
```

Kerry then provided his readers with an account of the highlights of his visit to the mission. He began with a description of the mission itself and the priest who was in charge of it, Father Quinn. Then came accounts of side trips that his group made during the week to rancheros and barrios in the area. He also wrote about Bean Day, a day when beans were given to people who came to the mission:

```
            The last day we spent was a shocker to all of us.
    We had Bean Day. Bean Day is where we give beans to as
    many people that can get to the mission. People start
    filling the church the night before. We started at 6:00.
    Once the church was empty Father Quinn would take a
    bunch of guys to let the people outside of the church
    in. We made a human chain and extend outward letting the
```

> people between the two chains in. It was an amazing
> feeling to know that all these people were going to be
> helped by the little thing we did. Total I would guess
> we gave beans and flour to near 5,000 people.

Kerry ended his first draft with this paragraph:

> The trip to Saltillo does miraculous things. You
> leave with a bunch of strangers and return with friends
> you could never part with. It seems kind of humorous
> looking back on my trips to Mexico. While you are there
> you are hot, dirty, smelly, and wishing you were home.
> Spending all week praying to be home as soon as I walk
> in my door I wished I was back in Saltillo.

Kerry felt satisfied with this full and accurate account of his trip.

The next day Kerry read his essay aloud to a group of his class-mates and got their mildly positive response. "Yeah, sounds like a good trip," one of the students in Kerry's group commented, but another pointed out that the essay didn't seem to have a thesis—a main idea or main point. Still, Kerry left class feeling relieved—his first essay written and his first peer response session over.

Before the writing class met again, Kerry was expected to revise his essay, so he wrote it out again, correcting some spelling and punctuation errors, adding and deleting a few words, changing a few phrases, and writing more neatly, but he didn't change the essay in any significant way. He turned the essay in and put it out of his mind.

When Kerry read his instructor's comments a few days later, he was disappointed because she didn't tell him the essay was fine, just as it was, nor did she tell him exactly how to change it. She had written only, "Kerry, your essay has some wonderful bits and pieces but lacks a clear focus. Let's talk briefly after class." After class she suggested that Kerry was attempting too much and should focus as he revised on the part of his trip that had been most meaningful to him.

That night Kerry read his essay again. Not having seen it for several days, he read it with a new perspective. He began to see what the student in the response group and his teacher had seen: the essay lacked a clear focus. He had included too much and had not really explained anything fully. Thinking back to the trip, Kerry tried to remember what had happened and how he had felt. Although the whole week had been exciting, and he had learned a great deal about Mexican culture, the experience of giving people food on Bean Day was his most vivid memory.

Taking some clean paper from a notebook, Kerry began a new draft of his essay. He decided to scrap the introductory paragraph because it was too general and not very clear. The new introduction focused on his Bean Day experience:

> To the average American citizen a scoop of beans means no more than a bad supper. However, I've learned not to take beans or any food, for that matter, for granted.

After writing a completely new introduction, Kerry decided to keep the next few paragraphs, which provided background information about the trip and the mission. Then he cut the paragraphs about the side trips to the neighboring rancheros and barrios. He hated to get rid of such a big chunk of his essay, but he realized now that this information didn't add anything; in fact, it detracted from what he really wanted to accomplish.

Rereading the original paragraph about Bean Day, Kerry realized how skimpy and unclear it was. He wrote a new description of that experience, a description that grew from a paragraph to almost five handwritten pages. When he was ready to end the essay, he didn't hesitate to cross out the old conclusion and write a new one that reflected his new focus. When Kerry read the new draft through, he realized that in this revision he had improved his essay about 100 percent.

EDITING THE TEXT.   When his teacher read the new draft, she agreed that he had written a much stronger essay. At this point, the essay went into Kerry's working portfolio. When the time came for Kerry to decide which essays he wanted to include in his final portfolio, he selected the Bean Day essay as one. Rereading the essay several months after he had written it was a strange experience. He could see some minor errors he had not noticed before, but he still liked the essay and felt it communicated clearly something that had been important to him.

In order to edit the essay, he reread it carefully, correcting the errors he identified and marking anything he thought might be an error. He also changed a few phrases and rewrote a couple of sentences so they would be clearer or easier to read. Later he asked his instructor about the sentences that he suspected might include errors and asked a friend to read the essay over to see if he had missed anything. Then, confident that he had done what he could to ensure his essay was clearly written and free of errors, he typed it in its final form and placed it in his portfolio. Here is that essay:

Bean Day

To the average American citizen, a scoop of beans means no more than a bad supper. However, I have learned not to take beans, or any food, for granted.

During the summer of 1992, I joined a church group on a journey to a small mission in Saltillo, Mexico. The mission is supported by the Diocese of Biloxi, and is visited by their youth groups during the summer. These groups help Father Quinn, an older man with sun-beaten skin, silver hair, and a heart of gold. Father Quinn volunteered to run the mission for three years. Now, 30 years later, he is still in charge of the mission.

The mission is a large area around a church with a big courtyard. During the day, the children from the city came to the mission to play. When we came in from the ranchos and barrios, where we passed out food and clothing, we would have time to play in the courtyard with the children. We learned a lot about history and people playing with those kids. Many of the games they play are similar to ones played in the United States. I believe that is what was so remarkable about our playing. We expected those kids to be different from us, and they had thought we were different from them. It turned out we are a lot alike, which showed in the way we picked up each other's games quickly and in the way they understood the games we taught them.

There were a lot of faces in the yard, no one face really remembered. It was the time spent with the dirty little faces that will always be special to me.

The last day we were at the mission was a surprise to all of us. We were there during the week of "bean day." Father Quinn has beans trucked into the mission all during the month, and on one Friday of the month he gives them out. We called this "bean day." People from all over the city and surrounding towns came for those beans that would feed their families for a couple of weeks. They started showing up the afternoon before bean day and sat in the church. When the church was filled, Father closed the doors and people waited out by the street. During the night the people held an all-night vigil. As we slept in the dorms, we could hear the rosary being prayed in the church.

By the time the side door to the church was opened the next morning, people had begun to pass out from the heat and the long wait. The calm crowd dashed madly to the six stations we had set up. We shoveled beans into anything the people had that would hold them. We could only give them two scoops full of beans. After that, we asked them to move on, but some of them just sat there asking for more. It is hard to say "no" to a sad face asking for more than just two scoops of beans. But, it would have been even harder to say "We have no more" to the last person in that line.

When the church was empty, Father Quinn asked the adult men and some of the older boys to help him get the people still outside into the church. If the doors were just opened, the fight to get in would crush people into the doors. That is why Father Quinn needed us. We made a human fence on each side of the door. Father told us when he opened the door to walk out and hold onto the gate and to let only the people inside the two fences in.

When he opened the door, the number of people was shocking. We walked out and people were pushing and hitting to get in. The best comparison I can make is

this: If a rock concert were to have a fire, the fight
to get to the door would be much like this fight to get
food. When one part was cleared, we would open another
one. We worked for over an hour until everyone was in
the courtyard getting beans or waiting in the church.

This experience was an eye-opener for me, but the
one picture I will always remember is one of an old
lady. After all the beans were gone and the people had
cleared out of the courtyard, there the old lady was,
down on all fours, going from station to station looking for beans that had been dropped.

There were a lot of things that I took for granted
in my life. Sometimes, I still do take things for
granted. But now, when I find myself doing that, I
think about the pain I saw on this lady's face. A lady
scrounging for beans that would, most likely, feed her
children and her grandchildren, for a while longer.

You will probably discover, as Kerry did, that you cannot march
through the writing process in a neat, sequential fashion. Don't expect
a writing (or reading) project to be orderly. Your mental image of
what you are writing will probably change as you write, and each
time your ideas change, you will have to change what you have written as well.

Even so, overall you will progress through several stages. You
usually begin a writing project by *planning*—thinking about what you
are going to write, discovering new ideas, making connections and
gaining new insights, researching for additional information, organizing your thoughts, and considering your purpose and audience.
During this stage, you expand your initial idea of your text, and this
developing idea starts to grow into some kind of plan. Planning
involves writing as well as thinking; in fact, the two are inseparable
throughout the writing process.

When you have some idea of what you want to write, you are
ready to begin *constructing* your written text. Constructing a written
text involves not only thinking and writing but also reading and revising. Throughout this part of the writing process you must often move
backward to go forward. You must think about what you want to
write, write it, read it over to see if it corresponds to what you are
thinking, and then change it or your mental image of your text so that

they agree. In other words, you are going to change your mind frequently, rethinking what you want to write as you write it. This is a normal, productive part of the process. Eventually, you will produce a piece of writing that satisfies you, or you will simply run out of time.

Next you turn your attention to *editing* your written text—to making it more readable and more correct. By the time you begin to edit your text, its focus, development, and organization should satisfy you. In editing, you pay attention to accuracy and appearance. This is the time to make sure that each sentence is well structured, that each word is correctly used, that each punctuation mark is appropriate. If you are using a computer, you make final decisions about format and run the spell check. To edit is to polish or refine what you have written. Your main concern during this stage is the final preparation of your manuscript.

When we write about this progression from planning to writing to editing, the process seems sequential and linear, but your own writing experiences tell you otherwise. You may begin to write before you have finished planning, or you may revise even before you actually begin writing your text. And after you have produced a written text, you may still be changing your plans, just as Kerry changed his essay from a general description of his entire trip to Mexico to an essay about one experience he had there. At any point in the process you may be planning, writing, or revising—shuttling back and forth among these three activities.

Reading

Like writers, readers move backward—rereading, reconfirming, and rethinking—as well as forward—anticipating what is to come and connecting the new and different information with what they already know. Readers as well as writers construct texts. A writer begins with a mental image of the text and constructs a written text; a reader begins with a written text and constructs a mental image of it. Like writers, readers move back and forth between the two forms of the text—the one on the page and the one in their head.

To understand the reading process better, we'll follow a group of students who read this excerpt from Joseph Campbell's book about myths entitled *The Hero with a Thousand Faces*:

Whether we listen with aloof amusement to the dreamlike
mumbo jumbo of some red-eyed witch doctor of the Congo, or
read with cultivated rapture thin translations from the sonnets

of the mystic Lao-tse; now and again crack the hard nutshell of an argument of Aquinas, or catch suddenly the shining meaning of a bizarre Eskimo fairy tale: it will be always the one, shape-shifting yet marvelously constant story that we find, together with a challengingly persistent suggestion of more remaining to be experienced than will ever be known or told.

Throughout the inhabited world, in all times and under every circumstance, the myths of man have flourished; and they have been the living inspiration of whatever else may have appeared out of the activities of the human body and mind. It would not be too much to say that myth is the secret opening through which the inexhaustible energies of the cosmos pour into human cultural manifestation. Religions, philosophies, arts, the social forms of primitive and historic man, prime discoveries in science and technology, the very dreams that blister sleep, boil up from the basic, magic ring of myth.

(*The Hero with a Thousand Faces*,
Princeton UP, 1949: 3)

When the students initially read this passage, they found it confusing and complex. After a single reading, few of them were sure what Campbell meant. Asked to write a sentence that expressed Campbell's main idea, one student, Tanya, wrote that the main idea was "All of life's beliefs and understandings of life were derived from early myths." This summary reflects only part of Campbell's meaning. After rereading the passage, this time underlining what she considered the key terms and phrases, Tanya revised her summary statement to reflect more accurately the scope and meaning of Campbell's passage. This time she wrote, "The writer tells us that old myths and religions have inspired our activities throughout history." Tanya has now incorporated into her own version of Campbell's text his idea that behavior as well as beliefs derive from myths. After reading the passage a third time and discussing it with two classmates, Tanya formulated a third summary statement: "The writer tells us that activities of both the past and present are based on myths." Two important modifications make the new version more accurate. Tanya states that human actions *are based on* myths rather than merely *are influenced by* myths and she includes, as does Campbell, both the present and the past.

Tanya's final summary statement reflects her increased understanding of Campbell's words. By returning repeatedly to the text, marking it to emphasize key words and phrases, and discussing it with other people, Tanya reduced a difficult text to a clear idea that she could make her own.

Readers do not construct the same text as the writer's, but the writer's text significantly shapes the reader's mental image. In presenting precise information, building specifications or instructions for assembling a bookcase or operating a computer, for example, writers work hard to minimize the difference between their written texts and the mental images their readers construct. Poets and novelists, on the other hand, may actually encourage readers to construct mental images that are only loosely based on the written text. But no matter what writers intend, readers form their own images of the texts they read.

The students who read the Campbell excerpt about myths differed as to its meaning. One, Jennifer, concluded that the main idea was "There is more to the world than we know, and humans attempt to explain the unexplainable through myths." Another student, Suzanne, wrote that "everything we do and are is based on ancient myths and stories." Although these summaries are similar to Tanya's and reflect Campbell's text, each is also slightly different. Each reader developed a personal and unique version of the text.

Readers, like writers, use individual processes, but we can still generalize about the overall process of reading and can suggest some strategies that usually make the process, especially of reading difficult texts, more productive.

REREADING.   First, as the group of students who read the Campbell text discovered, rereading is essential. Even the most experienced readers must frequently reread, especially when they lack background information on the text they are reading. The more you know about a subject, the easier you find it to understand a difficult text on that subject. Rereading a text compensates to some extent for lack of background information, because each reading after the first builds on a slowly growing foundation of information.

Rereading is also necessary because a reader's attention can easily drift. You may think you have read every word on a page but have no idea what you have read. Everyone has had this experience. Perhaps you are thinking about an idea from the previous page or just daydreaming. Whatever the reason, the answer is to reread.

Sometimes a text is so complex that even a reader who is paying attention must reread to sort out complicated relationships, figure out complex ideas, or just wade through the author's impenetrable prose. Rereading is not a sign of failure but an essential part of the process.

ANNOTATING.   Experienced readers use a second strategy: annotating the text. To annotate simply means to mark a text—to write on the pages so that, in effect, you create a text of your own that merges with the one you are reading. How you mark a text really doesn't matter. That's up to you. The important thing is that you respond to the text in writing as you are reading it. For example, Tanya annotated her copy of the passage on myths by underlining key phrases and sentences and by writing notes in the margin.

Whether we listen with aloof amusement to the dreamlike mumbo jumbo of some red-eyed witch doctor of the Congo, or read with cultivated rapture thin translations from the sonnets of the mystic Lao-tse; now and again crack the hard nutshell of an argument of Aquinas, or catch suddenly the shining meaning of a bizarre Eskimo fairy tale: it will be always the one, shape-shifting yet marvelously constant story *?* that we find, together with the challengingly persistent suggestion of more remaining to be experienced than will ever be known or told.

Are myths just stories? What about dreams? Throughout the inhabited world, in all times and under every circumstance, the myths of man have flourished; and they have been the living inspiration of whatever else may have appeared out of the activities of the human body and mind. It would not be too much to say that myth is the secret opening through which the inexhaustible energies of the cosmos *Important* pour into human cultural manifestation. Religions, philosophies, arts, the social forms of primitive and historic man, prime discoveries in science and technology, the very dreams that blister sleep, boil up from the basic, magic ring of myth.

VERBALIZING.   Finally, readers need to put into words, either orally or in writing, their response to what they have read. Ideally, this response takes the form of a conversation, or dialogue, with another person who has read the same text. Such conversations enable readers to articulate their responses and test them, one against the other. In this process, the two readers argue for their own mental version of the text but also rethink and even reshape their version in light of the other reader's responses.

Because reading partners are not always conveniently present when you read, you may have to summarize what you have read for the benefit of the person to whom you are talking. Even if you have no one to discuss your readings with, you can discuss them with yourself. Hold a dialogue with yourself, articulating the main points of what you have read. Better yet, *write* a summary of what you have just read. Then, you can extend the dialogue by responding to these main points, agreeing, disagreeing, engaging with them to fix them in your mind. The important thing is to put into words your mental image of the text. Doing that gives you a sure grasp of the text.

CONCLUSION

In both writing and reading, a text is constructed by a process that involves moving back and forth between a written and a mental text. Nothing is more important to both reading and writing than these mental, interior parts of the processes. The time you spend thinking about what you are going to write is never time wasted. Don't rush into actually putting words on paper or into the computer. Of course, you can't put off writing forever, but what goes on in your mind before you write and as you write is essential to the process. This means that you should allow time between drafts to let what is in your head shape your written text and to let your written text reshape what is in your head. Finally, it means that you do not stop thinking when you begin writing: writing and thinking occur simultaneously, one stimulating the other in an ongoing process.

If you clearly understand what is going on as you read and write, you will gradually gain control of these processes. Writing is not a special talent given to some people nor a mysterious process that you cannot possibly understand; nor is it a simple one-two-three process. Constructing a text, whether you are a reader or a writer, is an interactive, meaning-making process that involves both the written text and your mental image of that text. The interaction between your mind and the text *creates* meaning.

Joshua Sheldon

▼

PART TWO

PURPOSES

Douglas Olson, *Detail, Door*

2

▼

WRITING
TO
EXPLORE

The reason I write is to find out what I mean.

LESLIE MARMON SILKO

One of the most important reasons for writing is to discover what you have to say on a subject. For some reason, the act of writing helps bring back information, sensations, impressions, and emotions—in other words, to retrieve from memory things you may have forgotten you even knew. But you can also write to explore in order to forge new connections or construct new information—to see the past in terms of the present or select from your memories certain data and combine them with present information to create new knowledge. Writing can help you recall individual bits of information and relate them to one another, to see them not just as bits but as a new whole. For readers to see the relationships, connections, implications, and meaning of what you write, you must first be able to see them for yourself. In this chapter's reading selections, you will learn about writers as they explore themselves and their writing experiences.

You are often asked to write in order to show what you know, as on a test or in a research paper. But you may be less familiar with writing to explore—writing to find out what you know rather than to prove you know something. (In a sense, each time you write, you write to explore because writing is always an act of discovery. Even when you think you know exactly what you are going to write, you may surprise yourself, writing something other than what you had planned.) When you write to explore, you can find out what you want to say and how you want to say it, to see how much you remember, to discover where your words lead you and if that is where you want to go.

Exploratory writing may be impermanent—a fleeting image on a computer screen, a note written and then destroyed, a rough draft later revised, a brainstorming list produced by a group or an individual and used to generate ideas. But many people have kept their written explorations in some permanent form, sometimes to be read later by others. Exploratory writing in the form of diaries, journals, notebooks, and commonplace books enriches the world, as you will see in this chapter's reading selections.

Exploratory writing can be private—stuff you really don't want anyone else to read, at least not right now, but that you want to write down. Or it can be preliminary—writing that leads to other writing. For example, some people freewrite (that is, write quickly and freely) on a subject before they actually begin to compose what they want to say. Peter Elbow, a well-known writing teacher and theorist, believes that "free exploratory writing," as he calls it, can work powerfully to overcome the fear of writing or inability to write that afflicts everyone at times. Elbow describes the process of freewriting this way:

> Just write and keep writing. (Probably best to write on only one side of the paper in case you should want to cut parts out with scissors—but you probably won't.) Just write and keep writing. It will probably come in waves. After a flurry, stop and take a brief rest. But don't stop too long. Don't think about what you are writing or what you have written or else you will overload the circuit again. Keep writing as though you are drugged or drunk. Keep doing this till you feel you have a lot of material that might be useful; or, if necessary, till you can't stand it any more—even if you doubt that there's anything useful there.

> (*Embracing Contraries*,
> Oxford UP, 1986: 49–50)

Because writing to explore is an important part of becoming an experienced writer, we suggest you keep a journal, a separate notebook or computer file for your written explorations. You can use this journal to freewrite, to record your thoughts and feelings, to practice your writing, to explore new topics, to analyze your own writing behavior as do the journal-keepers in this chapter's reading selections, or to take notes for writing assignments. Your instructor may suggest other ways to use your journal and may want to evaluate it in some way.

One reason to keep a journal is that each chapter in this book has several informal writing assignments in which you are asked to make entries based on the reading selections. Sometimes you will react specifically to what you read; at other times you will explore a related topic or issue. You could, of course, write these entries without recording them in a notebook. But a journal provides you with a record of your writing and reading experiences, becoming a text you may later enjoy reading for other purposes—to remember what it was like to be a student, to look up something you have forgotten, to compare the writer you become to the one you used to be.

▶ R E A D I N G   W R I T T E N
E X P L O R A T I O N S

Because much exploratory writing is personal if not private, when you read someone else's journal you may feel like an accidental audience—someone who is reading something not intended for him or her. True, people often keep a diary or journal without a clear sense of who the reader will be. Diarists often claim they are writing only for themselves, but even if they are writing only for their future selves, people who write in a journal or diary always have a sense of audience. By its very nature, writing is a communicative act. Writing connects a writer and a reader, even if the reader is the writer.

In his book about diaries entitled *A Book of One's Own*, Thomas Mallon, a prolific diarist himself, analyzes his own sense of audience and argues that people who keep diaries are always writing for a "you" as well as for themselves:

> Is that the only person I'm writing for—myself when older? Or is there someone else? Who is this "you" that's made its way more and more often into these pages in the last few years, this odd pronoun I sometimes find myself talking to like a person at the other end of a letter? Sometimes when I'm writing on the right-hand leaf of a notebook I catch sight of a spelling or grammatical mistake I made on the left one the night before, and I correct it. For "you"?
>
> I can say without a trace of coyness that I have no idea who "you" is. I don't know if "you" is male or female, met or unmet, born or unborn, tied to me by blood or accident. But I do know that "you" has come to stay. What's more, I now realize that he or she has been hovering around . . . from the beginning.

> (Ticknor & Fields, 1984: xvi)

Mallon's argument gains support from the number of people who eventually publish their diaries or journals. The writer Anne Lindbergh, wife of the aviator who made the first solo nonstop transatlantic flight, published several collections of her diaries, and in the introduction to one explains why she thinks people publish journals and diaries:

Why do people publish diaries and journals? If they have had interesting lives, they may feel they can add a tiny segment to the history of their times or put a missing fragment of mosaic in the picture. In terms of the individual there is the wish to give testimony to a journey taken by one human being which might amuse, enlighten, or explain other individuals to themselves. In the case of an individual who has lived somewhat in the public eye, there is always the hope of clarifying a record that has been obscured by rumors and blurred by distorted images. And finally, perhaps, the writer seeks some kind of personal summation in order to discover for himself the true essence of a life.

(*Bring Me a Unicorn*, Harcourt, 1971, 72: xv)

How should you read published diaries and journals? Much as you would any other piece of writing. However, a diary, whether it is published or unpublished, always seems to be an honest revelation of the writer's thoughts and actions. It may not occur to you as a reader of a diary to question the truth or accuracy of what has been written. Yet diarists and journalists are only recording their perception of what happened, and, like most writers, they usually want to present themselves in a good light. Before publishing his diary, Evelyn Waugh, a famous English novelist of the early twentieth century, deleted entries that didn't reinforce the impression of wit and humor he cultivated. Anäis Nin, a Paris-born American writer whose six volumes of diaries describe her life among the wealthy and the literary in Paris in the 1920s and 1930s, embellished her already exotic and extravagant life in her diaries to create the story she wanted to live.

Reading a journal or diary is, for the most part, like reading other kinds of texts. Be aware of the writer behind the text and try to decide what his or her purposes may have been. Read critically, weighing evidence and argument. And finally, know your own purpose for reading. If that purpose is to understand the writer of the diary or journal, then you need to know that the person presented in the text (the persona) is not necessarily the person who wrote it, any more than you can assume that a character in a novel is an accurate reflection of the novelist.

And what if you are reading your own diary or journal? People often keep diaries and journals so they can reread them at a later time. Does being a reader of your own writing change the way you read a diary or journal? Not as much as you might think. Again, the purpose for reading is the most important factor. If you are reading a journal you kept when you were a child, you probably want to understand who that child was just as you would if you were reading a diary or journal written by a child you did not know. Since you are no longer the child you once were, you are still trying to glimpse the figure behind the words on the page.

People also read their own journals to remember what happened, to check on some bit of information, to relive experiences that have faded with time, to rekindle ideas or stimulate thinking. In the following reading selections, for example, imagine Lord Lugard rereading his East Africa journals as an old man, or picture Virginia Woolf turning to her journals to refresh her memory about the writing plans she often described in them. Similarly, you may often find yourself rereading the journal you keep in this course, especially if you use it to explore ideas and take notes for writing assignments.

READINGS FOR WRITING

This chapter's reading selections show writers exploring the subject of themselves *as writers* in their personal journals. These journal entries open a window on the way the writers construct a text and on their attitudes toward their own writing.

ON WRITING

Jim Whorton

As a member of a composition class, Jim Whorton was required to keep a writing journal. Since Whorton is a creative writing major, he focused mainly on his experiences in writing short stories, using his journal to explore how he feels about writing and himself as a writer. As you read, notice the abundant specific details that Whorton includes as he describes his own writing process and the delightful "side trips" he takes as one idea leads him to another.

September 9

My girlfriend Kathryn and I were just discussing writing. I mentioned the required typing of all assignments in some composition classes. She vehemently argued that she would require all essays to be handwritten, and if they were illegible she'd fail them unhesitatingly. Her position is that writing is a dying skill and it should be maintained. People in college should be able to write by hand. My position is similar but different too. I honor the tradition of writing in script, of having a handwriting. I like the idea of each of us having a signature that identifies us, even though individual samples are not themselves identical. If a student likes to write by hand, and takes care to do it well, I say more power to the student. I am less militant than Kat, though—I would not fail illegible papers, but return them to be recopied or typed.

I'm left considering the physicality of writing. A member of USM's English faculty told me that composition must always be done LONGhand, because the motion of hand over paper fuels the imagination. Of course in typing there is as much physical activity or more than in longhand. I have a computer I like to write on, but the ever-present possibility of an electric surge or slip-up eradicating my work makes me nervous. That's why I got this Remington Noiseless, a relic from the Thirties, according to the man who sold me the ribbon. Design changed very little in the early decades of mass-produced typewriters. You can tell the pre-WWII models by their lack of color. They are black. It was just after WWI that tipewryters were mass produced in the US. Factories that had produced guns for the war, such as Remington, Smith and Wesson, became Remington Tipewryters and Smith-Corona respectively. I paid just ten dollars for this very heavy piece of equipment at a thrift store called Bargains and Blessings. It works well except for the bell, which dings not.

3   I am rambling, but this is how I often write, therefore I judge whatever comes into my head self-evidently apropos. Since this is a journal whose concern is writing . . .

October 22

4   Got a story due for the workshop on the 25th. I decided to go with the new one, which I just started but is more interesting to me right now. So I'm hoping I'll get a late rush of energy and do something worthwhile with this story. I don't put a whole lot of stock in the idea of inspiration—I try to resist the idea because it seems too mystifying. So it's not that I expect the last-minute pressure to inspire me with great thoughts. But it might provoke me to greater exertion.

October 31

5   What I was saying above seems unnecessarily vague. The kind of inspiration I value and use is really just a feeling of freshness, or strangeness, that lets you see things and talk about them in a fresh way. This fresh feeling can be achieved just by doing something a little unusual, like getting up two hours early one morning, or staying up extra late, or taking a walk at a different time of day, or eating in an unfamiliar restaurant. The strangeness heightens your sensitivity to the familiar too.

6   So what I did to finish the new story was stay up late. Burn incense (which always seems *flaky* to me, and always will, but that's partly why I like it). Drink one glass of wine, maybe, a small glass only. Coffee maybe. Get worked up. Put the dogs to bed and sit there in the quiet with your computer screen. My suspicion of everything mystical helps me out, because it heightens the artificiality of the mood I'm creating for myself to write in.

7   But, this doesn't always work. Sometimes this flops.

8   Certainly you can't rely on this method for consistent success. Though maybe it is important to always be doing things that make you

feel weird. That sounds fruity, but it works, and it's the best way to live even if you're not writing. I don't mean scaring people, knifing yourself, driving cross-country. I do mean going into junk stores and touching bugs, tasting banana peel, etc.

December 3

It's not a simple matter, writing. I could make a list of things I've 9 learned but then I might make another list that contradicts the first but is also persuasive. . . .

Am I too touchy about words? Am I too meticulous? Are words 10 too precious to me? Is there a danger of ineffectualness in my language? One of the true low points of my semester was when I listened to a recording of myself reading my own writing and I was bored by it. The care and precision did not pay off.

What a drag that was. 11

Maybe I'm not as precise as I'd like to be. 12

Maybe I'm overly stodgy. . . . 13

I worry some about grades but I don't understand how people 14 can get through school doing work JUST to get good grades. How can they stand the boredom. I'm sounding pretty snooty along about now—maybe I should back up and clarify what I'm talking about.

1) I'm interested in the most tedious aspects of language 15

2) I'm worried that this is not a good thing to be interested in 16

3) I'm worried I'll bore others 17

4) I'm worried I'll look up one day and find myself totally boring, 18 as has happened recently

5) I'm trying to justify the presence of all this stuff here in my 19 composition journal. Perhaps this is the most pressing issue of all.

QUESTIONS TO CONSIDER ◀

1. Whorton is clearly concerned with the physical as well as the mental process of writing. Does the "physicality of writing"—the physical method a writer employs to create a text—influence what is written? For instance, have you noticed differences in your writing process when you use a computer rather than a typewriter or a pen and pencil?

2. Whorton is also concerned about boring his readers. Should writers worry about boring their readers? Why or why not? How can you determine if what you have written is boring?

3. Whorton mentions several things he does to gain a fresh perspective when he writes. Can you think of other ways to force yourself to see things in new ways?

▶ WRITING ACTIVITIES

Individual: Explore your own writing process by freewriting about it, describing in detail exactly what you do when you write. Do you observe any particular rituals when you write? Do these rituals vary depending on what you are writing?

Collaborative: Working with a group of students, compare your writing processes. Discuss how your writing methods, habits, and rituals are the same and how they are different. Then, based on your analysis of your individual processes, decide if there is a basic process that all of you seem to go through when you write. If so, describe that process.

Computer: To test the effect of the "physicality of writing," write a paragraph about yourself as a writer using pen (or pencil) and paper. Then, using a computer, write another paragraph about the same subject. Compare these two writing experiences. Was one easier? More satisfying? Faster? Did one result in a stronger, more interesting piece of writing?

❖❖❖❖❖

HARD G, SOFT G

Tobi Gillian Sanders

In 1968 a Barnard College English class had the following assignment: "The members of the class will keep daily journals and work up the material in finished papers, fiction and nonfiction." Two of the members of that class, Joan Frances Bennett and Tobi Gillian Sanders, later published their journals in a book entitled Members of the Class Will Keep Daily Journals. *The following excerpts from Sanders's journal focus on a story she is writing, for her*
English class, based on her experience as a waitress in a restaurant

owned by a man named Artur. Her journal entries tell of the problems she has in writing the story and the response of her classmates to it. As you read, notice the emotional ups and downs Sanders experiences as she struggles to write the story for her writing class.

7 March 1968 (Thursday)

Still trying to work out a pattern for my story due on the 18th. I was put down by Mrs. Dobkin tenderly and tactfully. She was right. A story on Tom and me would not work—the restaurant is where it will have to be. . . . 1

10 March 1968 (Sunday)

I had planned to spend tonight writing a good deal of my story, but too much happened. Mentally I am entirely gone; physically, I'm just plain period-achy and pooped. 2

Mum called tonight. Tom's father died suddenly. The funeral is Tuesday (4:30) at the First Unitarian Church. 3

I just had some grapefruit. The bitter-acid taste in my mouth is not from that. 4

21 March 1968 (Thursday)

I must admit, it's good to be writing daily entries again. The story drained me of absolutely everything, especially when the class and Mrs. Dobkin seemed to fail to grasp what I was trying to do. Perhaps it was my fault. I realize a good part of it needs revision, but the structure, the deliberate choice of words, motifs, everything seemed to fall upon the deaf. I don't think I can look at *Artur's Restaurant* for a while. I didn't even go to work tonight. 5

One last thing about the story—I will not change the basic style or tone. I see no reason to cripple myself. Oh, shit, I've got a long way to go. . . . 6

24 April 1968 (Wednesday)

I've found my style, holy shit, at last I've found my style and it was right there all the time only like a knucklehead I kept trying to mask it. Wow, I'm satisfied with what I've done—it's the beginning. The a-g-o-n-y of sitting in that class today drugged from no sleep and when no one cracked a smile, I thought I'd jump out of the window. Then, like a domino miracle, one person chuckled, another giggled and soon everyone plain guffawed out loud. LOUD! . . . 7

13 May 1968 (Monday)

8 I really did mean to re-do *Artur* this weekend but it proved impossible. Friday night I Anya-sat. Saturday was her shower. Saturday night was show-down night with Stephen and Sunday was a Happy Mother's Day for all.

9   Just for the record, this afternoon our writing class met at Mrs. Dobkin's apartment in observance of the STRIKE and a joyous time was had by all. It was nice—I hated to leave, but was feeling sickly. . . .

17 May 1968 (Friday)

10 I _____ do hereby swear that the short story concerning Artur and his restaurant will be revised and pronto-ly special delivered to one Mrs. Dobkin before June has done all her busting out. Due to circumstances (mainly the inability to read through the 10 or so pages, plus a campus riot thrown in for diversion/procrastination) beyond the above's control, a revision before the end of the semester is impossibly out of any question. . . .

11   Therefore the signee hopes that Mrs. Dobkin will honor her request for AMNESTY. The signee will under no condition consider a STRIKE.

▶   **QUESTIONS TO CONSIDER**

1. Who is the audience for this journal? Does Sanders seem to be writing for herself, her teacher, or someone else? Do you think she knew when she wrote the journal that she would someday publish it?

2. How does the teacher affect Sanders's writing process and her attitude toward herself as a writer? Does Sanders perceive of her teacher as her primary audience? Why or why not? What effect do the reactions of her classmates have on her and how she feels about her story?

3. How long does Sanders work on the story she describes in her journal? When the journal entries end, is the story finished? Do you think she ever finished it? Why or why not?

4. What differences do you see in Sanders's two assignments: writing in her journal and writing the story? Which is easier for her to write?

Why? From which does she derive more satisfaction? Why? From which assignment does she seem to learn more? How does she use her journal to help write her story?

5. Compare Sanders's and Whorton's journals. How are they alike and how are they different?

WRITING ACTIVITIES

Individual: Explore your attitude toward yourself as a writer by freewriting about your perceptions of what kind of writer you are.

Collaborative: Discuss what Sanders means when she says she has "found her style." How would you describe her style of writing as it is reflected in her journal entries?

Computer: Using your word-processing program, rewrite the May 17 journal entry changing the formal style Sanders adopted in that entry to the informal style of her other entries. Be sure to convey the same information even though you change the **style and voice** of the entry.

STYLE AND VOICE, PAGE 596

❖❖❖❖❖

JOURNALS FROM THE LATE FORTIES AND FIFTIES

John Cheever

John Cheever, notable American novelist and short story writer, often wrote about life in America's affluent suburbs. His novels include The Wapshot Chronicle *(1957) and* Falconer *(1977). His collection* The Stories of John Cheever *won the Pulitzer Prize in 1978. Like many professional writers, Cheever kept a journal in which he recorded not only his daily thoughts and activities but also his reflections on his own writing. Cheever wrote the entries here when he was in his thirties and forties and an established writer but not yet the eminent success that he would become later in his life. In 1990*

(Cheever died in 1982), parts of his journal were published in The New Yorker *magazine, from which these excerpts come. This reading selection consists of a series of entries in which Cheever reflects on himself as a writer and evaluates his writing. As you read, notice how dissatisfied Cheever seems to be with his work even though it had already received great attention and would receive more in the future.*

1   As I approach my fortieth birthday without having accomplished any one of the things I intended to accomplish—without ever having achieved the deep creativity that I have worked toward for all this time—I feel that I take a minor, an obscure, a dim position that is not my destiny but that is my fault, as if I had lacked, somewhere along the line, the wit and courage to contain myself competently within the shapes at hand. I think of Leander and all the others. It is not that these are stories of failure; that is not what is frightening. It is that they are dull annals; that they are of no import; that Leander, walking in the garden at dusk in the throes of a violent passion, is of no importance to anyone. It does not matter. It does not matter . . .

2   I have recounted my unsuccessful stories over again and again, planned to revise them and felt that this was aiming below the mark, and so have waited for something better, but nothing better has come and I must look on these stories as a business venture and finish them off, as second-rate as they seem. I will have "The Reasonable Music." This should be revised again and sent off.

3   There is "Vega," this lacks some intrinsic drama. I want to dramatize the irresponsible interference of the intellectual. I can't seem to breathe fire into Atcheson. I will read that over again, at once, and see what I have.

4   There is "Christmas Is a Sad Season for the Poor." This can be a reasonably funny story.

5   There is "Emma Boynton." This is slight, but it might sell.

❖

6   Nov. 27th. Snowing.

❖

7   Dec. 5th. Partly at my wife's suggestion I've given the Saul Bellow novel a thorough reading. Here is the blend of French and Russian that I like, the cockroach and peeling wallpaper described with precision and loathing. The principal force of the work I think is

poetic. Some of it ("I stand upon bones," etc.) is bad poetry. I think some of it is very good. I have always been pleased with light and I am always pleased with descriptions of it. Through the desperate choices of my own unhappy mind I have developed, and struggled to discard, a detailed method, but I find Bellow's detail impressive. It comes back to trying to find justification for the sentiment, carnality, and melodrama in my own work.

My style seems ruminative and soft; my descriptive powers are not what I would like them to be. I want to let some air and light into this room; waking up this morning I thought that I could use a brisk fistfight. I would like to write a story but not the New Jersey night, not the man in Columbus Circle, nothing overbalanced with morbidity, something with bulk and power. Not the heat wave. The news that it was snowing in Berlin.

8

As a part of moving I have had to go through some old manuscripts and I have been disheartened to see that my style, fifteen years ago, was competent and clear and that the improvements on it are superficial. I fail to see any signs of maturity, of increased penetration; I fail to see any deepening of my grasp. I was always in love. I was always happy to scythe a field and swim in a cold lake and put on clean clothes. I was more exuberant and naive about both this and love than I am now, but this is not a change for the better. There are thousands of notes, thousands of pages of description, thousands of striking conversations, and because they all lack an inner logic, because they lack passion, they are of no import.

9

To bring out a collection of short stories this fall: "Torch Song," "O City of Broken Dreams," "Emma Boynton," "The Day the Pig Fell Into the Well," "The Enormous Radio," "The Season of Divorce," "The Sutton Place Story," "The Pot of Gold," perhaps "The Radio Man," I mean "The Elevator Man," and to write a couple of stories to complement the collection, a couple of long pieces with no dying fall. Read at the office yesterday most of the stories I've written in the last five years and was, quite incidentally, exhilarated and happy to leave the office for the open streets at five. The stories didn't seem too good. The war stories are spoiled with chauvinism, a legitimate weakness. I also found pitiful evidences of poorly informed snobbism, an exaggerated wish to impress my knowledge of Army prose upon the reader, and associated with this a tendency to use verbatim conversation rather than the remarks that should be made by my characters. Some of the best of it seems to be the set of descriptions of character: Emma

10

Boulanger had the soul of a housemaid, etc. This I picked up from Flaubert and it is showing signs of turning into a bad characteristic of generalization. I can use these set pieces if they are integrated into a crisis. My interim narrative style needs a lot of work. Love of sorts is reasonably well described. There are too many scornful and fine phrases.

❖

11   The strain of debt; the difficulty of trying to write one's way out of it. There are seven more days, six more days, etc. Once in New Hampshire for three months I tried unsuccessfully to rip a story out of my brain or to patch together a series of incisive notes with no success at all. I have at times been able to sweat out a story, at times I've failed.

12   It helps to be relaxed.

❖

13   There is a time to write and a time to walk and a time to reflect and a time to act and I come unwillingly to this journal today, wanting to do something less reflective and feeling that I sometimes strip myself of my most reasonable attributes, bent over this machine. However, any feeling of good health ought to be able to withstand a little looking into. . . .

► QUESTIONS TO CONSIDER

1. Basing your opinion on these journal entries, how would you describe Cheever as a person and as a writer? What does he think of himself and his work?

2. Why do you think Cheever is so negative and discouraged about his writing? Is he more or less negative than Whorton and Sanders, who at the time they were writing were young unpublished writers?

3. Cheever indicates in one of his entries that he is writing to get out of debt. Other than this economic purpose, what seems to motivate him to write?

4. Using the information provided by these journal entries, describe Cheever's writing process. Does it ever vary? When and how?

5. Why do you think Cheever kept a journal? What purpose did it serve? Who was his audience? Was he writing just for himself or did he anticipate that his journal would one day be published?

WRITING ACTIVITIES   ◀

Individual: Compare Cheever's writing process, as it is revealed in these entries, to your own.

Collaborative: Have one member of your group read aloud one entry from Whorton, Sanders, and Cheever. Then, as a group, discuss each one's writing **style and voice**. Write an imaginary conversation that might have taken place among Whorton, Sanders, and Cheever on the subject of writing. Try to make each character's voice distinctive. When you have finished writing your conversation, assign each character to a different member of your group and read your conversation aloud to the other members of your class.

STYLE AND VOICE, PAGE 596

Computer: For the conversation described in the collaborative activity, use your computers to conduct the dialogue between the characters. Working in pairs, with each person adopting the voice of one of the authors (Whorton, Sanders, or Cheever), talk to each other on the subject of writing, using the tone and style of your adopted author. If your computers are networked, you can conduct your dialogue through network mail. If not, you can exchange monitor screens or keyboards so you and your partner read each other's screens as you type, rather than reading your own screen.

❖❖❖❖❖

A WRITER'S DIARY

Virginia Woolf

Like John Cheever, the English novelist and essayist Virginia Woolf produced volumes of diaries during her lifetime. Her diaries are filled not only with glimpses of her daily life but also with musings and observations about herself as a writer—how she writes, what she has already written, what she plans to write. Clearly, Woolf used her diaries to explore as well as record ideas. In one entry, written on March 9, 1920, she imagines herself reading her own diaries years later:

*In spite of some tremors I think I shall go on with this diary for the
present. . . . I fancy old Virginia, putting on her spectacles to read
of March 1920, will decidedly wish me to continue.*

*The excerpts here from Woolf's diary were written over a period of two
years, from 1928 to 1930, during which time she thinks about and
then writes a novel she initially calls* The Moths *but later changes to*
The Waves. *As you read, notice how the novel takes shape in her mind
and then gradually becomes a written text.*

Saturday, August 12th, 1928

1   Shall I now continue this soliloquy, or shall I imagine an audience,
which will make me describe? This sentence is due to the book on
fiction which I am now writing—once more, O once more. It is a
hand to mouth book. I scribble down whatever I can think of about
Romance, Dickens etc. must hastily gorge on Jane Austen tonight and
dish up something tomorrow. All this criticism however may well be
dislodged by the desire to write a story. *The Moths* hovers somewhere
at the back of my brain. But Clive yesterday at Charleston said that
there were no class distinctions. We had tea from bright blue cups
under the pink light of the giant hollyhock. We were all a little
drugged with the country; a little bucolic I thought. It was lovely
enough—made me envious of its country peace; the trees all standing
securely—why did my eye catch the trees? The look of things has a
great power over me. Even now, I have to watch the rooks beating
up against the wind, which is high, and still I say to myself instinc-
tively "What's the phrase for that?" and try to make more and more
vivid the roughness of the air current and the tremor of the rook's
wing slicing as if the air were full of ridges and ripples and rough-
nesses. They rise and sink, up and down, as if the exercise rubbed
and braced them like swimmer's in rough water. But what a little I
can get down into my pen of what is so vivid to my eyes, and not
only to my eyes; also to some nervous fibre, or fanlike membrane in
my species.

Wednesday, November 28th, 1928

2   As for my next book, I am going to hold myself from writing till I have
it impending in me: grown heavy in my mind like a ripe pear; pen-
dant, gravid, asking to be cut or it will fall. *The Moths* still haunts me,
coming, as they always do, unbidden, between tea and dinner, while

L. plays the gramophone. I shape a page or two; and make myself
stop. Indeed I am up against some difficulties. Fame to begin with.
Orlando has done very well. Now I could go on writing like that—the
tug and suck are at me to do it. People say this was so spontaneous,
so natural. And I would like to keep those qualities if I could without
losing the others. But those qualities were largely the result of ignoring
the others. They came of writing exteriorly; and if I dig, must I not
lose them? And what is my own position towards the inner and the
outer? I think a kind of ease and dash are good—yes: I think even
externality is good; some combination of them ought to be possible.
The idea has come to me that what I want now to do is to saturate
every atom. I mean to eliminate all waste, deadness, superfluity: to
give the moment whole; whatever it includes. Say that the moment is a
combination of thought; sensation; the voice of the sea. Waste, deadness, come from the inclusion of things that don't belong to the
moment; this appalling narrative business of the realist: getting on
from lunch to dinner: it is false, unreal, merely conventional. Why
admit anything to literature that is not poetry—by which I mean saturated? Is that not my grudge against novelists? that they select nothing?
The poets succeeding by simplifying: practically everything is left out. I
want to put practically everything in: yet to saturate. That is what I
want to do in *The Moths.*

Thursday, March 28th, 1929

Perhaps I ought not to go on repeating what I have always said about   3
the spring. One ought perhaps to be forever finding new things to say,
since life draws on. One ought to invent a fine narrative style.
Certainly there are many new ideas always forming in my head. For
one, that I am going to enter a nunnery these next months; and let
myself down into my mind; Bloomsbury being done with. I am going
to face certain things. It is going to be a time of adventure and attack,
rather lonely and painful I think. But solitude will be good for a new
book. Of course, I shall make friends. I shall be external outwardly. I
shall buy some good clothes and go out into new houses. All the time
I shall attack this angular shape in my mind. I think *The Moths* (if that
is what I shall call it) will be very sharply cornered. I am not satisfied
though with the frame. There is this sudden fertility which may be
mere fluency. In old days books were so many sentences absolutely
struck with an axe out of crystal: and now my mind is so impatient, so
quick, in some ways so desperate.

Tuesday, May 28th, 1929

4   Now about this book, *The Moths.* How am I to begin it? And what is it
to be? I feel no great impulse; no fever; only a great pressure of difficulty. Why write it then? Why write at all? Every morning I write a little
sketch, to amuse myself. I am not saying, I might say, that these
sketches have any relevance. I am not trying to tell a story. Yet perhaps it might be done in that way. A mind thinking. They might be
islands of light—islands in the stream that I am trying to convey; life
itself going on. The current of the moths flying strongly this way. A
lamp and a flower pot in the centre. The flower can always be changing. But there must be more unity between each scene than I can find
at present. Autobiography it might be called. How am I to make one
lap, or act, between the coming of the moths, more intense than
another; if there are only scenes? One must get the sense that this is
the beginning; this the middle; that the climax—when she opens the
window and the moth comes in. I shall have the two different currents—the moths flying along; the flower upright in the centre; a perpetual crumbling and renewing of the plant. In its leaves she might see
things happen. But who is she? I am very anxious that she should have
no name. I don't want a Lavinia or a Penelope; I want "she." But that
becomes arty, Liberty greenery yallery somehow: symbolic in loose
robes. Of course I can make her think backwards and forwards; I can
tell stories. But that's not it. Also I shall do away with exact place and
time. Anything may be out of the window—a ship—a desert—London.

Sunday, June 23rd, 1929

5   However, I now begin to see *The Moths* rather too clearly, or at least
strenuously, for my comfort. I think it will begin like this: dawn; the
shells on a beach; I don't know—voices of cock and nightingale; and
then all the children at a long table—lessons. The beginning. Well, all
sorts of characters are to be there. Then the person who is at the table
can call out anyone of them at any moment; and build up by that person the mood, tell a story; for instance about dogs or nurses; or some
adventure of a child's kind; all to be very Arabian Nights; and so on:
this shall be childhood; but it must not be *my* childhood; and boats on
the pond; the sense of children, unreality; things oddly proportioned.
Then another person or figure must be selected. The unreal world
must be round all this—the phantom waves. The Moth must come in;
the beautiful single moth. Could one not get the waves to be heard all
through? Or the farmyard noises? Some odd irrelevant noises. She
might have a book—one book to read—another to write in—old let-

ters. Early morning light—but this need not be insisted on; because there must be great freedom from "reality." Yet everything must have relevance.

Wednesday, September 25th, 1929

Yesterday morning I made another start on *The Moths*, but that won't   6
be its title; and several problems cry out at once to be solved. Who thinks it? And am I outside the thinker? One wants some device which is not a trick.

Friday, October 11th, 1929

And I snatch at the idea of writing here in order not to write *Waves* or   7
Moths or whatever it is to be called. One thinks one has learnt to write quickly; and one hasn't. And what is odd, I'm not writing with gusto or pleasure: because of the concentration. I am not reeling it off; but sticking it down. Also, never, in my life, did I attack such a vague yet elaborate design; whenever I make a mark I have to think of its rela-tion to a dozen others. And though I could go on ahead easily enough, I am always stopping to consider the whole effect. In particu-lar is there some radical fault in my scheme? I am not quite satisfied with this method of picking out things in the room and being reminded by them of other things. Yet I can't at the moment divine anything which keeps so close to the original design and admits of movement. Hence, perhaps, these October days are to me a little strained and surrounded with silence.

Saturday, November 30th, 1929

I fill in this page, nefariously; at the end of a morning's work. I have   8
begun the second part of *Waves*—I don't know. I don't know. I feel that I am only accumulating notes for a book—whether I shall ever face the labour of writing it, God knows. From some higher station I may be able to pull it together—at Rodmell, in my new room. Reading the *Lighthouse* does not make it easier to write . . .

Sunday, January 12th, 1930

Sunday it is. And I have just exclaimed: "And now I can think of noth-   9
ing else." Thanks to my pertinacity and industry, I can now hardly stop making up *The Waves*. The sense of this came acutely about a week ago on beginning to write the *Phantom Party*: now I feel that I can rush on, after 6 months' hacking, and finish: but without the least cer-

tainty how it's to achieve any form. Much will have to be discarded: what is essential is to write fast and not break the mood—no holiday, no interval if possible, till it is done. Then rest. Then re-write.

Wednesday, April 23rd, 1930

10 This is a very important morning in the history of *The Waves*, because I think I have turned the corner and see the last lap straight ahead. I think I have got Bernard into the final stride. He will go straight on now, and then stand at the door: and then there will be a last picture of the waves. We are at Rodmell and I daresay I shall stay on a day or two (if I dare) so as not to break the current and finish it. O Lord and then a rest; and then an article; and then back again to this hideous shaping and moulding. There may be some joys in it all the same.

Tuesday, April 29th, 1930

11 And I have just finished, with this very nib-ful of ink, the last sentence of *The Waves*. I think I should record this for my own information. Yes, it was the greatest stretch of mind I ever knew; certainly the last pages; I don't think they flop as much as usual. And I think I have kept starkly and ascetically to the plan. So much I will say in self-congratu-lation. But I have never written a book so full of holes and patches; that will need re-building, yes, not only re-modelling. I suspect the structure is wrong. Never mind. I might have done something easy and fluent; and this is a reach after that vision I had, the unhappy sum-mer—or three weeks—at Rodmell, after finishing the *Lighthouse*.

P.M.   And I think to myself as I walk down Southampton Row, "And I have given you a new book."

▶   QUESTIONS TO CONSIDER

1. In the first entry, Woolf mentions that a new novel *(The Moths)* "hovers somewhere in the back of [her] brain." How many months does Woolf spend thinking about the novel before she actually begins to write? How does her construction of her mental text pre-pare her for the construction of the written text?

2. Woolf seems to construct a text by focusing first on different images rather than characters and plots. What are the dominant images that shape her mental text?

3. What role does Woolf's diary seem to assume in the construction of this novel?

4. Woolf was forty-eight years old when she finished *The Waves*, an older and more experienced writer than Cheever was when he wrote the entries we included from his journal. How does Woolf's journal reflect her maturity and experience as a writer?

WRITING ACTIVITIES

Individual: Select an idea from Woolf's diary that surprises you or contradicts your impression of how novelists write. In a journal entry, identify the idea you selected and explore why the idea surprises you.

Collaborative: Outline a schedule that reflects the construction of Woolf's novel (i.e., when did she begin it, how much time did she spend thinking about it, writing it, and rewriting it?).

Computer: Freewrite on screen about how you think using a computer would have changed Woolf's writing process.

❖❖❖❖❖

THE DIARIES OF LORD LUGARD

Frederick Lugard

 *From November 1889 to December 1890, Lord Lugard, an English adventurer, explorer, and big-game hunter, was employed by the Imperial British East Africa Company to command an expedition to Uganda. Lugard led a caravan that explored the routes in this region and established a series of stations. One of his responsibilities was to submit to the Company regular reports and maps of the region he was exploring. Lugard kept detailed accounts of his experiences in East Africa in a series of diaries, which were published after his death. In the following excerpts from one of these diaries, he describes the adverse circumstances he endured as he was writing one*

of his routine reports. As you read, notice the pleasure that Lugard seems to take in his writing task even though he is plagued by absolutely dreadful working conditions. If anyone ever had a good excuse for not writing, it was Lord Lugard.

1 . . . my left arm is now in a *very* bad state, a large purple lump has formed (*above* the wound strangely) and throbs and smarts dreadfully. It will burst if not lanced for it appears to be separate from the open channel thro' which a small amount of matter is daily discharged since I left England. The doctor wants to cut it open and extract dead bone. I declined, with thanks. I prefer nature to take her course to be[ing] experimented upon by young doctors, and the fact of the abscess being *above* the wound makes me think it *possible* that it arises from an inflammation of the sinews only, due to over-use, and exertion, and bad living, but I *think* there is dead bone. I have to wear it in a sling and it is of course quite useless, and very painful. So I should not be able to do much in the swimming line in case of an upset!

2 Now, however, I hope to sit tight here and work hard at the map and report. I have got into a spare room in a wooden house, but the situation is so exposed that it rocks with the constant hurricane, and I can rarely open door or window or everything is blown away, and the rain drives in. Consequently the ventilation is very bad, and the doctor says I am poisoning myself with Carbonic Acid gas!—which accounts for chippiness and headache.

3 I paid off the men who brought in my things. That scoundrel Matari, who up to the day we got here was so keen to redeem himself, and whom I brought down partly on that account, finding his master had gone into the interior declined to pay the ransom and claimed his full pay. After all I have done for him, and understanding as he does the whole question, it is 'base ingratitude.' However I did not feel justified in withholding the money, tho' it was only due to the fact that I told his master he had agreed to pay the ransom that he was not seized when down at the coast before. So he has more than stultified me, and made me appear a liar to the Arabs. I almost regret now I did not withhold the money, but I told him not to let me see his face again unless he wanted me to go for him &c.!

4 My little cat gets on wonderfully, it is as savage as a tiger at feeding time, and can't be touched. But at other times it is very affectionate and licks my hand and knows me, . . . I 'correct' it pretty severely (with my hand or a slipper) continually for it must learn obedience, and *must fear* me. As it is, a guttural sound of disapproval from me causes it to drop any mischief and scamper away, or prepare itself for

a fight if it will not part with its object. Then, after a good licking, it is conquered and retires and a minute or two afterwards has clean forgotten all about it—quite unlike the dog tribe in this respect. No amount of licking will cow it, and it will fight with teeth and claws a long time before giving in, and forget immediately! I am very fond of it indeed.

My skins are full of insects, and much spoilt. It is impossible to get them thoroughly dried in this pouring rain, and I am afraid they will not be worth anything by the time they get to England after all my trouble. I gave Mackenzie a good slab of the rhino hide for a little table. The big tortoise shell is a failure. All the pieces of 'tortoise' are coming off in sections, and the shell is merely of bone. The horns and heads are being macerated in water.   5

Hard at work at the map and report. Have completed the latter, and sent it to be copied. The map is made under great difficulties. The ink is thick, the light so bad I can hardly see, the house rocks with the wind, and I am interrupted every moment—so much so that nearly all of it has been done by lamp light at night. I have, however, a huge drawing board, and a piece of tracing paper which takes in the whole thing, and am making a nice bit of work of it, spite of difficulties. The Sabaki and route run diagonally from one corner to the other. In the large space left empty at the top right hand side, I have put three square spaces about 12 inches by 14 inches each, for the three plans of forts which I have made. That of Machakos I have put in, the other two, one of Makongeni and one of the intermediate forts, I have not time for nor have I the accurate measurements. Below there were tables of notes on the country around the stockades, reasons for selecting these points, structure of stockades &c. In the left bottom corner was the scale &c. and a long table of the bearings. I completed both the map (to this point) and the report by the return of the steamer on the [blank in diary].   6

QUESTIONS TO CONSIDER ◀

1. What are the conditions under which Lord Lugard is writing his report? Which of these conditions seem to you the most distracting?

2. What does Lugard's attitude toward these adverse conditions seem to be? How do they affect his writing task? What is his attitude toward the report and map he is constructing? Does Lugard view this writing task as a chore or does he seem to enjoy this work?

3. Who is the audience for Lugard's report? Do you think he imagines an audience for his diary? Support your answer with evidence from the entries you read.

4. How does Lugard's journal differ in purpose, content, and tone from those written by Whorton, Sanders, Woolf, and Cheever?

▶ WRITING ACTIVITIES

Individual: Freewrite about distractions or conditions that have discouraged or prevented you from writing at some time in the past and tell how you overcame them.

Collaborative: Discuss Lugard's attitude toward writing and how it differs from that of the other writers included in this chapter. Whorton, Sanders, Cheever, and Woolf all mention some distractions or difficulties that interfere with their writing. Make a list of these distractions and identify those that seem to be legitimate reasons for procrastination as opposed to excuses.

Computer: Type a list of writing distractions from your individual freewriting activity into a computer file. Then, using the block and move features of your word-processing program, create a brief outline in which you identify several categories (e.g., real reasons for not writing, legitimate distraction, fanciful distractions, mere excuses). Next, expand your outline into a brief essay on writing procrastination.

❖❖❖❖❖

W R I T I N G   T O   E X P L O R E

When you write to explore, there are no rules. In fact, one of the car-dinal guidelines of writing to explore is that anything goes. You don't have to worry about making errors or even making sense. You are writing to see what happens—what you know, remember, or think about a subject. Written explorations are musings, unchartered journeys, experiments and, as such, should not be structured or constrained. Just try to discover as much as possible.

Understanding the Guidelines

Don't be intimidated by the idea of writing without rules. Written ex-plorations, like freewriting exercises, are not supposed to be perfect, as you can see from this chapter's reading selections. Three suggestions can help you write to explore, especially if you have never tried it before:

- ❖ Take risks.
- ❖ Get the details down.
- ❖ More is better.

TAKE RISKS.   When you write to explore, don't play it safe. Forget the rules, experiment, surprise yourself. For instance, take the side of an argument with which you would normally disagree. Try out a new writing voice. Write about something you usually avoid thinking about. The whole idea of writing to explore is to see what happens. If you try to be careful and constrained, not much will happen. If you let your-self be adventuresome and free, you may make some exciting discov-eries about your subject or yourself as a writer.

GET THE DETAILS DOWN.   The most valuable part of what you write in a journal is not the big generalization ("My last essay was terrible!") but the small details ("My essay consisted of about fifteen different ideas stuck together in two impossibly long paragraphs"). Details feed read-ers' minds, forming images and recreating experiences. Details feed readers' imaginations, encouraging them to form images and recreate in their minds their own experiences. Collectively, details often lead you to discover a generalization that can evolve into a sound argu-ment. On her first visit to Mexico, overcome by this exotic new land, Anne Lindbergh wrote this in her diary:

> The best I can do is to piece together painstakingly the small superficial details, all—everything I can remember, everything no matter how little—and blindly hope that a miracle will happen, that this conglomerate, patched collection of fragments may ignite somehow—at least for me—and that some glimmering of the indescribable feeling may be relit in me.
>
> (*Bring Me a Unicorn:* 88)

If you write vaguely and nonspecifically in your journal, the entries may not make a lot of sense to you or anyone else when they are read later. At the time you are writing, you may know exactly what you mean when you say that something is great or dreadful, but later you will need the details. You won't be able to make much use of vague generalizations in the future, and settling for them now will not improve your present writing skills. Using specific details, on the other hand, will benefit you as both present writer and future reader. Whatever your subject, get the details down when you write to explore.

MORE IS BETTER.   Force yourself to go beyond your usual length limits, to write more than you initially think you can or normally do. First attempts at writing to explore can be obvious and trite, little more than conventional responses. When you force yourself to keep writing, however, you begin to produce ideas that go beyond the simple and superficial. So probe deeply into your subject by continuing to write even after you think you have emptied your mind of everything you have to say on the subject. The more you write and the more often you write, the more likely you are to learn more about yourself, your writing, and your world.

W R I T I N G   A S S I G N M E N T

Begin your journal (either in a notebook or on a computer disk) by describing your best or worst experience with writing. This experience may have occurred in school or out, it may pertain to something you were required to write or something you wrote because you wanted to, it may concern something you wrote recently or a long time ago.

Planning Your Text

Begin this assignment by brainstorming. Quickly list as many different writing experiences as you can remember, beginning with the earliest (a Mother's Day card you labored over when you were six) and working toward the present (a senior term paper in your last high school English course or a letter of application for a job). Then review this list, thinking about which of these experiences were good and which were bad. Perhaps in the fifth grade you had to write a research paper on the Olympic Games and in the process became interested in gymnastics. Or maybe you enjoyed writing for the school newspaper when you were in high school. On the other hand, perhaps you were once forced to stay after school and write on the board "I will not chew gum in school" five hundred times or to write thank-you notes to all of your relatives each Christmas when you were a child. As you review your list, think about what made these experiences good or bad (see **invention**).

INVENTION, PAGE 529

Constructing Your Text

DRAFTING.   Once you have selected an experience you want to write about, write as much as you can on the subject. Write quickly and steadily, not worrying about anything other than how much you can recall about this experience. Write until you have squeezed your memory dry. Try to remember how you felt and describe the experience as completely and exactly as you can, including every specific detail you can remember about the incident.

READING.   Read what you have written, trying to picture in your mind the experience as it occurred. Have you captured the feelings you had when this experience took place? How do you feel now about this experience? Has it affected your attitude toward yourself as a writer in any way?

REVISING.   Because this is a journal entry, you may not want to revise it. If you are not satisfied, however, revise what you have written—for example, adding more details or explaining more clearly and specifically what happened and how you felt.

Editing Your Text

In future assignments you will edit your written text, but this assignment requires nothing other than recording in your journal your memory of this experience and how it affected you. Later you may want to reread this entry to see if your attitudes about writing and yourself as a writer have changed.

Front porch of the home of author Flannery O'Connor.
Glynne Robinson Betts/Photo Researchers

3

WRITING TO RECONSTRUCT EXPERIENCE

One writes out of one thing only—one's own experience.

JAMES BALDWIN

One of the oldest and most compelling reasons for writing is to reconstruct experiences in words. Long before they could write, people reconstructed their experiences in gestures and oral language, narrating stories about what they had done and describing what they had seen or how they felt.

NARRATION, PAGE 558

DESCRIPTION, PAGE 456

Although occasionally writers use one and not the other, **narration** and **description** nearly always occur in combination. Writers narrating stories often describe scenes or sounds or emotions. They may occasionally use description by itself, for example, in a poem or a description of a mechanism, but it occurs most often with other types of discourse, especially narration.

You automatically use narration and description to weave the stories you tell, probably without conscious awareness of what you are doing rhetorically or linguistically. Telling stories is as natural as talking. That is, you don't think, "I'm going to tell a story now." You just tell it. Like any other familiar routine of daily life, you have internalized the patterns and conventions associated with storytelling.

Almost all discourse, both written and oral, is based to some extent on reconstructions of experience. From birth, you have been immersed in the stories family and friends tell, the stories you see on television and film, the stories you read in books and magazines. In this chapter, writers reconstruct their experience of holidays, some familiar, others not.

Why are stories so important to tell and listen to? To write and read? One reason is that stories—both those you create and those you read and hear—help you to understand your own experiences. Because stories, or narratives, are reconstructions of experience, they enable you to reflect on your experiences and thus to make some meaning of your life.

Reconstructions of experience take many different forms and serve both aesthetic and pragmatic purposes. Recollections of experience such as memoirs, personal experience essays, and autobiographies serve primarily aesthetic purposes; that is, they exist for their own sake much as a piece of sculpture or a musical composition does. Even more clearly aesthetic are novels, plays, short stories, and poems—many of which are also, at least indirectly, based on personal experience. In contrast, reconstructions of experience such as travelogues and diaries have pragmatic purposes: A travelogue provides readers with information; a diary provides a record of the writer's experiences.

You may not recognize some narratives as stories. The scientist's account of how a seed evolves into a plant is a story. So is the historian's reconstruction of a historical event, the psychologist's case study of a client, the manager's report of what happened to sales, and the engineer's analysis of a mechanical process. Other reconstructions of experience take forms that may not even *look* like stories. For example, résumés reconstruct a person's professional experiences and many poems and song lyrics reconstruct human experience.

Because life is filled with stories, you probably feel quite comfortable with them. A technical report or a textbook or a set of instructions or a poem may be intimidating, but even if a story doesn't begin with the words "Once upon a time," you usually recognize it almost immediately as a story and know intuitively how to read it. You know, for example, it will be based on chronological order, moving through time and relating events in a more or less accurate reflection of the experiences it seeks to reconstruct.

READING RECONSTRUCTIONS OF EXPERIENCE

In reading texts that reconstruct a writer's experiences, you may have various purposes. Sometimes you want to share vicariously in the writer's experiences, especially if they seem exciting or amusing or if they remind you of experiences you have had yourself. At other times, you want to learn from the writer's experiences, to gain information or insights that the writer articulates or that you can infer. At still other times, you may read about a writer's experiences because they are familiar and therefore comforting. For example, certain types of experience have special meanings that go beyond the actual plot. Success stories and love stories tend to make us feel hopeful; war stories often inspire feelings of patriotism and pride; and stories about families remind us of those who created and cared for us.

Your purpose in reading about a writer's experiences will, therefore, determine to some extent how you read a text. Reading for pleasure usually means that you read in a more casual and less focused way than you do if you are reading for information. However, whatever your purpose or purposes, when you read to reconstruct experiences, you are always viewing these experiences from the writer's perspective. The writer, however objective he or she may strive to be, has constructed a personal, subjective version of what happened. As a reader, therefore, you must read to understand not only what has happened but also how the writer has interpreted the real event and shaped it into a narrative. That is, the writer always stands between you and the reality of the subject; the narrative you read can never be an absolutely accurate representation of the events that occurred.

Recognizing Objective and Subjective Points of View

Your awareness of the writer's role as interpreter is an important factor in how effectively you read reconstructions of experience. Some writers reconstruct their experiences *subjectively*. What they write is filtered through their own experiences and unabashedly viewed from their own perspective. In this chapter's reading selections, Jesse Stuart and Maya Angelou make no attempt to be objective. One of their purposes here is to reveal their personal views about the experiences they are relating. In effect, they are the main characters in the stories they tell. They want you to understand their points of view and make no attempt to minimize their subjectivity. Lillian Ross, on the other hand, appears to be very objective and unbiased as she begins her account of Halloween but becomes increasingly subjective as she continues. Her apparent objectivity is a strategy. Kenneth Read is perhaps the most objective of all the writers included in this chapter, but even he does not attempt to efface himself entirely. Although his account is part of an anthropological study intended for readers who want to know more about different cultures and how they are alike and different, Read is very much a character in the story he tells—but a less important character than Stuart or Angelou in the stories they tell.

One question you should ask yourself when you read narratives based on the writer's experiences is just how important objectivity is. Do you think a narrative account is less valuable if it focuses primarily on the writer's own reactions rather than on the event itself? Again, the issue here is mainly one of purpose. For example, Angelou's purpose in describing the African celebration is not just to provide readers with details about the celebration—so different from our own Thanksgiving rituals—but to tell of her response to it, of how she was caught up in the event and became a participant rather than merely an observer. Although she doesn't articulate a **thesis**, or main idea, her story sug-THESIS, PAGE 599gests that she identifies with these Africans and their unfamiliar rituals perhaps even more than she does the familiar but in many ways more alien rituals of white-dominated North American society. Angelou serves her purposes by moving from a rather detached, objective stance initially to an obviously subjective response as she relates her own emotional reactions to the celebration.

Should writers be objective or subjective in telling their stories? That depends on their purpose. Either stance is legitimate. A problem exists only if writers *pretend* to be objective and readers do not detect the pretense—do not understand this relationship between a writer's presence in a text and his or her purpose. If you believe a writer is objective but that writer is only pretending to be objective, you may not read a text accurately. Such a misreading is most likely if the writer uses as narrator an objective persona (character) who seems to represent the writer. In such cases, readers may attribute the persona's objectivity to the writer.

Likewise, as a reader, you need to realize that total objectivity is a myth, that all writers are subjective because they can view experience only from their own perspective even if they are writing something as seemingly objective as a scientific report. Writers may eliminate all references to themselves and report the experience as if they are relating only the facts, but reconstructions of experience are essentially subjective however the writer presents them. When you read a writer's version of what happened, be aware of the writer and his or her purposes as a significant presence in the narrative. Often, the writer's presence is your main reason for reading such a narrative. You are not primarily interested in the events being described so much as you are interested in the writer—what he or she felt or thought or did. For example, most of the authors included in this chapter are well known writers, celebrities of a sort, and they provoke interest for that very reason. On the other hand, student writer Warren Slay, who wrote about his family's Thanksgiving, is not yet famous; therefore, his story provokes interest largely because many readers can identify in some way with the experience he reconstructs. Not incidentally, Slay's story is interesting primarily because he is very much a presence in it—not as a famous person but as a person whose voice is real and believable.

Recognizing Narration as Argument

In reading reconstructions of experience, be aware that writers usually have a purpose beyond simply telling a good story. Although they may not state a thesis explicitly, a controlling idea usually shapes their story and the way they tell it. They are, in a sense, trying to convince readers of something they believe is important. Among the authors included in this chapter, Stuart believes it is important for a family to have continuity and a sense of the past. Galarza believes it is important for people to understand how it feels to grow up in the midst of an alien culture. Ross believes children are growing up too fast and are acquiring the wrong values. Angelou and Read believe it is important for people to understand and respect cultures other than their own. If you read reconstructions of experience merely as stories, you may be amused or entertained or interested or even enlightened, but you may also miss the larger point. Storytellers often have more than a single purpose, and the less obvious purposes may be the most important.

The following reading selections all narrate the writer's personal experience with a holiday. Although we like to think of holidays as happy affairs, times when families get together and people feel good about themselves and their lives, holidays can also be difficult times. Many people dread holidays or become depressed or even ignore them because they are so painful. Other people look forward to holidays only to be disappointed when the reality does not meet their expectations. Thus the following reading selections are not all stories of families happily celebrating joyous occasions together, nor are they all accounts of traditional American holidays. Rather they tell of people's often complex emotions in response to holidays, describe possibly unfamiliar holidays, and explore relationships between holidays and the cultures in which they exist.

DECEMBER: FROM THE YEAR OF MY REBIRTH

Jesse Stuart

Jesse Stuart was a schoolteacher, administrator, and writer. Known as a regional writer, he wrote primarily of the people who live in the mountains of eastern Kentucky, capturing in his fiction and poetry not only the struggles and hardships of their lives but also their humor and humanity. During his period of recuperation following a heart attack, Stuart wrote a memoir entitled The Year of My Rebirth. *In the following excerpt, he writes of a quiet Christmas he spent with his wife Naomi and daughter Jane that year. Notice as you read how Stuart focuses on his fireplace in this account, using it as both a symbol of his family's endurance and a unifying feature of his discourse.*

I have just closed the kitchen door so Jane and Naomi Deane won't   1
hear the noise of my typewriter. I am afraid if they hear me writing
into the night they will not be able to sleep. Then there is another

thing I would like to do by closing this door. I can't, but I like to pretend. I'd like to close this door to preserve in this kitchen our happiness, our love, the words that we have spoken tonight. I'd like to keep it all in this kitchen fastened up forever. I wish there could be another time when all this would unfold to other ears like voices from a record. In some future day and time I'd like others to hear the words spoken, the Christmas carols sung, the laughter, friendship, and family love that lived before our little fireplace in the corner of our kitchen tonight.

2   I know that I cannot reproduce these sounds, this love, with cold symbols on a printed page. But I am going to sit here and write down what I can. Actually nothing extraordinary happened at all. Our family of three lived for one evening in our kitchen.

3   First, about our kitchen. We have a fireplace in the corner. We don't have to have a fireplace now. We could close it, for we don't need it for either cooking or heat. We have hot-water heat which comes through convectors around our kitchen wall and produces an efficient even heat all over our house. Our four fireplaces could never do this. We know this is true, for in winters here, before the heater was installed, we had all four fireplaces going, and parts of this house were still cold.

4   But we will never close up any of the fireplaces, even the one in the kitchen. We like to sit before an open fire to watch the flames leap up from the wood, to warm our feet on the fender. We like to pull the red-hot coals from the grate and cook cornbread in a skillet, covered with a lid to hold the steam inside to give the cornbread flavor. We like to roast sweet potatoes, which we grow in our small creek bottoms, in the ashes. We like to hold an old-fashioned popcorn popper over the flame and watch the little grains jump up in the pan to pop open like big white flakes of falling snow. We like to boil sorghum with butter and pour it over the popcorn, which makes the best molasses popcorn balls in the world. Once we used to reboil our sorghum into a thick syrup, then put butter on our hands and pull it while it was still warm into long sticks of brown sorghum candy. We shaped it into brown twists similar to those of tobacco.

5   Sometimes we roast apples, which come from our trees, by putting them in a pan and putting the lid down tight under hot ashes. We like to sit a comfortable distance back from the fire holding long willow wands with marshmallows on their tips over the blaze until they start turning brown. We laugh and talk as we watch them swell

with heat. When they catch fire, we jerk our long wands back in a hurry and blow the flames out.

Now, how can one do this sort of thing with furnace heat, or with coal in a grate? This is the reason why we have not closed any of our four fireplaces. They will not be closed as long as Naomi and I continue to live here. If Jane lives on here after we go, since she has grown up in the tradition of the family around the open fireplace in the evening, I believe she will always have some wood to burn and a little fire, even if she is living in the year 2000 and is warmed by atomic heat.

6

On this very spot where I am using this typewriter, my mother and father used to sit around a table in their kitchen. Four of their seven children, for two were dead and one was born later, sat with them. Here we planned and talked and laughed. Only we didn't have an open fireplace. We had a big cookstove we called a wood range. It burned wood like a fireplace, and heat danced above its flat top like sunlight over a tin roof on a midsummer afternoon. Dad used to cut the stovewood for this range, and I carried armfuls inside the kitchen and put them inside the woodbox. In the mornings while Mom got breakfast, I used to go to the kitchen long before daylight and sit on the woodbox close to the stove while the kitchen got warm. But after the stove got really hot, we couldn't stay in this kitchen, no matter if it was twenty below outside, unless we raised a window to let the heat out.

7

Naomi and I rebuilt the fireplace and chimney in the old living room after we began housekeeping here. We figured that where this hearth stands is a great tradition of family life around the open fire. At least twenty families have lived here in the century and a half this house has stood. I can remember eight of these families myself. We estimated that six or seven thousand people, young and old, have sat before a blazing winter fire here and laughed, talked, joked, ate, and lived life joyously and fully in the years that have passed.

8

Before we tore down the old stone chimney, made by Eric Brickey, a stonemason of another century, the elements had eroded many of these large stones until they were so thin there was danger of the chimney's falling. Heat escaping from this chimney melted the snow for a radius of twenty feet around. This frightened us, so we tore it down and replaced it with one made of bricks. But this was not breaking any old tradition, for the stone chimney had replaced an even earlier one made of sticks and mud. And the bricklayer

9

who made our chimney, Sam Brickey, was a grandson of Old Eric, who had built the stone chimney and fireplace almost a hundred years ago.

10 I wish the doors had been shut for each family in the century and a half past, and we could open them to look in on evenings of long ago when a man with buckskin moccasins on his feet and a coonskin cap on his head stood before the wood fire in a fireplace built of clay and sticks. I wish we could see his wife and their young children, the long rifle hanging to a joist and a powder horn on the wall. Captain George Naylor Davis (1781-1847) belonged to that time. He trained a company of men near here and took them by boat down the Ohio and Mississippi to help Andrew Jackson in the Battle of New Orleans. Later he served on Andrew Jackson's staff, for the General took a fancy to him. Now Captain George Naylor Davis lies buried in Brick Union's rural churchyard, which is six miles from here. There were no roads then, no schools, no work but hunting, fishing, clearing of land, building, and trading furs with Indians.

11 Then, like turning the pages of a book, I would like to see each family that shared this fireplace up until the present. I myself can remember back to 1915.

12 Eric Brickey made the big chimney and fireplace so large it took a mule to pull a backstick for it. It took several men to roll one over the floor to get it in behind the andirons. Sam Brickey told us that his grandfather, Eric Brickey, called his stone chimneys, so many of which he built in this area, his "living monuments." Sam, in turn, called our new brick chimney one of his "living monuments." His living monument, too, would pass away when another age developed new chimney materials. But the tradition of the open fire would not pass away if we could do anything to keep it alive.

13 If we could close the kitchen doors to perpetuate what took place before our fireplace tonight, here is what we would pass along to some future inhabitants of this house.

14 It was after dinner, and we were drying the dishes. Naomi had already brought extra wood for the fire and filled the brass kettle that stands in the corner. I stopped drying long enough to put an extra stick of wood on the grate.

15 Naomi joined Jane in a Christmas carol, and while we finished the dishes and the flames leaped up through the wood in our kitchen fireplace, we sang "Silent Night." Christmas was a week or two off, but its spirit always precedes it. I remembered that this same song was

sung before this same fireplace in the years from 1915 to 1918. And I am sure others sang it here long before then.

We sang "God Rest Ye Merry, Gentlemen" as we sat before the fire. Naomi got up to find a nutcracker, and I went to the woodshed to fetch a peck of hickory nuts and the two bricks which we keep for this purpose. I laid them on the hearth. Naomi was going to bake a hickory-nut cake, and we had to have the kernels. Jane used one of the bricks while I used the other to crack the hickory nuts. We put them in Naomi's lap, and she took the kernels from the nuts. We then threw the nuts, clean of their kernels, into the blazing fire.   16

We worked slowly cracking our thin-shelled hickory nuts. Naomi, Jane, and I had gathered them in October from a tall hickory tree that grows about a hundred yards up the valley at the edge of the pine grove. We had gathered ourselves plenty for the long winter but had left enough for our squirrels. Now, by the time we had filled the crock with hickory-nut kernels, we had cracked a peck. We had sung all the Christmas carols we knew, including some we didn't know too well. Jane had recited "The Night before Christmas" without a halt. We had each recited a poem. Then Jane popped corn for herself and her mother, and we finished with an evening cup of tea and a piece of angel-food cake.   17

That was all, except for the talk and the gaiety and the love that I will not try to put down here.   18

Now Jane and Naomi are fast asleep. I have been sitting here thinking about life in front of this fireplace over the century and a half. The fire in the fireplace is now a bed of embers.   19

QUESTIONS TO CONSIDER ◀

1. As Stuart begins this account, he is quite explicit about his intention to recreate what went on in his kitchen on this particular evening a few days before Christmas. And he follows through on this intention, reconstructing in great detail the activities of the evening. But he also achieves a larger purpose, one he does not state explicitly. As he tells of how his "family of three lived for one evening" in their kitchen, he also reveals much about the history of his family and its values. What values does Stuart emphasize most in his account of his family, past and present?

NARRATION, PAGE 558

DESCRIPTION, PAGE 456

2. Notice Stuart's skillful use of both **narration** and **description**. Reread the first few pages to identify which sentences or paragraphs are descriptive and which are narrative. Then reread these pages once more, this time reading just the narrative portions. How effective is the narration without the description? What does the description add?

3. In reconstructing his experiences in this memoir, do you think Stuart's purpose is primarily aesthetic or pragmatic? That is, does this story help the reader accomplish anything or is it rather an aesthetic artifact, something a reader appreciates or enjoys reading? What was your reaction to it?

4. How does Stuart's use of specific details and concrete language contribute to his narrative? For example, in the fourth paragraph he describes in detail some of the foods the family cooks in their fireplace. What effect would it have on this narrative if Stuart merely stated that they used the fireplace for cooking?

▶   **W R I T I N G   A C T I V I T I E S**

Individual: Write a journal entry in which you reconstruct in careful detail one particular holiday you remember well. Focus on a single detail, as Stuart focuses on the fireplace, making this detail the central image in your narrative.

Collaborative: Working with a group of your peers, discuss and list the multiple purposes that Stuart may have had in writing this story as part of his memoir. Then explain in a brief paragraph what you think his main purpose is, illustrating your explanation with evidence from the story. Compare your explanation with those of the other groups.

Computer: Using a computer, make two outlines. First, on the left side of the screen, outline the story that Stuart tells of the evening he spent in the kitchen with his family. Next, on the right side of the screen, outline the history of the fireplaces. Most word-processing programs allow you to create columns, which will make this process much easier. Or, if your word-processing program has a split-screen feature, you can use it to set up your two outlines. Then, viewing the two outlines simultaneously, determine how Stuart combines the two stories by making one outline of the two. Why do you think Stuart intertwined the two stories in the way he did? Do you see other possibilities?

❖❖❖❖❖

HALLOWEEN PARTY

Lillian Ross

Lillian Ross, a longtime regular contributor to The New Yorker, *wrote this piece about Halloween for the magazine's "Talk of the Town" column. In it Ross gives a mother's perspective of a child's holiday. As you read, notice how Ross describes in precise detail the expenses incurred in giving a Halloween party, how each guest is costumed, and what each says and does. Compare this seemingly objective account to the subjective narrative of Stuart.*

A letter has arrived from a woman we know: 1

My thirteen-year-old son gave a Halloween costume party for a   2
bunch of boys and girls. I became his financier as he talked endlessly about his Count Dracula costume. Count Dracula seems to have been the most popular Halloween costume for the past ten years—a black satin Count Dracula cape ($18.95), Count Dracula fangs ($1.25), clown whiteface makeup ($2), and Zauders stage blood ($2). The menu for the party included fried chicken, spaghetti, Cokes, salad, and cupcakes with orange or chocolate icing (cost per guest: $7). The candy, for visiting trick-or-treaters as well as for the guests, was orange and black jelly beans, sugar pumpkins, Candy Corn, Tootsie Rolls, Raisinets, Almond Joys, Nestlé Crunch, Baby Ruths, Milky Ways, Heide Jujyfruits, Peanut Chews, and Cracker Jacks (total: $38.65). My son also had eight cookies, six inches in diameter and decorated with black cats ($1.25 each); eight little plastic pumpkins full of hard candies, each with a trembly plastic spider on top ($2.50 each); eight orange-colored balloons that blew up to resemble cats (eighty-five

cents each); eight orange-colored lollipops with jack-o'-lantern faces (seventy cents each); a large paper tablecloth showing a black witch standing over a black caldron with spiders popping out of the caldron ($2.25); matching napkins ($1.10); matching paper cups ($2); matching paper plates ($1.75); a "HAPPY HALLOWEEN" sign ($1.25); a dancing skeleton ($3.99); something called a Happy Spider ($4); a classic jack-o'-lantern, made of a real pumpkin ($4, plus labor). Total investment in props: $181.59. Total investment of labor in jack-o'-lantern, kitchen cleanup, and laundry: $35. Total investment in emotion and puzzlement: indeterminable.

3   I watch the guests arrive. The first one, A, comes as Darth Vader, of "Star Wars." B comes as Luke Skywalker, of "Star Wars." C comes as The Incredible Hulk. D comes as a tramp. E comes as a ghost. F comes as a ballerina. G comes, in one of her mother's old evening gowns, as Bette Midler. All are in an advanced stage of hysteria. A pulls at C's costume. G immediately starts throwing sugar pumpkins at E. They've given themselves an hour before they move the party out to ring doorbells and see what they get. They tear into the fried chicken, most of them eating three bites and wasting the rest. They sprinkle jelly beans on the chicken and on the spaghetti. They pick at the spaghetti, which is on the menu because my son said everybody likes spaghetti. They eat it one strand at a time, dropping a strand on the floor for each strand they consume. They gulp down the Cokes, another "must"—their appetite for the caffeine insatiable. And what are they talking about, these eighth graders who are eying each other fishily? They are talking about their *careers*. They are talking about getting into Exeter. They are talking about Yale and Yale Law School. They are talking about how to get in here and how to get in there. They are talking about who makes more money, the president of Chase Manhattan or the president of General Motors. Nobody is talking kid talk. Nobody is talking about the present time and what to do with it. Nobody is talking about learning. Nobody sounds *young*. A, a pudgy boy who tries to find out the marks of every other child in his class, wants to be "a successful corporation lawyer." He doesn't say just "corporation lawyer." It's success that he's bent on. He informs my son that he intends to have more money than his uncle, who is a corporation lawyer in Philadelphia. Next, A tells my son that he wants to go to Exeter. Why? "Because Exeter is a stepping-stone to Harvard," he says. Not Exeter for the wonders of Exeter but Exeter because it will be useful *after* he leaves it.

B, with his mouth full of Almond Joy, is asking the others a question: "Do you want to be a little fish in a big pond or a big fish in a little pond?"

What has that got to do with getting an education? How about the excitement of learning algebra? How about the wonderful grammar teacher who showed you how to recognize the participle absolute? Why aren't you talking about your French teacher's getting you to speak French with an accent that would wow them in Paris? I want to butt in with my questions, but I keep my mouth shut.

Now A is talking. His mother, he is saying, has taken him rock climbing, because rock climbing is an impressive activity to put down as his "interest" on the application to Exeter.

"But you *hate* rock climbing!" says D, who is a mischief-maker with the face of an angel under his tramp makeup. "You hate to move your *ass*," D adds.

All right, who else is here? C, who is wearing a mask of The Incredible Hulk. C is the jock of the group. He has been in training since the age of two in the craft of giving nothing away. He's wary and tight and already immunized to the teeth against charity for its own sake. He, too, wants to be a corporation lawyer; so do B and D. The girls, though—the ballerina and Bette Midler—both want to be big-corporation presidents. They are both relaxed, being well aware of what women's lib has done for them. E, the ghost, is the only one with a simple costume, made of a sheet. A, talking to B, points out that E doesn't have to bother about a costume, because he's rich, very rich. His grandfather lives in Texas and owns real oil wells—not new ones but very old and very productive oil wells. E wants to be a movie director and has promised to give my son, who at the moment wants to be an actor, a starring part in his first movie. They are pals. Both of them are regarded with suspicion by the ones who want to be corporation lawyers.

What else are they saying? They're still talking about Exeter. Apparently, A is obsessed by Exeter—it is he who keeps bringing the conversation back to it.

"They ask you to write a 'personal letter' to them," this little busybody says. "They say, 'This letter should represent you as accurately as possible.' But then they tell you in the catalogue what they want, so all you have to do is tell it back to them."

C finally talks. "The way *you* always figure out what the teacher wants and give it right back to *him*," he says.

12   D squirts a little Coke at A, and the future lawyers get up and make for the door. They cram their loot bags with the orange and black jelly beans, the Candy Corn, the cookies, the trembly spiders, the balloons, the jack-o'-lantern lollipops, and the rest. They make a big point of thanking me loudly. The girls amble out, smiling knowledgeably at each other. E and my son run to catch up to them. They, too, thank me extravagantly. And they all go off, in their disguises, to do their tricks and get their treats. I am left wondering what it's all about.

▶   QUESTIONS TO CONSIDER

THESIS, PAGE 599   **1.** Ross does not state her **thesis** and ends her account of the party by saying, "I am left to wonder what it's all about." Yet her attitude is clear. How would you characterize her attitude toward Halloween? The party? The guests? What is Ross suggesting about the younger generation in general?

2. Is Ross as objective as she appears to be, or is she assuming this detached tone to create the illusion she is recording objectively and accurately the expenses and activities of this party—much as an accountant or reporter would do? What else does she do to create this illusion? Why does she want to create this illusion? How does it reinforce the point she is making about young people?

3. This narrative can be viewed as an argument that Halloween, and by extension all holidays, have become hopelessly commercialized. It can also be interpreted as an argument against the type of young people our society is producing. How does Ross portray young people? Is there a connection between her argument about the commercialization of holidays and her argument about young people? Does one reinforce the other, or does Ross weaken both arguments by combining them?

4. Ross uses a number of direct quotations in her narrative. How does her reproduction of the young people's comments and conversation strengthen her argument? Notice how she punctuates these direct quotations.

WRITING ACTIVITIES ◀

Individual: Write an account of a recent holiday, being as objective as you can by giving only the facts—the setting, what happened, who was there, what they did and said, and so on.

Collaborative: Working in your assigned group, compare your objective holiday descriptions. Then, generalizing from the information you have each included, write one statement that seems to be true of all holidays. Compare your statement with those composed by the other groups.

Computer: Enter into your computer or copy to a new file your objective account of a recent holiday (see Individual Writing Activity). Then revise that account so that it is subjective by using first-person point of view (I or we) and inserting specific details that provide readers with a sense of how you personally experienced this holiday.

❖❖❖❖❖

GRANDPA'S OLD ROCKER

Warren Slay

The student who wrote this essay grew up in a small town. His narrative of the last Thanksgiving he spent with his grandfather not only tells what happened on that particular day but also suggests why his grandfather was special to him. As you read this story, notice how Slay uses dialogue and specific details to reconstruct this occasion—to help his readers experience the occasion as he experienced it and to evoke the setting in which the story occurred.

The old house was packed with people. All three of my mother's   1
sisters and their families were there. It was Thanksgiving at Grandma and Grandpa's. All of the women were out in the kitchen. They were putting the food on Granny's old Masonite-topped table and laughing about who knows what. Most of the men, and us boys, were out on

the old wooden front porch talking about hunting and how to make more money. Most of us on the porch were clad in camouflage overalls, coveralls, orange caps, and rubber boots because we had just got back from hunting. Going hunting on Thanksgiving morning was a time-honored tradition among us.

2   Grandpa was sitting there in the old rocking chair he had made years ago. He was doing what he said was the only thing he was expert at, grinning and rocking. His old overalls were faded and a little too short, and his leather work boots looked like they had just about walked their last mile. It's not that he didn't have better clothes; he just didn't wear them. When Granny would get on him about it, he'd just say, "Annie Lee, I'm an old man. I can wear old clothes if I want to." He wasn't able to go hunting anymore, but he sat there and listened to our stories and told some pretty good ones himself.

3   Finally Granny shuffled to the door and said, "Coy, ya'll come eat." Then, we all got up and went to the kitchen. After someone said the blessing, we "men" fixed our plates and returned to the porch to eat and let Uncle Wayne finish his story, so we'd all quit wondering if he got unlost or not. After we finished, we gave all the scraps to Little Mike, my dog. Then the older men went into the small living room to watch football on the tiny black and white T.V. while all us little ones stayed outside in the yard to play.

4   That was the Thanksgiving of 1979. I was only seven, but I can still vaguely remember that Thanksgiving. A few of the missing parts have been filled in by stories from family, but I remember sitting on Grandpa's lap and talking to him after everyone else had left to go home. It was in conversations such as these that I learned many of the things a little boy should know—like how to catch gopher hole crickets and whistle.

5   It wasn't but a few months after this Thanksgiving that things changed. Grandpa got sick and just got worse until April 19th, when he passed on. At my young age I was not really affected by this happening. I was sad, and I knew I would miss him and all, but it wasn't until a few Thanksgivings later that I realized what I really had lost.

6   We all still gather at Grandma's as we have for years and years. Now, there are more grandkids and greatgrandkids than before, but we do the same things we have always done. The only difference is that Grandpa is not there.

7   I can't really say that Thanksgiving is a sad day for me now because all of the family is together and good old Grandma is still here, but I do catch myself staring at that old rocking chair every now and again. As I look back in my mind, there is a lot I have forgotten

about Grandpa Coy, but I still remember that Thanksgiving. So, when Thanksgiving rolls around now, I have those memories to fill the emptiness in Grandpa's old rocker.

QUESTIONS TO CONSIDER

1. How does Slay's emphasis on his grandfather's rocking chair compare to Stuart's use of the fireplace as a symbol? How many references to the chair can you find in the story?

2. One of the strongest features of this story is the writer's authentic voice. How does he achieve the impression that he is speaking directly and honestly to his readers?

3. Do you find this story too sentimental? That is, does the writer too obviously appeal to your emotions? Or do you like this quality of the story? Which images and statements contribute to the sentimentality? Do you view sentimentality as a positive or negative feature? Compare the degree of sentimentality in this story to that in Stuart's narrative. Can you come to any conclusions about when sentiment is appropriate?

4. In the first part of the story, the narrator is a young boy; in the last part he is a young man. How does Slay indicate this shift in time and perspective?

5. In his story Slay includes dialogue he remembers from that Thanksgiving Day. Whom does he quote? Do you think he remembered the exact words that were spoken? Is Slay able to suggest another person's voice when he quotes them? What does his use of dialogue add to his narrative?

WRITING ACTIVITIES

Individual: Write an evaluation of this narrative, pointing out both its strengths and its weaknesses.

Collaborative: As a group, discuss the strengths and weaknesses of this narrative. Do you find it more or less interesting than the selections by professional writers that are included in this chapter? Compose a note to the author, Warren Slay, suggesting specific ways he might revise his essay.

Computer: Working with a partner, select a topic and conduct an on-line dialogue. You can exchange disks or use a network program. Incorporate your computer conversation into a brief narrative, carefully punctuating each response to indicate who said what.

❖❖❖❖❖

THE SIXTEENTH OF SEPTEMBER

Ernesto Galarza

In Mexico, the Sixteenth of September is celebrated as Independence Day, the day when Mexico gained its independence from Spain in 1821. Often people from Mexico who migrate to the United States continue to celebrate this holiday. In his account of growing up in a Los Angeles barrio, Ernesto Galarza includes the following story about a party that was held to celebrate this holiday.

As you read, compare the customs that Galarza describes with those we observe when we celebrate the Fourth of July.

1   In the family parties, the funerals, the baptisms, the weddings and the birthdays, our private lives continued to be Mexican. And there was a public affair that once a year brought the *colonia* together, the celebration of the Sixteenth of September.

2   The year José was chosen a member of the committee to arrange the program for the Sixteenth, I was drafted to assist as interpreter in obtaining from the American authorities permits of one kind or another. As José's aide-de-camp I also helped decorate the hall with streamers of green, white, and red crepe paper and the colored portrait of Don Miguel Hidalgo hung under a large Mexican flag.

3   The program went along smoothly. The hall was crowded, family style with whole clans in attendance from babies to grandparents. There was a short speech by the president of the Comisión Honorifica; the crowning of the queen, elected with votes paid for by her admirers; the singing of the national anthem; a poetic reading; and one hour before midnight *El Grito*, the call to arms in remembrance of the cry of the Illustrious Father of the Nation, the rebel Catholic priest, Don Miguel Hidalgo y Costilla.

For those between fifteen and thirty the real business of the   4
Sixteenth was the dance. After *El Grito*, the floor was cleared, the
mothers and elders sitting on chairs and benches along the walls, a
stolid line of chaperons, the girls in a double row in front of them.
Across from them the young men stood, like runners at the starting
line of a hundred-yard dash. On the first downbeat of the band leader,
they rushed across the floor, each man headed for his favorite girl
who, according to the rules, accepted her partner on a first come first
served basis.

During the early rounds of the dancing the rushes created no   5
problems. I watched them from a back corner of the bandstand, my
duty post as assistant to the floor manager. There were intermissions
for soft drinks and beer.

But it wasn't the coca-cola or the brew that gradually enlivened   6
the festival. It was the trips to the men's toilet for short nips from
flasks of tequila and other fiery stuff.

By one o'clock in the morning a good deal of tequila had been   7
consumed. Everybody knew, of course, that a Mexican's honor
became more sensitive the more nips he had. In the presence of the
choicest girls of the *colonia*, there are some things a man cannot tolerate. And in one of the rushes one of these things happened. Two
young men collided within reach of the girl they both wanted for the
dance. Like perfect gentlemen they picked themselves up from the
floor paying no heed to the giggles of the girls and the owlish grins of
the old folks. I saw them rush out of the ballroom, my uncle at their
heels. When I caught up with him in the toilet it was too late. The two
bantams were in a corner, squared off and slugging it out, my uncle
taking cuffs from both as he tried to separate them.

Instantly, word of the fight reached the dance floor and the men   8
rushed to see it, first as spectators and then as partisans of the fighters.
With Mexican honor now running hot through their veins, they
insulted one another until the free-for-all began in earnest. I watched
the *chicanos* pair off, pushing each other against the walls and swinging wildly. Two of them were on the floor kicking and rolling, half
hidden under the swinging door of a toilet. A beer bottle crashed
through a window.

José slugged his way through the melee to my corner, yanked me   9
by the arm, and we headed for the ballroom. A policeman was already
at the door of the toilet looking in bewilderment for a way to take
hold of a roomful of rioting Mexicans.

The ballroom was emptying fast. Mothers were herding their   10
daughters through the hall and out into the street. The elders gathered

on the sidewalk waiting to group their families and hasten away. My uncle ordered the band to play on, "to restore the calm," as he said. But it was the police and not the music that restored the calm. Someone with more experience than José had yelled in the hall, "La Julia," and before the paddy wagon appeared in the street and a pair of cops walked in, the hall was deserted, except for ourselves and the musicians.

11   It was nearly dawn before we finished taking down the decorations, mopping up the spilled beer, scrubbing the blood on the toilet floor, sweeping up broken glass, and heaping the cigarette butts in a pail. The colored portrait of Don Miguel was the last thing we took down.

▶   **QUESTIONS TO CONSIDER**

1. Who is Galarza's intended audience? Is he writing for other Mexican Americans, people who know something about the history of Mexico and life in a barrio, or for people who know nothing of these things? What specific clues do you find in his narrative that help you identify his audience? How does his choice of an audience shape his narrative? Does Galarza idealize what went on at the celebration in order to impress his audience, or does he give an objective account? Can an author, especially one who is writing about his own people and culture, really be objective?

2. How does this celebration compare to American Fourth of July celebrations? Do Fourth of July celebrations sometimes get out of hand also? If so, how and why?

3. According to Galarza, Hidalgo was a "rebel Catholic priest" who helped the Mexican people win their independence from Spain. What effect does Galarza's mentioning the picture of Hidalgo at both the first and last of his account of the celebration have on you as a reader? Is it more or less effective than Stuart's similar use of the fireplace in his story? How might Galarza have used this image more effectively?

▶   **WRITING ACTIVITIES**

Individual: Write a journal entry in which you tell of an exuberant celebration that included potentially dangerous activities. Include as many specific details as you can remember.

Collaborative: With the members of your group, discuss your individual responses to Galarza's narrative, focusing on whether your response was primarily positive or negative. Then discuss whether you think your responses conform to Galarza's intention. That is, what response do you think he wanted you to have? Finally, identify and make a list of the features of the narrative that influenced your group's responses most strongly. Compare your list with those produced by the other groups.

Computer: Key your journal entry that describes an exuberant celebration into a computer file. (If your journal is on a computer file, simply move this entry into a new file.) Then share your account with your classmates by using a network program or by exchanging disks. Once you have all read one another's descriptions, conduct an on-line discussion about such events and their potential dangers.

❖❖❖❖❖

A Thanksgiving Feast in Aburi

Maya Angelou

Maya Angelou, the African-American writer who wrote and delivered a poem for President Clinton's inauguration, describes in the following narrative a celebration that took place in Aburi, Ghana, while she was visiting there. We can compare this holiday to Thanksgiving, just as we compared the Sixteenth of September holiday to our Fourth of July. As you read, note the differences between our own Thanksgiving and the African feast.

1   The music of the Fanti language was becoming singable to me, and its vocabulary was moving orderly into my brain.

2   Efua took me to a durbar, a thanksgiving feast in Aburi, about thirty miles from Accra. Thousands of gaily dressed celebrants had gathered, waving, singing and dancing. I stood on the edge of the crowd to watch the exotic parade. Hunters, rifles across their shoulders, marched in rhythm to their own drummers. Soldiers, with faces set in grim determination, paced down the widened roads behind their drummers while young girls screamed approval. Farmers bearing scythes and fishermen carrying nets were welcomed loudly by the throng.

3   The annual harvest ritual gave each segment in the society its opportunity to thank God and to praise its workers and their yield.

4   I was swaying to the rhythm when the drums stopped, and the crowd quieted. The restless air steadied. A sound, unlike the other sounds of the day, commenced in the distance. It was the harsh tone of hundreds of giant cicadas grinding their legs together. Their rasping floated to us and the crowd remained quiet but edgy with anticipation. When men appeared out of the dust scraping sticks against corrugated dry gourds, the crowd recovered its tongue.

5   "Yee! Yee! Awae! Awae!"

6   The scrapers, like the paraders who preceded them, gave no notice to the crowd or to the small children who ran unceremoniously close to their serried ranks.

7   Rasp, Rasp. Scrape! Scrape, Scour, Scrunch, Scrump. Rasp, Rasp! Scree! The raspers faded into a dim distance.

8   The deep throb of royal drums was suddenly heard in the distance and again the din of celebration stopped. The people, although quiet again, continued to move, sidle, exchange places and wipe their brows. Women adjusted the clothes which held babies securely to their backs. Rambunctious children played tag, men and women waved at each other, smiled, but kept looking toward the sound of the drums.

9   Efua touched my shoulder and offered me a large white handkerchief.

10   I said, "Thank you, but I'm all right." She kept her hand extended. I took the handkerchief.

11   Men emerged out of the dim dust. One set had giant drums hefted onto their shoulders, and others followed in splendid cloth, beating the drums with crooked sticks. The powerful rhythms rattled my bones, and I could feel the vibrations along the edges of my teeth.

12   People began clapping, moving their feet, their hands, hips and heads. They shouted clamorously, "Yee! Yee! Aboma!" And there was still a sense of anticipation in the turbulence. They were waiting for a climax.

13   When the first palanquin hove into view, I thought of a Chinese junk on the Yangtze (which I had never seen), and a ten ton truck on a California freeway (which I knew well). Long poled hammocks, sturdy as Conestogas, were carried by four men. In the center of each conveyance sat a chief, gloriously robed in rich hand-woven Kente cloth. At his side (only a few chiefs were female) sat a young boy, called the Kra, who, during an earlier solemn ceremony, had received

the implanted soul of the chief. If the chief should die during the ritual, there would be no panic, for his people would know that his soul was safe in the young boy's body and, with the proper ritual, could be placed into the body of the chief's successor.

The drums beckoned, the kings appeared, and the air nearly collapsed under the weight of dust and thudding drums and shouting jubilation. 14

Each chief was prouder than the one preceding him. Each dressed in more gold and richer colors. Each black beyond ebony and shining with oil and sweat. They arrived in single file to be met by the adoring shouts of their subjects. "Na-na. Na-na." "Yo, Yo, Nana." The shouting united with the thumping of the drums and the explosion of color. Women and men bounced up and down like children's toys, and children not tall enough to see over the crowd were lifted by the nearest adults to see their passing royalty. 15

A flutter of white billowed over that excited scene. Thousands of handkerchiefs waving from thousands of black hands tore away my last reserve. I started bouncing with the entranced Ghanaians, my handkerchief high above my head, I waved and jumped and screamed, "Na-na, na-na, na-na." 16

QUESTIONS TO CONSIDER ◀

1. Angelou's reaction to the celebration changes as it progresses. What is her initial reaction? Her final reaction? Would this final response have occurred had she been watching the celebration from a distance? At what point in her narrative does her role change from observer to participant? How does her narrative reflect this change?

2. Unlike Galarza, Angelou is describing a celebration that she does not understand well. She is writing for an audience who is even less knowledgeable than she is about Ghana and its customs, so she explains what occurs during the celebration carefully. But her primary purpose is not merely to inform her readers about this strange celebration. What is her primary purpose?

3. Notice the descriptive details that Angelou includes in her narrative. Her account of the celebration consists of a series of vivid images. To what senses (sight, sound, etc.) do these images appeal? Which is the strongest image for you as a reader?

▶ WRITING ACTIVITIES

Individual: Rather than focusing primarily on the sense of sight, as writers often do, write a journal entry in which you describe in detail sounds or odors you associate with a particular holiday.

THESIS, PAGE 599 **Collaborative:** Angelou does not include a stated **thesis**, but her main idea can be inferred. With the members of your group, write a brief introduction for this story in which you state the thesis. Do you think this introduction makes the narrative more or less effective? Why or why not?

Computer: Describe an event to which you responded strongly, for example, a graduation, a marriage (or divorce) ceremony, a parade, a sporting event, or a church service. In your first account of this event, begin with a thesis that states exactly what your response was. Next copy your text to a new file and revise it so the thesis statement appears at the end. Finally, copy the original text again (to a third file) and revise it once more, omitting the thesis statement entirely but including images and details that clearly suggest your main idea. Print all three versions of the text and consult with the members of your peer response group to discover which one they prefer. Or if you have a network program, post all three versions to your class network so that your classmates can respond on line, indicating which version they prefer.

❖❖❖❖❖

IDZA NAMA

Kenneth E. Read

Anthropologist Kenneth Read lived among the Gahuku, an aboriginal tribe of New Guinea, to study their culture. This description of one of their celebrations is from The High Valley, *Read's book about his experiences. Thus this account is essentially an anthropological report. As such, its purpose (to inform readers about this particular culture) is more pragmatic than the other narratives included in this chapter. Notice as you read, however, that Read's account includes many of the same features found in the other narra-*

tives: it is detailed, it includes vivid images, it is arranged in chronological order, and it gives the reader a sense of the writer's subjective reactions to his experiences.

I awakened one morning with the feeling that something new had been added to a familiar situation. The village was completely silent, yet the air seemed to vibrate uneasily against my ear, prompting me to recall the unidentified sound that had broken into my sleep. For a while I lay still and listened intently for anything that would give it a recognizable shape, but there was nothing to which I could fasten an explanation. The day had barely begun. It was far too early for any movement in the houses, and the sound that had left its track on my mind must have come from outside the settlement. I started to dismiss it as imagined when suddenly it came again, lifting me up to my elbows with a sense of shock. 1

In later months the same notes came at many times of day, but they always carried the quality of this first encounter—the predawn air chilling my arms and shoulders, the glimmer of light in the empty street, and the whole valley lying exposed and unsuspecting as it slept. Their sound eludes description. It had too many different elements and contradictions, and the music was based on an entirely alien scale. The clear air offered it no resistance, and the notes, coming from a distance, seemed to wind at will through an echoing void, tracing such a capricious path that their origin was successfully concealed. They struck with a hollow, pulsing beat in the bass register, a continuous explosion of notes like a cry of hunger torn from a distended, disembodied throat. More shrill calls played in and out of this rhythmic background in repetitive patterns that after a while could be identified as tunes. Both elements were deliberately joined, contrasting and complementing, designed to produce a unified effect. The shrill notes fluttered avidly around the deeper cries, possessed of the same need and urging the stronger on to fulfill it like cultures wheeling in a cloudless sky, dependent on their predatory fellows. 2

Even as the first calls troubled the morning air people began to stir. Currents of speculation ran through the village, subsiding gradually into a listening silence. Outside my room the predawn light grew slowly more intense; then the strange cries ceased as abruptly as they had begun, leaving only a momentary echo on the threshold of day. 3

In the street later, I found that the sounds were the principal topic of conversation. There was no doubt what they were or where they came from. They were the sacred flutes of Gama, and at this time 4 of year their appearance could mean only one thing, that the Gama had decided to hold the greatest of Gahuku festivals, the *idza nama*.

5   These festivals were a complex of activities; their principal components were male initiation and the ceremonial exchange of enormous quantities of pigs, the principal measure of traditional wealth. They occurred infrequently, at intervals of five to seven years, timed to coincide with the maturation of each succeeding group of adolescent boys, but also dependent upon the state of the group's resources, for they were competitive displays of strength, a celebration and affirmation of the values that gave life its characteristic shape and tone. No other activity took so long to arrange, engaged such a large number of people at one time, or involved so much visiting. Secondary ceremonies signified the completion of various stages in the preparations and pointed to the climactic events with which they closed. Each one of them provided an opportunity for self-display, a chance to stress the dominance of men and the bonds uniting their sex, to assert the wealth of tribe and clan, and to obtain prestige and influence. All the richness of their lives found expression in this context, played out in the flashing, gaudy colors of paint and feathers and towering decorations that added several feet to the normal height of a man. And when the festival was over and people returned to their routine tasks, a whole pattern of existence had been displayed.

6   Adding to the extraordinary character of the events, indeed, sanctifying and setting them apart, the sacred flutes invested them with the mysterious power of the supernatural. From the moment that their first dawn cries served notice of the group's decision their calls marked the beginning of every day, beat against the tight, dry air of noon, and wound a magic thread through the silver silence of the nights. Gahuku are not philosophers or theologians. They had no priesthood devoted to the interpretation of doctrine, the preservation of dogma, or the management of ritual. Their religious beliefs are not formulated precisely, not stated in a more or less coherent system that is available for objective examination and discussion. No other side of their life proved so difficult to penetrate, was so elusive, less amenable to definite statements yet also so pervasive, so intrinsically a part of the world as it is seen through their eyes and minds. Inference was almost the only key to entering this realm of thought.

7   In Gahuku religion there are no gods to whom men are responsible and few demons, apart from some bogeymen—horribly deformed simulacra of human beings who are encountered sometimes by solitary individuals. Yet the world and everything within it depend on supernatural force, an impersonal power operating as the

force of life, having no name nor any specific location, vaguely ancestral in character, and ultimately the source of all success, indispensable for everything men hope to achieve. The religious quest is
essentially a search for this power, an effort to tap it and control it, to
discover its source, and to enlist its aid in securing a bountiful life. It
is a search beset by fundamental uncertainties; for the nature of the
power sought is not known completely, and it is possible that there
are alternative ways of obtaining access to it, some giving a more certain control and bringing more abundant rewards than others.
Individuals, even whole groups of people, may differ in the efficacy
of the methods they employ, in their knowledge of the source of
power, and their control over its operation, but everyone has need of
it. This force is not malevolent; it neither punishes nor condemns.
There are, however, potentially harmful spirits who entice women
away from the paths and gardens, seduce them, and after intercourse
reveal their true identity by spitting in the women's faces. Death
results from these encounters, and sometimes illness is caused by the
ghosts of the recently dead who feel neglected or displeased by
behavior that failed to show them proper respect.

    Ritual is the means men use to tap the fountainhead of power   8
and to divert it to man's ends. In periodic cycles spanning the better
part of a generation the villagers renew their whole lives in it, building
the ozaha neta whose meaning had been so difficult for me to ascertain. The unspectacular object fashioned from stakes and roughly
hewn timber is like a flume thrust into an invisible stream, drawing it
off and channeling it down to men, establishing a supernatural reservoir whose mystical influence sustains them through the following
years. This rite is the supreme act of faith and aspiration, the dual
impulse of fallible human nature lying at the heart of all religion. But
the crude table and the bleached bones almost concealed by sprouting
leaves speak less clearly of the continuing concern with power than
the pulsing cries of the flutes echoing along the paths of morning.

    These sounds are explained to women as the calls of mythical,   9
carnivorous birds, *nama*, which abide periodically in the men's house
and carry off the adolescent boys during the crisis of initiation. It is a
graphic and pertinent description of the effect produced by the bamboo instruments, and sitting behind the closed doors of the houses,
whenever the flutes are played in the open street, the air seems to be
roiled by the beating of invisible wings. Yet the nama are more than a
symbol of male dominance, a picturesque way of telling women their
proper place, and the simple deception, which possibly fools only
children, is one of their less important features.

10   On a characteristic occasion, I was with a procession of twenty villagers returning along the ridge to Susuroka from the floor of the valley below Ekuhakuka, where the morning and early part of the afternoon had been spent feasting at a secluded garden dwelling. While the men gossiped or slept in the shade, the nama rested in pairs inside the house on a bed of colored leaves and flowers. They were unremarkable instruments, hollow sections of bamboo closed at one end, about two feet six inches long and six inches in diameter, with a small round hole that a player held to his mouth. There was no external decoration and they had so little material value that they were broken and burned at the end of the festival. In spite of their ceremonial bed and their food, salt and cooked pork placed in each mouthpiece, it was difficult to associate them with the extraordinarily moving cries that began and closed each day at the height of the festival season. But it was the tunes that carried their wealth of symbolic implication.

11   It was nearing midafternoon when we returned from the floor of the valley to the ridge. The climb to Ekuhakuka was short but steep, and I was out of breath when we reached the crest, thankful for the brief pause as the men formed a single file just beyond the dilapidated, empty settlement. For a mile or so, from here to the outskirts of Gohajaka, the ridge was narrow, falling away abruptly on either side of the path. The grass was stunted in many places and the slopes were gashed with the red and chocolate scars of recent slides that had carried away the covering of crotalaria, leaving the track completely exposed, almost miraculously suspended in light and air, so open that anyone moving along it was plainly visible from the gardens below, their figures silhouetted on the breathless arch of sky. As we reached these barren heights the men nearest the flute players extended branches of leaves to hide them from sight, though even this attempt at concealment must have seemed a trivial subterfuge to any curious eyes directed upward from the gardens by the sound of the music. The men were absorbed by the performance, speaking only when the flutes were passed to a new group of players. It was impossible for me to tell what they felt, though the startling brightness was a perfect match for their rapt expressions. I was struck by the thought that they may have wanted to be seen, that they were aware of the effect they made, that each step filled them with a mounting pride and drew them closer together in the bonds of a common emotion.

12   A short distance from the entrance to Gohajaka, Gapiriha, holding a formidable length of cane, pushed his way to the front of the procession, going ahead in order to clear the street for our progress through the village. He was running past the houses as we entered the street,

beating against the barred doors, scattering the terrified chickens perched on the thatched roofs and the ubiquitous pigs scavenging near the fires. The music of the flutes rose to a new pitch of intensity as the players seemed to double their effort, inspired by the submissive, unseen audience behind the walls, the throaty shouts of the other men who had followed the example of their herald, and the answering welcome of old Alum whose age allowed her the privilege of staying outside her house, where she leaned against her staff and faced the nama, her eyes closed fast and her thin, bent body shaking with shrill cries.

Later, back in my house with the flutes laid carefully on the floor, 13 the men were like contestants in a game that had tested their strength and concentration to the limits of their endurance. They were almost drunk with excitement, balanced on the edge of exhaustion, their nervous energy so recently strung to its highest pitch seeking to return to its normal level through incessant talking. Hunehune's eyes were bright with feeling. His voice trembled perceptibly, like his hand, which rested lightly on a pair of flutes, while he tried to make me understand and share the wonder of the sound we had heard. The aesthetic thrill he hoped to explain was closely linked to the fact that each tune required two flutes, bass and treble, point and counterpoint, melody and rhythm, joined as parts within a whole. One without the other carried no emotional charge whatever, but played together, complementing yet intertwined, the effect was magical, a mystery for which he had no adequate words. Gesturing helplessly with his hands, Hunehune turned to Bihore and remarked that his playing had so deranged him that if he had been a woman he would have had to come to Bihore's house. There was no mistaking the implication of his words, the attribution of sexual qualities to the nama. Male sexuality was a manifestation of power, the very force of life, the basis of existence; the flutes not only symbolized power in its most inclusive sense but also linked it to the structure of relationships that bound each man to his fellows.

Each tune was the common property of a different subclan, that 14 group of men who were descended through males from a common ancestor. Passed down, according to tradition, from the most remote ancestral times, they stood for the continuity of this group and the inviolate character of its bonds and associated attitudes, internal harmony, mutual support, and solidarity before the world at large. In the tunes of the nama each subclan expressed and experienced its common purpose and identity, celebrated the goals it sought, and the invisible medium of power in which it was steeped.

In the following weeks the sounds of the nama were threaded 15 through the background of every day. The Gama flutes could be heard quite clearly from Susuroka, but as the season progressed other tribes and villages signified their intention to hold the festival, and on any morning the calls seemed to speak to each other from a dozen different places harshly insistent from the grasslands to the south, thin and troubled like the last notes of an echo, from the hanging valleys in the western mountains. Though they became a customary part of experience, I was never able to sleep through their cries, always waking as their notes beat at the threshold of dawn and carrying the memory of them in my mind as I waited for them to return in the blue and golden air of evening. Their inaudible vibration hung upon the intervening hours, pulsing in the sunlight and the purple underside of clouds, following a breeze along the leaves of the cane fences, filling the whole landscape with the quickening tempo of life.

▶   QUESTIONS TO CONSIDER

1. Although Read participates in the celebration and includes his subjective reaction to some of its rituals, he remains primarily an observer. Thus as a narrator, he is both, or alternately, subjective and objective—at times describing his own sensations and feelings and at other times describing with detailed detachment exactly what happened. Do you see Read as a character in the story or as a scientist carefully observing and recording the events? Do you find this combination of subjective and objective points of view effective or disconcerting? Why? Would his account have been more effective had he remained entirely objective throughout?

2. Because he is a scientist, Read not only narrates and describes but also interprets, explaining not only what happened but why. He seems especially concerned that his readers understand the significance of the rituals he describes. Why do you think he is concerned about his readers' understanding of these rituals? What might readers' reactions be if he did not interpret and explain the events?

3. The celebration Read describes is intended primarily to celebrate male superiority. Although he explains this purpose and discusses its significance, he does not reveal his own feelings about it. That is, he is not judgmental. Why do you think he avoids making a judgment about whether the idea of male superiority is valid or appropriate for this culture? How do you react to this idea as it relates to this unfamiliar culture? Would your reaction differ if the culture were your own?

4. What is your general reaction to the culture you glimpse through Read's narrative of this particular celebration? Is it a place you would like to live? To visit? Why or why not?

WRITING ACTIVITIES

Individual: Describe a celebration or a holiday for an audience that knows your culture well. For example, you might describe how your family observes Christmas or Hanukkah or some other holiday to someone who also celebrates that particular holiday. Focus on those details that make your observation of this holiday unique.

Collaborative: Discuss with a group of your classmates how an objective observer might describe a football game or other sporting event in our society much as Read describes the Gahuku celebration. Could this ritual be viewed as a celebration of male superiority or a renewal of life? Write a brief description of a sporting event, such as a football game, depicting it as a ritual, especially a ritual of male dominance.

Computer: Enter into your computer or copy to a new file the text of your individual writing activity, in which you described how you observe a particular holiday for a reader who is familiar with that holiday. Then revise that description so it is appropriate for a reader who is *not* familiar with the holiday you are describing.

▶ WRITING RECONSTRUCTIONS OF EXPERIENCE

Although writing to explore often involves reconstructing your own experiences, when you write to reconstruct your experiences for an audience, you have a different purpose. Rather than writing primarily to discover, you are writing to communicate something to someone, using your own experiences as the raw material for your text.

Making the Experience Real

In reconstructing your own experiences, you depend on your memory to provide you with the basic structure of your narrative—who did what when. This structure must be clear so that readers can reconstruct the experience in their own minds. But to make your experiences vivid and real for your readers, you need more than just the basic facts. Three strategies can help you make your experience real:

- ❖ Use specific details.
- ❖ Use concrete language.
- ❖ Use analogies.

USE SPECIFIC DETAILS.   Make your narrative vivid and interesting by using specific details in telling your story. For example, describing a car as red is better than just saying "a car," but calling the car a "bright red 1958 Dodge sedan with tail fins and a white roof" is even better. Telling your readers that an experience was exciting doesn't convey what you really felt, but providing a detailed account of an experience such as scaling the jagged stone face of a 15,000-foot mountain during a blinding snowstorm will probably convey to them something of the thrill you experienced.

USE CONCRETE LANGUAGE.   Convincing narratives require more than specific details. They also require the use of concrete language—words that create a specific image in the mind of your reader. For example, *ambling, strolling, sauntering, strutting, slouching, hurrying, tiptoeing, wobbling,* and *weaving* are all more precise choices than *walking.* And describing someone as red-faced and trembling with indignation gives a more vivid picture than merely saying the person was angry. Anger is an abstraction, a sterile concept that provides a reader with intellectual understanding. In contrast, concrete language creates an image of the way in which a person experiences anger, allowing the reader to visualize the reality of the anger.

The instruction to use evocative language doesn't mean merely to slap more adjectives into your sentences. You cannot convince a reader just by intensifying general statements. To tell readers that climbing the mountain was "very exciting" accomplishes no more than using "exciting" alone (and "exciting" doesn't evoke much!). Read the following two versions of the same experience and determine which is more convincing:

First Version

My mother's decision to divorce my father ruined Christmas for me that year. When she told me she planned to leave us and move into an apartment, I was devastated. I will never feel the same about Christmas.

Second Version

"I am going to divorce your father," my mother said. "I am moving to another apartment next month." For several seconds her words hung in the air like frozen water drops, ready to fall down to the floor and break into thousands of pieces. I was standing in front of her in the Christmas-decorated living room, feeling the stable ground beneath my feet starting to tremble. With two simple sentences my mother had just torn apart the only place of safety I knew in this world—my home.

In the second version, specific details and images convince; they create a context that makes the writer's assertions believable. Without these vivid details and images, a reader may understand the writer's point, may even agree or sympathize with that point, but will not be able to reconstruct the experience. Good writing of any kind—whether a story or not—includes a wealth of specific details, and the more specific the better.

USE ANALOGIES.   **Analogies**—comparing one thing to something else— ANALOGY, PAGE 413
also increase specificity and evoke images. For example, stating that your steak was overcooked is not as convincing as saying it tasted like a well-seasoned rubber tire. But stale overused analogies only deaden your prose. Comparing something that is hard to a rock or a hammer

doesn't accomplish anything. Comparing the same hard object to the heart of a Wall Street broker or a ten-carat diamond would be much more effective. For example, in the preceding paragraph the student writer says her mother's words "hung in the air like frozen water drops, ready to fall down to the floor and break into thousands of pieces." This analogy is not only original but also poignantly echoes the writer's feelings.

Developing a Personal Writing Voice

Abundant specific details and evocative language help to make narrative accounts real to a reader, and a personal writing voice can convince a reader that what is being said is not only real but significant. The voice you adopt in a narrative depends on your purpose, on the kind of narrative you are writing, and on your attitude toward your subject. If, like Jesse Stuart or Warren Slay, you idealize or sentimentalize your subject, then your writing voice will reflect these sentiments. You will include details that are affirming, even flattering, and will use words that evoke and reinforce these sentiments.

On the other hand, if you feel ambivalent toward your subject, as Maya Angelou does toward the African celebration in the first part of her essay and as Ernesto Galarza seems to toward the Sixteenth of September celebration, your voice will also reflect this ambivalence. An ambivalent voice differs from the objective stance assumed by Kenneth Read in his description of the Gahuku ritual. Ambivalence involves both positive *and* negative feelings, whereas objectivity involves neither.

Finally, you may have a negative attitude toward your subject, as Lillian Ross has in her description of the Halloween party. If so, your writing voice may range from detached to critical to hostile.

The degree of formality you adopt toward your subject also determines your writing voice. In general, a less formal approach sounds more intimate and personal, whereas a more formal treatment results in a more distant, impersonal voice. An informal writing voice evokes the sense of someone talking; it is conversational, identified with a specific person, and often with a particular situation or context. In contrast, a formal writing voice seems to exist apart from any particular person, place, and time—outside of a personal context. Your writing's level of formality usually depends on such features as word choice (diction), person (use of *I* or *we* versus *you* versus *he, she, it,* or *they*), and sentence structure. Content—what you say as well as how you say it—also affects formality. For example, the intimate details that

Galarza, Stuart, and Slay include make their narratives seem less formal than Read's or Ross's.

You may not always think consciously about the voice you plan to use before you begin to write. Rather, the subject about which you are writing, your attitude toward that subject, the audience for whom you are writing, and your purpose in writing usually determine the voice you will adopt. As you gain experience as a writer, you will probably develop a fairly consistent voice. However, because you may not yet have found your writing voice, you may need to give this issue deliberate thought when you write (see **style and voice**).

STYLE AND VOICE, PAGE 596

W R I T I N G   A S S I G N M E N T

Holidays can be happy affairs, with people celebrating a specific occasion in distinctive ways. Holidays can also be disappointing, even depressing. For this assignment, write about a holiday you experienced that disappointed you in some way or that was different from your usual celebrations. Explain not only what happened but *why* you were disappointed or sad on this particular occasion and *how* this disappointment affected you. In effect, you are assuming the role of historian. That is, you are going to record what happened and then interpret these events for a reader who does not know you.

Planning Your Text

Begin your narrative by brainstorming about (i.e., making a list of) holidays you routinely celebrate. Once you have completed this brainstorming list, look for ideas in it that might serve as the subject for an essay about a disappointing holiday. Although you may have listed holidays or celebrations you usually enjoy, you may have included an idea that will lead to a topic you can write about. Perhaps some of the holidays you listed have become less enjoyable as you have gotten older. Do you enjoy Christmas or Valentine's Day as much now as you did when you were a child? Begin to compare various holidays and to think about why you enjoy some more than others. If you moved to this country from another one, do you enjoy the celebrations of holidays in this country as much as you did those in your native country? Or has something happened in your family, a death or perhaps even the birth of a younger sister or brother, to change your experiences at certain holidays? At this point, don't try to reach a definite decision about your topic. Just let some ideas take shape in your mind.

Then choose from this list a holiday that at some time was a disappointment for you and freewrite about it. Write whatever comes to your mind on the subject. Don't try to be organized or even coherent; rather, free-associate on paper or on your computer screen, writing anything and everything that occurs to you. For example, if you chose the most recent Fourth of July as the holiday you were going to write about, you would try to remember everything that happened to you on this occasion and how you felt about what was happening. At this point, don't be concerned about correctness—how you spell or where you put punctuation marks. Just write to get information and ideas on paper. Freewriting is not a draft of an essay; it is just a way to generate ideas by recalling information that has been stored in your long-term

INVENTION, PAGE 529 memory. So write as rapidly and as freely as you can (see **invention**).

Once you have formed a mental image of the essay you plan to write, even if that image is still rather vague, you can begin to think more specifically about your text. Since this assignment asks you to write about a personal experience, you will probably structure this essay as a narrative; that is, you will probably tell a story about one particular holiday that disappointed you in some way. Before you begin to write, spend a few minutes thinking about what you want your readers to understand about your experience. Essays based on personal experience often do not include an explicit statement of the writer's

THESIS, PAGE 599 **thesis**; the main idea is implied rather than stated. But, as a writer, *you* need to be aware of the point you want to make. Your thesis may change, in both substantive and incidental ways, as you construct your text (in fact, it probably should change), but you should at least give the matter some thought. You can decide later whether you want to include a thesis statement in the introduction or conclusion of your essay, but for now just be sure that the story you plan to tell has a main idea—that it makes a point beyond the mere telling of the story.

Constructing Your Text

DRAFTING.   Your freewriting should have warmed you up to start drafting your essay. Because this assignment involves writing a narrative, you may not need a formal introduction. You may just want to begin telling your story. Most of the readings included in this chapter just seem to begin at the beginning. They do not have traditional introductions in which the writer tells the reader what to expect. If you feel the need to sum up your story in some way, making its thesis explicit, you may find that your conclusion is the place for this type of direct commentary.

Some people sit down and write their entire text in a single session. As one student put it, "Usually, I sort of spit up words and get done with it." Other writers write one or two paragraphs, and then rewrite what they have written before moving on to the next part. You will have to discover your own drafting pattern. If you need to feel satisfied with your first paragraph before writing anything else, fine, do that. If you prefer to get the whole thing down before revising, that's also fine. There is no single right or even best way to draft a text. The important thing is to get something on paper or your computer screen so you can rethink and resee the text in your head and later reshape and revise your written text more effectively.

READING.   Reading your own text objectively and perceptively—the key to good writing—is also one of the most difficult parts of the process. Because you have written the text, you will have difficulty reading it objectively. Instead, you will see what you think is there, your mental text obscuring your perception of your written text. If you want to learn to revise your texts so they become better and better with each successive draft, learn to read each draft perceptively.

The first step to becoming an effective reader of our own writing is to slow down the process. Don't read your text as soon as you have finished writing it; you won't see what is really there. Wait until the mental text has faded somewhat before trying to read your written text. The longer the better, but at least wait a few hours (an entire day is much better). Then read your text as if you are a "dumb reader"—as if you know nothing about the subject other than what is on the paper (or screen) before you. In the case of a narrative, this is especially difficult. Since you were, of course, actually present to experience what you are writing about, it is not easy to pretend you are ignorant of what happened. But try.

Read first to determine if your story has a single clear focus. In telling a story, you are always selective because you cannot tell everything that happened. Be sure what you have chosen to include reinforces the point you want to make. If you have included information or details that do not contribute to your main idea, indicate on your text that this material may later need to be deleted (but do not delete anything hastily—especially if you are working on a computer).

Next read to see if the story you are telling is clear. Can a reader who was not there understand what happened? Do you include enough information about who did what where and when? Do you provide necessary background information? Do you identify characters and places adequately? Making these assessments can be difficult because you know so much about your subject. Here you must try hard to view your text through your reader's eyes; imagine you are seeing it for the first time and know nothing about the experience.

Read again to determine if you have made the story real and interesting by including enough specific details—especially sensory details about how things look and feel and taste and sound and smell. No matter how exciting its plot, a story will not interest a reader unless that reader can experience it. The main way to help readers experience your story is to include specific details that help them to see and hear and feel and smell and taste what you experienced. Don't include meaningless details, and don't overwrite by using a string of adjectives or adverbs to modify every noun and verb you use. But do include pertinent, vivid, specific details to make your story come alive for your readers.

Additional readings can focus on whether you used concrete language and fresh analogies in telling your story and on whether your writing voice is natural, direct, and real (as opposed to stilted, vague, and contrived—a voice that doesn't sound like you or anyone else the reader might want to know). As you become a more experienced writer and a more skilled reader of your own text, you can focus on many of these elements at the same time.

How many times should you read and reread your written text as you revise? Initially, you may have to reread many times, focusing on a separate aspect of your text each time. As you gain more experience as a writer and as a reader of your own writing, you may be able to accomplish several purposes in a single reading. Plan to read your written text many times and on many different occasions. Don't shortchange this essential part of the process.

You may also want to ask someone else—a classmate, a writing center tutor, roommate, friend, or family member—to read your story and respond to it. Your instructor may divide your class into pairs or small groups so you can read one another's texts. Any reader's response is valuable. Don't let your reader get by with just telling you that your story is good or interesting. Demand a more critical response; ask for specific details about what is good and what is less good, clear and unclear, interesting and dull. One of the best ways to learn about reading your own texts, is to ask other people to read and respond to what you have written.

As you read and reread your story, your mental version of it will inevitably change. You may have surprised yourself by writing something other than what you planned to write, or you may have written exactly what you planned to write only to find it dull and trite. After reading your written text, you can reevaluate your original idea of your text. Was it too ambitious, too vague, too obvious? Are there problems you didn't anticipate, weaknesses you failed to predict? Don't be afraid to abandon your initial version if it now seems unrealistic or unworkable. Readjust your thinking to conform to the reality that confronts you in the form of the written text you have produced.

On the other hand, you may want to stay with your earlier idea if you think it is taking shape but just needs more work or if you still feel it is a good idea in spite of the failure of this draft. You must be the judge about what needs changing as you try to function as both writer and reader. Don't be afraid to take risks and experiment: it's not too late to try something new. Let the two forms of your text—what is in your mind and what is on the paper or computer screen in front of you—shape each other.

REVISING.   Revising is an ongoing part of the writing process, but when you have completed a draft of your text, you are ready to focus on revising. The term *revise* is rather abstract and vague. Just what does it mean to revise a text? The word comes from a Latin term that means "to visit or see again." Literally, the term means to resee what you have written. But in practice, revising is limited to three functions: you can delete, add to, or rearrange what you have written. In this respect, you are like a computer.

Why delete material you have just struggled to write or write more, especially if you already have the required number of words or pages? The best answer to these questions is to put yourself in the place of your reader. Have you given your reader nonessential information, information that destroys the focus of your story and does not support your main idea? If so, it has to go, even if it includes the most brilliant sentence you have ever written. Or have you failed to give your readers essential information or enough details to make your story come alive? If so, you need to add to what you have written—not just so you will have more words or pages but so your readers can construct in their minds the experience you are reconstructing in your narrative.

Because you are writing a narrative, you may not need to rearrange any of the parts of your story. But you might consider rearranging the

CAUSE AND EFFECT, PAGE 418

events in the story so they do not follow the exact chronological order in which they occurred. Variations on strict chronological order can be an effective way to focus readers' attention on a particular part of the narrative or to suggest a strong **cause-and-effect** relationship. For example, you could begin with the ending, tell what happened or how you felt at the end, and then go back and tell what led to this outcome. You can, in fact, begin at any point in your narrative as long as you do not confuse your readers.

Editing Your Text

Editing is not the same as revising. When you revise, you focus on meaning and content, whereas when you edit, you focus on style, readability, and correctness. Don't turn your full attention to editing until you feel fairly confident that you have finished revising. There is no point in worrying about the punctuation of a sentence that is in a paragraph you may delete. However, when you have a written text that satisfies you, turn your attention to matters of style, readability, and correctness.

CREDIBILITY, PAGE 443

Editing is a courtesy to your reader, whether that reader is your instructor or your peer, an employer or a colleague, an individual or an audience of thousands. More important, a well-edited manuscript helps to establish your **credibility** as a writer. No matter how informed, exciting, or significant your content, your credibility also depends on whether you construct a text that readers can easily read—a clear, correct, and well-written text.

The problem is that recognizing what needs to be edited and knowing how to do it are in large measure matters of experience. One of the purposes of this book is to help you become a better editor. Each chapter focuses on different editing concerns and suggests ways for you to improve your editing skills. Here are four basic guidelines that will help you take responsibility for the readability and correctness of your text:

* Trust your instincts.

* Trust your peers.

* Trust your instructor.

* Wait to proofread.

1. TRUST YOUR INSTINCTS. Writers can usually sense problems with style, readability, and correctness even if they do not know what the problem is, what to call it, or how to fix it. If you suspect that a problem exists, it probably does. For example, if you stumble over a sentence as you read your text aloud or have to reread a sentence if you are reading silently, that sentence probably needs some editing.

2. TRUST YOUR PEERS.   Let several classmates read what you have written. Ask them to point out unclear or hard-to-read sentences, misspelled or inappropriate words, incorrect punctuation. Discuss with them how you might make these sentences easier to read.

3. TRUST YOUR INSTRUCTOR.   When instructors invite you to come by and talk to them about your writing, they mean it. Yes, they are busy, but they respect students who are concerned enough to come by for a conference. A brief conference with your instructor can not only clear up a great many editing problems in a given text but can also provide you with the information you need to avoid the same problems in the future.

4. WAIT TO PROOFREAD.   Don't trust yourself to proofread effectively immediately after you have finished writing your text. Reading aloud or pointing to each word as you read it may help alter your normal reading process and thus allow you to see what is really on the page, as opposed to what you expect to be there, but waiting until your text is cold is the best strategy. Even then, don't confuse reading and proofreading. When you read something, even something you have not written, you do not read every word, only those that are necessary to predict meaning. To proofread (or "goofread") effectively, you must alter your normal reading process to force yourself to see exactly what is there. This takes time and perseverance and even then is not easy. But a good writer is nearly always a good proofreader (see **revising and editing** and **proofreading**).

REVISING AND EDITING, PAGE 593

PROOFREADING, PAGE 585

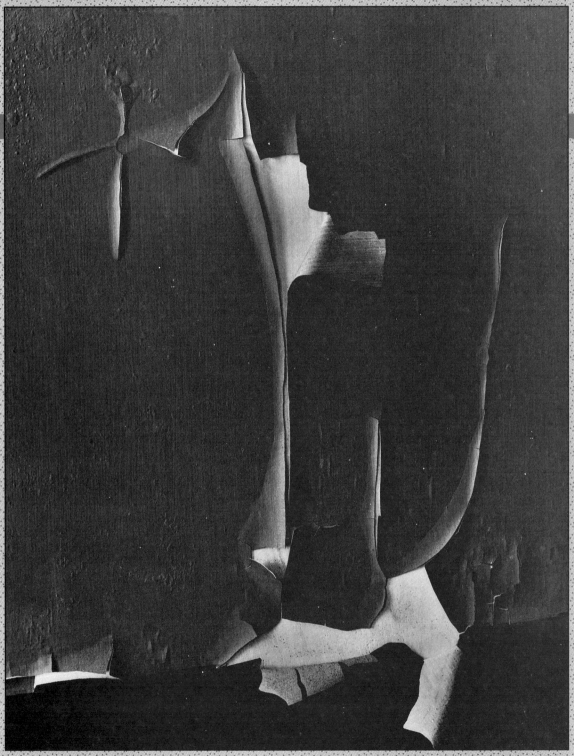

4

WRITING TO INFORM

101

Information has become perhaps the world's fastest growing and most important business.

ALVIN TOFFLER

Another reason for writing, to share information with others, may seem to you a less compelling purpose than writing to explore or writing to reconstruct experience. Most of your experience in writing to inform has probably come in academic writing—exercises, reports, tests, assignments designed to prove that you *have* certain information. But writing to inform can also give you the chance *to share* information with an interested reader, as the writers in this chapter do, sharing information about change. Although you may at times have voluntarily written to explore or to reconstruct your own experiences, you may have written to inform only when someone (usually a teacher) required you to do so.

But you live in a society that runs on information. People want to know what is happening with the stock market and the weather, in sports and education, in politics and entertainment. They want to know the latest gossip about famous people, to learn about the scandals and successes of the rich and powerful. They read histories and biographies, cookbooks and travelogues, self-help books and reference books—everything from autobiographies to zoology texts. They soak up televised information, which was writing to inform at some stage, too. Newspapers, magazines, journals, brochures, reports, letters, memos, scripts, and countless books pour forth as writers feed information to readers. Libraries overflow with information; computer databases give users access to incomprehensible amounts of information; filing cabinets across the nation bulge with neatly and not so neatly alphabetized information. Whether the field is business, education, medicine, law, engineering, finance, or government, staggering amounts of information are being produced so rapidly that storing and retrieving it becomes more difficult than assembling it.

Why do writers painstakingly gather bits and pieces of information about some subject, interpret and analyze it, and then incorporate it into their own writing in order to inform a reader? Similarly, why are readers interested in such information? Of course, humans are curious animals who like to know how things work and what has happened.

Information allows its consumers to understand the world better. Beyond simple curiosity, however, lies another reason. Increasingly in this society, information is power. People in a society as complex as ours require enormous amounts of information in order to function. As a result, information is a valuable commodity in this world, and the ability to communicate information clearly and effectively is a valuable skill.

Plainly, then, now and later you need to know how to write to inform—how to explain something to someone who wants or needs information you have. Although every discipline and profession has its own communication conventions, its own way of presenting information, you can use this chapter's general principles of effective informative writing whatever your plans for the future.

R E A D I N G   T O   B E   I N F O R M E D

You are already an experienced reader of informative writing, since most textbooks fall into this category. You have probably also had some experience in reading magazines written primarily to inform, whether *People*, *Rolling Stone*, or *Science News*. You have also read newspapers, brochures, and miscellaneous nonfiction books that include vast amounts of information. In fact, you may have already encountered so much informative writing that you read it almost automatically, sifting through the information quickly and casually to find the author's main point.

However, you need to be aware that not all information is equal. That is, some information is better—more reliable, more accurate, more up-to-date, or from better sources—than other information. You cannot take information for granted. Just because an author includes facts, specific details, statistics, even charts and graphs, you cannot assume that information always equals truth.

How Information Is Used

Information is usually a means to an end rather than an end in itself. Authors rarely provide information without using it in some way—to illustrate a point, draw a conclusion, or support an argument. Exceptions exist, or course. For example, financial reports and weather bulletins in the daily paper (or on the radio or television) are usually pure information—just the facts. The daily television guide and the scores of athletic events also fall into this pure information category. Similarly, the report of crimes committed on a college campus shown on the next page is pure information. Readers of this report are left to draw their own conclusions: For example, most violations (26) involve vehicles; the campus is a relatively safe one (no violent crimes); and property should be protected (14 instances of vandalism and theft).

But most information exists in a larger context, and that context usually has some purpose beyond merely providing you with information. For example, in this chapter's reading selections, Beth Bailey's sociological study of courtship includes information to support her theories about why certain changes have occurred and the effect of these changes on our society. Even information based on the writer's own experience, as in the essay by the student writer Morgan Hands and in *The New Republic* article by Stanley Kauffmann, should not be accepted without question.

Evaluating Information When You Read

Reading informative writing, therefore, involves not just understanding but also evaluating the information presented. Reading to be informed should always be a process of constantly evaluating the accuracy and quality of the information included. Facts and figures can and do lie. Therefore, in reading to be informed, you need to question three aspects of the information included:

* What is its source?

* Is it relevant?

* Is it accurate?

WHAT IS ITS SOURCE?   First, you need to question the author's sources: Where does the information come from? Has the author presented information that comes from unreliable or biased sources? For example, can you really trust information about gun control if the only source is the American Rifle Association or information about the effects of smoking on health if the only source is the tobacco industry?

IS IT RELEVANT?   Second, you need to question whether the information pertains to the arguments it is intended to support. For example, does the author use national statistics to support an argument about a local problem? Or analyze the causes of drug addiction among teens with information that pertains to adults? Or cite migratory patterns of

Police Report

Below is a summary of the criminal events reported to the Department of Public Safety as having occurred on the university campus; and certain significant activities of Department of Public Safety officers from 3 September through 16 September 1991.

Alcohol Related Arrests, Citations, Events, Public Drunk	1
Annoying/Obscene/Threatening Phone Calls, etc.	5
Assault, Simple	3
Bicycle Theft	3
Collision Vehicular	10
Disorderly Conduct	1
Disturbance (Noise, Fireworks, etc.)	1
Disturbance, Domestic (Problems)	5
Exhibitionist	1
Fire (Trash Can)	2
Larceny (Grand)	6
Larceny (Petit)	1
Malicious Mischief	2
Medical Assist	8
Police Assist	3
Recovered Stolen Motor Vehicle	1
Suspicious Person, Report of	4
Traffic Violations, Citations, Arrests, etc.	16
Vandalism	7
Total	80

geese in Minnesota to explain the migration of egrets in Florida? Be sure the information included supports the assertions being made. Also be sure the information is current. Does the author use information about urban problems in the 1950s as if it were directly relevant to urban problems today? In general, dated information is suspect unless the author shows how it is appropriate.

IS IT ACCURATE?   Third, you need to question whether the information is true to its source. Has the author been careless or dishonest in presenting the information? Such evaluations can be difficult to make. You cannot very well check all information you read by going back to the author's sources. But you can be aware that discrepancies can and do exist. You can become a skeptic—reading with a doubting, questioning attitude, refusing to accept information at face value just because it is in print. And when your instincts tell you information is dubious, you can and should check the source to verify its accuracy.

Also evaluate the arguments and conclusions that writers derive from the information they present. Even if the information is accurate, the author's conclusions may be invalid. A clear and logical relationship should exist between the information presented and the conclusions drawn. As a reader, it is your responsibility to test the arguments you read, weighing the author's conclusions against the evidence (information) presented. Whether that information is derived from the writer's own experiences or from other sources, it should clearly and logically support the assumptions made, the arguments presented, and CREDIBILITY, PAGE 443 the conclusions drawn (see **credibility**).

R E A D I N G S   F O R   W R I T I N G ◀

This chapter's reading selections, all written primarily to inform, focus on something that has changed. As Alvin Toffler points out in *Future Shock*, "the vast majority of people, . . . , find the idea of change so threatening that they attempt to deny its existence" (21). Because the idea of change is threatening to us, we seek explanations of how and why things change and the effects that result from the change. The authors of the reading selections in this chapter not only describe how something or someplace has changed but also explore why the change occurred and what the results have been.

A BLESSING SENT FROM HEAVEN?

Morgan Hands

The author of the following essay, a student writer in a freshman composition course, views change as problematic. Describing the changes that occurred in his hometown of Eunice, Louisiana, after the oil bust in the late 1980s, Morgan Hands suggests that the affluence and progress of the boom period may have changed the town too quickly and too drastically. His comparison of the town before and after the decline in oil prices provides readers with the information they need to understand how the town changed.

Eunice would tell a sad tale if it could speak. Like many of its neighboring cities, Eunice was once a thriving community—new buildings being built, new businesses opening, everyone working, and plenty of cash circulating. But one look at the city today and it is clear those days are gone forever.   1

Eunice, like many other cities in southern Louisiana, was almost entirely built around petroleum revenues. The petroleum revenues either directly or indirectly affected almost everything in Eunice. Obviously the petroleum revenues directly affected businesses such as gas stations, pipe companies, oil-field equipment specialists, and welders. But what is not so obvious is the fact that all the town's businesses, whether directly associated with the oil field or not, depend on petroleum-generated revenues. Take the average John Doe who earns a thousand dollars a week working for AWI workover-rigs. As a result   2 of John's prosperity, he decides that he deserves a new watch or ring from the local jeweler. Maybe next month he can afford to buy that new 27-inch, color stereo television from Perry's Home Electronics. And if John plays his cards right, he may even be able to afford that new pickup truck by the end of the year. It is not hard to see just what a dominant role petroleum revenues had on Eunice's economy.

3   Eunice was once a tiny farming community just southeast of Lafayette. Then the oil business came to town. Black-gold fever struck Eunice. Before the townspeople knew what was going on, they had all caught the fever. Most of the people around Eunice had been living off the land just as their ancestors had done centuries before them. A hard day's work only yielded a small return. But now the returns were much larger with oil at stake instead of rice or beans. Farmers began using their equipment to perform tasks for oil-related businesses. Some even sold their land and farm equipment to buy oil-field products and machinery. The petroleum era had begun. It was a blessing sent from heaven. Or was it?

4   Numerous new oil-related businesses started opening up around town and strengthening the other local businesses. They strengthened the economy so much, in fact, that the whole town began to rely almost entirely on these businesses for the revenues they generated. It was an excellent time for financial gain. The banks were giving loans to almost any and everyone. Small family-owned businesses began popping up all over town. Everyone was earning money as well as spending it. The city was literally flooded in cash and flourished with big department stores and expensive restaurants. Suddenly, yesterday's farmers were high rollers, cruisin' in Jaguars, Benzes, and Porsches. Everyone was living it up.

5   But an airplane can only fly so high before it starts on its crashing descent. The Middle East moved into the picture and began to dominate the petroleum industry. There wasn't much anyone could do about it. The federal government did what it could by placing additional taxes on imported oil. But it wasn't enough to stop the determined Middle Eastern countries. They had no trouble underselling the United States' marketers. Within no time, they had driven the U.S. oil-field business into the ground. People had no choice but to file for bankruptcy and give up on the businesses to which they had given their lives. The Middle Eastern countries crushed the U.S. market and started a domino effect of bankruptcies that continues even today. Eunice had relied so greatly on the petroleum revenues that the crash affected not only oil-field-related businesses but every

business. Because no matter what type of business it was, it relied on customers. And who employed most of these customers? The oil-related businesses.

One look at the main street in Eunice today and you'll see a   6
strong-spirited community desperately trying to get back on its feet. You may even catch a glimpse of one of the big shots of yesterday. But don't bother looking for the Porsches or Jaguars; most of them have been repossessed. Now the big shots of yesterday drive the same cars they owned ten years ago, before black-gold fever struck. Those are the lucky ones. Some have seen the empires they created destroyed before their eyes and have never recovered from such a devastating blow.

Black gold created and destroyed a number of businesses and the   7
men who built them. Black gold provided a roller coaster ride for the once boring town of Eunice, Louisiana. The ride was full of ups and downs, a definite thriller for those who were brave enough to ride.

QUESTIONS TO CONSIDER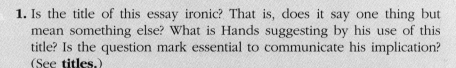

1. Is the title of this essay ironic? That is, does it say one thing but mean something else? What is Hands suggesting by his use of this title? Is the question mark essential to communicate his implication? (See **titles.**)

TITLES, PAGE 604

2. Hands gives his readers three views of Eunice: he describes the town before it became prosperous from oil revenues, while it enjoyed that prosperity, and after it suffered the loss of those revenues. Which period of time does he describe most fully? Why does the writer emphasize this period in the town's history? Does the information he provides about the other two periods give you a clear basis for comparison? That is, can you understand from the information Hands includes how drastically the town changed?

3. What is the primary source of the information Hands includes in this essay? Is this information relevant?

WRITING ACTIVITIES ◀

Individual: Write a journal entry in which you describe some change that has occurred in your hometown or in some town you know well.

Collaborative: Working in groups, brainstorm about the economic changes that have occurred in the United States during the past decade. Then formulate a general statement about economic change that reflects all of the changes you have listed.

Computer: List the main changes that have occurred during your lifetime in your hometown (or some town you know well). Identify those changes that are related and formulate a general statement expressing the nature of these changes, why they occurred, or the result of the changes on the town. Next delete from your list those changes that are not related and rearrange the remaining items into an informal outline.

❖❖❖❖❖

Two Cities
Stanley Kauffmann

This reading selection, which first appeared in The New Republic, *focuses on the changes that have occurred in New York City during the author's lifetime. New York, of course, is very different from Eunice, Louisiana, and the author, Stanley Kauffmann, is very different from Morgan Hands. For one thing, Kauffmann is a professional writer, journalist, and editor, whereas Hands is a college student. For another, Kauffmann is past middle age (born in the 1920s) whereas Hands is young (born in the 1970s). But Kauffmann, like Hands, is describing the changes that have occurred in his hometown during his lifetime. It just so happens that his hometown is New York City.*

1   A young friend asked me recently what it's like to live in the city where I grew up. The question startled me. I never think of New York that way. True, when I walk along certain streets, I remember things that happened there, but the same city?

2   When I went to grammar school in the mid-1920s on 63rd Street between Second and Third Avenues—now a chic residential neighborhood bristling with high apartment houses—I passed a blacksmith shop on the way from the corner to the middle of the block. I can still hear the hiss of the white-hot horseshoes being plunged into a bucket of water, can still sniff the burny smell of the hoof to which a warm shoe was fixed. I used to hitch rides to and from school on the back

step of horse-drawn ice wagons. I used to go shopping with my mother in the pushcart market that lined both sides of Second Avenue from 70th Street to 76th. Those pushcarts were under the Second Avenue El. We lived on 68th Street near the corner of Second, and if one of us was on the phone when an El train came along, we had to halt the conversation until it passed. (Other boroughs still have Els, but people under 50 can't imagine one in mid-Manhattan.)

In those 1920s, near the end of the great immigration wave, my schoolmates were mostly Italian Catholic and Eastern European Jewish, the children of foreign-born parents or foreign-born themselves. Both of my parents had been born in New York, as had both of my grandmothers. My schoolmates called me, semi-derisively, "the Yankee." Once a teacher asked me to carry a note to the principal. In his outer office, an Italian woman, mother of one of the students, was waiting to see him. While waiting, she was unembarrassedly nursing a baby. I remember a blue vein in her very white breast.

Radio was still new in those days, wondrous. Many of my schoolmates came from families too poor to own a set. I became something of a school celebrity because of radio and my father. He was a dentist, and in the professional society to which he belonged, he was in charge of a series of talks on dental hygiene that the society presented on the municipal radio station WNYC—fifteen minutes at midday once a week. Usually he invited other dentists to speak, but one week he did the talk himself. My mother wrote a note to my teacher asking that I be excused a half-hour before lunchtime that day, so that I could come home and hear my father. It was granted. I heard him, and I bragged. Some of my friends, especially the foreign-born ones, could hardly believe it. They actually knew someone whose father's voice had been broadcast all around New York City. One of them, probably quoting a parent, said," Only in America."

Earlier, until I was 7 years old, we lived in Washington Heights, near the northern tip of Manhattan. A photographer used to come around with a pony on which children would sit to have their picture taken. I still have mine taken at 4. (My future wife, then unknown to me, had her picture taken on the same pony a few years later.) In the summer, a truck came around with a small carousel on the back. The driver turned the carousel by hand. There was a big iron wheel at the side, and he pumped up and down while six or eight children rode around. I loved it. (My wife, a few years later, loved it too.) A man occasionally wandered through the streets, garments draped over his shoulder, calling out, "I cash clo'. I cash clo'." He bought old clothes, usually men's, that people wanted to get rid of, and then sold them somewhere. Opposite our apartment house was a large vacant lot that had never been built on. It was surrounded by apartment houses, but the lot itself was untouched. I used to clamber over rocks and climb trees that Indians had known. This was true of Central Park, too, I knew, but that was for the city. This was for me and my friends, our own Indian territory.

6   I don't live in that city anymore.

7   Is New York worse now? Of course, and not just because many of my mementos are gone. We have an average of six murders a day, often including children. We have tens of thousands of homeless men and women, some of them mentally incompetent. We have a horrific drug problem. We share those miseries with other cities; one title we hold alone. New York streets are dirtier than those in any American city I've seen (let alone London or Paris).

8   But the greatest single change in New York in my lifetime is in the view of equality. Blacks are no longer required to "know their place"—at any rate, not comparably with the rigors of the past. At least lip service is now paid to the idea of absolute equality. ("Assume a virtue, if you have it not," says Hamlet.) After World War II, Puerto Ricans flocked to New York. Soon came other Hispanics. Equality for them, too. The cash machine in my bank now asks, after I've inserted my card, whether I want my instructions in English or Spanish. New York has become, perhaps less willy than nilly, a gigantic testing ground for the idea that America has been mouthing for 200 years. This, too, is true of other American cities, but New York is the hugest crucible. Insofar as inherited hates and prejudices—in *all* of us—will permit, we are finding out whether equality can be more than a catch-word, whether equality is possible in race, religion, sexual preference, gender. (Female police officers, for example. Fully uniformed and packing pistols, they still avoid eye contact with a passing man, just like other women.) New York is at the head of the parade that is being asked to put its money where its Fourth-of-July mouth is.

9   The process is expensive. It costs everybody something. It abrades those who grew up in a stratified New York. It harries those, particularly black or Hispanic, who are on the frontier and must bear both the resentments in others and the frustrations in themselves. Surely crime rates and drug abuse are connected to the tauntings of unfulfilled equality. Surely the decline in civic pride is connected to those same frustrations.

"Superb-faced Manhattan!" sang Whitman. "Comrade Americanos! to us, then at last the Orient comes." Was he foreseeing sushi bars, Korean grocers and nail shops? Walt continued:

To us, my city,
Where our tall-topt marble and iron
   beauties range on opposite sides, to walk
   in the space between,
To-day our Antipodes comes.

10

Will the vast experiment succeed? I'll never know; but the fact that it is
happening helps to reconcile me to this dirty and dangerous city, this
second New York of my life.

11

QUESTIONS TO CONSIDER

1. How does Kauffmann use comparison and description in his article
to support his argument that New York has changed?

2. Kauffmann, like Morgan Hands, uses his own experiences as a
source of information. Especially in his description of the New York
in which he grew up, he relies on his own story—the sights and
sounds and odors that were part of his childhood experience. Are
writers justified in using their own experiences to support their assertions? That is, are personal experiences a valid form of information?

3. Kauffmann's description of the New York of his childhood seems
almost idyllic. But he begins his description of the city as it is now
by asking "Is New York worse now?" He then answers his own
question by replying, "Of course, . . ." But he concludes the article
by pointing out one important change that he views as positive:
racial equality is increasingly recognized in the city. Does
Kauffmann imply that this one positive change somehow makes up
for all of the negative changes that have occurred? Do you agree or
disagree with this position?

4. Kauffmann includes in his essay several literary allusions (see **allusion**). In his final paragraph, for example, he refers to the nineteenth-century poet Walt Whitman, who often celebrated in his
verses the worth of the individual and the kinship among humans.
The quotation Kauffmann includes is from Whitman's poem "A
Broadway Pageant." To understand this quotation, you need to know
the word *Antipodes* (an tip' po dez), which means "exact opposite"
and is often used to refer to something that is on or from the opposite side of the earth. Reread the final paragraph of the article. Do
you think Kauffmann's inclusion of this quotation strengthens his

ALLUSION, PAGE 403

argument and makes his conclusion more effective? What does his use of Walt Whitman suggest about the audience for whom he is writing?

▶ WRITING ACTIVITIES

Individual: Write a journal entry in which you describe some way in which race relations have changed in your lifetime.

Collaborative: With a group of your classmates, discuss ways in which race relations have changed for the better in recent years and ways in which they have changed for the worse. Write a brief statement that expresses clearly your group's conclusions.

Computer: Revise your journal entry so it is addressed to your classmates. If your computers are networked for text sharing, send your revised statement out to the class. While your message is being read by your classmates, read those written by them and sent to you. If time permits, respond to any of your classmates' messages that interest you. Then, after you have read the responses sent to you, revise your own message so it is an appropriate editorial for your school newspaper.

PROGRESS

John Sterling Harris

Most writing to inform is prose rather than poetry. However, poets also write to inform, including in their poetry factual information as well as imaginative descriptions and figurative language. Although the primary purpose of poetry is to create—to construct in language a work of art—poetry also communicates. The following poem by John Sterling Harris, a poet who is also a technical writer, describes how an old church was torn down and replaced by more modern, "progressive" structures. As you read, try to determine the poet's attitude toward the changing scene he describes.

The old church is down,
And where it stood
Lie scattered chunks of plaster
On dry rough-graded ground
Shielded from the rain a hundred years;   5
The dump trucks hauled away the scraps
Of age-darkened wood with
Many layers of white and ivory paint;
The bricks of the new addition,
Only half a century old,   10
Were carefully scraped of mortar
And stacked in cubical piles—
There is good demand for antique brick
To build the prosperous houses on the hill;
The huge old ceiling beams   15
And the rough-sawn red pine rafters,
Too big to use, too hard to cut,
Will make fence rails
And cattle shelters somewhere;
But the handmade adobe bricks   20
Of the chapel's yard-thick walls
Have no modern use;
The dozer knocks them down,
Not easily, but still too quickly
To return to the earth they came from.   25

It was always there,
And the schools and stores came later,
Because it was there;
Now the street is naked for its loss.

The officials point with pride   30
To the bright glass replacement up the street,
Praise the classrooms,
The long carpeted hallways
And the tall aluminum steeple
That has no bell;   35
They walk with relief over the old site
With its fearsome past all hauled away
And talk with the service station man
About his plans.

▶ QUESTIONS TO CONSIDER

1. The title of the poem, "Progress," is ironic. That is, the poet is saying one thing but means another. Although the word *regress* is the literal opposite of *progress* when it is used as a verb, there is no word that means the opposite of *progress* when it is used, as it is here, as a noun (*regression* just doesn't mean the same thing as lack of progress). Can you think of another word or phrase that would more accurately reflect the poet's attitude toward the destruction of the old church? Would this nonironic title be as effective as the ironic one the poet has chosen? Why or why not?

2. The poet states that the church "was always there." What effect does this overstatement create?

3. The poet suggests the church was responsible for the creation of the town. Is this an instance of overstatement or an accurate reflection of the town's history?

4. To what new uses will the various parts of the demolished old church be put? What type of structure is going to replace the old church? Contrast these new uses and plans with the role the church played in the past.

▶ WRITING ACTIVITIES

Individual: Change is often confused with progress. That is, we sometimes think any type of change involves progress, that simply changing something makes it better. Describe some incidence of change that supposedly represented progress but which you found counterproductive, foolish, or sad.

Collaborative: Meeting in small groups, compare the incidents you described in the individual writing activity. Then formulate two definitions of the term *progress*: one that reflects popular thinking on the subject and one that represents the group's idea of what constitutes meaningful progress.

Computer (1): Choose one of the two definitions of *progress* that your group formulated and enter it into the computer. Below the definition list examples that support it. Then revise the definition so it can serve as the topic sentence of a paragraph. Expand several of the examples you have listed into sentences that support your topic sentence.

Computer (2): Using your word-processing system, write a prose summary of the poem "Progress." Try not to leave out any of the ideas that are included in the poem, but paraphrase those ideas into straightforward prose in your own words. Share your prose version with a peer and discuss what the differences are between the poetic and the prose versions.

❖❖❖❖❖

LIFE ON THE NEW FRONTIER: EDGE CITY

Joel Garreau

Joel Garreau, a reporter for the Washington Post, *has written a book entitled* Edge City *(1991), in which he argues that the new frontiers—the places we are now settling and developing—are the edges of our cities. Neither a suburb nor a city, Edge City is a new urban center where people live and work and shop. Sprawling, modern, convenient, usually unplanned, and often ugly, these new centers of population increasingly overwhelm the cities that give birth to them. In this reading selection, taken from the first chapter of his book, Garreau defines Edge City and how it is changing the world we live in.*

Americans are creating the biggest change in a hundred years in how we build cities. Every single American city that *is* growing, is growing in the fashion of Los Angeles, with multiple urban cores. 1

These new hearths of our civilization—in which the majority of metropolitan Americans now work and around which we live—look not at all like our old downtowns. Buildings rarely rise shoulder to shoulder, as in Chicago's Loop. Instead, their broad, low outlines dot the landscape like mushrooms, separated by greensward and parking lots. Their office towers, frequently guarded by trees, gaze at one another from respectful distances through bands of glass that mirror the sun in blue or silver or green or gold, like antique drawings of "the city of the future." 2

3   The hallmarks of these new urban centers are not the sidewalks of New York of song and fable, for usually there are few sidewalks. There are jogging trails around the hills and ponds of their characteristic corporate campuses. But if an American finds himself tripping the light fantastic today on concrete, social scientists know where to look for him. He will be amid the crabapples blossoming under glassed-in skies where America retails its wares. We have quaintly if accurately named these places after that fashionable tree-lined promenade created in the late 1600s—the Mall in London's St. James Park. Back then, its denizens even had a name for the hour when the throng of promenaders "giggling with their sparks" was at its height. They called it High Mall. Pity we've not picked up that usage. We have certainly picked up the practice, because malls usually function as the village squares of these new urbs.

4   Our new city centers are tied together not by locomotives and subways, but by jetways, freeways, and rooftop satellite dishes thirty feet across. Their characteristic monument is not a horse-mounted hero, but the atria reaching for the sun and shielding trees perpetually in leaf at the cores of corporate headquarters, fitness centers, and shopping plazas. These new urban areas are marked not by the penthouses of the old urban rich or the tenements of the old urban poor. Instead, their landmark structure is the celebrated single-family detached dwelling, the suburban home with grass all around that made America the best-housed civilization the world has ever known.

5   I have come to call these new urban centers Edge Cities. Cities, because they contain all the functions a city ever has, albeit in a spread-out form that few have come to recognize for what it is. Edge, because they are a vigorous world of pioneers and immigrants, rising far from the old downtowns, where little save villages or farmland lay only thirty years before.

6   Edge Cities represent the third wave of our lives pushing into new frontiers in this half century. First, we moved our homes out past the traditional idea of what constituted a city. This was the suburbanization of America, especially after World War II.

7   Then we wearied of returning downtown for the necessities of life, so we moved our marketplaces out to where we lived. This was the malling of America, especially in the 1960s and 1970s.

8   Today, we have moved our means of creating wealth, the essence of urbanism—our jobs—out to where most of us have lived and shopped for two generations. That has led to the rise of Edge City.

9   Not since more than a century ago, when we took Benjamin Franklin's picturesque mercantile city of Philadelphia and exploded it

into a nineteenth-century industrial behemoth, have we made such
profound changes in the ways we live, work, and play.

    Good examples of our more than two hundred new Edge Cities are: 10

❖ The area around Route 128 and the Massachusetts Turnpike in   11
the Boston region that was the birthplace of applied high technology;

❖ The Schaumburg area west of O'Hare Airport, near which Sears
moved its corporate headquarters from the 110-story Sears
Tower in downtown Chicago;

❖ The Perimeter Center area, at the northern tip of Atlanta's Belt-
way, that is larger than downtown Atlanta;

❖ Irvine, in Orange County, south of Los Angeles.

    By any functional urban standard—tall buildings, bright lights,   12
office space that represents white-collar jobs, shopping, entertainment,
prestigious hotels, corporate headquarters, hospitals with CAT scans,
even population—each Edge City is larger than downtown Portland,
Oregon, or Portland, Maine, or Tampa, or Tucson. Already, two thirds
of all American office facilities are in Edge Cities, and 80 percent of
them have materialized in only the last two decades. By the mid-1980s,
there was far more office space in Edge Cities around America's largest
metropolis, New York, than there was at its heart—midtown
Manhattan. Even before Wall Street faltered in the late 1980s there was
less office space there, in New York's downtown, than there was in
the Edge Cities of New Jersey alone.

    Even the old-fashioned Ozzie and Harriet commute from a con-   13
ventional suburb to downtown is now very much a minority pattern,
U.S. Census figures show. Most of the trips metropolitan Americans
take in a day completely skirt the old centers. Their journeys to work,
especially, are to Edge Cities. So much of our shopping is done in
Edge Cities that a casual glance at most Yellow Pages shows it increasingly difficult in an old downtown to buy such a commodity item as a
television set.

    These new urban agglomerations are such mavericks that every-   14
one who wrestles them to the ground tries to brand them. Their list of
titles by now has become marvelous, rich, diverse, and sometimes
unpronounceable. The litany includes: urban villages, technoburbs,
suburban downtowns, suburban activity centers, major diversified centers, urban cores, galactic city, pepperoni-pizza cities, a city of realms,

superburbia, disurb, service cities, perimeter cities, and even peripheral centers. Sometimes it is not clear that everybody is talking about the same thing. My heart particularly goes out to the San Francisco reporter who just started calling whatever was seething out there, past the sidewalks, Tomorrowland.

15   The reasons these places are tricky to define is that they rarely have a mayor or a city council, and just about never match boundaries on a map. We're still in the process of giving each Edge City its name—a project, incidentally, that could use more flair. In New Jersey, for example, there is one with only the laconic designation "287 and 78." The reason there are no "Welcome to" signs at Edge City is that it is a judgment call where it begins and ends.

16   Take the traditional measure of urban size—population. The out-counties where Edge Cities now rise are almost by definition larger than the cores they surround. After all, these places we thought of until recently as suburbs are where the majority of Americans have been living for decades. Fairfax County, Virginia, is more populous than either Washington, D.C., or San Francisco. Ninety-two percent of the people in the New York metropolitan area do not live in Manhattan.

17   A more narrow, and I think more accurate, comparison is to take Edge City—that acreage where the huge growth in jobs and other truly urban functions is centered—and compare it with the old central business district, the old downtown. Even by that tight measure, Edge City is almost always more populous. How many people in America, after all, live right in the old downtown? Fewer than live within sight of that Edge City landmark—the office monument so huge it would have been unthinkable to build one anywhere but downtown only thirty years ago.

18   That is why I have adopted the following five-part definition of Edge City that is above all else meant to be functional.

19   Edge City is any place that:

20   ❖ *Has five million square feet or more of leasable office space—the workplace of the Information Age.* Five million square feet is more than downtown Memphis. The Edge City called the Galleria area west of downtown Houston—crowned by the sixty-four-story Transco Tower, the tallest building in the world outside an old downtown—is bigger than downtown Minneapolis.

❖ *Has 600,000 square feet or more of leasable retail space.* That is the equivalent of a fair-sized mall. That mall, remember, probably has at leas three nationally famous department stores, and eighty to a hundred shops and boutiques full of merchandise

that used to be available only on the finest boulevards of
Europe. Even in their heyday, there were not many downtowns
with that boast.

* *Has more jobs than bedrooms.* When the workday starts, people
  head toward this place, not away from it. Like all urban places,
  the population increases at 9 a.m.

* *Is perceived by the population as one place.* It is a regional end
  destination for mixed use—not a starting point—that "has it all,"
  from jobs, to shopping, to entertainment.

* *Was nothing like "city" as recently as thirty years ago.* Then, it was
  just bedrooms, if not cow pastures. This incarnation is brand new.

An example of the authentic, California-like experience of   21
encountering such an Edge City is peeling off a high thruway, like the
Pennsylvania Turnpike, onto an arterial, like 202 at King of Prussia,
northwest of downtown Philadelphia. Descending into traffic that is
bumper to bumper in *both* directions, one swirls through mosaics of
lawn and parking, punctuated by office slabs whose designers have
taken the curious vow of never placing windows in anything other
than horizontal reflective strips. Detours mark the yellow dust of heavy
construction that seems a permanent feature of the landscape.

Tasteful signs mark corporations apparently named after Klingon   22
warriors. Who put Captain Kirk in charge of calling companies Imtrex,
Avanor, and Synovus? Before that question can settle, you encounter
the spoor of—the mother ship. On King of Prussia's Route 202, the
mark of that mind-boggling enormity reads MALL NEXT FOUR LEFTS.

For the stranger who is a connoisseur of such places, this Dante-   23
esque vision brings a physical shiver to the spine and a not entirely
ironic murmur of recognition to the lips: "Ah! Home!" For that is precisely the significance of Edge Cities. They are the culmination of a
generation of individual American value decisions about the best ways
to live, work, and play—about how to create "home." That stuff "out
there" is where America is being built. That "stuff" is the delicate balance between unlimited opportunity and rippling chaos that works for
us so well. We build more of it every chance we get.

If Edge Cities are still a little ragged at the fringes, well, that just   24
places them in the finest traditions of Walt Whitman's "barbaric yawp
over the rooftops of the world"—what the social critic Tom Wolfe calls,
affectionately, the "hog-stomping Baroque exuberance of American
civilization." Edge Cities, after all, are still works in progress.

25   They have already proven astoundingly efficient, though, by any urban standard that can be quantified. As places to make one's fame and fortune, their corporate offices generate unprecedentedly low unemployment. In fact, their emblem is the hand-lettered sign taped to plate glass begging people to come to work. As real estate markets, they have made an entire generation of homeowners and speculators rich. As bazaars, they are anchored by some of the most luxurious shopping in the world. Edge City acculturates immigrants, provides child care, and offers safety. It is, on average, an *improvement* in per capita fuel efficiency over the old suburbia-downtown arrangement, since it moves everything closer to the homes of the middle class.

26   That is why Edge City is the crucible of America's urban future. Having become the place in which the majority of Americans now live, learn, work, shop, play, pray, and die, Edge City will be the forge of the fabled American way of life well into the twenty-first century.

27   There are those who find this idea appalling. For some who recognize the future when they see it, but always rather hoped it might look like Paris in the 1920s, the sprawl and apparent chaos of Edge City makes it seem a wild, raw, and alien place. For my sins I once spent a fair chunk of a Christmas season in Tysons Corner, Virginia, stopping people as they hurried about their holiday tasks, asking them what they thought of their brave new world. The words I recorded were searing. They described the area as plastic, a hodgepodge, Disneyland (used as a pejorative), and sterile. They said it lacked livability, civilization, community, neighborhood, and even a soul.

28   These responses are frightening, if Edge City is the laboratory of how civilized and livable urban America will be well into the next century. Right now, it is vertigo-inducing. It may have all the complexity, diversity, and size of a downtown. But it can cover dozens of square miles, and juxtapose schools and freeways and atria and shimmering parking lots with corporate lawns and Day-Glo-orange helicopter wind socks. Its logic takes a while to decode.

29   Will we ever be proud of this place? Will we ever drag our visiting relatives out to show off our Edge City, our shining city on the hill? Will we ever feel—for this generation and the ones that follow—that it's a good place to be young? To be old? To fall in love? To have a Fourth of July parade? Will it ever be the place we want to call home?

30   Robert Fishman, a Rutgers historian who is one of the few academics successfully to examine Edge City, thinks he knows the answer. "All new city forms appear in their early stages to be chaotic," he reports. He quotes Charles Dickens on London in 1848: "There were a hundred thousand shapes and substances of incompleteness, wildly

mingled out of their places, upside down, burrowing in the earth, aspiring in the earth, moldering in the water, and unintelligible as in any dream."

That is also the best one-sentence description of Edge City extant.   31

Edge City's problem is history. It has none. If Edge City were a   32 forest, then at maturity it might turn out to be quite splendid, in triple canopy. But who is to know if we are seeing only the first, scraggly growth? I once heard an academic with a French accent ask Fishman, seriously, what the *ideal* of an Edge City was. What a wonderfully French question! Who *knows* what these things look like when they grow up? These critters are likely only in their nymphal, if not larval, forms. We've probably never *seen* an adult one.

If Edge City still gives some people the creeps, it is partially   33 because it confounds expectations. Traditional-downtown urbanites recoil because a place blown out to automobile scale is not what they think of as "city." They find the swirl of functions intimidating, confusing, maddening. Why are these tall office buildings so far apart? Why are they juxtaposed, apparently higgledy-piggledy, among the malls and strip shopping centers and fast-food joints and self-service gas stations? Both literally and metaphorically, these urbanites always get lost.

At the same time, Edge City often does not meet the expectations   34 of traditional suburbanites, either. Few who bought into the idea of quarter-acre tranquility ever expected to take a winding turn and suddenly be confronted with a 150-foot colossus looming over the trees, red aircraft-warning beacons flashing, its towering glass reflecting not the moon, but the sodium vapor of the parking lot's lights.

The question is whether this disorienting expectation gap is per-   35 manent or simply a phase, a function of how fast we've transformed our world. I discussed this with scholars who had examined the history of Venice. Venice today is venerated by American urban planners as a shrine to livability. What was Venice like when it was new?

"People forget that Venice was built by hook or by crook,"   36 replied Dennis Romano, a social historian of the early Renaissance. "Venice was just as mercantilist as Tysons. It was full of land speculators and developers. The merchants' primary concern was the flow of goods, of traffic. Those who now romanticize Venice collapse a thousand years of history. Venice is a monument to a dynamic process, not to great urban planning. It's hard for us to imagine, but the architectural harmony of the Piazza San Marco was an accident. It was built over centuries by people who were constantly worried about whether they had enough money."

37   In his plan for the urban future that he christened Broadacre City, that most relentlessly American of urban visionaries, Frank Lloyd Wright, anticipated with stunning accuracy many of the features of Edge City.

38   "Nonsense is talked by our big skyscraperites in the blind alley they have set up, defending urban congestion by obscuring the simple facts of the issue," he trumpeted in the 1950s in *The Living City*. "Their skyscraper-by-skyscraper is . . . the gravestone of . . . centralization."

39   Wright viewed as interchangeable the concepts of individualism, freedom, and democracy. He saw them as fundamentally in opposition to the despised, exploitative "monarchy" of the old downtowns. He yearned for a system in which all men fled the evils of big capital, big authorities, big cities—troglodytes of every stripe—for a connection with nature, the earth, the ground. He thought an acre per person was about right. He saw individuals newly freed coming back together in totally modern agglomerations, on new terms, stronger, growing together "in adequate space." He saw the automobile and aircraft as the glorious agents of that dispersion and reintegration, and he knew exactly what would happen when inexorably, we blew Edge City out to their scale:

40   "After all is said and done, *he*—the citizen—is really the city. The city is going where he goes. He is learning to go where he enjoys all the city ever gave him, plus freedom, security, and beauty of his birthright, the good ground."

41   How *about* that. We've done it! Just as he said. But are we in our new Edge Cities ever going to reap the benefits of what he knew we'd sow?

42   "Try to live . . . deep *in* nature," he exhorted us. "Be native as trees to the wood, as grass to the floor of the valley. Only then can the democratic spirit of man, individual, rise out of the confusion of communal life in the city to a creative civilization of the ground."

43   Edge City has quite clearly released us from the shackles of the nineteenth-century city—out into that valley and wood, just as Wright foresaw. It is common for a first-generation Edge City to arise ten miles from an old downtown, and a next-generation one twenty miles beyond that, only to attract workers from distances forty-five minutes beyond that. At this rate, it is easy to see how a field of Edge Cities can easily cover more than ten thousand square miles. This is why the San Francisco area now statistically is measured as halfway across California, pulling commuters out of Stockton, in the Central Valley, into its Edge Cities east of Silicon Valley.

44   Whether that spatial liberation leads to Wright's "creative civilization of the ground," however, came to be my main concern, for it is

central to the battles being fought in America today over such amorphous essentials as "growth" and "quality of life."

The forces of change whose emblem is the bulldozer, and the 45
forces of preservation whose totem is the tree, are everywhere at war in this country. The raging debate over what we have lost and what we have gained, as we flee the old urban patterns of the nineteenth century for the new ones of the twenty-first, is constant. Are we satisfying our deepest yearnings for the good life with Edge City? Or are we poisoning everything across which we sprawl?

Getting to the bottom of those questions leads directly to issues 46
of national character, of what we value. They come down to who we are, how we got that way, and where we're headed. It is why, when the reeling feeling caused by Edge City finally subsides, I think it is possible to examine the place as the expression of some fundamental values. Nowhere in the American national character, as it turns out, is there as deep a divide as that between our reverence for "unspoiled" nature and our enduring devotion to "progress."

In *The Machine in the Garden*, the cultural historian Leo Marx 47
writes about our complicated attitudes toward utilitarian versus pastoral landscapes. For Americans, he observes,

> regenerative power is located in the natural terrain: access to
> undefiled, bountiful, sublime Nature is what accounts for the
> virtue and special good fortune of Americans. It enables them
> to design a community in the image of a garden, an ideal
> fusion of nature with art. The landscape thus becomes the symbolic repository of value of all kinds—economic, political, aesthetic, religious . . . .
>
> A strong urge to believe in the rural myth along with an
> awareness of industrialization as counterforce to the myth—since
> 1844, this motif appears everywhere in American writing . . . It is
> a complex distinctively American form.

One springtime, over lunch near his MIT office, Marx observed 48
that Edge City represents "an escape from the negative aspects of civilization. Too much restraint, oppression, hierarchy—you justify building out there in order to start again and have another Garden. You want the best of both worlds. This would be Thomas Jefferson's Virginia; he very explicitly wanted a land that is midway between too much and too little civilization."

In fact, says Marx, the whole thing goes back to the very dawn of 49
our civilization. Captain Arthur Barlowe, captain of a bark dispatched by Sir Walter Raleigh, described Virginia in 1584 in what became a car-

dinal image of America: an immense garden of incredible abundance. Virginia is a land of plenty; the soil is "the most plentifull, sweete, fruitfull, and wholsome of all the worlde"; the virgin forest is not at all like the "barren and fruitles" woods of Europe. We "found shole water," Barlowe wrote, "wher we smelt so sweet and so strong a smel, as if we had bene in the midst of some delicate garden abounding with all kinde of odoriferous flowers . . ."

50   What Barlowe was describing, of course, was Eden. That image inflamed the popular imagination as the first English settlement succeeded in America, in Jamestown, Virginia, 1607. It drove Shakespeare when, three years later, he wrote *The Tempest.*

51   What is so striking about these reports depicting Virginia as Paradise Regained—tapping a deep and persistent human desire to return to a natural idyll—is how sharply they conflict with the views of the second set of Englishmen to show up in America to stay. Those were the Pilgrims of the Massachusetts Bay. When the *Mayflower* hove to off Cape Cod in November 1620, what William Bradford saw shocked him. He described it as a "hidious and desolate wilderness, full of wild beasts and willd men." Between the Pilgrims and their new home, he saw only "deangerous shoulds and roring breakers."

52   This wasn't heaven. Quite the opposite.

53   "Which way soever they turnd their eys (save upward to the heavens) they could have litle solace or content . . . The whole countrie, full of woods and thickets, represented a wild and savage heiw."

54   His people, said Bradford, had "no friends to wellcome them, nor inns to entertaine or refresh their weather beaten bodys, no houses or much less townes to repaire too, to seeke for succoure."

55   There was, in short, no civilization. Bradford found this void horrifying, hellish.

56   Here, then, is established the enduring divide in the way Americans have related to their land ever since. The hideous wilderness appears at one end of the spectrum, and the Garden at the other. These are such antithetical ways for man to understand his relation to his environment that Leo Marx calls them "ecological images. Each is a kind of root metaphor, a quite distinct notion of America's destiny." These vastly different systems of value, noted Ralph Waldo Emerson, would "determine all their institutions."

57   It comes to this. One vision of the American natural landscape was that it had inherent value and should be treasured for what it already was and had always been. The other saw in the land nothing but satanic wastes; there could be placed on it no value until it was bent to man's will—until civilization was forced into bloom.

The history of America is an endless repetition of this battle. We   58
are fighting it to this day, nowhere more so than in our current frontier, Edge City. In the unsettled, unsettling environment of Edge City,
great wealth may be acquired, but without a sense that the place has
community, or even a center, much less a soul. And the resolution of
these issues goes far beyond architecture and landscape. It goes to the
philosophical ground on which we are building our Information Age
society. It's possible that Edge City is the most purposeful attempt
Americans have made since the days of the Founding Fathers to try to
create something like a new Eden.

Edge City may be the result of Americans striving once again for   59
a new, restorative synthesis. Perhaps Edge City represents Americans
taking the functions of the city (the machine) and bringing them out to
the physical edge of the landscape (the frontier). There, we try once
again to merge the two in a new found union of nature and art (the
garden), albeit one in which the treeline is punctuated incongruously
by office towers.

If that is true, Edge City represents Americans once again trying to   60
create a new and better world—lighting out for the Territory, in the
words of Huckleberry Finn. If that new world happens to be an
unknown and uncharted frontier, well, that's where we've headed
every chance we've had—for four hundred years. Frank Lloyd Wright
genuinely believed that Americans continued to be the sons and daughters of the pioneers. He called us "the sons of the sons of American
Democracy." Wright saw us as heading out of our old cities, freed from
old verities, creating a new spiritual integrity in community. The enduring, exhilarating, and frightening themes to be examined in Edge Cities
are if, whether, and how we are pulling the Utopian vision off.

This goes to the ultimate significance of Edge City. The battles we   61
fight today over our futures do not have echoes only back to 1956,
when Dwight D. Eisenhower changed America forever with the creation of the interstate highway program. Nor does it go back only to
the New Deal of the 1930s, during which Franklin Delano Roosevelt
shaped America into a society of homeowners. It goes to the core of
what makes America America, right back to the beginning, with the
Pilgrims in 1620 and the Virginia Cavaliers of 1607.

It addresses profound questions, the answers to which will rever-   62
berate forever. It addresses the search for Utopia at the center of the
American Dream. It reflects our perpetually unfinished American business of reinventing ourselves, redefining ourselves, restoring ourselves,
announcing that our centuries-old perpetual revolution—our search for
the future inside ourselves—still beats strong.

63   It suggests that the world of the immigrants and pioneers is not dead in America; it has just moved out to Edge City, where gambles are being lost and won for high stakes. It adds another level of history to places already filled with ghosts. That is why one day Edge City, too, may be seen as historic. It is the creation of a new world, being shaped by the free in a constantly reinvented land.

▶   **QUESTIONS TO CONSIDER**

1. According to Garreau, what are the defining features of Edge City? Based on your own experience with these new urban centers, what other features would you add?

2. Garreau uses comparisons, examples, and descriptions to define Edge City. Find examples of his use of each of these strategies and evaluate how well they help you grasp the concept of an Edge City.

3. What is Garreau's attitude toward Edge City? Do you think his attitude is unbiased and objective? Why or why not?

4. Compare Edge City to Eunice, Louisiana, and New York City. Also compare Garreau's attitude toward Edge City to Morgan Hand's attitude toward Eunice and Stanley Kauffmann's attitude toward New York City. Can you imagine a person who lives in an Edge City thinking of it as a hometown? Why or why not?

ANALOGY, PAGE 413   **5.** Garreau compares Edge City to a frontier. Is this an appropriate **analogy**? How is an Edge City like a frontier and how is it not?

6. Much of Garreau's information derives from his own observations, but he also cites a variety of other sources—everyone from Frank Lloyd Wright to Walt Whitman. Which do you find more relevant: his own observations or his quotations from well-known people? Why?

▶   **WRITING ACTIVITIES**

Individual: Describe a particular Edge City you know well. Use the defining features that Garreau identifies as the basis for your description.

Collaborative: Discuss how living in Edge City is different from living in a rural area, a medium-sized or small town, a suburb, or an inner city. Decide if these changes represent progress.

Computer: Using your word-processing program, write a brief poem about Edge City. One way you might begin your poem is

America has moved to Edge City,
A new frontier where . . .

Look back at the poem "Progress" for ideas on how you might structure your own poem. Use the features of your word-processing program (such as indent, bold, underline, spacing, font styles, etc.) creatively to highlight words and phrases in your poem.

❖❖❖❖❖

FROM FRONT PORCH TO BACK SEAT

Beth L. Bailey

This reading selection is the first chapter of a sociological study of courtship in twentieth-century America. The author, Beth Bailey, focuses on a different type of changing scene. Bailey points out that courtship has literally moved from the front porch of the girl's home to the back seat of the boy's car, "from woman's sphere to man's sphere." In supporting her thesis, Bailey provides her readers with a wealth of information about dating, including how the word date *entered our vocabulary, why dating began, and what effects it has had on courtship in the United States.*

One day, the 1920s story goes, a young man asked a city girl if   1
he might call on her. We know nothing else about the man or the girl—only that, when he arrived, she had her hat on. Not much of a story to us, but any American born before 1910 would have gotten the punch line. "She had her hat on": those five words were rich in meaning to early twentieth-century Americans. The hat signaled that she expected to leave the house. He came on a "call," expecting to be received in her family's parlor, to talk, to meet her mother, perhaps to have some refreshments or to listen to her play the piano. She expected a "date," to be taken "out" somewhere and entertained. He ended up spending four weeks' savings fulfilling her expectations.

2   In the early twentieth century this new style of courtship, dating, had begun to supplant the old. Born primarily of the limits and opportunities of urban life, dating had almost completely replaced the old system of calling by the mid-1920s—and, in so doing, had transformed American courtship. Dating moved courtship into the public world, relocating it from family parlors and community events to restaurants, theaters, and dance halls. At the same time, it removed couples from the implied supervision of the private sphere—from the watchful eyes of family and local community—to the anonymity of the public sphere. Courtship among strangers offered couples new freedom. But access to the public world of the city required money. One had to buy entertainment, or even access to a place to sit and talk. Money—men's money—became the basis of the dating system and, thus, of courtship. This new dating system, as it shifted courtship from the private to the public sphere and increasingly centered around money, fundamentally altered the balance of power between men and women in courtship.

3   The transition from calling to dating was as complete as it was fundamental. By the 1950s and 1960s, social scientists who studied American courtship found it necessary to remind the American public that dating was a "recent American innovation and not a traditional or universal custom." Some of the many commentators who wrote about courtship believed dating was the best thing that had ever happened to relations between the sexes; others blamed the dating system for all the problems of American youth and American marriage. But virtually everyone portrayed the system dating replaced as infinitely simpler, sweeter, more innocent, and more graceful. Hardheaded social scientists waxed sentimental about the "horse-and-buggy days," when a young man's offer of a ride home from church was tantamount to a proposal and when young men came calling in the evenings and courtship took place safely within the warm bosom of the family. "The courtship which grew out of the sturdy social roots [of the nineteenth century]," one author wrote, "comes through to us for what it was—a gracious ritual, with clearly defined roles for man and woman, in which everyone knew the measured music and the steps."

4   Certainly a less idealized version of this model of courtship had existed in America, but it was not this model that dating was supplanting. Although only about 45 percent of Americans lived in urban areas by 1910, few of them were so untouched by the sweeping changes of the late nineteenth century that they could live that dream of rural simplicity. Conventions of courtship at that time were not set by simple

yeoman farmers and their families but by the rising middle class, often
in imitation of the ways of "society."

By the late nineteenth century a new and relatively coherent   5
social group had come to play an important role in the nation's cultural
life. This new middle class, born with and through the rise of national
systems of economy, transportation, and communication, was actively
creating, controlling, and consuming a national system of culture.
National magazines with booming subscription rates promulgated middle-class standards to the white, literate population at large. Women's
magazines were especially important in the role of cultural evangelist.

These magazines carried clearly didactic messages to their reader-   6
ship. Unlike general-interest (men's) magazines, which were more
likely to contain discussions of issues and events, women's magazines
were highly prescriptive, giving advice on both the spiritual and the
mundane. But while their advice on higher matters was usually
vaguely inspirational, advice on how to look and how to act was
extremely explicit.

The conventions of courtship, as set forth in these national maga-   7
zines and in popular books of etiquette, were an important part of the
middle-class code of manners. Conventional courtship centered on
"calling," a term that could describe a range of activities. The young
man from the neighboring farm who spent the evening sitting on the
front porch with the farmer's daughter was paying a call, and so was
the "society" man who could judge his prospects by whether or not
the card he presented at the front door found the lady of his choice "at
home." The middle-class arbiters of culture, however, aped and elabo-
rated the society version of the call. And, as it was promulgated by
magazines such as the *Ladies' Home Journal*, with a circulation over
one million by 1900, the modified society call was the model for an
increasing number of young Americans.

Outside of courtship, this sort of calling was primarily a woman's   8
activity, for women largely controlled social life. Women designated a
day or days "at home" to receive callers; on other days they paid or
returned calls. The caller would present her card to the maid (common
even in moderate-income homes until the World War I era) who
answered the door, and would be admitted or turned away with some
excuse. The caller who regularly was "not received" quickly learned
the limits of her family's social status, and the lady "at home" thus, in
some measure, protected herself and her family from the social confusion and pressures engendered by the mobility and expansiveness of

late nineteenth-century America. In this system, the husband, though generally determining the family's status, was represented by his wife and was thereby excused from this social-status ritual. Unmarried men, however, were subject to this female-controlled system .

9   The calling system in courtship, though varying by region and the status of the individuals involved, followed certain general outlines. When a girl reached the proper age or had her first "season" (depending on her family's social level), she became eligible to receive male callers. At first her mother or guardian invited young men to call; in subsequent seasons the young lady had more autonomy and could bestow an invitation to call upon any unmarried man to whom she had been properly introduced at a private dance, dinner, or other "entertainment." Any unmarried man invited to an entertainment owed his hostess (and thus her daughter[s]) a duty call of thanks, but other young men not so honored could be brought to call by friends or relatives of the girl's family, subject to her prior permission. Undesired or undesirable callers, on the other hand, were simply given some excuse and turned away.

10   The call itself was a complicated event. A myriad of rules governed everything: the proper amount of time between invitation and visit (a fortnight or less); whether or not refreshments should be served (not if one belonged to a fashionable or semi-fashionable circle, but outside of "smart" groups in cities like New York and Boston, girls *might* serve iced drinks with little cakes or tiny cups of coffee or hot chocolate and sandwiches); chaperonage (the first call must be made on daughter and mother, but excessive chaperonage would indicate to the man that his attentions were unwelcome); appropriate topics of conversation (the man's interests, but never too personal); how leave should be taken (on no account should the woman "accompany [her caller] to the door nor stand talking while he struggles into his coat").

11   Each of these "measured steps," as the mid-twentieth-century author nostalgically called them, was a test of suitability, breeding and background. Advice columns and etiquette books emphasized that these were the manners of any "well-bred" person—and conversely implied that deviations revealed a lack of breeding. However, around the turn of the century, many people who did lack this narrow "breeding" aspired to politeness. Advice columns in women's magazines regularly printed questions from "Country Girl" and "Ignoramus" on the fine points of calling etiquette. Young men must have felt the pressure of girls' expectations, for they wrote to the same advisers with questions about calling. In 1907, *Harper's Bazaar* ran a major article titled "Etiquette for Men," explaining the ins and outs of the calling system.

In the first decade of the twentieth century, this rigid system of calling was the convention not only of the "respectable" but also of those who aspired to respectability.

At the same time, however, the new system of dating was emerging. By the mid-1910s, the word *date* had entered the vocabulary of the middle-class public. In 1914, the *Ladies' Home Journal*, a bastion of middle-class respectability, used the term (safely enclosed in quotation marks but with no explanation of its meaning) several times. The word was always spoken by the exotica, the college sorority girl—a character marginal in her exoticness but nevertheless a solid product of the middle class. "One beautiful evening of the spring term," one such article begins, "when I was a college girl of eighteen, the boy whom, because of his popularity in every phase of college life, I had been proud gradually to allow the monopoly of my 'dates,' took me unexpectedly into his arms. As he kissed me impetuously I was glad, from the bottom of my heart, for the training of that mother who had taught me to hold myself aloof from all personal familiarities of boys and men." 12

Sugarcoated with a tribute to motherhood and virtue, the dates—and the kiss—were unmistakably presented for a middle-class audience. By 1924, ten years later, when the story of the unfortunate young man who went to call on the city girl was current, dating had essentially replaced calling in middle-class culture. The knowing smiles of the story's listeners had probably started with the word *call*—and not every hearer would have been sympathetic to the man's plight. By 1924, he really should have known better. 13

Dating, the great American middle-class institution, was not at all a product of the middle class. Dating came to the middle class through the upper classes—and from the lower. The first recorded uses of the word *date* in its modern meaning are from lower-class slang. George Ade, the Chicago author who wrote a column titled "Stories of the Streets and of the Town" for the *Chicago Record* and published many slang-filled stories of working-class life, probably introduced the term to literature in 1896. Artie, Ade's street-smart protagonist, asks his unfaithful girlfriend, "I s'pose the other boy's fillin' all my dates?" And in 1899 Ade suggested the power of a girl's charms: "Her Date Book had to be kept on the Double Entry System." Other authors whose imaginations were captured by the city and the variety of its ihabitants—Frank Norris, Upton Sinclair, O. Henry—also were using the term by the first decade of the twentieth century. 14

The practice of dating was a response of the lower classes to the pressures and opportunities of urban-industrial America, just as calling was a response of the upper stratas. The strict conventions of calling 15

enabled the middling and upper classes to protect themselves from
some of the intrusions of urban life, to screen out some of the effects
of social and geographical mobility in late nineteenth-century America.
Those without the money and security to protect themselves from the
pressures of urban life or to control the overwhelming opportunities it
offered adapted to the new conditions much more directly.

16   Dating, which to the privileged and protected would seem a system of increased freedom and possibility, stemmed originally from the
lack of opportunities. Calling, or even just visiting, was not a practica-
ble system for young people whose families lived crowded into one or
two rooms. For even the more established or independent working-
class girls, the parlor and the piano often simply didn't exist. Some
"factory girls" struggled to find a way to receive callers. The *Ladies'
Home Journal* approvingly reported the case of six girls, workers in a
box factory, who had formed a club and pooled part of their wages to
pay the "janitress of a tenement house" to let them use her front room
two evenings a week. It had a piano. One of the girls explained their
system: "We ask the boys to come when they like and spend the
evening. We haven't any place at home to see them, and I hate seeing
them on the street."

17   Many other working girls, however, couldn't have done this even
had they wanted to. They had no extra wages to pool, or they had no
notions of middle-class respectability. Some, especially girls of ethnic
families, were kept secluded—chaperoned according to the customs of
the old country. But many others fled the squalor, drabness, and
crowdedness of their homes to seek amusement and intimacy elsewhere. And a "good time" increasingly became identified with public
places and commercial amusements, making young women whose
wages would not even cover the necessities of life dependent on
men's "treats." Still, many poor and working-class couples did not so
much escape from the home as they were pushed from it.

18   These couples courted on the streets, sometimes at cheap dance
halls or eventually at the movies. These were not respectable places,
and women could enter them only so far as they, themselves, were not
considered respectable. Respectable young women did, of course,
enter the public world, but their excursions into the public were cushioned. Public courtship of middle-class and upper-class youth was at
least *supposed* to be chaperoned; those with money and social position
went to private dances with carefully controlled guest lists, to theater
parties where they were a private group within the public. As rebels
would soon complain, the supervision of society made the private par-

lor seem almost free by contrast. Women who were not respectable did have relative freedom of action—but the trade-off was not necessarily a happy one for them.

The negative factors were important, but dating rose equally from the possibilities offered by urban life. Privileged youth, as Lewis Erenberg shows in his study of New York nightlife, came to see the possibility of privacy in the anonymous public, in the excitement and freedom the city offered. They looked to lower-class models of freedom—to those beyond the constraints of respectability. As a society girl informed the readers of the *Ladies' Home Journal* in 1914: "Nowadays it is considered 'smart' to go to the low order of dance halls, and not only be a looker-on, but also to dance among all sorts and conditions of men and women. . . . Nowadays when we enter a restaurant and dance place it is hard to know who is who." In 1907, the same magazine had warned unmarried women never to go alone to a "public restaurant" with any man, even a relative. There was no impropriety in the act, the adviser had conceded, but it still "lays [women] open to misunderstanding and to being classed with women of undesirable reputation by the strangers present." Rebellious and adventurous young people sought that confusion, and the gradual loosening of proprieties they engendered helped to change courtship. Young men and women went out into the world *together*, enjoying a new kind of companionship and the intimacy of a new kind of freedom from adult supervision. 19

The new freedom that led to dating came from other sources as well. Many more serious (and certainly respectable) young women were taking advantage of opportunities to enter the public world— going to college, taking jobs, entering and creating new urban professions. Women who belonged to the public world by day began to demand fuller access to the public world in general. City institutions gradually accommodated them. Though still considered risqué by some, dining out alone with a man or attending the theater with no chaperone did not threaten an unmarried woman's reputation by the start of the twentieth century. 20

There were still limits, of course, and they persisted for a long while. Between 1904 and 1907, *Ladies' Home Journal* advisers repeatedly insisted that a girl should not "go out" with a young man until he had called at her home. And in the early 1920s, Radcliffe girls were furnished with a list of approved restaurants in which they could dine with a young man. Some were acceptable only before 7:30 p.m.; others, clearly, still posed a threat to reputations. These limits and condi- 21 tions, however, show that young men and women of courting age were *expected* to go out—the restrictions were not attempts to *stop* dating, only to control it.

22   Between 1890 and 1925, dating—in practice and in name—had gradually, almost imperceptibly, become a universal custom in America. By the 1930s it had transcended its origins: Middle America associated dating with neither upper-class rebellion nor the urban lower classes. The rise of dating was usually explained, quite simply, by the invention of the automobile. Cars had given youth mobility and privacy, and so had brought about the system. This explanation—perhaps not consciously but definitely not coincidentally—revised history. The automobile certainly contributed to the rise of dating as a *national* practice, especially in rural and suburban areas, but it was simply accelerating and extending a process already well under way. Once its origins were located firmly in Middle America, however, and not in the extremes of urban upper- and lower-class life, dating had become an American institution.

23   Dating not only transformed the outward modes and conventions of American courtship, it also changed the distribution of control and power in courtship. One change was generational: the dating system lessened parental control and gave young men and women more freedom. The dating system also shifted power from women to men. Calling, either as a simple visit or as the elaborate late nineteenth-century ritual, gave women a large portion of control. First of all, courtship took place within the girl's home—in women's "sphere," as it was called in the nineteenth century—or at entertainments largely devised and presided over by women. Dating moved courtship out of the home and into man's sphere—the world outside the home. Female controls and conventions lost much of their power outside women's sphere. And while many of the conventions of female propriety were restrictive and repressive, they had allowed women (young women and their mothers) a great deal of immediate control over courtship. The transfer of spheres thoroughly undercut that control.

24   Second, in the calling system, the woman took the initiative. Etiquette books and columns were adamant on that point: it was the "girl's privilege" to ask a young man to call. Furthermore, it was highly improper for the man to take the initiative. In 1909 a young man wrote to the *Ladies' Home Journal* adviser asking, "May I call upon a young woman whom I greatly admire, although she had not given me the permission? Would she be flattered at my eagerness, even to the setting aside of conventions, or would she think me impertinent?" Mrs. Kingsland replied: "I think that you would risk her just displeasure and

frustrate your object of finding favor with her." Softening the prohibi-
tion, she then suggested an invitation might be secured through a
mutual friend. She had been even stricter two years before, insisting
that "a man must not go beyond a very evident pleasure in a woman's
society, by way of suggestions." Another adviser, "The Lady from
Philadelphia," put a more positive light on the situation, noting that
"nothing forbids a man to show by his manner that her acquaintance is
pleasing to him and thus perhaps suggest that the invitation [to call]
would be welcome."

    Contrast these strictures with advice on dating etiquette from the   25
1940s and 1950s: An advice book for men and women warns that
"girls who [try] to usurp the right of boys to choose their own dates"
will "ruin a good dating career. . . . Fair or not, it is the way of life.
From the Stone Age, when men chased and captured their women,
comes the yen of a boy to do the pursuing. You will control your
impatience, therefore, and respect the time-honored custom of boys to
take the first step."

    One teen advice book from the 1950s told girls never to take the   26
initiative with a boy, even under some pretext such as asking about
homework: "Boys are jealous of their masculine prerogative of taking
the initiative." Another said simply: "*don't ask*," and still another
recounted an anecdote about a girl who asked a boy for a date to the
Saturday-night dance. He cut her off in mid-sentence and walked
away.

    Of course, some advisers stressed that women were not without   27
resource. Though barred from taking the initiative, nothing forbade
women from using tricks and stratagems, from showing by a friendly
manner that they would welcome an invitation for a date.

    This absolute reversal of roles almost necessarily accompanied   28
courtship's move from woman's sphere to man's sphere. Although the
convention-setters commended the custom of woman's initiative
because it allowed greater exclusivity (it might be "difficult for a girl to
refuse the permission to call, no matter how unwelcome or unsuitable
an acquaintance the man might be"), the custom was based on a
broader principle of etiquette. The host or hostess issued any invitation; the guest did not invite himself or herself. An invitation to call
was an invitation to visit in a woman's home.

    An invitation to go out on a date, on the other hand, was an invi-   29
tation into man's world—not simply because dating took place in the
public sphere (commonly defined as belonging to men), though that
was part of it, but because dating moved courtship into the world of
the economy. Money—men's money—was at the center of the dating

system. Thus, on two counts, men became the hosts and assumed the control that came with that position.

30   There was some confusion caused by this reversal of initiative, especially during the twenty years or so when going out and calling coexisted as systems. (The unfortunate young man in the apocryphal story, for example, had asked the city girl if he might call on her, so perhaps she was conventionally correct to assume he meant to play the host.) Confusions generally were sorted out around the issue of money. One young woman, "Henrietta L.," wrote to the *Ladies' Home Journal* to inquire whether a girl might "suggest to a friend going to any entertainment or place of amusement where there will be any expense to the young man." The reply: "Never, under any circumstances." The adviser explained that the invitation to go out must "always" come from the man, for he was the one "responsible for the expense." This same adviser insisted that the woman must "always" invite the man to call; clearly she realized that money was the central issue.

31   The centrality of money in dating had serious implications for courtship. Not only did money shift control and initiative to men by making them the "hosts," it led contemporaries to see dating as a system of exchange best understood through economic analogies or as an economic system pure and simple. Of course, people did recognize in marriage a similar economic dimension—the man undertakes to support his wife in exchange for her filling various roles important to him—but marriage was a permanent relationship. Dating was situational, with no long-term commitments implied, and when a man, in a highly visible ritual, spent money on a woman in public, it seemed much more clearly an economic act.

32   In fact, the term *date* was associated with the direct economic exchange of prostitution at an early time. A prostitute called "Maimie," in letters written to a middle-class benefactor friend in the late nineteenth century, described how men made "dates" with her. And a former waitress turned prostitute described the process to the Illinois Senate Committee on Vice this way: "You wait on a man and he smiles at you. You see a chance to get a tip and you smile back. Next day he returns and you try harder than ever to please him. Then right away he wants to make a date, and offer you money and presents if you'll be a good fellow and go out with him." These men, quite clearly, were buying sexual favors—but the occasion of the exchange was called a "date."

33   Courtship in America had always turned somewhat on money (or background.) A poor clerk or stockyards worker would not have called upon the daughter of a well-off family, and men were expected

to be economically secure before they married. But in the dating system money entered directly into the relationship between a man and a woman as the symbolic currency of exchange in even casual dating.

Dating, like prostitution, made access to women directly dependent on money. Quite a few men did not hesitate to complain about the going rate of exchange. In a 1925 *Collier's* article, "Why Men Won't Marry," a twenty-four-year-old university graduate exclaimed: "Get Married! Why, I can't even afford to go with any of the sort of girls with whom I would like to associate." He explained: "When I was in college, getting an allowance from home, I used to know lots of nice girls. . . . Now that I am on my own I can't even afford to see them. . . . If I took a girl to the theatre she would have to sit in the gallery, and if we went to supper afterward, it would be at a soda counter, and if we rode home it would have to be in the street cars." As he presents it, the problem is solely financial. The same girls who were glad to "go with" him when he had money would not "see" him when he lacked their price. And "nice girls" cost a lot.

In dating, though, the exchange was less direct and less clear than in prostitution. One author, in 1924, made sense of it this way. In dating, he reasoned, a man is responsible for all expenses. The woman is responsible for nothing—she contributes only her company. Of course, the man contributes his company, too, but since he must "add money to balance the bargain" his company must be worth less than hers. Thus, according to this economic understanding, she is selling her company to him. In his eyes, dating didn't even involve an exchange; it was a direct purchase. The moral "subtleties" of a woman's position in dating, the author concluded, were complicated even further by the fact that young men, "discovering that she must be bought, [like] to buy her when [they happen] to have the money."

Yet another young man, the same year, publicly called a halt to such "promiscuous buying." Writing anonymously (for good reason) in *American Magazine*, the author declared a "one-man buyer's strike." This man estimated that, as a "buyer of feminine companionship" for the previous five years, he had "invested" about $20 a week—a grand total of over $5,000. Finally, he wrote, he had realized that "there is a point at which any commodity—even such a delightful commodity as feminine companionship—costs more than it is worth." The commodity he had bought with his $5,000 had been priced beyond its "real value" and he had had enough. This man said "enough" not out of principle, not because he rejected the implications of the economic model of courtship, but because he felt he wasn't receiving value for money.

34

35

36

37   In all three of these economic analyses, the men are complaining about the new dating system, lamenting the passing of the mythic good old days when "a man without a quarter in his pocket could call on a girl and not be embarrassed," the days before a woman had to be "bought." In recognizing so clearly the economic model on which dating operated, they also clearly saw that the model was a bad one—in purely economic terms. The exchange was not equitable; the commodity was overpriced. Men were operating at a loss.

38   Here, however, they didn't understand their model completely. True, the equation (male companionship plus money equals female companionship) was imbalanced. But what men were buying in the dating system was not just female companionship, not just entertainment—but power. Money purchased obligation; money purchased inequality; money purchased control.

39   The conventions that grew up to govern dating codified women's inequality and ratified men's power. Men asked women out; women were condemned as "aggressive" if they expressed interest in a man too directly. Men paid for everything, but often with the implication that women "owed" sexual favors in return. The dating system required men always to assume control, and women to act as men's dependents.

40   Yet women were not without power in the system, and they were willing to contest men with their "feminine" power. Much of the public discourse on courtship in twentieth-century America was concerned with this contestation. Thousands of sources chronicled the struggles of, and between, men and women—struggles mediated by the "experts" and arbiters of convention—to create a balance of power, to gain or retain control of the dating system. These struggles, played out most clearly in the fields of sex, science, and etiquette, made ever more explicit the complicated relations between men and women in a changing society.

▶   QUESTIONS TO CONSIDER

CAUSE AND EFFECT,
PAGE 418

1. Bailey explores both the **causes and effects** of dating in this first chapter of her book. What are some of the factors Bailey claims led to the practice of a couple's dating as opposed to visiting in the girl's home? What effects has dating had on courtship in the United States?

2. A sociological phenomenon such as dating is open to interpretation. That is, no one knows absolutely why it came into existence or how it has affected our society. In this chapter, Bailey is, in effect, arguing for her interpretation. Using factual information that she has

gathered through a process of research, she pieces together her narrative about what has happened to courtship practices during this century. Bailey attempts to persuade her readers not by insisting on her view but by supporting it with information. As a reader, do you find her evidence convincing and her arguments sound? Why or why not?

3. Bailey cites the increasing independence and freedom of females as one of the reasons that dating came into existence. Ironically, she also points out that dating changed the balance of power between males and females to give males the advantage. Why did dating give males an advantage? Do males still have an advantage in dating?

4. Bailey argues that dating is "clearly an economic act" and even compares it to prostitution. Is this comparison, or analogy, appropriate? Effective? Do you agree with her on this point?

5. In her conclusion, Bailey assumes a feminist stance, arguing that dating allows "men always to assume control" and forces "women to act as men's dependents." Do you find these final arguments appropriate? Convincing?

WRITING ACTIVITIES

Individual: Describe one way in which dating has changed in your lifetime.

Collaborative: Discuss with a group of your classmates the ways in which age, location, race, economic background, education, and technology seem to affect dating practices. List all the factors that affect dating and identify the one you think is most significant.

Computer: Although Bailey presents an economic rather than a romantic view of dating, her arguments are predicated on the assumption of a very traditional model in which the male takes the female out and pays for all expenses. Write a paragraph in which you argue for or against this traditional model. Then, by posting your argument to your class network or by exchanging disks, share your argument with your classmates and respond to their arguments.

❖❖❖❖❖

▶ WRITING TO INFORM

When you write to reconstruct your own experiences, you focus primarily on yourself. Whether the result is fiction or nonfiction, your purpose is primarily to allow readers to know and understand you—to see the world and share certain experiences through your eyes. Conversely, when you write to inform, you focus primarily on your *subject*, piecing together information that you have derived from various sources, which may include but are not limited to your own experiences. When your purpose is to inform, your goal is to help readers understand not you but the subject. Although Stanley Kauffmann writes about being in grammar school and other personal experiences in his article on New York City, he is focusing not on himself but on the changes in the city. Beth Bailey, on the other hand, has probably had numerous experiences with dating, but she does not mention her own experiences in her discussion of how dating replaced visiting as the primary form of courtship.

When you write to inform, if you want to include your own experiences, that's fine. Personal experiences and observations are a valid form of information and can be used effectively to support your ideas and opinions. But remember to keep the focus on your subject. When your purpose is to inform, subordinate yourself to your subject.

Using Patterns of Development in Writing to Inform

When you wrote a reconstruction of an experience, the narrative probably controlled the way you organized the story. Most likely, you used chronological order to relate the events you were narrating. You may decide to use narration again as you write to inform, or you may choose one or more different strategies. Here are strategies you will find useful when you write to inform:

* Use narration.

* Use comparison/contrast.

* Use cause and effect.

* Use exemplification.

USE NARRATION.   Because people like to hear and tell stories and feel comfortable telling them, it is natural to adapt **narration** to accommodate the need to understand, explain, and communicate information.

NARRATION, PAGE 558

Narrative reconstructions of information, like stories, use chronological structure. Also, like stories, they benefit from your using specific details. Whether they are found in a novel or a report, narration and description are only as good as the specific details they include.

But there are also differences between the story you write about your first encounter with the registration process at your school and a report about that same process. In the story, you want to include your own subjective reaction to what you experienced, to give your readers some background information about yourself, and probably to exaggerate the length of the waiting line and the number of times you had to return to your adviser for a signature. In the report, you want to include other people's experiences with the process, to emphasize the process rather than yourself, and to be as accurate, factual, and objective as possible.

Another difference is that stories often do not have an explicit **thesis statement**, whereas narrative reconstructions of information nearly always do. If you are writing to inform, you usually want your readers to know your main point very soon after they begin reading. Stating your main idea clearly in the introduction ensures that the information you are providing is meaningful to your readers. A complicated narrative may also use a **forecasting statement** in the introduction to explicitly summarize the story's major events or stages before getting into the details. The overview that a clear thesis and forecasting statement provide helps readers make sense of the information you include.

THESIS, PAGE 599

FORECASTING STATEMENT, PAGE 503

USE COMPARISON/CONTRAST.   In addition to narration and description, you will want to use other patterns of development in writing to inform. One of the most useful patterns for informative writing is **comparison/contrast**. Because the common theme of this chapter's reading selections is the changing scene, each selection compares or contrasts at least one thing with something else. The authors compare what was to what is, most of them explicitly. Stanley Kauffmann describes the New York of his childhood and then compares it to the New York he lives in today. Joel Garreau contrasts the old downtown areas of cities to the present phenomenon of suburbs.

COMPARISON/CONTRAST, PAGE 437

This comparison/contrast pattern can effectively develop and amplify your subject for an informative purpose. If you are comparing something your readers know well to something they know less well, you can use their knowledge of the one to increase their understand-ANALOGY, PAGE 413ing of the other. (For a particular type of comparison, see **analogy**.) A primary way people learn is to use existing knowledge to acquire new knowledge, old information to understand new information. If you are comparing two things that are equally known or unknown, the problem is rather more difficult. By comparing two things, however, you can help your readers form a clearer understanding of both. Morgan Hands, for example, successfully communicates the changes in Eunice, a town that few readers outside of Louisiana would know, by comparing the town as it was during its prosperous days to the way it was after it had fallen on hard times.

Comparison/contrast presents you with certain arrangement options to choose from. Are you going to give all of the information about one subject and then shift to the other (topic by topic, as Kauffmann does, writing first about his childhood New York and then about New York now)? Or are you going to intersperse the information about both subjects throughout your text (point by point, as Bailey does)? The "first one and then the other" model (topic by topic) is easier to write, but it is not always the more effective. If you select the interspersed model (point by point), in which you go back and forth a number of times, you must be sure that your readers can follow your zigging and zagging from one point to the other. Point-by-point com-TRANSITIONS, PAGE 612parisons usually require clear **transitions** and careful organization so that your readers will not become confused.

For example, in the following paragraph Joel Garreau compares new urban centers, which he calls Edge Cities, to more traditional urban centers. Notice that he provides his readers with clear signals so they can follow his movement from one to the other.

> Our new city centers are tied together *not* by locomotives and subways, *but* by jetways, freeways, and rooftop satellite dishes thirty feet across. Their characteristic monument is *not* a horse-mounted hero, *but* the atria reaching for the sun and shielding trees perpetually in leaf at the cores of corporate headquarters, fitness centers, and shopping plazas. These new urban areas are marked *not* by the penthouses of the old urban rich or the tenements of the old urban poor. *Instead,* their landmark structure is the celebrated single-family detached

dwelling, the suburban home with grass all around that made
America the best-housed civilization the world has ever known.
[italics added]

Be sure to signal your readers clearly each time you zig or zag from
one topic to the other.

USE CAUSE AND EFFECT.   In a way, **cause and effect** is just a variation
of narration. In explaining causes and effects, the writer tells a story—
because this happened, this and this and this happened (cause and
effect); or this and this and this happened because this happened
(effect and cause). All the writers in this chapter use this pattern to
some extent: John Harris tells what happened when the old church
was torn down; Morgan Hands tells what happened when Eunice went
from boom to bust; Stanley Kauffmann tells what happened when
New York changed from the place he knew as a child to the place
where he now lives; Beth Bailey tells what happened when "calling
on" was replaced by dating; and Joel Garreau describes the effects of
life in Edge City on civilization.

CAUSE AND EFFECT,
PAGE 418

    As with comparison/contrast, cause and effect provides you with
choices. You must decide whether you want to begin with causes and
than explain effects or vice versa. You must decide whether to emphasize causes or effects or both. You must decide how much information
your readers need about your subject in order to understand the causal
relationship you are emphasizing.

USE EXEMPLIFICATION.   Like comparison/contrast and cause and effect,
exemplification helps writers develop and amplify a subject. Using a
specific example to explain a general statement is one of the best and
most natural ways people have to clarify difficult, abstract, vague concepts. Examples enable readers to understand information that would
otherwise be incomprehensible. To say that it is hot in Nevada in the
summer is meaningless to someone who has never been there. But to
provide readers with an example of the heat (you can't walk 10 blocks
without becoming shaky-kneed and light-headed, all without feeling a
drop of instantly vaporizing sweat) gives them a basis for comparing
their own experience of summer heat with that of someone in Nevada
and a concrete image that allows them to see and feel the heat.

EXEMPLIFICATION, PAGE 488

    If you have real examples to use, as Beth Bailey does in her
study of courtship, by all means use them. But if you cannot cite actual
instances to illustrate the point you are making or to clarify the con-

cept you are explaining, you can make one up. For example, Bailey also uses a hypothetical example, that of the 1920s gentleman caller, to illustrate her theory about the changes in courtship practices, and Morgan Hands cites the example of the fictitious John Doe as a representative example of the citizens of Eunice, Louisiana. If you do use hypothetical examples, be sure they are based on valid information.

Should you use predominantly one pattern to structure and amplify your entire essay, or should you use more than one? Although you may want to emphasize one pattern, in general several patterns in combination produce a more complex, interesting, fully developed piece of writing. The authors of the selections included in this chapter, for example, all use multiple patterns of development—narration, description, comparison/contrast, exemplification, and cause and effect.

Evaluating Information When You Write

In deciding what information to use, ask yourself the questions you keep in mind when you read written information:

❖ What is its source?

❖ Is it relevant?

❖ Is it accurate?

WHAT IS ITS SOURCE?   Is the information from a reliable, unbiased source? Advertisements, for example, are usually not regarded as reliable sources of information. A magazine such as *Consumers' Guide*, a professional journal, or a government publication is generally a more reliable source.

IS IT RELEVANT?   Because information can become dated and thus irrelevant quickly, you should derive your information primarily from periodicals, which are published daily, weekly, monthly, or at least every few months, rather than from books, which require years to be published. (Of course, for general background information or for researching a subject from the past, such as early U. S. automobiles, you can rely on the information in books, even old books.)

IS IT ACCURATE?   Make careful notes or obtain a photocopy of the material you plan to use so you can later confirm that the information you include in your text conforms to the source material.

Also be sure that the conclusions you draw are supported by the information you include. Do not go beyond the information you have cited to make claims that are illogical and unsupported.

WRITING ASSIGNMENT

For this assignment you are informing your readers about something that has changed. You may want to write about a place that has changed—a place such as your hometown, your grandparents' home, a familiar vacation spot, a room you particularly like, or a favorite hangout or place to eat. Or you may want to write about an event, a relationship, or a pattern in your life that has changed. For example, how has your relationship with your parents changed as you and they have grown older? Or, if you have a child of your own, how has that relationship changed? Like Beth Bailey, you may want to write about some social custom that has changed. For example, our eating habits, exercise patterns, clothing fashions, child-rearing practices, race relations, and attitudes toward the countries that made up the former Soviet Union have all undergone dramatic changes in recent years.

If an idea for a topic does not immediately come to you, freewrite about the changes you have experienced in your lifetime or about the changes you observe in our society. From this freewriting, choose a single idea to use as a topic. Once you have chosen your topic, you may want to freewrite again, this time focusing on the topic you have chosen (see **invention**).

INVENTION, PAGE 529

This assignment can take the form of an essay or, if you prefer, a report. An essay usually includes more specific references to the writer's own experiences and opinions, whereas a report is not only more factual and objective but also usually has a more limited audience and purpose. In either case, your audience will be your classmates unless you wish to specify a different audience.

Planning Your Text

Once you have discovered a topic, you can begin to plan your essay or report. In writing to inform, as in all writing, one of your first concerns is to formulate a tentative thesis. What is the point you wish to make? A thesis differs from a topic in that it makes an assertion about the topic. In this assignment, your thesis will probably involve the idea of change, but try to be more specific than just saying that something has changed. Define the change, analyze and evaluate it, or describe its result. For example, instead of merely stating that women's attitudes about housework have changed, you might say that women's attitudes about housework have become more casual or that women's changing attitudes about housework have resulted in messier homes but happier children.

Remember that your initial thesis is not necessarily the one you will stay with until you complete your essay or report. An initial thesis is always tentative—a hypothesis you may modify slightly or drastically or even discard once you begin to write. In fact, some writers prefer to begin writing before they formulate even a hypothesis, knowing their thesis will emerge as they write. However, most writers begin writing with at least a tentative idea of the point they plan to make. But don't hesitate to change this initial thesis—to refine, narrow, and revise it—as you continue constructing your text. Your preliminary thesis is at most a guide, perhaps merely a point of departure, but never a binding contract (see **thesis statement**).

THESIS STATEMENT, PAGE 599

Most informative writing involves some form of research. You may think immediately of the library when research is mentioned. And **library research** is an excellent resource for writers, providing abundant information on an amazing variety of topics. If you are writing about the U.S. relationship with the countries of the former Soviet Union, for example, and want to know how it has changed in the past few years, you will need library resources, especially periodicals but also books (histories, reference books, and others) to provide you with background information.

LIBRARY RESEARCH, PAGE 534

But don't think only of the library. **Field research** can be equally or even more appropriate. For example, if you plan to write about how something in your own life has changed, you may need to spend some time observing what you are writing about or interviewing someone who can give you information about your subject. Suppose, for example, you are writing about how gas stations have changed from full service filling stations with an icebox full of soft drinks out front to pump-your-own-gas mini-shopping centers that sell a little of everything but provide no services. The library will probably not help you much on this one, but talking to the owner of a gas station who has experienced these changes would probably provide you with lots of good information. Even if you are working on a topic such as the one about how U.S. relations with the countries of the former Soviet Union

FIELD RESEARCH, PAGE 493

have changed, you might want to interview a family member who remembers how strained those relations were in the 1950s or a history professor who has done research in this area. Or you might survey the students in your composition class to see how many of them think the former communist countries are still a threat to the United States.

Research, like writing, is an ongoing process. You will probably want to complete preliminary research before you begin writing, but as you write you may think of other forms of research that will provide evidence to support your thesis. The important thing is to think of research as broadly as possible—as any possible source of information. Don't limit your research to looking up your subject in the card catalog at the library. Think in terms of what will provide you with the information you need and pursue that information in any way possible.

Constructing Your Text

DRAFTING.   You might want to begin your text by writing a discovery draft in which you are primarily testing your hypothesis to see if it is one you can support. In this draft, merely sketch out the broad points you want to make and write what comes into your mind about them. Let your essay take shape by allowing your writing to lead you where it will. A discovery draft is only a few steps removed from freewriting. You have a topic and a general idea of your thesis (a hypothesis), but you don't really know what you want to say. The important thing at this point is to get something on paper or in a computer file.

On the other hand, if you have a fairly good idea about what you want to write, have done some preliminary research on the subject, and have at least a vague plan in mind, you can write a different type of rough draft—one that reflects the mental image you have already formed. This draft is not complete, and it certainly may be rough, but it is more than a tentative exploration: it is a step down a path you have already chosen. Several drafts may be needed to shape your essay or report into the text you want it to be, but the first draft is an important step in that direction.

As you write, you are faced with countless options and decisions (what to include and exclude, which words to use, how much evidence to present, and more). Some of these decisions you will make unconsciously. Some will be determined by your audience and purpose. Many are made even before you begin to write. But others must be made consciously, as you write. One of these conscious decision is

NARRATION, PAGE 558

CAUSE AND EFFECT, PAGE 418

EXEMPLIFICATION, PAGE 488

AMPLIFICATION, PAGE 404

how you should develop your thesis. Do you want to explain the changing scene you are writing about by telling a story, by comparing what was to what is, by providing examples that illustrate the change, or by explaining its causes and effects? These are important decisions and need to be made consciously if you do not discover them in the process of writing (see **narration**, **cause and effect**, **exemplification**, and **amplification**).

READING. As you read what you have written, you will want to determine first of all if your thesis works. That is, do you have a clear focus—a main idea that controls the content of your essay or report? To be sure that what you have written supports and develops your thesis clearly, write a one-sentence summary of each paragraph (the topic sentence may serve as a summary of the paragraph). Now write your thesis and the sentence summaries after it. If you are using a computer, you can accomplish the same thing by making a copy of your text on a new file and then deleting everything but your thesis and the topic sentence of each paragraph. The idea is to construct an outline of what you have written so you can determine if your essay or report is well focused. Keep this outline so you can refer to it when you revise.

Once you are satisfied that your essay or report is unified and well focused, read it again, this time paying attention to the information you have included. Have you included the information your readers will need? For example, if you are writing about the ways in which basketball has changed since you were a child, you will need to provide your readers with information about what the game was like then and what it is like now. You cannot assume your audience will all know as much about the game as you do. Some of your class members may know very little about the game, but all of them will know certain things (such as what a basketball and goal look like and that the game involves five players trying to get the ball through the goal while another five players try to prevent them from doing this). Read your essay carefully to determine if you have included too much or too little information. The amount of information you include, its appropriateness, and its clarity are essential when you are writing to inform. If you decide that you need more information and if that information is not already known to you, you may need to research your subject further—talk to a ballplayer, attend a ball game, read an article about the sport or players.

As you read, consider also whether **graphics** would make the GRAPHICS, PAGE 519 information in your essay or report clearer or more understandable to your readers. Simple illustrations, graphs, and tables provide information in an alternate form that reinforces your written explanations. A picture may not be worth a thousand words, as the Chinese proverb claims, but it can certainly be valuable when you are writing to inform.

Finally, ask someone else to read what you have written. A reader is always useful when you are writing because that person invariably sees your text from a different perspective. No matter how carefully you read your own text, you cannot view it as a reader will because you know it too well. What you need at this point is a pair of fresh eyes—someone who is not reluctant to say "I don't understand what you mean here" or "This point confuses me" or "I need more information about this." Your instructor may arrange for you to work in pairs or groups, responding to one another's texts. If not, find someone who will read what you have written and give you an honest response.

REVISING.   After reading your essay or report several times, you will have some ideas about what you need to do as you revise. However, as you revise, you should continue reading and rereading what you have written. Possible revisions will keep occurring to you as you read and write, write and read, and read yet once more. You will find, in fact, that the more experienced you become as a writer, the more you will probably revise. Rather than learning to get it right the first time, you will discover that you are learning to revise until you get it right.

If you are using a computer, revising is much easier because you can make changes as often as you like without having to rewrite the entire essay or report. But be sure that you are not just tinkering with your text—making minor changes and adjustments rather than making more substantive changes in the content, development, and organization of your text. Remember that you can rearrange entire blocks of text if the order in which you have presented your ideas is not logical, add sentences and even paragraphs if more development is needed, deleting not only words but large chunks of material if they do not support your thesis.

Now is a good time to go back and look at the outline of your text suggested earlier. Are there paragraphs that should be omitted? Is the order of your paragraphs logical? Use this outline as a revision guide. It will help you view your text more objectively.

HEADINGS, PAGE 526
FORMAT, PAGE 505

Since you are writing to inform in this assignment, you might consider adding headings to your text as you revise (see **headings** and **format**). Headings help readers to understand and access the information you are presenting. For example, if you are writing about the changes in automobile design, you might want to include the following headings:

Changes in Appearance

Changes in Performance

Changes in Safety Features

Headings are usually placed flush with the left margin and emphasized by the use of <u>underlining</u>, **boldface type**, or ALL CAPS. The idea is to set them off in some way from the rest of the text. But don't overdo it by using all three. If you have subheadings as well as headings, you will need to distinguish between the two in some way.

Remember that your purpose is to inform, so your text should not only be clear and readable but also accurate. Revise with this goal in mind. Check carefully on the accuracy of all your information. If you are giving only a rough estimate, indicate this to your reader. If you include dates, verify them. If you cite statistics, be sure to check them against your source. And if you are using information from other sources, such as interviews or written sources, be sure to include the name and/or title of the source in your text. Your instructor may not insist on formal documentation of sources, but you do need to acknowledge any source you use (see **documentation** and **library research**).

DOCUMENTATION, PAGE 460
LIBRARY RESEARCH,
PAGE 534

Editing Your Text

If possible, ask someone to read your completed text and point out any errors or omissions you have failed to notice. Copyeditors often perform this service for professional writers. Most experienced writers have a colleague, friend, or spouse who helps them edit. The point is that every writer needs someone to function as an editor. Your instructor may arrange for your class to edit one another's papers. If not, find someone yourself, ideally someone with a good knowledge of the conventions of written English, to help you clean up your text.

If you are writing with a computer, editing programs may be available to assist you. Text-editing programs can point out certain types of problems and give you an objective view of your text. For example, some programs provide a readability level for a text; others point out excessive use of passive voice; still others indicate sentence length. This information can be useful; take advantage of such programs if they are available to you. However, no software is capable of really editing your text, so don't put your faith in a computer program when you edit. Even spell-check programs cannot identify all misspelled words. Because they can identify only words that are not included in their dictionaries, they cannot catch a real word used wrongly. For example, if you use the word *accept* when you mean *except* or *use* when you need *used*, a spell-check program will not alert you to this kind of error.

Readers and editors can certainly help you improve your text, but in the final analysis you must assume responsibility for what you write. Most important, of course, is whether what you have written is accurate, complete, and readable. But correctness and appearance also play a significant role in how others perceive a text. Readers may ignore even a useful text if it is carelessly written. Your text is a reflection of you and should present you at your best (see **revising and editing**).

REVISING AND EDITING, PAGE 593

Joshua Sheldon

5

▼

WRITING TO INSTRUCT AND ADVISE

155

The reasonable thing is to learn from those who can teach.

SOPHOCLES

In every society experienced older members teach inexperienced younger members how to live—how to conduct themselves, relate to one another, survive in their particular environment. These instructions take many forms; the most basic are transmitted through observation. Children watch their elders and imitate what they see. More explicit are oral instructions such as "Don't touch," which is one of the first instructions that children hear. Oral instructions continue to be a life-long source of learning. But in literate societies, written instructions become vital once a person learns to read. For example, in this chapter's reading selections writers offer instructions and/or advice about some aspect of college life. As computer technology expands, you will also be reading on-line instructions and advice.

So far, your experience with instructions has probably been more that of reader than writer. You have read instructions in your textbooks that tell you how to write an essay, solve an equation, conduct an experiment. You have read instructions to hook up a stereo system, bake chocolate-chip cookies, pass a driver's license exam. You have probably also read articles dispensing advice on everything from how to pass a college entrance exam to how to find a mate.

NARRATION, PAGE 558 In one sense, all instructions are narratives because they are arranged chronologically (see **narration**). Instructions always involve a process, and a process is, in effect, a story of what happens next. Whether a simple series of steps (how to withdraw money from an automatic teller machine), a complicated procedure (how to install a car radio), or a serious lesson in life (how to be a success), a process is usually presented in chronological order.

But some instructions actually are narratives—stories that teach a lesson. Much of what we have all learned in our lives has come from these instructive stories, usually called parables or fables, that offer instruction in its most palatable, seductive form. These lessons clothed in narrative fabric—like the story of the Prodigal Son, the tortoise and the hare, and the little boy who cried "Wolf"—instruct indirectly, slipping the lesson into a narrative framework that is easy to listen to, easy to understand, and easy to remember.

In writing and reading instructions, you will use many of the same patterns you used in writing to reconstruct experience and writing to inform. The difference is not in the structure, but in the purpose and the format. In writing to instruct, you are presenting information and reconstructing experiences, but your primary purpose is to teach your readers how to do something or advise them about something.

READING INSTRUCTIONS AND ADVICE

Good written instructions are easy to read, easy to follow, and easy to remember. Unfortunately, they are also rare, so the reader's task becomes more difficult. Everyone has had the frustrating experience of trying to follow badly written instructions that leave out important information, that assume too much knowledge on the part of the reader, or that do not explain clearly what needs to be done in a straightforward manner. When you read instructions, therefore, you must often compensate for what the writer of the instructions did not do well.

Two types of instructions exist: (1) specific instructions that outline the steps in a process that the reader follows immediately and (2) general instructions and advice that offer suggestions for the readers' consideration but do not assume immediate action on their part. You should read each type of instruction differently.

Reading Specific Instructions

When you read specific instructions, your primary purpose is nearly always to accomplish some task. Most people read instructions only if they are interested in performing the process described. Thus reading instructions is usually a means to an end, a way of accomplishing a task you want to perform, whether that task is changing the filter in your air conditioner or testing a smoke alarm or installing a new stereo system in your car. Few other types of reading are so focused and specific in purpose.

Look at the simple set of instructions for using a floppy disk mailer on the following page. These brief directions include all of the elements of a good set of instructions: numbered steps; appropriate use of imperative verbs; an illustration that reinforces the written instructions; and warnings ("Do not bend or fold. Avoid exposure to all magnetic fields.") But simple and brief as they are, they are not as

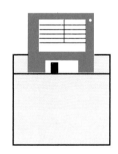

1. Insert disk into mailer with metal shutter end first.
2. To assure proper sealing remove tape and press <u>firmly</u> along entire flap.

FLOPPY DISK MAILER
Do not bend or fold. Avoid exposure to all magnetic fields.

clear and complete as they might be. In step 1 the term *metal shutter end*, which some readers may not understand, is not explained, and the illustration does not indicate this feature. Further, the instructions do not make clear why it is important to insert the metal shutter end first. In step 2 readers are not told to *fold* the top flap of the mailer down after removing the tape. Finally, the warnings are intended for a different audience—mail handlers rather than disk senders—but nothing indicates this shift. As a result, the warning about not bending or folding could confuse senders of disks about whether to fold down the top flap of the mailer to seal it. And the warning about exposure to magnetic fields fails to define magnetic fields or give readers examples of what constitutes a magnetic field or tell *why* they should be avoided. Thus even this simple set of instructions could be improved to ease the reader's task.

Because readers of specific instructions often are hurrying to perform a task, they may read the instructions quickly and carelessly. Cursory, hasty reading can have unfortunate consequences (an inedible casserole, a nonfunctioning stereo, a rickety bookcase, or a damaged computer disk), especially if the instructions are also badly written. The combination of a poorly written set of instructions and a hurried reader can result in a lot of frustration if not a complete disaster. To get the best results from instructions you are reading, follow four guidelines (which are themselves general instructions):

* Read before you begin.

* Study illustrations.

* Read each step again.

* Pay attention to warnings.

READ BEFORE YOU BEGIN.   Read the instructions through completely at least once before you begin the task. It is important to have an overview of the process before you begin. If you start the process before you have an idea of what is involved, you may start your cake before you realize that you are going to need a springform pan, a utensil you not only do not own but have no idea where to locate. Or you may begin to assemble a desk before you realize you are going to need a Phillips head screwdriver, a tool missing from your toolbox.

STUDY ILLUSTRATIONS.   Whenever diagrams or illustrations are included, study them carefully. Graphics can often be more important than the text accompanying them. Study each one until you are sure you recognize everything represented in it. If you cannot identify everything in the diagram, following the written instructions will probably be difficult.

READ EACH STEP AGAIN.   This time, follow the outlined procedure in each step carefully as soon as you have finished reading about it.

Don't try to rush the process by skipping steps or guessing what comes next. Even simple instructions can become complicated if you do not take them in the proper order.

PAY ATTENTION TO WARNINGS. If instructions include notes of warning or caution, *always* read them carefully and be sure you understand the potential problem or danger. Even if you don't understand why you are not to do something in a certain way, don't do it. Trust the writer of the instructions to know more about the possible pitfalls.

Reading specific instructions is not the most fascinating reading you will ever do. Instructions are usually straightforward and unamusing, but being able to read and follow them matters. You may never have to read a set of instructions about how to inflate your life jacket on a sinking ship, but you should be prepared for such an emergency.

Reading General Instructions and Advice

This chapter's reading selections provide general instructions and advice. The authors are instructing you about broad and ongoing action to be undertaken in the future rather than instructing you specifically how to perform an exact task now. For example, John Bear is encouraging readers to be bold about seeking financial backing for college; Nikki Giovanni is offering advice to African-American students who may be planning to attend a predominantly white school. These articles, like most of the many how-to books on the market, provide readers with general guidelines and advice rather than explicit instructions.

Read articles and essays that provide general instructions or advice not as you read a set of instructions that tells you how to make a long-distance call using your telephone credit card but rather as you would any general article or essay. Evaluate the instructions or advice given. Is the author a known authority on this subject? If not, does he or she explain convincingly why the advice should be followed? In this chapter, Joshua Halberstam is a college professor, so you may assume he knows what college students should do to succeed. Stacey Colino, in contrast, is not a known authority on her subject, campus crime, but she establishes her credibility by citing other sources and including statistics that support her theories.

Often you will find specific and general instructions combined. That is, an article or essay may offer general advice on a subject but also include fairly specific instructions. Nikki Giovanni begins her article for African-American students who choose to attend predominantly white colleges with general advice and then includes at the end more specific instructions.

READINGS FOR WRITING ◀

As a college student, you often seek the advice of others—teachers, administrators, counselors, and more experienced students. You may also occasionally seek written advice. This chapter's reading selections tell you, as a college student, how to do something or offer you advice about something pertaining to college life. Each one was written to instruct.

GETTING MONEY FROM PECULIAR SOURCES AND OFF-THE-WALL SCHEMES

John Bear

One of the first concerns for most college students is how they will finance their education. John Bear has written an entire book, Finding Money for College, *on this subject. The chapter included here focuses on unusual sources of funding—those you would not think of on your own. Bear's suggestions for pursuing these rather outrageous sources are only half-serious. That is, his purpose is to amuse as well as to instruct. Bear doesn't tell his readers specifically how to pursue these avenues of funding (i.e., how to apply for the scholarships or how to approach an eccentric millionaire to ask for money) because different scholarships have different application procedures and different millionaires have different eccentricities. But he does suggest that, in spite of being longshots, these approaches sometimes pay off, and he does provide readers with the basic information they need to pursue this unconventional approach.*

With certain broad restrictions, a person has the right to bequeath his or her money for any purpose whatsoever, no matter how peculiar or unusual. And that is why we have a whole raft of peculiar and unusual scholarships.   1

Many of them are not of broad interest. In fact, they are of such narrow interest that there may only be a small handful of people in the U.S. who would qualify for them—and have an interest in going to college.   2

Peculiar Scholarships

3   **Convicted prostitutes in Seattle.** A judge established this fund, which was, oddly, very little used.

4   **People named Baxendale, Borden, Pennoyer, or Murphy.** Scholarships available at Harvard.

5   **People born on June 17, 1979.** When they get old enough, 150 of them can claim a $1,500 scholarship from the Rochester Institute of Technology.

6   **Former caddies from New Jersey.** Scholarship from the New Jersey State Golf Association.

7   **Children of glass blowers**. Four $2,000 awards a year from the Glass Bottle Blowers Association of Media, PA.

8   **Wonder Woman Scholarships.** Dozens of awards in the $2,000 to $5,000 range each year, to celebrate Wonder Woman's 40th birthday, for talented women over 40, from the Wonder Woman Foundation, 1290 Sixth Ave., New York NY 10019.

9   **Abstainers.** $3,000 a year for students attending Bucknell University who don't use alcohol, drugs, cigarettes, or engage in strenuous sports.

10   **Female helicopter pilots.** $4,000 from the Whirly-Girls of Washington, D.C.

11   **Needy lefties.** Four small scholarships for suchlike attending Juniata College.

12   **Calf-roping scholars.** $500 a year from the University of Arizona for people with high marks and calf-roping experience.

13   **People named Defores or Leavenworth**. $1,000 is waiting at Yale University.

14   **Needy people interested in golf course turf.** 25 awards of $500 from the Golf Course Superintendents Association.

The Chutzpah Approach

15   Chutzpah is nerve. Cheek. Outrageous brashness. One Yiddish anthology defines it by the case of the man who killed his mother and father, then pleaded for mercy because he was an orphan.

In the world of scholarships, it could be defined by the young 16
man who, on a cold winter day in East Lansing, Michigan, in the late
1950's, dashed off a letter to Doris Duke that said, in effect, "It just
isn't fair. There you are the richest woman in the world, who can buy
anything you want, and here I am the poorest student in the world,
who can't even afford the car I desperately need, much less next
quarter's tuition."

The first thing that happened was a call from the local car 17
dealer, saying, "I've got a brand new Dodge for you, paid for by Doris
Duke." The second thing was that his tuition was also paid from the
same source.

I have known four or five super-rich people in my life. All but 18
one said that even though they were quite well shielded from financial
requests of all kinds, every so often some approach *did* break through
to them, and whether because of the extreme cleverness of the
approach, or often because of the extreme worthiness of the need,
they actually did loosen their pursestrings.

Nothing but time, energy, very modest cost, and perhaps damage 19
to the ego, to be lost by trying. (Each year, *Forbes* magazine lists and
describes the 400 richest people in America—and most of their
addresses can be found in *Who's Who in America*.)

QUESTIONS TO CONSIDER ◀

1. Which of his purposes—to instruct or to amuse—does Bear attain
more successfully?

2. This selection is informative as well as instructive. The author provides you with the information he thinks you need to follow his
advice. Is the balance of instruction and information effective or do
you need more of one or the other?

3. Does Bear convince you that appealing to a wealthy individual or
an organization to help you finance your college career is a good
idea? Why or why not?

4. Is the information in this selection useful in itself, or is its main
strength the suggestion that you try unusual approaches in order to
obtain financing for your education? What other outrageous but
potentially rewarding approaches can you suggest?

▶ WRITING ACTIVITIES

Individual: Write a letter to someone who wants to attend your college or university explaining to him or her the fixed and variable costs involved. Be sure to include living expenses as well as tuition, fees, and books. Make the letter as clear and detailed as possible.

Collaborative: Compare the letters that each of you has written. Do you agree in general about costs? Then write a set of instructions for people who might be interested in attending your college, telling them how to calculate what their expenses will be.

Computer: Enter into a computer the set of instructions that your group composed and format these instructions so your intended audience can not only read them clearly but also refer to them easily. Some of the format features you may want to use include indent, bold, underline, italics, and different font styles (see **format**).

FORMAT, PAGE 505

CAMPUS RACISM 101

Nikki Giovanni

Nikki Giovanni is a well-known African-American poet as well as a college professor. In this article, first published in Essence, *a magazine directed primarily at black readers, Giovanni gives advice to African-American students who attend or who are thinking about attending predominantly white universities. Notice as you read how Giovanni convinces her readers she is qualified to instruct them on this subject.*

1   There is a bumper sticker that reads: "Too bad ignorance isn't painful." I like that. But ignorance is. We just seldom attribute the pain to it or even recognize it when we see it. Like the postcard on my corkboard. It shows a young man in a very hip jacket smoking a cigarette. In the background is a high school with the American flag waving. The caption says: "Too cool for school. Yet too stupid for the real world." Out of the mouth of the young man is a bubble enclosing the

words "Maybe I'll start a band." There could be a postcard showing a jock in a uniform saying "I don't need school. I'm going to the NFL or NBA." Or one showing a young man or woman studying and a group of young people saying "So you want to be white." Or something equally demeaning. We need to quit it.

I am a professor of English at Virginia Tech. I've been here for four years, though for only two years with academic rank. I am tenured, which means I have a teaching position for life, a rarity on a predominantly white campus. Whether from malice or ignorance, people who think I should be at a predominantly Black institution will say, "Why are you at Tech?" Because it's here. And so are Black students. But even if Black students weren't here, it's painfully obvious that this nation and this world cannot allow white students to go through higher education without interacting with Blacks in authoritative positions. It is equally clear that predominantly Black colleges cannot accommodate the numbers of Black students who want and need an education. 2

Is it difficult to attend a predominantly white college? Compared with what? Being passed over for promotion because you lack credentials? Being turned down for jobs because you are not college-educated? Joining the armed forces or going to jail because you cannot find an alternative to the streets? Let's have a little perspective here. Where can you go and what can you do that frees you from interacting with the white American mentality? You're going to interact; the only question is, Will you be in some control of yourself and your actions, or will you be controlled by others? I'm going to recommend control. 3

What's the difference between prison and college? They both proscribe your behavior for a given period of time. They both allow you to read books and develop your writing. They both give you time alone to think and time with your peers to talk about issues. But four years of prison doesn't give you a passport to greater opportunities. Most likely that time only gives you greater knowledge of how to get back in. Four years of college gives you an opportunity not only to lift yourself but to serve your people effectively. What's the difference when you are called a nigger in college from when you are called a nigger in prison? In college you can, though I admit with effort, follow procedures to have those students who called you nigger kicked out or suspended. You can bring issues to public attention without risk of your life. But mostly college is and always has been the future. We, neither less nor more than other people, need knowledge. There are discomforts attached to attending predominantly white colleges, 4 though no more so than living in a racist world. Here are some rules to follow that may help:

5   **Go to class.** No matter how you feel. No matter how you think the professor feels about you. It's important to have a consistent presence in the classroom. If nothing else, the professor will know you care enough and are serious enough to be there.

6   **Meet your professors.** Extend your hand (give a firm handshake) and tell them your name. *Ask them what you need to do to make an A.* You may never make an *A* but you have put them on notice that you are serious about getting good grades.

7   **Do assignments on time.** Typed or computer-generated. You have the syllabus. Follow it. And turn those papers in. If for some reason you can't complete an assignment on time, let your professor know before it is due and work out a new due date—then meet it.

8   **Go back to see your professor.** Tell him or her your name again. If an assignment received less than an *A*, ask why, and find out what you need to do to improve the next assignment.

Yes, your professor is busy. So are you. So are your parents who are working to pay or help with your tuition. Ask *early* what you need to do if you feel you are starting to get into academic trouble. Do not wait until you are failing.

9   **Understand that there will be professors who do not like you;** there may even be professors who are racist or sexist or both. You must discriminate among your professors to see who will give you the help you need. You may not simply say "They are all against me." They aren't. They mostly don't care. Since you are the one who wants to be educated, find the people who want to help.

10 **Don't defeat yourself.** Cultivate your friends. Know your enemies. You cannot undo hundreds of years of prejudicial thinking. Think for yourself and speak up. Raise your hand in class. Say what you believe no matter how awkward you may think it sounds. You will improve in your articulation and confidence.

11 **Participate in some campus activity.** Join the newspaper staff. Run for office. Join a dorm council. Do *something* that involves you on

campus. You are going to be there for four years, so let your presence be known, if not felt.

You will inevitably run into some white classmates who are troubling because they often say stupid things, ask stupid questions—and expect an answer. Here are some comebacks to some of the most common inquiries and comments:

Q   *What's it like to grow up in a ghetto?*   12
   A   I don't know.   13

Q   *From the teacher: Can you give us the Black perspective on Toni Morrison, Huck Finn, slavery, Martin Luther King, Jr., and others?*   14
   A   I can give you *my* perspective. [Do not take the burden of 22 million people on your shoulders. Remind everyone that you are an individual, and don't speak for the race or any other individual within it.]   15

Q   *Why do all the Black people sit together in the dining hall?*   16
   A   Why do the white students sit together?   17

Q   *Why should there be an African-American–studies course?*   18
   A   Because white Americans have not adequately studied the contributions of Africans and African-Americans. Both Black and white students need to know our total common history.   19

Q   *Why are there so many scholarships for "minority" students?*   20
   A   Because they wouldn't give my great-grandparents their 40 acres and the mule.   21

Q   *How can whites understand Black history, culture, literature and so forth?*   22
   A   The same way we understand white history, culture, literature and so forth. That is why we're in school: to learn.   23

Q   *Should whites take African-American–studies courses?*   24
   A   Of course. We take white-studies courses, though the universities don't call them that.   25

Comment: When I see groups of Black people on campus, it's really intimidating.   26

27   **Comeback: I understand what you mean. I'm frightened when I see white students congregating.**

28   **Comment:** It's not fair. It's easier for you guys to get into college than for other people.

29   **Comeback: If it's so easy, why aren't there more of us?**

30   **Comment:** It's not our fault that America is the way it is.

31   **Comeback: It's not our fault, either, but both of us have a responsibility to make changes.**

32   It's really very simple. Educational progress is a national concern; education is a private one. Your job is not to educate white people; it is to obtain an education. If you take the racial world on your shoulders, you will not get the job done. Deal with yourself as an individual worthy of respect, and make everyone else deal with you the same way. College is a little like playing grown-up. Practice what you want to be. You have been telling your parents you are grown. Now is your chance to act like it.

▶   **QUESTIONS TO CONSIDER**

1. The first part of this article establishes Giovanni's credibility and authority. How does she convince readers that she is qualified to write on this topic?

2. The second part of the article gives specific steps for African-American students to follow in order to succeed on a predominantly white campus. Would these same steps be equally appropriate for all students?

3. The third part of the article focuses on the questions that African-American students are sometimes asked and gives suggested responses for these inquiries. Do you think the responses Giovanni suggests are appropriate? What other responses might be given to the same questions?

4. This article is persuasive as well as instructive. What do you think Giovanni is trying to persuade her readers to do? How effective do you think she is? Can you offer some ways in which Giovanni might be more persuasive?

WRITING ACTIVITIES ◀

Individual: Write a journal entry in which you write about an experience you have had as a minority. For example, perhaps you are the only female or male in a class you are taking, or the only one from a rural background in your sorority or fraternity, or the only one in your carpool who smokes. How do you feel in these situations? Are your feelings the result of what the other people (the majority) actually say and do or what you imagine they think about you?

Collaborative: Working in a group, compose another set of "stupid" inappropriate questions and the answers that could be given to them. Compare your answers with those written by other groups.

Computer: Notice the format of Giovanni's article—the use of indention, spacing, boldface type, and so on. Using your computer, design a format that makes the rules, or instructions, given in the last part of the article clearer and easier to read.

❖❖❖❖❖

CLASS IN THE CLASSROOM
Joshua Halberstam

Joshua Halberstam, who teaches ethics at New York University, has written a book entitled Acing College, *in which he gives students a professor's-eye view of how to succeed in college. The subtitle of the book is* A Professor Tells Students How to Beat the System. *In this selection from the book, Halberstam advises students about classroom behavior. Notice, as you read, his slightly cynical tone and direct, no-nonsense advice. Does this approach increase his credibility?*

Kid knocks on my office door. He looks vaguely familiar. "My name is Scott," he says. "I'm in your logic class." Yes, that's why I recognize him; he's the fellow who showed up a couple of times at the beginning of the semester. Sat in the back, I think.

"So where have you been all term?" I ask with genuine curiosity. "Well," the student fumbles, "I'm taking this tough course in organic chemistry, and well, uh, like I got this lazy attitude, I admit. Anyway, I'd like an extension on my term paper deadline. And would you reconsider my midterm grade?"

3   I listen, but I don't listen sympathetically. I'm certainly not inclined to reward this student for his lack of interest in my class. It's not a matter of an official policy—I don't take attendance. But I don't have to do favors either, and I rarely do for students who don't show up to class.

4   "The most important thing in life is showing up," says Woody Allen. That's true, too, with regard to your classes.

5   In this chapter we'll discuss how to make the most of your time when you're in class. But these guidelines are useful only if you're there to use them.

SHOWING UP

6   On any given school day, you could probably think of seven thousand more fun things to do than go to class. One compelling alternative is to just stay in bed. In fact, staying in bed will loom as one of the greatest temptations of college life.

7   I take it for granted that if you aren't thoroughly dull or irrecoverably compulsive, you will miss class on occasion. What does it take for you to decide "forget it, I'll skip class?" A blah, rainy day? A gorgeous, sunny day? Students' cutting patterns get fixed pretty early in their college career. The question is not whether you will miss class, but how often.

8   Some professors include attendance as part of their course requirements. These professors usually carry out their threat. The more stringent ones will even fail the A student who has accrued too many absences. Unfair? I agree. In fact, I find this outrageous. With few exceptions (labs, for example), I favor abolishing all attendance requirements. College students are adults and should decide for themselves whether or not they want to come to class. If you never show up, you risk flunking your tests—but that's *your* problem. On the other hand, if you never show up and get A's on your exams, you should receive an A for the course.

9   Why do professors require attendance? Many will tell you it's because students need to attend their lectures to understand the material. And they quickly emphasize the need for an "attendance requirement" for those students who lack sufficient discipline to show up regularly without this externally imposed threat.

Hogwash. Professors require attendance, in most cases, because   10
they are insecure. They're afraid that if they don't take attendance, no
one will show up—and they're usually right. Not surprisingly, it's most
often the dull teachers who force their students to suffer through their
dreary lectures.

What can you do about these attendance requirements? Nothing.   11
Maybe you can do something later when you become the college
president, but until then, if you have an attendance requirement, show
up. You have no choice.

But even if you don't have an attendance requirement, it's impor-   12
tant to show up regularly.

If you want to ace your classes, cut out cutting. You might   13
think your case is different. But I can only assure you of what all my
colleagues and I see: A students show up to class regularly, and F students don't. Here's why.

Objectively

You'll learn more. Nothing beats being there. When you study   14
without having been to class, you're learning the material for the first
time. When you study after you've been to class, you're reviewing.
What a difference!

You learn what the professor considers essential. Professors   15
test you on what they consider important. What did the professor put
on the blackboard? What did he emphasize? What did he repeat?

You can't get this information from another student's notes, or   16
even a tape recording. You need to observe firsthand your professor's
delivery: you need to know not only *what* was said but *how* it was said.

Subjectively

In the subjective realm of grading, attendance always counts.   17
Professors respond positively toward students who come to class regularly. Repeated absences will lose you the benefit of the doubt when it
comes to grading—and you might very well need that benefit.

College teachers are as sensitive as anyone else. Most people like   18
to believe they are good at what they do, and college teachers like to
think of themselves as good teachers. Your consistent cutting tells your
teacher that you consider him a failure: he isn't sufficiently interesting

to get you to come to class. And your teacher—at least on some level—will take it personally. He might take it out on you personally.

19   **Attendance is especially important in seminars, language, math, and science classes.** The smaller the class, the more your absences are noticed, so if you have to play hooky, cut a large lecture class. The worst classes to skip are seminars where student participation is expected. Cutting seminars undermines the whole class.

20   It's also essential to show up regularly to math, science, and language classes. If you are facile with words and know the tricks of extemporaneous writing, you might get by with absences in some of your humanities and social science classes. Math, science, and language classes are different: here, learning is cumulative, with each class building on the previous class. If you fall behind, it becomes increasingly difficult to catch up.

If You Do Cut

21   Don't make a big deal about it. Professors who require attendance might require a doctor's note or some other justification for your absence. Professors who don't take attendance don't care why you were out.

22   I never could understand why students bother bringing me notes explaining why they missed a class. I don't read them and I suspect few professors do. (It's another matter if you miss an exam.) Nor do I understand why students bother to tell me they will miss the next class. Why call attention to an absence?

DO THE READINGS

Prepare for Class

23   I know this sounds like more obvious professor talk but believe me, preparation is far from common.

24   All students are "rah rah" the first week of class. They do the assigned readings and come to class rearing to go. Then the slack-off begins. By the end of the first month a sizable contingent have stopped coming to class prepared. By the end of the second month, you can count on one hand the number of students who read the material before coming to class. By the middle of the third month, forget it; the student who still prepares is now a rarity.

Read the assignments all through the semester and con-   25
sider yourself an extraordinary phenomenon. College homework
is a term-long affair. In high school you did your homework only
when it was assigned and when you expected it to get checked. In
college, you have to rely on your own schedule and discipline.

Figure it this way: you have to read the material eventually any-   26
way, so you may as well read it before class. It's much more effective
that way: even boring classes are improved, and you can contribute to
the class.

The big hurdle is reading those stupefying assignments that seem   27
to have been written as prescriptions for sleeping pills. To get these
assignments done, you've got to make class preparation part of your
daily routine.

But if You Don't Prepare

You won't always come to class prepared. Perhaps you have a   28
test in another class. Or a heavy date the night before. Or a heavy date
coming up. What then?

Try not to walk into class totally oblivious of the assignment.   29
Cultivate the art of intelligent skimming; when you get good at it—and
like everything else it's a matter of practice—you can pick up lots of
information very quickly.

Okay, it was a *very* heavy date. Not only weren't you able to scan   30
the assigned material, you can now barely keep your eyes open. In this
situation, it isn't your eyes that matter, it's your mouth. Keep it shut.

Few displays of student behavior are as annoying to teachers as   31
students spouting about subjects they know nothing about—but
should, had they done the assigned reading. Don't fool yourself and
make a fool of yourself in the process. If you haven't read the article,
you don't know it. And if you don't know the assignment, don't adver-
tise that you don't.

WHERE TO SIT

In some large lectures, your seating arrangement is alphabetically   32
determined, so this isn't an issue. But in most classes you have a
choice. Where should you sit? Which seat is most conducive to getting
the A?

33   **Sit where the action is.**

34   Writers on power often talk about "power centers" in a room. Every class has its corresponding power center. It's the section that carries the weight of the class.

35   Watch your teacher's movements. (If your teacher is any good, you won't find her sitting behind her desk.) Speakers respond to the section of the audience that responds to them. If one side of the class reacts more vocally to the teacher than the other side, before long, the teacher will be addressing that part of the room more often. Move to that side.

36   Front or back? You can get an A or an F from the front or the back of the room, but in general, front or toward the front is better.*

37   Sitting up toward the front has two main advantages:

38   ❖ **Your professor notices you.** Bad enough that you're a name-less name in the crowd; why be a faceless face in the crowd? Also, teachers tend to think—justifiably or not—that students who sit up front are more conscientious.

39   ❖ **You insure your participation.** Sitting in the professor's eye-line forces you to behave. Your absences are noticed, so you'll make sure to show up in class. You are also less likely to read, talk, or sleep during even the most boring class. If the class is especially important or particularly dreary, sit up front. You'll need all the help you can get, and this helps.

40   The worst seat? It's the back corner seat near the door. You seem uninvolved. **If you are stuck in the back, make sure to speak up in class.**

A FEW NOTES ON TAKING NOTES

41   Unless you have a photographic memory, you need to take some notes. You certainly can't expect to remember during final exam week in May what your professor said back in March.

42   But don't confuse taking notes with stenography. A good lecture gets you to *reflect* during class. You can't listen, think, and respond if you're busy playing secretary.

---

*Students inform me that some of their professors look out above the first row into the class beyond, so a row or two up might be the best of all.

Write down key phrases and ideas that will get you to remember   43
what was discussed (in some classes that will mean a lot of writing, in
others very little writing).

Many study guides offer instruction on how to take notes effec-   44
tively. These guides are a waste of time. You take notes to help *you* review when preparing for exams; what helps you might not help others.

A few of the more compulsive of these study guides recommend   45
that students rewrite their notes after each class. They also suggest that
you write a summary at the end of each class, restating the essential
points of the lecture. Sure, and I recommend that you do a triathlon
every morning and read one play by Shakespeare with dinner every
evening. Who are we kidding?

The Old Blackboard Reflex

When I feel mischievous in the middle of a lecture, I sometimes   46
turn and write on the board a word such as "ineluctable," or the
phrase "the cat's meow," or whatever comes to mind. I look up at the
class and, invariably, I see dozens of students earnestly copying my
words into their notebooks. The assumption: if it's on the blackboard,
it's important.

Agreed, instructors do use the blackboard to highlight important   47
points. But not everything on the board merits special attention; professors will use the board gratuitously, as the whim strikes them.
Sometimes they use it just to show the correct spelling of some
obscure word.

Remember, too, that much that isn't on the board appears on the   48
test. Use your judgment, not your reflexes.

Other People's Notes

If you missed class, it's a good idea to borrow someone's notes,   49
especially in cumulative classes, the kind where each class builds on
the previous one.

Make sure, though, to borrow the notes immediately after   50
the missed class. If you wait until exam time, two things will happen.
First, the notes lose their context, and you'll have an awful time trying
to make sense of them. Second, getting the notes will be a battle. Your
new friends won't eagerly part with them the night before the final.

51   Remember, too, not to trust completely in your classmate's notes. She may have gotten it down wrong. She might have been lost in a sweet fantasy just when the important stuff was discussed. She might have that photographic memory and not bother with careful notes.

Private Ruminations

52   In a later chapter, I encourage you to keep a journal of your personal thoughts, a sort of intellectual diary. You should also save a section in the back of your notebook for class-related meditations. Something your professor or a classmate said might trigger an interesting idea. Jot it down. These notes can become extremely helpful when you review for an exam.

LEAVE A MESSAGE
AND WE'LL GET BACK TO YOU

53   When tape recorders first started showing up on my students' desks, I had this terrifying image of lecturing to a classroom empty of people but dotted with little tape recorders on every desk. At the end of this imaginary lecture, my students would come to pick up their tape recorders. After a while, I figured that since no one was responding during class, I might as well just tape my lectures. So I'd bring in my tape recorder, set it up on the lectern, hit "play," and leave; all the other tape recorders would dutifully record my words of wisdom.

54   An old-fashioned nightmare. Soon, I suppose, video cameras will appear on desks to record lectures. Professors will have to take acting lessons, which, come to think of it, isn't such a bad idea.

55   Why tape record the class? I suppose that students use tape recorders as a security blanket. They're afraid they might miss something important and feel reassured knowing that the vital information is trapped in that little box, caught forever on a magnetic strip.

56   Beware: not even narcissistic professors like having their classes taped. Having your lecture recorded is like having your classes audited by your boss. It kills spontaneity: you're always afraid you might say something incriminating or dumb.

57   For those who insist on bringing a tape recorder to class, here are a few rules:

❖ Get your teacher's permission first. It's rude to record anyone   58
without telling him, and rudeness toward the person who grades
you isn't clever.

❖ Don't use a tape recorder if it inhibits you from participating in   59
class. Some students who would otherwise speak up will shut
down when they're being recorded.

❖ Don't rely on the recording. Gestures convey crucial information.   60
Your tape recorder can't capture the body language.

Since you have to listen to the class anyway, why not just pay   61
attention the first time?

CLASS PARTICIPATION

Want to get an A? Participate.   62
As I've said, showing up to class is essential, and not showing up   63
will hurt your grade. But coming to class isn't enough. According to a
recent survey, only 20 percent of the average class asks questions, and
you should join this minority if you want to secure the A.
Professors seek, need, and appreciate student involvement in   64
their class. We need applause, and the applause of the classroom is
animated discussion. Even the most thick-skinned professor knows
when he's not setting his class on fire. Students who make professors
feel successful are rewarded with better grades.

Too Shy?

Are you uncomfortable speaking up in a group? What are you   65
going to do about it? Resign yourself to spending four years in silence,
masquerading as part of the classroom furniture?
Perhaps you are reluctant to speak up because you don't want to   66
sound like those annoying classmates who blabber inanities in class. You
fear that you don't have anything of substance to add to the proceedings.
I know it's difficult, but try not to worry about what your class-   67
mates think of you. They won't judge you: they're too busy thinking
about their own brilliant comments. Some people are too self-con-
scious to dance on a crowded floor in a discotheque. There too, no
one notices.

68   A tinge of nervousness before speaking in a group is perfectly normal. Just bear in mind that making a comment in class is no major undertaking—your contribution counts as much as any of your classmate's. And rest assured, it gets easier with practice.

69   You will need to speak in public when you are out in the world. The college classroom affords a wonderful opportunity to become good at it.

Don't Lecture

70   About that blabbering classmate: every class has one. He thinks his classmates are paying money to hear him, not the professor, lecture. He has opinions about everything and makes sure everyone knows them. He considers himself provocative—but the only thing he provokes is a conspiracy to lynch.

71   Typically, this student loves to argue; he argues for the sake of arguing. He's not about the courage of his conviction; he's about contrariness: tell him it's raining and he'll say it's snowing, tell him it's snowing and he'll call it a beach day.

72   He believes belligerence is endearing, but everyone finds him immature, boring, and self-defeating.

73   If you genuinely disagree with your professor—and if you aren't catatonic, you'll disagree plenty of times—by all means, voice your objection. But challenging your professor's dominance for the sake of the challenge alone is a no-win strategy. The classroom is the professor's turf, his territorial imperative. **Attempts to undercut his authority bring you only one result: a lower grade.**

74   Another, milder class nerd is the student who insists on treating the class to private, boring anecdotes about his life. This clod isn't interested in asserting his brilliance; he just considers his personal life endlessly fascinating to everyone. So we have to listen to tales about how his mother tortured him as a child, how his uncle became a Bedouin in the Sahara, how he stopped a mugger on the subway, and how his roommate ripped off the telephone company. Somebody should tell him that **nobody is interested.**

75   These students don't just irritate their classmates by using the classroom for their personal forum, they deflect the class discussion away from the direction the professor intended. Professors respond by lowering these students' grades.

Questions Are Better Than Comments

Teachers like comments that move the discussion along. They   76
like questions even better, and among the best questions are requests
for clarification.

"Could you explain that again?" is not an appropriate question if   77
you didn't understand the discussion because you were busy doing the
Sunday crossword puzzle. It is an excellent question if you paid attention and need to have a point repeated. This sort of question does
your classmates a service. If you didn't follow what was said, the
chances are that many of your classmates didn't either.

Requests for elucidation also help your grade. It shows you care   78
about the material and want to understand the class discussion. But
don't overdo it. You don't want to seem obstructive or slow.

Ask Questions about an Upcoming Exam

Has your professor told the class little or no information about   79
the upcoming test? Ask. Wait till the end of class (some professors prefer questions at the end of the class period) and ask your professor
what to expect: an essay or short-answer test, or a cumulative, open
book exam? Sometimes your instructor doesn't tell the class because
she simply forgets to, and your question is a welcome reminder.

Dress

I'd rather not believe that professors factor in a student's appear-   80
ance in the determination of his or her grade, but studies indicate otherwise. Especially at the grade-school and high-school levels,
good-looking students are graded more leniently than ugly students.

I think you are pretty safe dressing as you like in college, and I   81
think you should dress as you like in any case. Don't be surprised, however, if you run into that professor who takes you—and your work—less
seriously than you'd like because you wear outlandish clothing.

DEALING WITH BOREDOM

Fact one: You will have to sit through boring classes. Fact two: If   82
you are unlucky, you will sit through many boring classes.

83   This is the fourth class in which you've discussed the symbolic role of birds in early Anglo-Saxon literature. Moreover, you're a computer science major with less than zero interest in birds, real or symbolic, and you're only taking this class to meet a humanities requirement. You've been good. You've contributed your insights on the relationships between bird chirps and microchips. And you're bored out of your wits.

84   Don't read. Don't talk. Your professor can see your face, so look alive. Bored or not, the grade counts.

85   It's time for creativity. Play mind games. Count how many times your teacher uses the word *impact*. Decide who are the three best-looking students in the class. Check out the other students' accents. Picture your professor as a five-year-old . . . as an eighty-year-old.

86   If you're inventive, you can come up with dozens of mind games that keep you entertained and, at the same time, keep your attention focused on what's happening in class. This has the advantage of making it appear as if you're interested in the class; how could your professor know that when you are looking at him, you're imagining him with a pacifier in his mouth?

THOU SHALT NOT

87   Here's a review of behavior you must avoid. Etiquette is not the concern here (though that counts too). The concern is how to avoid a lower grade than you deserve.

88   ❖ **Never badmouth the subject matter.** A quick and sure way to get a lousy grade in a class: ridicule the subject you're studying. You, a twenty-year-old undergraduate, have decided that economics is "bull," or that psychology is all smoke, or that Henry James can't write for beans.

89   Your professor has devoted his life to the subject and will judge you to be an ignorant, impudent brat. He will also welcome the opportunity to grade your work as severely as he can.

90   ❖ **Never study for an exam in another class.** This suggests to the professor that you worry more about the other class than her own. It's insulting.

91   ❖ **Avoid coming late or leaving early.** In college, you are largely anonymous. To get A's, you need to stand out. But that doesn't include standing out like a sore thumb—arriving late and leaving early are the wrong ways to call attention to yourself.

Don't stare at your watch, pack your books or put your coat on 92
five minutes before the end of the class. These maneuvers disrupt
the class and offend your professor. If you have to leave early,
tell your professor before class starts and sit near an exit.

❖ **Never read in class.** Textbooks from other classes are bad 93
enough, but magazines and newspapers are particularly offensive.

❖ **Don't sit at your desk without a notebook.** Bring paper and pen 94
even if all you do is doodle. Pretend you are a serious student.

❖ **Don't yack in class.** It's rude and makes you seem adolescent. 95

QUESTIONS TO CONSIDER ◀

1. Did you find Halberstam's straightforward approach convincing?
Why? Do his cynical tone and brusque style fit your stereotype of a
college professor? How many of your professors actually conform to
this stereotype?

2. What one piece of advice did you find most useful? Why do you
think this advice is valuable? Do you think following Halberstam's
advice would make you more successful in college? That is, do his
insider's tips actually provide you with valuable information you
would otherwise not know?

3. How does Halberstam's advice differ from the standard advice given
to students by parents and teachers? Did you learn anything from
this selection that you did not already know?

4. *Acing College*, the title of the book from which this chapter was
taken, suggests that the reason to read (and/or buy) the book is to
learn how to make good grades in college. In fact, above the title
on the cover of the book is written "Studying is not enough to guarantee A's." Should making A's be the most important goal of a college student? What other goals do you consider equally or more
important? Would Halberstam's advice help you attain these goals?

5. Identify examples of the following formatting features that Halberstam uses: main headings, subheadings, bullets, boldface type, and
italics (see **headings** and **format**). How do these features improve
the readability of his text?

HEADINGS, PAGE 526

FORMAT, PAGE 505

▶ **WRITING ACTIVITIES**

Individual: Describe yourself as you appear and act in a particular class. How do your appearance and actions differ from those recommended by Halberstam? Have you ever used any of Halberstam's suggestions successfully to get a better grade? Have you ever attempted one of Halberstam's suggestions and had it backfire on you?

Collaborative: Compare your classroom behavior with that of a group of your classmates. Then decide on a set of instructions for ideal classroom behavior from a student's point of view. Make your instructions brief and specific.

Computer: Choose one instruction from the list your group compiled and revise it, amplifying (see **amplification**) it with personal experiences and examples, so that it becomes a piece of advice rather than an item from a set of instructions. Your **style and voice** should reflect the personal, informal way in which students communicate with one another.

AMPLIFICATION, PAGE 404

STYLE AND VOICE, PAGE 596

❖❖❖❖❖

CRIME ON CAMPUS

Stacey Colino
With Tina Oakland and Maryann Jacobi

This selection appeared first in Seventeen, *a magazine written primarily for a young female audience. Notice that the author begins by providing her readers with information. In fact, this first part of the essay is both informative (this is what has been going on) and persuasive (something should be done about it). The next part of the article consists of a series of questions and answers. The last part of the essay is clearly instructive. As you read, decide how the first two parts of the essay contribute to the effectiveness of the final instructions.*

1   Early on the morning of January 17, 1988—hours after the Winter Formal—University of Georgia sophomore Dana Getzinger woke up when a man tried to smother her in bed with a pillow. Wearing a ski

mask and gloves, the intruder had broken into the off-campus apartment she shared with her roommates through a sliding glass door. As Getzinger fought him off, she felt what she thought was a punch in the stomach; as it turned out, she'd been stabbed. Several people who were staying in the apartment heard the intruder leaving and came to Getzinger's rescue.

After she recovered, Getzinger learned of four similar incidents that had occurred on campus. Each attack happened a month apart and within a one-mile radius of her apartment; all of the women had been raped. The man who committed at least two of the other crimes was caught, but Getzinger still doesn't know if he's the one who attacked her. What really angered her was that none of the crimes had been publicized to students. "We had no idea that this was going on," Getzinger says now. "We were living with such a false sense of security."   2

That's the way it's been for years at most colleges and universities across the country. In the past, these institutions haven't been required by law to report campus crimes to students, parents, employees, prospective students, or the government. And because they're competing for applicants, colleges and universities have little incentive to voluntarily report just how dangerous their campus might be. After all, a school would rather stand out in a prospective student's mind for its academic standing or its idyllic setting than for its crime rate.   3

"Colleges and universities are in a highly competitive market for students, for enrollment, for appropriations, and for gifts," says Michael Clay Smith, professor of criminal justice at the University of Southern Mississippi and author of *Coping With Crime on Campus* and *Wide Awake: A Guide to Safe Campus Living in the 90s.* "I don't accuse most college administrators of bad faith, but it is considered anathema to talk about negative aspects of campus life. An institution that says we don't have a campus crime problem, however, is either lying or ignorant. Students can only protect themselves if they comprehend the reality of the problem by seeing actual numbers at the schools."   4

"It's a really vulnerable time for students," says Dana Getzinger. "They've just stopped living with Mom and Dad, and they're on their own for the first time. So many people think that because they haven't heard about crimes, they don't exist. People need to be told; otherwise they're even more vulnerable."   5

The news is that the situation is about to change. A federal law passed last fall will require colleges and universities to do what's in the best interest of their students: publish annual statistics on campus crime, publicize their campus safety policies, and submit an annual copy of campus crime figures to the Secretary of Education. (Similar   6 laws in some states already require colleges and universities to provide this information upon request.) Under the federal law, schools will have to disclose how many incidents of murder, rape, robbery, aggravated assault, burglary, and motor vehicle theft occur on their campus every year. Called the "Student Right-to-Know and Campus Security Act," the measure will also require colleges and universities to publish the number of arrests for liquor law violations, drug violations, and possession of weapons.

7   Once the law takes effect on September 1, 1992, it will enable prospective students to size up a school more accurately. It will also serve to alert current students to what's going on at their own school and encourage them to take precautions. The hope is that forewarned will mean forearmed.

8   It took the determination of victims like Dana Getzinger and two devastated parents, Connie and Howard Clery, to finally bring national attention to the pressing problem of slack campus security. In one of the most widely publicized cases, freshman Jeanne Ann Clery was raped and murdered in her dorm room at Lehigh University, in Bethlehem, Pennsylvania, by a fellow student in 1986. The dormitory was protected by a series of heavy doors that locked automatically, but students had propped them open that night to allow people to come and go. Since then, Clery's parents have formed Security on Campus, Inc., and lobbied hard for state and federal legislation.

9   One obstacle has been that because colleges and universities haven't been required to report campus crimes, it's been difficult to gauge just how serious the problem is—or whether it's been getting worse. Right now, only 15 percent of colleges and universities report their crime rates to the FBI, and the ones that do are mostly state universities. Also, at many schools there are fraternity and sorority houses, as well as student houses and apartments, that are considered off-campus. Dana Getzinger's assault wasn't reported as a campus crime because she lived in an off-campus apartment—as do most University of Georgia upperclassmen. Then, too, there's the reluctance of schools to show themselves in a bad light.

10   Yet even the statistics that are reported are alarming. In 1989 there were 2 murders, 243 rapes, 552 robberies, 1,675 aggravated assaults, and 105,994 property crimes reported on 360 of the nation's campuses. By some estimates, two to ten times as many crimes actually occur as are reported to police.

11   Contrary to popular belief, 80 percent of criminal activity on campuses is committed not by outsiders, but by students. Towson State University's Center for the Study and Prevention of Campus Violence

found that of the 639 sexual assaults that were reported on campuses in 1988, 80 percent were perpetrated by an acquaintance.

College administrators say they often face an impossible task when it comes to protecting students. "Parents send children to colleges and universities and expect they'll be protected from everything around them," says Kathleen Curry Santora, vice president for operations of the National Association of Independent Colleges and Universities. "But now colleges are trying to achieve a balance between giving students the freedom they want and protecting them. People have very high expectations of colleges, and I don't see why we should be held to a higher standard than the rest of the country."   12

Indeed, crime on college and university campuses may simply be a reflection of society's ills, though there are experts who argue that schools are crime magnets. The real problem now is that students don't always understand that just because you're on campus doesn't mean you're safe. As nice as the quad looks, as friendly as fellow students seem, as much fun as it can be to run around at all hours and have no rules—campuses are potential crime areas, and students have to take precautions just like anyone anywhere.   13

While the federal legislation will help with the reporting of campus crimes, it won't stop the violence or theft. According to campus safety experts, colleges and universities need to do three things in order to fulfill their duty to students: alert them to the dangers around them, provide better security, and teach crime prevention. Most colleges and universities now offer a variety of safety programs, including escort services, after-dark shuttle buses, security systems in dormitories, and emergency call boxes strategically located on campus, in addition to roving security guards.   14

As a result of the Clery murder, Lehigh has introduced a security program in certain dormitories and sororities that includes electronic systems that signal when doors aren't properly secured. Plus, many schools now offer programs to boost student awareness of crimes like acquaintance rape. Trained student volunteers have been leading sessions on sexual victimization at the University of Florida since 1981, at the University of Michigan since 1986, and at the University of Colorado since 1987.   15

"It happens to a lot of people," says Judy Buck, coordinator of Colorado's Dare to Stop Rape program, "but they don't always know there's a name for it or recognize what it is. After we do a presentation, the phone calls to our counseling center vastly increase."   16

"Schools need to teach students more about crime prevention in such a way as to change the behavior of perpetrators as well as vic-   17 tims," says criminal justice professor Smith. "If we can do a better job of teaching what it means to live in a community with others, we *can* change behavior."

18   As many as one in six college women is a victim of rape or attempted rape each year. Some of these rapes are "stranger rapes," where an unknown man sneaks up on his victim, but more than half are acquaintance rapes, where the rapist and victim know each other. These statistics may seem overwhelming, but there are steps you can take to greatly increase your safety—on campus or off.

19   Each of the following questions describes a common situation that can easily lead to assault. Decide which option would be the safest in each situation.

20   **1.** The nice guy who sits next to you in calculus asks you out for next Saturday night. When you accept, he suggests going to a movie and then taking a drive. You
(a) agree with his plan, despite feeling uncomfortable about the drive.
(b) suggest going out with your roommate and her boyfriend.
(c) tell him the movie sounds great, but you'd like to save the drive for another time.
(d) agree, but plan to fake a headache and go home right after the movie.

Answer: *c*

21   If you agree to go for a drive with a guy you hardly know, you're placing yourself in a potentially dangerous situation. The majority of date rapes occur on a first or second date, on a weekend evening, in an isolated place like a car, a dorm room or apartment, the woods, or the beach. The single most important step you can take to protect yourself is to avoid being alone with a guy or guys you don't know well.

22   Option *c* offers a safe way to go out with a guy you like. To be safest, you may want to restrict your first few dates to public places like movie theaters or restaurants that you can get yourself to and from. That way you can avoid being alone in a car with him, and you can leave if he behaves badly.

23   If you choose *b* and arrange a double date, make sure you all stay together. Option *d* is a bad idea, because it can make you seem unsure of yourself or passive, and a lot of rapists know how to take advantage of that. You need to communicate from the beginning what your rules and limits are and that you're in charge of what you do.

2. You're at a fraternity party. After dancing with a guy you've met   24
there, you have a few glasses of punch to cool off. It tastes okay, but
you soon start to feel dizzy and nauseous. You
(a) ask a friend to take you home.
(b) ask the guy you've been dancing with to take you home.
(c) accept his offer to go into a nearby room and lie down until you
feel better.
(d) slip outside by yourself to get some fresh air and clear your head.

Answer: *a*

  This is a very common date rape situation. Chances are your drink   25
was spiked (maybe even with grain alcohol, which is extremely potent
and very hard to detect). Many, perhaps most, date rapes occur when one
or both people have been drinking. When you've been drinking, your
natural good judgment and intuition are impaired, and you may take risks
you wouldn't otherwise take. You're also less able to defend yourself.

  Your goal in this situation is to get help from a reliable person as   26
quickly as possible, so option *a* is your safest bet. It's unfortunate but
true that some guys will offer assistance with the hidden goal of luring
you into an isolated place, such as another room in the fraternity
house or a car or your dorm room. For this reason, avoid options *b*
and *c*. If you wait, you may become disoriented and even pass out, so
you probably shouldn't attempt to just slip out or go home alone.

3. You've been researching a term paper, and it's almost midnight   27
when you're ready to leave the library. The campus is practically
deserted. You
(a) walk quickly or jog back to your dorm or apartment.
(b) wait until a male student walks by and ask him for an escort.
(c) wait until a female student walks by and ask her for an escort.
(d) call the campus security service.

Answer: Probably *d*

  Many colleges offer escort services to help students get around   28
campus safely after dark. If there's one available on your campus, consider using it.

  Options *a, b,* and *c* are also reasonable responses. You have to   29
select the one that feels right to you at the time, though you're safest
asking another girl to walk with you. While it might feel safer to ask a
guy, this can lead to trouble (see question 5). If you go home by yourself, jog or walk assertively to avoid looking like an easy target.

30 **4.** Shortly before your psychology midterm, a guy in your class you'd like to know better asks if you want to study together. You accept enthusiastically. "Great," he says. "Come by my apartment around seven tonight." He explains that the library is too crowded and the student union too noisy for studying. You

(a) accept without reservation—you prefer to study at home, too.

(b) tell him to come to your place instead.

(c) ask him if he has a roommate, and decline if he doesn't.

(d) tell him you don't want to go to his apartment and suggest another place you can study together.

Answer: *d*

31   Like most situations that can lead to date rape, this one is hard to read. He may be a serious student who does his best work at home or even just a guy who'd like to be alone with you, but would never hurt you. Nonetheless, going alone to his apartment—whether or not there's a roommate—can be dangerous. You probably wouldn't go to his apartment for your first date with him, so don't let a study session be any different.Turning the tables and inviting him to your place isn't necessarily any safer, unless your roommates promise to stick around. Your safest option is *d*. Chances are he'll be understanding—and would you really want a relationship with him if he weren't?

32 **5.** You're at a football game with a group of friends, and you've all had some beers. After the game, a guy you've just met offers to walk you back to your dorm, which is on the other side of campus. You

(a) accept with pleasure—it's a nice gesture.

(b) tell him you appreciate the offer, but decline politely.

(c) accept, but ask a friend or two to join you.

(d) accept, but tell him that you're in a hurry and really need to go straight home.

Answer: *b* or *c*

33   Chances are you've met a nice guy who wants to get to know you, but the combination of alcohol and isolation can lead to a bad situation. When you've been drinking, your problem-solving skills are weaker than usual, so if problems develop, you may have a hard time dealing with them.

34   In this case, your safest options are *b* and *c*. By asking some friends to join you, you can get better acquainted with this guy without isolating yourself. Option *d* may *sound* good, but it really doesn't protect you, and it can make you sound unsure of yourself.

6. You've been having a great time at a party in an apartment complex   35
next to campus. There were more guys than girls to begin with, so
you've been dancing nonstop for hours. You could keep going, but
you look around and notice there are only three girls and about nine
or ten guys left. You
(a) leave immediately.
(b) ask another girl to let you know when she's leaving, so you can
leave with her.
(c) keep an eye on the situation, but don't overreact—these are guys
from your college, not strangers you met in a bar.
(d) ask both of the other girls to leave with you right away.

Answer: *d*

    Girls who are the last to leave a party are at increased risk for   36
rape, particularly gang rape, especially if everyone's been drinking.
Some guys may assume that you want sex because you stayed behind
after most others left. It's definitely time to leave this party, but try not
to desert the other girls: Leave together if possible. For this reason, the
best option is *d*. Option *b* may seem reasonable, but it has the disadvantage of prolonging your time in a risky situation. Option *a* is an
okay choice, but it's probably best not to head out on your own.

7. Finally, this guy you've had a crush on has asked you out. You're   37
thrilled and spend the whole afternoon getting ready. He shows up on
time, looking great. But as you're headed out to dinner, he puts his
arm around you, pulls you close, and runs his hand over your back in
a way that makes you feel weird. You
(a) tell him angrily to get his hands off you.
(b) pull away, pretending to tie your shoelace or adjust your contact
lens—he'll probably get the hint.
(c) tell him that you don't want him—or anyone you don't know
well—to put his arm around you.
(d) decide not to do anything unless the situation escalates—he may
not really mean anything by it.

Answer: *c*

    It's possible your date is so pleased to see you that he's showing   38
some spontaneous affection. On the other hand, he could be testing
you to see how pliable you are. If you let him continue to touch you
in a way that is suggestive and that makes you uncomfortable, you risk
sending him subtle signals that you can be easily manipulated. Another

kind of testing behavior is asking inappropriate questions, such as whether your roommates will be home after dinner or about your past sexual experiences.

39 　All too often, women discount their discomfort in such situations to avoid "making a scene"; it may also seem better to quietly endure his advances than to risk insulting him or embarrassing yourself.

40 　Most girls who were date rape victims, however, recall trying to ignore a variety of testing behaviors because they felt they were being "oversensitive." Direct, assertive, and firm refusals to allow a guy to touch you or speak to you in ways that are too familiar—option *c*—are more likely to prevent a date rape. If he persists or doesn't take you seriously, resort to option *a*.

41 　**8.** You decide to start running—at least three times a week. The safest time for you to plan to go is
(a) early morning, varying your route.
(b) midday, varying your route.
(c) midday, following the same route.
(d) early evening, following the same route.

Answer: *None of the above*

42 　Any time of day can be dangerous. Regardless of what time you want to run, map out some safe routes in advance that avoid isolated or wooded areas and stick to brightly lit, clear, and well-traveled pathways. Ideally, you should vary your route and the time you run to reduce the likelihood that someone could lie in wait for you. Best of all, jog with a friend: it's safer, and you're more likely to exercise regularly, too.

43 　To stay safe, follow these guidelines:

44 　**Trust your instincts.** If someone's making you uncomfortable or afraid, take immediate action. You are the best judge of what's appropriate in a given situation. It's better to overreact and risk embarrassment than to ignore your intuition and risk assault. Listen to your inner voice.

45 　**Watch where you're going.** Don't end up alone or with a guy you don't know well in an isolated place. If you're out of the sight of others (even if they're only a dorm room away), your chances of being raped or assaulted increase greatly.

46 　**Be assertive.** Don't let a guy touch you or talk to you in a way that makes you feel uncomfortable. Be firm about your objections.

Be careful about drinking. Remember that it will impair your   47
judgment and reactions. If you plan to drink, stay with your friends.

Whatever happens, don't blame yourself. If you are raped or   48
assaulted, what you need is counseling and medical attention, not self-
accusation. The student health service, women's center, dorm adviser,
campus security service, police, and dean of students should all know
what to do. You owe it to yourself to get help.

QUESTIONS TO CONSIDER

1. Colino, like Roberts, begins with a narrative. What does this true story
   of a University of Georgia student's experience add to the article?
   Why do you think the author continues to refer to this story throughout her essay?

2. What purpose does the series of questions and answers serve?

3. The article ends with five briefly stated instructions to help women
   avoid sexual assault. Would these instructions be as effective if they
   were presented by themselves rather than in the context of the
   essay? Why or why not?

WRITING ACTIVITIES

Individual: Write a journal entry in which you describe an experience
you or an acquaintance has had with campus crime.

Collaborative: Discuss with a group of your classmates one type of
crime that seems to occur often on your campus. Then write a set of
specific instructions telling students how to avoid this type of campus crime. Choose a **format** that is appropriate and easy to read.   FORMAT, PAGE 505

Computer: Enter into a new computer file the set of specific instructions that your group wrote in the collaborative activity. Then, using
your computer network or sharing disks, read and edit one
another's instructions. Finally, combine and format all the instructions into a brief handbook on how to avoid being the victim of
campus crime for new students.

A STUDENT AT ANY AGE

Tammy Adams

Tammy Adams is married, has a child, and works full time in a university. She is also a student. She wrote this essay in a freshman composition class in response to an assignment that directed the students to write to instruct. Because she was a returning student, one who had been out of school for a number of years, she decided to write an essay giving advice to other returning students.

1   For most students, entering college is exciting. It means leaving home for the first time and beginning a new life as an adult. However, for adult students who are returning to school, it is often a time of insecurity. These adult students have been in the "real world" for some time. Some are homemakers, some are mothers or fathers, and most are employees. Adults often enter school with feelings of fear and insecurity, questioning whether they can handle an already full load of adult responsibilities and at the same time compete with the younger traditional college students. As an adult student myself, I would like to give some words of advice to adult students who are planning to enter college.

2   First of all, turning in an application to the school should not be your first step. Your first step should be turning in an application at home. Adult students who succeed at completing their education usually have the cooperation of family members who help them reach the goal of completing their degree. Most of you who are returning to school have either a spouse or children or a combination of both. Whatever your situation may be, your success as a student depends on the cooperation you receive from your family. For example, an adult student I know recently told me she was withdrawing from school for the semester because her husband had demanded that she withdraw. As an adult student myself, I know the advantage of having a supportive spouse. There are plenty of times that my husband takes over in the evenings to do supper and take care of our daughter so I can study. On weekends he frequently entertains the little one so I can write a report or prepare for exams.

3   Second, as an adult student, coming back to school after years of not being a student, you should be prepared to ask a lot of questions. The adult student often tends to be reluctant to ask questions. After all,

adults are supposed to know everything. Right? This reluctance generally stems from the age difference between the traditional young students and yourself. Although you may feel intimidated when it comes
to asking questions, students, regardless of their age, should never
hold back from asking questions. Assuming how something will be,
rather than asking questions, generally results in your making a bad
decision. For example, during my first semester I registered for a night
class that was canceled due to the lack of students in the class. I
assumed that since the course was canceled by the department, it was
not my responsibility to drop the course from my schedule. However,
not only did I not receive a refund for the course but on my grade
report there was an "F" for the course. After making several phone
calls, walking all over campus getting permission to drop after the
deadline, and standing in a long line at the registrar's office, I had
learned a very valuable lesson. Now I always call my department to
verify procedure rules and regulations.

Finally, as an adult student, you need to take advantage of pro-   4
grams that are designed to help you. In the past decade universities and
colleges have experienced a significant increase in the number of adult
students. In the beginning nothing was done to try to help these particular students adjust to their new academic world. However, now there are
many different programs to help the adult student adjust. One of the
main programs available to you is the counseling center. Counseling centers usually offer counseling services, tests to help you determine a major,
and lists of academic tutors available to help you during the semester.

Once you begin to feel in place, instead of out of place, you can   5
concentrate on academics rather than your fears and feelings of insecurity. The reason most adult students give for feeling that they are out
of place is their age. However, with time you will begin to see that
being older is not a disadvantage but rather an advantage. You will
eventually realize that, while it is true that you have more difficulty
finding study time because of work or family obligations, you have
several advantages over the traditional student. Your life experiences
will play a large part in your academic success. Because of your age,
you will have more experiences to give in class discussions. The most
interesting classes I have been in have been the classes in which there
was a large variety of students, including older students. A friend of
mine taking business management classes has found it easier to understand the course's content because most of what she is studying is similar to situations she deals with in her job. In a history class I took,
those of us over 25 years had much more to contribute to class discussions, especially discussions on politics and world affairs.

6   There is no age limit on getting an education. If you have the desire and motivation, you can succeed as a student at any age. Once you overcome your fears and feelings of inadequacy, you may very well discover that you do extremely well in your new world of academics.

▶   **QUESTIONS TO CONSIDER**

1. According to Adams, what are the advantages and disadvantages of starting college after you have been out of high school for a number of years? Can you think of others?

2. Does Adams keep her audience (adult returning students) in focus throughout her essay? Identify instances in which it is clear she is writing for this audience.

3. Is the essay by Adams interesting to all readers or just to those to whom it is primarily addressed? Is the advice that she gives adult students also useful to younger students? In what way?

4. Adams states that adult students have been in the "real world." How does the real world differ from the academic world? In what way is the academic world unreal? Is this a useful distinction for Adams to make in her introduction?

5. If you are a returning student, do you find Adams's advice clear? Useful? Reassuring? What other advice might she have included?

▶   **WRITING ACTIVITIES**

Individual: Write a set of specific instructions for someone who is registering for classes in your college or university for the first time. Be brief and specific. Write your instructions in the form of a numbered list.

Collaborative: Compare the instructions for registering that each of you wrote. Then compose a new set of instructions combining the best features of your individual lists.

Computer: Expand the specific set of instructions that your group wrote into an article that gives general advice about how to register at your school. You may want to make your advice humorous. Share your article with your peers on your computing network.

❖❖❖❖❖

WRITING INSTRUCTIONS AND ADVICE

Writing a good set of instructions is much harder than it looks. You may think that since instructions are usually rather brief and straightforward, they are not difficult to write. After all, how difficult can it be to tell someone how to groom a dog, file an income tax return, or use a computer program? The answer is, probably more difficult than you think.

Determining Your Purpose

The purpose of instructions or advice is to explain to your readers how to do something. If you are writing specific instructions, your readers will be performing the task in question even as, or immediately after, they read what you have written. If you are giving general instructions or advice, your readers may not be immediately engaged in the task or process, but they probably are interested in doing the thing you are writing about at some future time. In either case, your instructions or advice should be easy to read, adequately explained and illustrated, and formatted so that information is accessible to a reader who needs to go back and reread parts of the instructions.

To do this, you must know your audience well. Teaching a computer systems analyst how to run a particular software program requires a very different set of instructions from those a beginning computer user needs to run the same program. Instructions tend to be more audience-specific than any other type of writing. For example, if you are writing an article on how to apply eye makeup, you are probably writing for females rather than males, and you had better know if your audience is young or old if you want to give them the appropriate advice. The audience for some instructions can be large and varied (readers of driver's license manuals, for example). But most instructions are written with a smaller and less generic audience in mind. The first, and possibly the most important, rule for writing good instructions is "Know your audience." You should know not only who your readers are but also, if possible, what they are capable of understanding, their general intelligence and background experience with the subject, if they are biased toward the subject in any way, how they feel about the task at hand, and how much time they will likely be able to spend on the task.

The following questions will help you analyze your audience:

1. Who will my primary reader(s) be?

2. What is their specific knowledge of the subject?

3. What is their age, gender, education, and so on?

4. What biases may they have?

5. What is their purpose in reading my text?

Structuring Instructions

It is the writer's responsibility to structure instructions so that the reader's task is as uncomplicated as possible. Sometimes a narrative structure accomplishes this goal, but instructions often take other forms. For example, specific instructions are often structured as a list:

1. Do this,

2. Then do this,

3. Finally, do this.

The structure of written instructions depends to a great extent on whether the instructions are intended to guide the reader through an immediate and specific task (such as installing new software or assembling a bookcase) or to give the reader advice about how to do something general in the future (how to choose a career, win an argument, improve a tennis serve, or dress for success). Instructions should be structured so that readers can easily recognize the different steps, locate specific information, and backtrack to reread important information (also see **format**). For example, if a reader needs to reread one step in the instructions, that step should be easy to find—numbered, set off from the other steps, or perhaps in boldface type or capital letters.

FORMAT, PAGE 505

Establishing the Appropriate Voice

Specific instructions are often written impersonally and objectively, and the writer's voice is usually that of an anonymous expert. Someone who is trying to install a smoke alarm doesn't need to know who wrote the instructions as long as they are clearly and accurately written. Exceptions exist, of course; some bestselling cookbooks have been written by authors, such as Julia Child, who intrude effectively into the instructions. But most instructions of this type are limited to essential information presented clearly and anonymously.

In contrast, instructions that offer readers advice are usually more discursive. Often authors who are advising their readers use an essay or narrative structure, embedding the advice in a context rather than presenting it in isolation. In this type of instruction, the author's persona and **credibility** are important factors. Readers do not accept advice from just anyone. The writer must be perceived as knowledgeable, experienced, even wise, if the advice is to be accepted.

CREDIBILITY, PAGE 443

Understanding General Guidelines

Six general guidelines can help you write effective instructions:

❖ Clarity is everything.

❖ Amplify, amplify, amplify.

❖ Don't overload readers' minds.

❖ Use the imperative mood.

❖ Format instructions for reading ease.

❖ Use graphics to reinforce words.

Although these general guidelines are primarily for writing specific instructions, many of them also apply to writing advice or general instructions.

CLARITY IS EVERYTHING.   In most kinds of writing, clarity is desirable but not essential; in certain types of poetry and fiction, for example, ambiguity may even be a virtue. But unclear instructions are worthless and sometimes even dangerous. Remember too that clarity means more than being clear to you, the writer; the instructions must be clear to your readers. Reread the instructions you write repeatedly, and also ask other people to read them to be sure they are clear and unambiguous.

AMPLIFY, AMPLIFY, AMPLIFY.   Instructions should, of course, be brief and to the point. Readers who are primarily reading to accomplish some task do not want to read any words that are unnecessary. However, instructions can also be too brief. Skimpy instructions lacking in details and examples are not very useful for readers. Writers of instructions often assume that their readers will know as much about the subject as

AMPLIFICATION, PAGE 404

they do and thus provide too little information. Be sure, if it is needed, that you amplify each step of the instructions so your reader knows exactly what you want him or her to do (see **amplification**).

DON'T OVERLOAD YOUR READERS' MINDS.   Give readers a chance to respond to each command or suggestion before going on to the next one. In specific instructions this means giving readers only one command per sentence. If an instruction needs to be amplified, allot a single paragraph to the command plus the amplification it requires. In more general instructions and advice, discuss only one step or suggestion per paragraph.

USE THE IMPERATIVE MOOD.   Teachers often caution composition students against using second person, *you*, when they write, but when you are writing instructions, *you* is appropriate and effective. Whether you are writing specific instructions or general advice, writing directly to your readers makes it easier for you to tell them what to do and easier for them to understand what to do. For example, "You turn the knob to the right" is much easier to understand than "The knob should be turned to the right," which can be a description of a static condition (a knob that is pointing to the right) or an option (it *should* be turned to the right but doesn't necessarily have to be turned to the right) as well as an instruction. Often you can omit the pronoun *you* and just say "Turn the knob to the right." You are using the imperative mood when the pronoun *you* is understood rather than stated.

Even if you are writing general advice rather than specific instructions, you can use *you*. Trying to stay in the third person can become very awkward when you are telling someone how to do something even if that person is not going to do anything immediately. However, if you are describing a process, *how* something is done, you may find third person more appropriate.

Example

When *you* are making a decision about which college to attend, *you* must always consider cost.

When *students* begin the process of selecting a college, *they* usually consider cost an important factor.

FORMAT INSTRUCTIONS FOR READING EASE.   Especially if you are writing specific instructions, remember that the arrangement of the text on the page can make it more readable. The point of using lists, numbers, bullets, and different typefaces is not to decorate your text but to make it easier for readers to understand and to locate specific information within your text. If you are working on a computer, try different formats to find one that is attractive and that helps readers access important information easily (see **format**). For example, simply arranging the steps of instructions in a numbered list makes them easier for a reader to follow.

FORMAT, PAGE 505

USE GRAPHICS TO REINFORCE WORDS.   A picture may actually be worth more than a thousand words. Often you can illustrate a complex step with a simple diagram or illustration much better than you can by describing the process in words. Fortunately, you do not have to choose between words and pictures; use both. Graphics don't replace words; they reinforce them. Thus tell your reader to insert the computer disk into the mailer, and also provide a diagram illustrating this instruction. Keep graphics uncomplicated and label them clearly (see **graphics**).

GRAPHICS, PAGE 519

Whether you are writing simple instructions or giving profound advice, your readers need to feel confidence in you and what you have written. When you write clear, complete, direct, and appropriately illustrated instructions, you will gain your readers' confidence and gratitude.

W R I T I N G   A S S I G N M E N T

As a college freshman, you have already had experiences that taught you how to survive as a college student. You have selected a college and enrolled, worked out a class schedule, registered for classes, and learned your way around campus. You may also have applied for financial aid, moved into a dorm, adjusted to a roommate, decided which organizations to join, and figured out how to manage your money, meet new friends, get along with a variety of people, and still get your laundry done each week. In this writing assignment, you are to instruct or advise new students about something you have learned. For example, you might tell new students how to do something specific, like registering by phone or using the key-word search function of the on-line catalog in the library. Or you might give them general advice about such subjects as how to eat at the cafeteria without gaining weight, how to reduce stress, how to get along with professors, how to study for an exam, or how to avoid problems with drugs and alcohol.

Offer advice that is creative and specific to your experiences. For example, if you have been out of school for a number of years, you may want to advise other returning students about how to adjust to being a student again. If you are a foreign student, you may choose to advise other international students about how to overcome language difficulties or adjust to a new culture. If you attended a small high school, you may want to advise other students how to make the transition from a small high school to a large college or university.

Planning Your Text

Your choice of a topic should include a decision about audience. Are you writing to all college freshman, only to those at your own school, or to a special group or type of entering college freshmen? Spend some time thinking about your audience—their previous experiences, background information (what they do and do not know about college), ages, expectations, and attitudes.

Remember, your readers will be entering freshmen who have not shared your experiences as a college freshman. Try to remember how you felt when you first arrived on campus, a new student who did not know how to read a college bulletin or schedule of classes, how to purchase a meal ticket or find the registrar's office, what to wear or where to go. Your audience will probably be like you in significant ways but at the same time will not have had the recent experiences you have had. You are the expert on how to schedule classes so you have enough time to prepare for each one, how to find time to work as well as go to school, how to figure out which professors are good, or how to manage your money so you don't run out by the middle of the month. Your readers are intelligent people who have chosen to pursue their educations, but they are not as knowledgeable as you are about such matters.

The purpose of your instructions will determine whether they are specific or general. If you expect a reader to perform the task you are describing while reading your instructions, then they will be specific. If you expect a reader to apply what you have written at a later time, the instructions will be general. Although you may choose a topic that lends itself to specific instructions, many topics are more appropriate for general instructions or advice. Make this decision too before you begin to write.

Once you have chosen a topic, analyzed your audience, and decided whether your instructions will be specific or general, you are ready to think about the form the instructions will take. If you are writing specific instructions, you will need to identify the steps you want to include and determine what graphics to use. If you are writing general instructions, you may want to jot down the main points you wish to make. In either case, you need to give some thought to what information your readers will need, the order in which it should be presented, and the format that will make it most accessible.

Finally, you may want to gather information from other sources that will supplement your own experiences. For example, talking to someone who works in the registrar's office would provide you not only with additional information about the registration process but also with a different perspective on it. You might discover why the different steps in the process are necessary and how the current process evolved. If you consult other students, you might learn some shortcuts that you overlooked or some strategies you have not yet discovered. A brief survey of selected students might also reveal such information as the average time required to register, the chances of getting the classes preferred, and the role of faculty advisement in the process (see **field research**).

FIELD RESEARCH, PAGE 493

Constructing Your Text

DRAFTING.   You may want to begin with a simple outline of the steps you want to include or the points you want to make. Then you can expand on each, amplifying it until it is fully developed. Or you can begin with an introduction in which you address your audience directly, explaining what your topic is (how to get enough exercise) and why it is important (to keep from gaining weight and to relieve stress) and establishing your own credibility as an expert on this topic (you've figured out how to incorporate exercise into a hectic student schedule). Eventually, you will need both an introduction and the steps or points that will form the body of your text, but it is up to you to decide which to write first.

As you begin to write, try to communicate directly with your audience. Your readers are students like yourself but with less experience. Your purpose is not to impress them but to assist them as they make the difficult transition to becoming college students. Your writing voice should be fairly informal and direct.

At this point, you do not need to be concerned about format. You can make decisions about format later as you revise. But make every effort from the first to write as clearly as possible and to include the information your readers will need. Remember, they will not have been through the same processes and experiences, so they will need careful explanations of things that seem very familiar to you.

Be sure to tell your readers not only *what* to do but *why* to do it as you suggest. Advice gains acceptance when its rationale is clear. For example, if you advise your readers to schedule a conference with each professor during the first few weeks of school, also give them reasons why: to get to know the teacher, to make themselves known, to establish their seriousness as a student, to obtain additional information about their courses, and so on.

Remember to include any appropriate warnings and cautions. Instead of just telling students to be sure to pay their fees on time, for example, warn them of specific consequences such as being dropped from the class rolls and having to repeat the entire registration process at a time when most classes are full.

READING.   As you read what you have written, focus on clarity and completeness. Remember, unclear or incomplete instructions and advice are worthless. Be sure to read your instructions with your readers' needs in mind. They will not have yet had the experiences about which you are writing and will, therefore, need careful explanations of each step or point. For example, if you are advising students about how to establish a good working relationship with their teachers, you may need to explain different types of teachers (teaching assistants, part-time instructors, untenured assistant professors, tenured full professors, and so on). Reading your instructions may even convince you that you need more information in order to make them useful to a reader. Though you have written a draft, rereading it may show you that you need to talk with some of your teachers to get their viewpoints or to ask more experienced students if they agree with what you have written.

Let the instructions you have written get cold before you reread them. If you try to read them immediately after you have finished writing them, you will only see what you think is there rather than what is really there. When you do read them, pretend to be an uninformed reader—to anticipate how even the most confused and inexperienced student might react to them. Also ask several other people to read. Ideally, one of these people will be someone who is not already familiar with your subject and thus will read it from the perspective of a new student. Make it clear to those you ask to read your instructions that you want more than a pat on the back and that you are really interested in knowing how to make these instructions as clear and complete as possible.

REVISING.   You will probably revise your text several times. The first time you revise you might focus on improving the clarity and completeness of your text. For example, you may add more information, explanations, and examples to your earlier draft, developing your ideas so your reader will have no difficulty in understanding your instructions. Or you may have decided in reading your instructions that much of what you have included was not really pertinent. As a result, you may now need to delete the extraneous material and expand the remaining points so they are more fully developed. And you definitely need to examine the sequence of the steps or points you have included. Even if your instructions are general rather than specific, sequence is often crucial. A step that is omitted or not in the correct order can cause readers serious problems.

Another way of assuring that your instructions are clear is to provide your readers with good signals that help them perceive the basic structure, recognize the major steps or points, and anticipate what is to come. There are several ways to accomplish these goals:

1. Use numbers (as in this list) to designate major steps or points.

2. Use headings and subheadings to indicate major and minor parts of your text (see **headings** and **format**).

HEADINGS, PAGE 526

FORMAT, PAGE 505

3. Use **forecasting statements** and other clear signals, such as **transitions** (*first, second, third, next, then,* and *finally*), to help your reader anticipate and recognize various sections of the instructions. Depending on his or her needs, your reader may be interested in reading only certain parts of the instructions. The more likely it is that readers may need a specific part of the instructions, the more you should provide for selective access to information.

FORECASTING STATEMENTS, PAGE 503

TRANSITIONS, PAGE 612

4. Use paragraph structure to indicate different sections clearly. In general, discuss only one step or point in each paragraph.

Writers often use a combination of these strategies. For example, clear transitional signals can reinforce appropriate paragraphing, and numbered lists can fall in sections introduced by headings. Remember, instructions usually require stronger formatting features than most other texts because readers often need to reenter the text in order to reread a certain section or to locate one particular bit of advice. You don't want a cluttered, overly formatted text, but you do want one that readers can easily read and follow.

After you are sure your written instructions are clear to your readers and provide them with the information they need to follow your instructions or advice, consider whether a graphic—map, picture, diagram, table, chart—would further help them. For example, a map of your campus might provide your readers with useful points of reference if you are writing about the location of several different buildings. If you decide a graphic is appropriate, be sure to make it clear and effective. A poorly drawn diagram, inaccurate map, or blurred illustration may confuse readers. Also be sure to integrate any graphic into your text, referring to it at specific points rather than just tacking it on at the end (see **graphics**).

GRAPHICS, PAGE 519

Finally, at some point in revising, consider whether to include specific warnings. You don't want to alarm your readers needlessly, but if you know of pitfalls they should avoid, alert them to these dangers (selecting too many fat-rich foods at the cafeteria, waiting too late to register, being late to class, joining a fraternity when they can't afford it, and so on). In specific instructions, warnings can be set off from the text in some way (indented, marked by a bullet, star, or asterisk, underlined, placed in a box, or highlighted) to attract readers' attention. In general instructions and advice, warnings should usually be explained in a separate paragraph rather than merely stuck on as the final sentence of a paragraph. Always explain to your readers the consequences of ignoring your warning. Readers are much more likely to follow your advice if they understand why you have given it.

Editing Your Text

Instructions should be written correctly, because errors and inconsistencies in your text will almost certainly confuse your readers and may convince them you are not a knowledgeable, credible writer they can trust. Be sure your text is free of misspelled words and errors in punctuation and usage. In addition, edit your text carefully for the following:

- ❖ Parallel structure.
- ❖ Consistent point of view.

USE PARALLEL STRUCTURE. Items in a series should be in parallel form. For example, if you include a numbered list of steps, structure all the steps the same way. Examine the steps listed here, which are not parallel:

a. Notes should be taken in class.

b. You should always write a summary of your notes.

c. Read your summary before attending the next class.

Now, read this revised list, noticing its more direct and readable parallel structure:

a. Take notes in class.

b. Write a summary of your notes.

c. Read your summary before attending the next class.

KEEP A CONSISTENT POINT OF VIEW.   Specific instructions are nearly always written in second person. That is, the writer is speaking directly to the reader, often using the imperative mood, in which the pronoun *you* is understood but not stated. In writing general instructions or advice, writers often combine third-person point of view (writing *about* the situation, process, and so on, as well as *to* the reader). For example, read the following paragraph, with its inconsistent shifts from first- to second- to third-person point of view:

> You cannot appreciate the difficulty of being a student while also working until you have experienced it. We have to juggle these two parts of our lives, changing roles constantly as we shift from work to school and back again. The roles we assume as students and employees are often quite different. In class students are expected to be subordinate to the teacher and to assume a rather passive role. But if you are employed in a competitive, aggressive environment, you must assume a very different role.

Consistency is generally important to good writing. In fact, publishers provide copyeditors to help their authors achieve consistency. But consistency is especially important in writing to instruct. When you write instructions, act as your own copyeditor, making sure you have not needlessly and illogically shifted from one point of view to another (also see **revising and editing**).

REVISING AND EDITING, PAGE 593

Here is the paragraph above after the shifts in point of view have been corrected. Notice the improvement when the point of view is consistent:

> You cannot appreciate the difficulty of being a student while also working until you have experienced it. You have to juggle these two parts of your lives, changing roles constantly as you shift from work to school and back again. The roles you assume as a student and an employee are often quite different. In class you are expected to be subordinate to the teacher and to assume a rather passive role. But if you are employed in a competitive, aggressive environment, you must assume a very different role.

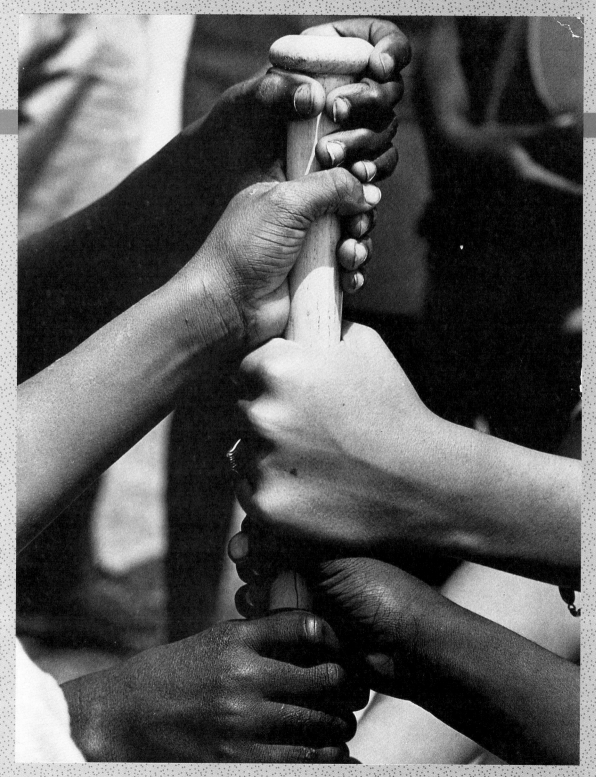

Bruce Roberts/Rapho/Photo Researchers

6

▼

WRITING
TO
SOLVE
PROBLEMS
AND
PRESENT
SOLUTIONS

207

A problem well put is half solved.

JOHN DEWEY

Writing to solve problems, like writing to explore, is a way of thinking on paper (or on the computer screen)—a way to find out what you already know, to organize your thoughts, to visualize a problem, and to make connections between what you know and what you need to know or do. The more complicated the problem, the greater the need to write. Writing helps you think, enables you to view a problem from different perspectives, to see relationships that you had previously overlooked, and ultimately to discover solutions.

Once you have solved the problem, you usually need to convince someone that your solution will work. Writing to present a solution and convince readers of its value is more formal and structured, more like writing to inform or instruct than writing to explore. Your purpose is no longer to solve the problem but rather to persuade readers that a problem can or should be solved in a certain way. In this chapter, writers offer solutions to complex and compelling problems in human relations.

Writing to convince readers that a particular solution will work abounds, especially in business, government, and education. Reports in which an individual or a committee defines a problem, evaluates various solutions, and argues in favor of one are common forms of communication whether the problem is related to transportation, urban decay, deficit spending, or curriculum design.

Writing to solve problems takes other forms too. Editors, columnists, politicians, researchers, and experts in every field from cosmetics to aeronautics often argue for a specific solution to a particular problem, whether the problem is how to conceal dark circles under the eyes or how to design a safer aircraft. Fiction, drama, and poetry frequently focus on solving problems as well. Typically, the protagonist faces a problem and eventually solves it. Although the author may not overtly advocate a particular solution, he or she usually suggests a certain response or form of behavior as a type of solution.

When you propose a solution in the professional or business world, you usually write a rather formally structured memo or report.

These reports, often called recommendation reports, or proposals, generally have the following elements:

* Definition of the problem
* Identification of alternative solutions
* Evaluation of alternative solutions
* Argument for proposed solution

Even informal reports usually include most of these elements. But almost endless variations are possible. If you are writing for a general audience rather than a professional audience, you may decide not to identify or evaluate alternative solutions. You may decide not to define the problem because you know your readers are familiar with it. Or you may decide that defining the problem is more important than a long discussion of the easily understood solution. In general, however, writing to solve problems and reading problem-solution writing involves consideration of these four elements.

READING PROBLEM-SOLUTION WRITING

When you read to find a solution to a problem, you probably already know something about the problem; otherwise, you wouldn't be reading about it. The information and experience you already have on the subject enable you to evaluate the proposed solution effectively. You must assume that the writer of a problem-solution text is biased in favor of the solution he or she is proposing, and so you must correct for this bias as you read. To do this, you should evaluate each of the four elements typically included in a problem-solution text.

Evaluating the Definition of the Problem

First, decide whether the problem is really a problem. For example, is the depletion of the ozone layer of the earth's atmosphere really a problem? Scientists, environmentalists, politicians, and manufacturers of ozone-destroying products disagree not only about the seriousness of the problem but about whether a problem actually exists. A report or article on this issue should probably include a discussion of the different points of view as well as convincing evidence that ozone depletion constitutes a problem that requires a solution.

Second, determine whether the writer has defined the problem accurately and clearly. What is his or her experience or knowledge of this problem? What sources are cited? What evidence presented? A well-defined problem is one that you can understand clearly. You should have no questions about why the problem exists, what its consequences are, and who will be affected. You should also be able to determine from the author's discussion whether the problem is likely to become more serious and, if so, how soon. In other words, the author's definition of the problem should leave no doubt in your mind as to what caused the problem and what effects it will have.

Third, be alert to the possibility that the writer's view of the problem may be biased or unfair. Does it suit the writer's purpose to minimize or exaggerate the seriousness of the problem? Defining a problem is more often a matter of interpretation than a totally objective, scientific process. For example, a male may not view sexual harassment or gender-biased language as a significant problem, whereas a female may. In contrast, a female may not view affirmative action policies as a serious problem, whereas a male, especially a white male, may. In other words, as a reader, you often need to know not just what writers say but who they are and then factor in their possible biases as you evaluate the problem. In some instances, you may recognize the writer's name, the organization he or she represents, or the position he or she holds. Often this information is provided for you, as in the biographical information on each of the writers in this book. In other instances, the book or journal in which the text appears may offer clues about who the writer is and what possible biases he or she may hold. For example, *The New Republic* is generally acknowledged to have a neo-liberal political view. If you have no idea who the author is and what his or her biases may be, you may need to research the writer's background by asking somebody knowledgeable in the field or by looking in one or more biographical dictionaries or encyclopedias.

Evaluating Alternative Solutions

The most important consideration in evaluating the writer's discussion of alternative solutions is to determine if obvious solutions have been omitted and, if so, why. Most writers feel obliged to acknowledge other solutions, at least briefly, before arguing in favor of their own solution. However, writers are not obliged to include (nor could they) a complete list of possible solutions. Expect selectivity. For example, one of this chapter's reading selections focuses on problems males and females often have in communicating. One possible solution is to create courses in elementary schools to prevent different communication styles from developing. But the author, Frank Cedeño, doesn't include this solution, calling instead for "men and women . . . to educate themselves by becoming aware of their different approaches . . ."

As a reader, you should decide whether the writer has included the most plausible alternative solutions and has presented them fairly and accurately. An author's failure to do so suggests that the proposed solution compares unfavorably to the omitted solutions.

Evaluating the Assessment of Alternative Solutions

If alternative solutions are included, decide whether they are fairly and accurately evaluated. Unless writers present alternative solutions objectively and fairly, they are not being responsible to their readers. Obviously, the alternative solutions are not the ones the writer favors, but he or she still has an obligation to discuss them as objectively as possible. If a writer dismisses alternative solutions cavalierly or discusses them only superficially, you should probably be suspicious that he or she is not fully informed about the alternative solutions or not willing to evaluate them fairly for fear that readers will prefer them to the proposed solution.

For example, suppose you are reading an article on the problem of providing adequate health care for people who live in the United States. You notice that the writer denigrates and then casually dismisses the Canadian health-care model as a possible solution. Perhaps the writer claims that in the United States people would never tolerate the lack of choice inherent in the Canadian system and then doesn't discuss that solution further. What should you conclude? That the Canadian system is inadequate and does not deserve a more thorough evaluation? That the Canadian system is workable in Canada but not here? Or simply that the writer favors his or her proposal and doesn't want to discuss the pros and cons of alternative programs fully?

Evaluating the Proposed Solution

Finally, evaluate the proposed solution. The first question to ask is whether the proposed solution is presented clearly. If it is not, it is useless. If you cannot understand how the solution works, what it consists of, and what effects it will have, then you cannot evaluate it fairly.

The next question to ask is whether it will work. Even a brilliant solution is worthless if it is not workable. In effect, you must decide if the solution being proposed will solve the problem that has been defined. In addition, you must determine if it is practical, if it will cost too much, and if it is reasonable or even possible. For example, the U. S. health-care problem could probably be solved fairly easily if cost were not a consideration. But a solution that bankrupts the nation is not acceptable. Similarly, the problem would be solved if physicians treated patients at cost but not for profit. However, such an idealistic solution is unlikely.

You should also beware of solutions that solve only part of the problem. For example, if all employers, by law, had to offer health-care insurance to their employees, the problem of universal health care would still not be solved because many people are unemployed or cannot afford health insurance even if it is available.

The last question to ask is whether the proposed solution is ethical. A solution may be feasible and still not be ethical, and a writer who proposes a solution may be more interested in pragmatics than in ethics. For example, waste-disposal problems are often solved at the expense of powerless people or at great cost to the environment. Dumping dangerous waste materials in a sparsely populated rural area may solve the problem of waste disposal but is hardly fair to the people, even if they are few, who live in the area. Similarly, dumping garbage in a river or harbor solves the disposal problem but damages the environment. People concerned about protecting the environment would not consider that solution ethical. So in the final analysis a solution is acceptable only if it is considered ethical as well as workable.

Don't expect to find the four elements usually included in recommendation reports treated equally in every problem-solution text you read. The attention devoted to each depends on a number of factors, one of the most important of which is the writer's sense of who his or her readers will be. If readers do not need extensive information about the problem, writers do not provide it. If readers need extensive information about alternative solutions, writers include a full discussion of what else might be done before arguing for their own solution. In other words, a writer's sense of audience shapes the text he or she constructs. This is true of all writing but especially true of problem-solution texts.

READINGS FOR WRITING ◀

This chapter's reading selections focus on human-relations problems. Human relationships are fragile even under the best of circumstances. Even family members and friends sometimes have problems getting along together. Not surprisingly, then, human-relations problems usually increase when the people involved differ in some way. Thus problems exist between males and females, employers and employees, the educated and the uneducated, Democrats and Republicans, and even (or perhaps especially) children and parents. People of different ages, races, ethnic backgrounds, religions, and economic levels may have difficulty understanding one another. In fact, many of the most serious problems we face, as individuals and as a nation, result from these differences. Each author in this chapter focuses on one of these problems and proposes a solution.

THE EDUCATION OF A DIVORCED DAD

Dudley Clendinen

Dudley Clendinen is a former national correspondent for The New York Times *and a contributing editor for* Lear's, *in which the following story appeared. Clendinen writes in this personal account about his difficulties establishing a relationship with his young daughter after he and his wife divorced. Although he is telling his own story, he is also suggesting that other men may have similar problems and might benefit from knowing how he solved his. This primarily narrative text, a reconstruction of Clendenin's own experiences, describes an increasingly common predicament and indirectly argues for a particular solution.*

In the early part of 1984, over a drink at home in Boston, I had what I thought of, then, as a sincere and solemn talk with my wife. Life was conversational, I thought, an exercise in logic. Talk mattered. I mattered. I was work consumed. I was a national correspondent for *The New York Times*, and I had been asked to cover the presidential campaign all through that year. It was important, the kind of thing that I should do. "I know I've been gone a lot," I said. "But if I do this, I'm *really* going to be gone. I don't even know how much. More than either of us can imagine now."

1

2   My wife looked at me with large, serious brown eyes. She understood, she said. It wasn't that she approved, but she agreed, and shortly, the campaign travel began.

3   The person not present at that conversation was the person who would be most affected by my absence: our daughter. At least I don't think she was present. It was past her bedtime. But the point is, I'm not sure. Dimly—very dimly—I think I recall a second conversation, a miniature of the first. I do not have so much a memory of that conversation as I do an image of her face as I talked—small, pale, fading, illumined like a snowflake sinking in the dark. "Uh huh," she may have said, eyes big, not understanding. "Oh-kay."

4   She was just a little girl then, and not that good at the kind of conversations I was used to having. It didn't occur to me until later that I wasn't much good at the kind of conversation she was used to having. She was bright. She was funny. She had little teeth and the darkest shining eyes, a silver giggle, and a wonderfully piquant and whisperingly confidential voice. Those are the things I remember. I carry them like a picture and a recording in my mind. She was three and a half. Life was her mommy, play school, the neighborhood, her best friend, Hillary, an immense daily run of unfolding mysteries and secrets, and her daddy here and there.

5   Her world was one of feelings, not of conversation. She had me there. Secrets, I was familiar with. They were always crowding up through the manholes of my life. Feelings were my mystery.

6   That winter, I followed the campaign as it began to move and flow and acquire a kind of madcap form and flawed, eccentric force on its rush toward election day. Madcap on the Democratic side, of course. The Reagan campaign was as smooth and certain as a monolith. Iowa, New Hampshire, Massachusetts, Georgia, Florida, Oklahoma. I know how much I was gone because at some point, cornered into filing expense reports by the accounting office in New York, I went with tired fingers—tired fingers, tired spirit, tired mind—through the codelike entries in my calendar and appointment book. Michigan, Illinois, Pennsylvania, Louisiana, Texas, West Virginia. And I discovered that in the first three months, I had been home six nights. There were six more months to go.

7   When I was away, when the deadline for my story of the day didn't carry me past her bedtime (deadlines were extremely important), I called. I conceived the beginning of these conversations as a kind of geography lesson: "Hey, little Pooh. This is Daddy. Do you know where I am?"

8   "Nooo," she'd say in her breathy voice.

"Des Moines, Iowa," I'd say. Or Houston, or Philadelphia, or Charleston, West Virginia. "Do you know where that is?"   9

"Nooo," she'd say. "Whish one is thuh cidy, an' whish one is thuh stayt?" And I would tell her, thinking of myself, I guess, as Daddy the Teacher, bringing her awareness of the country beyond her neighborhood closer to her by tying faraway cities and towns to me.   10

What I was probably doing, by tying myself to places she had never heard of and couldn't visualize, was making myself more distant. I had been doing that all her short life, and she tired of it after a time. It wasn't her game. I think she didn't want to have to guess where her daddy was, or when she would see him, or why he wasn't home. Her voice sounded small.   11

And then one night she said something that summed up all I had taught her—I, her daddy, the occasional voice on the phone. It haunted me for years.   12

I was feeling the distance between us, I think, and without a clue of how to close it, I reached for an image. "Night, night, little Pooh," I said. "Sleep tight. In your own little bed."   13

"Night, night, Daddy," she said, her voice whispering through the night. "You sleep tight, too. Wherever you are."   14

And she hung up. The words had come a thousand miles down the line through the dark, or off a satellite in space. I don't know. But they left me hunched and dazed beneath a desk lamp, staring at a phone, in a hotel room far away.   15

Those words, that breathless, innocent voice, echoed in my head for years. *Wherever you are wherever you are wherever you are wherever you are you are you are . . .*   16

I was my work. That's what I was. That's where I was—wherever the writing was, wherever I needed to be. I lived not in my life but in my head, absorbed with whatever story I was researching and writing there: with the things I didn't yet know, the schedule I had to keep, the people I had to persuade to let me interview them. That's what journalists do, by and large: We write about other people, great issues, other lives. Things that take us out of ourselves.   17

It's a convenient side step to one's own life, particularly if life isn't something you know how to do. By *do* I mean knowing who you are and what you feel, how you make others feel, and being honest about that with yourself and them. I didn't have a clue. I could write a story about the pain and resolution of other lives, in which you could trace the feelings as finely as the smaller veins beneath your skin. I simply couldn't get beneath my own skin.   18

19   And the one person whose skin was mine, in whose veins my blood ran, was a child I didn't know how to love. Not that she wasn't deserving or lovable. God, she was a heart squeeze. I had been present at her birth, and waltzed her through her colic, marveled at the unfolding of her mind and the softness of her cheeks. She was, as I kept telling her, regularly, persistently, as she got older, my prettiest, fastest, smartest, funniest, most athletic, artistic, balletic, gymnastic, and lovable daughter. "Daddy (giggle), *stop* saying that!" Right. Men are such dopes.

20   I could talk about feelings, articulate them and hold them up to the light, turn them fondly, poignantly, the way a traveling salesman might hold a glass in his hand and raise it to home and family far away. But it's the sad romance my kind of traveling salesman drinks to, not the love itself: the image of love, the distance, the unclosed space. How sad. It's for themselves—ourselves, I think—that drunks, egomaniacs, and romantics feel sad or happy. The only people we end up feeling for is us. And if that's uncomfortable we have another glass. And the feelings ebb away.

21   I have another memory, also dim, but I think it's from that year. It is night in the house outside Boston, after her bedtime. It is a substantial brick house on a curve of lawn a block from the Charles River, and its windows, I think now, must have given out the warm and yellow glow that has always tugged my romantic heart when I pass such windows on walks at night—the lamplit glow that emanates, one imagines, from the snug and familial life inside. The lamplit glow of home.

22   In my memory I have come home. I am still dressed—bow tie, suit coat perhaps, or dark robe—and for some reason she is up, running in blind terror through the rooms on the second floor of the house. I don't know what has awakened her, but something is chasing her in her mind, some monster that has roused her. I try to catch and comfort her, but each time I get close, her terror expands, and she breaks and runs. I cannot catch and hold and quiet her. She runs as if from me. Finally, her mother sweeps her up, holds her, and carries her to bed, and gradually, over long minutes, soothes her to sleep.

23   My daughter has a different memory, perhaps of the same night. While I was gone covering the presidential election, her nursery school class one week learned about strangers and kidnappers. On a night soon after, she fell asleep in bed with her mommy. And when I came home from the airport and picked her up to carry her off to her own bed, she woke up screaming that she was being taken by a

stranger. "That's no stranger," she remembers her mother saying. "That's your dad."

When I left the house for good, more than three years ago—a bigger house, in Atlanta, a deeper curve of lawn—I called back on the second day to hear my wife say that my daughter hadn't even noticed I was gone.   24

I had made no regular presence at home—not during my daughter's waking hours. And I had been gone through Christmas, gone through New Year's, to one of those places where grown-ups go when things get out of whack, when they haven't grown as people in proportion to their lives.   25

But she and I had begun to talk. Or rather, I had begun to try. I cannot speak for her or for her mother, only for myself. And this isn't about marriage. Difficult as it is to separate the two, this is about fatherhood.   26

"Tell her that you're going away to try to learn to be a better daddy," my wife had suggested.   27

Was that true? I wondered. If going away should bring an end to a marriage that seemed impossible, could I be a better daddy? How could that be if I might not be there?   28

I had never been able to divide my child from her mother, to grow a feeling for my daughter that was separate from my complex emotions for my wife. The one was webbed to the other, and I couldn't imagine how this was going to work. I couldn't think it through. I only knew it could not get worse.   29

It wasn't, of course, a mental question. It was an emotional one, a matter of relationship built on honest feeling, of responsibility asserted and claimed. And so I made a small beginning at emotional truth. We had another conversation, again about my being away. I told her I was going to try to learn to be a better daddy, at a place something like a hospital, with doctors and diet. I wouldn't drink.   30

And I called her, and I wrote. She listened, and she read the letters, and when I asked her questions, she responded. This was real. I described the place to her, and what I learned.   31

"Alcohol can make you preoccupied and distracted," I said. Did I seem distracted?   32

"Are you kidding?" she asked.   33

"And impatient," I said. "Irritable. Remember?"   34

"Yes," she said.   35

And angry. I especially remembered one morning before school. "You hurt my arm," she said.   36

37   I had hoped she wouldn't have that memory. But now I was half glad she did. There was something I could do. "I'm sorry," I said.

38   The more we did that, the better we got. Her mother and I had each told her that there were things we didn't agree about, and that when I got back we might live apart.

39   For two days I stayed in a blank room in a nowhere motel at an exit off the interstate, trying to focus. And then I leased space in a recycled Days Inn, two blocks farther down the access road. It was a complex of transients: lower-middle business types transferred to Atlanta; families on their way up or down; single women aswirl in crying children and daytime soaps; old people with no life to hold them; drug dealers, it seemed to me; and newly separated men.

40   The living room had a double sofa bed for my daughter, and she came and stayed there, bringing stuffed animals and sometimes a friend. She thought it was an adventure, kind of neat. It was the first space we had defined together. We commenced to do things like going bowling and playing ball. But the place seemed bleak to me, and dreary, and I found a two-bedroom apartment in town, in an old neighborhood of Victorian houses and sighing trees.

41   Some days I picked my daughter up from school. Sometimes she'd walk right by me, picture of wary apprehension lest I try to do some obnoxious thing like hug her, and I would have to trail her down the sidewalk to the car. Down the road, a mile or so, down the afternoon, half an hour or so, if I didn't push it, she'd relax. The marital house and school seemed edgy grounds, but our own space got more comfortable. Gradually, I learned not to ask questions, just to try to be open, and easy, and steady.

42   She spent some nights, but she didn't like being transient—she got tired of eating out. So I began to cook. We went to the movies, played checkers, and on some weekends ate our lunch in the park. This was not bucolic. This was tentative, accumulating, incomplete. And there was never precisely one day, or a week, or even a particular month when the decision was made, but gradually it dawned on me that I was discovering something precious, and that if I left I would lose it, and her, forever. Increasingly, she was what I cared about.

43   Work, however, had always been the source of worth and definition in my family. "Oh?" my mother said one day, when I told her on the phone that I had not accepted a job in Washington. (I had been up there and had put a deposit on a rental house in Georgetown.) No. I wasn't sure I wanted to leave the Pooh yet, I said. There was a steely, deliberate pause as she digested this unwelcome news. "But don't you want her to respect you?" she finally said.

"No," I said. "I want her to know that I love her." 44

And there it was. If I left now I would be the kind of father I had 45
been before, the kind of father my own father had been, and I realized that there was more to fathering than I had known. More I still
had to give.

The apartment began to feel small, and while I liked the neigh- 46
borhood, its eclectic population included robbers who rummaged
through my neighbors' apartments and my car. I decided to move and
bought an old house with two rental apartments and a cottage behind
it nestled in a patch of ivy. I moved into the cottage. It had a big
kitchen in which I put my writing desk and a round table that I placed
beside glass doors overlooking the ivied slope. My daughter would do
her homework at it on afternoons when I picked her up from school.

We built a schedule of about 45 hours a week together, and on 47
the little deck out back, after waffles and bacon in the mild breeze of
spring one Sunday morning, I talked to her about different kinds of
love between people and why a successful marriage was not possible
between me and her mother.

She hung upside down from my lap as I went on, her head and 48
face out of my sight, down in the dappled shade between the table
and the deck. Once or twice I asked if she were listening. "Yes," she
said. Then we settled down to Monopoly.

She had become the focus of my life. And she developed this 49
wonderful equilibrium. When her mother decided that they would
move back to where we came from, way down south, my daughter at
first was sad and then excited. And I was mournful, and angry, too.

"I know this must be devastating for you," her mother said. 50
Which was nice of her. And true. But it was freeing, too, for all of us.
My now former wife needed to have her own life, I needed mine, and
our daughter needed not to be burdened with parents who sacrificed
the content of their lives for her.

They moved south and bought a house with a yard and a room 51
and playroom for our daughter on the second floor. I went north to a
job in Baltimore and bought a row house with a room and bath for her
on the third floor. I'd fly down to see her. She came up once when it
was supposed to snow; she loves the snow from our Boston days. She
liked her room, the house, the neighborhood, the restaurants, breakfast
in the morning, and beating me at checkers. But it didn't snow.

One morning a few weeks later, when I looked out the window, 52
I called and caught her just before she left for school. "Guess what?" I
said, eager to report. "It's snowing."

There was a pause. "That's not fair," she said. 53

54   I gave her the other news. I had caught Splatter, the gerbil who always gets out of her cage when I leave town, and put her back with Nosey. I had run out of their food but was giving them Special K. It had the desired effect.

55   "Dad, you're so dumb!" she wailed in mock despair. "You can't give gerbils Special K!"

56   We had met the week before in Atlanta, visiting friends for Thanksgiving. She had relented with elaborate sighs of accommodation to fit me into her busy schedule.

57   "I might not want to," she had warned.

58   "I know," I had said.

59   On the weekend of Thanksgiving we had gone bowling and to dinner and to a play. She had brought a friend. I had, too. Now we talked briefly about Christmas, and she mentioned that she had been to the dentist. "How many big teeth do you have?" I asked.

60   "Let's see," she began. "One, two, three, four, five, six . . . no . . . one, two, three, four, five, six, seven, eight, nine, ten. I have ten, but two of them in the bottom, on the back, are just halfway up."

61   "How many cavities do you have?" she asked.

62   "One," I told her. "I got it when I was forty-two."

63   "I have none," she sniffed.

64   "That's good," I said.

65   "I know," she said. "I'm special. I have your teeth."

66   I looked out the kitchen window, watching the snow float down, and smiled. "I know," I said.

▶   **QUESTIONS TO CONSIDER**

1. How does the author's divorce affect his relationship with his daughter? Did the divorce cause the problems with his relationship with his daughter or merely make him aware of them?

2. How does Clendinen solve his problem? Is his solution one that is available to every man in similar situations? What factors in the author's life contribute to the success of his solution?

3. Clendinen does not discuss alternative solutions. Would such a discussion have strengthened the article?

4. Problems in human relations are never solved finally and completely. What other problems may develop between Clendinen and his daughter as she grows older? Will the same or similar solutions work?

5. This essay is primarily a reconstruction of the author's experiences. Translate the author's personal narrative into a general statement of his thesis. That is, summarize in your own words what the author is proposing as a solution to the problem that divorced fathers often have in maintaining good relationships with their children.

WRITING ACTIVITIES

Individual: Write about a family problem that you have experienced.

Collaborative: Using your journal entries as a point of departure, discuss the problems you identified. Select one problem that you think is common to most families and suggest a solution.

Computer: Enter into your computer your journal entry about a family problem. Post your entry to the computer network so that interested classmates can suggest possible solutions. Then write an evaluation of these alternative solutions.

❖❖❖❖❖

BRIDGING THE COMMUNICATION GAP

Frank Cedeño

Frank Cedeño, the writer of this problem-solution essay, spent a semester as a freshman composition student researching the differences between male and female communication styles. As a result of his research, Cedeño was able to define the problem that males and females often have in communicating with each other—the "gap" referred to in the title. He devotes much less attention to the solution he proposes because it, in effect, depends on an understanding of the problem. Thus, in explaining the problem carefully, Cedeño is hoping to solve it.

Much research has been done on the different conversation styles of men and women and the misunderstandings that result from these differences. These misunderstandings about what is really being said can cause serious problems in relationships between men and women.

1

Perhaps these differences can best be understood by examining the different rules that govern the conversation game men and women play.

2   Rule number one of the conversation game states that men seek status while women simply need support. Charles Derber, a sociologist at Boston College, has discovered that men will often shift conversations to their preferred topics (qtd. in Kohn, "Girl Talk" 65). Men grow up thinking of conversation as a contest. Their goal is to achieve the upper hand or at least avoid being pushed around. Women, however, typically use conversation to exchange confirmation and support. A woman is better able to respond supportively. Alfie Kohn states in *Psychology Today*, "The wife gives more active encouragement to her husband's talk about himself while the husband listens less well and is less likely to actively 'bring her out' about herself and her own topics" ("Girl Talk" 65).

3   Deborah Tannen, a linguistics professor at Georgetown University, cites an example of this difference in her article, "Can't We Talk?" A married couple had jobs in different cities. When friends commented that this arrangement must be difficult for them, the wife accepted their sympathy. The husband became irritated and would explain that the situation had advantages, which included long weekends and vacations together. Although his statement was true, it still puzzled his wife. To him, he explained, the comments implied: "Yours is not a real marriage. I am superior to you because my wife and I have avoided your misfortune" (20). The wife saw that her husband was viewing the world as a place where people tried to achieve and maintain status. She, on the other hand, saw the world as a network of connections in which people seek consensus.

4   Rule number two states that women struggle to preserve intimacy but men tend to focus on establishing independence. These differences in communication can cause serious conflicts in the way a situation is viewed. Consider the following scenario: Joe receives a phone call from an old friend saying he will be in town soon. Joe invites the friend to spend several days with him and his wife Linda. Later that evening he tells Linda, and she is upset. She wonders why Joe has not checked with her first. He angrily replies, "I can't say I have to ask my wife for permission!" Joe feels that checking with Linda would make him seem like a child or that he is not free to act on his own. Linda, however, feels that if the situation were reversed, checking with Joe would only show that her life is involved with her husband's (Tannen 21-22).

5   Rule number three states that men give advice whereas women only want understanding. For example, often women complain to men about feeling physically unattractive. When this happens, men usually

feel challenged to find a solution to this problem. But often women are only looking for emotional support. A compliment is needed more than a solution. If a woman tells a man that she is getting too fat, the last thing she wants to hear is that she ought to go on a diet! On the other hand, men avoid seeking help, advice, or consolation altogether. They resist the intimacy of discussing their feelings because it implies a need for advice (Adler 74). Their goal is to remain in control. Perhaps this is why so many men refuse to ask for directions when in a strange place. To ask for help is to put oneself in a position of inferiority (Adler 74).

According to rule number four, a woman's proposal is often inter-   6
preted by a man as an order. Most men resist being told what to do. When men react in this way, women are confused because they feel they are only making suggestions when they say, "Let's park closer to the store" or "Let's clean up before lunch." Their indirect style of talking is viewed by them as just a way of getting others to do what they want (Tannen 24).

Such proposals, suggestions, and questions are distinctively char-   7
acteristic of women's conversation. Robin Lakoff, a linguist at the University of California, Berkeley, has pointed out several characteristics of this indirect style:

1. Women ask more questions (nearly three times as many as men)

2. Women make statements in a questioning tone

3. Women use more tag questions (statements such as "Don't you think?" or "Isn't it?")

4. Women lead off with questions that ensure a listener's attention ("Hey, y'know what?")

5. Women use more "hedges" or qualifiers and rely on intensifiers (such as "kinda" or "really")

Lakoff also notes that the use of intensifiers suggests women feel they are not persuasive, so they add intensifiers to make sure their listeners understand the importance of what they are saying (qtd. in Kohn, "Girl Talk" 66).

Rule number five ordains that men face conflict head on while   8
women tend to compromise. Most women try to avoid confrontation even if it means going against their own beliefs. However, according to Tannen, "At times it's far more effective for a woman to assert herself, even at the risk of conflict" (24). Women find they are labeled as unfeminine by women as well as men if they speak assertively and

directly. On the other hand, if they avoid conflict and adopt a more traditional role, they are not taken seriously and are considered unintelligent. Lakoff states it best, "A woman is damned if she does and damned if she doesn't" (qtd. in Kohn, "Girl Talk" 66).

9   Finally, and most importantly, rule number six states that men communicate primarily for information whereas women speak mainly to exchange feelings or emotions. Women become upset and are hurt when men don't talk to them. This is frustrating to men because they don't know why they have disappointed their partners. Tannen has found that women spend much of their time throughout their lives stating their feelings to friends and relatives. To them, this expression of emotion denotes involvement and caring. On the other hand, men keep their innermost thoughts to themselves to preserve an image of masculinity, communicating mainly to share information.

10   Barbara Langstern, in her article "Your Well-Being," sums up this communication conflict best. She feels the division between men and women frequently leads to extremes that are intolerable. She explains,

> The woman aches for emotional companionship and validation. She no longer wants to express all the feelings for the couple. But attacking the man's passivity usually causes him to retreat. He, uneasy expressing emotions, hardly will take his first step into an emotional tempest. (27)

11   Based on the communication differences discussed in this paper, one might conclude that it is useless for men and women to attempt to talk with each other. Mary Kay Blakely suggests in her article, "Why Can't Men and Women Speak the Same Language?" that the most effective solution may be to cease talking altogether (152). This solution, however, is not only impractical but unrealistic. Perhaps if men and women become conscious of their differences in conversation styles, less grief will occur. If they become aware that these gender differences in speech are simply reflections of the power struggle between men and women, better understanding can result (Kohn, "Kinder Sex" 34). Understanding how the other sex will probably react can prepare both men and women to avoid conflicts. Once they educate themselves by becoming aware of their different approaches to communication, they will have a better chance of preventing disagreements from spiraling out of control (Tannen 24). This awareness of basic differences in conversation styles could provide the bridge across the communication gap that separates men and women.

LIST OF WORKS CITED

Adler, Jerry. "When Harry Called Sally . . . " *Newsweek* Oct. 1, 1990: 74.

Blakely, Mary Kay. "Why Can't Men and Women Speak the Same Language?" *Glamour* Nov. 1988: 151-52.

Gibson, Janice T. "Are Boys and Girls Really So Different?" *Reader's Digest* Oct. 1988: 15.

Kohn, Alfie. "The Kinder Sex." *Health* Sept. 1990: 32, 34.

———. "Girl Talk, Boy Talk." *Psychology Today* Feb. 1988: 65-66.

Langstern, Barbara. "Your Well-Being." *Vogue* Jan. 1988:41.

Tannen, Deborah. "Can't We Talk?" *Reader's Digest* Dec. 1990: 19-24.

QUESTIONS TO CONSIDER

1. Cedeño defines the problem that males and females have in communicating by explaining that men and women both see conversation as a game with certain rules but they play by different rules. Of the six rules he includes, which one accounts for the most serious communication problem between males and females?

2. Do you agree with Cedeño that being aware of the problem (i.e., the different styles of communication) will solve it? Why or why not?

3. What other solutions does Cedeño include? What other solutions might he have included?

4. Do you agree that male-female communication styles are different? If so, were you aware of these differences before reading this essay or did Cedeño convince you that males and females follow different conversational rules? If so, how did he convince you?

WRITING ACTIVITIES

Individual: In a journal entry, describe your own conversational style. How many of the rules that Cedeño includes accurately describe your conversational pattern? How difficult would it be to change your conversational style?

Collaborative: Discuss the six rules of conversation that Cedeño uses to structure his essay. Be sure you understand clearly the different *perceptions* that he claims males and females tend to have on each of these points. Then, to solve the problems created by these different perceptions, revise each rule so it is a compromise—a rule for effective communication that both males and females could follow comfortably.

Computer: Conduct a network conversation on the topic of male-female communication styles. Do not identify yourself or your gender. Then, as a class, analyze the computer conversation to determine if the participants' gender can be identified by their conversation styles.

❖❖❖❖❖

THE AGGRESSORS

Melvin Konner

Melvin Konner is an anthropologist, a physician, and a professor. In the following essay, which was published in the New York Times Magazine, *Konner describes the problem of male aggression and offers a solution based on his belief that males are biologically programmed to be more aggressive than females.*

1   Dr. Dan Olweus knows the bullies in Norway; at least those 8 to 16 years old in a population of 140,000 in 715 public schools. Olweus, a professor of psychology at the University of Bergen, was asked by the Norwegian Government to get a handle on the bullying problem. Concluding his recent study, he estimates that of the 568,000 Norwegian schoolchildren, 41,000, or 7 percent, bully others regularly. The bullies were far more likely to be male: more than 60 percent of the girls and 80 percent of the boys victimized in grades 5 to 7 were bullied by males. The tendency of girls to bully declined with age; in boys, it rose: a twofold difference in the second grade widens to fivefold in the ninth.

2   Many studies, even of remote, primitive societies, show that males predominate overwhelmingly in physical violence. Pick your behavior: grabbing and scratching in toddlers, wrestling and chasing in nursery-school children, contact sports among teen-agers, violent crime in adulthood, tank maneuvers in real, grown-up wars. In 1986, Alice H. Eagly and Valerie J. Steffen, then of Purdue University, published a survey of 63 psychological studies. They emphasized that no category

existed in which women were more aggressive than men, and they said the tendency to produce pain or physical injury was far more pronounced in men. Joining a distinguished line of social and psychological researchers, Eagly and Steffen concluded that these differences "are learned as aspects of gender roles and other social roles."

That belief, a tenacious modern myth, becomes less justified with every passing year: sex difference in the tendency to do physical harm is intrinsic, fundamental, natural—in a word, biological. 3

Olweus, in a smaller study—one of scores contributing to this new conclusion—selected 58 boys aged 15 through 17, and compared blood levels of testosterone, the male sex hormone, to aggression. He found a strong effect of testosterone on intolerance for frustration and response to provocation. The puzzle of aggression is not yet solved, but it seems increasingly apparent that testosterone is a key. However, it is testosterone circulating not only post-pubertally, as has been commonly thought, but also during early development—specifically, during fetal life, at the stage when the brain is forming. The first clues to this process came from animal studies. In 1973, G. Raisman and P. M. Field reported a significant sex difference in a part of the rat's brain known as the preoptic area—a region that, in females, helps control the reproductive cycle; certain brain cell connections in this area were more numerous in females. Most interestingly, castration of males at birth, or early treatment of females with testosterone, abolished the adult brain difference. 4

This was the first of many similar studies showing that the differentiation not only of the brain but of behavior—especially sexual and aggressive behavior—depends in part on early testosterone exposure. This has proved to be true of rats, mice, hamsters, rabbits and monkeys, among other species. Clear anatomical differences have been found in the hypothalamus and amygdula regions of the brain as well as the preoptic area. 5

One ingenious study showed that the tendency to fight in adult mice, although greater by far in males, differs among females, depending on whether they spent their fetal life near males or other females in the womb. Females with males on each side in utero grew up to be fighters, but those with only one adjacent male were less pugnacious as adults. Those flanked by two other females in the womb became the least aggressive adults. Separate evidence indicated that the three groups of females also differed in their degree of exposure to intrauterine testosterone—which had evidently come from the blood of the nearby males. 6

No experimental evidence is available for humans, of course, but some clinical studies are suggestive. Sometimes human fetuses are 7 exposed to hormones that have effects similar to those of testosterone—for example, synthetic progestins, used to maintain pregnancy. June M. Reinisch, now director of the Kinsey Institute, studied 25 girls and boys with a history of such exposure and found them more aggressive than their same-sex siblings, as indicated by a paper-and-pencil test. This finding was in line with studies of monkeys and other animals exposed to male sex hormones in utero. Females with such exposure engaged in more rough-and-tumble play during development than other females. As in the human study, the differences became apparent before puberty.

8   Some years ago, there was a bitter controversy over whether men with an extra male-determining Y chromosome—the XYY syndrome—were hypermasculine. One not-so-subtle humorist wrote in to *Science* that it was silly to get so excited over the extremely rare XYY syndrome, when 49 percent of the species was already afflicted with the XY syndrome—an uncontroversial disorder known to cause hyperactivity and learning disabilities in childhood, premature mortality in adulthood and an egregious tendency to irrational violence throughout life. "Testosterone poisoning," a colleague of mine calls it.

9   Is there no contribution of culture, then, to the consistent male excess in violence? Of course there is; but it acts on an organism already primed for the sex difference. Cultures can dampen it or exaggerate it. The role of modeling in encouraging aggression is well proved. Give a girl a steady diet of Wonder Woman and lady wrestlers while her brother gets Mr. Rogers, and you may well push them past each other on the continuum. But we now have a pretty good answer to Margaret Mead's famous question: What if an average boy and an average girl were raised in exactly similar environments? We don't know, she said. Now we do. The boy would hit, kick, wrestle, scratch, grab, shove and bite more than the girl and be more likely to commit a violent crime later in life.

10   Mead became famous for her elegant demonstrations of cultural variation in sex roles. Among the Tchambuli, a New Guinea fishing society, the women, "brisk, unadorned, managing and industrious, fish and go to market; the men, decorative and adorned, carve and paint and practice dance steps." Among the Mundugumor, river-dwelling cannibals, also in New Guinea, "the women are as assertive and vigorous as the men; they detest bearing and rearing children, and provide most of the food. . . ." These quotations from her 1949 book "Male and Female" helped provide the basis for the modern conception of the tremendous flexibility of sex roles—as well they should have. But the Tchambuli men, when they finished their dance steps, went headhunting. And note that Mead's own words following her often-cited quote

on the Mundugumor are: *"leaving the men free to plot and fight."* In every known society, homicidal violence, whether spontaneous and outlawed or organized and sanctioned for military purposes, is committed overwhelmingly by men.

The conclusion would seem to be that women should run the world. If we can agree that the greatest threat to human survival over the long haul is posed by human violence itself, then the facts of human violence—the sex difference, and its biological basis—can lead nowhere else. But what of Margaret Thatcher, Indira Gandhi, Golda Meir; what of Catherine the Great and Elizabeth I, in earlier eras? They are no use as test cases. All were women who clambered to the tops of relentlessly male political and military hierarchies. They could scarcely restrain the surges of all those millions of gallons of testosterone continually in flux under their scepters. And again: the categories overlap; the consistent differences are in averages. The gauntlets those five women ran to get to the top and stay there can scarcely be said to have been at the least-aggressive end of the female spectrum. And women in a male world often find themselves outmachoing the men—to gain credibility, to consolidate power, to survive.   11

Those negative examples notwithstanding, a steady, massive infusion of women into positions of power, in a balanced way, throughout the world, should in fact reduce the risk that irrational factors—"Come on, make my day" sorts of factors—will bring about an end to life on earth. Political scientists and historians often argue as if there were no resemblance between fistfights and war. Anthropologists and biologists know better.   12

Interestingly, that same Norway that sent Dan Olweus off to study—and try to diminish—bullying, appears to be in the vanguard. Not only the Prime Minister, but 8 of the 18 members of the Cabinet, are currently free of testosterone poisoning. In an almost all-male, consistently violent world of national governments, this little boat of the Norwegian Cabinet may run into some high seas. But it is a far cry from the Viking ships of yore, and I, for one, am keeping a hopeful eye on its prow.   13

QUESTIONS TO CONSIDER ◀

1. Do you agree that male aggression is an innate biological characteristic? If so, how is Konner's evidence persuasive? If not, what evidence could Konner provide that would be more persuasive? What factors other than biological ones influence male aggression?

2. Evaluate the author's proposed solution to the problem of male aggression. How workable is this solution? Will it solve the problem? Is it practical? Is it ethical?

3. Konner includes no alternative solutions to the problem he defines. Can you think of alternative solutions?

4. This article appeared in the *New York Times Magazine*, which is read primarily by fairly well-educated, economically secure readers in the Northeast. How might the author have approached this same topic if he were writing for a medical journal, *Ladies' Home Journal*, or *Esquire?*

▶   W R I T I N G   A C T I V I T I E S

Individual: Write about the difference between male and female aggression. What problems can develop as a result of each?

Collaborative: Discuss the problems that can develop as a result of male or female aggression. Briefly define one of these problems, identify alternative solutions, and argue in favor of one solution.

Computer: Respond on your computer network to Konner's argument that "women should run the world." Your response should include a summary of Konner's argument, an evaluation of his argument, and your reaction to his solution.

❖❖❖❖❖

AIDS ISSUES HAVEN'T GONE AWAY

Nancy L. Breuer

This article appeared in Personnel Journal, *a professional journal for personnel managers. The author, Nancy L. Breuer, is a Los Angels-based writer and business consultant specializing in health and safety education. She describes a problem that did not exist a few years ago but that faces many employers now— how to deal with employees who are HIV positive. As you read, evaluate the solution that Breuer proposes.*

Driving into the parking lot one morning, the human resources   1
director of a New York-based department store found employees
milling around the back door, refusing to enter the building. She knew
a longtime employee had called to say that he'd be returning to work
that day after being hospitalized for *Pneumocystis carinii* pneumonia
and wanted his co-workers to know his diagnosis. She put two and
two together and reached a depressing conclusion: No one wanted to
work with a colleague who had AIDS.

What happened next, however, surprised her. When the returning   2
employee reached the parking lot, his co-workers wouldn't go inside
until each person had offered him a hug, a card, flowers, or some balloons. Astonished and laden with tokens of his co-workers' goodwill
and compassion, the AIDS-diagnosed employee began one of the best
days of his working life.

Is this a fantasy or an event masterminded by management? No, it   3
actually happened—spontaneously. Could it happen in your company?

Most people in American workplaces in the 1990s work beside   4
people who have HIV infection or AIDS. The virus is found most often
in people of working age; so far, its heaviest toll has been among people in their 20s, 30s and 40s. Because therapies constantly improve,
HIV-infected people will be able to work longer and with greater productivity as the decade progresses. Even after bouts of serious illness,
people who have HIV infection will return to work more often and for
longer periods than has been true in the past.

Do most American workers have any reliable training to help   5
them cope with this reality? The intensity and nature of the conversation following basketball star Magic Johnson's announcement that he's
HIV-positive suggest that they don't. Many employees remain ignorant
and fearful. If the fear and ignorance aren't addressed, they're likely to
worsen.

Thanks to the leadership of businesses that have provided work-   6
place HIV education since the late 1980s, there are models that illustrate the value of making AIDS education ordinary.

The Prudential Insurance Company, Western Home Office, has   7
been providing employee AIDS education seminars every six months
since 1987, distributing a copy of the company's AIDS policy with
employee orientation materials and handling reasonable accommodation matters and cases of AIDS-related discrimination quietly.

Dick Hunt, vice president for administration and a 39-year   8
employee with the company, explains: "The longer you spend in
human resources, the better nose you have for a bad situation and the
better your batting average for avoiding them becomes. It was a matter

of realizing that, if we did nothing, our first AIDS case would happen, and some people would panic out of ignorance." The Prudential made employee HIV training part of the regular human resources training menu; they made it ordinary.

9   Morrison & Foerster, an international law firm, took the same course and began employee HIV training in 1987. By now, says Personnel Manager Gene Bendel, when the firm announces an employee HIV training date, some employees ask, "Again? I thought I had that training last year." The company provides annual seminars so employees will be aware of new information about the epidemic. HIV training has become ordinary.

10   So far, the firm hasn't faced any HIV-related work disruptions or discrimination cases, even though the firm has faced employee HIV infection. "This is preventive education," Bendel reminds the firm. Even if there's no one with AIDS in the office today, "what about tomorrow?"

11   Dr. Ann Lewis, medical director for the Prudential at the Western Home Office, agrees. She points to the contrast between the company's first case and its most recent case as a dramatic example of the power of HIV education.

12   When the first case developed, Dr. Lewis had a stream of fearful employees in her office, afraid of contact and posing hypothetical questions. People didn't want to work in the same environment with a person rumored to have AIDS. Emotions ran high, productivity suffered and the myths about HIV transmission complicated efforts to communicate valid information.

13   Recently there was another case of symptomatic HIV infection in the same environment. Although co-workers are saddened by the waning energy of their colleague, no one is afraid to work beside the employee. No one questions the accommodation of installing a computer and printer in the affected employee's home to allow telecommunicating as a less fatiguing option to full, on-site work days. After several years of regular training, these employees know they aren't at risk and are simply concerned for their colleague.

14   Some companies resist training because of a fear that current medical information may be incomplete, that there may be ways of transmitting HIV that are yet unknown. Such fears, given free reign, aggravate the problem.

15   Although many individuals acknowledge that an HIV-infected person at work doesn't pose a risk to co-workers unless they're sharing needles or having sex, they're afraid the person becomes a threat when he or she becomes symptomatic. These people worry that the

infected person's skin lesions, persistent cough and diarrhea might be passed along to their co-workers.

According to David Dassey, deputy medical director for AIDS programs in the Los Angeles County Department of Health Services, such fears are unfounded. Only people who have impaired immune systems fall ill with the specific infections that affect people who have HIV infection or AIDS. Each person carries many of the infections that make HIV-infected people ill. A healthy immune system suppresses such latent infections as herpes or mononucleosis and fights off such environmental infections as candidiasis (yeast infections). Other AIDS-related infections are caused by organisms common in the environment. A damaged immune system can't fight them off, and the person becomes ill. 16

The only exception is tuberculosis, an infection that afflicts many people, including some HIV-infected people. Any employee—HIV-infected or not—who has active tuberculosis shouldn't be at work during the days the TB is infectious. After a physician releases a tubercular patient to return to work after he or she has begun responding to treatment, the person poses no risk to co-workers. 17

In 1992, it's quite clear that someone who has AIDS poses no risk at work. There's no medical evidence to the contrary. But what about the argument that the workplace might be dangerous to an HIV-infected person because of all the germs to which he or she is exposed? 18

Employees sometimes worry that their colds or flu will make an HIV-infected co-worker sick. That isn't the case, Dassey explains. Those infections are handled easily by the part of the immune system that isn't seriously damaged by HIV, so controlling colds or flu is no more difficult for an HIV-infected person. 19

Even if HIV transmission or other infections isn't a workplace risk, there's a very real risk that employees will be paralyzed by their own panic. Often managers delay or avoid workplace HIV training to try to avoid provoking that fear. Is this a good idea? Not at all, says Bendel. He points out that strategic planning is used to anticipate business issues, and HIV *is* a business issue. 20

What would businesses that are providing HIV education say to those that aren't? Nissan Motor Corporation felt that the epidemic "had given rise to a number of critical human relations and legal issues" and decided it was "imperative to provide managers and supervisors some training on how to respond properly when confronted with the issues the crisis raises in the workplace," according to Ernest Stroman, manager of EEO and affirmative action programs at the U. S. headquarters 21 office. "We found there's no need for any company to be apprehensive about providing this kind of training. Our managers and supervisors were extremely positive about it, and went so far as to recommend that the training be provided for all employees. Approximately 90% indicated their awareness of how the disease is transmitted was enhanced greatly and their apprehensions about contracting the disease were relieved substantially," Stroman says.

22   Bendel points out that many employers, often working with their health insurance providers, discuss drug addiction and alcoholism routinely in employee training programs, viewing it as a health issue that has a profound impact on the workplace. He encourages managers to fold HIV education into the same series of seminars.

23   Projections from the World Health Organization and the Centers for Disease Control in Atlanta tell us that we're only on the edge of this epidemic. Sadly, working effectively with HIV in the workplace is a necessary business skill for the '90s. Refusing to yield to fear is one way to reduce its impact and ease the pain—and to benefit from the courage of Magic Johnson and other HIV-infected people.

▶   QUESTIONS TO CONSIDER

1. Do you personally know someone who is HIV positive or actually suffering from AIDS? What is your reaction to this person? Is your reaction primarily rational or emotional?

2. The author introduces the problem she is addressing by telling a story. Is this narrative an effective way to introduce this rather sensitive subject? Why or why not?

3. How well does Breuer define the problem of HIV-infected employees? From whose perspective does she primarily view this problem? The AIDS victim? Fellow employees? The employer(s)? What is the effect of using this perspective?

4. Breuer does not include alternative solutions in her article. Should she have? What alternative solutions can you suggest? Are these solutions feasible? Legal? Ethical?

5. How well does Breuer argue her case for educating all workers about AIDS as the solution to the problem of HIV-positive people in the workplace? Again, note the perspective she is taking. Whom does she cite? What evidence does she present? Whom is she trying to convince?

WRITING ACTIVITIES

Individual: In a journal entry, analyze your reaction to AIDS and the people who have it.

Collaborative: Discuss how Breuer's article would have differed had she been writing for a different audience. Make a list of changes you would make if you were revising this article for employees rather than employers.

Computer: Using the list of changes generated by your group in the preceding collaborative activity, revise the introduction (paragraphs 1-5) to this article so it is appropriate for an audience of employees rather than employers.

❖❖❖❖❖

RACE AGAINST TIME

The Editors of The New Republic

This editorial appeared in The New Republic *the week after the Los Angeles riots that followed the acquittal of four police officers for beating a suspect named Rodney King. Like journalists across the nation, these editors were attempting to identify the problems that caused the riots and to suggest solutions that would prevent them from happening again. Their solutions are of two types. First, they identify attitudes and assumptions that must be changed, and, second, they suggest actions that must be taken if we are to avoid similar riots in the future. As you read this editorial, mark in your text the solutions that these editors propose.*

Denial will soon set in. But what we have just witnessed in Los   1
Angeles is a glimpse of a racial and urban crisis in this country that is
steadily growing in intensity. Neither Republican neglect nor traditional
Democratic liberalism comes close to solving it. It's time to start over.

We should start with a rejection of the crasser simplifications that   2
have been aired over the past few weeks. The Rodney King verdict

and the riots in South Central Los Angeles do not necessarily reflect an utterly polarized country, or a society defined solely by differences of race. In many areas—most particularly in the workplace—American life is far more racially integrated than it was two generations ago. Our public culture is saturated with various racial and ethnic influences in which minority tastes are, if anything, dominant. Our major cities, once divided clearly into black and white, are increasingly a jumble of new ethnic groups in which the black-white divide is a fragment of a more complex immigrant drama. Black Americans constitute a smaller and smaller part of the racial mix in our major cities; and South-Central Los Angeles is a case in point: African Americans now make up some 55 percent of the population, compared with 65 percent a decade ago; whites have increased their presence slightly; those identified in the Census as Hispanic have jumped threefold. This social transformation has created ineluctable tensions, misunderstandings, and breakdowns; but these breakdowns have been a function of greater, not lesser, access of one kind of American to another. We are witnessing as much the wages of social nearness as the wages of social distance. And alienation from those nearby is especially combustible.

3   Moreover, these complexities operate within races as well as among them. The emergence of a large and powerful black middle class, in some ways more horrified than its white counterpart by the pathologies of the inner city, has transformed the sociology of race. Thirty years ago James Brown performed on television to help defuse a race riot; in 1992 Hammer spent the weekend after the L.A. conflagration at the Kentucky Derby. For many blacks, the riots took place in another world. Similarly, what job you have and where you live are far more accurate predictors of racial attitudes among whites than they were thirty years ago. We do scant justice to the efforts and the experiences of millions of white Americans who have come a long way since the 1960s if we equate them all with the jury of Simi Valley.

4   The lessons of the Rodney King verdict, furthermore, are not reducible to the race of the jurors; fair and decent verdicts are to be expected even from "racially unbalanced" juries. The verdict was owed, rather, to a cultural and economic divide between the most secluded of suburbs and the inner city. Moving the trial out of its original neighborhood turned the central meaning of the American jury on its head. The original point of the constitutional guarantees of trial by jury in this country was not to protect a defendant's right to be judged by his peers (as in England), but to protect the right of local communi-

ties to be represented on popular bodies that could check overreaching by governmental officials. The Sixth Amendment requires a jury "of the district wherein the crime shall have been committed," because many Anti-Federalists wanted an explicit guarantee that juries would be organized around local rather than statewide communities, which they thought would be more alert to abuses by central authorities. The result in the King case confirms this original republican insight: if the community's voice is not represented in the jury box, it will be heard in the streets. We hope the federal civil rights case against the police officers in the Rodney King beating is pursued vigorously, and in the district where the incident occurred, an area with a large black and Latino population.

Many, of course, will seize on the King verdict as a sign that   5
American society must become more race-conscious, not less: that we should have more racially contrived juries and judges, more racially determined electoral boundaries, more "multicultural" political and cultural and educational arrangements. Republicans have a history of cooperating on this front, happy to exploit whiter and whiter ghettos as their permanent political power base, and cynically accepting the permanence of racial prejudice and suspicion. Right now the Supreme Court is deciding a case that will determine whether criminal defendants can strike prospective jurors simply because of their race. In a related case, Justices Rehnquist and Scalia recently argued in a dissent that a defendant has a right to be judged by a jury of his own race but has no right to object to the exclusion of jurors of another race. (In other words, the government can't exclude black jurors from the trial of a black defendant, but it can automatically exclude white jurors.) Scalia and Rehnquist would recognize the "undeniable reality" that all racial groups tend to be sympathetic to members of their own race, and hostile to members of others. The separatist assumption of their logic—that justice is inseparable from race—is, of course, shared by many on the political left. Caught in the pincers of this strange political alliance, the cause of colorblind justice will have a hard time surviving.

We do not mean to argue, of course, that the American criminal   6
justice system is not prone to racial bias, or that in general American society does not display lingering and intense signs of racism. We simply believe that the positive developments of the last thirty years suggest that, with time, these elements are superable; that the complex racial dynamics of our society are not easily summed up by blanket

assertions of racism; that immigration is continuing to transform the racial—and social—balance of this country, often for the better; that the answer to the problem of racism, in any case, is not to compound it with more racist assumptions.

7   Moreover, the notion that a civil rights agenda is always the solution to a race-based problem is profoundly faulty. It wasn't even true in the 1960s, when race riots followed civil rights legislation rather than preceded it. Today the disjunction is even more acute. At the root of much of the disturbance in Los Angeles is not an inherently corrupt criminal justice system, but a phenomenon that underpins much of the discussion of race in this country: the black underclass. We say black underclass, because for all the elaborate statistical arguments that can be made, it is still a predominantly black phenomenon. In 1980 blacks constituted some 58 percent of those living in neighborhoods with extreme social problems, and over 60 percent of those on welfare for a long time. The levels of family breakdown are, moreover, far higher among blacks than whites. Even Andrew Hacker (see "The Myths of Racial Division," TNR, March 23) concedes that 56.2 percent of black families are headed by single women, compared with 17.3 percent of white families.

8   The black underclass perpetuates racial division in this country in several ways. It has helped weaken the American city, speeding up white flight to the suburbs and decreasing the level of black-white geographic contact. Where black-white mixing does occur, the powerful image of the black underclass—underscored by the events of the last week—has served to stigmatize the vast majority of middle-class blacks, and to powerfully perpetuate the racism of whites.

9   Any analysis of race in this country has to grapple directly with this problem. It did not emerge yesterday; nor is it, as some Democrats would have it, a simple creation of the Reagan-Bush era, although, heaven knows, neither Reagan nor Bush showed much interest in alleviating it. We do not believe that even the proposals we make here will fundamentally change life in South-Central Los Angeles within the next generation. But we are equally convinced that they cannot be postponed any longer.

10   We should begin by recognizing that even the underclass is not monolithic. Within its ranks there are both the truly disadvantaged and the truly deviant. We have seen plenty of both groups in the last week. The former are quite often—and most typically—the victims of the lat-

ter, and no attempt to break underclass culture can ignore the presence of this black-on-black violence. When black civil rights leaders said the lesson of the Rodney King case was that no black man was safe on the streets from white policemen, they revealed just how out of touch they are. The real person the black inner-city inhabitant has to fear is another black inhabitant. The vast majority of inner-city crime is black-on-black, and the scope of it is terrifying. In the District of Columbia, some 42 percent of black males between 18 and 35 are enmeshed in the criminal justice system.

Since the 1960s the progressive response to these thugs has been to develop new alternatives to incarceration (or, as probation and parole are now called by academic faddists, "intermediate sanctions"). Today more than 3 million convicted criminals are serving their sentences on the streets, not behind bars. We've tried this approach every which way (intensive supervision, community service, boot camps), and it simply doesn't work. The data on all such probation and parole programs are now in, and they're damning. Whatever you call it, "community-based corrections" spells higher crime and higher social costs than you get from incarcerating street criminals for all or most of their sentences.

The answer, however, is not to lock up the truly deviant and throw away the key. With 42 percent of the young black male population in the inner city involved in crime, the prisons simply aren't large enough. Rather, the answer is more aggressive community policing. Real community policing means lots of cops on the streets working with community leaders, talking to residents, and living in the neighborhoods they patrol. The federal government should provide the funds and training necessary to increase the manpower of all major big-city police departments by at least 20 percent. All of the additional cops should be deployed in the inner cities, and all should be trained, retained, and promoted according to the precepts of community policing. The cost of such a program, according to John DiIulio of Princeton, would be about $2 billion.

Second, the federal government should promote and pay for first-rate prison-based drug treatment programs. In prison or out, the key to successful drug treatment is staying with the program. All the data show that certain types of prison-based programs work very well, especially when there's an after-care, post-release component. The federal prison system is developing a full menu of drug treatment programs for federal prisoners. The feds should mandate, fund, and provide the technical assistance necessary to implement such programs in every state prison system in the country. Just as important is making drug treatment available for those members of the underclass who have managed to stay out of prison.

14   A far more powerful governmental weapon in the battle to break underclass culture, however, is already in the hands of the federal government. It's the welfare system. The coup de grace last week in L.A. was the sight of lines forming to receive welfare checks the Friday after the meltdown. This, for many, was the return to normal. We don't believe, as some conservatives do, and as Marlin Fitzwater continues to assert, that welfare created the underclass crisis in these communities. Nor do we believe that family breakdown was created by welfare or that fiddling with monetary incentives could put those families back together. We merely hold, as TNR senior editor Mickey Kaus argues in his forthcoming book, *The End of Equality* (New Republic Books), that at this point welfare is the critical sustaining element in the life of the underclass. If we are to break through this culture of idleness, poverty, illegitimacy, and crime, we have to cut off its lifeline.

15   This does not mean a perpetuation of Republican neglect. The panaceas of "empowerment"—homeownership, tenant-management schemes, and the like—however beneficial in themselves, fail to address the gravity of the situation. Even Jack Kemp, the only member of this administration who shows the slightest empathy for the inner-city poor, admits that it is hard to pull yourself up by your bootstraps when you don't have any boots. Enterprise zones are illusionary in the best of circumstances, and the inner city is not the best of circumstances. Trickle-down economics has never trickled down this far. The culture of dependency is so great that even times of economic boom, such as the mid-1980s, have left the structures of unemployment and despair largely intact.

16   Our alternative proposal—and Kaus's—is a radical one: to return to Franklin Delano Roosevelt's commitment to "preserve not only the bodies of the unemployed from destitution but also their self-respect, their self-reliance and courage and determination." We propose replacing all financial payments to the able-bodied poor (including Aid to Families with Dependent Children, "general relief," Food Stamps, and housing subsidies) with a simple offer of a government-provided job. This radical shift from the welfare model is the only proposal with a hope of changing the way the underclass thinks and acts; shifting the paradigm of people's lives; relating actions—such as childbearing—to

their immediate costs. It has the benefit of not merely encouraging responsibility, but of making it the only option available.

Such a proposal would cost a great deal of money and be an administrative headache. Kaus's best estimate of the cost is somewhere between $40 billion and $60 billion. That's a sum beyond the imagination of today's Washington establishment, but one that could be raised by a simple hike in the gas tax to levels Europeans would dream about, or a claw-back of middle-class entitlements, or a combination of both. In a sane government, given the events of the last week and the developments of the last two decades, it would be approved with dispatch.   17

It's no panacea, of course, and it requires greater elaboration than we have space for here. The point of the proposal, however, is extremely simple: that only the experience of work can integrate the underclass poor back into our society; that only government can accomplish this task; that, without this effort, we are not only committing more generations to misery and violence, we are poisoning the rest of our society as well.   18

Our conviction that something this drastic must be attempted is motivated by a belief that what is at stake in the events in Los Angeles is the entire notion of a common American citizenship that can transcend race and class and connect one civic obligation to another civic need. The liberal welfare state, for all its good intentions, has done much to undermine this notion of citizenship. The liberal obsession with purely racial paradigms has weakened it still further. Conservative cynicism has compounded its demise. If the flames of Los Angeles do not spur us to recover it, nothing will.   19

QUESTIONS TO CONSIDER   ◀

1. The authors begin their editorial by referring to the racial and urban crisis that resulted in the L.A. riots. However, their third sentence shifts the focus from problem to solution. Why do the authors devote so little attention to defining this problem? Do they focus on the problem again in their discussion of solutions? Would you prefer that the editorial were arranged so that all discussion of the problem occurs first, followed by a discussion of the solutions? What would be gained and lost by this type of organization?

2. The editors use the word *crisis* rather than *problem*. What difference do you perceive between a problem and a crisis? Are the editors justified in using the word *crisis* in this context?

3. Do you think the editorial shows a pronounced bias? Are the editors placing the blame for the riots on liberals, conservatives, or both? On whites, blacks, or both? On social, religious, or political factors, or all three?

4. What role do the editors suggest race played in the L.A. riots?

5. What role do they suggest economic factors played?

6. What actions do they suggest should be taken by government? Do you think these actions would solve the problems that caused the riots? Why or why not?

7. This editorial was a collaborative effort. It was written by an unspecified number of editors rather than a single editor. What process do you think these experienced professional writers employed to produce this single text? In other words, what form do you think the collaboration took?

 WRITING ACTIVITIES

Individual: A significant period of time has now elapsed since the L.A. riots. From your present perspective, write an evaluation of this editorial. Did the writers understand the problem and assess it accurately? Were the solutions suggested in the editorial ever implemented and, if so, were they effective?

Collaborative: Using your own words, list each solution proposed in this editorial. Then write a one-paragraph summary of the editorial.

Computer: Enter into your computer the paragraph summary written in the collaborative writing activity. Underline all important words in your paragraph. Then, using the thesaurus on your computer, change any neutral or bland words into more powerful or more emotional words (such as the word *problem* to the word *crisis*). What difference do these changes in words make in your summary's tone?

❖❖❖❖❖

W RITING   TO   P RESENT ◀
S OLUTIONS

Like writing to instruct, writing to present solutions falls into two general categories: writing for readers who plan to take immediate action and writing for readers who just want to think about the problem and consider the proposal as a possible long-range solution. Before writing to present a solution to a problem, you must decide which of these two purposes you are pursuing. If you are writing to propose a solution to be implemented now, you will probably write a letter, memo, or report. If you are writing to emphasize a problem or to suggest a possible solution for the reader's consideration (but not immediate action) you will more likely write an editorial, article, or essay.

Let's say the hard part is done: you have recognized a problem, figured out a solution, and determined the type of document to write. How do you write a memo, report, essay, or editorial that convinces readers to adopt or at least try your solution? Answering the following questions will help:

❖ Who is my audience?

❖ What should I include and emphasize?

❖ What organization plan should I use?

Determining Your Audience

First, you must decide who your readers will be and then analyze their qualifications, needs, and expectations. You will be able to make many writing decisions based on this analysis.

Decisions about audience go beyond merely deciding who is interested in solving the problem. A more important consideration is, who has the power to solve the problem? For example, suppose you are a human-resource specialist in a utilities company and have been asked by your supervisor, the personnel director, to recommend a plan to eliminate 75 employees. Your report will obviously be directed to your supervisor, but you should be aware that his or her managers will also read it, so you should consider them part of your audience too. These secondary readers actually have the power to implement your solution. In addition, there may be a third set of readers—the employees who would be affected by the plan's implementation. Although you will write primarily for the personnel director, don't forget your other readers' needs and perspectives.

In contrast to being told to solve a problem, you may sometimes volunteer to solve a problem; that is, you may offer an unsolicited solution. The question of audience is even more complex in this situation. Suppose you want to suggest a way to improve the relationship between your community's police and the rest of its citizens. You could, of course, write a letter to the editor of your local newspaper or a guest editorial for the Sunday edition. Your proposed solution might have a wide readership if you presented it in the newspaper. However, unless an election or referendum related to this issue were about to take place, your solution might have little effect. Even though you might persuade the readers of the newspaper that your solution was workable, even brilliant, few of them would have the power to implement your solution. In such a situation, you would probably accomplish more if you wrote a letter to the chief of police or the local governing body. Not only are these people interested in the problem created by a bad relationship between the police force and the community, but they have the power to do something about it.

In contrast, if you merely want to point out such a problem, you might very well choose to write a letter to the editor of your local newspaper. In this case, you would be writing primarily to the people of the community, attempting to persuade them that a problem exists and that they need to be concerned about it. Such a letter might also get the attention of people who have the power to change the situation, because no one likes to be criticized, and these people might eventually attempt to solve the problem you identify.

You can see why decisions about audience affect later decisions—the type of document you write, your purpose in writing it, what you say, and the way in which you say it. Identifying your readers, the ones who will read what you have written and who have the power to solve the problem, is an essential first step.

The second step is to analyze your reader or readers. As experienced writers often do informally and almost automatically, you should learn to question yourself about your readers. For example, simple demographics are important. What is the age, gender, economic status, education level, and profession of the reader(s)? Beyond these basic facts, what are the interests, attitudes, and biases of those to whom you are writing? What do these people have to gain or lose by the solution you are proposing? Such considerations should shape the text you eventually produce.

Deciding What to Include and Emphasize

Once you know and understand the person(s) to whom you are writing, you should be able to answer the next question about what to include and emphasize. Think in terms of the four elements introduced at the start of this chapter:

Definition of the problem

Identification of alternative solutions

Evaluation of alternative solutions

Argument for proposed solution

The attention you devote to each of these elements depends primarily on your audience and purpose. If you are writing a letter to the editor because you want to call attention to a problem (say the problem of police-community relations), you will probably want to emphasize the problem. You might mention that some of the police commissioner's efforts to solve this problem have been ineffectual or that a total reorganization of the police force is necessary, but your primary purpose is just to make people aware that a problem exists.

In contrast, if you are the personnel director who has been asked to devise a plan to reduce the number of employees in your company, you may say very little about the problem, which is probably all too well known by your employers. Instead, you will emphasize the solution you are proposing.

It is said that if there are no alternatives, there is no problem. In other words, if there is only one course of action, that is obviously the solution. However, in writing to present solutions, you must decide not only if alternative solutions exist but also whether to present them and, if so, how much attention to give them.

The decision about whether to include alternative solutions depends primarily on who your audience is. If your readers already know about other solutions, there is no need to discuss them extensively, although you may want to mention them briefly. For example, the utilities company management knows that one way to solve their problem is simply to fire the 75 employees. You don't need to remind them of this solution. But you might want to include and evaluate other solutions (early retirement, voluntary part-time employment, salary reductions, and so on) before arguing for your proposed solution of reorganization and reassignment.

The authors of this chapter's reading selections vary widely in what they emphasize and include. Some focus almost exclusively on the problem. For example, Frank Cedeño discusses the solution he proposes in just one paragraph, and he omits alternative solutions entirely. Others emphasize their solutions and say very little about the problems. Breuer, for example, assumes that her audience understands the problem of AIDS victims in the work force and is primarily concerned about a solution. Still others balance the two, devoting almost equal attention to problem and solution.

Deciding on a Plan of Organization

In writing to present a solution, you may want to follow the plan of organization suggested by the four key elements of a problem/solution document. That is, you may want to begin with a definition of the problem, move on to a discussion of alternative solutions, and then conclude with arguments that support your own solution. This plan has the virtue of meeting your readers' expectations because it is the most common pattern for writing to present a solution. However, you shouldn't feel bound by this organization plan. Variations are possible and even desirable. For example, why not present your own solution before discussing alternative solutions? If you do this, you might want to discuss your solution again briefly in your conclusion in order to refocus your reader's attention on it.

Different organizational patterns appear in this chapter's reading selections. Although the *The New Republic* editorial on the Los Angeles riots begins with a reference to the riots (i.e., the problem), after two sentences the authors mention alternative solutions—Republican neglect and Democratic liberalism—and even more quickly (after only one sentence) progress to their own solution. However, they intersperse additional discussion of both the problem and alternative solutions in the long discussion of their solution. The result is a rather discursive, conversational, reflective text that invites readers to consider and reconsider, to reflect rather than act. The authors' purpose in writing this editorial was not to bring about immediate action but rather to change public opinion. Their readers are people who are concerned about national attitudes and public policy but who are not necessarily in positions of power that enable them to make direct decision about such matters. That is, they are not readers who must make a decision the next day about what to do about racial strife. Rather they are readers who want to be informed and who have the leisure and education required to read a magazine such as *The New Republic.*

In contrast, Breuer, writing for a journal read primarily by personnel specialists, follows a straightforward, simple plan of organization. First she briefly discusses the problem of HIV-infected employees in the workplace, and then argues for her solution, providing her readers with numerous examples of companies that have successfully implemented this solution (i.e., educating all employees about the disease and its effects). What if Breuer had organized her text more loosely, moving freely from problem to solution as the writers of *The New Republic* editorial did? Her readers might have become frustrated and impatient with this organization, for they need an immediate, workable solution to a problem that is only going to get worse in the near future. They are in a position to take action and need information to do so.

Often readers interested in solving a problem merely skim the first part of an article or report, focusing most of their attention on the solution. For such readers, you might want to include **headings** that HEADINGS, PAGE 526 identify the different sections of your memo, report, or article. Headings enable readers to read more quickly and efficiently. They are especially appropriate when you are writing to present a solution to someone who is going to make an immediate decision about your proposal. Also when you write for such a reader, you should organize your text in the most direct, straightforward manner possible, including each element in the expected order. Also include strong transitions that indicate clearly each major section of your text. If you are writing for someone who is merely interested in the problem and wants to think about it, feel free to vary the usual pattern. As always, audience and purpose are the determining factors.

WRITING ASSIGNMENT

For this writing assignment select a problem involving human relations—how people do or, in this case, do not get along—and write an essay, editorial, memo, or report proposing a specific solution. For example, you might write about the problem of working on collaborative assignments with other students or about the problem of being a smoker in an office of nonsmokers. Or you might write about problems that often exist between older and younger generations, between native and non-native students, or between males and females.

In general, the more specific you are, the better the results will be. For example, if you are an athlete, write about the problems athletes have in getting to know nonathletes at your school rather than writing about this problem in general. Or if you are writing about the problem of date rape, you should probably focus on the problem as it exists on your own campus (although you might want to include some statistics about the problem nationwide or mention that the problem is not limited to your school).

However, if you choose to write about a topic such as parent-child or male-female relationships, you should probably not focus on yourself exclusively. Remember that you are writing for an audience, not yourself. Write about your own personal relationships only if you can meet the following standards:

1. You can discuss the problem objectively.

2. You can solve the problem.

3. Both the problem and solution are generalizable—that is, they can appropriately be applied to other people and other situations.

In other words, in choosing a problem to write about, you must strike a delicate balance. You will probably want to focus on a specific problem that you know a great deal about and think you can actually solve. But you don't want to be too personal—to write about a problem affecting just you and not pertaining to other people.

Even so, remember that these are guidelines, not iron-clad rules that must be followed regardless of your interests and inclinations. Some people like to tackle big issues like race, parent-child, or male-female relations, for example. Most of the reading selections in this chapter do just that. If you want to write about such a topic, be sure you know the problem well (perhaps even firsthand) and have a viable solution to propose. Realize, however, that such a problem is more challenging—more difficult to write about convincingly and more difficult to solve.

Whatever problem you choose to write about, be sure you have a plan that can solve it. Even if you do not have an immediate solution, you should have a serious proposal to present to your readers— something they can consider as an eventual or possible solution. Ideally, your solution should be as specific as your problem. Just telling your readers that the people in question should get along better is a poignant hope but not a solution.

Planning Your Text

Once you have chosen a problem you want to write about, you need to think about your audience. In general, you want to write for readers who need to be aware of the problem or can solve it or both. In addition, you need to decide if you are proposing an immediate solution, one that you expect your readers to implement in the near future, or merely suggesting a long-range solution for readers to consider. If you have selected a problem that does not lend itself to these considerations about audience, you probably need to rethink that decision. Perhaps you can narrow or refocus the problem, but you may need to abandon it and pursue another altogether.

Be very specific about identifying your audience. "Anyone who is interested" or "someone who can solve the problem" will not do. You need to know, if not the exact person or persons, at least something about the type of person who will be your reader. For example, suppose you are writing about the problems you have experienced and observed working with other students on collaborative assignments. You might write a memo to a specific instructor who requires group work, to a department chair or dean who supervises faculty members who frequently include collaborative assignments in their courses, or to a professional education journal. Although you might know only the instructor personally, the other possible readers are also knowable. You know, for example, the approximate education and economic levels of chairs and deans as well as the fact that they tend to be busy administrators. The readers of a professional journal are less easily knowable, but you can generalize that such readers are probably teachers and are reading a journal because they want to improve their teaching or keep abreast of new developments in their profession.

The audience you identify will determine to a great extent what you say and how you say it. Audience analysis usually involves identifying certain of your readers' characteristics. For example, answering the following questions will help you learn more about your readers(s):

- ❖ Who is your audience?

- ❖ Where do they live?

- ❖ What do they do?

- ❖ How much eduction do they have?

- ❖ How much information do they have about the problem?

- ❖ Do they have the power to solve your problem?

- ❖ Are they likely to be reading hurriedly or leisurely, carefully or superficially?

- ❖ Are they likely to be hostile or friendly readers?

- ❖ What do they have to gain or lose by your proposal?

In addition to selecting a problem and identifying your audience, you may want to learn more about the problem before you begin to write. For example, you could observe a situation in which the problem exists or interview people who are familiar with the problem but have perspectives different from your own. You may also want to

FIELD RESEARCH, PAGE 493

LIBRARY RESEARCH, PAGE 534

obtain additional information from written documents (see **field research** and **library research**).

Constructing Your Text

DRAFTING. You can begin writing by constructing an outline based on the different elements usually included in a problem/solution text:

Definition of the problem

Identification of alternative solutions

Evaluation of alternative solutions

Argument for proposed solution

As you develop each of these elements, you may well discover that you want to omit one or more or that one will be much longer than the others. That's fine. Just let your text take shape as it will, growing naturally as you expand and develop each section.

The traditional methods of development are your best strategies for developing your text. Let's see how each section of a problem/solution text might use various methods of development.

❖ *Definition of the Problem.* In defining the problem you are addressing you may use almost any method of development. For example, Breuer and Clendinen begin their problem definitions with **narration**. More typically, however, you might use **description**, **exemplification**, **comparison/contrast**, or **cause and effect**. Cause and effect is perhaps the method of development most frequently used in defining a problem. Readers typically want to know what caused a certain problem and what its effects are likely to be. However, all of the methods of development mentioned here could be used appropriately. For example, suppose you are writing about the problem that some students have in relating to their instructors. You might want to describe a bad student-teacher relationship, compare it to a good student-teacher relationship, illustrate each, and then discuss the cause and/or effect of this problem in terms of student performance.

NARRATION, PAGE 558

DESCRIPTION, PAGE 456

EXEMPLIFICATION, PAGE 488

COMPARISON/CONTRAST, PAGE 437

CAUSE AND EFFECT, PAGE 418

❖ *Identification of Alternative Solutions.* If you identify alternative solutions in your text, you may want to develop them (briefly) by using one or more of the same methods you used to define the problem: description, exemplification, comparison and contrast, or cause and effect, depending on how much information your readers need to understand each one. In addition, you might also want to use **classification**. If, for example, you are identifying a number of different alternative solutions, help your reader by classifying the solutions in some way (e.g., those that are temporary and those that are permanent; those that involve reorganization and those that involve personnel; those that are favored by one group and those that are supported by another group).

CLASSIFICATION, PAGE 422

❖ *Evaluation of Alternative Solutions.* If you not only identify alternative solutions but evaluate them, you will, of course, use comparison and contrast, but you might also want to use classification and/or cause and effect. Although you might conceivably need to devote as much attention to alternative solutions as you do to your own, in general keep this section brief and to the point.

❖ *Argument for Proposed Solution.* You can use a variety of development methods in arguing for your own solution. In fact, it is difficult to think of one that could not be used. You will, of course, need to describe the solution you are proposing, perhaps providing your readers with examples (exemplification). And, just as you need to discuss cause and effect when you define a problem, you will probably also want to point out the effects you anticipate if your solution is implemented. You may also want to compare and contrast your solution with the alternative solutions you have included or even to classify it so your readers can see how it relates to other solutions. Finally, you may want to tell a story (narration) in order to persuade your readers that your solution should be accepted. Reconstructions of personal experiences can be compellingly persuasive. In deciding how extensively to develop each section of your text, remember to keep your purpose in mind. Your primary purpose is to present your own solution and argue for its implementation.

READING. Allow some time to elapse after you finish a draft of your text and before you read it. Of course, you will read your text, at least in bits and pieces, many times as you are drafting it. But when you have finished a draft, let it rest for a day or so (longer, if possible) before reading it through carefully. Then try to put yourself in your intended reader's place—try to imagine how a reader will respond to what you have written. This trick of pretending you are the intended reader takes practice. It is much easier to read from your own point of view. As the writer, you know all about the problem and understand perfectly how the solution is supposed to work. However, your readers will not have these advantages, so you must try to gain their perspective.

Because you identified your audience specifically in the planning stage, you should know exactly who your readers are. Imagining yourself as a specific reader should be much easier than imagining yourself as a vaguely defined, nebulous reader.

In this imagining-yourself-as-reader process, be sure to carefully consider the possible attitudes of your intended reader toward the problem you are discussing. Is this a friendly reader or an indifferent reader or a hostile reader? A busy, impatient reader or a leisurely reader? Is this person convinced a problem exists, or do you need to persuade him or her? Does this person want a solution? If so, is he or she biased in favor of another solution? Here are other questions to ask yourself as you read:

- Is my problem well defined?

- Have I represented other solutions fairly?

- Is my solution workable? Practical? Ethical?

- Is my text clear and easy to read?

As you read, write notes to yourself on the text so you will remember what you want to do when you begin to revise. For example, suppose you discover that you need to reorganize your text. You can bracket or circle the material to be moved and draw an arrow indicating the position in the text where you want to insert it. If you decide that one section needs to be developed more fully, write a note to that effect. If some material needs to be deleted, scratch it out. In other words, don't rely on your memory. Annotate your text as you read it so you know exactly what you want to do when you revise.

REVISING.   If you have made good notes as you read your text, you should know what you need to do as you revise it. In addition, carefully consider the organization of your text at this point. Would your text be more interesting if you began with your solution? Do you really need to include alternative solutions? Would a less structured plan of organization be more appropriate? Would a more structured plan of organization be more appropriate? Would headings help your reader?

Also, carefully evaluate the development of your text now. Have you assumed too much knowledge on the part of the reader and omitted necessary information? It is easy to assume your reader knows as much as you do about the problem and views the problem exactly as you do. But this may not be the case. You may also have assumed that your reader will be able to see the good sense of your proposed solution even though you have given him or her very few details. Especially if you are expecting your reader to implement your proposal at once, be sure you have given that person enough information to make a decision. A decision to act is not easily made. If you do not give your reader sufficient information, it will not matter how persuasively you have written.

Editing Your Text

STYLE AND VOICE, PAGE 596

A text that persuades your readers the problem you are addressing needs to be solved and that you have the best solution requires not only effective organization and adequate information but also appropriate **style and voice**. A brusque no-nonsense voice and formal style may be exactly what some readers want, whereas others prefer a personal, easygoing voice and informal style.

Editing for style and voice is not easy because these qualities of a text seem so abstract and nebulous. Just what constitutes style and voice? How do you know if your style and voice are appropriate? Style and voice indicate your relationship with your reader. If you want that relationship to be familiar, even personal, you reveal yourself freely in your text, using first-person point of view, giving your opinions freely, even including information about yourself (as Dudley Clendinen does, for example). If you want that relationship to be impersonal and more formal, you reveal very little about yourself (as Nancy Breuer, Frank Cedeño, Melvin Konner, and *The New Republic* editors do).

In making these decisions, you must once again consider your audience. Who are your readers? What would be an appropriate relationship for you to have with them? If you are writing to other students, for example, you can be rather personal and fairly informal. In contrast, if you are writing to an administrator, the readers of a newspaper, or your employer, you will want to maintain a certain level of formality and not intrude on your text.

Once you have determined the appropriate relationship, read your text to see if its style and voice reflect the relationship. The following questions may help you determine whether your style and voice are appropriate:

❖ Have you referred to yourself or your experiences?

❖ Have you used first-person point of view (I)?

❖ Have you addressed the reader(s) directly as *you*?

❖ Are your sentences short and fairly simple?

❖ Have you used colloquial or slang expressions?

❖ Have you used humor?

❖ Would you describe your text as chatty, friendly, or personal?

❖ Will your reader know you as a person better after reading your text?

If you answered "yes" to most or all of these questions, you have probably written in a very personal voice and informal style. If you answered "yes" to only a few of these questions, you have probably written in a somewhat personal voice and informal style. If such a voice and style do not reflect an appropriate relationship with your intended reader(s), you probably need to edit your text so it is more formal and less personal (see **revising and editing**).

REVISING AND EDITING, PAGE 593

Minor White, *Windowsill Daydreaming*, 1958. Reproduction courtesy
The Minor White Archive, Princeton University.
Copyright © 1982 by The Trustees
of Princeton University. All rights reserved.

7

WRITING
TO
PERSUADE

The art of writing has for its backbone some fierce attachment to an idea.

VIRGINIA WOOLF

In the broadest sense of the word *persuade*, all writers write to persuade regardless of what they are writing. Thus the poet writes to persuade a reader that his love is like a red rose, the chef writes to persuade a reader that her recipe for clam chowder is the most succulent, and the technical writer writes to persuade a reader that a computer should be operated in a certain way. Writers do not have to write an editorial or a legal brief to be concerned about convincing readers of something. The writers of this chapter's reading selections use letters, books, magazines, and free-standing essays to persuade readers that appearance does not always equal reality.

Why is almost every type of writing to some extent persuasive? One answer may be that persuasive writing is a socially acceptable version of humans' innate aggressiveness. Most people usually channel those aggressive instincts into civilized, productive forms of behavior, using words, most of the time, rather than weapons to persuade others to agree with them.

People also use persuasive writing to get things done. Social, political, and economic action depends on persuasive discourse. Whether a society is a democracy or a dictatorship, whether the goal is consensus or compliance, political leaders use language to govern, and the language they use is most often persuasive. The forms and methods of rhetorical persuasion may differ from one culture to another, but the persuasive purpose is the same.

Advertisers also use language to persuade. In fact, the entire U.S. economic system depends on the ability of industry and business to persuade people to use their products and services. As a result, everyone from General Electric to the local video store tries to entice people to buy something or use something or do something. And in turn people must constantly make decisions about whom to believe, what to do, and when to act.

Writers use a wide variety of rhetorical tools and strategies to persuade a reader of the validity of their arguments. Some arguments are forceful and direct; others are subtle and indirect. Some are objective and impersonal; others are subjective and highly personal. Some command; others cajole. In general, writers use anything that works to persuade their audience to believe and, in some cases, to act on their arguments.

As a reader, your responsibility is to evaluate the writer's argument. And, since the persuasive purpose is at least a secondary aim in almost all writing, you should be prepared to recognize and evaluate arguments in whatever you read, whether a textbook, a comic strip, or a brochure. Otherwise, you give up your right to defend yourself against the writer's arguments.

R E A D I N G   P E R S U A S I V E ◀
D I S C O U R S E

Much of what you have already learned about reading texts that inform, instruct, evaluate, explore, and reconstruct experience also applies to persuasive texts. For example, you must carefully evaluate the accuracy of any information in persuasive writing. You must be satisfied that the information is current, relevant, and accurate before you can accept any arguments based on it. If a writer cites inaccurate, dated, or irrelevant information, you will probably not be persuaded by his or her arguments (see Chapter 4, "Writing to Inform").

But reading persuasive texts intelligently requires more than just evaluating information. An argument is a complex form of discourse that operates on several levels at the same time. Aristotle explained persuasive discourse by identifying the three kinds of appeals that a writer can make to a reader:

* *Logos*, the appeal to logic

* *Pathos*, the appeal to emotion

* *Ethos*, the appeal to credibility

A strong argument usually includes all three kinds of appeals.

Understanding Appeals to Logic

An effective argument usually makes a strong appeal to the audience's sense of reason—to what is true or at least plausible. An illogical argument—that is, one that does not ring true to those who hear or read it—will probably be rejected. Thus when writers write to persuade, they often base their arguments on logical premises, on statements that are generally accepted as true. For example, if a writer is arguing that the decline in traditional family structure in recent years is responsible for many of our social problems, he or she might build the following argument:

1. If the family units that make up a society do not function well, then the society will not function well.

2. Therefore, since our society is not functioning well, the problem must lie with the families that comprise it.

Now this argument may or may not be true. Someone could argue the other way around just as easily—that because society is not functioning well, the family is having trouble. Both statements are based on logical arguments. That is, each statement is based on another statement that is generally perceived to be true. In this case, both arguments are also based on the underlying assumption that a close **cause and effect** relationship exists between a society and the families in it.

CAUSE AND EFFECT,
PAGE 418

It is important to realize that logical arguments are not necessarily true. They just follow a pattern of reasoning that Western tradition has deemed logical, but logic does not necessarily equal truth. A logical argument is merely one that appeals to the audience's sense of what *could be* true, what is possible or reasonable.

As a reader, you may be strongly influenced by a logical appeal, but you must still analyze the argument and evaluate its worth. For example, a writer might argue that if the traditional family fails, then society will fail. This statement sounds logical. But a reader's acceptance of this assertion depends on his or her interpretation of what the writer means by words such as *family, traditional,* and *fail.* Family structure varies from age to age and from society to society. Many societies have endured without having so-called traditional family structures. And evaluating the failure of a family and of a society may require different criteria for and definitions of failure.

Like the pattern of proving one assertion by citing another, the use of examples constitutes a common method of logical persuasion. For instance, it can be argued that because a certain number of non-traditional families exists, the traditional family structure must no longer be the norm. Many careful scientific and statistical studies are based on this type of research. Researchers examine a large number of individual phenomena and then generalize their findings to the society at large. For example, if a government survey indicates that more than half the families participating in the survey are nontraditional in structure, the researchers might legitimately conclude that the traditional family consisting of two parents (one male and one female) and several children is no longer the norm in our society.

However, this form of reasoning can be misused and misleading. If the number of specific phenomena examined is too small or not typical of the population at large, the results may not be accurate and should not become the basis of a generalization. For example, a writer who cites several apparently healthy, successful people from nontraditional families can legitimately argue that nontraditional families *sometimes* produce healthy, productive offspring. But, on the basis of these few examples, the writer should not claim that nontraditional families are as effective as traditional families in this respect or that *all* children reared in nontraditional families are healthy and successful. Citing a few examples simply does not support a general claim. A few examples can be used effectively to support an argument, but you need to be skeptical when a writer or speaker makes broad general claims on the basis of a few examples (see **exemplification**).

EXEMPLIFICATION, PAGE 488

As a reader, you should certainly value reasonable arguments, but you must analyze and evaluate logical appeals just as carefully as you would any appeal. Sometimes this analysis means examining closely the language of the argument. What terms does the writer use and what do they mean in this particular context? If terms are not clearly defined, consensus is rarely possible. Even a seemingly simple term such as *family* can have different meanings. Is a couple a family? Can this couple be two males or two females and still be considered a family? Does a single parent plus children constitute a family?

Your responsibility as a reader, therefore, is not only to determine that arguments are logical or reasonable but also to evaluate the truth of the logic. Remember, a logical argument is not necessarily true. To be logical usually means only that a particular reasoning process was used to reach the conclusion. This process can result in inaccurate, misleading, or simply untrue arguments. Thus in reading any persuasive text, from a few lines of advertising to a book-length interpretation of ideas or events, you must evaluate the writer's logical appeals. On the basis of your evaluation, you can then accept or reject the writer's arguments.

Understanding Appeals to Emotion

In an ideal world, perhaps all arguments would be based exclusively on logic; that is, arguments would appeal only to the sense of reason. In this ideal world, reasonable people would argue logically and rationally, and the most reasonable argument would triumph over less reasonable arguments. But in the real world, people are persuaded by emotion as well as by logic and reason.

You may find it hard to accept the idea of emotion as a valid appeal in persuasive discourse. You may consider emotional appeals as unworthy, even downright unfair. Certainly, unscrupulous emotional appeals abound. Too many politicians appeal to people's greed, pride, and prejudices in order to gain power. Too many advertisers appeal to people's insecurities and desires to be attractive, successful, or comfortable.

One of the most terrifying examples of unscrupulous emotional appeal was Adolf Hitler's appeal to the German people's pride and nationalism, as he invoked claims of racial superiority in order to gain power in the 1920s and 1930s. Using emotional appeals, Hitler aroused feelings in some people that ended in heinous crimes against others. Rejecting emotional appeals entirely is easy if you think of Hitler's use of them as the standard.

But not all emotional appeals are illegitimate. People are, after all, emotional as well as rational creatures. The emotional appeal can be just as valid as the logical appeal, depending on how it is used and to what purpose.

An editorial appealing to your sense of responsibility toward others in order to persuade you to support local charities is legitimate. Likewise, a politician's appeal to your pride in democracy in order to convince you to vote is valid.

Interestingly, the same emotion can be used in both valid and invalid appeals. For example, those who are writing or speaking to persuade often use appeals to fear. Politicians evoke fear that their opponents will raise taxes, evangelists evoke fear of divine punishment, doctors evoke fear of disease; and environmentalists evoke fear of ecological disaster. Appeals to fear are not in themselves invalid. In each case you must look at the writer's or speaker's purpose.

Even when you examine their purpose, you may find it hard to evaluate emotional appeals. A politician's primary purpose may be to be elected president, but he may also believe that higher taxes will harm the economy. An evangelist may preach about hell and damnation to increase donations but may also sincerely believe that people need to hear this message. A doctor may want people to fear disease enough to take care of themselves (be inoculated, get regular check-ups, eat right, etc.) and/or may also want more patients in order to become rich. And an environmentalist may engender fear of global warming in order to save people and the planet and/or to get more money from the government.

Although you may have a hard time evaluating emotional appeals, at least try to be aware of them. As you read a text, you should determine if emotional appeals are being used to manipulate you. Is the emotional appeal being used to evoke illogical fears or reprehensible emotions? Are your emotions being aroused about improbable events or behaviors? Does an emotional appeal attempt to obscure the lack of valid arguments? If so, be wary of the arguments based on these appeals. Emotional responses are a normal part of the reading process, and it is important for you to be aware of what you are feeling as well as what you are thinking when you read. In fact, what you are feeling may well determine what you are thinking. Emotional appeals are a powerful and valid persuasive strategy, and most effective arguments appeal to the emotions as well as to the intellect. But you need to be aware of your emotional reactions and to evaluate those feelings as part of your assessment of the arguments you are reading.

Understanding Appeals to Credibility

Ethos is an appeal to the reader's belief in the writer's or speaker's **credibility**. In other words, one of the reasons you accept or reject an argument is your belief in the writer's or speaker's trustworthiness. If you perceive the writer or speaker as honest, intelligent, informed, and well intentioned, then you probably will accept that person's arguments. If, in contrast, you perceive the writer or speaker as dishonest, stupid, uninformed, inexperienced, self-serving or malicious, you are not likely to accept his or her arguments regardless of how brilliant, logical, or emotionally charged they may be. Ultimately, then, the reader's perception of the writer determines the effectiveness of an argument.

CREDIBILITY, PAGE 443

Some writers and speakers have established their credibility even before they write or speak: that is, their audience knows them, either personally or by reputation. In a small town, for example, if a teacher writes a letter to the editor of the local newspaper arguing that education is underfunded, the readers of that letter probably know the teacher and have previously formed an opinion of him or her. The readers will respond to the teacher's letter on the basis of their opinion of the teacher as much as, or more than, they will on the basis of what the teacher writes in the letter. Or when well-known actor Charlton Heston argues against gun control, readers react not only on the basis of what he says but also on the basis of their perception of him as a strong, honest, trustworthy man. That this perception may be based solely on the roles Heston has played rather than on who he really is may not occur to many readers.

Even people you do not really know anything about may seem trustworthy because they have certain credentials. They may teach at a prestigious university, have written thirteen books, have an impressive title or degree attached to their name, or have had experiences that lend them credibility. For example, Sir Edmund Hillary and Tenzing Norgay, the first people to scale Mt. Everest, had enormous credibility when they wrote about mountain climbing.

Writers also establish their credibility by citing familiar and respected sources. If a writer supports arguments with sources the reader knows and respects, the reader will often transfer the source's credibility to the writer. Politicians who are trying to appeal to African-Americans, for example, will often cite Martin Luther King, Jr., and Jesse Jackson.

All writers, whether known to their readers or not, struggle to establish their credibility as they construct their texts. As a reader, you are a judge of that credibility. You need to be aware as you read texts intended to persuade that your perception of the writer influences your perception of the arguments you are reading. Remember too that in most instances you are dealing with just a perception. You may know the writer by reputation, but seldom do you really know the person who is writing. A skilled writer can create a very believable persona (a role that is assumed in the text) to convince readers of the validity of his or her arguments. The persona may reflect the real author, but you shouldn't assume it to be the same as the author. It is your responsibility to evaluate the effect of this persona on your response to the writer's arguments.

Understanding Underlying Assumptions

Analyzing and evaluating the arguments in a persuasive text also means identifying the underlying assumptions on which the arguments are based. What is the writer assuming that he or she does not necessarily state? For example, in the argument about the decline in traditional family structure, the writer is assuming that biological father-mother-children families are the best type of family structure.

Often what is *not* stated is more important than what is stated. Implicit in almost every argument is one or more unstated assumptions on which the argument is based. The writer assumes you agree with him or her on this point but doesn't state the point explicitly. For example, if a writer is arguing that traditional families are no longer the norm and that children are being neglected as a result, the assumptions are that families should take care of children and that traditional families perform this function best. If you share the writer's assumptions, you will probably accept the argument. If, in contrast, you believe that the government should share in the responsibility for children by providing adequate day-care facilities or that nontraditional families can also effectively nurture children, you may reject this writer's argument.

Stephen Toulmin, an English logician, has devised a system for analyzing arguments that includes the unspoken assumptions connecting the evidence provided and the assertion (or claim) based on the evidence. These unspoken assumptions, or *warrants* as Toulmin calls them, reveal (make explicit) the relationship between the evidence and the claim.

For example, examine the following diagram of an argument:

Evidence	**Claim**
The driver had consumed seven cans of beer in the previous two hours.	→ His friends should not have allowed him to drive.

This argument involves the following unspoken assumptions:

1. Seven cans of beer in two hours will make a person incapable of operating an automobile safely.

2. Driving after consuming that amount of beer in that time span is dangerous, against the law, and so on.

3. Friends should be responsible for one another.

To analyze the argument, a reader must evaluate not only the stated evidence and claim but also the unstated assumptions on which the argument is based. Most people would probably agree on the example's first two assumptions even though some might point out that the alcoholic content of beer differs greatly and that different people's tolerance for alcohol also varies. Some readers might not readily accept the third assumption, that friends should be responsible for one another. They might argue that people are responsible only for themselves or that there are degrees of friendship.

You need to be aware that all arguments include unarticulated, implicit beliefs—whether they are called assumptions or warrants—on which the arguments depend. Often these unspoken assumptions involve value judgments that tell you more about the writer's basic orientation and beliefs than the arguments themselves. For example, if someone argues that protecting the timber industry is more important than protecting forests, the underlying assumption is that economic wellbeing now is more important than the environment and that a choice must be made between the two. Whether or not you agree with these assumptions, you should realize that they are the foundation of the argument. To understand an argument completely, you must identify the underlying, unspoken assumptions on which it is based.

R E A D I N G S   F O R   W R I T I N G   ◄

This chapter's reading selections all deal with appearance versus reality. Each writer begins by explaining a misapprehension or myth, something generally accepted as true that is, at least in the writer's opinion, inaccurate or invalid. The writer then proceeds to argue in favor of his or her version of reality—what is really true as opposed to what seems to be true. This convention of first presenting a myth or distortion and then correcting it is a common and effective strategy many writers use to initiate arguments that seek to persuade.

BEAUTY AT ANY PRICE

Rebecca Williams

While a student in a freshman composition course, Rebecca Williams wrote the following essay about her experience as a beauty contestant. This experience changed her perception of beauty contests and her idea of what constitutes beauty. In her essay Williams argues that beauty contests are not the equitable and joyful competitions they seem to be. Ironically, Williams did not win the beauty contest, but her essay won first place in an essay contest.

For many years, I dutifully watched the televised Miss U.S.A. and   1
Miss Texas-U.S.A. pageants. I always saw the productions as exciting shows which quite naturally ran perfectly. I assumed that they were produced by volunteers who were simply interested in honoring the best young woman in the country (or state). I pictured the contestants as sweet, intelligent young women who willingly gave up a year of their lives to represent their home towns and participate in those exciting live telecast pageants. Being a contestant-at-large in the 1987 Miss Texas-U.S.A. Pageant was an experience which changed my views about not only the pageants but also the contestants in them.

The overwhelming impression I formed while in San Antonio for   2
the pageant is that pageants are a money-making business. In the case of Miss Texas-U.S.A., the system has been fully controlled by two men for thirteen years. Richard Guy and Rex Holt formed GuyRex Associates, Inc., which not only produces the pageant, but also markets expensive dresses for its contestants and manages its winner.

GuyRex Associates, Inc. is getting rich, mainly because so many young women are willing to make a huge investment to compete for a major title. Each one of the 109 contestants in the 1987 pageant spent between $3,000 and $30,000 on evening gowns, other clothes, and professional training in preparation for the pageant. One thousand dollars of the total amount spent by each was mailed directly to GuyRex Associates for the contestant's entry fee. Since all pageant accommodations, food, prizes, and television time were provided by official sponsors, it isn't too difficult to guess who ended up keeping the $109,000.

3   Since the success of the pageant is largely dependent on television ratings, the producers willingly sacrifice realism and, in some cases, honesty in order to stage a spectacular pageant which will draw millions of viewers and thus bring in more "big bucks." A viewer of a televised pageant is often led to believe that the entire performance and competition are spontaneous and live. I found it very interesting to be backstage and see just how much time was spent memorizing cue cards, learning to lip-synch the words of professionally pre-recorded music, and pre-taping actual segments of the supposed live telecast itself. All orchestral music, singing, and applause were done by professionals and are taped long before the pageant week ever begins. Most pageants also televise the judges and official auditor hard at work on the night of the pageant. The image of these people working on the actual pageant night is almost totally false, since their work is already done. For example, in the 1987 Miss Texas-U.S.A. Pageant, the winner had known that she was to win shortly after preliminary judging, two days prior to the live telecast.

4   The producers weren't the only people trying to make a profit at the Miss Texas-U.S.A. Pageant. The winner was to receive over $100,000 in cash and prizes, so competition was fierce. No longer did I see the contestants as friendly young women honored to represent their communities, but rather as professionals in the cut-throat business of beauty. I watched while many perfectly beautiful girls ruined their appearance by becoming engrossed with the desire to win, and by looking out for only themselves. These were not the sweet women I remembered seeing on television. They were indeed professionals, who invested not only thousands of dollars per year on pageant fees and evening gowns, but also years of their lives, all in order to compete for a title and the monetary rewards which go along with it.

5   After spending ten days behind the scenes of a pageant as one of the 109 contestants, I learned that what a viewer sees on television is only a show. Pageants are not the magical, suspense filled dream-shows that many young girls see them as being. They are the result of

some entrepreneur's desire to become rich. Unfortunately, this wealth comes at the expense of the contestants who expend so much time, hope, and money, as well as the winner who, although she may enjoy it for a while, is often exploited by her new managers and sponsors.

Competing in the pageant also made me realize that the contestants and winner of the pageant were really no more beautiful than many other women in Texas. I've found that beauty is more than a perfect set of teeth or a 5′11″ frame carrying only 130 pounds. Beauty radiates from the inside of a person and is seen not in the way someone applies her make-up or in the clothes she wears but through her willingness to share her true beauty with everyone around her.

6

QUESTIONS TO CONSIDER

1. How does Williams establish her credibility? Why is she qualified to write about beauty contests?

2. Williams begins her essay by describing her perception of beauty contests before she was a participant. She devotes only one paragraph to this description. Would more information about her earlier perceptions strengthen her essay? Why or why not?

3. Williams's essay includes both logical and emotional appeals. Give examples of each.

4. Does the fact that Williams's experience was limited to a single contest weaken her argument? Why or why not?

5. Williams's main argument is that beauty contests are money-making businesses that are staged to impress television viewers. What other objections could she have raised to beauty contests? Would these objections have been appropriate given her purpose in this essay?

WRITING ACTIVITIES

Individual: In a journal entry, write about your reaction to beauty contests as viewer or participant.

Collaborative: Make a list of the pros and cons of beauty contests. Then write down one logical and one emotional appeal you could use to support each position. Compare your arguments with those of the other groups.

Computer: Choose one of the arguments from the pro/con list generated by your group in the collaborative activity. Enter this argument into a new computer file and then develop it by adding supporting evidence. Share your argument with classmates through a network program or by exchanging disks. Respond to at least three of your classmates' arguments.

❖❖❖❖❖

ON NATURAL DEATH

Lewis Thomas

Noted scientist and essayist Lewis Thomas argues in this essay that all deaths are natural. This essay is part of a collection of Thomas's essays entitled The Medusa and the Snail: More Notes of a Biology Watcher. *Like Williams, Thomas begins this essay by setting forth a common misperception—namely, that death is "an extraordinary, even an exotic experience" for humans. He then proceeds to argue against this view of death.*

1   There are so many new books about dying that there are now special shelves set aside for them in bookshops, along with the health-diet and home-repair paperbacks and the sex manuals. Some of them are so packed with detailed information and step-by-step instructions for performing the function that you'd think this was a new sort of skill which all of us are now required to learn. The strongest impression the casual reader gets, leafing through, is that proper dying has become an extraordinary, even an exotic experience, something only the specially trained get to do.

2   Also, you could be led to believe that we are the only creatures capable of the awareness of death, that when all the rest of nature is being cycled through dying, one generation after another, it is a different kind of process, done automatically and trivially, more "natural," as we say.

3   An elm in our backyard caught the blight this summer and dropped stone dead, leafless, almost overnight. One weekend it was a normal-looking elm, maybe a little bare in spots but nothing alarming, and the next weekend it was gone, passed over, departed, taken.

Taken is right, for the tree surgeon came by yesterday with his crew of young helpers and their cherry picker, and took it down branch by branch and carted it off in the back of a red truck, everyone singing.

The dying of a field mouse, at the jaws of an amiable household cat, is a spectacle I have beheld many times. It used to make me wince. Early in life I gave up throwing sticks at the cat to make him drop the mouse, because the dropped mouse regularly went ahead and died anyway, but I also shouted unaffections at the cat to let him know the sort of animal he had become. Nature, I thought, was an abomination. 4

Recently I've done some thinking about that mouse, and I wonder if his dying is necessarily all that different from the passing of our elm. The main difference, if there is one, would be in the matter of pain. I do not believe that an elm tree has pain receptors, and even so, the blight seems to me a relatively painless way to go even if there were nerve endings in a tree, which there are not. But the mouse dangling tail-down from the teeth of a gray cat is something else again, with pain beyond bearing, you'd think, all over his small body. 5

There are now some plausible reasons for thinking it is not like that at all, and you can make up an entirely different story about the mouse and his dying if you like. At the instant of being trapped and penetrated by teeth, peptide hormones are released by cells in the hypothalamus and the pituitary gland; instantly these substances, called endorphins, are attached to the surfaces of other cells responsible for pain perception; the hormones have the pharmacologic properties of opium; there is no pain. Thus it is that the mouse seems always to dangle so languidly from the jaws, lies there so quietly when dropped, dies of his injuries without a struggle. If a mouse could shrug, he'd shrug. 6

I do not know if this is true or not, nor do I know how to prove it if it is true. Maybe if you could get in there quickly enough and administer naloxone, a specific morphine antagonist, you could turn off the endorphins and observe the restoration of pain, but this is not something I would care to do or see. I think I will leave it there, as a good guess about the dying of a cat-chewed mouse, perhaps about dying in general. 7

Montaigne had a hunch about dying, based on his own close call in a riding accident. He was so badly injured as to be believed dead by his companions, and was carried home with lamentations, "all bloody, stained all over with the blood I had thrown up." He remembers the entire episode, despite having been "dead, for two full hours," with wonderment: 8

9   It seemed to me that my life was hanging only by the tip of my lips. I closed my eyes in order, it seemed to me, to help push it out, and took pleasure in growing languid and letting myself go. It was an idea that was only floating on the surface of my soul, as delicate and feeble as all the rest, but in truth not only free from distress but mingled with that sweet feeling that people have who have let themselves slide into sleep. I believe that this is the same state in which people find themselves whom we see fainting in the agony of death, and I maintain that we pity them without cause . . . In order to get used to the idea of death, I find there is nothing like coming close to it.

10   Later, in another essay, Montaigne returns to it:

> If you know not how to die, never trouble yourself;
> Nature will in a moment fully and sufficiently instruct you; she
> will exactly do that business for you; take you no care for it.

11   The worst accident I've ever seen was on Okinawa, in the early days of the invasion, when a jeep ran into a troop carrier and was crushed nearly flat. Inside were two young MPs, trapped in bent steel, both mortally hurt, with only their heads and shoulders visible. We had a conversation while people with the right tools were prying them free. Sorry about the accident, they said. No, they said, they felt fine. Is everyone else okay, one of them said. Well, the other one said, no hurry now. And then they died.

12   Pain is useful for avoidance, for getting away when there's time to get away, but when it is end game, and no way back, pain is likely to be turned off, and the mechanisms for this are wonderfully precise and quick. If I had to design an ecosystem in which creatures had to live off each other and in which dying was an indispensable part of living, I could not think of a better way to manage.

▶   QUESTIONS TO CONSIDER

1. Because Thomas is a well-known scientist as well as a writer, many readers recognize his name and thus know he is qualified to write on the subject of death. However, even readers who do not recognize Thomas's name usually find him believable. How does he establish his credibility in this essay?

2. Thomas supports his argument by citing his own personal experiences and observations. Is his evidence convincing? Is he justified in making the claim that all death is natural on the basis of the evidence he cites?

3. What appeals does Thomas use most effectively in this essay? What assumptions does he make?

4. This essay, as Thomas readily admits, is largely speculative. That is, he does not pretend to know for sure that what he is arguing is actually true. Is the speculative nature of the essay one reason why Thomas does not include logical appeals? Is Thomas successful in convincing you of his arguments even though they are mainly speculation? Why or why not?

5. What does Thomas mean by *natural* death? Define the term as he uses it.

6. Do you agree with Thomas that the death of a person is like the death of an animal or plant?

WRITING ACTIVITIES

Individual: Write a journal entry in which you describe the death of a person, animal, or plant that you have closely observed. On the basis of your observations, come to some conclusion about death.

Collaborative: Discuss Thomas's argument that all death is natural. Make a list of the evidence that Thomas uses to support his argument. Then analyze the evidence on the list to decide if it is valid. Write a brief conclusion, stating whether your group accepts or rejects Thomas's argument and why.

Computer: Using the journal entry in which you described the death of a person, animal, or plant that you closely observed, freewrite at the computer, focusing on the feelings generated by this experience. Concentrate on emotions rather than logic as you write. Then reread your freewriting and identify one sentence that seems to express most accurately how you feel about this experience. Using this sentence as a topic sentence, develop and simplify this idea into a paragraph or brief essay.

THE DAY CARE DEMONS:
MAKE YOUR OWN STATISTICS

Susan Faludi

*This selection is part of a book by Susan Faludi enti-
tled* Backlash: The Undeclared War Against American
Women. *Faludi's book is one of many feminist books
to appear in recent years. Faludi argues in this piece
that statistics about day care have been used irresponsibly by both politicians and the press. But
Faludi's larger purpose is to argue that this misrepresentation of day-care studies and statistics has been
used to discourage females from entering the work
force—to keep them in the home.*

1   The anti–day care headlines practically shrieked in the '80s:
"MOMMY, DON'T LEAVE ME HERE!" THE DAY CARE PARENTS DON'T SEE. DAY CARE
CAN BE DANGEROUS TO YOUR CHILD'S HEALTH. WHEN CHILD CARE BECOMES
CHILD MOLESTING: IT HAPPENS MORE OFTEN THAN PARENTS LIKE TO THINK. CREEP-
ING CHILD CARE . . . CREEPY.

2   The spokesmen of the New Right, of course, were most denunci-
atory, labeling day care "the Thalidomide of the '80s." Reagan's men
didn't mince words either, like the top military official who pro-
claimed, "American mothers who work and send their children to faceless centers rather than stay home to take care of them are weakening
the moral fiber of the Nation." But the press, more subtly but just as
persistently, painted devil's horns both on mothers who use day care
and day care workers themselves.

3   In 1984, a *Newsweek* feature warned of an "epidemic" of child
abuse in child care facilities, based on allegations against directors at a
few day care centers—the most celebrated of which were later found
innocent in the courts. Just in case the threat had slipped women's
minds, two weeks later *Newsweek* was busy once more, demanding
"What Price Day Care?" in a cover story. The cover picture featured a
frightened, saucer-eyed child sucking his thumb. By way of edifying
contrast, the eight-page treatment inside showcased a Good Mother—
under the title "At Home by Choice." The former bond seller had
dropped her career to be home with her baby and offer wifely assis-

tance to her husband's career. "I had to admit I couldn't do [every-thing]," the mother said, a view that clearly earned an approving nod from *Newsweek*. Still later, in a special issue devoted to the family, *Newsweek* ran another article on "the dark side of day care." That story repeatedly alluded to "more and more evidence that child care may be hazardous to a youngster's health," but never got around to provid-ing it. This campaign was one the press managed to conduct all by itself. Researchers were having a tough time linking day care with deviance. So the press circulated some antiquated "research" and ignored the rest.

At a press conference in the spring of 1988, the University of New   4
Hampshire's Family Research Laboratory released the largest and most comprehensive study ever on sexual abuse in day care centers—a three-year study examining the reported cases of sexual abuse at day care facilities across the country. One would have assumed from the swarm of front-page stories on this apparent threat that the researchers' findings would rate as an important news event. But the *New York Times* response was typical: it noted the study's release in a modest article on the same page as the classifieds. (Ironically, it ran on the same page as an even smaller story about a Wisconsin father beating his four-year-old son so brutally that the child had to be institutional-ized for the rest of his life for brain injuries.) Why such little interest? The study concluded that there was no epidemic of child abuse at day care centers. In fact, if there was an abuse crisis anywhere, the study pointed out, it was at home—where the risk to children of molestation is almost twice as high as in day care. In 1985, there were nearly 100,000 reported cases of children sexually abused by family members (mostly fathers, stepfathers, or older brothers), compared with about 1,300 cases in day care. Children are far more likely to be beaten, too, at the family hearth, the researchers found; and the physical abuse at home tends to be of a longer duration, more severe and more traumatic than any violence children faced in day care centers. In 1986, 1,500 children died from abuse at home. "Day care is not an inherently high-risk locale for children, despite frightening stories in the media," the Family Research Laboratory study's authors concluded. "The risk of abuse is not sufficient reason to avoid day care in general or to justify parents' withdrawing from the labor force."

Research over the last two decades has consistently found that if   5
day care has any long-term effect on children, it seems to make chil-dren slightly more gregarious and independent. Day care children also appear to be more broad-minded about sex roles; girls interviewed in

day care centers are more likely to believe that housework and child rearing should be shared by both parents. A National Academy of Sciences panel in 1982 concluded that children suffer no ill effects in academic, social, or emotional development when mothers work.

6   Yet the day care "statistics" that received the most press in the '80s were the ones based more on folklore than research. Illness, for example, was supposedly more pervasive in day care centers than in the home, according to media accounts. Yet, the actual studies on child care and illness indicate that while children in day care are initially prone to more illnesses, they soon build up immunities and actually get sick less often than kids at home. Day care's threat to bonding between mother and child was another popular myth. But the research offers scant evidence of diminished bonds between mother and child—and suggests that children profit from exposure to a wider range of grown-ups, anyway. (No one ever worries, it seems, about day care's threat to paternal bonding.)

7   With no compelling demographic evidence to support an attack on day care for toddlers, critics of day care turned their attention to infants. Three-year-old toddlers may survive day care, they argued, but newborns would surely suffer permanent damage. Their evidence, however, came from studies conducted on European children in wartime orphanages and war refugee camps—environments that were hardly the equivalent of contemporary day care centers, even the worst variety. One of the most commonly quoted studies in the press wasn't even conducted on human beings. Psychologist Harry Harlow found that "infants" in day care suffer severe emotional distress. His subjects, however, were baby monkeys. And his "day care workers" weren't even surrogate adult monkeys: the researchers used wire-mesh dummies.

8   Finally in 1986, it looked as if day care critics had some hard data they could use. Pennsylvania State University psychologist and social researcher Jay Belsky, a prominent supporter of day care, expressed some reservations about day care infants. Up until this point, Belsky had said that his reviews of the child development literature yielded few if any significant differences between children raised at home and in day care. Then, in the September 1986 issue of the child care newsletter *Zero to Three*, Belsky proposed that placing children in day care for more than twenty hours a week in their first year of life may pose a "risk factor" that could lead to an "insecure" attachment to their mothers. The press and conservative politicians hurried to the scene. Soon Belsky found himself making the network rounds—"Today,"

"CBS Morning News," and "Donahue"—and fielding dozens of press calls a month. And, much to the liberal Belsky's discomfort, "conservatives embraced me." Right-wing scholars cited his findings. Conservative politicians sought out his Congressional testimony at child care hearings—and got furious when he failed to spout "what they wanted me to say."

Belsky peppered his report on infant day care with qualifications, strongly cautioned against overreaction, and advised that he had only a "trickle," "not a flood," of evidence. He wrote that only a "relatively persuasive *circumstantial* [all italics are his] case can be made that early infant care *may* be associated with increased avoidance of mother, *possibly* to the point of greater insecurity in the attachment relationship." And he added, "I cannot state strongly enough that there is sufficient evidence to lead a judicious scientist to doubt this line of reasoning." Finally, in every press interview, as he recalls later, he stressed the many caveats and emphasized that his findings underscored the need for better funding and standards for child care centers, not grounds for eliminating day care. "I was not saying we shouldn't have day care," he says. "I was saying that we need *good* day care. Quality matters." But his words "fell on deaf ears." And once the misrepresentations of his work passed into the media, it seemed impossible to root them out. "What amazed me was the journalists just plagiarized each other's newspaper stories. Very few of them actually read my article."

What also got less attention in the press was the actual evidence Belsky used to support his tentative reassessment. He focused on four studies—any of which, as he himself conceded, "could be dismissed for a variety of scientific reasons." The first study was based on one center that mostly served poor welfare mothers with unplanned pregnancies—and so it was impossible to say whether the children were having trouble because they went to day care or because they had such grim and impecunious home lives. Belsky said he had evidence from more middleclass populations, too, but the authors of the two key studies he used later maintained that he has misread their data. University of North Carolina psychologist Ron Haskins, author of one of the studies on the effects of day care on aggression, flatly stated in a subsequent issue of *Zero to Three* that "my results will not support these conclusions." Belsky alluded to a final study to support his position that infants in day care might be "less compliant" when they get older. But he failed to mention the study's follow-up review, in which the authors rather drastically revised their assessment. Later behavioral problems, the researchers wrote, "were not predicted by whether the toddler had been in day care or at home" after all. In response, Belsky says that it all depends on how one chooses to read the data in that study. Like so many of the "findings" in this politically charged field of research, he says, "It is all a question of, is the glass half full or half empty?"

11   Social scientists *could* supply plenty of research to show that one member of the American family, at least, is happier and more well adjusted when mom stays home and minds the children. But that person is dad—a finding of limited use to backlash publicists. Anyway, by the end of the decade the press was no longer even demanding hard data to make its case. By then the public was so steeped in the lore of the backlash that its spokesmen rarely bothered to round up the usual statistics. Who needed proof? Everybody already believed that the myths about '80s women were true.

▶   QUESTIONS TO CONSIDER

1. Does Faludi convince you that statistics can be used irresponsibly and unscrupulously? Why or why not?

2. Does she convince you that the irresponsible use of day-care statistics has been motivated by the "backlash" against women? Why or why not?

3. Faludi states that one study concluded "that there was no epidemic of child abuse at day care centers." What constitutes an epidemic of child abuse? What connotations does the word *epidemic* have? What other term or terms could she have used to express this concept more precisely and more neutrally?

4. Faludi identifies most of the studies and articles she cites only partially. In one case, for example, she merely refers to "actual studies on child care and illness" rather than telling her readers exactly which studies. Under what circumstances would a reader need more exact information about her sources? Would more exact information have been more convincing? More useful? Why or why not?

5. Faludi is clearly arguing that existing studies of day care are seriously flawed and, even worse, misrepresented. She uses the word *evidence* frequently—criticizing those whose evidence is not valid or accurate. What evidence does Faludi include to support her own arguments?

WRITING ACTIVITIES   ◀

Individual: Write a letter to Faludi, agreeing or disagreeing with her position.

Collaborative: Discuss your individual responses to this selection. Then, as a group, identify the major strengths and weaknesses of Faludi's arguments and write a paragraph summarizing your conclusions.

Computer: Type into a computer the summary paragraph generated by your group for the collaborative activity. Expand your group's paragraph into your own individual critique of Faludi's arguments. Format the group paragraph by separating each sentence from the rest of the paragraph with several line spaces. Use each of these summary sentences as the topic sentence for a new paragraph that elaborates on the major strengths and weaknesses of Faludi's arguments.

LETTER FROM BIRMINGHAM JAIL

Martin Luther King, Jr.

Martin Luther King, Jr., was a clergyman and writer but is best known as a leader of the civil rights movement in the 1960s. He was awarded the Nobel Peace Prize in 1964 in recognition of his efforts to end segregation and to ensure the civil rights of African-Americans in the United States. King was assassinated in 1968 in Memphis, Tennessee.

King's effectiveness as a leader was in no small part the result of his ability to speak and write persuasively. He wrote the following letter in response to a public statement issued by eight Alabama clergymen following a peaceful civil rights demonstration in Birmingham in which a number of the demonstrators, including King, were arrested. In the statement, the clergymen deplored the "unwise and untimely" demonstrations led by "outsiders" and encouraged African-Americans to "withdraw support from these demonstrations, and to unite locally in working peacefully for a better Birmingham." King's letter explains, patiently and persuasively, his view of this situation—his vision of what had happened and why it had to happen as it did.

Public Statement
by Eight Alabama Clergymen

April 12, 1963

1   We the undersigned clergymen are among those who, in January, issued "An Appeal for Law and Order and Common Sense," in dealing with racial problems in Alabama. We expressed understanding that honest convictions in racial matters could properly be pursued in the courts, but urged that decisions of those courts should in the meantime be peacefully obeyed.

2   Since that time there had been some evidence of increased forbearance and a willingness to face facts. Responsible citizens have undertaken to work on various problems which cause racial friction and unrest. In Birmingham, recent public events have given indication that we all have opportunity for a new constructive and realistic approach to racial problems.

3   However, we are now confronted by a series of demonstrations by some of our Negro citizens, directed and led in part by outsiders. We recognize the natural impatience of people who feel that their hopes are slow in being realized. But we are convinced that these demonstrations are unwise and untimely.

4   We agree rather with certain local Negro leadership which has called for honest and open negotiation of racial issues in our area. And we believe this kind of facing of issues can best be accomplished by citizens of our own metropolitan area, white and Negro, meeting with their knowledge and experience of the local situation. All of us need to face that responsibility and find proper channels for its accomplishment.

5   Just as we formerly pointed out that "hatred and violence have no sanction in our religious and political traditions," we also point out that such actions as incite to hatred and violence, however technically peaceful those actions may be, have not contributed to the resolution of our local problems. We do not believe that these days of new hope are days when extreme measures are justified in Birmingham.

6   We commend the community as a whole, and the local news media and law enforcement officials in particular, on the calm manner in which these demonstrations have been handled. We urge the public to continue to show restraint should the demonstrations continue, and the law enforcement officials to remain calm and continue to protect our city from violence.

We further strongly urge our own Negro community to withdraw   7
support from these demonstrations, and to unite locally in working
peacefully for a better Birmingham. When rights are consistently
denied, a cause should be pressed in the courts and in negotiations
among local leaders, and not in the streets. We appeal to both our
white and Negro citizenry to observe the principles of law and order
and common sense.

Signed by:

C. C. J. Carpenter, D.D., LL.D.,
Bishop of Alabama
Joseph A. Durick, D.D.,
Auxiliary Bishop, Diocese of Mobile, Birmingham
Rabbi Milton L. Grafman,
Temple Emanu-El, Birmingham, Alabama
Bishop Paul Hardin,
Bishop of the Alabama-West Florida Conference
of the Methodist Church
Bishop Nolan B. Harmon,
Bishop of the North Alabama Conference
of the Methodist Church
George M. Murray, D.D., LL.D.,
Bishop Coadjutor, Episcopal Diocese of Alabama
Edward V. Ramage,
Moderator, Synod of the Alabama Presbyterian Church
in the United States
Earl Stallings,
Pastor, First Baptist Church, Birmingham, Alabama

Letter from Birmingham Jail

April 16, 1963

My Dear Fellow Clergymen: 1
        While confined here in the Birmingham city jail, I came across
your recent statement calling my present activities "unwise and
untimely." Seldom do I pause to answer criticism of my work and
ideas. If I sought to answer all the criticisms that cross my desk, my
secretaries would have little time for anything other than such corre-

spondence in the course of the day, and I would have no time for constructive work. But since I feel that you are men of genuine good will
and that your criticisms are sincerely set forth, I want to try to answer
your statement in what I hope will be patient and reasonable terms.

2   I think I should indicate why I am here in Birmingham, since you
have been influenced by the view which argues against "outsiders
coming in." I have the honor of serving as president of the Southern
Christian Leadership Conference, an organization operating in every
southern state, with headquarters in Atlanta, Georgia. We have some
eighty-five affiliated organizations across the South, and one of them is
the Alabama Christian Movement for Human Rights. Frequently we
share staff, educational and financial resources with our affiliates.
Several months ago the affiliate here in Birmingham asked us to be on
call to engage in a nonviolent direct-action program if such were
deemed necessary. We readily consented, and when the hour came we
lived up to our promise. So I, along with several members of my staff,
am here because I was invited here. I am here because I have organizational ties here.

3   But more basically, I am in Birmingham because injustice is here.
Just as the prophets of the eighth century B.C. left their villages and
carried their "thus saith the Lord" far beyond the boundaries of their
home towns, and just as the Apostle Paul left his village of Tarsus and
carried the gospel of Jesus Christ to the far corners of the Greco-
Roman world, so am I compelled to carry the gospel of freedom
beyond my own home town. Like Paul, I must constantly respond to
the Macedonian call for aid.

4   Moreover, I am cognizant of the interrelatedness of all communities and states. I cannot sit idly by in Atlanta and not be concerned
about what happens in Birmingham. Injustice anywhere is a threat to
justice everywhere. We are caught in an inescapable network of mutu-
ality, tied in a single garment of destiny. Whatever affects one directly,
affects all indirectly. Never again can we afford to live with the narrow, provincial "outside agitator" idea. Anyone who lives inside the
United States can never be considered an outsider anywhere within
its bounds.

5   You deplore the demonstrations taking place in Birmingham. But
your statement, I am sorry to say, fails to express a similar concern for
the conditions that brought about the demonstrations. I am sure that
none of you would want to rest content with the superficial kind of
social analysis that deals merely with effects and does not grapple with

underlying causes. It is unfortunate that demonstrations are taking place in Birmingham, but it is even more unfortunate that the city's white power structure left the Negro community with no alternative.

In any nonviolent campaign there are four basic steps: collection   6
of the facts to determine whether injustices exist; negotiation; self-purification; and direct action. We have gone through all these steps in Birmingham. There can be no gainsaying the fact that racial injustice engulfs this community. Birmingham is probably the most thoroughly segregated city in the United States. Its ugly record of brutality is widely known. Negroes have experienced grossly unjust treatment in the courts. There have been more unsolved bombings of Negro homes and churches in Birmingham than in any other city in the nation. These are the hard, brutal facts of the case. On the basis of these conditions, Negro leaders sought to negotiate with the city fathers. But the latter consistently refused to engage in good-faith negotiation.

Then, last September, came the opportunity to talk with leaders   7
of Birmingham's economic community. In the course of the negotiations, certain promises were made by the merchants—for example, to remove the stores' humiliating racial signs. On the basis of these promises, the Reverend Fred Shuttlesworth and the leaders of the Alabama Christian Movement for Human Rights agreed to a moratorium on all demonstrations. As the weeks and months went by, we realized that we were the victims of a broken promise. A few signs, briefly removed, returned; the others remained.

As in so many past experiences, our hopes had been blasted, and   8
the shadow of deep disappointment settled upon us. We had no alternative except to prepare for direct action, whereby we would present our very bodies as a means of laying our case before the conscience of the local and the national community. Mindful of the difficulties involved, we decided to undertake a process of self-purification. We began a series of workshops on nonviolence, and we repeatedly asked ourselves: "Are you able to accept blows without retaliating?" "Are you able to endure the ordeal of jail?" We decided to schedule our direct-action program for the Easter season, realizing that except for Christmas, this is the main shopping period of the year. Knowing that a strong economic-withdrawal program would be the by-product of direct action, we felt that this would be the best time to bring pressure to bear on the merchants for the needed change.

Then it occurred to us that Birmingham's mayoral election was   9
coming up in March, and we speedily decided to postpone action until

after election day. When we discovered that the Commissioner of Public Safety, Eugene "Bull" Connor, had piled up enough votes to be in the run-off, we decided again to postpone action until the day after the run-off so that the demonstrations could not be used to cloud the issues. Like many others, we waited to see Mr. Connor defeated, and to this end we endured postponement after postponement. Having aided in this community need, we felt that our direct action program could be delayed no longer.

10   You may well ask: "Why direct action? Why sit-ins, marches and so forth? Isn't negotiation a better path?" You are quite right in calling for negotiation. Indeed, this is the very purpose of a direct action. Nonviolent direct action seeks to create such a crisis and foster such a tension that a community which has constantly refused to negotiate is forced to confront the issue. It seeks so to dramatize the issue that it can no longer be ignored. My citing the creation of tension as part of the work of the nonviolent-resister may sound rather shocking. But I must confess that I am not afraid of the word "tension." I have earnestly opposed violent tension, but there is a type of constructive, nonviolent tension which is necessary for growth. Just as Socrates felt that it was necessary to create a tension in the mind so that individuals could rise from the bondage of myths and half-truths to the unfettered realm of creative analysis and objective appraisal, so must we see the need for nonviolent gadflies to create the kind of tension in society that will help men rise from the dark depths of prejudice and racism to the majestic heights of understanding and brotherhood.

11   The purpose of our direct-action program is to create a situation so crisis-packed that it will inevitably open the door to negotiation. I therefore concur with you in your call for negotiation. Too long has our beloved Southland been bogged down in a tragic effort to live in monologue rather than dialogue.

12   One of the basic points in your statement is that the action that I and my associates have taken in Birmingham is untimely. Some have asked: "Why didn't you give the new city administration time to act?" The only answer that I can give to this query is that the new Birmingham administration must be prodded about as much as the outgoing one, before it will act. We are sadly mistaken if we feel that the election of Albert Boutwell as mayor will bring the millennium to Birmingham. While Mr. Boutwell is a much more gentle person than Mr. Connor, they are both segregationists, dedicated to maintenance of the status quo. I have hope that Mr. Boutwell will be reasonable

enough to see the futility of massive resistance to desegregation. But
he will not see this without pressure from devotees of civil rights. My
friends, I must say to you that we have not made a single gain in civil
rights without determined legal and nonviolent pressure. Lamentably,
it is an historical fact that privileged groups seldom give up their privi-
leges voluntarily. Individuals may see the moral light and voluntarily
give up their unjust posture; but, as Reinhold Niebuhr has reminded
us, groups tend to be more immoral than individuals.

We know through painful experience that freedom is never vol-   13
untarily given by the oppressor; it must be demanded by the
oppressed. Frankly, I have yet to engage in a direct-action campaign
that was "well-timed" in the view of those who have not suffered
unduly from the disease of segregation. For years now I have heard
the word "Wait!" It rings in the ear of every Negro with piercing familiarity. This "Wait" has almost always meant "Never." We must come to
see, with one of our distinguished jurists, that "justice too long delayed
is justice denied."

We have waited for more than 340 years for our constitutional   14
and God-given rights. The nations of Asia and Africa are moving with
jetlike speed toward gaining political independence, but we still creep
at horse-and-buggy pace toward gaining a cup of coffee at a lunch
counter. Perhaps it is easy for those who have never felt the stinging
darts of segregation to say, "Wait." But when you have seen vicious
mobs lynch your mothers and fathers at will and drown your sisters
and brothers at whim; when you have seen hate-filled policemen
curse, kick and even kill your black brothers and sisters; when you
see the vast majority of your twenty million Negro brothers smother-
ing in an airtight cage of poverty in the midst of an affluent society;
when you suddenly find your tongue twisted and your speech stam-
mering as you seek to explain to your six-year-old daughter why she
can't go to the public amusement park that has just been advertised
on television, and see tears welling up in her eyes when she is told
that Funtown is closed to colored children, and see ominous clouds
of inferiority beginning to form in her little mental sky, and see her
beginning to distort her personality by developing an unconscious bitterness toward white people; when you have to concoct an answer
for a five-year-old son who is asking: "Daddy, why do white people
treat colored people so mean?"; when you take a cross-country drive
and find it necessary to sleep night after night in the uncomfortable
corners of your automobile because no motel will accept you; when

you are humiliated day in and day out by nagging signs reading "white" and "colored"; when your first name becomes "nigger," your middle name becomes "boy" (however old you are) and your last name becomes "John," and your wife and mother are never given the respected title "Mrs.", when you are harried by day and haunted by night by the fact that you are a Negro, living constantly at tiptoe stance, never quite knowing what to expect next, and are plagued with inner fears and outer resentments; when you are forever fighting a degenerating sense of "nobodiness"—then you will understand why we find it difficult to wait. There comes a time when the cup of endurance runs over, and men are no longer willing to be plunged into the abyss of despair. I hope, sirs, you can understand our legitimate and unavoidable impatience.

15   You express a great deal of anxiety over our willingness to break laws. This is certainly a legitimate concern. Since we so diligently urge people to obey the Supreme Court's decision of 1954 outlawing segregation in the public schools, at first glance it may seem rather paradoxical for us consciously to break laws. One may well ask: "How can you advocate breaking some laws and obeying others?" The answer lies in the fact that there are two types of laws: just and unjust. I would be the first to advocate obeying just laws. One has not only a legal but a moral responsibility to obey just laws. Conversely, one has a moral responsibility to disobey unjust laws. I would agree with St. Augustine that "an unjust law is no law at all."

16   Now, what is the difference between the two? How does one determine whether a law is just or unjust? A just law is a man-made code that squares with the moral law or the law of God. An unjust law is a code that is out of harmony with the moral law. To put it in the terms of St. Thomas Aquinas: An unjust law is a human law that is not rooted in eternal law and natural law. Any law that uplifts human personality is just. Any law that degrades human personality is unjust. All segregation statutes are unjust because segregation distorts the soul and damages the personality. It gives the segregator a false sense of superiority and the segregated a false sense of inferiority. Segregation, to use the terminology of the Jewish philosopher Martin Buber, substitutes an "I–it" relationship for an "I–thou" relationship and ends up relegating persons to the status of things. Hence segregation is not only politically, economically and sociologically unsound, it is morally wrong and sinful. Paul Tillich has said that sin is separation. Is not segregation an existential expression of man's tragic separation, his awful

estrangement, his terrible sinfulness? Thus it is that I can urge men to obey the 1954 decision of the Supreme Court, for it is morally right; and I can urge them to disobey segregation ordinances, for they are morally wrong.

Let us consider a more concrete example of just and unjust laws.   17
An unjust law is a code that a numerical or power majority group compels a minority group to obey but does not make binding on itself. This is *difference* made legal. By the same token, a just law is a code that a majority compels a minority to follow and that it is willing to follow itself. This is *sameness* made legal.

Let me give another explanation. A law is unjust if it is inflicted on   18
a minority that, as a result of being denied the right to vote, had no part in enacting or devising the law. Who can say that the legislature of Alabama which set up that state's segregation laws was democratically elected? Throughout Alabama all sorts of devious methods are used to prevent Negroes from becoming registered voters, and there are some counties in which, even though Negroes constitute a majority of the population, not a single Negro is registered. Can any law enacted under such circumstances be considered democratically structured?

Sometimes a law is just on its face and unjust in its application.   19
For instance, I have been arrested on a charge of parading without a permit. Now, there is nothing wrong in having an ordinance which requires a permit for a parade. But such an ordinance becomes unjust when it is used to maintain segregation and to deny citizens the First-Amendment privilege of peaceful assembly and protest.

I hope you are able to see the distinction I am trying to point   20
out. In no sense do I advocate evading or defying the law, as would the rabid segregationist. That would lead to anarchy. One who breaks an unjust law must do so openly, lovingly, and with a willingness to accept the penalty. I submit that an individual who breaks a law that conscience tells him is unjust, and who willingly accepts the penalty of imprisonment in order to arouse the conscience of the community over its injustice, is in reality expressing the highest respect for law.

Of course, there is nothing new about this kind of civil disobedi-   21
ence. It was evidenced sublimely in the refusal of Shadrach, Meshach and Abednego to obey the laws of Nebuchadnezzar, on the ground that a higher moral law was at stake. It was practiced superbly by the early Christians, who were willing to face hungry lions and the excruciating pain of chopping blocks rather than submit to certain unjust laws of the Roman Empire. To a degree, academic freedom is a reality today

because Socrates practiced civil disobedience. In our own nation, the Boston Tea Party represented a massive act of civil disobedience.

22   We should never forget that everything Adolf Hitler did in Germany was "legal" and everything the Hungarian freedom fighters did in Hungary was "illegal." It was "illegal" to aid and comfort a Jew in Hitler's Germany. Even so, I am sure that, had I lived in Germany at the time, I would have aided and comforted my Jewish brothers. If today I lived in a Communist country where certain principles dear to the Christian faith are suppressed, I would openly advocate disobeying that country's antireligious laws.

23   I must make two honest confessions to you, my Christian and Jewish brothers. First, I must confess that over the past few years I have been gravely disappointed with the white moderate. I have almost reached the regrettable conclusion that the Negro's great stumbling block in his stride toward freedom is not the White Citizen's Counciler or the Ku Klux Klanner, but the white moderate, who is more devoted to "order" than to justice; who prefers a negative peace which is the absence of tension to a positive peace which is the presence of justice; who constantly says: "I agree with you in the goal you seek, but I cannot agree with your methods of direct action"; who paternalistically believes he can set the timetable for another man's freedom; who lives by a mythical concept of time and who constantly advises the Negro to wait for a "more convenient season." Shallow understanding from people of good will is more frustrating than absolute misunderstanding from people of ill will. Lukewarm acceptance is much more bewildering than outright rejection.

24   I had hoped that the white moderate would understand that law and order exist for the purpose of establishing justice and that when they fail in this purpose they become the dangerously structured dams that block the flow of social progress. I had hoped that the white moderate would understand that the present tension in the South is a necessary phase of the transition from an obnoxious negative peace, in which the Negro passively accepted his unjust plight, to a substantive and positive peace, in which all men will respect the dignity and worth of human personality. Actually, we who engage in nonviolent direct action are not the creators of tension. We merely bring to the surface the hidden tension that is already alive. We bring it out in the open, where it can be seen and dealt with. Like a boil that can never be cured so long as it is covered up but must be opened with all its ugliness to the natural medicines of air and light, injustice must be

exposed, with all the tension its exposure creates, to the light of human conscience and the air of national opinion before it can be cured.

In your statement you assert that our actions, even though peaceful, must be condemned because they precipitate violence. But is this a logical assertion? Isn't this like condemning a robbed man because his possession of money precipitated the evil act of robbery? Isn't this like condemning Socrates because his unswerving commitment to truth and his philosophical inquiries precipitated the act by the misguided populace in which they made him drink hemlock? Isn't this like condemning Jesus because his unique God-consciousness and never-ceasing devotion to God's will precipitated the evil act of crucifixion? We must come to see that, as the federal courts have consistently affirmed, it is wrong to urge an individual to cease his efforts to gain his basic constitutional rights because the quest may precipitate violence. Society must protect the robbed and punish the robber.   25

I had also hoped that the white moderate would reject the myth concerning time in relation to the struggle for freedom. I have just received a letter from a white brother in Texas. He writes: "All Christians know that the colored people will receive equal rights eventually, but it is possible that you are in too great a religious hurry. It has taken Christianity almost two thousand years to accomplish what it has. The teachings of Christ take time to come to earth." Such an attitude stems from a tragic misconception of time, from the strangely irrational notion that there is something in the very flow of time that will inevitably cure all ills. Actually, time itself is neutral; it can be used either destructively or constructively. More and more I feel that the people of ill will have used time much more effectively than have the people of good will. We will have to repent in this generation not merely for the hateful words and actions of the bad people but for the appalling silence of the good people. Human progress never rolls in on wheels of inevitability; it comes through the tireless efforts of men willing to be co-workers with God, and without this hard work, time itself becomes an ally of the forces of social stagnation. We must use time creatively, in the knowledge that time is always ripe to do right. Now is the time to make real the promise of democracy and transform our pending national elegy into a creative psalm of brotherhood. Now is the time to lift our national policy from the quicksand of racial injustice to the solid rock of human dignity.   26

You speak of our activity in Birmingham as extreme. At first I was rather disappointed that fellow clergymen would see my nonviolent   27 efforts as those of an extremist. I began thinking about the fact that I stand in the middle of two opposing forces in the Negro community. One is a force of complacency, made up in part of Negroes who, as a result of long years of oppression, are so drained of self-respect and a sense of "somebodiness" that they have adjusted to segregation; and in part of a few middle-class Negroes who, because of a degree of academic and economic security and because in some ways they profit by segregation, have become insensitive to the problems of the masses. The other force is one of bitterness and hatred, and it comes perilously close to advocating violence. It is expressed in the various black nationalist groups that are springing up across the nation, the largest and best-known being Elijah Muhammad's Muslim movement. Nourished by the Negro's frustration over the continued existence of racial discrimination, this movement is made up of people who have lost faith in America, who have absolutely repudiated Christianity, and who have concluded that the white man is an incorrigible "devil."

28   I have tried to stand between these two forces, saying that we need to emulate neither the "do-nothingism" of the complacent nor the hatred and despair of the black nationalist. For there is the more excellent way of love and nonviolent protest. I am grateful to God that, through the influence of the Negro church, the way of nonviolence became an integral part of our struggle.

29   If this philosophy had not emerged, by now many streets of the South would, I am convinced, be flowing with blood. And I am further convinced that if our white brothers dismiss as "rabble-rousers" and "outside agitators" those of us who employ nonviolent direct action, and if they refuse to support our nonviolent efforts, millions of Negroes will, out of frustration and despair, seek solace and security in black-nationalist ideologies—a development that would inevitably lead to a frightening racial nightmare.

30   Oppressed people cannot remain oppressed forever. The yearning for freedom eventually manifests itself, and that is what has happened to the American Negro. Something within has reminded him of his birthright of freedom, and something without has reminded him that it can be gained. Consciously or unconsciously, he has been caught up by the *Zeitgeist*, and with his black brothers of Africa and his brown and yellow brothers of Asia, South America and the Caribbean, the United States Negro is moving with a sense of great urgency toward the promised land of racial justice. If one recognizes this vital urge that has engulfed the Negro community, one should

readily understand why public demonstrations are taking place. The Negro has many pent-up resentments and latent frustrations, and he must release them. So let him march; let him make prayer pilgrimages to the city hall; let him go on freedom rides—and try to understand why he must do so. If his repressed emotions are not released in non-violent ways, they will seek expression through violence; this is not a threat but a fact of history. So I have not said to my people: "Get rid of your discontent." Rather, I have tried to say that this normal and healthy discontent can be channeled into the creative outlet of nonvio-lent direct action. And now this approach is being termed extremist.

But though I was initially disappointed at being categorized as an   31
extremist, as I continued to think about the matter I gradually gained a measure of satisfaction from the label. Was not Jesus an extremist for love: "Love your enemies, bless them that curse you, do good to them that hate you, and pray for them which despitefully use you, and perse-cute you." Was not Amos an extremist for justice: "Let justice roll down like waters and righteousness like an ever-flowing stream." Was not Paul an extremist for the Christian gospel: "I bear in my body the marks of the Lord Jesus." Was not Martin Luther an extremist: "Here I stand; I cannot do otherwise, so help me God." And John Bunyan: "I will stay in jail to the end of my days before I make a butchery of my con-science." And Abraham Lincoln: "This nation cannot survive half slave and half free." And Thomas Jefferson: "We hold these truths to be self-evident, that all men are created equal . . ." So the question is not whether we will be extremists, but what kind of extremists we will be. Will we be extremists for hate or for love? Will we be extremists for the preservation of injustice or for the extension of justice? In that dramatic scene on Calvary's hill three men were crucified. We must never forget that all three were crucified for the same crime—the crime of extrem-ism. Two were extremists for immorality, and thus fell below their envi-ronment. The other, Jesus Christ, was an extremist for love, truth and goodness, and thereby rose above his environment. Perhaps the South, the nation and the world are in dire need of creative extremists.

I had hoped that the white moderate would see this need.   32
Perhaps I was too optimistic; perhaps I expected too much. I suppose I should have realized that few members of the oppressor race can understand the deep groans and passionate yearnings of the oppressed race, and still fewer have the vision to see that injustice must be rooted out by strong, persistent and determined action. I am thankful, however, that some of our white brothers in the South have

grasped the meaning of this social revolution and committed themselves to it. They are still all too few in quantity, but they are big in quality. Some—such as Ralph McGill, Lillian Smith, Harry Golden, James McBride Dabbs, Ann Braden and Sarah Patton Boyle—have written about our struggle in eloquent and prophetic terms. Others have marched with us down nameless streets of the South. They have languished in filthy, roach-infested jails, suffering the abuse and brutality of policemen who view them as "dirty nigger-lovers." Unlike so many of their moderate brothers and sisters, they have recognized the urgency of the moment and sensed the need for powerful "action" antidotes to combat the disease of segregation.

33   Let me take note of my other major disappointment. I have been so greatly disappointed with the white church and its leadership. Of course, there are some notable exceptions. I am not unmindful of the fact that each of you has taken some significant stands on this issue. I commend you, Reverend Stallings, for your Christian stand on this past Sunday, in welcoming Negroes to your worship service on a nonsegregated basis. I commend the Catholic leaders of this state for integrating Spring Hill College several years ago.

34   But despite these notable exceptions, I must honestly reiterate that I have been disappointed with the church. I do not say this as one of those negative critics who can always find something wrong with the church. I say this as a minister of the gospel, who loves the church; who was nurtured in its bosom; who has been sustained by its spiritual blessings and who will remain true to it as long as the cord of life shall lengthen.

35   When I was suddenly catapulted into the leadership of the bus protest in Montgomery, Alabama, a few years ago, I felt we would be supported by the white church. I felt that the white ministers, priests and rabbis of the South would be among our strongest allies. Instead, some have been outright opponents, refusing to understand the freedom movement and misrepresenting its leaders; all too many others have been more cautious than courageous and have remained silent behind the anesthetizing security of stained-glass windows.

36   In spite of my shattered dreams, I came to Birmingham with the hope that the white religious leaders of this community would see the justice of our cause and, with deep moral concern, would serve as the channel through which our just grievances could reach the power structure. I had hoped that each of you would understand. But again I have been disappointed.

I have heard numerous southern religious leaders admonish their   37
worshipers to comply with a desegregation decision because it is the
law, but I have longed to hear white ministers declare: "Follow this
decree because integration is morally right and because the Negro is
your brother." In the midst of blatant injustices inflicted upon the
Negro, I have watched white churchmen stand on the sideline and
mouth pious irrelevancies and sanctimonious trivialities. In the midst
of a mighty struggle to rid our nation of racial and economic injustice,
I have heard many ministers say: "Those are social issues, with which
the gospel has no real concern." And I have watched many churches
commit themselves to a completely otherworldly religion which makes
a strange, un-Biblical distinction between body and soul, between the
sacred and the secular.

I have traveled the length and breadth of Alabama, Mississippi   38
and all the other southern states. On sweltering summer days and crisp
autumn mornings I have looked at the South's beautiful churches with
their lofty spires pointing heavenward. I have beheld the impressive
outlines of her massive religious-education buildings. Over and over I
have found myself asking: "What kind of people worship here? Who is
their God? Where were their voices when the lips of Governor Barnett
dripped with words of interposition and nullification? Where were they
when Governor Wallace gave a clarion call for defiance and hatred?
Where were their voices of support when bruised and weary Negro
men and women decided to rise from the dark dungeons of complacency to the bright hills of creative protest?"

Yes, these questions are still in my mind. In deep disappointment   39
I have wept over the laxity of the church. But be assured that my tears
have been tears of love. There can be no deep disappointment where
there is not deep love. Yes, I love the church. How could I do otherwise? I am in the rather unique position of being the son, the grandson
and the greatgrandson of preachers. Yes, I see the church as the body
of Christ. But, oh! How we have blemished and scarred that body
through social neglect and through fear of being nonconformists.

There was a time when the church was very powerful—in the   40
time when the early Christians rejoiced at being deemed worthy to suffer for what they believed. In those days the church was not merely a
thermometer that recorded the ideas and principles of popular opinion; it was a thermostat that transformed the mores of society. Whenever the early Christians entered a town, the people in power became
disturbed and immediately sought to convict the Christians for being

"disturbers of the peace" and "outside agitators." But the Christians pressed on, in the conviction that they were a "colony of heaven," called to obey God rather than man. Small in number, they were big in commitment. They were too God-intoxicated to be "astronomically intimidated." By their effort and example they brought an end to such ancient evils as infanticide and gladiatorial contests.

41   Things are different now. So often the contemporary church is a weak, ineffectual voice with an uncertain sound. So often it is an arch-defender of the status quo. Far from being disturbed by the presence of the church, the power structure of the average community is consoled by the church's silent—and often even vocal—sanction of things as they are.

42   But the judgment of God is upon the church as never before. If today's church does not recapture the sacrificial spirit of the early church, it will lose its authenticity, forfeit the loyalty of millions, and be dismissed as an irrelevant social club with no meaning for the twentieth century. Every day I meet young people whose disappointment with the church has turned into outright disgust.

43   Perhaps I have once again been too optimistic. Is organized religion too inextricably bound to the status quo to save our nation and the world? Perhaps I must turn my faith to the inner spiritual church, the church within the church, as the true *ekklesia* and the hope of the world. But again I am thankful to God that some noble souls from the ranks of organized religion have broken loose from the paralyzing chains of conformity and joined us as active partners in the struggle for freedom. They have left their secure congregations and walked the streets of Albany, Georgia, with us. They have gone down the highways of the South on tortuous rides for freedom. Yes, they have gone to jail with us. Some have been dismissed from their churches, have lost the support of their bishops and fellow ministers. But they have acted in the faith that right defeated is stronger than evil triumphant. Their witness has been the spiritual salt that has preserved the true meaning of the gospel in these troubled times. They have carved a tunnel of hope through the dark mountain of disappointment.

44   I hope the church as a whole will meet the challenge of this decisive hour. But even if the church does not come to the aid of justice, I have no despair about the future. I have no fear about the outcome of our struggle in Birmingham, even if our motives are at present misunderstood. We will reach the goal of freedom in Birmingham and all over the nation, because the goal of America is freedom. Abused and scorned though we may be, our destiny is tied up with America's des-

tiny. Before the pilgrims landed at Plymouth, we were here. Before the pen of Jefferson etched the majestic words of the Declaration of Independence across the pages of history, we were here. For more than two centuries our forebears labored in this country without wages; they made cotton king; they built the homes of their masters while suffering gross injustice and shameful humiliation—and yet out of a bottomless vitality they continued to thrive and develop. If the inexpressible cruelties of slavery could not stop us, the opposition we now face will surely fail. We will win our freedom because the sacred heritage of our nation and the eternal will of God are embodied in our echoing demands.

Before closing I feel impelled to mention one other point in your   45
statement that has troubled me profoundly. You warmly commended the Birmingham police force for keeping "order" and "preventing violence." I doubt that you would have so warmly commended the police force if you had seen its dogs sinking their teeth into unarmed, nonviolent Negroes. I doubt that you would so quickly commend the policemen if you were to observe their ugly and inhumane treatment of Negroes here in the city jail; if you were to watch them push and curse old Negro women and young Negro girls; if you were to see them slap and kick old Negro men and young boys; if you were to observe them, as they did on two occasions, refuse to give us food because we wanted to sing our grace together. I cannot join you in your praise of the Birmingham Police Department.

It is true that the police have exercised a degree of discipline in   46
handling the demonstrators. In this sense they have conducted themselves rather "nonviolently" in public. But for what purpose? To preserve the evil system of segregation. Over the past few years I have consistently preached that nonviolence demands that the means we use must be as pure as the ends we seek. I have tried to make clear that it is wrong to use immoral means to attain moral ends. But now I must affirm that it is just as wrong, or perhaps even more so, to use moral means to preserve immoral ends. Perhaps Mr. Connor and his policemen have been rather nonviolent in public, as was Chief Pritchett in Albany, Georgia, but they have used the moral means of nonviolence to maintain the immoral end of racial injustice. As T. S. Eliot has said: "The last temptation is the greatest treason: To do the right deed for the wrong reason."

I wish you had commended the Negro sit-inners and demonstra-   47
tors of Birmingham for their sublime courage, their willingness to suffer and their amazing discipline in the midst of great provocation. One

day the South will recognize its real heroes. They will be the James Merediths, with the noble sense of purpose that enables them to face jeering and hostile mobs, and with the agonizing loneliness that characterizes the life of the pioneer. They will be old, oppressed, battered Negro women, symbolized in a seventy-two-year-old-woman in Montgomery, Alabama, who rose up with a sense of dignity and with her people decided not to ride segregated buses, and who responded with ungrammatical profundity to one who inquired about her weariness: "My feets is tired, but my soul is at rest." They will be the young high school and college students, the young ministers of the gospel and a host of their elders, courageously and nonviolently sitting in at lunch counters and willingly going to jail for conscience sake. One day the South will know that when these disinherited children of God sat down at lunch counters, they were in reality standing up for what is best in the American dream and for the most sacred values in our Judaeo-Christian heritage, thereby bringing our nation back to those great wells of democracy which were dug deep by the founding fathers in their formulation of the Constitution and the Declaration of Independence.

48   Never before have I written so long a letter. I'm afraid it is much too long to take your precious time. I can assure you that it would have been much shorter if I had been writing from a comfortable desk, but what else can one do when he is alone in a narrow cell, other than write long letters, think long thoughts and pray long prayers?

49   If I have said anything in this letter that overstates the truth and indicates an unreasonable impatience, I beg you to forgive me. If I have said anything that understates the truth and indicates my having a patience that allows me to settle for anything less than brotherhood, I beg God to forgive me.

50   I hope this letter finds you strong in the faith. I also hope that circumstances will soon make it possible for me to meet each of you, not as an integrationist or a civil-rights leader but as a fellow clergyman and a Christian brother. Let us all hope that the dark clouds of racial prejudice will soon pass away and the deep fog of misunderstanding will be lifted from our fear-drenched communities, and in some not too distant tomorrow the radiant stars of love and brotherhood will shine over our great nation with all their scintillating beauty.

Yours for the cause of Peace and Brotherhood,
Martin Luther King, Jr.

QUESTIONS TO CONSIDER

1. Although Martin Luther King, Jr., was well known to the clergymen he was writing to, they did not perceive him as a reasonable man who was acting wisely. Thus King attempts in this letter to convince his readers he is credible—that his actions were not "untimely and unwise" as they have charged. How does King accomplish this goal? Does the fact he is in jail argue for or against his credibility? Why or why not?

2. King methodically refutes each of the clergymen's claims: (1) that he is an outsider who should not have been involved; (2) that the demonstrations were "untimely," and (3) that they were "unwise." What arguments does he use to refute each of these claims? How effective are his arguments?

3. King uses several different methods of development in his letter. Identify examples of the following methods: cause and effect, exemplification, narration, description, classification, comparison/contrast, and definition.

4. Although he is writing to people who disapprove of what he has done, King does not treat them as adversaries. Rather he repeatedly attempts to identify with them and to point out areas of consensus. Identify several of these attempts.

5. Although King's tone is generally reasonable and even objective, there are times when he becomes impassioned. Reread paragraphs 14 and 29–30. In these passages, King makes strong emotional appeals. To what emotions is he appealing? How effective are these appeals? Would they be equally effective if they were not balanced by his appeals to reason and by his efforts to establish his own credibility?

6. How does King distinguish between just and unjust laws? Do you accept his distinction? Does this distinction help readers to recognize and question the unspoken assumption that *all* laws are just? Is this strategy effective in supporting his primary assertion that the demonstrations were not untimely or unwise?

7. Which of King's appeals—to reason, emotion, or his own credibility—do you find most persuasive? Why?

WRITING ACTIVITIES

Individual: In a journal entry, answer King's question, "How does one determine whether a law is just or unjust?"

Collaborative: Make a list of the underlying assumptions on which King bases his argument that the civil rights movement is the best way to avoid violent racial strife. Then decide which of these assumptions you accept and which you reject. Support your decisions.

Computer: Type King's last paragraph into a computer file. Rewrite the paragraph in an objective, matter-of-fact style, eliminating the colorful language and imagery of the original. Compare your rewrite with those of your peers and with the original. What differences are there?

❖❖❖❖❖

THE MYTHS OF RACIAL DIVISION

Andrew Hacker

Andrew Hacker teaches political science at Queens College, New York. This essay, which appeared in the March 23, 1992, issue of The New Republic, *is based on Hacker's research for his recent book,* Two Nations, *in which he argues that our nation is becoming increasingly divided by race. In this article, however, Hacker debunks "a variety of black-and-white myths," arguing that the differences frequently cited between African-Americans and whites are, in fact, really "grayer realities."*

1   The urge to emphasize racial division in America is hard to resist. Few nations have etched so deep a black-and-white separation as our own. Even South Africa allows for Coloureds, while Latin countries have mulattos and mestizos, as well as Creoles and quadroons. But here even children of mixed marriages end up regarded as black. And while citizens may cherish their European origins, being white retains

primacy in most of their minds. At times, race seems to surpass even gender as our major schism.

It shouldn't. We now have information about how much impact race has in areas such as school achievement, hiring, family life, and crime—and it should spur us to rethink the actual impact of race and ethnic separatism. If anything, there is evidence that race is becoming a *less* salient factor for growing groups of Americans. Here follows a brief debunking of a variety of black-and-white myths, which, upon inspection, turn out to be grayer realities.

The black family is disintegrating, while the white family remains intact. Since Daniel Patrick Moynihan's 1965 report found black families trapped in a "tangle of pathology," conditions seem to have gotten worse. Two-thirds of black babies are now born outside of wedlock, and more than half of black homes are headed by women. A majority of black youngsters live only with their mother; and in most of these households she has never been married.

Almost everyone agrees that the increases in non-marital births and female-headed households are causes for dismay. But why should race be the crucial variable? Readily available reports show that low income and education outweigh race in causing family instability. Absent fathers abound in depressed counties where the residents are almost wholly white. In rural Maine, for example, out-of-wedlock rates exceed those for blacks in several states.

As it happens, extramarital births and households headed by women are subject to social trends, which touch all races and classes in similar ways. The Census figures for female-headed families for the last four decades show that both black and white families have disintegrated at virtually identical rates. In 1950, 17.2 percent of black families were headed by single women, against 5.3 percent of white families (a black-white multiple of 3.2). In 1990, the figures are 56.2 percent and 17.3 percent respectively (a black-white multiple of 3.2). Plainly, what we have been seeing are not so much race-based differences as concurrent adaptations to common cultural conditions. True, the black figure has always been three times larger, and here is where "racial" reasons have an influence of their own. But those forces were at work well before 1950, prior to talk about "pathology." Of course, the current 56.2 percent rate for black households is depressingly high. But then the 1990 figure for whites is almost identical to the one for blacks lamented in Moynihan's report.

The point here is not whether family structure is important, but whether its dynamic over the last thirty years has been different along racial lines. It hasn't been. Given the ubiquity of absent fathers—black and white—little will be gained by lecturing one race on its duties. To call on black Americans to show greater discipline would seem to suggest that only they have deviated from national norms. Black families will become more stable when all households evolve a stronger structure.

7   Where out-of-wedlock births are concerned, there is actual racial convergence. What we hear most is that 66 percent of black births are to girls and women who are not married. However, close study of the figures reveals that the black-white multiple is less than half of what it was forty years ago. So while black out-of-wedlock births are at an all-time high, the white ratio has been ascending at a far faster rate. Even in typical mid-American cities such as Davenport, Iowa, and Dayton, Ohio, the current white figures are 27.8 percent and 31.4 percent. In 1950, 16.8 percent of black births were out of wedlock, while 1.7 percent of white births were (a black-white multiple of 9.9). In 1970, the proportions were 37.6 percent and 5.7 percent respectively (a multiple of 6.6). Today, the figures are 66 percent and 16 percent (a multiple of 4.1). The chief reason for the decrease in the multiple is the availability of abortion. Although black women constitute only 13 percent of women of childbearing age, they account for more than 30 percent of the pregnancies terminated each year.

8   *Blacks are far more likely to commit crimes than whites.* When we hear allusions to "crime," our first image tends to be of violent assaults—rape, robbery, murder—not insider trading or embezzling. And "black crime" conjures up Willie Hortons, whose acts of terror forever scar their victims' lives. By every measure we have, black felons commit far more than their share of the most dreaded crimes. While constituting only about 12 percent of the population, they account for 43.2 percent of arrests for rape, 54.7 percent of murders where the perpetrator is known, and 69.3 percent of reported robberies.

9   Does this mean that blacks on the whole are less law-abiding? Bruce Wright, a black New York judge, came close to saying just that when he argued that felons of his own race are simply breaking "a social contract that was not of their making in the first place." In fact, we know much less about offenses by whites, since their crimes tend to be office-based, or involve insurance claims or tax evasion, fewer of which are uncovered or apprehended. Although white-collar crooks can and do end up behind bars, many more do not. There is reason to believe that larcenous proclivities exist in members of every race but since more alternatives are open to whites, they have less need for

thievery that threatens physical harm. (Class constraints are also more likely to make whites repress hatred or rage that could propel them to rape or murder.)

Because we fear more for our bodies than our bank accounts, vio-   10
lent crimes are more apt to bring prison terms, which explains the disproportionate number of blacks behind bars. But how far is their race the reason? What we can say with some assurance is that people who end up as inmates tend to be lower class, and represent a rougher and tougher element within that economic stratum. The prison rolls in West Virginia and Idaho are overwhelmingly white, and most inmates were convicted of crimes that in other states tend to be associated with blacks. (While West Virginia's and Idaho's overall crime rates are relatively low, their ratios of violent to non-violent crimes do not differ significantly from those of states having larger black populations.)

Blacks now outnumber whites in our penal institutions, but this   11
was not always so. In 1930, 76.7 percent of inmates were white; as recently as 1970 the number was 60.5 percent. In contrast, blacks made up 22.4 percent of the prison population in 1930 and now make up a staggering 45.3 percent. This would suggest that black men were much more law-abiding half a century ago, since most then lived in the South, where they could have been sent to the chain gang with relative ease. In fact, controls exerted by churches, the authority of elders, and community pride combined to deter conduct that could land black men in trouble. Given the depth of poverty and endless humiliations, this discipline is all the more striking.

At the same time, the past had a much larger class of whites who   12
used or threatened violence. The Jimmy Cagneys of New York's Hell's Kitchen and the George Rafts who filled the cells at Sing Sing portrayed an actual segment of the population. Indeed, what is often seen today as "black crime" used to be predominantly white. Since those days many if not most whites have moved up to the middle class, so those who are drawn to larceny have less need to commit face-to-face felonies. The flip side is that blacks now constitute a much larger share of the poor, and more of them live in urban centers where earlier controls no longer apply. As a result, they preponderate among those being charged and imprisoned for the kinds of crimes poorer people are more likely to commit.

Blacks score less well on objective IQ tests. Ours is an age of   13
machine-graded tests, so much so that a single score can determine a person's future. The Scholastic Aptitude Test, which more than a million high school seniors take every year, is the first thing colleges con-

sider when assessing applicants. Do the tests discriminate? Quite obviously they do. Children from better-off families usually do better, since they go to schools that familiarize them with the format. Students with a mathematical bent usually score well throughout the SAT, as do those with a flair for solving puzzles at a one-a-minute rate.

14   The problem is that black Americans as a group do not do well on standardized tests. This holds true for job applicants and civil service promotions, even when special courses have been arranged. An analysis of the SAT results shows that blacks still lag behind other groups even when they come from homes with comparable incomes and parental educations. The average SAT scores for students whose parents earn between $50,000 and $60,000 are 955 for Asians, 947 for whites, 879 for Hispanics, and 790 for blacks. For those whose parents have a graduate degree, the average SAT scores are 1053 for Asians, 1018 for whites, 897 for Hispanics, and 830 for blacks. Can there be a bias in the SAT that hampers even privileged blacks?

15   The first answer is that if there is a bias, it is not "white" in character. As the scores show, Asians rank ahead of whites when backgrounds are held constant, just as Hispanics outperform blacks. Asians and Hispanics do better on this American test because they study longer and harder, pay attention to the rules, and are less likely to cavil about the oddities of the test. If there is a bias to the multiple-choice matrix, it favors what might be called a technocratic mentality, which is emerging in Seoul and Bogotá as much as in Seattle or Baltimore.

16   But why so visible a black gap at every social level? Here the causes are explicitly racial, in that they stem from the segregation that affects even black youngsters from professional homes. Simply stated, the intellectual processes most black children learn, which tend to be at odds with technocratic modes, are reinforced by spending much of their time among people of their own race. The persistence of segregation—residential and social—draws a sharp dividing line between blacks and whites of all classes. In consequence, black intellectual styles remain more discursive than linear, which can be a drawback when facing a multiple-choice format. Indeed, one of the early arguments for integration was that in mixed classes, black students would learn "white" modes of interpretation and analysis, thus eroding the SAT gap. Yet white scores have been on the decline for at least twenty years, so whites may not be the best model.

17   *Whites have been hurt by affirmative action.* Whether affirmative action involves "quotas" or "goals," in practice it means exempting

some people from customary requirements and qualifications. In fact, such policies have been around a long time. For example, colleges occasionally decide to admit some students from Montana, to ensure a diverse entering class. Even if their grades aren't very good, coming from a distant state is seen as a compensatory credential. And to make room for them, abler applicants from other states end up being turned down. Today affirmative action aims at raising black ratios in education and employment. As with coming from Montana, being black becomes a credential.

No one can say with certainty how many white Americans have been bypassed or displaced because of preferential policies. Alan Bakke sued a University of California medical school because he believed that a place he deserved had gone to a minority applicant. He obviously felt injured. But if his record was creditable, he would probably have been admitted to some other schools, which should have cushioned the blow. With this caveat in mind, we can try to gauge how far affirmative action has been edging out whites.   18

At last count, ten top-rated schools—Amherst, Brown, Cornell, Dartmouth, Harvard, MIT, Northwestern, Princeton, Stanford, and Yale—had a total of 9,555 black, Hispanic, and Native American students out of an overall 107,409 enrollment. Unfortunately, colleges do not report academic records for subgroups. So for present purposes, using nationwide SAT figures, I will assume that three-fifths of the minority students accepted had records that were inferior to those of other applicants who were turned away. Three-fifths of 9,555 works out to 5,733 unadmitted whites and Asians, who had to settle for lesser schools. (Had these colleges imposed their customary criteria, their aggregate minority ratio would have stood at 3.6 percent, rather than the 8.9 percent they attained through affirmative action.) Still, 101,676 whites and Asians *were* admitted, a fairly hefty number. And in many if not most cases, those rejected simply traded down within the Top Ten. It's also worth considering that not all admitted whites are potential Phi Beta Kappas. In addition to Montana residents, even the Iviest schools bend rules for alumni offspring, and even Harvard has been known to favor football players.   19

White displacement in employment is less easy to compute, since hirings and promotions are more apt to involve intangible judgments. Still, figures for occupations yield some answers. In most professional, white-collar, and craft fields, recent years have seen an increased bloc of blacks; and affirmative action has undoubtedly played some role. There is much talk about whites who feel they are   20 being bypassed, with not a few filing lawsuits. In the academic world, white men seeking instructorships have good reason to believe that their résumés will be relegated to the bottom of the pile. After all, it is hard to find a department that has not given high priority to recruiting a black colleague.

21   The blue-collar world has young men who aspire to careers as police officers or fire fighters, often to carry on a long family tradition. Although not usually studious, they cram hard for the tests; but those who pass at the margin see appointments going to blacks with lower scores.

22   But how typical are stories like these? The Census and Bureau of Labor Statistics collate figures on racial distributions within various occupations. As the accompanying table shows, despite all the efforts of medical schools and college faculties, the black proportions of physicians and professors have barely budged over twenty years.

Black Representation in Occupations

	1970	1990	Share of New Jobs
Physicians	2.2%	3.0%	3.8%
Lawyers	1.3%	3.2%	4.3%
College Professors	3.5%	4.5%	6.3%
Electricians	3.0%	6.2%	12.7%
Bank Tellers	4.3%	9.9%	16.3%
Bus Drivers	14.3%	24.4%	33.8%
Police Officers	6.3%	13.5%	41.1%
Total Work Force	9.6%	10.1%	11.0%

Indeed, blacks filled only 6.3 percent of the new faculty positions created between 1970 and 1990. So if white men haven't gotten posts, it wasn't due to extensive black hiring, but rather to a preference for women, who received more than half of the new academic openings. Among doctors and lawyers, black gains were even smaller, in part because expansions in both professions brought in even more whites. Nor are all advances by blacks due to preferential policies. There are more black bus drivers and bank tellers; while one reason is that blacks have been upgrading their skills, another may be that fewer whites find they are attracted to those jobs.

Although the percentage of black electricians doubled, it yielded   23
them little more than their overall share of new jobs, so hardly any
whites lost out. The real shift was in police selection, where blacks
received more than 40 percent of the 100,000 new posts in law
enforcement. Here, clearly, affirmative action has worked against white
applicants. Unlike the students rejected by Amherst, who go on to
Lehigh, whites who don't make it into the police haven't as consoling
a second option. But in the end black Americans remain a relatively
small minority, so there are limits to how many whites they can dis-
place even with aggressive affirmative action recruiting. At the college
level, the real competition for whites comes from Asians, who are win-
ning places not through preferential policies but on academic merit.

Overall, persons with racial identities—black and white   24
Americans—constitute a declining portion of the population. Since
1970 individuals of European ancestry, or Caucasoid stock, have
declined from 83.3 percent to 75.3 percent of the national total. And
during these decades, Americans of African ancestry, or the Negroid
race, rose by only one percentage point—from 10.9 percent to 11.9
percent—and that was largely due to new arrivals from the Caribbean.
By the next census, it is likely that blacks will have lost out to
Hispanics—whose share of the population has more than doubled in
the last twenty years—as America's largest minority group. Indeed, that
has already happened in twenty states, including Massachusetts,
California, and Colorado.

The nation's fastest-growing groups are rejecting racial designa-   25
tions. For example, we hardly ever hear allusions to the "yellow" or
"Mongoloid" race, just as "Oriental" has all but disappeared. Chinese
and Japanese and Koreans have chosen to emphasize their separate
national identities rather than evoke a common heritage. Unfortunately
the media have adopted the umbrella term "Asian," which tells us little
about those under it, since they could equally well be Afghans or
Laotians or Filipinos.

Hispanics are also finding no need for a racial category. This, too,   26
is a recent development. In responding to the 1970 census, fully 98
percent said they wanted to be classified as black or white. In 1990,
however, over half shunned those racial options and chose to check
"Other." By doing this, they were signaling that their Hispanic identity
was all they wanted or needed. Even less than Asians, Hispanics are
hardly a race. If anything, Latin America has been the world's leading
melting pot, yielding every possible mixture of European and African

and indigenous strains. Even Latino lobbyists limit themselves to calling for preserving regional histories, languages, and cultures rather than racial roots.

27   In the past, also, many persons of indigenous stock would report that they were white, perhaps hoping to gain such benefits as that designation might bring. Recently we have seen displays of pride among these groups, reflected in what they tell the census. Since 1970 persons listing themselves as Native Americans, Hawaiians, Aleuts, or Eskimos have increased by almost 90 percent, which comes to seven times the increase for the nation as a whole. Moreover, these affinities tend to be tribal or regional, rather than racial.

28   Of course, it could be argued that it doesn't much matter if the "disuniting of America"—Arthur Schlesinger's phrase—is along racial or other lines. Blacks and Puerto Ricans and Aleuts all claim preference under affirmative action; and supposed disadvantages can have varied sources. Still, my own observations have been that Asians and Hispanics and others who want to make it on their own have seen the harm that being "racial" can do. To define oneself as black or white—or to have those origins assigned to you—assigns overwhelming weight to a primordial ancestry. With race can come a genetic determinism, often suggesting higher or lower locations on an evolutionary ladder. Hence the choice of Asians to put their nationalities first, while Hispanics prefer to stress the culture they created and sustain as a matter of choice. They are also aware of the hostilities and tensions dividing blacks and whites, and have chosen not so much a middle ground as seats off to the side.

29   If the United States becomes less racial, does this mean it will emerge as a more "multiethnic" society? Don't bet on it. The great majority of recent immigrants, like their counterparts in the past, intend to become mainstream Americans. They did not make the trek here to change the rules and regimens of a society in which they want to succeed. Too much heed has been paid to Latino and kindred publicists, who make careers calling for the preservation of what are essentially folktales and folkways. (They get as much attention as they do by playing on white guilt, which regards tribal rites in the same vein as the spotted owl.)

30   Statistically, the advent of Hispanics and Asians—joined by new immigrants from the Middle East—will spell further white decline. Yet if most of those arriving have no wish to become white, not many see themselves as "people of color." They want their children to get traditional American educations and graduate to assimilated suburbs. As

recent books by Linda Chavez and Rosalie Pedalino Porter have shown, Hispanic students tend to be shunted into special classes by self-serving bureaucrats rather than at the behest of their parents. And the families of my immigrant students in Queens regard the borough as a way-station prior to a suburban move. Moreover, once they become middle-class, they will have little or no difficulty entering what were once all-white neighborhoods. (For that reason, they are at pains to dissociate themselves from black Americans; just listen to some of their remarks.) In return, middle-class America is prepared to absorb newcomers who show a willingness to adapt. Even George Bush boasts of his Hispanic daughter-in-law, and she is one of almost 30 percent of Hispanics who marry outside their culture. But that hardly matters, since most people come here to become Americans, and they have a good eye and ear for how and where to adapt.

QUESTIONS TO CONSIDER ◀

1. Hacker, like the other writers in this chapter, begins by describing what is perceived—in this case, racial differences—and then argues that this perception is not accurate. Do you agree that racial division is not a significant fact of life in our society, or do you think Hacker is manipulating statistics to support his argument?

2. Hacker divides his article into four main arguments in order to prove his primary assertion that racial divisions are becoming less important in our society. What are these arguments? Which of them do you find most convincing? Why? Which do you find least convincing?

3. Hacker's arguments are supported primarily by statistical evidence. In most cases, he does not cite the source of the statistics he includes. Do you doubt the accuracy of these statistics since you do not know their source, or do you trust Hacker? If so, why?

4. Hacker concludes his article with a final argument to support his thesis that the United States is becoming less race conscious. However, he does not include this argument in his list of myths and does not italicize the initial sentence of this section. What is this final argument? Is this argument more or less convincing than the other four?

5. Hacker does not include any obvious emotional appeals in his article. Would the article have been more or less convincing had he done so? Why?

▶ WRITING ACTIVITIES

Individual: Write a rebuttal to one of Hacker's arguments—the one you feel is weakest and least convincing. Begin your rebuttal by summarizing the argument and then argue against it, pointing out its weaknesses.

Collaborative: Working as a group, make a list of the unspoken assumptions on which Hacker bases his primary argument that race is becoming less important to most people. Then reevaluate his argument on the basis of these assumptions.

Computer: Statistical evidence is difficult to read because it requires readers to compute as well as comprehend. As a result, readers often accept statistics uncritically—sort of skimming over them without really examining them carefully. In your own case, what is your reaction to statistical evidence? Do you examine the figures carefully, following the mathematical calculations and understanding their implications, or do you merely assume the figures support the author's argument? Select a paragraph in which Hacker includes statistical evidence (e.g., 5, 7, 8, or 11) and examine the figures carefully. Then compose a simple graphic that illustrates the information provided by the statistics.

❖❖❖❖❖

W R I T I N G   T O   P E R S U A D E

When you write to persuade, you are attempting to convince your reader of something—that Reeboks are the best athletic shoes, that John F. Kennedy was or was not assassinated by Lee Harvey Oswald, that college entrance exams are unfair, or that a local recycling program is needed.

Constructing Logical Arguments

Although all writing can be viewed as persuasive, writing that is primarily persuasive usually takes the form of an argument. That is, the writer makes an assertion (a statement that is possible or even probable but open to question or debate) and then supports it in some way. The support is, in effect, the evidence that the writer presents to establish the validity of his or her assertion.

For example, you might assert that more women should be elected to Congress. You could support this assertion by using the following arguments:

1. More than half the population is female; therefore, at least half the congressional representatives should be female.

2. Men have not done a very good job in running the country, so women should be given a chance.

3. Women are most concerned with domestic affairs and, since many of our current problems are domestic rather than foreign, women would be more effective in solving them.

4. Women are more likely to compromise and negotiate than men and would be able, therefore, to reach consensus and pass legislation more often.

5. Women are less likely to become involved in sexual and financial scandals than men.

6. The women who have previously served in Congress have good records of achievement.

7. Men have been in control long enough; it's time to give women their chance.

8. Women are less aggressive than men and thus would be less likely to get us into another war.

Although some of these reasons are clearly better than others, they all support the assertion that more women should be elected to Congress.

Notice that each of these supporting statements is, in effect, another assertion that must in turn be supported. For example, you would need to provide evidence to prove your assertion that previously elected female representatives have been effective. You could, for example, cite their good attendance records, the number of times they have been reelected, or the number of bills they have introduced that have become laws. To support your assertion that female representatives would be less likely to involve the nation in war, you could cite generic studies indicating that males are typically more aggressive than females or law enforcement statistics showing that males commit more acts of physical aggression than females.

A good argument is erected by slowly and carefully supporting each assertion, one after another, until you have built a well-constructed interlocking network of arguments. When you write to persuade, you make a single *primary* assertion but support your primary assertion with secondary assertions and in turn support them with examples and evidence. In effect, you are building a network of arguments—assertions supported by other assertions that must also be supported. In effective argument, all the secondary arguments ultimately convince your reader of the validity of your primary assertion.

Using Emotional Appeals

The arguments you construct should be based primarily on logic—on reasonable conclusions that the reader can draw on the basis of the evidence you have presented. But arguments can also be supported by emotional appeals. For example, in supporting the assertion that more females should be elected to Congress, you could appeal to your readers' sense of fairness, arguing that for women not to be equally represented is unfair because they constitute more than half the population. You could also describe the position of women both today and historically as second-class citizens who have never been treated fairly. Or, becoming even more obviously emotional, you could characterize women as mother figures who want to nurture the nation as a whole but whose efforts have been rejected.

In general, use emotional appeals not as your main supporting arguments but rather as part of those arguments. If you use reasonable arguments to support your main assertion, you can then introduce an emotional appeal effectively as part of that argument. For example,

James Herriot, the British veterinarian and writer who wrote *All Creatures Great and Small*, has written convincingly about the difference between what he was taught in school and what he actually encountered once he began to practice veterinary medicine. Herriot graphically describes lying on the cold, hard, dirty barn floor struggling with a cow that is calving, and contrasts this image with one in his medical textbook of a white-coated doctor delivering a calf in a sterile room. Although these images *logically* support his argument, providing convincing evidence and example, they also make a subtle but strong emotional appeal. The reader *feels,* or vicariously experiences, what Herriot is describing as well as recognizes the information as reasonable proof of his argument. Herriot does not have to point out explicitly that real life in this case is dirtier, harder, and more uncomfortable than the textbook version. The details he includes accomplish this goal as convincingly as any assertion he might make on the subject. Because of his vivid description, readers respond empathetically, understanding on an emotional as well as an intellectual level Herriot's point.

A fine line separates an effective, legitimate emotional appeal from one that clearly tries to play on the reader's emotions. It is usually better to use subtle and restrained emotional appeals, as Herriot does, simply suggesting an appropriate emotional response rather than crudely evoking it. Arguments won solely on the basis of inappropriate emotional appeals do little to help people reach a consensus or to work out satisfactory solutions to problems. Pictures of dead fetuses and accounts of women butchered by illegal abortionists have probably not advanced either side of the abortion issue, for example, and they certainly have not lessened the ugly conflicts characterizing that volatile issue.

Establishing Your Credibility

You will also want to support your arguments by establishing your **credibility** as a person whose words can be trusted. Four qualities can help establish this type of confidence:

CREDIBILITY, PAGE 443

- ❖ Be well informed.

- ❖ Be accurate.

- ❖ Be reasonable.

- ❖ Be correct.

BE WELL INFORMED.   Accurate, pertinent, clear information is one of the most compelling forms of evidence you can use to support your assertions. The information must, of course, be directly related to the assertion you are making. You support your arguments by providing your readers with the appropriate information and then, if necessary, explaining the relationship between the information and your assertion. For example, in supporting the assertion that more females should be elected to Congress, you might provide your readers with statistical information about how many females now serve in Congress, what the total population of the United States is, and what percentage of that population is female. Then you could discuss the relationship among these statistical data, explaining how they support your assertion.

All the writers included in this chapter depend on information to support their assertions. Rebecca Williams gives very specific information about a beauty pageant to prove that such contests are not what they appear to be. Andrew Hacker supports his assertion that racial separatism is a myth with an abundance of statistical information. Susan Faludi cites statistical misinformation to prove her point that day care has been unjustly maligned. Lewis Thomas uses information derived from his own observations of nature and life to argue that the last stage of dying is probably painless and thus natural.

You will probably research some of the information you use, but much of it may come from you own general knowledge of the subject and your own experiences and observations. Information comes in many forms. Often the most valuable information is that which you have obtained from your own experiences. In fact, most writers do not write about a subject unless they have some information of their own to contribute (see also **library research** and **field research**).

LIBRARY RESEARCH, PAGE 534

FIELD RESEARCH, PAGE 493

BE ACCURATE.   Whatever the source of your information, be sure it is accurate. Nothing destroys your credibility as completely as being wrong. If you are not sure of the information you are using, try to verify it. Then, if you are still not convinced of its accuracy, don't include it or, at least, qualify it appropriately. Qualifiers such as *approximately, usually, in general, sometimes,* and *often* can help you make the point you want to make without running the risk of being inaccurate.

Another way of being accurate is to carefully define any terms you use that are subject to various interpretations or that might be misunderstood. You and your reader should agree as completely as possible about what you mean when you use such terms as *day care, child abuse, equality,* or *natural death.* If readers do not understand your particular use of a term, even if they are familiar with its general definition, they may not know if they agree with you or not. Precise, accurate definitions are an important part of any argument (see **definition**).

DEFINITION, PAGE 452

BE REASONABLE.   Impassioned arguments, often dramatic, can be effective when the writer's passion is anchored in reason. However, they are seldom convincing when they become overly dramatic or when a writer becomes so impassioned that he or she becomes unreasonable or even aggressive. Just as listeners do not usually respond well to being yelled at, readers do not respond well to the written equivalent of yelling—to insistent, hysterical, unreasonable verbal aggression. Martin Luther King, Jr., is quietly impassioned in his "Letter from Birmingham Jail," but he is even more clearly reasonable and courteous in what he says and how he says it. A writer's credibility depends to a great extent on the reader's perception of him or her as a reasonable person, one who weighs evidence, takes a balanced view, and sees both sides.

One of the most effective ways to establish yourself as reasonable is to acknowledge opposing arguments, treating them with respect even as you refute them, as King does in his letter to the clergymen. Scorn, sarcasm, and harsh criticism usually alienate readers rather than convince them. Your goal in persuasive writing should be to prove your own point—not by convincing your readers that they are wrong but by persuading them that your own argument is superior.

One way to do this derives from Carl Rogers's nondirective approach for counseling therapy. Rogers, a noted psychologist, encouraged therapists to create an accepting and empathetic environment for their clients, to reassure them that their feelings were acknowledged and accepted before trying to convince them to change those feelings. You can use the same strategy successfully when you are writing to persuade. By establishing common ground, accepting other views, compromising on key issues, and acknowledging the validity of other positions, you convince readers who would otherwise remain resistant and alienated.

Remember, verbal persuasion is not like an athletic contest. You don't win just by beating your opponents. Rather you work toward consensus, negotiating with your readers not only by refuting their arguments but also by compromising with their position.

In acknowledging opposing viewpoints, however, you must be careful to focus clearly on your own. Explaining the opposing position as carefully and extensively as you do your own will only confuse your readers. Your readers should always know which side you are on. You will usually acknowledge other positions by merely evaluating their strengths and weaknesses. Or you can point out the similarity between an opposing position and your own to create some common ground. In some instances, you may even want to devote more space to opposing positions, as Susan Faludi does, but be sure if you adopt this strategy that you are clearly refuting these arguments. Acknowledge other positions, establish common ground and points of consensus, even be generous, but keep the focus on your own arguments.

If readers perceive you as a reasonable person, willing to see both sides of an issue but ready to defend your own position, you will probably have some effect on their convictions and possibly even their actions. But don't expect too much. Most arguments are neither won nor lost completely; small gains are what you can realistically expect.

BE CORRECT.   Correctness in terms of spelling, punctuation, and usage may seem an insignificant factor in persuading someone of the validity of your assertion. However, observing the conventions that guide standard language usage can play an important role in establishing your credibility—no matter that knowing how to spell *environment* correctly has absolutely nothing to do with your being qualified to write on this subject. Readers will expect you to spell the word correctly (and punctuate sentences correctly, use verbs correctly, and so on), and they will find you less convincing if you do not meet these expectations.

In many places in the United States, a female politician who wears gaudy makeup and revealing clothes is probably not going to be elected to the U.S. Senate. Likewise, a stockbroker who talks too loudly and drives a flashy sports car is probably not going to have many financially conservative clients. It doesn't matter if the candidate and stockbroker are brilliant, honest, and well qualified. They may, in fact, be all those things, but their credibility suffers because they violate conventions.

The same is true of the image of yourself you create when you write. Because most of your readers will know you only by what they see in your text, you must be careful to present the best possible image of yourself. Readers will make a judgment based on errors in your text without even evaluating your arguments. It is much easier to spot a misspelled word than to evaluate a complex argument. So don't sabotage your own arguments by discrediting yourself as a careful, knowledgeable writer. Errors are certainly not a moral issue, and a compelling argument could be written entirely in misspelled words and sentence fragments. But you will often be judged by the way you write as well as by what you say, and many readers do not generously overlook writing errors.

WRITING ASSIGNMENT

For this writing assignment, persuade your readers that something is not as it appears to be. Like the authors of this chapter's reading selections, argue against a popular perception, a myth, or an accepted view of what seems to be. Your arguments will, in effect, persuade your readers of your view of reality. You may, for example, argue that college is not what you were led to expect, that your generation is not what it is generally perceived to be, that being an only (or oldest, youngest, or middle) child is not as good (or bad) as it is thought to be, that marriage (or dating or living away from home or being a parent) is not as much fun as you had expected, that small towns (or large cities) are not bad places in which to grow up, or that prejudice, class consciousness, materialism, or indifference does not characterize the place where you live in spite of the publicity found in the press (or movies or television).

You should deal in some way with the difference between appearance and reality, at least, your version of reality. You can focus on the difference between television ads and real-life situations, between storybook romances and realistic male-female relationships, between political promises and post-election realities. Your purpose is to persuade your readers that your viewpoint is more honest and accurate than some other viewpoint.

Be sure to choose a topic you know something about rather than something you have just heard about. Although you may want to research your subject also (by reading, or perhaps by questioning, observing, and interviewing—see **field research**), you should have some personal experience or basic information to begin with. When writers try to persuade an audience they have not identified about a subject they know nothing about, the result is usually a very general and superficial text, an academic exercise that hasn't engaged the writer and so cannot engage a reader. Writers are much more persuasive when they write about something they have some firsthand knowledge or experience of and direct their arguments to a specific audience.

FIELD RESEARCH, PAGE 493

To find something you can write about comfortably and competently, you may want to make a list of things that seem to you not what they appear to be. Force yourself to make a fairly long list. Then choose one of the topics on the list to explore in some depth. For example, suppose you are an athlete and think you might want to write about why college athletes do not actually have the privileged positions they are thought to hold. You would write "Being a college athlete" at the top of a sheet of paper or your computer screen and then list the ways in which being a real athlete is different from the general perception. If you think of a number of differences between the reality as you know it and the popular idea of athletes as college heroes, then you can assume that this subject will be one you can write about convincingly (see also **invention**).

INVENTION, PAGE 529

Be sure to identify the audience you are writing for—other college athletes, high school students trying to decide whether to accept athletic scholarships, college students who don't know what an athlete's life is like, college administrators, and so on. Instead of an essay, you may want to write an article for your school newspaper, an editorial for a local or state newspaper, or (as Martin Luther King, Jr., did) a letter to someone who holds a different viewpoint.

Planning Your Text

After you have decided what you will write about and have identified some of the differences you want to include, you are ready to start constructing your argument. Your primary assertion, or **thesis**, can simply be that a difference exists—that whatever you are writing about is not what it is commonly supposed to be. However, a stronger argument can be built if you go one step further to make an explicit statement about your topic. For example, Rebecca Williams did not just say that beauty contests are not what they appear to be; she also stated clearly that they are profit-hungry businesses. It is this idea of the beauty contest as a money-making proposition that gives her essay a clear focus. She is not just identifying random differences she noticed; rather she focuses on the argument that beauty contests are primarily businesses that sacrifice honesty and the contestants' well-being to the profit motive.

THESIS, PAGE 599

For example, if you are writing about college athletes, your primary assertion might be that they are abused rather than privileged. Then you can refer to your list of differences and select those that support this assertion. You will probably also be able to think of other ways in which college athletes are abused once you have established this focus.

It is also good to think in advance about your main supporting arguments—about what type of evidence you plan to introduce to support your primary assertion. If you have chosen your subject wisely, you will already have a great deal of information on it. But to write solely from your own experiences and information is to limit the scope of your text to a single perspective. Now is the time to begin thinking about other sources of information. For example, if you are writing about the misperception of college athletes, you might survey other athletes to get their opinions on certain issues or interview several of them on this subject. You could also talk with coaches and teachers to gain their perspectives and read in some current magazines and journals about problems associated with college athletes (steroid use, stress, time management, etc.). You could also try to discover how many athletes actually graduate from your school after four years and how many drop out after one year or never graduate. Your own information, observations, and experiences should form the basis, or foundation, of your argument, but it will be a more convincing argument if it has a broader perspective (see **field research**).

FIELD RESEARCH, PAGE 493

Constructing Your Text

DRAFTING.   At this point you should have a general plan in mind for your argument. You should have at least a tentative hypothesis to use as your primary assertion and have identified several supporting arguments for that assertion. You should also have collected information to use as evidence in your supporting arguments.

As you write an initial draft, try to include as much information as possible, for this information is your most compelling evidence. Don't just mention a piece of information; give your readers details—lots of specific, concrete, abundant details. For example, don't just say that athletes are overscheduled; provide a full schedule of a day in the life of a typical college athlete, a blow-by-blow, minute-by-minute account of classes, practices, study sessions, and visits to the trainer's room.

The arguments you present will be only as strong as the detailed information you include to support them. Merely asserting that college athletes are overstressed, overscheduled, and overrated is not enough. You must convince your readers that your assertions are valid, and abundant information is the best way to accomplish that goal.

One way to generate additional information and gain new perspectives on your subject is to use a variety of methods of development as you write. You will, of course, begin with a comparison of your view to the common perception. But you can use other comparisons as you develop your arguments. For example, you could compare athletes to music majors (who are similarly overscheduled) or to students who have a very light schedule. Or you could compare athletes to the gladiators of ancient Rome, who were exploited for the pleasure of those who watched them perform.

Comparing or contrasting your subject to something else allows you to establish connections in the mind of your reader—to control the associations that the reader will make. For example, by comparing modern college athletes to ancient gladiators, whose abuse by the Romans is generally acknowledged, you strengthen your argument that college athletes are abused. Comparisons can appeal to your readers' emotions as well as to their sense of logic. The gladiator comparison obviously includes both appeals.

However, to be effective, the comparison must be appropriate and reasonable. You can compare college athletes to gladiators even though there are significant differences between the two because gladiators, like athletes of today, participated in athletic contests. In contrast, comparing college athletes to soldiers or slaves or women would not be as effective, even though it can be argued that they, like athletes, have often been abused or sacrificed for the pleasure of others. In other words, be sure to establish the fundamental similarity between your subject and whatever you are comparing or contrasting it to. Also, consider carefully the connotations and associations the comparison is likely to evoke in your reader. You want the comparison to work for, not against, your argument (see **comparison/contrast**).

COMPARISON/CONTRAST, PAGE 437

Another method of development effective for persuasive writing is cause and effect. Arguing that something will have certain consequences (effects), either good or bad, can be very convincing. For example, you could argue that continued abuse of college athletes will not only hurt individual athletes but also eventually hurt an athletic program. Then, of course, you would have to support this assertion also. One of the ways to do this would be to provide examples of athletic programs that have suffered because their athletes failed to pass and were ineligible to play, because they dropped out of school due to financial problems, or because they did not perform well as a result of pressure (see **cause and effect** and **exemplification**).

CAUSE AND EFFECT, PAGE 418

EXEMPLIFICATION, PAGE 488

You could also support your assertion about the consequences of continued abuse of college athletes by using narration or description. You could, for example, describe in detail the effects of these abuses on the athletes themselves or the program in general. Or you could tell a story, either true or hypothetical, about a single athlete or a single program (see **narration** and **description**).

NARRATION , PAGE 558

DESCRIPTION, PAGE 456

You can see that several methods of development can be used to support a single assertion. Use them in conjunction with one another to support your arguments. The web of arguments you weave—primary assertion supported by other assertions, which must in turn be supported and amplified by details and evidence—is largely composed of combinations of these different methods of development.

READING.   Reading your own efforts to persuade is often like patting yourself on the back. Your arguments reflect your own convictions, so when you read them it is difficult not to find them convincing. They will make perfect sense to you, especially if you read them just after you have written them. Therefore, try to gain some distance, both temporal and psychological, before reading what you have written. Wait until your rough draft is cold before reading it. Reread some of the information you collected or, better yet, an opposing argument before you attempt to evaluate your own arguments.

If possible, also read some of your classmates' arguments and, even more important, ask them to read yours. Your instructor may arrange for you to do this in class; if not, do it on your own. It is important to have another reader when you are writing to persuade. You need someone else's viewpoint—another person's reaction to your arguments.

However, if you let some time lapse before reading the draft you have constructed and read it with specific purposes in mind, you should be able to evaluate it in certain ways. For example, you can read it once to evaluate the balance of emotional and logical arguments you have used. Remember that logical arguments should dominate but that subtle, indirect emotional arguments can also be effective. Read it again focusing on the persona you have created in your text. Just how credible will a reader find you on this particular subject? Have you attempted to create a climate of consensus in your text by identifying points of agreement and acknowledging the validity of other views?

You might devote another reading to identifying the implicit assumptions on which your assertions rest. To accomplish this, you can make a list of each assertion included in your text and then write beside it the assumption(s) implied by the assertion. For example, if you argue that female athletes are not valued at your school, you are assuming that athletes should be valued and that females should be valued equally with males. Are you sure your readers will share these assumptions? Should you argue these points explicitly? Weak arguments are often those that assume too much—that fail to articulate and support all the assumptions the writer makes.

REVISING.   Reading the early draft or drafts of your text may have revealed significant weaknesses in your argument. Your first (or even your second or third) draft may be fairly rough because you often don't know what you need in the way of supporting evidence until you have attempted to construct your argument. You may have discovered a number of weak links in the chain of assertions and support you have constructed thus far. Now is the time to strengthen those weaknesses, to create a tightly constructed, well balanced, and clearly focused argument.

You might begin your revision by constructing an informal outline of your text. The purpose of your outline should be to reveal not only the organization of your text but also the basic links between assertions and support. Begin by writing your thesis, the primary assertion you are making, at the top of a sheet of paper or your computer screen. Beneath this primary assertion, list each supporting argument. Then beneath these supporting arguments, indicate the evidence or support you have included. Whether the resulting outline looks like a simple list, a tree diagram, or a flow chart, it should show the order in which you present each argument and the evidence and/or secondary assertions you are using to construct each argument.

This visual representation of your text should help you see its strengths and weaknesses more clearly. Is the order of your arguments the most effective way to arrange them? (Most writers place their strongest argument last.) Is your primary assertion (thesis) supported adequately? Is each individual argument well developed? Is your argument as a whole well constructed, held together by strong, well-forged links that progress logically from one point to the next?

Revising, when you write to persuade, usually involves multiple drafts. You will probably need to revise, reread, and revise again many times before you have constructed a clear and convincing argument.

Editing Your Text

Because your credibility is so important when you write to persuade, you should edit your text carefully. Four kinds of errors particularly damage reader confidence:

- Spelling errors

- Sentence boundary errors

- Agreement errors

- Unwarranted shifts

SPELLING ERRORS.   If you are using a computer, be sure to use a spell-check program. If not, verify the spelling of any word that you are not absolutely sure you have spelled correctly.

SENTENCE BOUNDARY ERRORS.   You can often detect fragments and run-on sentences if you read your text backward, sentence by sentence, so that you are examining the sentences out of their usual context.

A simple test that sometimes helps identify fragments is to add a tag question to each sentence.

> College athletes often drop out of school after a single semester—don't they?

If the resulting construction (sentence plus tag question) makes sense, then the sentence is probably not a fragment. For example, try to add tag questions to the following fragments:

> Dropping out of school after an initial semester characterized by frustration, exhaustion, and failure.

> If athletes were told in advance what to expect—how much time, physical effort, and energy would be required of them.

> An outstanding athlete, one who performs brilliantly time after time under incredible pressure and with very little financial reward.

Run-on, or fused, sentences can be more difficult to recognize, but it sometimes helps to identify all the nominative-case personal pronouns (*I, we, you, he, she, it, they*) you have used. Run-on sentences often occur when the second sentence begins with a personal pronoun. It is as though the writer did not believe an insignificant-looking word such as a personal pronoun could function as a sentence subject.

> The student entered the class **late she** took a seat near the door.

You can correct this error in any of the following ways:

> The student entered the class **late. She** took a seat near the door.

> The student entered the class **late; she** took a seat near the door.

The student entered the class **late and took** a seat near the door.

The student entered the class **late, and she** took a seat near the door.

Because the student entered the class late, she took a seat near the door.

Entering the class late, the student took a seat near the door.

Another word to look for in identifying run-on sentences is *then*. This little word is often used to begin a new sentence, or independent clause, as in the following example.

Athletes have to make all of the adjustments typical of college **freshmen *then* they** must also adjust to the very stressful world of college athletics.

Then is a conjunctive adverb (like *however, therefore,* and *consequently*) rather than a coordinating conjunction (like *and, but,* and *so*). When it is used to introduce a complete sentence, it must either follow a semicolon or begin a new sentence.

Athletes have to make all the adjustments typical of college **freshmen; then** they must also adjust to the very stressful world of college athletics.

Athletes have to make all the adjustments typical of college **freshmen. Then** they must also adjust to the very stressful world of college athletics.

AGREEMENT ERRORS. In the world of edited American English, subjects must agree with verbs and pronouns must agree with antecedents in both number and case. Number refers to singular and plural. Case refers to whether a word is used as a subject or an object (*they* versus *them* and *who* versus *whom*). If you know you have not mastered these conventions, proofread your text carefully to identify the subject and verb of each independent clause in your text. If you are not sure about their agreement, ask your teacher or someone else whose mastery of these conventions you trust. You can then do the same with the pronouns in your text. Underline each pronoun and identify its antecedent and its case function. You can then ask someone if any pronouns seem problematic.

UNWARRANTED SHIFTS.   Unnecessary shifts in tense and point of view distract readers. Be sure that if you begin in the present tense, for example, you don't needlessly and illogically shift to the past tense. Similarly, if you begin with a third-person point of view (*he, she, it,* and *they*), don't suddenly shift to second person (*you*). Change tense and point of view when a change is justified and logical. For example, if you include a narrative of something that took place in the past, you will logically shift to the past tense. But avoid unnecessary, illogical shifts.

Errors, especially those we have discussed, can distract a reader and can damage your credibility. Learning to edit carefully can, therefore, make your arguments more persuasive. Here is valuable general advice about editing:

- Be aware of the types of errors you are likely to make and look especially for these when you edit.

- Take the time to edit and proofread carefully. (Everyone makes errors, but careful writers take the time and care to look for errors and correct them.)

- Seek assistance when you need it.

The most effective way to improve your editing skills is to edit your own text carefully. Identifying your own errors and learning how to correct them will eventually result in your learning the correct conventions (see **revising and editing** and **proofreading**).

REVISING AND EDITING, PAGE 593

PROOFREADING, PAGE 585

8

ARGUING FROM SOURCES

The writer . . . is careful of what he reads, for that is what he will write. He is careful of what he learns, for that is what he will know.

ANNIE DILLARD

Whatever your writing purpose, you may decide to research your subject and report on the results of that investigation. Research enables you to learn more about a subject, to provide readers with additional information and multiple viewpoints, to gain credibility in the eyes of your readers, and to reinforce and confirm or sometimes to disprove and abandon your own ideas and arguments. When you report on your research, you may want to focus primarily on the sources you have discovered, objectively reporting the results of your investigation. More often, however, you will use your sources to develop and support your own arguments, as the writers in this chapter do in writing about environmental issues.

Researching a topic or issue and using the results of that research in your own text enable you to establish a dialogue with others who have written about the subject. When you include other sources in your text, you enter an ongoing conversation—responding to what has been said and contributing to the body of knowledge that exists on that subject. For example, Vice President Al Gore, one of the authors whose work is included in this chapter, mentions in the introduction to his book *Earth in the Balance* the influence that an earlier work by Rachel Carson had on him:

> I particularly remember my mother's troubled response to Rachel Carson's classic book about DDT and pesticide abuse, *Silent Spring*, first published in 1962. My mother was one of many who read Carson's warnings and shared them with others. She emphasized to my sister and me that this book was different—and important. Those conversations made an impression. . . . (3)

In this statement, Gore acknowledges his debt to Carson. His book on the environment continues a conversation that she initiated thirty years before.

Using outside sources makes special demands on both writer and reader, for they are constructing a text that includes not one voice but several. Most writers who use additional sources don't just report what others have written or said about a subject but *integrate* and *synthesize* the sources' ideas and information with their own ideas and knowledge. Speaking in their own voices and adding others, writers must present these multiple voices distinctly and yet blend them into a whole that makes sense to a reader. Even though a writer uses valuable information from impressive sources, the writer's own voice should dominate. The clear, strong voice of the writer unifies a text, giving it direction, coherence, and ultimately meaning.

Readers of a text in which the writer uses additional material to develop and support arguments encounter information from a variety of sources—and hear many voices, not just one. Readers must evaluate multiple viewpoints, not just the writer's ideas, information, arguments, analyses, and recommendations, but also the sources'.

Your first introduction to this type of writing is likely to be a research paper—a common assignment that requires you to research a subject and report on it. But reporting on research is more than an academic exercise. Such reports are common in business, government, and science. Recommendation reports and grant proposals, for example, nearly always involve the results of the writer's investigation of his or her subject. And research is not limited to science, government, and business. Reviews of books, music, art, and film also use other sources. In fact, *most* experienced writers use a variety of sources, including their own experiences, when they construct texts. Such writers see research and investigation as an essential, natural part of their writing process.

In a way, you always include other sources in your own writing, without being aware of doing so. What you know derives from long-forgotten sources that have become part of your general knowledge base. Your opinions, beliefs, ideas, and attitudes, too, have been shaped by diverse sources you may no longer remember. But when you knowingly and deliberately use other sources, you are obligated to acknowledge those sources appropriately. Not to do so is to plagiarize.

This chapter focuses on the processes of evaluating sources, selecting sources to support your argument, integrating sources effectively into your own text, and acknowledging those sources appropriately (see **documentation** and **library research**).

DOCUMENTATION, PAGE 460

LIBRARY RESEARCH, PAGE 534

READING ARGUMENTS THAT USE SOURCES

In one sense, all texts are based on research. All writers use not only their own experiences but what they have learned from other sources—from other texts and from other people—when they construct a text. However, writers often deliberately investigate a subject and include the results of that investigation in their texts to develop and support their own ideas and arguments. When readers confront such a text, they comprehend and react to it in different ways than they do when they read a text that does not explicitly include the results of the writer's research.

Understanding Why to Evaluate Sources

A writer's use of several sources provides a reader with different viewpoints and more information. But because skillful writers usually select and structure their sources to reinforce their own viewpoints, readers may accept these source-supported arguments without analyzing the role those sources assume in the argument. Even readers who are not swayed by the sheer number of sources may succumb to the authority of the sources the writer has included. For example, if an article on the enforcement of environmental laws includes supporting evidence from a Supreme Court justice, the attorney general of the United States, and several district judges, readers may accept the writer's arguments primarily because they are impressed with the cumulative authority of these sources.

It is also easy to be unduly impressed with arguments supported by research studies. If a writer argues that "research indicates that . . . ," readers may uncritically accept this vague reference to research as proof rather than evaluate the evidence. However, research studies do not always yield accurate, correctly interpreted results. Even careful research—honestly and accurately designed, conducted, and evaluated—may be flawed. Medical researchers who undertake extensive research, much of it well-executed, frequently have to revise their research findings in the light of subsequent research. Remember the on-again, off-again benefits and dangers of oat bran, caffeine, cholesterol, exercise, and aspirin?

Some readers also equate the results of polls with proof that an argument is sound. Yet each week, especially during election years, new polls appear that make previous ones obsolete. Polls are, after all, only collected opinions. Many are limited in scope and purpose yet reported as if they were a valid representation of national, if not global, reality.

Knowing How to Evaluate Sources

How then does a careful reader navigate these dangers of misinformation and misrepresentation when reading a source-based text? The following five guidelines can help:

❖ Consider context.

❖ Correct for bias.

❖ Question sources' accuracy and relevance.

❖ Scrutinize documentation of sources.

❖ Focus on the argument.

CONSIDER CONTEXT.   Out of context, a person's words can easily be misrepresented. Responsible writers never deliberately take a person's words out of context in a way that changes their meaning; unscrupulous writers often do. For example, a politician may state in a speech that she believes "national health care would benefit every level of society but no one more than the average working-class American." Parts of this statement, taken out of the full context, could read as follows:

> Senator Anne Hawkins argued that "national health care would benefit . . . no one. . . ."

So beware of snippets—a few words taken out of their original context and placed in the writer's own sentence—because they are incomplete and may be misleading.

CORRECT FOR BIAS.   When you are reading a text that includes multiple sources, you must be aware of not only the writer's possible bias but also that of the sources. For example, if a report on environmental issues cites only sources known to be concerned that the Earth's ecology is being harmed (Audubon Society, Sierra Club, Natural Resource Defense Fund, and so on) and ignores opposing viewpoints of government, industry, and others, you can assume that the sources are probably biased. Likewise, if the sources for an article on animal rights consist only of reports of research funded by the cosmetic and fur industries, you can assume they are probably not objective.

QUESTION SOURCES' ACCURACY AND RELEVANCE. Don't accept any source without question. Research studies can be misleading, polls are seldom scientific, and even authorities can be misquoted, quoted out of context, or simply wrong. Just because someone with a long title after his or her name says that something is so, it is not necessarily so. Even though most sources can be trusted, don't assume all sources can be trusted. Examine all sources carefully, noting especially their relevance and timeliness. The writer may have quoted a physician as saying that moderate amounts of alcohol are not harmful to most adults, but this opinion is not relevant if the issue is whether females should consume alcohol during pregnancy. Similarly, this same statement in a journal article published twenty-five years ago—even in the most reputable scientific journal—would not be valid today because only recently have medical researchers determined the effects of alcohol on the unborn fetus.

SCRUTINIZE DOCUMENTATION OF SOURCE. It is increasingly common to find undocumented sources (that is, material from sources that are not appropriately acknowledged) in popular magazines and journals. Although scholarly and academic journals still require careful **documentation**, popular books, magazines, and newspapers frequently include references to unnamed sources ("a recent study indicates . . . ," "a high-ranking official confirmed . . . ," "an eyewitness reports . . . ," and so on). Even more common is the practice of citing a source by name but not providing full documentation—the details that permit a reader to find out where, when, and even why the statement was made.

DOCUMENTATION, PAGE 460

The reason for omitting such information may be stylistic. That is, the writer may not want to include formal documentation because it would be intrusive or would alter the tone of the text. In such cases, the writer should take responsibility for providing readers with basic information such as the name of the source and the title (and, if possible, the date) of the work from which it is taken or a description of the occasion on which it was spoken (personal interview, speech to Congress, and so on). You should be skeptical of all sources that are not documented at least informally.

FOCUS ON THE ARGUMENT.   All texts are at some level persuasive. The writer is attempting to persuade readers of something—that a certain product is best, a particular method superior, a recent movie or book terrible; that an issue should be resolved this way or that way; that something is wrong, something is right, everything is wrong; and so on. When writers research a subject and present their findings, sometimes they are merely sharing with you the results of their research as objectively, accurately, and fairly as possible; more often they are using their research to support their own arguments.

As a reader, you need to focus on the writer's arguments rather than on the sources. However, evaluating those sources—why they are there and how they are being used and what effect they are having on you—should be part of your analysis of the writer's argument. What role are the sources playing in the writer's argument? Is the argument valid in itself, or does it depend entirely on the authority of the sources used to support it? Examples of weak arguments supported by strong sources abound. Advertisements often use a beautiful woman's name in association with a cosmetic product to help convince readers that the product brings beauty to the user, and having a successful man endorse a car helps persuade readers that the car somehow ensures success.

Whatever you are reading, be aware that the writer is trying to persuade you of something and that one of his or her most powerful weapons is the use of sources. Although most writers try to be accurate and responsible in reporting the results of their research, some writers use sources irresponsibly, even unethically. Readers must make every effort to tell the difference between the two.

▶ R E A D I N G S   F O R   W R I T I N G

The reading selections in this chapter focus on environmental issues—whether, and if so how, humans are damaging and perhaps destroying Earth. Some of these issues are controversial. Environmental protection groups, government officials, and industrial leaders seldom agree about which environmental problems need to be addressed and practically never agree about what action, if any, to take. As you read these selections, think about your own position on these issues.

All the reading selections include the results of the writers' research. As you read, notice how the writers use their sources to support and develop their own arguments, how they integrate their sources into their own writing so the two are effectively blended, and how they acknowledge their sources.

The Earth's Green Mantle

Rachel Carson

Rachel Carson's book Silent Spring *was one of the first to call attention to ongoing environmental damage. Even though her book was published over thirty years ago, in 1962, it is still pertinent because the environmental issues she identified still exist. In his recent book on the environment,* Earth in the Balance, *Vice President Al Gore refers to* Silent Spring *as a "classic." In this selection from her book, Carson argues that the destruction of native plants has serious consequences. As you read, notice that Carson establishes her argument primarily by describing the effects that the destruction of sagebrush has had on animal life in the West. That is, she argues that because the sagebrush is being destroyed, the wildlife it supports will also be destroyed (cause and effect). Carson uses not only her own observations and knowledge but also supports her argument by citing a study by late Supreme Court Justice William O. Douglas that tells of a similar instance of ecological destruction.*

1   Water, soil, and the earth's green mantle of plants make up the world that supports the animal life of the earth. Although modern man seldom remembers the fact, he could not exist without the plants that

harness the sun's energy and manufacture the basic foodstuffs he depends upon for life. Our attitude toward plants is a singularly narrow one. If we see any immediate utility in a plant we foster it. If for any reason we find its presence undesirable or merely a matter of indifference, we may condemn it to destruction forthwith. Besides the various plants that are poisonous to man or his livestock, or crowd out food plants, many are marked for destruction merely because, according to our narrow view, they happen to be in the wrong place at the wrong time. Many others are destroyed merely because they happen to be associates of the unwanted plants.

The earth's vegetation is part of a web of life in which there are intimate and essential relations between plants and the earth, between plants and other plants, between plants and animals. Sometimes we have no choice but to disturb these relationships, but we should do so thoughtfully, with full awareness that what we do may have consequences remote in time and place. But no such humility marks the booming "weed killer" business of the present day, in which soaring sales and expanding uses mark the production of plant-killing chemicals. 2

One of the most tragic examples of our unthinking bludgeoning of the landscape is to be seen in the sagebrush lands of the West, where a vast campaign is on to destroy the sage and to substitute grasslands. If ever an enterprise needed to be illuminated with a sense of the history and meaning of the landscape, it is this. For here the natural landscape is eloquent of the interplay of forces that have created it. It is spread before us like the pages of an open book in which we can read why the land is what it is, and why we should preserve its integrity. But the pages lie unread. 3

The land of the sage is the land of the high western plains and the lower slopes of the mountains that rise above them, a land born of the great uplift of the Rocky Mountain system many millions of years ago. It is a place of harsh extremes of climate: of long winters when blizzards drive down from the mountains and snow lies deep on the plains, of summers whose heat is relieved by only scanty rains, with drought biting deep into the soil, and drying winds stealing moisture from leaf and stem. 4

As the landscape evolved, there must have been a long period of trial and error in which plants attempted the colonization of this high and windswept land. One after another must have failed. At last one group of plants evolved which combined all the qualities needed to survive. The sage—low-growing and shrubby—could hold its place on the mountain slopes and on the plains, and within its small gray leaves 5 it could hold moisture enough to defy the thieving winds. It was no accident, but rather the result of long ages of experimentation by nature, that the great plains of the West became the land of the sage.

6   Along with the plants, animal life, too, was evolving in harmony with the searching requirements of the land. In time there were two as perfectly adjusted to their habitat as the sage. One was a mammal, the fleet and graceful pronghorn antelope. The other was a bird, the sage grouse—the "cock of the plains" of Lewis and Clark.

7   The sage and the grouse seem made for each other. The original range of the bird coincided with the range of the sage, and as the sagelands have been reduced, so the populations of grouse have dwindled. The sage is all things to these birds of the plains. The low sage of the foothill ranges shelters their nests and their young; the denser growths are loafing and roosting areas; at all times the sage provides the staple food of the grouse. Yet it is a two-way relationship. The spectacular courtship displays of the cocks help loosen the soil beneath and around the sage, aiding invasion by grasses which grow in the shelter of sagebrush.

8   The antelope, too, have adjusted their lives to the sage. They are primarily animals of the plains, and in winter when the first snows come those that have summered in the mountains move down to the lower elevations. There the sage provides the food that tides them over the winter. Where all other plants have shed their leaves, the sage remains evergreen, the gray-green leaves—bitter, aromatic, rich in proteins, fats, and needed minerals—clinging to the stems of the dense and shrubby plants. Though the snows pile up, the tops of the sage remain exposed, or can be reached by the sharp, pawing hoofs of the antelope. Then grouse feed on them too, finding them on bare and windswept ledges or following the antelope to feed where they have scratched away the snow.

9   And other life looks to the sage. Mule deer often feed on it. Sage may mean survival for winter-grazing livestock. Sheep graze many winter ranges where the big sagebrush forms almost pure stands. For half the year it is their principal forage, a plant of higher energy value than even alfalfa hay.

10   The bitter upland plains, the purple wastes of sage, the wild, swift antelope, and the grouse are then a natural system in perfect balance. Are? The verb must be changed—at least in those already vast and growing areas where man is attempting to improve on nature's way. In the name of progress the land management agencies have set about to satisfy the insatiable demands of the cattlemen for more grazing land.

By this they mean grassland—grass without sage. So in a land which nature found suited to grass growing mixed with and under the shelter of sage, it is now proposed to eliminate the sage and create unbroken grassland. Few seem to have asked whether grasslands are a stable and desirable goal in this region. Certainly nature's own answer was otherwise. The annual precipitation in this land where the rains seldom fall is not enough to support good sod-forming grass; it favors rather the perennial bunchgrass that grows in the shelter of the sage.

Yet the program of sage eradication has been under way for a number of years. Several government agencies are active in it; industry has joined with enthusiasm to promote and encourage an enterprise which creates expanded markets not only for grass seed but for a large assortment of machines for cutting and plowing and seeding. The newest addition to the weapons is the use of chemical sprays. Now millions of acres of sagebrush lands are sprayed each year.   11

What are the results? The eventual effects of eliminating sage and seeding with grass are largely conjectural. Men of long experience with the ways of the land say that in this country there is better growth of grass between and under the sage than can possibly be had in pure stands, once the moisture-holding sage is gone.   12

But even if the program succeeds in its immediate objective, it is clear that the whole closely knit fabric of life has been ripped apart. The antelope and the grouse will disappear along with the sage. The deer will suffer, too, and the land will be poorer for the destruction of the wild things that belong to it. Even the livestock which are the intended beneficiaries will suffer; no amount of lush green grass in summer can help the sheep starving in the winter storms for lack of the sage and bitterbrush and other wild vegetation of the plains.   13

These are the first and obvious effects. The second is of a kind that is always associated with the shotgun approach to nature: the spraying also eliminates a great many plants that were not its intended target. Justice William O. Douglas, in his recent book *My Wilderness: East to Katahdin*, has told of an appalling example of ecological destruction wrought by the United States Forest Service in the Bridger National Forest in Wyoming. Some 10,000 acres of sagelands were sprayed by the Service, yielding to pressure of cattlemen for more grasslands. The sage was killed, as intended. But so was the green, life-giving ribbon of willows that traced its way across these plains, following the meandering streams. Moose had lived in these willow thickets, for willow is to the moose what sage is to the antelope. Beaver had lived there, too, feeding on the willows, felling them and   14 making a strong dam across the tiny stream. Through the labor of the beavers, a lake backed up. Trout in the mountain streams seldom were more than six inches long; in the lake they thrived so prodigiously that many grew to five pounds. Waterfowl were attracted to the lake, also. Merely because of the presence of the willows and the beavers that depended on them, the region was an attractive recreational area with excellent fishing and hunting.

15   But with the "improvement" instituted by the Forest Service, the willows went the way of the sagebrush, killed by the same impartial spray. When Justice Douglas visited the area in 1959, the year of the spraying, he was shocked to see the shriveled and dying willows—the "vast, incredible damage." What would become of the moose? Of the beavers and the little world they had constructed? A year later he returned to read the answers in the devastated landscape. The moose were gone and so were the beaver. Their principal dam had gone out for want of attention by its skilled architects, and the lake had drained away. None of the large trout were left. None could live in the tiny creek that remained, threading its way through a bare, hot land where no shade remained. The living world was shattered.

▶   **QUESTIONS TO CONSIDER**

1. Carson's main argument is that water, soil, plants, and animals form a "web of life" and that the delicate balance of this carefully woven web is upset when one element is destroyed or even changed (cause and effect). Is the logic of her argument sound? Do your own observations and knowledge of life on Earth support this theory? Try to refute Carson's argument by (1) thinking of exceptions to this theory, (2) proving the logic is unsound, or (3) arguing there is a greater good involved (i.e., raising plants to support cattle for human consumption is more important than preserving antelope and grouse).

2. Carson supports her argument by describing in detail numerous examples of the effects the destruction of sagebrush has had on animal life in the West. Would her argument have been equally convincing had she used fewer examples? Why or why not?

3. Carson also supports her argument by citing a book by former Supreme Court Justice William O. Douglas. What specifically does she use from Douglas's study? Why is this source an effective support for her argument?

4. Carson's argument is emotional as well as logical. How does she evoke emotion in her reader? Is this emotional appeal effective? Would the use of statistics indicating how much damage insecticides have done in the United States have been more or less effective than her description of what is happening in particular areas? Why or why not?

WRITING ACTIVITIES

Individual: Select a particular feature of nature and write an imaginative account of what would happen if it were destroyed.

Collaborative: Assume the role of one of the bad guys (government agent, rancher, manufacturer of chemicals used to kill plants, etc.) and write a brief defense of the destruction of sagebrush in the West, responding specifically to Carson's argument.

Computer: Interview one of your classmates on this issue, recording verbatim several statements that he or she makes. Ask the person you are interviewing to read the statements you have recorded (on screen) to verify their accuracy. When the interview is over, summarize it briefly, inserting the direct quotations appropriately (see **documentation**).

DOCUMENTATION, PAGE 460

❖❖❖❖❖

WAR AND THE ENVIRONMENT

Michio Kaku

Michio Kaku, a professor of nuclear physics at the City University of New York, frequently writes and lectures on the environment. In this article, which he wrote for Audubon, *an environment-friendly magazine, Kaku argues that "the Gulf War was the greatest environmental setback in years" and that wars in general not only bring death and misery to humans but also cause devastating environmental damage. He begins and ends his argument by citing* Hiroshima, *a well-known novel by John Hersey, which movingly describes the effects of the atomic bomb on Hiroshima, Japan, at the close of World War II.*

1   In the aftermath of World War II, after the raucous tickertape parades down Broadway and the spontaneous outbursts of joy and relief had subsided, a disturbing series of articles appeared, first in *The New Yorker* magazine and eventually as John Hersey's landmark book, *Hiroshima.*

2   At once moving and deeply unsettling the book chronicled to an unsuspecting world the birth of a powerful new technology. From then on the victory celebrations were tempered with the frightening knowledge that a new weapon with almost Biblical implications had been unleashed on the planet.

3   Perhaps no book as powerful as Hersey's will emerge in the aftermath of the Gulf War. But after the fanfare surrounding Desert Storm fades, perhaps a more sober, thoughtful analysis of the Gulf War will take hold in the public's consciousness, and with it, the realization that victory in war has meant a devastating defeat for the environment. For by almost any yardstick, the Gulf War was the greatest environmental setback in years.

4   It is not an exaggeration to compare the environmental and human destruction unleashed in Iraq and Kuwait to the atomic bombing of Hiroshima.

5   In Hiroshima the atomic bomb released the explosive equivalent of 13,000 tons of TNT. By comparison the cumulative bombing of Iraq and Kuwait by U.S. forces totaled 88,500 tons of explosives, or roughly seven times the destructive force of the Hiroshima bomb. Although most Americans remember the Gulf War as the first "clean" Nintendo war in history, the Pentagon now admits only 7 percent of the bombs dropped in the Gulf were "smart" bombs; fully 93 percent were gravity bombs, or "dumb" bombs, with no midcourse guidance systems whatsoever. Overall, 70 percent of the bombs missed their targets. The "clean" war was a myth. The astonishing video tapes aired during the war were a victory of editing and public relations over truth.

6   In Hiroshima over 100,000 Japanese perished because of the radiation and fire of the atomic bomb. Yet perhaps as many as 150,000 to 200,000 Iraqis lost their lives in the Gulf War, according to the estimates of the Sunday *London Times* and the Chaldean Catholic Church of Iraq. And a Harvard medical team reported in May that tens of thousands of children might later die because of the United Nations embargo and the collapse of basic sanitation and the medical infrastructure.

7   In Hiroshima the radioactive fallout was limited because the bomb was detonated high in the atmosphere. But in Kuwait, there is a

massive plume fed by the burning of 1,250 oil wells, nearly 500 of which still blaze. The plume's effects have spread more than 1,500 miles, darkening parts of Kuwait and Iran during the day, sending temperatures plunging 20 degrees in some areas, and creating acid rain as far away as Bulgaria, India, and Pakistan.

The fire may be spewing out as much as 50,000 tons of sulfur   8
dioxide and 100,000 tons of sooty smoke per day. The pollution created by the burning of about five million barrels of oil per day is difficult to grasp. By the estimates of some scientists it is ten times the oil-related pollution generated by the entire United States.

Our planet has now become a laboratory for atmospheric scien-   9
tists: Physicists are already analyzing the distribution and size of the particles of soot. Some scientists even subscribe to the "nuclear winter scenario." (Fortunately, preliminary studies show that most of the soot has not yet flooded the upper atmosphere, where it may trigger serious planetary disturbances.)

In Hiroshima radioactive levels began to drop dramatically after   10
the first few weeks. However, in the Gulf, the fires may rage anywhere from two to four years. Capping them proceeds at an agonizing snail's pace: Only one oil well can be capped per crew, per week. Furthermore, the pollution caused by the massive slick in the Persian Gulf, which is several times the size of the Exxon Valdez oil slick, may last decades. Because the Persian Gulf has an average-depth of only a few hundred feet and is partially sealed off at the Strait of Hormuz, it may take as long as a century before all the oil is completely washed out. But within a few years, many of the roughly 450 species of animal life in the Gulf may be wiped out, leaving a dead sea.

Equally ominous is the precedent set by the U.S. Air Force's de-   11
struction of two Iraqi nuclear reactors and chemical plants. In future wars, nuclear power plants will be fair game to the military. Ironically, the United States has most to lose by this: In particular, the new rules may open the country up to an increased threat of attacks against its 111 commercial nulcear plants. The nuclear ash contained within a single commercial U.S. nuclear plant (over 10 billion curies per plant) is several hundred times larger than the fallout released by a large hydrogen bomb.

The Hiroshima bombing had at least one positive legacy: Its hor-   12
rific damage created a deep psychological inhibition against the wanton use of nuclear weapons.

It is to be hoped the Gulf War will likewise serve as a grim warn-   13
ing to military planners who view the devastation of the environment

and civilians as mere "collateral damage." If environmentalists can successfully educate the public about the massive ecological impact of the Gulf War, then planners will be forced to consider the environment as a factor in the calculus of war.

14   Encouragingly, there are small, hopeful signs of a new era emerging. Throughout recorded history, nations have engaged in predatory wars in the quest to secure power, resources, and wealth. But we may now be seeing the dawning of a New Environmental Order, where the overarching necessity of controlling worldwide pollution and environmental desecration will force unwilling nations to cooperate on an unprecedented basis.

15   Pollution knows no boundaries. Greenhouse gases, ozone, acid rain, and the destruction of the rainforest have forced nations to re-examine priorities, such as energy use, consumption, industrialization, and social development. These are all pressing issues pushing nations to engage in cooperation, not confrontation.

16   For example, vivid satellite pictures of the large atmospheric hole above the South Pole have galvanized previously reluctant nations to restrict domestic use of chlorofluorocarbons. Most developed nations have agreed to stop CFC use by the year 2000, and most developing nations are set to stop soon afterward.

17   However, the transition to the New Environmental Order is still very fragile and must be nurtured carefully. Like John Hersey after World War II, environmentalists must now alert the public to the profound threat the world's vast military arsenal poses to the environment.

18   As with Hiroshima, this may be the real legacy of the Gulf War— rather than getting ready for the next war, perhaps we will become determined to prevent it.

▶   QUESTIONS TO CONSIDER

1. One important way Kaku develops his argument is by comparing the devastation of the Gulf War to that caused by the dropping of an atomic bomb on Hiroshima. Identify other methods of development that he uses.

2. Is the comparison between the damage caused by a single atomic bomb at Hiroshima and the entire Gulf War a fair **analogy**?

ANALOGY, PAGE 413

3. Kaku supports his argument by using John Hersey's novel as a source, summarizing the novel briefly and reviewing its effect on readers when it first appeared as a series of articles in *The New Yorker* magazine. What effect does Kaku create by using this source? How does it contribute to his own argument?

4. Kaku also mentions other sources—the Pentagon, the *London Times*, the Chaldean Catholic Church of Iraq, a Harvard medical team, and "some scientists." However, he does not supply enough information about these sources to allow readers to verify them. In other words, the author assumes his own credibility (as a teacher, scientist, writer, and environmentalist) is good enough that readers will trust him to represent his sources accurately and honestly. Is his assumption valid? What effect would it have had on his own credibility if he had cited these sources more explicitly? What effect would it have had on the **style and voice** of the article?   STYLE AND VOICE, PAGE 596

5. The author refers to the Gulf War as the "first 'clean' Nintendo war." Explain what you think the author means by this remark. What reaction do you think this "Nintendo effect" had on those who viewed the war on television? Do you think the Nintendo effect was the inevitable result of new technology or was deliberately created by our government to make the war more acceptable to the American public?

WRITING ACTIVITIES

Individual: Summarize Kaku's arguments briefly and then argue for or against the idea that war will become obsolete in the future because it is too dangerous to our environment.

Collaborative: Discuss Kaku's argument that the Gulf War's military and political goals were overshadowed by the environmental destruction it caused. List your reasons for agreeing or disagreeing with this assertion.

Computer: Answer the following question: Is war worth its environmental costs? Share your answer with your peers through a computer network program (or by sharing disks). Respond to at least three of your classmates' answers.

CRIME AND PUNISHMENT

Patricia A. Parker

This article by free-lance writer Patricia A. Parker appeared in Buzzworm: The Environmental Journal. *The readers of this magazine are typically people who are concerned about the environment, whose minds are made up on environmental issues. Yet Parker's article is objective and balanced. Without appearing to be strongly biased on this subject, she provides readers with considerable information about environmental crimes and how they are prosecuted. One of the ways she achieves this objective tone is to use a variety of sources representing not only proenvironment organizations but also government and industry. As you read, notice the great number of sources Parker uses in her report (the magazine calls it an eco-report), how she introduces and identifies her sources, and how she uses them to give readers an overview of this complex issue.*

1   Crime: An unjust, senseless or disgraceful act. Robbery, murder . . . and environmental destruction? That's right. It's not nice—or legal—to foul Mother Nature. Those who do could wind up behind bars. That goes for corporate executives and individual citizens alike.

2   Traditionally, punishment for environmental violations meant a slap on the wrist. Now, federal, state and local governments are training their police, prosecutors and regulatory personnel to identify and preserve criminal evidence in hopes of increasing incarceration sentences. In its Enforcement Strategy for the 1990s, the US Environmental Protection Agency (EPA) says that sentencing courts are more willing to "view environmental crime for what it really is—a crime of violence and an egregious departure from responsible citizenship."

3   Already, the state of New Jersey has demonstrated its aggressive enforcement crackdown with the establishment of the first environmental prosecutor's office in the country. A number of states will probably follow suit as they continue to enact tougher environmental legislation.

4   "There is no question that 20 years after the EPA's inception, criminal enforcement is EPA's most effective deterrent," says Earl Devaney, EPA's new director of criminal enforcement. "Unlike a civil

or administrative monetary penalty, jail time is one cost that the environmental criminal cannot pass on to customers or the public."

That's a 180-degree turn for the EPA, a 21-year-old environmental   5
knight in shining armor tarnished over the years by a fouled environment. Prior to 1970, the general public had no real protection from hazardous waste impacts. Even after EPA's inception in 1970, enforcement was virtually nonexistent until 1977, when the agency referred 143 civil cases to the US Department of Justice. By 1978, that number reached 262, then remained below that level until 1985. Since then, the number has gradually risen to 375 in 1990, and EPA officials say civil penalties are getting tougher.

For instance, EPA assessed a $15 million civil penalty against   6
Texas Eastern Pipeline in 1990. In May 1991, Wheeling-Pittsburgh Steel Corporation of Wheeling, West Virginia, agreed to pay a civil penalty in excess of $6 million—the largest penalty of its kind under the Clean Water Act.

The largest criminal fine for a hazardous waste violation under   7
the Resource Conservation and Recovery Act was $3.75 million assessed to United States Sugar in December 1991. Fines for more heinous violations have soared higher. For example, the *Exxon Valdez* settlement resulted in a $900 million civil penalty and a $100 million criminal fine, although environmentalists say that wasn't enough.

Until recently, criminal enforcement was a particularly low prior-   8
ity. It wasn't until 1984 that the Justice Department finally granted law-enforcement power to 23 special agents in EPA. Since then, roughly 2 percent of the agency's enforcement efforts have been devoted to criminal violations. When William Reilly took over in 1988, however, EPA steadily increased its criminal enforcement, recognizing criminal sanctions as its most powerful tool.

In 1990, 100 defendants (individuals and corporations) faced   9
charges for environmental crimes—the largest number in EPA's history. Of those, 55 received sentences for environmental crimes, including imprisonment. According to the Department of Justice, more than half of the individuals convicted for environmental crimes during 1990 received prison sentences, and nearly 85 percent of those are serving time, with an average sentence in excess of one year.

But environmentalists are cautious about the new effort.   10

"When a corporation gets involved in ripping off money, some-   11
how those crimes are dealt with more severely," says Brian Lipsett, research analyst with the Citizen's Clearinghouse for Hazardous Wastes. "Environmental crimes shouldn't be treated any differently

than fraud or tax evasion. Rich people's money is no more important than employees' lives, and the laws need to recognize that."

12   Federal laws are starting to do just that, says Barry Hartman, acting assistant attorney general at the Department of Justice. With the changes in laws during recent years, "it was obviously the desire of Congress that we prosecute serious violations to obtain serious penalties," Hartman says.

13   All of EPA's environmental laws authorize the use of criminal sanctions against firms or individuals who knowingly or willfully violate environmental standards.

14   A major advantage for the Department of Justice was the US Sentencing Commission's 1987 Sentencing Guidelines, which changed most environmental offenses from misdemeanors to felonies for individuals. Subsequently the Commission's 1991 Sentencing Guidelines accomplished the same for businesses. A felony means violators are more likely to face mandatory imprisonment that extends beyond one year. Felonies also lead to loss of civil rights while promising a criminal record. That can destroy future business contracts with the government and other entities.

15   Furthermore, these recent guidelines remove the discretionary power of judges and bind them to a point system within certain ranges for sentencing. Now federal prosecutors have the ammunition they need to lock violators away.

16   Currently, Hartman has an indictment against a Utah oil recycling company, which has allegedly dumped recylced oil into gas tanks and stored it illegally while making a profit. If the president of the company is found guilty, Hartman says, he faces 45 years in prison. To date, about 40 company presidents have been indicted by the Department of Justice.

17   "Our philosophy is to follow the evidence where it leads," says Hartman. "If it takes us to the boardroom, so be it."

18   "There's absolutely no oversight, and Congress lacks any spine when it comes to standing up to the lobbyists, industry and the EPA when they interpret the laws in a way which is detrimental to the environment," Lipsett says. "EPA likes to stock its enforcement list with a bunch of penny-ante enforcement actions against small-timers who don't have the political clout or financial might to fight EPA. Big companies—the ones with political clout and a revolving door into EPA—get a slap on the wrist at the very worst."

19   Hartman disagrees and says the track record over the last few years proves otherwise.

"It's not illegal to be in big business, but I have a hard time   20
understanding an argument that says we're not suing enough big companies," says Hartman. "We find them, we sue them, we treat them like
everyone else, and we try to get a fine that's commensurate with the
violation and the business."

Nearly every Fortune 500 company has been sued either crimi-   21
nally or civilly by the Justice Department over the last four or five
years, according to Hartman. Among those are International Paper,
Marathon Oil, Pillsbury, Ocean Spray, GM and Du Pont. Last year,
nearly 80 percent of the Department of Justice's indictments were
against corporations and their top officers.

One other legislative effort, the Pollution Prosecution Act of 1990,   22
should benefit EPA in identifying violators and collecting evidence.
This act requires that EPA quadruple its criminal investigators from the
current 55 up to 200 by the end of 1995. Two-thirds of EPA's cases fall
under the Clean Water Act and the Resource Conservation and
Recovery Act, accounting for the bulk of prosecutions. The remaining
one-third relate to the Clean Air Act and the laws governing pesticides
and toxics.

"The more investigators you have, the more cases you're able to   23
handle, or the more people you're able to place on bigger cases," says
Hartman.

"It sounds great to quadruple, but when you think about what   24
EPA has now, that's one investigator per state," says Jack Doyle, senior
analyst for technical and corporate policy at Friends of the Earth.
"There are 500 big companies—the Fortune 500—so, right now, that's
about 10 companies per inspector."

Currently, several companies are suggesting they will conduct   25
voluntary environmental audits—analyses of their operations for environmental compliance—with the hope that they won't be criminally
prosecuted. Doyle says this is "absurd" because companies should voluntarily comply as a "function of their charter for conducting business
in this country." Recent public opinion polls classified environmental
crime as more serious than insider trading or price fixing.

In addition to enforcement efforts at the federal level, a number   26
of state and local efforts are under way. New Jersey's visionary thinking led to the country's—and possibly the world's—first statewide
environmental prosecutor's office. In 1990, Governor Jim Florio created an executive order to coordinate the resources of environmental
enforcement agencies, including New Jersey's Department of Environ-

mental Protection, Department of Health, Solid and Hazardous Waste Unit, as well as others.

27   What's so special about a separate environmental prosecutor's office? In New Jersey, civil, criminal and regulatory jurisdiction reside under one roof with a central coordinator.

28   "I can cross all different department and division lines to get the job done," says Stephen J. Madonna, a New Jersey state environmental prosecutor. "That means I can structure a solution knowing I don't have to cajole, convince or outmaneuver another bureaucrat—no matter how well-intentioned—who has his own jurisdiction and turf and assesses the situation differently."

29   In 1990, nine people went to jail in New Jersey for environmental violations, with sentences as high as five years and as low as five months.

30   "It is essential as a prosecutor that the regulated community understands that you are fair," says Madonna, "but that you shoot on target and shoot with a cannon."

31   Last year, his office was instrumental in obtaining an additional $5 million in criminal fines and $10 million in civil penalties from Exxon for its 1990 inter-refinery pipeline rupture, placing the final resolution package near $59 million.

32   Because of New Jersey's tough stance, the "Wild West" days of dropping hazardous drums along the roadside have basically disappeared. A number of criminals have been driven from the area. Entering its second decade of enforcement, the state is reevaluating the "environmental criminal in New Jersey" to once again define the most efficient approaches and tactics.

33   Madonna would like to see other states become more assertive. The National District Attorney's Association is conducting a needs assessment on enforcement, but Madonna says the group doesn't seem to share his "sense of urgency and immediacy" because action is more critical than studies at this point. He's been encouraging such efforts since 1980, when he assisted the attorneys general of 11 northeastern states in developing the Northeast Hazardous Waste Project, now comprising 14 states.

34   The goal? To counter interstate activities of hazardous waste violators by 1) promoting and coordinating investigations among member states, 2) providing technical assistance, 3) providing an information bank for all public record information regarding the hazardous waste industry,

4) developing a law-enforcement partnership and 5) providing annual training to all levels of government on environmental enforcement.

Since 1980, three similar projects have emerged: the Midwest Environmental Enforcement Association, the Western States Hazardous Waste Project and the Southern Environmental Enforcement Network. Funded by the EPA and the 46 participating states, all four regional projects bring together law enforcement and regulatory representatives.   35

Membership in the regional networks has increased from 23 states to 46 states in just a three-year period, including the Canadian provinces of Ontario and Alberta. Last year alone, these four groups trained nearly 850 people.   36

Enforcement officials say so much additional training is under way by various groups that no one really has a handle on it right now. That should improve with the creation of EPA's National Environmental Training Institute, mandated by the Pollution Prosecution Act of 1990.   37

Another key player in the training arena is the Federal Law Enforcement Training Center in Glynco, Georgia. Since 1987, over 500 investigators and regulatory personnel have been trained in environmental crime scene evidence and investigative techniques. New Jersey's Madonna was instrumental in developing this program, too.   38

Police officers often stumble upon hazardous environmental conditions in their communities, but how prepared are they to recognize and preserve evidence? In the early 1980s, only four states—New Jersey, New York, Louisiana and Michigan—established dedicated environmental-crime units. Since then, nearly 30 states have formal criminal environmental-crime units at the state law-enforcement level, but most municipal police departments lack the resources for such units.   39

"When I was a cop, I used to drive around barrels, and I never knew what they meant because my training centered on murders, breaking and enterings, homicides and assaults," says Thomas Flanagan, administrator of investigations for New Jersey's environmental prosecutor. "Back in the early 1970s, I was never told what to look for."   40

It seems police agencies are still lagging behind, and many illegal and dangerous operations could worsen unless state and local agencies become more knowledgeable. Certainly, the Federal Law Enforcement Training Center and regional networks are valuable, but in New Jersey, Madonna is working to weave environmental enforcement into the curriculum of police academies.   41

But environmental enforcement can't exist without environmental statutes. More states are thinking along those lines, especially   42 with the guidance of the four regional networks. At least 10 states that did not have environmental-crime programs at the time of membership in one of the networks have since established them. Several states have already developed tough legislation, including New Jersey, California, Ohio and Pennsylvania, while others are working toward change.

43   What do corporations make of this crackdown? "If someone is sent to jail just because of lack of control, you have to wonder," says Joe Mayhew, director of environmental programs for the Chemical Manufacturers Association. "Often a plant manager or another employee has the power. The Department of Justice shouldn't overlook how a company is structured, because they may end up getting the wrong people in their effort to get to the top."

44   Because of the decentralized structures within industry, executives rely on employees to handle the regulatory details, says Mayhew. Corporate officers who are several steps removed from a violation worry that they might miss something "just because of too much to do."

45   He says prosecutors need to look where the power lies. If the wrong people are punished, the deterrent won't be effective. Enforcement needs to be rational, but jail time should be assigned only for "deliberate action," he says.

46   The Justice Department's Hartman says he intends to criminally prosecute those officers who knowingly and willfully commit violations. The selected avenue for penalties and imprisonment revolves around state of mind. Madonna says his office tends to think "more civilly as the conduct shifts away from intentional conduct."

47   "We're not crazies," adds Madonna. "We're very reasonable people, but we want reasonable, responsible environmental compliance."

48   Chemical manufacturers have not exactly experienced a love relationship with environmentalists and the public over the years.

49   "It's no secret that the chemical industry has received a bad reputation on the environment," says Thomas J. Gilroy, spokesman for the Chemical Manufacturers Association. "At first, a lot of people in the industry looked at it just as an undeserved reputation, but I think lately companies have more or less said that if people don't trust us . . . we have to change—by performance—what they think of us."

50   Chemical manufacturers and other corporations, however, will remain under the watchful eye of leery environmentalists. Citizen's Clearinghouse for Hazardous Wastes' Lipsett says a number of corporations are attempting to "green wash" by cleaning up their images

through slick public relations when they "should be cleaning up their act." The corporate responsibility project at Friends of the Earth will assist in keeping the "green marketing" claims in check. In fact, Doyle just completed a comprehensive evaluation of Du Pont's practices, entitled "Hold the Applause," in recognition of the company's recent commercial promoting double-hulled tankers.

"While the advertisement has been running since September 1990, Du Pont has amassed penalties for out-of-court settlement fees of an average $1 million per month," says Doyle. "That's a very conservative estimate of the fines and infractions and settlements against Du Pont and Conoco because, thanks to our wonderful, decentralized enforcement mechanism at EPA and the Justice Department, it's impossible to get a good snapshot of the enforcement record of any one company in the United States."   51

Generally, environmentalists seem to agree that a move to expand criminal enforcement is a step in the right direction.   52

"More and more environmental enforcement agencies are working to penetrate the corporate veil and pin criminal activity on executives in the corporation," Lipsett says. "The day we start putting people in jail will be the day we start to move on this stuff. But it will only happen because people in the communities demand it."   53

Amid the new enforcement effort, corporate lawyers are scurrying to land business contracts by promising to "fashion deals" and develop "safe harbor provisions" for clients.   54

"It will be a travesty if we start seeing these kinds of quid pro quos made for backing off on enforcement," says Doyle. "We're at a very important juncture, and public opinion is very strong on enforcement and executive responsibility for environmental offenses. We need this as a deterrent. Nothing sends shock waves through a corporate culture like CEOs going to jail."   55

Will more corporate officers go to jail in the next decade? Federal, state and local officials say yes.   56

"That will reset the tone to where the regulated community will understand that this is serious business," says Madonna. "Then you'll see a shift to more responsible programs, but you must have criminal enforcement in order to give credibility to the overall regulatory network of enforcement. Violators have to know that behind the civil regulatory enforcement scheme is somebody ready, willing, able and actually waiting to pounce on people who think they're going to buck the system."   57

QUESTIONS TO CONSIDER

1. Because she is writing for an environmental journal, Parker assumes her audience is knowledgeable about environmental issues and sympathetic to environmental causes. Thus she spends little time persuading her readers that environmental crimes *should* be punished. Rather she focuses on providing information from various sources about the increasing use of jail sentences to punish those who commit crimes against the environment. What would be the effect of this article on a reader who has never thought about appropriate sentences for environmental offenders or who has no particular sympathy for environmental causes?

2. This article reveals very little about the author. Parker's voice remains fairly anonymous throughout. Is her self-effacement appropriate for her purpose in writing this report? Or would the article have been more effective if the author's own ideas and opinions played a larger role?

3. Does Parker identify her sources adequately? Can you distinguish between the sources she interviewed and those she took from other texts (newspapers, magazines, reports, government documents, etc.)? Should she have provided readers with more information so they could verify or locate her sources should they desire to do so? Why or why not?

WRITING ACTIVITIES

Individual: Discuss in a journal entry which is the more serious crime—the taking of a single human life or the pollution of a water supply.

Collaborative: Select five of the sources that Parker uses and analyze them. Consider, for example, the following: (1) Is the source credible? (2) Is the source sufficiently documented? (3) Is the source biased? (4) Is the source quoted out of context?

Computer: Compose a brief argument for or against punishment for environmental crimes. Using your computer network program, share your argument with your peers and respond to their arguments. Then revise your argument by integrating into it one or more of your peers' responses.

❖❖❖❖❖

THE WASTELAND

Al Gore

Vice President Al Gore, formerly a U.S. senator from Tennessee, is a noted environmentalist. In his book, Earth in the Balance, *published in 1992, he discusses his concerns about the environment and proposes solutions to these problems. In the following selection from his book, he argues that "the way we think about waste is leading to the production of so much of it that no method for handling it can escape being completely overwhelmed." As you read, note each of the sources that Gore uses and how these sources support his argument.*

One of the clearest signs that our relationship to the global environment is in severe crisis is the floodtide of garbage spilling out of our cities and factories. What some have called the "throwaway society" has been based on the assumptions that endless resources will allow us to produce an endless supply of goods and that bottomless receptacles (i.e., landfills and ocean dumping sites) will allow us to dispose of an endless stream of waste. But now we are beginning to drown in that stream. Having relied for too long on the old strategy of "out of sight, out of mind," we are now running out of ways to dispose of our waste in a manner that keeps it out of either sight or mind.   1

In an earlier era, when the human population and the quantities of waste generated were much smaller and when highly toxic forms of waste were uncommon, it was possible to believe that the world's absorption of our waste meant that we need not think about it again. Now, however, all that has changed. Suddenly, we are disconcerted— even offended—when the huge quantities of waste we thought we had thrown away suddenly demand our attention as landfills overflow, incinerators foul the air, and neighboring communities and states attempt to dump their overflow problems on us.   2

The American people have, in recent years, become embroiled in debates about the relative merits of various waste disposal schemes, from dumping it in the ocean to burying it in a landfill to burning it or taking it elsewhere, anywhere, as long as it is somewhere else. Now, however, we must confront a strategic threat to our capacity to dispose of—or even recycle—the enormous quantities of waste now being   3 produced. Simply put, the way we think about waste is leading to the production of so much of it that no method for handling it can escape being completely overwhelmed. There is only one way out: we have to change our production processes and dramatically reduce the amount of waste we create in the first place and ensure that we consider thoroughly, ahead of time, just how we intend to recycle or isolate that which unavoidably remains. But first we have to think clearly about the complexities of the predicament.

4   Waste is a multifaceted problem. We think of waste as whatever is useless, or unprofitable according to our transitory methods of calculating value, or sufficiently degraded so that the cost of reclamation seems higher than the cost of disposal. But anything produced in excess—nuclear weapons, for example, or junk mail—also represents waste. And in modern civilization, we have come to think of almost any natural resource as "going to waste" if we have failed to develop it, which usually means exploiting it for commercial use. Ironically, however, when we do transform natural resources into something useful, we create waste twice—once when we generate waste as part of the production process and a second time when we tire of the thing itself and throw it away.

5   Perhaps the most visible evidence of the waste crisis is the problem of how to dispose of our mountains of municipal solid waste, which is being generated at the rate of more than five pounds a day for every citizen of this country, or approximately one ton per person per year. But two other kinds of waste pose equally difficult challenges. The first is the physically dangerous and politically volatile material known as hazardous waste, which accompanied the chemical revolution of the 1930s and which the United States now produces in roughly the same quantities as municipal solid waste. (This is a conservative estimate, one that would double if we counted all the hazardous waste that is currently exempted from regulation for a variety of administrative and political reasons.) Second, one ton of industrial solid waste is created each week for every man, woman, and child—and this does not even count the gaseous waste steadily being vented into the atmosphere. (For example, each person in the United States also produces an average of twenty tons of CO_2 each year.) Incredibly, taking into account all three of these conservatively defined categories of waste, every person in the United States produces *more than twice his or her weight in waste every day.*

6   It's easy to discount the importance of such a statistic, but we can no longer consider ourselves completely separate from the waste we

help to produce at work or the waste that is generated in the process of supplying us with the things we buy and use.

Our cavalier attitude toward this problem is an indication of how hard it will be to solve. Even the words we use to describe our behavior reveal the pattern of self-deception. Take, for example, the word *consumption*, which implies an almost mechanical efficiency, suggesting that all traces of whatever we consume magically vanish after we use it. In fact, when we consume something, it doesn't go away at all. Rather, it is transformed into two very different kinds of things: something "useful" and the stuff left over, which we call "waste." Moreover, anything we think of as useful becomes waste as soon as we are finished with it, so our perception of the things we consume must be considered when deciding what is and isn't waste. Until recently, none of these issues has seemed terribly important; indeed, a high rate of consumption has often been cited as a distinguishing characteristic of an advanced society. Now, however, this attitude can no longer be considered in any way healthy, desirable, or acceptable.

The waste crisis is integrally related to the crisis of industrial civilization as a whole. Just as our internal combustion engines have automated the process by which our lungs transform oxygen into carbon dioxide (CO_2), our industrial apparatus has vastly magnified the process by which our digestive system transforms raw material (food) into human energy and growth—and waste. Viewed as an extension of our own consumption process, our civilization now ingests enormous quantities of trees, coal, oil, minerals, and thousands of substances taken from their places of discovery, then transforms them into "products" of every shape, kind, and description—and into vast mountain ranges of waste.

The chemical revolution has burst upon the world with awesome speed. Our annual production of organic chemicals soared from 1 million tons in 1930 to 7 million tons in 1950, 63 million in 1970, and half a billion in 1990. At the current rate, world chemical production is now doubling in volume every seven to eight years. The amount of chemical waste dumped into landfills, lakes, rivers, and oceans is staggering. In the United States alone, there are an estimated 650,000 commercial and industrial sources of hazardous waste; the Environmental Protection Agency (EPA) believes that 99 percent of this waste comes from only 2 percent of the sources, and an estimated 64 percent of all hazardous waste is managed at only ten regulated facilities. Two thirds of all hazardous waste comes from chemical manufacturing and almost one quarter from the production of metals and machinery. The remaining 11 percent is divided between petroleum refining (3 percent) and a hundred other smaller categories. According to the United Nations Environment Programme, more than 7 million chemicals have now been discovered or created by humankind, and several thousand new ones are added each year. Of the 80,000 now in common use in significant quantities, most are produced in a manner that also creates chemical waste, much of it hazardous. While many kinds of hazardous chemical waste can be managed fairly easily, other kinds can be extremely dangerous to large numbers of people in even minute quantities. Unfortunately, there is such a wide range of waste labeled "hazardous" that the public is often misled about what is really dangerous and what is not. Most troubling of all, many of the new chemical waste compounds are never tested for their potential toxicity.

10   In addition, we now produce significant quantities of heavy metal contaminants, like lead and mercury, and medical waste, including infectious waste. Nuclear waste, of course, is the most dangerous of all, since it is highly toxic and remains so for thousands of years. Indeed, the most serious waste problems appear to be those created by federal facilities involved in nuclear weapons production. These problems may have received less attention in the past because most federal facilities are somewhat isolated from their communities. In contrast, the public has become outraged by the dumping of hazardous waste into landfills, because numerous studies and disastrous events have shown that the practice is simply not safe. Basically, the technology for disposing of waste hasn't caught up with the technology of producing it.

11   Few communities want to serve as a dumping ground for toxic waste; studies have noted the disproportionate number of landfills and hazardous waste facilities in poor and minority areas. For example, a major study, *Toxic Wastes and Race in the United States*, by the United Church of Christ, came to the following conclusion:

12   Race proved to be the most significant among variables tested in association with the location of commercial hazardous waste facilities. This represented a consistent national pattern. Communities with the greatest number of commercial hazardous waste facilities had the highest composition of racial and ethnic residents. In communities with two or more facilities

or one of the nation's five largest landfills, the average minority percentage of the population was more than three times that of communities without facilities (38% vs. 12%).

It's practically an American tradition: waste has long been   13
dumped on the cheapest, least desirable land in areas surrounded by less fortunate citizens. But the volume of hazardous waste being generated is now so enormous that it is being transported all over the country by haulers who are taking it wherever they can. A few years ago, some were actually dumping it on the roads themselves, opening a faucet underneath the truck and letting the waste slowly drain out as they crossed the countryside. In other cases, hazardous waste was being turned over to unethical haulers controlled by organized crime who dumped the waste on the side of the road in rural areas or into rivers in the middle of the night. There is some evidence that we have made progress in addressing these parts of the problem.

However, the danger we face as a result of improper waste haul-   14
ing is nothing compared to what happens in most older cities in America every time it rains heavily: huge quantities of raw, untreated sewage are dumped directly into the nearest river, creek, or lake. Since the so-called storm water sewers in these cities were built to connect to the sewer system (before the combined pipes reach the processing plant), the total volume of water during a hard rain is such that the processing plant would be overwhelmed if it didn't simply open the gates, forget about treating the raw sewage, and just dump it directly into the nearest large body of water. This practice is being allowed to continue indefinitely because local officials throughout the country have convinced Congress that the cost of separating the sewers that carry human waste from the sewers that carry rainwater would be greater than the cost of continuing to poison the rivers and oceans. But no effort has been made to calculate the cost of the growing contamination. Could it be because Congress, and indeed this generation of voters, seem to feel that this practice is acceptable because the cost of handling the waste properly will be borne by us, and much of the cost for fouling the environment can be shunted off on our children and their children?

Though federal law purports to prohibit the dumping of munici-   15
pal sewage and industrial waste into the oceans by 1991, it is obvious that the increasing volumes being generated and the enormous cost of the steps required to prevent ocean dumping will make that deadline

laughably irrelevant. Currently, our coastal waters receive 2.3 trillion gallons of municipal effluent and 4.9 billion gallons of industrial wastewater each year, most of which fails to pass muster under the law. Nor are we the only nation guilty of this practice. Germany's river system carries huge quantities of waste toward the sea each day. Most rivers throughout Asia and Europe, Africa and Latin America, are treated as open sewers, especially for industrial waste and sewage. And, as previously noted, the first major tragedy involving chemical waste in the water was in Japan in the 1950s, at Minimata. International cooperative efforts have focused on regional ocean pollution problems, such as the Mediterranean, the North Sea, and the Caribbean.

16   The disposal of hazardous waste has received a good deal of attention in recent years, though there is still much to be done. For one thing, how do we know which waste is truly hazardous and which isn't? We produce more industrial waste than any other kind, but do we really know enough about it? Most industrial waste is disposed of on sites owned by the generator, often next to the facility that creates the waste. The landfills and dumps used by industry are therefore often far from public view and—especially because these companies create jobs—their waste is usually noticed only when it escapes from the site by means of underground water flow or dispersal by the winds.

17   Much more difficult to hide are the landfills used for municipal solid waste. Many of us grew up assuming that although every town and city needed a dump, there would always be a hole wide enough and deep enough to take care of all our trash. But like so many other assumptions about the earth's infinite capacity to absorb the impact of human civilization, this one too was wrong. Which brings us to the second major change concerning our production of waste: the volume of garbage is now so high that we are running out of places to put it. Out of 20,000 landfills in the United States in 1979, more than 15,000 have since reached their permanent capacity and closed. Although the problem is most acute in older cities, especially in the Northeast, virtually every metropolitan area is either facing or will soon face the urgent need to find new landfills or dispose of their garbage by some other means.

18   Those landfills still in operation feature mountains of garbage that are reaching heroic proportions: Fresh Kills Landfill on Staten Island, for instance, receives 44 million pounds of New York City garbage

every single day. According to a study by a *Newsday* investigative team, it will soon become "the highest point on the Eastern Seaboard south of Maine." It will soon legally require a Federal Aviation Administration permit as a threat to aircraft.

Dr. W. L. Rathje, a professor of anthropology at the University of Arizona and perhaps the leading "garbologist" in the world, testified to the epic scale of these modern landfills before one of my subcommittee hearings: "When I was a graduate student, I was told that the largest monument ever built by a New World civilization was the Temple of the Sun, constructed in Mexico around the time of Christ and occupying thirty million cubic feet of space. Durham Road Landfill near San Francisco is two mounds compiled since 1977 solely out of cover dirt and the municipal solid waste from three California cities. I can still remember my shock when my students calculated that each mound was seventy million cubic feet in volume, a total of nearly five Sun Temples. Landfills are clearly the largest garbage middens (i.e, refuse heaps) in the history of the world."   19

What is in these mountains? Various forms of paper, mostly newspapers and packaging, take up approximately half the space. Another 20 percent or so is made up of yard waste, construction wood, and assorted organic waste, especially food. (Rathje found that 15 percent of all the solid food purchased by Americans ends up in landfills.) An unbelievable conglomeration of odds and ends accounts for the rest, with almost 10 percent made up of plastic, including the so-called biodegradable plastic. (Starch is added to the plastic compound as an appetizer for microorganisms, who will theoretically disassemble the plastic as they consume the starch.) Rathje dryly noted that he was skeptical of such claims: "In our landfill refuse from decades past we have uncovered corncobs with all their kernels still intact. If microorganisms won't eat corn-on-the-cob, I doubt whether they will dig cornstarch out of plastics."   20

But much organic waste does ultimately decompose, in the process generating a great deal of methane, which poses a threat of explosions and underground fires in older dumps that do not have proper venting or control. More significant, it contributes to the increased amount of methane entering the atmosphere. As we now know, rising levels of methane are one reason that the greenhouse effect has become so dangerous.   21

As existing landfills close, cities throughout the United States are desperately searching for new ones. And they are not easy to find. In   22 fact, in my home state of Tennessee, to take one example, the single hottest political issue in the majority of our ninety-five counties is where to locate a new landfill or incinerator. Since these problems have customarily been addressed at the local level, they have not been defined as national issues, even though they generate more political controversy nationwide than many other issues. Now, however, the accumulation of waste has gotten so out of hand that cities and states have begun shipping large quantities across state lines. The Congressional Research Service has estimated that more than 12 million tons of municipal solid waste were shipped across state lines in 1989. Although some of this volume is due to the fact that some major cities are next to a state line and some is due to formal interstate compacts for regional disposal facilities (which can be among the more responsible alternatives), there is an enormous growth in shipments by private haulers to landowners in poorer areas of the country who are ready to make a dollar by having garbage dumped on their property.

23   I remember the day that citizens from the small Tennessee town of Mitchellville (pop. 500) called me to complain about four smelly boxcars dripping with garbage from New York City that had been sitting in the hot sun for a week on a railroad siding in their town. "What worries me," said one resident to a reporter from the *Nashville Banner*, "is that so many germs are carried through the air, viruses and this type of thing. When that wind is blowing that stuff all over town, them little germs are not saying, 'Now, we can't leave this boxcar, you know we've got to stay here.'" Mitchellville's vice mayor, Bill Rogers, said, "A lot of the time you can see water, or some kind of liquid, dripping out the bottom of the cars, and some of them contain pure New York garbage." As it turned out, the mayor had agreed to let the hauling company, Tuckasee Inc., bring trash from New York, New Jersey, and Pennsylvania to a landfill thirty-five miles from the railroad siding for a fee of $5 per boxcar, which looked like a good deal for a city whose annual budget is less than $50,000.

24   Small communities like Mitchellville throughout the Southeast and Midwest are being deluged with shipments of garbage from the Northeast. Rural areas of the western United States are receiving garbage from large cities on the Pacific coast. No wonder that bands of vigilantes have formed to patrol the highways and backroads in areas besieged by trucks of garbage from larger population centers. One of my favorite spoofs on *Saturday Night Live* was a mock commercial for a product called the Yard-a-Pult, a scaled-down model of a medieval

catapult, just large enough for the backyard patio, suitable for the launching of garbage bags into your neighbor's property. No need for recycling, incineration, or landfills. The Yard-a-Pult is the ultimate in "out of sight, out of mind" convenience. Unfortunately, the fiction is disturbingly like the reality of our policy for dealing with waste.

      Sometimes truth is even stranger than fiction. One of the most bizarre and disturbing consequences of this considerable shipment of waste is the appearance of a new environmental threat called back-hauling. Truckers take loads of chemical waste and garbage in one direction and food and bulk liquids (like fruit juice) in the opposite direction—in the same containers. In a lengthy report, the *Seattle Post-Intelligencer* found hundreds of examples of food being carried in containers that had been filled with hazardous waste on the first leg of the journey. Although the trucks were typically washed between loads, the drivers (at some threat to their jobs) described lax inspections, totally inadequate washouts, and the use of liquid deodorizers, themselves dangerous, to mask leftover chemical smells. In 1990, Senators Jim Exon, Slade Gorton, and I joined with Congressman Bill Clinger to pass legislation prohibiting this practice.   25

      But no legislation, by itself, can stop the underlying problem. When one means of disposal is prohibited, the practice continues underground or a new method is found. And what used to be considered unthinkable becomes commonplace because of the incredible pressure from the mounting volumes of waste.   26

QUESTIONS TO CONSIDER ◄

1. Gore's purpose is clearly to persuade readers of the growing problems associated with waste disposal. He uses cause and effect as his primary method of development. What other methods does he use to develop his argument?

2. Gore uses a wide range of sources to support his argument—everything from a study by the United Church of Christ to a complaint by a resident of Mitchellville, Tennessee, about New York's garbage being sent to Mitchellville. Mark each source included in this selection and determine how effective it is in supporting Gore's argument. How convincing would his argument be had he not included these sources?

3. As you learned in the previous chapter, when people write to persuade, they typically appeal to their readers' sense of what is logical, to their emotions, and to their belief in the writers' credibility. Which of these appeals does Gore use?

4. As a former senator and presidential candidate and the current vice president, Gore has a strong ethos—a great deal of credibility with readers. However, being a politician and a government official hardly qualifies a person as an authority on the environment. How does Gore establish his **credibility** as an environmentalist?

CREDIBILITY, PAGE 443

5. Waste disposal is not a very attractive subject. It is, in fact, something that most of us would rather not think about. How does Gore convince readers that waste disposal is a significant, if not an appealing, problem?

6. In selecting the title "The Wasteland," Gore is not only predicting our future but also alluding to a poem by that title by T. S. Eliot. Eliot's poem describes the modern world as a spiritual and cultural wasteland—a desert void of everything except the most sterile and arid forms of life. Gore's image, in contrast, is of a literal wasteland, a land overflowing with waste. Compare these two images and explain how Eliot's image reinforces Gore's even though the two are different.

▶ WRITING ACTIVITIES

Individual: Make a list of everything that you have thrown away or discarded in the last twenty-four hours. Then write a statement generalizing about how much waste you personally produce and how you dispose of it.

Collaborative: Compare your individual lists of waste; then brainstorm about how our society might reduce the amount of waste we generate by repackaging, reusing, or recycling what we now discard. Write a brief proposal in which you suggest one way in which the amount of waste that must be disposed can be reduced. Address your proposal to the class.

Computer: Enter the proposal written by your group into your computer if you do not already have it on a file. Then revise it so it is appropriate for a different audience—for example, a college administrator, city official, or state or national legislator. Quote Senator Gore at least once in your proposal to support your arguments.

❖❖❖❖❖

THE END IS NOT AT HAND

Robert J. Samuelson

The following article, which first appeared in a 1992 issue of Newsweek *magazine, challenges the basic, often unspoken, assumption that we are creating environmental problems that will eventually destroy our planet. Economist Robert Samuelson argues that environmental rhetoric is overblown and that the planet will survive regardless of what we do or do not do. As you read, weigh Samuelson's arguments and evidence against those of the other authors you have read in this chapter.*

Whoever coined the phrase "save the planet" is a public-relations genius. It conveys the sense of impending catastrophe and high purpose that has wrapped environmentalism in an aura of moral urgency. It also typifies environmentalism's rhetorical excesses, which, in any other context, would be seen as wild exaggeration or simple dishonesty.   1

Up to a point, our environmental awareness has checked a mindless enthusiasm for unrestrained economic growth. We have sensibly curbed some of growth's harmful side effects. But environmentalism increasingly resembles a holy crusade addicted to hype and ignorant of history. Every environmental ill is depicted as an onrushing calamity that—if not stopped—will end life as we know it.   2

Take the latest scare: the greenhouse effect. We're presented with the horrifying specter of a world that incinerates itself. Act now, or sizzle later. Food supplies will wither. Glaciers will melt. Coastal areas will flood. In fact, the probable losses from any greenhouse warming are modest: 1 to 2 percent of our economy's output by the year 2050, estimates economist William Cline. The loss seems even smaller compared with the expected growth of the economy (a doubling) over the same period.   3

No environmental problem threatens the "planet" or rates with the danger of nuclear war. No oil spill ever caused suffering on a par with today's civil war in Yugoslavia, which is a minor episode in human misery. World War II left more than 35 million dead. Cambodia's civil war resulted in 1 million to 3 million deaths. The great scourges of humanity remain what they have always been: war,   4 natural disaster, oppressive government, crushing poverty and hate. On any scale of tragedy, environmental distress is a featherweight.

5   This is not an argument for indifference or inaction. It is an argument for perspective and balance. You can believe (as I do) that the possibility of greenhouse warming enhances an already strong case for an energy tax. A tax would curb ordinary air pollution, limit oil imports, cut the budget deficit and promote energy-efficient investments that make economic sense.

6   But it does not follow that anyone who disagrees with me is evil or even wrong. On the greenhouse effect, for instance, there's ample scientific doubt over whether warming will occur and, if so, how much. Moreover, the warming would occur over decades. People and businesses could adjust. To take one example: farmers could shift to more heat-resistant seeds.

7   Unfortunately, the impulse of many environmentalists is to vilify and simplify. Critics of environmental restrictions are portrayed as selfish and ignorant creeps. Doomsday scenarios are developed to prove the seriousness of environmental dangers. Cline's recent greenhouse study projected warming 250 years into the future. Guess what, it increases sharply. This is an absurd exercise akin to predicting life in 1992 at the time of the French and Indian War (1754-63).

8   The rhetorical overkill is not just innocent excess. It clouds our understanding. For starters, it minimizes the great progress that has been made, especially in industrialized countries. In the United States, air and water pollution have dropped dramatically. Since 1960, particulate emissions (soot, cinders) are down by 65 percent. Lead emissions have fallen by 97 percent since 1970. Smog has declined in most cities.

9   What's also lost is the awkward necessity for choices. Your environmental benefit may be my job. Not every benefit is worth having at any cost. Economists estimate that environmental regulations depress the economy's output by 2.6 to 5 percent, or about $150 billion to $290 billion. (Note: this is larger than the estimated impact of global warming.) For that cost, we've lowered health risks and improved our surroundings. But some gains are small compared with the costs. And some costs are needlessly high because regulations are rigid.

10   **Balance:** The worst sin of environmental excess is its bias against economic growth. The cure for the immense problems of poor countries usually lies with economic growth. A recent report from the World Bank estimates that more than 1 billion people lack healthy water supplies and sanitary facilities. The result is hundreds of millions of cases of diarrhea annually and the deaths of 3 million children (2

million of which the World Bank judges avoidable). Only by becoming wealthier can countries correct these conditions.

Similarly, wealthier societies have both the desire and the income   11
to clean their air and water. Advanced nations have urban-air-pollution levels only a sixth that of the poorest countries. Finally, economic growth tends to reduce high birthrates, as children survive longer and women escape traditional roles.

Yes, we have environmental problems. Reactors in the former   12
Soviet Union pose safety risks. Economic growth and the environment can be at odds. Growth generates carbon-dioxide emissions and causes more waste. But these problems are not—as environmental rhetoric implies—the main obstacles to sustained development. The biggest hurdle is inept government. Inept government fostered unsafe Soviet reactors. Inept government hampers food production in poor countries by, say, preventing farmers from earning adequate returns on their crops.

By now, everyone is an environmentalist. But the label is increas-   13
ingly meaningless, because not all environmental problems are equally serious and even the serious ones need to be balanced against other concerns. Environmentalism should hold the hype. It should inform us more and frighten us less.

QUESTIONS TO CONSIDER   ◀

1. Samuelson concedes that "up to a point" environmental concern has been a positive force because it has tempered our "mindless enthusiasm for unrestrained economic growth." Does this concession strengthen his argument by making him appear more reasonable or does it weaken his argument by making him appear less firm in his resolve? What other strategies does Samuelson use to establish his credibility as a reasonable person? How effective are these strategies? What is their purpose?

2. Samuelson states that "there's ample scientific doubt over whether [global] warming will occur and, if so, how much" and argues that "people and businesses could adjust." What evidence does Samuelson use to support this assertion?

3. Samuelson compares predictions about future environmental consequences to predictions about what life is like now that were made "at the time of the French and Indian War (1754-63)." Is this comparison valid? Why or why not?

4. How does Samuelson portray environmentalists? How does he contrast their position and attitude with his own? Does he suggest that they are calculating and have ulterior motives or that they are merely naive and overly enthusiastic?

5. Samuelson criticizes environmentalists for their "rhetorical excesses." What does he mean by this phrase? Is this criticism valid? Support your answer with examples from other reading selections.

▶   **WRITING ACTIVITIES**

Individual: Discuss in a journal entry which of Samuelson's arguments you find most convincing and why.

Collaborative: Evaluate Samuelson's arguments by applying them to those of Rachel Carson, Michio Kaku, and Al Gore. Then write a brief statement in which you argue that Samuelson's thesis is valid or not valid on the basis of your research.

Computer: Create a debate dialogue between Samuelson and one of the other authors in the chapter. In one document window, list all of Samuelson's criticisms of environmentalists; then in the other document window, refute each one, responding from the point of view of one of the other authors in the chapter.

THE NECESSITY FOR GREENPEACE

Paige Snyder

Paige Snyder was a college freshman when she wrote the following essay about the environmental organization Greenpeace, with which she had worked. In her essay, Snyder defends the methods used by Greenpeace, in particular the method known as direct action. Like Martin Luther King, Jr. ("Letter from Birmingham Jail," Chapter 7), whom she cites in her essay, Snyder argues that nonviolent direct action is justified as a method of resistance because it is a means to a justifiable end, in this case the preservation of the planet.

Greenpeace is an effective environmental group, for it raises the 1
public's awareness concerning environmental issues, in addition to
concerning itself with the awesome task of making our world clean
and safe for those who inherit it for the remainder of history. I know
from personal experience the numerous chores we face, the sociological changes that must come about, the new kind of enculturation we
must integrate into our world, to accomplish the goal of the earth
being indefinitely self-supporting and conducive to good health and
living. My work at Greenpeace has reinforced my knowledge that
Greenpeace and organizations like it are an important piece in the
puzzle of bringing about all these positive changes.

It is a simple task to set forth all the facts on environmental cata- 2
strophes. Numerous magazines like Greenpeace's (which is printed on
recycled paper) and responsible television like the Public Broadcasting
System are constantly informing the public on relevant issues. This is
one reason why I do not feel the need to dedicate this paper to persuading people that the environment is in trouble. For while there are
continuing debates among professionals as to the extent of some problems (such as the size of the hole in the ozone layer), there is agreement
that a new awareness must come about soon, because we are destroying our home. Another topic I will not debate is whether or not action
must be taken to prevent further ecological damage and repair past
abuse. This is simple, because if environmental crises are common
knowledge, then there can be no objections to taking care of the problems. Of course, this line of reasoning assumes that individuals are interested in propagating their species, as well as those of every other living
organism. So excluding those who do not believe life should continue
on earth, one must conclude that knowledge about our current condition would warrant education and change. Therefore, this paper will
focus on the methods that Greenpeace employs, especially the method
known as direct action. I will argue that, given the seriousness of our
environmental plight, the end in this case justifies the means.

Greenpeace was founded in 1971 by a handful of people 3
attempting to stop the testing of nuclear weapons. Since that time, it
has grown into a group numbering over 3.5 million members worldwide and is represented by offices in over 30 countries. The issues that
Greenpeace is involved in include ocean ecology (stopping the testing
of nuclear weapons under water, preventing the extinction of sea creatures), atmosphere and energy (finding new, clean alternatives for
energy, outlawing practices that destroy the ozone layer and actions
that increase the greenhouse effect), the rain forest (stopping the rap-
ing of the forests by eliminating the market for products made from

rainforest timber, helping the locals to retain their land and make money by practices which replenish the trees and undergrowth). These are several of Greenpeace's central campaigns. The philosophy of Greenpeace is that no one owns this planet. We only borrow it from the generation before us and must pass it on to those who follow us. And like anything that is borrowed, we must take better care of it than if it were our very own, especially when survival depends on it. In order to achieve its goals, Greenpeace's first tool is negotiation and discussion with environmental abusers. But more often than not, these offenders are large corporations, or even the government, and a request for them to change a major part of their operations usually goes unconsidered. So Greenpeace uses a tactic known as non-violent direct action. This philosophy has been used successfully for many years by people like Ghandi and Martin Luther King, Jr. And much like the wrath that their actions drew, Greenpeace has found itself on the defensive many a time against those who feel it is unnecessary to be so disruptive. But as Dr. King found, when people refuse to admit there is a problem, let alone be willing to discuss it, direct action can be the only peaceable way to bring all sides to the table. And so, Greenpeace organizes rallies, boycotts, and bans. In addition, they often block activities at places such as illegal nuclear testing sites or illegal dumping grounds.

4   I have faced much criticism of Greenpeace in my job as a canvasser but always thrived off of it. It was usually intelligent thinking from insightful people, and it made me continually question things, which I found made my convictions even stronger and myself more informed. Ironically, it was usually the members who asked the most questions and even criticized selected actions. Greenpeace is an organization of people, and thus is fallible to an extent. Not all 3.5 million members will agree on every decision made. But this essay is addressed to those who feel there is no need for a group like Greenpeace, or worse yet, those who feel Greenpeace causes more harm than good and is not constructive in its means of education, mediation, and direct-action campaigns. The essay "Greenpeace Wages Redwar" begins with this statement:

5   Because of the growing environmental fad of the last few years, much of the public has invested nearly blind faith in organizations claiming to play David to the Goliath of environmental exploitation. Among the leading beneficiaries of this public trust has been the international activist organization Greenpeace. (Ellison 7)

This statement gives very little credit to the millions of people   6
who donate their time and money to Greenpeace's efforts. I have
worked for Greenpeace at the grassroots level, going door to door
canvassing, enlisting new members, and visiting old members. More
than anyone else in the organization, the canvassers know who the
members are, where their heads are at, and how they view the organization they are investing in. I must first say that there are people who
join blindly, usually either to get me to leave their door, or because
they want to support the cause, but aren't interested in hearing about
what they are supporting. But out of thousands of members I met, this
"blind-faith" group constitutes only a handful. As I mentioned before,
it is the members, both prospective ones and those who have been
members for years, who ask most of the questions. They want to
know what we are currently involved in and what they can do to help
in other than financial ways.

My job at the grassroots level was not solely fundraising,   7
although that is one central objective. At any given time, we would be
running at least one letter campaign and a petition campaign. One
obstacle to the public's involvement in environmental legislation is
lack of knowledge concerning what bills are being proposed and
voted on. So Greenpeace finds out the calendar for Congressional vot-
ing, and in the months and weeks ahead of votes, educates the public
on those bills by going door to door. For example, last summer (1990)
Congress had legislation pending on the banning of CFCs. When I
went door to door, I carried on my clipboard a description of the bill
and presented it to anyone who expressed interest. They in turn could
write a letter to their Congressmen and Congresswomen expressing
how they wished their representatives to vote. Over the course of a
week, Greenpeace canvassers across the country would collect thousands of letters, which we would then send to Washington. Far from
preying on those with blind faith, Greenpeace needs and wants more
than financial support. It seeks to increase knowledge in and involvement by the public. I found this job so rewarding because people constantly thanked me for bringing them this information and giving them
the means to help change things.

But education, letter-writing, and petitions only accomplish so   8
much. Unfortunately, many companies do not respond to the public's
request to clean up their acts. And so we end up using the last resort,
which is direct action. In speaking of the necessity of using direct
action, I will be continually referring to Martin Luther King, Jr., most
specifically to his letter written while in Birmingham jail. Dr. King
speaks of the need for non-violent action where injustice exists and

when the opposition will not negotiate. In arriving at the decision to take such action, he speaks of the phases one must go through. "In any non-violent campaign there are four basic steps: collection of the facts to determine whether injustices exist; negotiation; self-purification; and direct action" (King 85). By the time Greenpeace arrives at the conclusion that direct action is required, its members have gone through these steps.

9   I feel now is the time to give an illustration of one such time when Greenpeace finally took a direct action, and what came as a result of that decision. Throughout the 1970s and early 1980s, the French government had been conducting illegal nuclear tests (atmospheric and underground) throughout the Pacific. These tests, conducted despite an international ban, resulted in widespread radiation leakage and protests from the citizens of Polynesia, where much of the testing was taking place. Despite these protests and the attempts of Greenpeace to make these tests known to the world, the international community did nothing. On July 7, 1985, Greenpeace sent its ship, the Rainbow Warrior, to New Zealand to prepare for a direct action against French nuclear testing in Mururoa. Greenpeace had been in the region previously, to attempt to draw attention to the illegal tests and to accumulate first-hand evidence, such as photographs (Danielsson 23-31). Chris Masters describes how the protest was to unfold and the risks that Greenpeace members were willing to take.

10   The Rainbow Warrior and the other protest boats would launch
          Zodiac inflatable speedboats from just outside the twelve-mile
          limit and attempt to land on the atoll. About a dozen Zodiacs
          would carry Greenpeace members of many different nationali-
          ties. They knew from experience the French would be forced
          to arrest the protesters and then face the embarrassing prospect
          of having to deport each of them to their home countries.
          (Danielsson 29)

11   Before the planned protest, the Rainbow Warrior was blown up
          by French agents, and a Greenpeace photographer was killed. Despite
          the tragedy, Greenpeace brought another environmental scandal to
          light. Masters writes, "the French media began to sense a Watergate and
          competed enthusiastically for new details of L'affaire Greenpeace"
          (Danielsson 29). The illegal testing stopped, and those responsible for
          exploding the boat were sentenced to ten years in prison.

12   While canvassing, I met resistance to direct action, much of
          which stemmed from ignorance. The above-mentioned incident was

remembered by many to be a case of Greenpeace blowing up a
French boat as part of its direct action campaigns. If violence were a
part of Greenpeace's philosophy or behavior, I would not feel secure
supporting it, nor would most of its 3.5 million members. I would now
like to speak to those who feel that non-violent direct action serves no
constructive purpose. Let me again refer to King's letter.

> Non-violent direct action seeks to create such a crisis and foster   13
> such a tension that a community which has constantly refused
> to negotiate is forced to confront the issue. It seeks so to dra-
> matize the issue that it can no longer be ignored. . . . The pur-
> pose of our direct-action program is to create a situation so
> crisis-packed that it will inevitably open the door to negotia-
> tion. (King 86–87)

    I know from experience that the corporations and governments   14
which are targets of these actions are usually those who believe the
actions are unnecessary. This is true for obvious economic and political
reasons, but also because it is the poor and minorities who face the
most immediate effects of environmental problems. They are the ones
who live next to the dumps and incinerators, who work in unsafe factories making chemicals and hazardous products. King realized that those
who do not directly see the injustice do not see the immediate need for
change. "Frankly, I have yet to engage in a direct-action campaign that
was 'well timed' in the view of those who have not suffered unduly. . . ."
(King 87). Those who are removed from the immediate effects of the
environmental crisis do not see it as a crisis. While canvassing in a nice
rural neighborhood in Massachusetts last summer, I came across a
woman who insisted that there was no problem where she lived and
that somehow this town was cleaner and healthier than those surrounding it. I asked her how this was possible, when she shared the air and
drinking water with a neighboring town which had severe health problems due to a toxic incinerator. To this she had no answer.
    Then there are the people saying, "I agree with you in the goal   15
you seek, but I cannot agree with your methods of direct action" (King
91). My answer is the same as Dr. King's: "Shallow understanding from
people of good will is more frustrating than absolute misunderstanding
of people of ill will" (91). What I found most difficult to comprehend
were those people who agreed with my every point, but felt I should
wait and not press the issue. Once again I agree with King, who proposes that "such an attitude grows out of a tragic misconception of
time, from the strangely irrational notion that there is something in the

very flow of time that will inevitably cure all ills" (92). But time did not magically alleviate racial injustice, and time will not mystically reverse all the damage humans have done and will continue to do to the environment. Fortunately, there are people who do see that only human perseverance will overcome human errors, and they do what they can do, like supporting such groups as Greenpeace, that take a stand and take action.

16   Greenpeace fills an essential role in educating the public and making changes in corporate and governmental behavior toward the environment. And more and more, the effectiveness of their philosophy is being recognized. A writer in a Japanese magazine expresses a desire to increase environmental activism in Japan:

17   The activities of the nongovernmental or citizen environmental organization that emerged in many nations over the past 20 years have led to continuous reforms in governmental policies and corporate behavior. . . . Greenpeace International has around 3.5 million supporters worldwide and an annual budget of about 125 million dollars, making it the largest "environmental pressure group." (Holliman 285)

18   Fortunately, more and more people in the United States and around the world see the urgent need for changes in environmental policies, as *Fortune* magazine reported in 1990.

19   The New York Times/CBS poll regularly asks the public if protecting the environment is so important that requirements and standards cannot be too high, and continuing environmental improvements must be made regardless of cost. In September 1981, 45% agreed and 42% disagreed with that plainly intemperate statement. Last June, 79% agreed and only 18% disagreed. For the first time, liberals and conservatives, Democrats and Republicans, profess concern for the environment in roughly equal numbers. (Kirkpatrick 46)

20   The same article also notes that "William Bishop, Proctor & Gamble's top environmental scientist, was an organizer of Earth Day in 1970 and is a member of the Sierra Club. One of his chief deputies belongs to Greenpeace" (47).

21   So change is coming about, and more people are aware of environmental problems and willing to take action on that knowledge. But these changes in thought did not occur by waiting for the truth to sink

in. The realization that something must be done to save our environment resulted from tireless campaigning and canvassing by Greenpeace and groups like it, who are bound and determined to make a difference, despite much indifference. And changes in policies that directly or indirectly affect our environment's well-being came about because of direct action campaigns, which forced the recognition of the problems and insisted on negotiation that would achieve positive change. While it is a good first step to acknowledge the environmental crisis this world is in, it is not enough. We must all be willing to do whatever is necessary to right our wrongs, including giving our time, money, and support for groups like Greenpeace, which persevere. They do what they must do, including taking direct action, and we must understand why, and be willing to do just as much. Let's continue the trend of awareness that is sweeping our world, and act on it.

WORKS CITED

Danielsson, Bengt. "Poisoned Pacific: The Legacy of French Nuclear Testing." *The Bulletin of the Atomic Scientists* 46.2 (1990): 23–31.

Ellison, Bryan J. "Greenpeace Wages Redwar." *The New American* 6.24 (1990): 7–12.

Holliman, Jonathan. "Environmentalism with a Global Scope." *Japan Quarterly* 37 (1990): 284–90.

King, Martin Luther, Jr. "Letter from a Birmingham Jail." *I Have a Dream: Writings and Speeches That Changed the World.* Ed. James M. Washington. San Francisco: HarperCollins, 1992. 83–100.

Kirkpatrick, David. "Environmentalism: The New Crusade." *Fortune* 12 Feb. 1990: 44–55.

QUESTIONS TO CONSIDER

1. Throughout the essay Snyder uses her personal experience as a canvasser for Greenpeace to support her arguments. Could her close association with the organization also be seen as a reason why she cannot effectively defend it? Why or why not?

2. Snyder states that "while there are continuing debates among professionals as to the extent of some problems . . . , there is agreement that . . . we are destroying our home." Can her assertion that there is agreement on this issue be challenged? How? Compare her assertion to Robert J. Samuelson's arguments in "The End Is Not at Hand."

3. Snyder clearly states that one of the basic assumptions in her pro-environmental action argument is that "individuals are interested in propagating their species." Is her assumption valid? Why or why not? Is Snyder's overt statement of this assumption an effective persuasive strategy?

4. Snyder bases her defense of nonviolent direct action on the arguments of Martin Luther King, Jr., as he articulated them in his "Letter from Birmingham Jail" (Chapter 7). As her main source, how does King strengthen Snyder's argument? Is he an effective source primarily because of what he says or who he is?

5. In addition to King, Snyder uses several other sources to support her arguments for Greenpeace's use of direct action. Which of these sources do you find most persuasive? Do you recognize the names of any of these sources? How important is it to use sources your readers know?

6. Snyder uses both examples from her own experiences and material from sources to support her argument. Do you find her own experiences or the source material more convincing? Is the combination of personal experience and source material effective? Why?

▶ **WRITING ACTIVITIES**

Individual: Snyder argues that time alone will not take care of the problems Greenpeace and similar environmental groups address and thus direct action is needed. Write a journal entry in which you agree or disagree with this argument.

Collaborative: Snyder compares environmental issues with civil rights issues. Discuss whether you think this is a valid comparison. Make a list of ways in which the two issues are alike and ways in which they are different.

Computer: Interview a classmate about whether he or she is for or against nonviolent direct action as a means of protecting the environment. Use your computer to record several exact responses of the person you interview. Then compose an account of the interview in which you include several of the quoted responses.

A R G U I N G   F R O M   S O U R C E S

Viewed most simply, research involves reading, talking, and observing. A literary scholar may spend years reading about a single author or work; a reporter may interview dozens of witnesses; and a scientist may observe the results of countless laboratory experiments. However sophisticated the results, their methods still involve reading, talking, and observing. In researching a topic, you will use these same basic methods (see **field research** and **library research**).

FIELD RESEARCH, PAGE 493

LIBRARY RESEARCH, PAGE 534

Although your immediate impulse may be to head for the library when you start a research project, be aware of other sources too. The books, popular magazines, scholarly journals, newspapers, and government documents in a library obviously provide a researcher with valuable information. But you may also want to read materials not kept in libraries: letters, brochures, pamphlets, instructions, guidelines, family records, and city and county records provide useful information too.

You can also learn a great deal about a subject by talking to people. Interviewing someone with knowledge or experience related to your subject can provide especially valuable material. If you interview someone, write down in advance the questions you plan to ask, but during the interview allow the person to digress from your questions. Digressions may, in fact, be more interesting or useful than the answers to your questions. When possible, and with the interviewee's permission, tape the interview. If this is not possible, carefully write down any statements you plan to quote. Ask the interviewee to read the statements as you have written them to verify their accuracy.

Finally, you can learn a lot about something by observing it. You will need to observe carefully and record in writing exactly what you see. For example, observing how your school disposes of its trash and waste products might provide useful information if you are researching the subject of waste management on your campus. For more about nonlibrary techniques for gathering information, see **field research.**

FIELD RESEARCH, PAGE 493

Thorough researchers use more than one method of investigation. They often read about a subject to gain some background knowledge of it, talk with other people (both in interviews and in informal conversations) to gain additional viewpoints and to test their own ideas, and then, if possible, also observe the phenomenon they are investigating.

For example, if you are investigating the effectiveness and practicality of solar energy as a source of heat, you might begin by reading articles, reports of energy studies, government documents, and builders' brochures on the subject. Then you might talk with an industrial or civil engineer with experience in this field, with the owner of a solar-heated house, and with a building contractor who installs solar energy systems. Finally, you might actually visit a home or building that uses solar energy to observe for yourself how well it works.

Throughout your research, keep careful records of all you read, hear, and observe. Notecards, notebooks, and research journals are traditional forms for recording the results of research. But most writers today also take advantage of photocopy machines. Duplicating an article or chapter is not a substitute for a careful summary, but well-annotated photocopies can be invaluable when the time comes to select quotations and to acknowledge sources. Computers can also be useful in recording and reporting on research. Keeping notes in a computer file can eliminate much recopying and rewriting because you can later work directly from the notes you have entered into the computer. Computers also enable you to expand outlines, experiment with different forms of organization, and insert quotations easily. Many software programs also have features that make it easy to document sources.

Formulating a Thesis

Research can be directionless until the writer develops a hypothesis (a tentative thesis). Although writers may begin research with only a general subject or question in mind, they usually formulate a hypothesis as soon as possible to guide their research into more specific channels. After completing their research, they can then formulate a definite thesis. Remember, in most reports of research, writers are not merely reporting on the results of their research but are using the information they have collected to develop and support their own ideas. For example, in the reading selections in this chapter, each of the authors is supporting a thesis: Rachel Carson's thesis is that when people destroy plant life, the balance of nature is upset; Michio Kaku's thesis is that wars destroy the environment; Patricia Parker's thesis is that those who destroy the environment should be prosecuted in the same way as those who destroy private property or human life; Al Gore's thesis is that unless we begin to control the waste we produce and the way we dispose of it, we will destroy our environment; Robert Samuelson's thesis is that environmentalists' hype causes all environmental concerns to be seen as equally urgent problems; and Paige Snyder's thesis is that Greenpeace is justified in using nonviolent direct action.

Each of these writers uses a strong thesis to give his or her text a clear focus. Without a single controlling idea, a report of research can become a meaningless exercise for the writer and a confusing, useless document for the reader. If you are not sure what your thesis is by the time you have completed your research, spend some time focusing on this important element of your report.

Writers formulate a thesis in different ways. Often the thesis exists in the form of a question before the research has even begun. For example, a writer investigating whether solar energy is an effective, practical source of heat knows the question from the first but learns the answer only after completing the research. That answer then becomes the writer's thesis: Although they are expensive to install, solar energy systems provide home owners in certain parts of the country with an effective source of heat.

Sometimes a thesis evolves out of the writer's convictions, which are at least partially shaped by doing the research. Many student writers begin a research project believing one thing but modify their beliefs as a result of their research. For example, a writer who initially believes that recycling is the answer to current waste disposal problems may discover that the problem is far larger than he or she thought. As a result, the thesis for the report may change from "Recycling is the answer" to "Recycling is an important step in solving an enormous problem" or even "Recycling isn't the answer."

Occasionally, however, students will not have a thesis even after researching an issue or topic. In this case, they must formulate a thesis from studying their sources. The best way to do this is to compare sources. What do they agree on and what do they not agree on? Points of disagreement usually offer the best opportunity for formulating a thesis because a strong thesis usually focuses on an issue on which people disagree. Consensus does not usually lead to a strong thesis. But if there is a difference of opinion, the writer can decide which position to take and base the thesis on that position. For example, if some sources claim that solar energy is expensive and some argue that it is cost effective, the writer can try to discover who is right and take that position as a thesis. In some cases, a thesis may voice a compromise position: Solar energy is initially expensive but in the long run can save money (see **thesis**).

THESIS, PAGE 599

Using Research to Inform Readers

Experienced writers use the results of their research in several ways. First, they use the information they have found to help their readers understand the subject they are reporting on. The results of the research thus become evidence to support the thesis. Because research nearly always results in more information than can possibly be included in a single report or essay, one of the writer's tasks is to decide what information to include. The following guidelines can help you with this important task:

❖ Use only pertinent information.

❖ Use only current information.

❖ Use only reliable information.

USE ONLY PERTINENT INFORMATION. Don't use everything you learn just to show how much research you have done. Regardless of how interesting the information is, if it doesn't directly support your thesis, leave it out. For example, in researching solar heating's potential, you may discover a detailed explanation of how to construct and install your own solar heating system. But if your purpose is not to teach readers how to build a solar energy heating system, don't include that information in your report. You might choose to mention in your discussion of initial costs that a do-it-yourself system is possible, and you could refer readers to the source of your information.

USE ONLY CURRENT INFORMATION. Unless your purpose is to provide your readers with background information or to focus on a historical topic, use only current sources that report up-to-date information. For example, you might want to include in a report on solar heating systems some background information about how early humans used the energy of the sun to keep warm. In fact, this information could be the basis of an effective introduction. But for the main part of your report you would not want to use sources from the 1960s, when there was great interest in solar energy but much current solar technology had not been invented. If your information is not up to date, you could misinform your readers about what is possible now.

USE ONLY RELIABLE INFORMATION. This guideline can be difficult to follow, for evaluating the reliability of sources can itself sometimes involve considerable research. However, by the time you have completed your research and are ready to report on it, you have become something of an expert on your topic. You probably know enough to become suspicious if certain information seems out of line. For example, if most of your sources indicate that the cost of purchasing and installing an effective solar heating system is approximately $10,000 but a brochure from your local electric power company gives the cost as considerably more, you are justified in suspecting that the electric power company's information may not be reliable. Similarly, if an article in an environmental magazine claims that the cost is $6,000 rather than the $10,000 estimate of most of your sources, you probably don't want to quote the lower figure. However, you might decide to give your readers the range of prices you have discovered, carefully explaining the source of each.

Using Research to Persuade Readers

Experienced writers also use the results of their research as evidence to support statements and ideas in their report. These supporting statements effectively reinforce the writer's arguments, especially if the sources are voices of authority. For example, even though Al Gore is a well-known political figure, his reputation as an authority on the environment is less well established. Thus he includes supporting statements from a major study on the disposal of hazardous waste by the United Church of Christ and supporting evidence from the United Nations Environment Programme, the Environmental Protection Agency, and a professor of anthropology he identifies as the "leading 'garbologist' in the world." These sources provide not only information for readers but also credibility for Gore. They situate him in a community of respected, knowledgeable authorities on the subject on which he is writing and, in doing so, help to convince readers that his arguments are valid.

Writers also use their sources to appeal to their readers' emotions and sense of logic. In this chapter's reading selections, Michio Kaku appeals to his readers' pity by citing a Harvard medical team's report that "tens of thousands of children" may die in Iraq even though the war has ended as a result of the "United Nations embargo and the collapse of basic sanitation and the medical infrastructure." In contrast, Patricia Parker uses the results of her research to appeal to her readers' sense of logic: if those who commit crimes against an individual are punished with jail sentences, why should crimes against the environment, which affect thousands of individuals, not be punished in the same way?

Don't ignore sources that do not support your thesis. Instead, acknowledge them, refute their arguments if possible, and try to find common ground with them. Few arguments outside a courtroom are won decisively by one side or the other. Changing someone's mind completely is extremely difficult, if not impossible. However, an effective argument can lead to a compromise or an agreement on certain aspects of an issue. If, for example, you find that your sources disagree on the general effectiveness of solar heating systems but agree that they have been most successful in the Southwest, you can argue that solar energy should be used in that region rather than trying to convince readers of its universal effectiveness.

In writing to persuade, you must analyze assumptions as well as the arguments of opposing positions. Assumptions are the givens—the deeply held beliefs, opinions, and values—that people *assume* are valid. Assumptions form the basis of every argument but are often not articulated. For example, Al Gore assumes that it is people's responsibility to save the world for future generations even though he doesn't explicitly articulate this belief. Many people, however, do not share this assumption. They believe that the future will take care of itself, that technology will provide whatever solutions are needed, that environmentalists are alarmists, or that present comforts outweigh future concerns. Gore must somehow reconcile his assumptions with those of his readers if he is to convince them that they must change the way they think about waste. For example, not everyone agrees that people have a moral responsibility for preserving the planet, but most will agree that it is in our interest economically to preserve those resources we need to maintain our current standard of living (see **credibility, field research, library research**).

CREDIBILITY, PAGE 443

FIELD RESEARCH, PAGE 493

LIBRARY RESEARCH, PAGE 534

Structuring and Developing Arguments

Experienced writers use various methods of development to structure the evidence they use from their sources. All the methods of development discussed throughout this book are appropriate for research-based arguments. You may compare and contrast (solar energy is safer and more economical than nuclear energy); show cause and effect (solar energy doesn't pollute the atmosphere or deplete resources); describe (solar energy is clean and inexpensive); classify (solar energy, like energy derived from wind and water, is a natural renewable source of energy); exemplify (solar energy has been used successfully in Arizona and New Mexico); and narrate (this is the way solar energy works).

Although you may use one method of development primarily, remember that most texts are developed through a combination of methods. Rachel Carson, for example, uses cause and effect as the primary method of development but also uses narration, description, exemplification, and comparison (see **narration, description, exemplification, comparison/contrast, classification**, and **cause and effect**).

NARRATION, PAGE 558

DESCRIPTION, PAGE 456

EXEMPLIFICATION, PAGE 488

COMPARISON/CONTRAST, PAGE 437

CLASSIFICATION, PAGE 422

CAUSE AND EFFECT, PAGE 418

W R I T I N G   A S S I G N M E N T

For this writing assignment you are to research and report on some arguable environmental issue. The reading selections in this chapter provide you with some useful background information on environmental issues, but you will want to select an issue that interests you in particular and research it thoroughly. Try to select an issue you have had personal or at least local experience with. For example, do you know what insecticides your city or local farmers use? How safe your local water supply is? Which animals, birds, or fish in your region are endangered species? How your city or school disposes of waste? Whether any hazardous waste products are being disposed of in your area?

Because the environment is a global as well as a local issue, you may choose to investigate a subject such as the effects of acid rain or oil spills, the depletion of the ozone layer or the disappearance of rain forests, the issue of global warming, or the issues involving endangered species. Many arguable (and argued) issues involve conflicts between environmental interests on the one hand and government and business interests on the other. For example, serious questions exist about the effects of environmental issues on the economy, the effectiveness of the Environmental Protection Agency in enforcing environmental policy, the effectiveness of laws in protecting the environment, and the roles of government and business in both creating and solving environmental problems.

Although you may initially begin with a very broad question, your research should help you focus on a more specific one. Further research will help you answer your initial question and formulate your thesis. The more you learn about the issue you are researching, the more focused your research will become.

Try to include interviews and observations as well as library research in your investigation. Even if you are researching a national or even international issue, you may be able to find someone at your school or in your city who can provide you with valuable information. Perhaps your college or university has an economist who studies the relationship between the environment and the economy. Or it may have a department or program of environmental science. Perhaps your city has an environmental organization such as a chapter of the Sierra Club or the Audubon Society. Local farmers and gardeners, hunters and outdoor enthusiasts also often have valuable knowledge about the regional animal and plant life. Local businesspeople may be able to give you a personal view of the impact of environmental regulation. Usually these people are willing to share their information. Requesting information from national organizations and agencies is also a possibility. A postcard or telephone call is often all it takes; sometimes a small fee is charged (see **field research**).

FIELD RESEARCH, PAGE 493

Of course, you will also depend heavily on available libraries. Try to locate current and unbiased information. Don't overlook such possibilities as government documents and statutes of law. In looking for magazine and journal articles, use indexes such as the *Humanities Index* and *Social Sciences Index* as well as *Readers' Guide*. For general background information, encyclopedias, especially specialized ones (e.g., *The Encyclopedia of Religion and Ethics, McGraw-Hill Encyclopedia of Science and Technology, The Encyclopedia of World Art*, etc.), can be useful, but don't rely on them for current information. Computer bibliographic searches are also useful. Don't hesitate to ask for assistance with your research. The librarians at the reference desk can tell you what research tools are available to you and direct you to those that are most likely to be productive (see **library research**).

LIBRARY RESEARCH, PAGE 534

Research is time consuming and requires great patience. Don't expect to investigate an issue in a few hours or even a few days. Allow plenty of time for this stage of the process. The more you learn, the more you will be able to learn. Each new source of information you discover will lead you to new sources, and the better you learn your way around the library, the more productive your research will become. Even after you have begun to construct your text, your research will probably continue, but don't rush through the initial stages. It is the foundation for your argument.

Planning Your Text

As in all writing tasks, before beginning a research project, you need to be clear about your audience and purpose. What is the purpose of your research and who will read the results? As a student in a writing course, you have one obvious purpose: to complete an assignment your instructor will read. But you should go beyond the obvious to explore other reasons and other audiences. Do you want to discover whether the river where you fish or where your community gets its drinking water is being polluted or how the use of insecticides may affect the health of people in your community? Even if you are researching a global issue, such as acid rain or global warming, you should determine in advance just what your purpose is.

Similarly, decide in advance who your readers will be—college administrators, a city or country official, state or national legislators, or a certain group of readers, such as sports enthusiasts, homemakers, businesspeople, pro- or anti-environmentalists, and so on. Whether you are writing to an industrialist or an environmentalist may make a difference not only in what you say but how you say it. It also makes a difference in the sources you use to support your point of view. Quoting a Sierra Club member will probably not impress the owners of timber companies, just as citing profit and loss statements will probably not impress a Sierra Club member.

READING AND KEEPING RECORDS OF YOUR RESEARCH.   Initially, you will not read your sources carefully but will merely *skim and scan* them—reading superficially just to get the gist of the source to determine if it is going to be useful to you. Don't take notes or photocopy a source until you are fairly sure it is pertinent. Then, if possible, *photocopy the source* so you will have an accurate copy of your own. Be sure to make a copy not only of the text itself but also of the publication information you will need to document the source if you eventually use it. Some magazines and journals include this information on each page, but many do not.

Once you have a good photocopy, you should *read the source carefully.* As you read, *annotate* your photocopy of the source thoroughly. For example, highlight the main points, mark information you think you may want to use later, underline statements you disagree with, circle sentences you may later want to quote, make comments in the margin, and so on (see Chapter 1).

Now is the time to take notes on what you have read. Whether you use notecards, a journal or notebook, or a computer, you need to *make a record* of your research. Here is an efficient and useful process:

1. Attach (stapling is best) a blank sheet of paper to the photo-copied source.

2. If your copy of the source does not include the information you will need to document it, write this information at the top of the sheet.

3. Summarize the entire source briefly in your own words.

4. Paraphrase important ideas you may want to use in developing your own arguments (indicate page numbers of the original source covered by your paraphrasing).

5. At the bottom of each sheet, write a brief note to yourself indicating how you plan to use this source in developing and supporting your own arguments (see also **library research**).

LIBRARY RESEARCH, PAGE 534

OUTLINING. Because research-based reports and essays are complex texts, you may want to use a preliminary planning outline to organize your ideas. Planning outlines can be as formal or informal as you like. A simple list will do. However, a fairly complete outline, showing not only the main points you want to make and the order you want to make them in but also how you plan to support those points, will be even more useful. You can indicate on this outline which sources you plan to use in developing each point.

Using a computer to make your outline may be the most efficient method because you can later revise and rearrange it, insert material into it (e.g., summaries, quotations, information), and expand it. In fact, if you have taken notes and then developed an outline on a computer, you can often build your report or essay by expanding the outline as you write.

Constructing Your Text

DRAFTING. One pitfall in writing a text based on research is relying too heavily on sources. It is easy to lose your own voice in your effort to make good use of your sources. For that reason, try beginning your text by writing a draft in which you do not include any source material. This initial draft can be rough and even fragmentary (you can fill in the blanks later), but it should establish your own voice and develop your own arguments. Later you can expand your arguments by including information and ideas from your sources, but let this first draft be all yours.

Once you have produced a rough draft on your own, you can write a second draft that includes appropriate source material. Be sure, however, that the sources you include directly support and develop your thesis. If you are using a computer, this step will be fairly easy because you can simply insert the source material where it is needed. If you are not using a computer, you will probably have to rewrite your initial draft.

As you insert quotations and specific information into your text, check them carefully against the original. Once something is copied into your text, you will tend to assume it was copied accurately. So carefully verify the accuracy of everything you include, especially if you are quoting someone.

You do not need to be concerned with complete documentation at this point, but it is a good idea to include the page numbers of the source material you use. You can, of course, wait until later to worry about these details, but it will be easier and more efficient to do it at this point than to do it later.

READING.   You will need to read your essay or report many times before it is finished. In some of those readings, concentrate on specific features:

❖ Read for focus.

❖ Read to evaluate development.

❖ Read for style.

Reading for focus involves determining whether your thesis and topic sentences clearly forecast the content that follows (see **forecasting statements**). Do you clearly state your thesis in the introduction? Does each topic sentence directly support the thesis? Topic sentences should guide your readers through your text, explicitly showing the direction each paragraph is taking. Ordinarily, none of your paragraphs should begin with quotations; you should firmly establish the point you are making in each paragraph before introducing source material, especially quoted source material.

FORECASTING STATEMENTS,
PAGE 503

You may want to copy your thesis and each topic sentence onto a separate sheet of paper so you can see their relationship to one another more clearly. These sentences, read together, should constitute a summary of your text. If you are using a computer, you can copy your text to a new file and then delete everything but the thesis and topic sentences to expedite this process.

Reading to evaluate development involves focusing specifically on the way you have developed each argument. Is the argument clearly articulated in your own words? Have you developed each argument with evidence from your sources and your own ideas? Could you expand and strengthen the development by using one of the traditional methods of development? For example, suppose one of your arguments is that Americans generate a tremendous amount of waste because they rely so extensively on fast foods. You could compare the waste involved in a meal consumed at home with one consumed at a fast-food restaurant, point out the effects of this type of waste, describe in detail all the paper that is wasted in a single fast-food meal, or give examples of the types of waste involved in fast-food merchandising.

You may also discover that some of your arguments need to be supported by additional source materials. In general, each argument should be developed by a combination of your own ideas and by ideas and information from your sources. If you discover that some of your arguments are not well supported, that you have not developed them adequately on your own or supplied adequate evidence from your sources, you may have to do further research. In fact, it is not until you read what you have written that this discovery is possible. Your sources may have seemed sufficient until you constructed a text. Now you may see clearly that you need more information.

Reading for style usually takes place rather late in the process of constructing your text. Is your own voice clear and distinct and appropriate for your audience? You do not want your sources to dominate your text. Rather, you want your readers to hear your own distinct, persuasive voice. In arguing from sources, you want to sound knowledgeable and well informed but not necessarily formal. In most research-based reports and essays, it is fine to use first person and even to use your own experiences if they support your arguments. Don't be reluctant to sound like you. Readers respond much better to a real person's voice than to a neutral-sounding, impersonal, anonymous voice. Although a few texts traditionally require the writer to "disappear," most disciplines and professions now encourage writers to speak as clearly and directly as possible.

In reading for style, you will also be concerned with whether your source material has been smoothly and effectively integrated into your own writing. Don't just plop a quotation into your own text without introducing it first or framing it to fit your own argument (see **library research**).

LIBRARY RESEARCH, PAGE 534

REVISING.   Each time you read your text, you will probably revise it some way. Some of these revisions may be substantive—rearranging sections of your text, deleting extraneous material, adding additional evidence—and some may be minor—rewriting an awkward sentence, correcting an error in subject-verb agreement, changing a word. Revision is an ongoing process. As long as you are constructing a text, you will be revising what you have written, making it clearer, more readable, more fully developed, more persuasive. Be sure to give special attention to the following features of your text:

* Focus

* Organization

* Development

If necessary, revise to sharpen focus. If you lose your readers as they attempt to read your text—if they can't trace the thread of your argument or see the relationship of what they are reading to your thesis—you will not convince them of anything. Readers are usually not willing to struggle with an unfocused text that wanders all over the subject and never makes a point. If your reading of your text doesn't reveal a clear, strong thesis, you must correct this flaw before you can hope to construct a good argument. However, including a strong thesis in your introduction doesn't always mean your text is well focused. If the arguments you include in the body of your text do not support your thesis, your text will still not be well focused. To be well focused a text must have a strong thesis *and* arguments that clearly and directly support it. Read the summary of your text that you created by combining your thesis with each of your topic sentences. If this summary does not have a clear focus, then you must suspect that your essay suffers from the same lack of focus.

If necessary, revise for more effective organization. Readers like to anticipate where your arguments are leading. Surprise endings may be popular in mystery stories, but they are usually not effective when your purpose is to persuade. To keep your readers on track, happy because they are following your arguments and that these arguments are leading to a logical conclusion, do two things. First, arrange your arguments so readers recognize the logic in your organization. One main point should lead naturally and logically into the next so readers have a clear sense of progression as they read. For example, if you are comparing the arguments for and against preserving a certain wilderness area, you do not want to discuss one and then the other haphazardly. It is more effective to discuss all the arguments for preservation and then those against preservation—or to organize the arguments point by point, discussing first the effects on wildlife, then the aesthetic arguments, and finally the economic considerations. Your arrangement of these main points depends on your point of view. If you are convinced that preserving the wilderness area is important and you think the aesthetic arguments are the strongest ones in support of this position, then conclude with this point. However, if you are against the preservation because you think the economic considerations—creation of new jobs, manufacturing development, and so on— override all others, then conclude with this point.

TRANSITIONS, PAGE 612

HEADINGS, PAGE 526

FORECASTING STATEMENTS, PAGE 503

The second thing you can do to help your readers perceive the logic of your organization is to tell them what is going on at strategic intervals. If you are progressing to a new point or even a new point of view, inform your readers by including a clear **transition** statement. Most often, writers make transitions as they begin new paragraphs. Clear topic sentences can not only announce the topic of the paragraph but also can lead the reader from the last point to the next one. You can also use **headings** to help readers perceive the organization of your text. Headings, and even subheadings, are especially useful in texts of five or more pages (see also **forecasting statements**).

If necessary, revise for better development. Now is also the time to look at the development of each of your main arguments. If these arguments are weak and underdeveloped, you may have to do further research. However, be sure your sources do not already dominate your arguments. Perhaps what is needed is further discussion and explanation of the sources you have already included or the expansion of your own arguments. *Remember, your sources are not your arguments; they are merely the evidence for your arguments.* Although you may arrive at your arguments as a result of the cumulative experience of the research you have done, they should be expressions of your own point of view articulated in your own words. If they are weak, sticking another source in may not be the solution. You may need to rethink the issue, do further reading, and talk to other people in order to strengthen and revise them.

Editing Your Text

In editing your text, focus on the uses you have made of source material. Especially important is how well you have integrated quotations into your own writing. Try reading your text aloud, even if no one is listening but you, to determine if the quotations you have used fit smoothly with and into your sentences. If a sentence sounds awkward to you, it probably is (see **documentation**).

DOCUMENTATION, PAGE 460

This is also the time to check the punctuation of quotations and the form of all your parenthetical citations and your list of works cited. Handled correctly, these details indicate that you are a careful researcher, a knowledgeable scholar, and a good writer. In other words, they can help to convince readers of your credibility and persuade them to accept your arguments.

Finally, and most important, check the accuracy of your documentation. Be sure each page number you supply is correct, each author's name is spelled correctly, every title is exactly like the original, and each date of publication is accurate. Also confirm the accuracy of each quotation you have used. This task will be fairly simple for sources you have photocopied. But even if you must go back to the library or must call someone you interviewed, take the time and make the effort. Inaccurate research suggests not just carelessness but dishonesty (see **revising and editing**).

REVISING AND EDITING, PAGE 593

▼

WRITING ESSAY EXAMINATIONS

You will probably write several essay examinations during your first year in college and perhaps dozens more before you graduate. Your instructors use essay examinations to test your knowledge of course content to be sure that you have acquired certain specific information and that you have read and understood assigned reading. But they want to test more than your ability to memorize material. They want to test your ability to express yourself, to organize material, to work with concepts, to make choices about what is important and unimportant information in a specific situation, and to convey knowledge in a focused, concise, and coherent manner under the pressure of time.

Your examination essays may provide instructors with the best evidence that you possess both the knowledge that you should have gained from the course and the ability to apply that knowledge to specific questions, problems, or situations.

Because essay examinations require a higher level of sophistication and a greater degree of independent thinking than do true-false, multiple-choice, and fill-in-the-blank examinations, they also require more extensive preparation. Preparation can be divided into three major stages:

- ❖ Long-range preparation
- ❖ Preliminary preparation
- ❖ Immediate preparation

There is specific work to be done at each stage, and done carefully.

Long-Range Preparation

Long-range preparation for essay examinations begins the first day of class and involves developing an intelligent approach to course work. Listen or read carefully when the instructor explains the purpose and scope of the course, the way your work will be evaluated, and the relative weight of examinations. If course materials include the objectives of the course, review them because they will give you some insight into what the instructor expects you to be able to do. Essay examinations are the opportunities you have to demonstrate that you can meet the objectives of the course.

Keep up with assigned readings and take notes in class. Learn important names, dates, events, places, and terms. Review the key concepts from your reading and from class lectures and discussions. Strive to make connections between various facts. For instance, to know that Shakespeare and Cervantes—the two greatest writers of their respective countries, England and Spain—died on the same day (April 16, 1616) is to possess a piece of trivial information. To realize that they were contemporaries and probably influenced by similar literary, religious, and philosophical ideas is to possess knowledge. If there are study questions at the end of chapters in your textbooks, use them. Questions on essay examinations may be based on these study questions or are likely to be similar kinds of questions. If necessary, ask your instructors about points that you do not fully understand. Above all, do not get into a situation where you have to cram several weeks of reviewing into a few hours.

As the quarter or semester goes along, broaden your information as much as possible by relating what you are studying to what you have learned in other courses. For instance, if you are studying the Great Depression of the 1930s in an American history course, review your reading and class notes from the American literature course in which you read John Steinbeck's *The Grapes of Wrath* to remind yourself of what happened to tenant farmers when corporations took over their farms. Or if you are reading Nelson Algren's *The Man with a Golden Arm* or William Burroughs' *Naked Lunch* for a literature course, review your notes on drug addiction from the sociology course you are also taking. This kind of preparation makes you more fully informed and will help you respond more intelligently and more interestingly to examination questions. You will be able to use more examples and take a wider view of issues as you synthesize information from several sources.

Preliminary Preparation

Preliminary preparation—dedicated study for a specific examination—should begin approximately a week before the examination. Make sure that you have a complete set of class notes. If you have missed class, ask other students about what was covered during your absence. If necessary, ask the instructor. Review your notes and readings to help you determine what you know and how well you can recall it. Find out if the instructor has provided previous examinations for students to review (many instructors do). Pay attention when the instructor discusses the upcoming examination (most instructors do). Be sure that you know what material the examination will cover.

Rehearse mentally for the examination. Study with two or three other students in the class who you believe will be prepared well, pooling your knowledge and resources and reviewing material and anticipating questions. In addition to studying previous examinations if your instructor makes them available, write out essay questions that you think might be on the examination. If you have taken previous examinations or written papers for the instructor, review them to see if the instructor's comments reveal certain interests or expectations. Take turns discussing what information and which strategies might best be used for answering each question.

Immediate Preparation

Immediate preparation occurs the day before or the day of the examination. Make sure that you have the correct equipment to write the examination and have whatever else is allowed—items such as a dictionary, a calculator, or a computer disk.

On the day of the examination, arrive early, find your favorite spot in the classroom—and try to relax. You may want to make a quick, last review of your notes. Being on time and well prepared will help lower the anxiety that sometimes occurs naturally just before an important examination.

Writing the Essay Examination

Instructors design their essay examinations carefully. They are not trying to trick you; they are trying to give you a fair chance to demonstrate your knowledge of the major concepts of the course. They carefully select what is to be covered, thoughtfully phrase their questions, and expect directions to be followed to the letter. So read all instructions and questions carefully to make sure you understand exactly what you are expected to do. If you have questions, ask the instructor or examination monitor.

Read through the examination before you begin so that you can determine whether you must answer every question or have a choice. Instructions usually will be simple and straightforward, as these two examples illustrate:

> *Instructions.* Read each question carefully, and answer *all* parts to each question. The point values are stated beside each question.

Instructions. Allow 30 minutes to answer *one* of the following essay questions (50 points).

Do not spend a lot of time deciding which questions to answer if you are given a choice. In general, choose to answer questions about which you have the most information and in which you have a definite interest. But do not spend more than a minute or two on this decision. Debating with yourself over which question to select takes time away from planning, writing, revising, and proofreading your answers. If you have to write on more than one question, begin with the easiest one—it will help you start quickly and will help you gain momentum and confidence. You will also be less likely to get hung up on the first question and run short of time.

Timing is important. Make sure that you allot enough time to answer all questions. Pay particular attention to the relative value of questions. Some questions may be worth more points than others. If so, give more time to them. You should not spend all your time on a question that covers only thirty percent of the exam.

Before you attempt to answer a question, take a minute to read it carefully and think about what it requires. Note phrases and words that may suggest what the instructor is expecting you to do. Look especially for verbs, such as *define, contrast, list, describe,* or *analyze.* These terms indicate what rhetorical response the teacher wants, the kinds of information you are being asked to provide, and the organizational strategies you can use in writing your answer. Here are a few suggestions on responding to questions.

If the question asks you . . .	*You should . . .*
to explain causes or effects or both	discuss what causes specific events, conditions, situations, acts, decisions, etc., to happen and/or the likely results or outcomes of the events, conditions, situations, acts, decisions, etc.
to compare or contrast or both	discuss two or more subjects by pointing out important similarities (comparing) and key differences (contrasting)
to classify	discuss subjects by categorizing them into groups, types, classes, etc.

to define	discuss a subject (usually a term or concept) by providing a logical definition and examples
to describe	discuss a subject in terms of its parts (mechanism, object, or abstract entity) or its stages, phases, or steps (process)

Watch for other cues as to what the instructor is expecting, such as admonitions to provide specific examples. If you do not provide the required specific examples, you are not fully answering the question and will lose some credit for your answer. Conversely, don't provide information you are told is not wanted. If, for example, a question asks you to explain three ways other than costs that a shear-type forage harvester is different from a flail-type forage harvester, you should identify three points of contrast and devote at least a paragraph to each one, detailing the specific differences and explaining the causes and the implications or significance of these differences. Since the question explicitly excludes cost as a consideration, don't waste your or your instructor's time writing about the difference in cost.

In answering a question, use a process of planning, writing, revising, and proofreading. Begin by taking a couple of minutes to make a few notes about what you plan to say or to outline the points you will discuss. The little time you spend doing this will probably pay good dividends as your write your answer. Place the most important points first in case you run short of time. Refer to your outline as you write, to assure that you include all the important points.

Because you will not have time to recopy your answers for neatness, doublespace your answer to allow for insertions or neat changes. You may not have a lot of time to do major revisions, but allow some time to reread and revise your answers. Check to make sure that you have covered the question and that you have supported your main points with specific evidence—facts, statistics, authoritative opinions, comparisons, examples.

Even proofreading will help. Instructors look for logical, well-supported, clearly organized answers and are fairly forgiving over a little sloppy punctuation and a misspelling or two (although less so if key terms or important names are misspelled or misused). But it is important to strive for correct usage, spelling, and punctuation for at least two reasons. First, faulty usage may produce unclear sentences. At the very least, it can annoy instructors by making them have to reread sentences. Second, even when clarity is not an issue, your image as a literate person is. Instructors want to see that you can write correctly even under the pressure of time.

You can demonstrate your grasp of a question and ability to work with concepts under time pressure by following these guidelines:

1. Rephrase the question as a thesis statement.

2. Use clear, strong topic sentences and transitions to indicate to the reader where the text is going.

3. Include specific information to support and develop each topic sentence.

4. Repeat key terms and phrases from the question and from the course.

To illustrate, here is an actual essay question and a student's response. Annotations point out effective aspects of the answer.

    Discuss the major areas of disagreement between capitalism and scientific socialism and explain how each was changed by the other.

The major area of disagreement between capitalism and socialism concerned who and what created industrial wealth and who was going to control it.

Capitalism was supported by the middle class. Its main proponent was Adam Smith, the eighteenth-century Scottish political economist.

Instructors want to see that the student understands the question. This answer comes straight to the point. The question is revised as an assertion that provides an overview of the answer the student intends to give—a good beginning.

The comparison of capitalism and socialism gets to the heart of the answer quickly. The last two sentences of the second paragraph state the controlling idea for the next several paragraphs and serve as a transition to the detailed discussion of Adam Smith and Karl Marx that follows. At this point the student shows that she knows where she is going with the answer and how she is going to get there.

The discussion contrasts capitalism and socialism in terms of conflicting economic interests between the capitalistic middle class and the socialistic working class. The paragraphs that follow provide sufficient detail without being wordy. The analysis of Adam Smith's laissez-faire economics and Karl Marx's social and

The middle class believed in the private owner-ship of wealth. Socialism was supported by the working class. Its main proponent was Karl Marx, the nineteenth-century social philosopher and political economist known as the founder of modern socialism. The working class believed in group or social ownership of wealth. Smith and Marx both had the same goals -- freedom, happiness, and progress. However, they had different ideas about how to accomplish these goals.

Smith (the spokesman for capitalism) wrote in *The Wealth of Nations* (1776) that people should be left alone to pursue their own economic self-interests and the natural laws of supply and demand and that competition should govern the institutions. Smith said that the state should only be involved in maintaining law and order and building what we today call infrastructures. He said this would result in greater wealth which would filter down through the classes and everyone could enjoy freedom, happiness, and progress.

The problem was that the wealth did not filter down. It remained in the hands of the middle class, the employers. The employers claimed this was because poverty would always be here and the poor were doomed to live a poor life. They based their claim on the theories presented by Thomas Malthus in Essay on the Principle of Population (1798)

economic philosophies, while brief, displays the student's familiarity with the important readings and the major concepts of the course. Throughout her answer, the student uses the important terminology of the course fairly well. The third and fourth paragraphs explain the main tenets of capitalism and its ultimate failure to create wealth for all members of society.

and David Ricardo in <u>Principles of Political Economy and Taxation</u> (1817).

The fifth and sixth paragraphs present the main principles of socialism and its theoretical weakness. The ability to cite specific political economists and social philosophers and the correct titles and dates of their relevant publications increases the student's credibility.

Marx, a German exile who lived in London in the middle of the nineteenth century, became the most influential socialist with the working class, because he identified the reason for their poverty as capitalism. He explained to them how they were kept poor by the middle class. He told them that they could free themselves from their exploiters by creating a classless society and abolishing private property. He also told them that they would eventually win. Marx based this claim on his theory of historical concept of Thesis vs. Anti-thesis = Synthesis. If an existing class (capitalism) were replaced by opposing class (socialism), a new class (communism) would be created. Marx wrote in *Das Kapital* (1867) that this would be the end of all strife because there would be no more classes.

The flaw in Marx's theory is that he misread human nature. His dream of giving according to one's means and taking according to one's needs never took place.

Marx's predictions about capitalism failing first in the industrialized countries (with England to be the first) were wrong. It was actually the less industrialized countries that became socialist. He was also wrong about capitalism. It did change. The wealth did filter down and the

In the last three paragraphs, the student responds specifically to the second part of the question—how capitalism and socialism influenced each other.

working class was better off, due primarily to the industrial expansion of the second half of the nineteenth century. Governments forced the wealth to filter down by passing laws concerning minimum wage, unemployment insurance, and health insurance.

Governments became involved because of the growing fear of violence from the working class and the growing size and electoral power of the working class. There was also a change in the liberal thinking of the capitalists. The government becoming involved was the main reason for the change in capitalism.

The change in socialism caused a split between the Social Democrats who no longer believed Marxist theories and did not want violence and the Revolutionary Socialists who believed that the only way that socialism could come to power was through violence.

As the student's answer illustrates, essay examinations require a broad knowledge of the subject, specific information, and clear, succinct writing. Use your knowledge of writing as a process when you write essay examinations:

1. Prepare thoroughly, both in the long-range and immediate stages.

2. Read the question carefully.

3. Plan and organize your answer before you write.

4. Revise the question to serve as the **thesis** of your answer.

5. Use clear **topic sentences, forecasting statements,** and **transitions.**

6. Include specific information and details.

7. Use key terms and phrases.

8. Revise and proofread carefully as time allows.

THESIS, PAGE 599

TOPIC SENTENCE, PAGE 609

FORECASTING STATEMENTS, PAGE 503

TRANSITIONS, PAGE 612

Douglas Olson, *Baskets and Boxes*

▼

PART THREE

STRATEGIES

Allusion

Amplification (Development)

Analogy

Cause and Effect

Classification

Coherence

Comparison/Contrast

Conciseness

Credibility

Definition

Description

Documentation

Emphasis

Exemplification (Illustration)

Field Research

Forecasting Statements

Format

Graphics

Headings

Invention (Prewriting)

Library Research

Narration

Pace

Paragraphs

Proofreading

Revising and Editing

Style and Voice

Thesis and Thesis Statement

Titles

Topic Sentence

Transitions

INTRODUCTION

Arranged in alphabetical order for quick access, these entries range from *allusion* to *transitions*. Each entry is intended to stand alone as a short, self-sufficient unit providing information that will be useful to you in thinking about and discussing a specific aspect of writing or reading. In no sense do we assume that this section offers a complete survey of all the concepts and strategies that are important to becoming a good writer or reader. It would take a much larger book than this one to do that, for the number of helpful and interesting things to know about these matters is practically limitless. Here we have concentrated only on what we consider some of the most important. You can read these entries in any sequence that serves your purpose or interest.

▶ You might want to refer to a particular entry while you are reading other parts of this book. Whenever a term that is discussed in this section is used elsewhere, it appears in boldface type and is repeated in the margin, where you will also find a page reference for its entry here in Part Three. When you encounter an unfamiliar term or a term that you want explained further that is marked by boldface type, you will know that you can find additional information about it in this section.

▶ You might scan through this section until you locate an entry that discusses a principle or a strategy with which you are working. At times as you write, you will be particularly aware of the need to refresh your memory or to learn more about a particular principle or strategy, whether you need an overview of a concept or merely want information on some small detail. The more you learn about a concept or strategy, the more intelligently you can use it to make the best choices among the available means for achieving an end.

▶ You might want to browse through this section until you discover an entry that deals with a concept you want to learn more about. An entry can be selected at random and read leisurely as a mini-essay, not just used as a quick reference while you grapple with your writing.

Each entry will help you explore a specific rhetorical concept, but one that is related to several others. While every entry is useful in itself, its greater value lies in its potential to be related to other entries. It is a starting point for further reading and thinking. The concepts and approaches in one entry can be useful in understanding others. The next entry that you read will probably depend on the associative trail that the first entry leads you to. In short, in using this section of the book, you can create your own pathway and move in any direction you want.

ALLUSION
▼

An allusion is a brief reference to a person, place, or event outside the text that adds richness and depth to a statement in the text. We have all noticed writers who have used allusions. T. S. Eliot's "The Love Song of J. Alfred Prufrock," for instance, is loaded with classical and Shakespearean allusions. At a pivotal moment in the poem, Prufrock reaches the decision not to assert himself, expressed in this line:

No! I am not Prince Hamlet, nor was I meant to be.

Eliot uses the allusion to Shakespeare's Prince Hamlet to bring into the text the associations and knowledge of a much larger idea about the capacity or incapacity to act forcefully, perhaps even heroically. Prufrock is a man divided, like Hamlet, between melancholia, tenderness, and hesitation on the one hand and assertive, perhaps even violent, action on the other. Unlike Hamlet, Prufrock lacks "the strength to force the moment to its crisis" and will not "dare disturb the universe." In a brief statement, the allusion compresses the complexity of Hamlet's character with that of Prufrock's. The allusion refers directly to Hamlet and indirectly to Hamlet's initial procrastination and eventual violent action. It also helps create great irony: Prufrock, unable to assert himself in a social situation, is contrasted to Hamlet, who is finally able to avenge his father's murder.

When writers use allusions, they are revealing their own education and learning, what information and ideas have influenced them and informed their thinking and feelings. Allusions come from philosophy, science, art, music, literature, and history and are specific to particular cultures. Native users of American English, like others whose backgrounds are informed by Judaism and Christianity, are influenced greatly by the Bible, perhaps more than by any other book or group of books. They frequently draw on the Bible for stirring quotations, vivid images, anecdotes, and illustrative examples. References to Lot's wife, the Tower of Babel, Armageddon, and statements such as "weighed in the balances and found wanting" and "handwriting on the wall" are only a few such allusions. Most writers are not classical scholars, but they have their store of cultural artifacts that enable them to allude to myths, classical history, and classical literature when referring to Achilles' heel, the Trojan horse, Titans, Helen of Troy, nemesis, and the tasks of Hercules or Sisyphus. Is there an experienced writer who has not used, or at least thought of using, this statement: "The subject, like ancient Gaul, is divided into three parts" (an allusion to Julius Caesar's *Gallic War*). Americans also have their own domestic reservoir of potential allusions in events such as Custer's last stand and Watergate, places such as Peoria, Mudville, and Valley Forge, and persons or characters such as Betsy Ross, Huck Finn, Babe Ruth, Huey Long, Oliver North, and Madonna.

Writers expect their readers to understand the allusions without explanation. They assume a shared body of knowledge and values between themselves and their readers and expect their readers to fill in the necessary details. When an allusion works, it taps into associations that readers already have, conveys a lot in only a few words by connecting, associating, or comparing one thing with another, and creates the pleasure of recognition. An allusion to Machiavelli or to Machiavellian strategies requires readers to associate what is being said with the manipulations of power explained in Niccolo Machiavelli's *The Prince*, a treatise on political power published in 1513. If the allusion is not recognized by readers, then their understanding of the text is limited. The desired effect will not only be lost, but readers may be baffled by the statement or even resentful that the writer is showing off his or her learning at their expense. So always ask yourself whether your readers will know enough about the allusion to get the associations you want to evoke.

AMPLIFICATION (DEVELOPMENT)
▼

Almost all writing can be regarded as amplification, which is the addition to or expansion of a point or an idea for clarification or proof. Writers are constantly involved in the painstaking, deliberate process of trying to anticipate when to leave a point or an idea undeveloped and when and how to develop it more fully.

Amplification strengthens writing three ways:

* ❖ It offers evidence to support assertions and arguments.

* ❖ It helps clarify any point that might not be immediately understood.

* ❖ It helps shape a thought, providing additional information that allows readers to adjust to an idea that might be unfamiliar or controversial.

Amplifying to Provide Support

Ideas, claims, statements, and assertions that are important require close examination and should not be made without some support. Probably 95 percent of the time, a point or an idea needs to be amplified. Although some readers grasp ideas quickly and easily, the writer should not stay on a general, abstract level for very long. Otherwise, readers will be left with only a vague impression of what is meant. Even relatively simple ideas may be abstract or vague in readers' minds. Take a look at the following, very general statement:

> The teeth of the rhinoceros are unlike the teeth of any other animal.

Unless this sentence is amplified, readers will be asking questions like these: What is so different about their teeth? Is it their size? Shape? Number? Location? Color? Durability? Use? Why is it important to know this? Amplification gives the details that translate the abstract and the general into the concrete and more accessible world of the senses.

Amplification helps us see. Here is the first line of John Keats's poem "The Eve of St. Agnes":

> St. Agnes' Eve—Ah, bitter chill it was!

The concrete language and the sensory details in the rest of the stanza build up a series of cold images and amplify the opening line to help readers see and feel the cold and to demonstrate the truth of the assertion that it was bitterly cold (St. Agnes' Eve is January 20, which according to folklore is the coldest day of the year).

St. Agnes' Eve—Ah, bitter chill it was!
The owl, for all his feathers, was a-cold;
The hare limp'd trembling through the frozen grass,
And silent was the flock in woolly fold:
Numb were the Beadsman's fingers, while he told
His rosary, and while his frosted breath,
Like pious incense from a censer old,
Seemed taking flight for heaven, without a death,
Past the sweet Virgin's picture, while his prayer he saith.

Notice in the following passage by Carol Bly, an essayist and fiction writer living in the small town of Madison, Minnesota, how the second paragraph amplifies and extends the idea of the first paragraph. The descriptive details of the second paragraph call up specific images that define more sharply what would have remained only a general impression had Bly continued to stay on the relatively abstract level of the first paragraph:

It is sometimes mistakenly thought by city people that grown-ups don't love snow. They think only children who haven't got to shovel it love snow, or only people like the von Furstenburgs and their friends who get to go skiing in exotic places and will never backslope a roadside in their lives: that is a mistake. The fact is that most country or small-town Minnesotans love snow. They relish snow in large inconvenient storms; they like the excesses of it, they like the threat of it, the endless work of it, the glamour of it.

Before a storm, Madison is full of people excitedly laying in food stocks for the three-day blow. People lay in rather celebratory food, too. Organic-food parents get chocolate for the children; weight watchers lay in macaroni and Sara Lee cakes; recently-converted vegetarians backslide to T-bones. People hang around the large Super-Valu window and keep a tough squinty-eyed watch on the storm's progress with a lot of gruff, sensible observations (just like Houston Control talking to the moon, very much on top of it all) like "Ja, we need this for spring moisture . . ." or "Ja, it doesn't look like letting up at all . . ." or "Ja, you can see where it's beginning to drift up behind the VFW." The plain pleasure of it is scarcely hidden.

—"Great Snows," in *Letters from the Country*
(New York: Harper & Row, 1981): 40-41.

Even texts that seem to consist of only narrative or descriptive details turn out, on closer examination, to be passages that move back and forth between general and specific statements. Here is a very brief passage in which each statement amplifies the statements that precede it:

> I locked the door, kept the world out; I vegetated, hibernated, remained in stasis, idled. No telephones, no television, no radio. Alone with the presence in the room. Who? Me, my psyche, the Shadow-Beast.

> —Gloria Anzaldua, *Borderlands/La Frontera;*
> *The New Mestiza* (San Francisco: Spinsters/Aunt
> Lute Book Company, 1987): 44.

Almost any idea or assertion a writer wishes to convey represents an invitation for amplification so that both the writer and the reader can think through a subject, examine it more closely, and come to know more fully what something is or means. Follow the development of the next passage, in which Louis L'Amour, a bestselling author of historical fiction of the American West, begins his reflections on the role of reading in learning.

> This is not the story of how I came to be in Singapore. That will be told elsewhere. This is a story of an adventure in education, pursued not under the best of conditions. The idea of education has been so tied to schools, universities, and professors that many assume there is no other way, but education is available to anyone within reach of a library, a post office, or even a newsstand.
> Today you can buy the *Dialogues* of Plato for less than you would spend on a fifth of whiskey, or Gibbon's *Decline and Fall of the Roman Empire* for the price of a cheap shirt. You can buy a fair beginning of an education in any bookstore with a good stock of paperback books for less than you would spend on a week's supply of gasoline.
> Often I hear people say they do not have time to read. That's absolute nonsense. In one year during which I kept that kind of record, I read twenty-five books while waiting for people. In offices, applying for jobs, waiting to see a dentist, waiting in a restaurant for friends, many such places. I read on buses, trains, and planes. If one really wants to learn, one has

to decide what is important. Spending an evening on the town? Attending a ball game? Or learning something that can be with you your life long?

Byron's *Don Juan* I read on an Arab dhow sailing north from Aden up the Red Sea to Port Tewfik on the Suez Canal. Boswell's *Life of Johnson* I read while broke and on the beach in San Pedro. In Singapore, I came upon a copy of *The Annals and Antiquities of Rajahstan* by James Tod. It was in the library of a sort of YMCA for seamen, the name of which I've forgotten but which any British sailor of the time would remember, for the British had established them in many ports, for sailors ashore.

—*Education of a Wandering Man* (New York: Bantam, 1989): 1-2.

The passage consists mostly of examples, details, facts and figures, qualifications, illustrations, and even questions that start bringing an idea to life and lead to a deeper and more extensive understanding of L'Amour's concept of education. Well before the end of the passage the reader knows that an education is available to anyone who chooses to read, that books are easily accessible, and that time is available for reading. The amplification also captures some of the notion that books bring excitement even when the reader is tired, lonely, and nearly broke.

As the Keats, Bly, Anzaldua, and L'Amour passages illustrate, amplification gets us deeper into a subject, primarily by providing details for clarifying and exploring ideas, for translating experience into richly specific feelings and images, for validating—even celebrating—the experience and knowledge embodied in ideas, and for arguing the truth claims of a proposition. Amplification can be almost anything and everything—facts, statistics, examples, anecdotes, comparisons, and restatements of those facts, statistics, examples, anecdotes, and comparisons. A text becomes meaningful primarily in terms of the details and repetition used to make it interesting and believable.

An underdeveloped passage that lacks the kind of amplification illustrated in the passages just cited reads like this:

Hardly a week goes by without some new example of attempts to enforce conformity on campus. At the California State University at Northridge, an offer by the Carl's Jr. fast-food chain to install a branch in the newly expanded bookstore was rejected last May. To Stephen Balch, Northridge's decision was outrageously intolerant.

How long would you keep reading something like this? Not long, we bet. The passage is boring and difficult to read. It is difficult to read because it is difficult to understand. It is difficult to understand because there is so little amplification. The lack of amplification makes the passage seem superficial, general, and disconnected. Readers yearn for the details that will make things clear and connected. They do not know why the fast-food chain's offer was rejected, why Balch believed the university's decision was objectionable, or even who Balch is. Too much information is missing for this passage to be interesting, clear, meaningful, or convincing.

A writer who does not amplify takes it for granted that readers will understand what has been written. But it is usually a mistake to assume that readers can fill in the details for themselves, for usually they are less familiar with the subject than the writer. The odds are overwhelmingly against readers understanding everything that is said, even when the writer thinks the text is absolutely clear and precise. All writers fail to amplify at times, particularly when they think that a meaning is as obvious to a reader as it is to them. But it is the writer's responsibility to provide the details that will give meaning to his or her ideas. To remain satisfied with broad generalizations is to run the risk of being or appearing to be a lazy thinker and an irresponsible writer.

Here's how the passage on enforcing conformity on campus actually was written for *Time* magazine:

> Hardly a week goes by without some new example of attempts to enforce conformity on campus. At the California State University at Northridge, an offer by the Carl's Jr. fast-food chain to install a branch in the newly expanded bookstore was rejected last May. The reason was not the quality or price of the chow but student and faculty objections to the conservative views of the chain's owner, Carl Karcher, who financially supports antiabortion groups such as the National Right to Life Action League. To Stephen Balch, Northridge's decision was outrageously intolerant. "You're not talking about Karcher doing anything on campus," he says. "You're not even talking about anything the fast-food chain did as a corporation. You're talking about something its owner did, certainly something he has a right to do, and something that a public institution should certainly not penalize people for."
>
> —John Elson, "Busybodies: New Puritans,"
> *Time* (August 12, 1991): 20.

The differences between the two versions are obvious, but the significance of these differences is especially important. The third, fifth, sixth, and seventh sentences clarify what is not stated and what is not already understood by most readers of the first version. The specific issues and proof are now there—who rejected the offer and why, and why Balch denounced the rejection.

However, these sentences illustrate only one level of development. There is another level of amplification within the third sentence, in which the writer amplifies several points further by identifying the views as conservative, giving the owner's name, labeling the support as financial, and providing an example of the kind of antiabortion group. This extensive amplification makes almost everything immediately clear. Probably the only question remaining for most readers after reading this paragraph is the identity of Stephen Balch. Extending the context provides the answer, for earlier in the text Balch is identified as president "of the National Association of Scholars, based in Princeton, N.J., which is dedicated to fighting lockstep leftism in academia." So the version published in *Time* does include all the information necessary for readers to understand the text.

Amplifying to Clarify a Point

The most important function of amplification is to provide information that makes ideas concrete, clear, and believable. What may not be obvious, however, is how much to amplify. Certainly writers must provide evidence to support their assertions. But how do writers know when enough is enough, when readers understand? There are no simple answers. It isn't easy to strike a balance between providing enough information but not too much.

Writers too often assume their readers know as much about the subject as they do. But when writers and readers do not share a common context, frame of reference, or basic assumptions, then more background information, more context building, and more explanation are required. Writers who are knowledgeable about their subjects legitimately fear being tedious and prolix. But for the most part their fear is unfounded. Up to a point, readers do not object to receiving familiar and sometimes redundant information. Often they are not able to recall immediately the information they already possess, and amplification triggers their memory and brings old information to the conscious level, as the writers do in this passage:

All computers, from the smallest to the largest, rely on a special class of mathematical logic developed in the 1850s by British mathematician George Boole. Named for its inventor, Boolean logic is a system for reducing a problem to a series of true or false propositions, which can be represented by zeros and ones. A problem-solver can then work out a solution with what is called binary mathematics.

—Stephen Bennett, Robert Hirshon, and Porter G. Randall, "Computers," in *The Almanac of Science and Technology: What's New and What's Known*, ed. Richard Golob and Eric Brus (Boston: Harcourt Brace Jovanovich, 1990): 229.

There are several points to be made about amplification in this passage. First, the degree of redundancy is very high—there is a lot of information overlap that most readers are not even aware of. But this kind of redundancy can improve comprehension. Examples of redundancies that most readers are unaware of occur in the first sentence: the plurality of the subject is conveyed by the adjective *all*, the *-s* ending on *computers*, and by the plural verb form *rely*. The phrase "from the smallest to the largest" is also redundant information added to "All computers." In case readers miss any of the plural markers, several other markers convey the same information. This kind of amplification makes information more readable for all readers.

Later in the passage the amplification is more noticeably redundant information for knowledgeable readers. For instance, readers are informed that Boolean logic is named for its inventor, George Boole. Much less obvious, but still redundant are the identification of Boole as a British mathematician and the point that Boole developed the system in the 1850s. But most readers of the encyclopedia-like publication from which this passage is taken would not perceive this information as overly redundant and might even regard much of it as new and helpful. One reason they read these kinds of publications is to acquire such basic information as contained in the details of the amplification. They are the readers for whom amplification pays off well. But even more knowledgeable readers will not find the redundancies objectionable. They will probably be pleased to have their knowledge confirmed and will appreciate what new information they glean from the passage. For example, many readers will know that naming something after its creator, inventor, or discoverer is a common practice but may not know that Boole was a British mathematician or when he developed the system.

What about fully informed persons who already know everything in the passage—all about Boolean logic, binary mathematics, and George Boole? They are not the intended readers for whom this text was prepared. The kind of information in a text tells a lot about whom the writer has in mind as his or her intended audience.

Amplifying to Allow Readers to Adjust to a New Idea

Amplification also helps readers link information (especially assertions and their support) and adjust to new ideas or ideas that they find controversial. Notice how Gilbert Highet accomplishes this in this paragraph in which he asserts that Winston Churchill's *The Second World War* is autobiography, not history:

> Sir Winston Churchill's six-volume *The Second World War* is really an autobiographical record. He himself says it is "the story as I knew and experienced it as Prime Minister of Defence of Great Britain." Therefore it cannot be called anything like a complete history of the war. For example, Churchill tells the story of one of the crucial events of this century—the reduction of Japan to impotence and surrender by intensive bombardment culminating in what he calls the "casting" of two atomic bombs—in only eight pages, while a greater amount of wordage is devoted to a reprint of a broadcast he made to British listeners on VE day.
>
> —*Talents and Geniuses* (New York: Oxford UP, 1957): 256-257.

Highet, professor of classics at Columbia University and chief literary critic for *Harper's* during his lifetime, begins his amplification by quoting Churchill in the second sentence, then restates his claim in the third sentence before adding a specific example to illustrate his claim. The second and third sentences allow the reader to remain on a relatively abstract level briefly before moving to the particular detail that Highet hopes is convincing. Those middle two sentences give the reader a bit more time to consider the claim before receiving the most specific evidence. Thus amplification is an important tactic for pacing information for readers.

Ultimately, the strength of a text depends on its amplification. Amplification is not just making a text longer or larger, but making it clearer. Development is not just adding more words but enlarging or elaborating a point to make it easier to understand. Virtually every idea is made more concrete, precise, and accessible by adding specific details. No less an authority than Cicero, the great Roman rhetorician who flourished just before the time of Christ, gives an excellent rationale for amplification in Book III of his *De Oratore*:

> Our orator will find great value in amplifying his statements, since audiences perceive this technique as an effort to clarify confusing matters.
>
> —quoted in Donovan J. Ochs, "Cicero's Classical Theory," in *A Synoptic History of Classical Rhetoric*, ed. James J. Murphy (Davis, CA: Hermagoras Press, 1983): 124.

Because no one strategy of amplification is sure to work, writers and speakers make their ideas accessible in a number of developing, reinforcing, restating, and supporting ways: **analogy, classification, comparison/contrast, description, exemplification**, and **narration**. These are only a few of the strategies for amplification and do not limit or determine the many possibilities of development and expansion.

ANALOGY
▼

An analogy is a special kind of comparison that shows ways in which two essentially different things are similar in important respects. It is a comparison between fundamentally different objects or concepts for the purpose of explaining or clarifying one of them.

Any new idea and certainly any new way of thinking develops in the context of existing habits of thought. Thus writers must be able to explain new information or obscure concepts in terms of what their readers already know. An analogy can be effective in constructing a bridge from existing knowledge to new knowledge, from the familiar to the unfamiliar.

Using Analogies to Clarify Difficult or Unfamiliar Subject Matter

Analogies are a primary means of explanation and are especially useful in helping readers to visualize the function, size, or structure of unfamiliar objects and to understand complex processes and concepts by showing their similarities to familiar objects, processes, and concepts. Visual analogies, especially those explaining concepts of shape, are commonly based on such things as Roman and Greek alphabetic letters (C clamp, I beam, Delta wing); anatomical parts (sawtooth, bottleneck, elbow joint); or other well-known objects (butterfly nut, kangaroo rat, kidney bean). Bicycle enthusiasts talk about brake shoes, drivetrains, eyelets, saddle seats, front forks, fork blades, fork crowns, gear teeth, spoke nipples, lock rings, mushroom clamps, and so forth—all parts of a bicycle that are named according to what they look like, or as in the case of brake shoes, what they used to look like. Most such analogies consist of only a word or two and are so common that writers are not necessarily aware that they use them. They write of "mining" the ocean for minerals, of "skimming" profits from gambling casinos, and of certain forms of life being "high on the food chain." So don't think of an analogy as an ornament of style used to make writing and speech colorful. Even the most ordinary language is saturated with word analogies.

Sometimes an analogy consists of a sentence, especially to clarify a difficult or new concept, as in "the finish of the automotive paint is orange peel" or "the human heart functions much like a pump." There are also longer analogies such as the following one by Victor Hugo in *Les Misérables* that uses a familiar object, the capital letter *A*, to describe the battlefield at Waterloo. The analogy provides a general visual impression that makes it easier to relate the details.

> Those who wish to form a distinct idea of the battle of Waterloo need only imagine a capital A laid on the ground. The left leg of the A is the Nivelles road, the right one the Genappe road, while the string of the A is the broken way running from Ohain to Braine l'Alleud. The top of the A is Mont St. Jean, where Wellington is; the left lower point is Hougomont, where Reille is with Jerome Bonaparte; the right lower point is la Belle Alliance, where Napoleon is. A little below the point where the string of the A meets and cuts the right leg, is La Haye Sainte; and in the center of this string is the exact spot where the battle was concluded. . . .
>
> The triangle comprised at the top of the A, between the two legs and the string, is the plateau of Mont St. Jean; the dispute for this plateau was the whole battle.
>
> —*Les Misérables*, Vol. 2, Book 1 (New York: Heritage Press, 1938): 12-13.

Hugo's comparison of the battlefield (the unfamiliar subject being discussed) to the shape of the capital letter *A* (the familiar object that it is being compared to) gives readers something to grasp by comparing the unfamiliar terrain with a shape they can easily imagine, helping them understand the movements of military units during the battle.

Effective analogies must fulfill three requirements.

▶ **Analogies should explain a complex or unfamiliar concept in terms of one that is simpler or more familiar to the reader.** It would not do to compare something to a colony of ants or to the flow of water through a pipe unless the reader or listener was familiar with the ways of ants or water pipes. It would be explaining the unknown in terms of yet another unknown. The very reason for using analogy is to make the unfamiliar more easily understood by comparing it to the familiar.

▶ **Analogies should be developed by detailing the points of similarity.** In what ways is a communal society (the concept to be explained) like an ant colony? Its function? Its organization? Its development? How is the flow of electricity through a wire (the concept to be explained) similar to the flow of water through a pipe? In its principle of operation? In the method of measuring the flow? The more characteristics an analogy can reveal, the better the analogy.

▶ **Analogies must not mislead by suggesting inappropriate or irrelevant features.** Comparing an object to a triangle (a two-dimensional object) is misleading and confusing if the object looks more like a pyramid (a three-dimensional object). For example, the earth is not just circular (two-dimensional feature). It is *spherical* (three-dimensional feature)—spherical with a slight depression at each of its poles. Good analogies make it easier to understand the features or aspects of the subject under discussion. Bad analogies mislead by ignoring important features or by implying features or aspects that the object of the analogy does not have.

Using Analogies in Argument

In argument, analogies are sometimes used to persuade readers that things not normally thought of as similar are, in fact, similar and that inferences can be based on those similarities. Handled well, an analogy can link ideas together—sometimes in surprising and pleasing ways, can build parallels between concepts, and can appeal to the reader's common sense and emotions. David Elkind, an eminent psychologist, uses an analogy in the fourth sentence (italicized) of the following passage to achieve exactly these effects in summing up his argument and clarifying his thesis that the education of children should be designed to meet their special needs as children rather than to hurry them into maturity:

> All children have, vis-a-vis adults, special needs—intellectual, social, and emotional. Children do not learn, think, or feel in the same way as adults. To ignore these differences, to treat children as adults, is really not democratic or egalitarian. *If we ignore the needs of children, we are behaving just as if we denied Hispanic and Indian children bilingual programs, or denied the handicapped their ramps and guideposts.* In truth, the recognition of a group's special needs and accommodation to those needs are the only true ways to insure equality and true equal opportunity.
>
> —*The Hurried Child: Growing Up Too Soon,*
> rev. ed. (Reading, MA: Addison-Wesley, 1988): 22.

A more extended analogy is developed by Malcolm X, the African-American civil rights leader of the early 1960s, in arguing that blacks who attempt to identify with whites undergo a painful experience both physically and psychologically. In *The Autobiography of Malcolm X,* written with the help of Alex Haley, he explains how as a teenager he used chemicals to redden and straighten his hair in seeking to conform to white standards of beauty. It was not until later in life that he realized the process of conking his hair was analogous to self-degradation.

> My first view in the mirror blotted out the hurting. I'd seen some pretty conks, but when it's the first time on your *own* head, the transformation, after the lifetime of kinks, is staggering.
>
> The mirror reflected Shorty behind me. We both were grinning and sweating. And on top of my head was this thick, smooth sheen of shining red hair—real red—as straight as any white man's.
>
> How ridiculous I was! Stupid enough to stand there simply lost in admiration of my hair now looking "white," reflected in the mirror of Shorty's room. I vowed I'd never again be without a conk, and I never was for many years.
>
> This was my first really big step toward self-degradation: when I endured all of that pain, literally burning my flesh to

have it look like a white man's hair. I had joined that multitude
of Negro men and women in America who are brainwashed
into believing that black people are "inferior"—and white people "superior"—that they will even violate and mutilate their
God-created bodies to try to look "pretty" by white standards.

—*The Autobiography of Malcolm X* (New
York: Grove Press, 1966): 54.

Handled poorly, argument by analogy can be risky because it
involves an inference. When an analogy is not logically sound—that is,
when it leads to false reasoning or is based on features that resemble
each other only in slight or remote ways—the argument is open to easy
attack. For example, an argument based on analogy might assert that
what happened once is likely to happen again, as follows: The graduate we hired from Ajax College did well in our accounting department;
therefore, we should hire another Ajax College graduate. Experience, of
course, should be considered in making decisions: people with similar
training or education are very likely to be able to perform similarly in
similar situations. But, in general, analogical resemblances are not adequate proof in argument. A decision to hire another Ajax College graduate because an earlier one succeeded on the job is as faulty as a
decision *not* to hire another Ajax College graduate because an earlier
one did poorly on the job. Such an argument is based on hasty generalization (one example of failure or success does not predict future failure or success) and non sequitur reasoning (it does not necessarily
follow that because one Ajax College graduate succeeded that another
will too, or vice versa).

Here is another analogy by Malcolm X, which is a little less successful than the one illustrated earlier. In a speech in which he criticized the participation of whites in the march on Washington, D.C., in
1962 for black civil rights, Malcolm X claims that whites took over the
leadership of the demonstration and instilled more moderate leaders,
consequently diluting its grass-roots nature:

It's like when you've got some coffee that's too black, which
means it's too strong. What do you do? You integrate it with
cream, you make it weak. But if you pour too much cream in
it, you won't even know you ever had coffee.

—"Message to the Grass Roots," in *Malcolm X
Speaks*, ed. George Breitman (New York: Grove
Weiderfeld, 1990): 16.

The cream-in-the-coffee image is striking and perhaps appropriately suggestive, but the analogy itself does not represent evidence that integration weakens a civil rights demonstration. If the context required a more logical argument, Malcolm X would have to offer more evidence that appointing a white millionaire as cosponsor of the march and inviting Walter Reuther, a white labor union leader, and several white members of the clergy to speak at the rally damaged the political movement.

Analogies can be useful in argument. But they can also be the weakest link in an argument. If an opponent is able to demonstrate that an analogy is strained or forced, hanging together by the slimmest of threads so to speak, or that the analogy leads to a hasty generalization, then the argument is likely to collapse like a house of cards.

CAUSE AND EFFECT

▼

When writers write about cause-and-effect relationships, they link events, attempting to show that one thing leads to another. They attempt to demonstrate why something is happening or has happened (why there has been an increase in the number of accidents in petrochemical plants in the United States, for instance) or to predict what is likely to happen (the federal government may develop regulations to establish safer plant procedures), or both.

Generally, cause-and-effect organization is straightforward. The writer looks back to determine why something is happening or has happened or looks into the future to what its likely consequences will be, or both. The writer may begin with the cause and then proceed to the effect or effects, or the writer may begin with the effect and work back to the cause or causes. The following three samples represent common cause-and-effect patterns.

Analyzing Causes

One pattern focuses on causes, on describing something that is taking place now, or has taken place, and explaining its causes. In *Forecast 2000*, George Gallup, Jr., president of the well-known Gallup Poll public opinion research firm, claims that the existence of the traditional American family is threatened and proceeds to identify several cultural trends that may be causing the change.

Twenty years ago, the typical American family was depicted as a man and woman who were married to each other and who produced children (usually two) and lived happily ever after. This was the pattern that young people expected to follow in order to become "full" or "normal" members of society. Of course, some people have always chosen a different route—remaining single, taking many partners, or living with a member of their own sex. But they were always considered somewhat odd, and outside the social order of the traditional family.

In the last two decades, this picture has changed dramatically. In addition to the proliferation of single people through divorce, we also have these developments:

❖ Gay men and women have petitioned the courts for the right to marry each other and to adopt children. . . .

❖ Many heterosexual single adults have been permitted to adopt children and set up single-parent families. . . .

❖ Some women have deliberately chosen to bear children out of wedlock and raise them alone. In the past, many of these children would have been given up for adoption, but no longer. . . .

❖ In a recent Gallup Youth Poll, 64 percent of the teenagers questioned said that they hoped their lives would be different from those of their parents. This included having more money, pursuing a different kind of profession, living in a different area, having more free time—and staying single longer.

    Most surveys show increasing numbers of unmarried couples living together. Also, there are periodic reports of experiments in communal living, "open marriages," and other such arrangements. . . .

❖ Increasing numbers of married couples are choosing to remain childless. . . .

So clearly, a situation has arisen during the last twenty years in which traditional values are no longer as important. Also, a wide variety of alternatives to the traditional family have arisen. Individuals may feel that old-fashioned marriage is just one of the many options.

—George Gallup, Jr., with William Proctor,
"The Faltering Family," in *Forecast 2000* (New
York: Morrow, 1984): 115-116.

Analyzing Effects

A second pattern of cause and effect focuses on effects, as Norman Cousins does in explaining the consequences of administering pain suppressants to professional athletes:

> Professional athletes are sometimes severely disadvantaged by trainers whose job it is to keep them in action. The more famous the athlete, the greater the risk that he or she may be subjected to extreme medical measures when injury strikes. The star baseball pitcher whose arm is sore because of a torn muscle or tissue damage may need sustained rest more than anything else. But this team is battling for a place in the World Series; so the trainer or team doctor, called upon to work his magic, reaches for a strong dose of butazolidine or other powerful pain suppressants. Presto, the pain disappears! The pitcher takes his place on the mound and does superbly. That could be the last game, however, in which he is able to throw the ball with full strength. The drugs didn't repair the torn muscle or cause the damaged tissue to heal. What they did was to mask the pain, enabling the pitcher to throw hard, further damaging the torn muscle. Little wonder that so many star athletes are cut down in their prime, more the victims of overzealous treatment of their injuries than of the injuries themselves.
>
> *—Anatomy of an Illness*
> (New York: Bantam, 1981): 92-93.

Analyzing Cause and Effect

A third pattern of cause and effect combines the first two. In the following passage, Joan Didion discusses the causes and effects of migraines:

> Almost anything can trigger a specific attack of migraine: stress, allergy, fatigue, an abrupt change in barometric pressure, a contretemps over a parking ticket. A flashing light. A fire drill. One inherits, of course, only the predisposition. In other words I spent yesterday in bed with a headache not merely because of my bad attitudes, unpleasant tempers and wrongthink, but because both my grandmothers had migraine, my father has migraine and my mother has migraine.
>
> No one knows precisely what it is that is inherited. The chemistry of migraine, however, seems to have some connec-

tion with the nerve hormone named serotonin, which is naturally present in the brain. The amount of serotonin in the blood falls sharply at the onset of migraine. . . .

Once an attack is under way . . . no drug touches it. Migraine gives some people mild hallucinations, temporarily blinds others, shows up not only as a headache but as a gastrointestinal disturbance, a painful sensitivity to all sensory stimuli, an abrupt overpowering fatigue, a strokelike aphasia, and a crippling inability to make even the most routine connections. When I am in a migraine aura (for some people the aura lasts fifteen minutes, for others several hours), I will drive through red lights, lose the house keys, spill whatever I am holding, lose the ability to focus my eyes or frame coherent sentences, and generally give the appearance of being on drugs, or drunk. The actual headache, when it comes, brings with it chills, sweating, nausea, a debility that seems to stretch the very limits of endurance. That no one dies of migraine seems, to someone deep into an attack, an ambiguous blessing.

—"In Bed," in *The White Album*
(New York: Simon & Schuster, 1979): 170-171.

Cause-and-effect relationships can be difficult to establish with certainty for several reasons, and you need to know what to do and what to watch out for when writing causal analysis. Here are two suggestions.

▶ **Know the basic pattern on which you are focusing—cause or effect or both.** When attempting to explain what caused something, you deal with a relatively known situation (the rate of accidents in petrochemical plants in the United States) but must research, analyze, and interpret a less well-known past (the age of the equipment in these plants, the level of training of employees, the financial condition of the industry, the level of production goals, and so forth) to determine the cause or causes of the present situation. When attempting to explain what will likely happen in the future as a result of a present situation, you deal with a relatively known situation but speculate on an unknown future (Will the petrochemical industry, which at present is allowed to set acceptable toxicity levels and plant safety procedures, develop more stringent standards, or will the federal government establish tougher standards and shift the responsibility of monitoring compliance to OSHA, the Occupational Safety and Health Administration?). Obviously, these two patterns can be combined when you are attempting to explain both causes and effects.

▶ Avoid the faulty conclusion known as the *post hoc fallacy*. Even when you believe you have accounted for causes and effects, there is always the possibility that some other, yet undiscovered, cause or causes exist or that some other unpredicted effect or effects will occur. For example, perhaps flaws in the design of new processing equipment are contributing significantly to the number of increased accidents, or perhaps better and more thorough reporting of industrial accidents has resulted in more accidents being reported rather than the rate of accidents increasing. If the latter is the case, perhaps no immediate corrective action is called for.

Cause-and-effect relationships are usually involved and complex, so avoid jumping to conclusions from just a few facts or slim evidence. The most common type of faulty conclusion involving cause-and-effect relationships is the one known as the *post hoc fallacy*, a mistake that many of us make from time to time. This is a conclusion based on the assumption that if one event follows another, the second event is caused by the first. (Did the Reagan administration's move in the early 1980s to get big government off the back of big business lead to the petrochemical industry, instead of OSHA, setting toxicity levels and safe plant procedures? Did the era of leveraged buyouts in the early 1980s cause companies to incur massive debts in an attempt to protect themselves from hostile takeovers? Did cost-cutting practices lead to using less trained personnel, to using aging equipment that should have been replaced, and to making other poor management decisions?)

Just because event B follows event A is not sufficient reason to conclude that A caused B. Proving a causal relationship requires evidence other than an association in time. However, despite the difficulties in analyzing causality, you constantly connect events in cause-and-effect relationships. Everybody assumes that events have causes and that events have consequences (effects).

CLASSIFICATION
▼

The ability to perceive resemblances that allow us to group similar things together is fundamental to our shaping a meaningful world. It is not surprising, then, that much writing uses classification, a systematic form of thinking in which the writer identifies a topic, arranges the information about the topic into groups or classes for convenience and order, and then explains each group or class in detail. When necessary, these groups can be subdivided into smaller categories.

Classification can be fairly casual and unrigorous, as used by Judith Viorst in an article titled "What, Me? Showing Off?" (*Redbook*, November 1982: 17-20). Viorst distinguishes between the unacceptable behavior of obnoxious show-offs and the acceptable behavior of what she regards as more acceptable show-offs. Viorst further classifies obnoxious show-offs as either competitive show-offs or narcissistic show-offs and the more acceptable show-offs as those who show off because they are basically insecure, those who say nothing about their achievements (Viorst treats these as a special kind of show-off), or those who exult in some charming fashion over their performances.

Classification can also be rigorous and complete, as shown in the following three-paragraph passage that describes three different systems for financing public education in the United States. Notice how the writers introduce the classification by mentioning three types of systems and then devoting a paragraph to each.

States use three types of school finance systems, the oldest and most prevalent being the foundation plan. States employing foundation plans establish a dollar level of per pupil expenditure that is guaranteed to all districts taxing a rate greater than or equal to some state-specified minimum rate. Districts wishing to spend above the minimal level may do so, although this places poor districts at a disadvantage. Some foundation plans have been criticized for setting the minimum funding level too low.

A second system of school finance is a district power-equalizing plan. Under such plans, states finance matching grants to ensure that poor districts may spend as much for education as if they had tax bases equivalent to those of wealthier districts. State-matching rates are tied directly to the fiscal capacity of school districts. Equivalent percentage tax rates will raise the same amount of revenue in both poor and wealthier districts, since the state supplements poor districts.

Some states, including Maine, Minnesota, Missouri, Montana, Texas, and Utah, have adopted a hybrid of the foundation and district power-equalizing plans. In these mixed systems, matching funds to locally raised revenues is applied by the state up to the foundation level of spending, but not beyond.

—Marcia Lynn Whicker and Raymond A. Moore, *Making America Competitive: Policies for a Global Future* (New York: Praeger, 1988): 71.

Some classifications are introduced by a direct statement that lists the different categories before each is discussed, as in the case of this discussion of types of bicycle storage bags:

Bags carried directly on the bike are of three kinds: saddle bags, handlebar bags and frame bags. The saddle bag . . . is so universally used in Britain that one wonders why it has not found its way to the U.S. in a comparable quality and variety. It is attached to the back of the saddle. That is no problem on a leather model with carrying eyelets, while other saddle types may require the installation of a special clamp. . . . It is also possible to install a handlebar bag, which is more widely available in the U.S., behind the seat post by means of a clamping bracket sold under the name Seat Post Thing.

Saddle bags exist in various sizes, ranging all the way from 10 liters, which is barely enough for the absolute essentials, to 30 liters (that's more than a cubic foot). The latter is big enough for a weekend trip if you don't go camping. A large saddle bag, especially if it is used on a bike with a relatively low saddle, should be supported by means of some kind of rack or bracket to keep it off the rear wheel and the rear brake. It should have side pockets for small items and straps on the top to carry your rain gear. Before buying such a bag, look at it very critically and ascertain that it is properly supported and will neither interfere with your movements nor drag on the rear wheel or the brake.

Handlebar bags are unreasonably popular in the U.S. and France, though I would put them at the bottom of my list of suitable bags. All right for carrying small items to which you want frequent access along the way, especially if it is of such a design that it can be easily removed from the bike. The only satisfactory models are those that are supported at the top by a bracket that fits on the handlebars, while the bottom of the bag is held down with elastic cords, preferably to the front fork-ends. A few external pockets and a transparent map compartment are helpful. Preferably it should open towards the rider. When buying this kind of bag, make sure it does not interfere with steering, braking or lighting. A special version of the handlebar bag is available to carry a camera and photographic accessories.

The frame bag . . . is a rare bird indeed. World travellers, who have to carry as much as possible, may find a use for a bag like that, in addition to every other bag that can be mounted on the bike. Trapezoidally shaped and tied between the frame tubes, it must be packed compactly to avoid its swelling to a thickness that interferes with the movement of your legs.

> —Rob Van der Plas, *The Bicycle Touring Manual,* rev. (San Francisco: Bicycle Books, 1988): 74-75.

The first sentence of the first paragraph sets up the classification by identifying the three types of bags. The rest of the first paragraph and the second paragraph deal with saddle bags. The third paragraph focuses on handlebar bags, the fourth on frame bags. The classification is ordered from the most familiar and common kind of bag, the saddle bag, to the least familiar frame bags. As you can see, once writers lay out a classification, they can use it as a framework for a clear and well-organized presentation.

Keep in mind these three important principles when you use classification to organize a presentation:

▶ **Use only one basis of classification at a time.** For example, the classification of saddle bags, handlebar bags, and frame bags is logical and consistent and lends itself readily as a structural principle for comparison. But the classification of saddle bags, handlebar bags, frame bags, synthetic-coated bags, and zipper bags is unworkable because the last two types are not parallel with the first three but may be subtypes of them.

▶ **Base the classification on a single feature which produces groups that are significant and explains similarities or differences worth thinking about.** For instance, classifying automobiles by their value is important to prospective buyers and to tax assessors (the value of the automobile determines the license fee). Classifying automobiles by color would not be important to tax assessors, but it might be to car buyers and to the persons who have to purchase the paint for the automobile manufacturer.

▶ **Make sure the classification is complete.** That is, the number of types, kinds, or classes should equal the whole topic. The classification of bicycle bags that attach directly to the bicycle is complete. If any of these types of bags is omitted, the classification is incomplete.

COHERENCE

▼

In a coherent text the ideas are linked together so they follow logically one after another. Unless there is some reason for surprising the reader, every sentence should logically follow the preceding one and lead normally into the next one.

Coherence in a Text

There are several ways to create coherence in a text:

- ❖ Give prominence to the main topic or subject of the text,
- ❖ Organize the text into a pattern that is easy to follow,
- ❖ Use transitions that show the relationship of one part of the text to another, and
- ❖ Relate new information to information you have presented earlier or the reader already knows.

▶ Perhaps the most basic strategy for establishing coherence in a text is to give prominence to its topic or subject. The frequency with which a topic appears cues readers to its importance, which in turn suggests that all information in the passage is related to that topic. In the following passage by Susan Orlean, the Bucklin Opera House in Elkhart, Indiana, is the main topic. Since it is the most prominent item in the passage, it persists as the subject of most sentences. It or its synonyms are the subject of five of the seven sentences: sentence 1, *Bucklin*; sentence 2, *The Bucklin Opera House*; sentence 3, *the opera house*; sentence 4, *the Bucklin*; and sentence 6, *it*. The repetition of this concept and its prominent subject position create a chain of subjects that keeps the focus on the old opera house, makes it easy to know what the passage is about, and helps predict how the information in subsequent sentences is likely to connect to the information already given in preceding sentences.

> Bucklin is the biggest lot downtown. The Bucklin Opera House, an imposing rococo stone structure built in 1884, used to stand on the site. In its day, the opera house was probably the swankiest recreational facility in town. After burlesque and vaudeville went out of fashion, the Bucklin showed movies, and then the movies moved to the mall. No other use of the building cropped up. Eventually, it fell into complete disrepair

and everyone gave up on it, so it was torn down. Some people in Elkhart consider the incident a shame, but as you might expect in a town of avid drivers, many others consider the parking lot a fine thing to have acquired in the deal.

> —"Cruising: Elkhart, Indiana," in *Saturday Night* (New York: Knopf, 1990): 8.

▶ Organizing text into a recognizable pattern is another basic strategy for establishing coherence. The particular pattern used is relatively unimportant, but it is vital to use some sequence that will hold together the ideas and sentences of the passage and be recognized by your readers. One of the most useful patterns is to arrange information from general to specific. As illustrated in the following passage, using specific examples is one of the most convincing means of supporting a generalization or abstract statement. This pattern directly provides evidence to back up the writer's assertion in the opening sentence, which is the **topic sentence** of the paragraph.

TOPIC SENTENCE, PAGE 609

Perhaps the most dramatic type of instinctive learning is imprinting. Young birds such as chickens, goslings, and ducklings show an inherited pattern of following, and normally follow their mother. In his famous study on geese, Konrad Lorenz got broods of newly hatched goslings to treat him as a mother figure and to follow him. Indeed, young goslings can imprint on almost anything that moves, including objects such as balloons. After a period of imprinting of only fifteen to thirty minutes, the young birds recognize and approach the moving object when they are exposed to it as long as several hours later.

> —Rupert Sheldrake, "Animal Memory," in *The Presence of the Past: Morphic Resonance and the Habits of Nature* (New York: Vintage, 1988): 172.

Another useful pattern is chronology, which was used by Susan Orlean in her brief history of the Bucklin Opera House in Elkhart, Indiana.

When there is no topic sentence or obvious organizational pattern, there is often a need to combine the pattern with a hierarchical order, giving an overall view of the whole before providing additional details, as Orlean does in the following description of the chapel of the Bowery Mission in lower Manhattan:

We got up and moved together into the chapel, and took seats in the back with the rest of the program men. The Bowery

Mission chapel is a long, narrow room faced with rough, beige stone. It has many rows of wooden pews, a high, arching ceiling, a simple altar, a piano, and an organ. It seems to be unconnected, in both architecture and ambience, to the harshly lit dining rooms and the rest of the building. The pews on the right side of the chapel were filled with men who had been waiting out on the sidewalk. One or two of them had fallen asleep, apparently just seconds after sitting down. Two women were seated in the front pew; one of them was pregnant and was missing one of her front teeth. The pews on the left side of the chapel were being saved for the Mennonites, who walked in after a moment and filed silently into their seats.

—"Praying: Lower East Side, New York, New York," in *Saturday Night* (New York: Knopf, 1990): 168.

One strategy that helps this passage cohere is the hierarchical network which presents the description in such a way that it helps build an image in the reader's mind. The details are not presented in a helter-skelter manner, but are arranged so the movement is from large features to more particular ones. And Orlean is in control of the hierarchy. After establishing her physical point of view, she first provides an overview of the chapel (the shape of the room, the design of the walls and ceiling, the style of the altar) before focusing on the pews and the persons sitting in them. Finally, she adds details about some of the individuals (men already sleeping and a pregnant woman with a front tooth missing). The hierarchy enables readers to follow Orlean's description easily—understanding clearly and quickly what the chapel looks like, how the pews are arranged, and which persons are the most interesting to her. Hierarchical networks that link details, such as Orlean employs in her description of the chapel, are among the most valuable cohesive strategies.

TRANSITIONS, PAGE 612

▶ Seldom is arrangement of information enough to achieve coherence; other devices are also necessary. **Transitions** are important to coherence because they signal explicitly the relationships among ideas and details. Readers are able to follow the history of the Bucklin Opera House easily because of the transitional phrases "in its day," "after burlesque and vaudeville went out of fashion," "and then the movies moved," and "Eventually." The passage, organized chronologically, proceeds in an even clearer and more obvious direction because these phrases tie the sentences together and highlight the sequence.

All details are important, but, as we have already seen in the description of the Bowery Mission chapel, usually the more general features or large concepts are explained first, then the more specific and smaller ones. The following passage begins with the main idea, then moves to a specific example, then to a detailed analysis of the example. The paragraph is structured to create the movement. The writer reveals this structure and movement by using transitions every time he moves from one idea to another. The transitions are in bold type.

> In **other** films, such as *The Left-Handed Gun, Bonnie and Clyde*, and *Little Big Man*, [Arthur] Penn created a version of the western or the gangster film in which traditional meanings were inverted, **but** the effect was tragic rather than humorous. In *Little Big Man*, **for example**, the conventional western opposition between Indian and pioneers serves as the basis for the plot, which embodies two of the most powerful western myths, the Indian captivity and the massacre. **However**, the conventional renderings of these myths pit the humanely civilizing thrust of the pioneers against the savage ferocity and eroticism of the Indians and thereby justify the conquest of the West. Penn reverses these implications. In his film it is the Indians who are humane and civilized, while the pioneers are violent, corrupt, sexually repressed, and madly ambitious. **By the end, when** Custer's cavalry rides forward to attack the Indian villages, our sympathies are all with the Indians. **From this perspective**, the conquest of the West is mythologized from the triumph of civilization into a historical tragedy of the destruction of a rich and vital human culture.
>
> —John G. Cawelti, "*Chinatown* and Generic Transformation in Recent American Films," in *Film Theory and Criticism*, 3rd ed., ed. Gerald Mast and Marshall Cohen (New York: Oxford UP, 1985): 515.

As the passage demonstrates, transitions help the reader understand how the ideas within the paragraph are related.

▶ Another means of tying sentences and ideas together is to apply what discourse analysts call the "given-new contract." This principle presents new information by connecting it with information the reader already knows, either from familiarity with the topic (due to experience or education) or from information given in preceding sentences or paragraphs. (We decided to go to sleep *early. By nine o'clock*, although it was not yet dark, all the lights were off and we were in bed.) In turn, readers will be able to relate any new information to what they already know. Thus there is always a familiar context or old information (the given) that makes the new information more easily accessible.

The given-new order always adds new information by tying it to information given in previous statements. The first sentence of a passage may contain all new information. Subsequent sentences will probably have a combination of given and new information. In a series of sentences, the information is arranged so most sentences begin with information that is tied to previous statements and move toward newer, less familiar information at the end.

To see the given-new contract in action, look again at the Susan Orlean passages about the Bucklin Opera House and the Bowery Mission chapel. In discussing the Bucklin parking lot, Orlean establishes in the first sentence that the topic is the Bucklin parking lot. The topic of the second sentence, "The Bucklin Opera House," is given information, tied to previous information—the subject of the first sentence—"Bucklin." The new information in the second sentence is that the opera house "used to stand on the site." In the third sentence the given information is "the opera house," a substitution for the subjects of the first two sentences; the new information is that the opera house was a swanky recreational facility, which in turn sets up the burlesque, vaudeville, and movies as the given information in the fourth sentence. In the fourth sentence the new information is that the movies have moved to the mall. In the fifth sentence the given information is the subject, "it," which refers to the vacant building; the new information is that the building remained vacant after the movies were no longer shown there. In the sixth sentence the new information is that the building was demolished. And so the sentences go in the passage—one growing out of the other—with the new information being accompanied by at least some of the old information already given in previous statements. Once mentioned, the new information becomes given information, and additional information can be linked to it. Every sentence in the passage begins where the preceding one leaves off.

Orlean's description of the Bowery Mission chapel is arranged in a similar given-new chain of sentences. Each sentence begins with a subject that repeats information from the previous sentences or has been anticipated by information in the previous sentences. Any new information is gradually added in the remainder of the sentence.

To summarize, here are the ways to achieve coherence within passages:

❖ State the topic explicitly—often in a topic sentence,

❖ Organize text according to appropriate patterns,

❖ Use transitions to signal the relationships among ideas and sentences, and

❖ Introduce new information in the context of familiar information.

These are also important methods of establishing coherence in even longer passages of text.

Coherence Within Longer Passages

Just as the elements within a short span of text must be joined together effectively, so in a longer passage the major sections must be organized so one section leads smoothly into another. Here we consider three strategies for achieving coherence within longer passages:

❖ Arrange the sections in a logical sequence,

❖ Use **forecasting statements** to present an overview of the main topics or ideas in a passage, and

FORECASTING STATEMENTS, PAGE 503

❖ Use grammatical parallelism to emphasize the parallelism of thought in a passage.

▶ Arranging the sections in a logical sequence is one of the most natural ways to achieve coherence. As we have seen with shorter texts, passages that are organized in some recognizable pattern—whether by topic, chronology, or space—are easier to understand and to remember. Regardless of pattern, the first topic should lead to the second topic, the second to the third, and so forth. Writers often use explicit topic sentences and transitions to connect the sections and indicate different directions the topic takes. In the following passage, Maria L. Muniz, a naturalized American citizen, describes her increasing sense of personal and cultural loss as she grew up in the United States separated from her extended family and her native culture. Since the content is strongly related to time, Muniz puts the paragraphs in a time sequence.

> And as I listened to this man talk of the Cuban situation, I
> began to remember how as a little girl I would wake up crying
> because I had dreamed of my aunts and grandmothers and I
> missed them. I remembered my mother's trembling voice and
> the sad look on her face whenever she spoke to her mother

over the phone. I thought of the many letters and photographs that somehow were always lost in transit. And as the conversation continued, I began to remember how difficult it often was to grow up Latina in an American world.

It meant going to kindergarten knowing little English. I'd been in this country only a few months and although I understood a good deal of what was said to me, I could not express myself very well. On the first day of school I remember one little girl's saying to the teacher: "But how can we play with her? She's so stupid she can't even talk!" I felt so helpless because inside I was crying, "Don't you know I can understand everything you're saying?" But I did not have words for my thoughts and my inability to communicate terrified me.

As I grew a little older, Latina meant being automatically relegated to the slowest reading classes in school. By now my English was fluent, but the teachers would always assume I was somewhat illiterate or slow. I recall one teacher's amazement at discovering I could read and write just as well as her American pupils. Her incredulity astounded me. As a child, I began to realize that Latina would always mean proving I was as good as the others. As I grew older, it became a matter of pride to prove I was better than the others.

As an adult I have come to terms with these memories and they don't hurt as much. I don't look or sound very Cuban. I don't speak with an accent and my English is far better than my Spanish. I am beginning my career and look forward to the many possibilities ahead of me.

—"Back, But Not Home," *New York Times*
(July 13, 1979): A25.

Each paragraph begins with a topic sentence and with references to Muniz's age. Major shifts at the end of the first, third, and last paragraphs are marked by additional references to time. Although this logical sequence should be apparent to readers, Muniz emphasizes the sequence by using explicit transitions.

▶ As a writer, you can reinforce coherence by using forecasting statements. By the time you have revised a passage, you have probably decided to arrange your content in a specific sequence. By providing a forecasting statement at the beginning of the passage that identifies the topics or ideas and the order in which they are to be taken up, you focus tightly on the upcoming information and make it easier for readers to understand. The chief characteristic of passages that contain forecasting statements is that they predict what is to follow. Thus, readers and listeners are able to anticipate how the passage is organized.

Sometimes the forecasting statement is scarcely noticeable as a preview of the coming topics until readers become aware of the ideas unfolding in the order established at the beginning. But as readers recognize the thread of continuity that has been provided, they begin to sense the wholeness of the passage. Elizabeth Gray Vining, the author of several novels and biographies, creates an effective brief overview of the details that follow in this passage from her autobiography, *Being Seventy*.

> There are two basically different ways of approaching what is so mincingly called the Later Years: the stick-it-out-in-the-world policy, and the duck-into-safety policy. The first one sounds so much more gallant, the second slightly craven.
>
> If you have a family, sons and daughters or devoted nieces and nephews, to step in and take responsibility if you fall in the bathroom and break your hip, then you can afford to live dangerously. If you are, as I am, entirely alone, I think you at least examine the second alternative.
>
> I have gone so far as to sign up as a "Founder" of Kendal, the Quaker Retirement Community now being built in Chester County near Longwood Gardens. I have paid half of the entrance fee for a one-bedroom apartment. I can still withdraw in the year that remains before it will be finished.
>
> —*Being Seventy: The Measure of a Year* (New York: Viking Press, 1978): 29-30.

In these three paragraphs, Vining identifies in broad terms two ways of approaching the challenges of old age, then devotes a paragraph to each way.

Vining is fairly subtle in cuing the reader to the progression of thought. At other times, writers use more explicit forecasting statements. The following is an excerpt from Colin Fletcher's classic guide to backpacking, *The Complete Walker III*, in which he clearly informs his readers that he is going to discuss four types of backpacks.

> Once you decide to stay out overnight or longer you'll find you must carry a genuine house on your back.
>
> A few years ago that house was virtually always a pack with a large and clearly visible tubular aluminum frame as its central feature: the kind of pack now called "external-frame." But soon after the last edition of this book appeared, so did successful

"internal-frame packs." They begat "travel packs." And now "ultralight packs" have arrived. So we need some definitions.

—*The Complete Walker III* (New York: Knopf, 1989): 101-102.

As readers read the last sentence of this opening, they anticipate that in just a few seconds they will be provided more specific information about each backpack in the order given. It would be a major mistake to present the information in a sequence other than the one forecast. Fletcher knows better than to make such a mistake. Following is the rest of the passage. Notice that Fletcher reinforces the topical order by arranging the illustrations in the same sequence given in the prose sentence and uses italics to highlight the key words at the beginning of each section. These strategies clearly display the coherence of the passage.

External-frame   Internal-frame   Travel Pack   Ultralightweight

External-frame packs evolved from the old wooden-frame Yukon packboards, and although aluminum tubing replaced the much heavier wood, their structure remained essentially unchanged: a roughly rectangular frame with a bag attached to one side and a harness to the other. Down the years variations have visited the frames (including a few departures from aluminum), the bags have matured (some to the brink of senility) and harnesses have grown far more sophisticated and efficient. But the E-frame's essential architecture endures.

Internal-frame packs evolved from long, soft, frameless, back-snuggling mountaineering packs that hampered a climber's free movement and delicate balance as little as the load permitted and had no protuberances to be damaged by or to interfere with the pack's being dragged up rockfaces—but which rode imperfectly and were abominably hot on the back. Then somebody inserted a rudimentary frame inside the pack bag to hold its forward surface just clear of the wearer's back yet still follow the back's contours. Today the frames remain rudimentary. Mostly, they consist of two flattened but curving aluminum stays arranged either in X form or running parallel up and down the back. Either arrangement radically improves the pack's ride and also holds it clear of your back so that cooling air can circulate—while retaining at least some of a mountaineering pack's clean-lined, nonsnagging qualities. Suspension systems on the best current I-frame packs are even more sophisticated and efficient than on equivalent E-frames.

Travel bags evolved from I-frames in response to the growing popularity of "adventure travel." The travelers' needs range wide. People planning backpack treks in distant places want something that will do the job on the trail but can without suffering or causing damage be slung hard and often into cab or bus and will even withstand the ravages of the human and mechanical gorillas who handle airplane baggage. At the other extreme are those "adventurers" who stride out for exotic, mildly roughing-it trips all over the world: their prime concern is luggage they can load without tears on dhow or camel or spaceship and can conveniently hump on their backs around airports or even along short trails. Intermediate demands abound. So we now face a continuous spectrum of devices ranging from near-expedition I-frame packs to modified suitcases.

Ultralightweight packs germinated with the New Wave. All therefore pare ounces to the practical limit, or beyond. Most are enlarged but gossamer day packs, with simple suspension systems and some back-contouring stiffener, such as a foam pad. But an emerging variation is a standard I-frame model shorn and abraded toward ethereality. At a guess, another wide spectrum of choices is about to materialize. Lightweight fanny packs form a subgenre.

—*The Complete Walker III* 102-103.

▶ Another method of creating coherence—and giving the coherence greater visibility—is to keep equivalent statements parallel. Parallel construction means putting statements with similar or identical functions into similar or identical form. For instance, Muniz uses similar grammatical structure for most of the sentences in the passage quoted on pages 431-432 to underscore the parallel thoughts.

You can also use parallelism to build up longer passages by linking paragraphs together with obvious repetition of structure and words in the topic sentences. In the following series of paragraphs, Marie Winn, who writes frequently on the subject of children and family life, uses several facts and examples to support her contention that childhood in America has in recent years undergone some disturbing changes. Her use of parallelism in the opening sentence of each paragraph not only makes it apparent that the paragraphs are dealing with the same topic (childhood), but also makes even more emphatic her views on various aspects of the topic (the joys of childhood, the limits of childhood, the image of childhood).

Something has happened to the joys of childhood. The child of a generation ago, observes the satirical magazine *National Lampoon*, spent his typical Sunday afternoon "climbing around a construction site, jumping off a garage roof, and onto an old sofa, having a crabapple war, mowing the lawn." The agenda for today's child, however, reads: "Sleep late, watch TV, tennis lesson, go to shopping mall and buy albums and new screen for bong, play electronic WW II, watch TV, get high." The bulging pockets of the child of the past are itemized: "knife, compass, 36¢, marble, rabbit's foot." The contemporary tot's pocket, on the other hand, contains "hash pipe, Pop Rocks, condom, $20.00, 'ludes, Merits."

Something has happened to the limits of childhood. An advertisement for a new line of books called "Young Adult Books" defines a young adult as "a person facing the problems of adulthood." The books, however, which deal with subjects such as prostitution, divorce, and rape, are aimed at readers between the ages of ten and thirteen, "persons" who were formerly known as children.

Something has happened to the image of childhood. A full-page advertisement in a theatrical newspaper showing a sultry female wearing dark lipstick, excessive eye-shadow, a mink coat, and possibly nothing else bears the legend: "Would you believe that I am only ten?" We believe it. For beyond the extravagances of show business lies the evidence of a population of normal, regular children, once clearly distinguishable as little boys and little girls, who now look and act like little grown-ups.

Something has happened to blur the formerly distinct boundaries between childhood and adulthood, to weaken the protec-

tive membrane that once served to shelter children from preco-
cious experience and sorrowful knowledge of the adult world . . .

—*Children Without Childhood* (New York:
Pantheon, 1981, 1983): 1-2.

COMPARISON/CONTRAST

▼

Comparison plays a substantial part in understanding or explaining almost any topic by exploring or describing the similarities and differences
between things. Most of the time, when we compare (see how things
are alike), we also contrast (see how things are different). Thus when
we compare one insurance plan to another, one school to another, one
philosopher's views or values to another's, or one president's foreign
policies to another's, we also contrast them. At times, though, we want
to emphasize either the similarities or the differences.

Comparison brings together subjects that are usually regarded as
different to show how they are similar. In the conclusion of a famous
article that contrasts the characters of Ulysses S. Grant and Robert E. Lee
as individuals and as symbols of their respective northern and southern
heritages, Bruce Catton—an authority on the American Civil War—shows
how the two generals were also alike. The first paragraph summarizes
the major differences between Grant and Lee; the second provides the
transition to the discussion of their similarities, which are arranged from
the least important to the most important similarity (climactic order).

So Grant and Lee were in complete contrast, representing
two diametrically opposed elements in American life. Grant
was the modern man emerging; beyond him, ready to come on
the stage, was the great age of steel and machinery, of
crowded cities and a restless, burgeoning vitality. Lee might
have ridden down from the old age of chivalry, lance in hand,
silken banner fluttering over his head. Each man was the perfect champion of his cause, drawing both his strengths and his
weaknesses from the people he led.

Yet it was not all contrast, after all. Different as they were—
in background, in personality, in underlying aspiration—these
two great soldiers had much in common. Under everything
else, they were marvelous fighters. Furthermore, their fighting
qualities were really very much alike.

Each man had, to begin with, the great virtue of utter tenacity and fidelity. Grant fought his way down the Mississippi Valley in spite of acute personal discouragement and profound military handicaps. Lee hung on in the trenches at Petersburg after hope itself had died. In each man there was an indomitable quality . . . the born fighter's refusal to give up as long as he can still remain on his feet and lift his two fists.

Daring and resourcefulness they had, too; the ability to think faster and move faster than the enemy. These were the qualities which gave Lee the dazzling campaigns of Second Manassas and Chancellorsville and won Vicksburg for Grant.

Lastly, and perhaps greatest of all, there was the ability, at the end, to turn quickly from war to peace once the fighting was over. Out of the way these two men behaved at Appomattox came the possibility of a peace of reconciliation. It was a possibility not wholly realized, in the years to come, but which did, in the end, help the two sections to become one nation again . . . after a war whose bitterness might have seemed to make such a reunion wholly impossible. No part of either man's life became him more than the part he played in their brief meeting in the McLean house at Appomattox. Their behavior there put all succeeding generations of Americans in their debt. Two great Americans—Grant and Lee—very different, yet under everything very much alike. Their encounter at Appomattox was one of the great moments of American history.

—"Grant and Lee: A Study in Contrasts," in *The American Story*, ed. Earl Schenck Miers (Great Neck, NY: Channel Press, 1956): 204-205.

Contrast examines subjects that are usually regarded as similar to show how they are different in significant ways. The following passage from a journal that has become an American classic, written by Richard Henry Dana, Jr., describes the little-known aspects of early nineteenth-century navy life by contrasting a sailor's life in steerage and in the forecastle.

In the midst of this state of things, my messmate S—— and myself petitioned the captain for leave to shift our berths from the steerage where we had previously lived, into the forecastle. This, to our delight, was granted, and we turned in to *bunk* and mess with the crew forward.

We now began to feel like sailors, which we never fully did when we were in the steerage. While there, however useful and active you may be, you are but a mongrel—a sort of afterguard and "ship's cousin." You are immediately under the eye of the officers, cannot dance, sing, play, smoke, make a noise, or *growl* (i.e. complain), or take any other sailor's pleasure: and you live with the steward, who is usually a go-between; and the crew never feel as though you were *one of them.*

But if you live in the forecastle, you are "as independent as a wood-sawyer's clerk" (nautice), and are a *sailor.* You hear sailor's talk, learn their ways, their peculiarities of feeling as well as speaking and acting; and moreover pick up a great deal of curi-ous and useful information in seamanship, ship's customs, foreign countries, etc., from the long yarns and equally long disputes.

No man can be a sailor, or know what sailors are, unless he has lived in the forecastle with them—turned in and out with them, eaten of their dish and drunk of their cup. After I had been a week there, nothing would have tempted me to go back to my old berth, and never afterward, even in the worst of weather, when in a close and leaking forecastle off Cape Horn, did I for a moment wish myself in the steerage.

—*Two Years Before the Mast* (Edinburgh: Adam & C. Black, 1869): 48-49.

Consider these two suggestions when you use comparison and contrast:

▶ Subjects being compared or contrasted must belong to the same gen-eral category and share some important characteristics. Otherwise, the analysis will resemble the proverbial comparison of apples and oranges. Robert E. Lee and Ulysses S. Grant were senior generals of their respective armies, but they differed in several distinctive ways. Thus they can be contrasted. But they also shared a number of signif-icant characteristics. Thus they can be compared. Likewise, the fore-castle and steerage are both working and living spaces on ships, but the lifestyle of each is significantly different. Thus daily experiences in the forecastle and in steerage can be contrasted.

▶ A comparison/contrast should make a point beyond the mechanical listing of similarities and differences. For instance, Pierre Boulle's novel *Bridge over the River Kwai* and the Oscar-winning movie based on it differ in a number of ways. Perhaps the most notable difference is their endings. In the novel, the allied commando team fails in its mission to destroy the bridge. The movie ends with the commandos succeeding in blowing up the bridge. Merely pointing out that the end-ings are different would not be very significant. However, the contrast could be used to illustrate Hollywood's romantic image, which pretty much dictates that the allied commandos will succeed in their mission. Use comparison and contrast not as an end in itself but as a strategy for making a point or clarifying an idea. See also **analogy**.

ANALOGY, PAGE 413

CONCISENESS
▼

Concise writing uses no more words than are necessary for clarity and good style. However, unless we are sending a telegram or are asked to state why we like Brand C "in 25 words or less," we usually are not concerned about how many words we use. We should be concerned, however, for unnecessary words take up space and the reader's time and do not provide new information, as the following examples illustrate.

wordy: She picked up the receiver, *put it to her ear,* and said "hello." [Where else would she put it? To her chin? Her elbow? Generally placing the receiver to the ear precedes speaking into it. Any reasonable reader would understand that at once, so the phrase *put it to her ear* is unnecessary.]

concise: She picked up the receiver and said "hello." [13 words reduced to 8)

wordy: The Planaria were *few in number* but reproduced in *a rapid manner.* [*Few* always refers to quantity, so *in number* is unnecessary, since it merely repeats the idea expressed in *few.* The adverb *rapidly* easily replaces *in a rapid manner* with no loss of meaning.]

concise: The Planaria were *few* but reproduced *rapidly.* [12 words reduced to 7]

wordy: *There was a total of* nine students in the class when the class was canceled. [*There was* is an expletive—like *it is, there are, here is,* and so on—that adds words to a sentence without adding or clarifying meaning. Nine already conveys the sense of *a total of.* The second *the class* unnecessarily repeats the first.]

concise: Nine students *were* in the class when it was canceled. [15 words reduced to 10]

No meaning or stylistic dignity is lost by cutting these words. But even if the more concise version is better, is cutting four of five words in each sentence worth the effort? A few words removed from one sentence may not appear to be much of an improvement. But if wordiness is a characteristic of your writing, then almost every sentence will pack a few unnecessary words. Cutting those unnecessary words could result in as much as 15 to 40 percent lightening of the text. Over several pages that can be noticeable. And if you learn to delete unnecessary words, you will probably soon avoid them as you write.

Four principles will help you write concisely.

▶ **Never use two or more words when one will do.** This principle is especially relevant to verb forms, for a lot of clutter exists around verbs. Verb phrases that begin with *be* (and its forms of *is, are, was, were*), *give, have,* and *make* and end with a noun ending with *-ion, -ment, -ity,* or *-al* are usually wordy.

wordy: Supervisors and workers *are in agreement* on the proposed work schedule.

concise: Supervisors and workers *agree* on the proposed work schedule.

wordy: Your adviser *is to give approval of* your course schedule before you register for classes.

concise: Your adviser *must approve* your course schedule before you register for classes.

Likewise, change *have a need for* to *need; take into consideration* to *consider; make a change* to *change; take an action* to *act.*

Many unnecessary words—especially prepositions—follow verbs. Some phrasal verbs (verbs followed by prepositions that have idiomatic meanings), such as *hold on* and *give in,* are acceptable, but most verbs are clear without a preposition:

wordy: We plan to *meet up with* John at the mall.

concise: We plan to *meet* John at the mall.

wordy: The new accounting program automatically *figures up* the costs.

concise: The new accounting program automatically *figures* the costs.

wordy: The game *was over with* at five o'clock.

concise: The gave *was over* at five o'clock (or The game *ended* at five o'clock).

Many adjectives and adverbs are also overused.

wordy: *The lot on the corner* was landscaped *in an appropriate manner.*

concise: *The corner lot* as landscaped *appropriately.*

wordy: The approach to the problem *which they used* was *carried out in an efficient way.*

concise: *Their approach* to the problem was *efficient* (or *They approached* the problem *efficiently*).

▶ Delete qualifiers and intensifiers that mean little. Many statements contain words which unnecessarily repeat a meaning that is already clear. For example, when the words *about* or *approximately* precede what is clearly stated as an estimate or approximation, they should be omitted.

wordy: The registrar estimated enrollment *at about* 20,000 students.

concise: The registrar estimated enrollment *at* 20,000 students.

wordy: The teacher assigned *about* 200 to 300 pages each week.

concise: The teacher assigned 200 to 300 pages each week.

Many inexperienced writers mistakenly believe that strong and emphatic writing depends on the use of intensifiers like *absolutely, definitely, extremely, greatly, really,* and *very.* In the following examples, the attempts to intensify *splendid, necessary,* and *interested* are defeated by the unnecessary qualifiers. Such thoughts are expressed more forcefully without an intensifier.

wordy: The party was *absolutely splendid.*

concise: The party was *splendid.*

wordy: It is *absolutely necessary* that we attend the committee meeting.

concise: It is *necessary* that we attend the committee meeting (or We *must* attend the committee meeting).

wordy: She was so *greatly interested* in the book that she could not *possibly lay* it down.

concise: She was so *interested* in the book that she could not *lay* it down.

Here are several other expressions that contain unnecessary qualifiers (the unnecessary word is italicized): *absolutely* essential, repeat *again,* resume *again*, *most* unique, cooperate *together*, *old* adage, small *in size*, many *in number*, *somewhat* tired, *totally* exhausted, *really* big, divide *in two*, *completely* unanimous. Because the meaning of the italicized words is included in the meaning of the other word, the italicized words are not needed.

▶ **Avoid overusing expletives (*there is*, *there are*, etc.) and *which* and *that* clauses.** Usually the expletive is unnecessary and adds nothing to the statement.

> *wordy:*   *There are* many folk dancers *who* make their own costumes.
> *concise:*   *Many folk dancers* make their own costumes.

> *wordy:*   Beside the hotel *there is* a parking garage.
> *concise:*   Beside the hotel *is* a parking garage.

Many *who*, *which*, and *that* constructions can be revised to more concise structures with no loss of meaning or force.

> *wordy:*   *Windows that are double insulated* conserve energy.
> *concise:*   *Double-insulated windows* conserve energy.

> *wordy:*   He wrote five *papers which consisted of about* 1,000 words each.
> *concise:*   We wrote five *papers of about* 1,000 words each.

Deleting *which consists* and *that are* takes away nothing important.

▶ **When you are drafting a text, do not worry about conciseness.** If you try too hard to be concise in writing your first draft, you may develop writer's block. But as you read over your draft, look for unnecessary words and expressions that inevitably crop up. If you are unsure about a word or expression, read the sentence without it. If your meaning is not affected, delete the word or expression.

CREDIBILITY
▼

Readers do not merely respond to a text; they respond to a text that is written by someone. Consequently, a text's impact depends greatly on how its audience responds to the personality of the writer that the text projects. A reader who believes in the writer's credibility and trustworthiness will not only be willing to read the text, but will also be inclined to believe and accept the writer's viewpoint. Readers who do not hold these beliefs will have so little confidence in the writer that their interaction with the text will be affected.

The bias toward one's own viewpoint is natural. You have credibility in your own eyes, for you have probably worked out your ideas and opinions fully in your own mind. But credibility is a matter of opinion and subjective judgment, and the reader's perception is the key to whether you connect with your audience. You possess high credibility if your readers perceive you as someone in whom they can have confidence, as someone who is intelligent, fair-minded, honest, and sincere, and as someone who is well disposed toward them (in effect, as someone who possesses the same qualities that they attribute to themselves). Perceiving these qualities of character, intelligence, and goodwill, readers will accept you as a reliable source of information. On the other hand, you possess low credibility if readers perceive you as someone who is uninformed, prejudiced, manipulative, or self-serving. Perceiving these qualities, readers will probably not consider your text worth reading.

Several factors can make your credibility rise or fall in the minds of your reader. Some of the factors help establish initial credibility; others help create derived credibility. Initial credibility refers to the reader's image of you just before she or he begins to read your text. Derived credibility refers to the reader's image of you as he or she responds to your test. (For a more complete discussion of initial and derived credibility, see James C. McCroskey, *An Introduction to Rhetorical Communication*, 3rd ed. [Englewood Cliffs, NJ: Prentice Hall, 1978]: 67-85. McCroskey uses the Greek term *ethos* in place of the more common term *credibility*.)

Initial credibility is based on your readers' prior knowledge of or prior experience with you even before they begin to read your text. The adage that your reputation precedes you is relevant here. Your initial credibility will be high if your readers regard you as trustworthy, educated, and well informed on the subject, open-minded and honest, or holding values similar to their own. Your initial credibility will be low if your readers perceive you as unreliable or dishonest, as close-minded and prejudiced, or as having suspect motives. Other factors also influence initial credibility. Something as simple as using good quality paper, typing or handwriting neatly, and appropriate format can increase your credibility. Evidence of unconcern—such as getting your text to the reader later than the established deadline or using cheap or otherwise inappropriate paper (such as odd-sized or strange-colored paper)—can lower it.

High initial credibility will assure that your ideas will be received, at least initially, by readers who are favorably disposed toward you. But initial credibility, though important, is not the most important factor on which your effectiveness as a writer depends. Usually you will be relatively unknown to your readers; therefore, you will have to build credibility with your text. And even if you are known by your readers, once they start responding to your text, what they read or hear will influence their perceptions even further. It is at this point that derived credibility becomes important because it can either confirm or raise questions about initial credibility.

Here are four strategies to enhance your derived credibility:

▶ Know what you are writing about. Don't pretend to know more than you actually do. Confine yourself to what you know is true and up to date, and know your subject inside and out before you try to tell somebody else about it. Misinformation and outdated information reduce your credibility considerably. Readers expect you to write with authority, not guess at facts or use old information. If you are unsure about some fact or statistic—such as which American city has the largest population of Asian Americans, or how many nuclear reactors are licensed for operation in Europe, or whether the headlights of jeeps during World War II were recessed into the grill—then check or double-check your sources for accuracy. If you are arguing the need to protect waterfowl from lead poisoning and are proposing that lead shot in shotgun shells should be illegal, make sure that such a law is not already in effect. The most basic procedures of credible research are to use up-to-date data and credible sources of information.

Since it is crucial that your readers have confidence in you as a source of valid information, you should attempt to establish your knowledge on the subject. Even persons who are likely to possess high initial credibility recognize that they must make their audience aware of their competence. C. Everett Koop, the surgeon general of the United Stated during the Reagan administration, attempted to make his audience aware of his competence to deal with the effects of violence on children by citing his years of experience as a pediatrician:

> . . . I believe the pediatrician has a unique relationship with children and with parents. You gain certain insights about individuals and families that other physicians may not have the chance to see.

I base that opinion, by the way, on the reflections of my own career of 35 years in pediatric surgery. Dealing with the young children who were my patients I saw firsthand the stresses of childhood and was aware of both the strengths and weaknesses of children trying to cope. I also had to understand the families of those children. I had to gain their confidence and win them as allies in the battle to help their children.

In the process, I think I began to understand a great deal about the contemporary family.

—"Violence and Public Health," in
Representative American Speeches, 1982-1983,
ed. Owen Peterson (New York: H.W. Wilson,
1983): 210-211.

Most of us are not recognized experts in the sense that Dr. Koop is, but we do have first hand experiences sometimes referred to as the "Hell, I was *there*!" claim to credibility. Firsthand reports have credibility, but don't overplay your hand. It is highly unlikely that you have personally experienced everything there is to know about a subject.

You will be credible when readers come to believe that you really know what you are writing about, you take painstaking care to be accurate, and your knowledge is up to date.

▶ Use the information you possess to support your ideas and propositions. This doesn't mean that every single fact you dig up will go into the final version of your text. Nor does it mean that every statement you make has to have evidence to back it up. But until you have a genuine working knowledge of your subject, you will not know what evidence to use in support of propositions that need it.

Most of the time when you write you are dealing with opinions—not absolute truths—and since you are attempting to persuade an audience to accept your claims, you have an obligation to try to prove to them that you are right. There are fewer indisputable matters of fact than most of us realize. Even if what you state is true, the truth is not automatically apparent. You must give readers reasons to believe you.

There are, of course, times when you can rely almost solely on your credibility to persuade readers to believe you. When you are already held in high regard by them or when they are already in agreement with a point you wish to make, you can state that something is true without having to prove it.

Unless your readers already agree with a point you want to make or are willing to take your statement at face value, you will need to provide support. Here is how Joyce Carol Oates, a professor of humanities at Princeton University and a prolific writer, backs up her statement that professional boxing is the most lucrative sport for its top athletes:

> There is something particularly American in the fact that, while boxing is our most controversial sport, it is also the sport that pays its top athletes the most money. In spite of the controversy, boxing has never been healthier financially. The three highest paid athletes in the world in both 1983 and 1984 were boxers: a boxer with a long career like heavyweight champion Larry Holmes—48 fights in 13 years as a professional—can expect to earn somewhere beyond $50 million. (Holmes said that after retirement what he would miss most about boxing is his million-dollar checks.) Dempsey, who said that a man fights for one thing only—money—made somewhere beyond $3,500,000 in the ring in his long and varied career. Now $1.5 million is a fairly common figure for a single fight. Thomas Hearns made at least $7 million in his fight with Hagler while Hagler made at least $7.5 million. For the first of his highly publicized matches with Roberto Duran in 1980—which he lost on a decision—the popular black welterweight champion Sugar Ray Leonard received a staggering $10 million to Duran's $1.3 million. And none of these figures takes into account various subsidiary earnings (from television commercials, for instance) which in Leonard's case are probably as high as his income was from boxing.
>
> —"On Boxing," *New York Times Magazine*
> (June 16, 1985): 37-38.

Oates has done two of the most important things that a writer can do to increase credibility. She has quoted two experts (boxers themselves) on the importance of money to boxers. And she has given several examples that illustrate her claim. Rather than just stating that the sport pays its top athletes more than any other sport does, Oates gives the reader several reasons to believe the claim.

Including evidence to support your assertions is effective in two ways: (1) it avoids depending so much on your initial credibility, and (2) it can even increase your credibility, especially if the evidence is new to your audience and comes from a source that they regard as authoritative.

▶ Refer to the opinions of others as evidence in support of your own points when you are expressing a view that contradicts something your reader believes. But not just any experts will do. Your credibility will rise or fall depending on whether your readers recognize the expert as a person or an organization that holds a credible opinion on the subject. In the following passage from an article that discusses women and drug addiction, the author uses two experts: a physician whose credentials as an authority are identified and a 29-year-old drug abuser.

> For women in the work place, alcohol and drug abuse is a multifaceted problem. "Many working women feel underpaid, undervalued, overworked, and overstressed; they're trying to juggle too many roles with too little reward. Some become frustrated and turn to alcohol or tranquilizers," says Reed Moskowitz, M.D., director of the Stress-Disorders Medical Services at New York University Medical Center. "Some women may also feel they lack the aggressiveness to compete in a male-dominated work place, and mistakenly think that drugs such as cocaine will give them that aggressive edge. Other women use drugs or alcohol to be one of the boys at business functions or while entertaining clients. The insecurities that make women feel they won't be accepted on their own terms also contribute to their addiction." And in such professions as entertainment and finance, where the energy level is frenetic and the stakes are high, the use of stimulants is even more common.
>
> "Cocaine was everywhere when I started out on Wall Street," admits Carol, twenty-nine. "Here I was, black, a brand new M.B.A., and the youngest woman at my level. Everyone had high expectations for me. My family had struggled to send me to college, then I got this fellowship to a top grad school. I was carrying some heavy baggage."
>
> Then an acquaintance turned Carol on to cocaine.
>
> "This business can be a pressure cooker," says Carol. "Cocaine seemed to keep me on track, help my concentration. But after a while, I would get wired—really tense—and to come down, I needed to take a drink or a Valium. Finally, I was taking so many drugs, I couldn't handle the job."

> —Rita Baron-Faust, "The Anatomy of Addiction," *Cosmopolitan* (June 1990): 220.

Baron-Faust increases her credibility by presenting more than her own opinion. She quotes an expert on drug treatment and uses the testimony of a former addict to give a specific, real example of the drug problem instead of merely describing a hypothetical situation.

A writer who is arguing in favor of legalizing drugs can strengthen his or her case by quoting such persons as conservative columnist William F. Buckley, Jr., well-known economist Milton Friedman, and former Secretary of State George Schultz, who have all argued at one time or another that the U.S. government's war on drugs is futile and misguided. The opinions of these persons are especially effective, because most readers would expect that these political and social conservatives would normally be hostile to the writer's or speaker's argument. On the other hand, someone who contends that the Holocaust never happened would damage his or her position by quoting information distributed by The Institute for Historical Review—an organization that has many neo-Nazi members—or by quoting the late George Lincoln Rockwell, the former leader of the American Nazi party, while ignoring information from the archives of the Nuremburg war crimes trials. Someone who is trying to ban the teaching of the scientific theory of evolution in public schools must use sources other than the old, largely discredited creationist's propaganda tracts. It is one thing to have admirable goals. It is quite another to use dubious arguments for attaining them. Since most readers would challenge the credibility of these sources on the grounds that they are biased, you should inform yourselves of the background and political leanings of sources you come across in your research.

▶ Regard your readers as people who are as intelligent, sophisticated, and well meaning as you are. Maintaining this attitude can be difficult when you are in the heat of an argument. But you can be confident in your position without being didactic, condescending, or close-minded. In fact, there is little chance that you can change the mind of people who disagree with you by showering ridicule and scorn on their position. Instead of looking at your readers as opponents, look at them as co-seekers of the truth.

When we argue a position we acknowledge that other positions exist, although we have a natural tendency to regard our own arguments highly and to undervalue those of our opponents. However, readers are more likely to believe you if you go beyond merely presenting your own viewpoint and the opinions of others who support your viewpoint. To be credible, you should also acknowledge opposing positions and, if possible, refute them.

Refutation involves anticipating or identifying the opinions of opponents and attempting to undermine the arguments that support them, either by rejecting the premises on which they are based or by objecting to the conclusions reached, or both. Refutation can involve some heavy hitting. Be careful not to dismiss an opposing idea by citing only a single poor illustration of it, misquoting or distorting an opponent's statement, or refuting an idea that your opponents never claimed.

A common method of refutation is to present arguments in support of your own beliefs first, then refute opposing views. Louis Nizer, one of America's best-known lawyers, in contending that legalizing drugs would reduce most of the problems associated with illegal drug use, makes his proposal, then acknowledges objections to it and directly refutes them point by point.

> There are several objections that might be raised against such a salutary solution.
>
> First, it could be argued that by providing free drugs to the addict we would consign him to permanent addiction. The answer is that medical and psychiatric help at the source would be more effective in controlling the addict's descent than the extremely limited remedies available to the victim today. I am not arguing that this new strategy will cure everything. But I do not see many addicts being freed from their bonds under the present system. . . .
>
> Another possible objection is that addicts will cheat the system by obtaining more than the allowable free shot. Without discounting the resourcefulness of the bedeviled addict, it should be possible to have Government cards issued that would be punched so as to limit the free supply in accord with medical authorities.
>
> —"How About Low-Cost
> Drugs for Adults?" *New York Times*
> 8 June 1986, sec. 4:23.

Nizer's credibility comes in part from the fact that he is open-minded enough to consider with respect other viewpoints and attempts to answer them. Don't be so steadfastly loyal to your own ideas that you fail to acknowledge and analyze the viewpoints of others.

However, while well-rounded arguments usually include some form of refutation, there are instances when refutation alone might be sufficient. For example, when opposing arguments are strong and well known, it might be a good strategy to meet the opposing arguments head on, focusing the argument on refuting the opposing viewpoints. In an article that appeared in *The New Republic*, Edward I. Koch, the former mayor of New York City and a strong advocate of the death penalty, presented his opinions by refuting point by point the major positions held by those with whom he disagrees: that the death penalty is barbaric punishment, that no other major democracy uses the death penalty, that an innocent person might be executed by mistake, that capital punishment is applied in a discriminatory manner, that the death penalty violates the biblical commandment "Thou shalt not kill," and that the death penalty is state-sanctioned murder ("Death and Justice," *The New Republic*, April 15, 1985: 12–15). In defending the death penalty, Koch attempts to show that these six beliefs are false, either because the evidence that supports them is incorrect or because the reasoning that leads to them is unsound. If Koch can convince his audience that those who oppose the death penalty have failed to make their case, he may convince his readers.

Above all else, your credibility depends on your not putting down those who disagree with you. Ranting and raving and showing disrespect for your audience, even when you may feel a sense of moral outrage, creates a negative image of yourself. Perhaps there is no more exemplary instance of a writer maintaining respect for those who hold opposing views than the opening of Martin Luther King's *Letter from Birmingham Jail.*

Disappointed at the lack of support from white and socially conservative clergy for his acts of civil disobedience and by charges that he was an extremist, King could have perhaps understandably erupted with a verbal equivalent of a volcano. But he knew he had to counter his image as an outside agitator, rabble-rouser, and perhaps even a criminal and establish himself as someone who has listened carefully to his critics and understands their position even though he doesn't agree with it.

> My Dear Fellow Clergymen:
> While confined here in the Birmingham city jail, I came across your recent statement calling my present activities "unwise and untimely." Seldom do I pause to answer criticism of my work and ideas. If I sought to answer all the criticisms that cross my desk, my secretaries would have little time for anything other than such correspondence in the course of the day, and I would have no time for constructive work. But since I feel that you are men of genuine good will and that your criticisms are sincerely set forth, I want to try to answer your statement in what I hope will be patient and reasonable terms.
>
> —*Why We Can't Wait* (New York: Harper & Row, 1963, 1964): 77.

King goes on to respond to his critics' questions and charges about his "unwise and untimely" activities in such a respectful manner that he was almost assured his readers (both the eight Alabama clergymen and the larger public audience he also had in mind) would consider the validity of his viewpoint and the justification of his actions. History indicates that he succeeded.

DEFINITION
▼

Meaning is created and agreement is negotiated through words. Thus writers must make sure that readers understand the concepts they are presenting and the words they are using to articulate those concepts. We should define a word we use when we believe that readers are not familiar with it or understand it differently.

Sometimes a concept or the word the writer uses to refer to the concept is basic to the understanding of a text. For instance, in his essay that explains the art of dubbing, Anthony Burgess provides these essential definitions early on:

> A whole collection of terms is applied to the artifice whereby synchronic sound and action are achieved by diachronic means, and the common term is *dubbing.*
>
> Strictly, *dubbing* implies not just the addition of sound to film shot silently. It presupposes an original sound track to be modified either partially or totally. In fact *dub* can be given three definitions: (a) to make a new recording out of an original tape or record or track in order to accommodate changes, cuts or additions; (b) to insert a totally new sound track, often a synchronized translation of the original dialogue; (c) to insert sound into a film or tape.

> —"Dubbing," in *The State of the Language,* ed.
> Leonard Michaels and Christopher Ricks
> (Berkeley: U of California P, 1980): 297.

These definitions enable readers to grasp the whole concept of dubbing as Burgess will discuss it.

We cannot discuss controversial issues constructively unless we and our readers agree on definition. In the following passage, Margaret Atwood, a Canadian essayist, poet, and novelist, explains clearly what she means by pornography. She knows that if her readers have a different concept of pornography, they will probably not agree with her that it is a serious cultural and social problem.

When I was in Finland a few years ago for an international writers' conference, I had occasion to say a few paragraphs in public on the subject of pornography. The context was a discussion of political repression, and I was suggesting the possibility of a link between the two. The immediate result was that a male journalist took several large bites out of me. Prudery and pornography are two halves of the same coin, said he, and I was clearly a prude. What could you expect from an Anglo-Canadian? Afterward, a couple of pleasant Scandinavian men asked me what I had been so worked up about. All "pornography" means, they said, is graphic depictions of whores, and what was the harm in that?

Not until then did it strike me that the male journalist and I had two entirely different things in mind. By "pornography," he meant naked bodies and sex. I, on the other hand, had recently been doing the research for my novel *Bodily Harm*, and was still in a state of shock from some of the material I had seen, including the Ontario Board of Film Censors' "outtakes." By "pornography," I meant women getting their nipples snipped off with garden shears, having meat hooks stuck into their vaginas, being disemboweled; little girls being raped; men (yes, there are some men) being smashed to a pulp and forcibly sodomized. The cutting edge of pornography, as far as I could see, was no longer simple old copulation, hanging from the chandelier or otherwise: it was death, messy, explicit and highly sadistic. I explained this to the nice Scandinavian men. "Oh, but that's just the United States," they said. "Everyone knows they're sick." In their country, they said, violent "pornography" of that kind was not permitted on television or in movies; indeed, excessive violence of any kind was not permitted. They had drawn a clear line between erotica, which earlier studies had shown did not incite men to more aggressive behavior toward women, and violence, which later studies indicated did.

—"Pornography Debate: Margaret Atwood on Pornography," *Chatelaine Magazine* (September 1983): 61, 118.

Since Atwood is aware that the word *pornography* means different things to different people, she knows it is crucial to define the term so there will be no misunderstanding. Readers for whom pornography means the explicit portrayal of nudity and sex will not understand Atwood's viewpoint. Her examples show the dangerous side of violent pornography that is far different from the "harmless" entertainment of nudity and sex.

What a word means is partly dependent on how a reader understands it, and you or the reader may have a meaning for a word that the other is not aware of. You cannot be expected to know all the meanings and private associations readers may attach to the words you use, but understanding that words and concepts have multiple meanings will make it easier for you to determine whether you should define your words and the concepts they stand for.

Here are three suggestions about definition to help you as you write:

▶ **Determine whether it is the word, the concept, or both that must be defined.** You can avoid too much defining by using simple and familiar words. Often readers are familiar with a concept but do not understand the word or words used to refer to the concept. For many, the term *recidivism* is unfamiliar even though they are familiar with the concept—the tendency of many ex-convicts to return to their former criminal behavior. If it is important to introduce an unfamiliar word to readers, define it the first time you use it.

EXEMPLIFICATION, PAGE 488

▶ **Rely on short, concise definitions when possible.** Several methods are available—formal definition, synonyms, **exemplification**, and etymology.

One of the most common methods of definition is to provide a formal, logical, three-part definition: the word to be defined, the class to which the word belongs, and the characteristics that differentiate the word from other members of the class. Dictionary definitions are commonly given this way, as this definition of *barometer* from *The American Heritage Dictionary* illustrates:

> word   class   differentiating characteristics
>
> A **barometer** is an **instrument** for **measuring atmospheric pressure, used in weather forecasting and in determining elevation.**

Another way is to provide a synonym, such as in this sentence in which both *anemia* and *hemoglobin* are defined parenthetically:

> Another common cause of nonspecific fatigue is anemia (a term applied to any condition in which the concentration of hemoglobin—the red oxygen-carrying pigment—in the blood is below normal).

A third common way to define a word is to provide examples (exemplification) to show what you mean by the word. Just make sure that readers are likely to be familiar with the examples and that the examples are typical of the concept being defined:

> Felines are animals belonging to the family Felidae, which includes lions, tigers, jaguars, pumas, and other wild and domestic cats.

A fourth common method of definition is to explain the etymology or derivation of a word. For instance, if you were discussing the relationship between heat and mechanical action, you would probably use the word *thermodynamics*, which is a combination of the Greek words "heat" and "power." Providing the etymology helps readers understand the word better. Most standard desk dictionaries include the etymology of a word as part of its definition. There are also several etymological dictionaries available, including *The Oxford English Dictionary*, if you want to trace the history of a word's meaning.

▶ If the concept is intricate, relatively abstract, or controversial, provide a more extended definition. For example, you can use not only such strategies as formal definition, synonyms, **exemplification**, and etymology, but also **analogy**, **cause and effect**, **classification**, **comparison/contrast**, **description**, and **narration.** Norman Cousins, who has written about the value of patients maintaining a positive attitude when faced with serious illness, defines *placebo* in the following passage. Cousins's definition makes it clear that a placebo is more than just a useless substance given to humor a patient. In many patients, a placebo triggers the body's own healing powers. The first paragraph provides the etymological definition of *placebo*; the second and third paragraphs contrast the negative and positive aspects of placebos; the fourth speculates on the process by which placebos affect the human body.

EXEMPLIFICATION, PAGE 488

ANALOGY, PAGE 413

CAUSE AND EFFECT, PAGE 418

CLASSIFICATION, PAGE 422

COMPARISON/CONTRAST, PAGE 437

DESCRIPTION, PAGE 456

NARRATION, PAGE 558

> The word placebo comes from the Latin verb meaning "I shall please." A placebo in the classical sense, then, is an imitation medicine—generally an innocuous milk-sugar tablet dressed up like an authentic pill—given more for the purpose of placating a patient than for meeting a clearly diagnosed organic need. The placebo's most frequent use in recent years, however, has been in the testing of new drugs. Effects achieved by the preparation being tested are measured against those that follow the administration of a "dummy drug" or placebo.
> For a long time, placebos were in general disrepute with a large part of the medical profession. The term, for many doc-

tors, had connotations of quack remedies or "pseudomedica-
ments." There was also a feeling that placebos were largely a
shortcut for some practitioners who were unable to take the
time and trouble to get at the real source of a patient's malaise.

Today, however, the once lowly placebo is receiving serious
attention from medical scholars. Medical investigators such as
Dr. Arthur K. Shapiro, the late Dr. Henry K. Beecher, Dr.
Stewart Wolf, and Dr. Louis Lasagna have found substantial evidence that the placebo not only can be made to look like a
powerful medication but can actually act like a medication.
They regard it not just as a physician's psychological prop in
the treatment of certain patients but as an authentic therapeutic
agent for altering body chemistry and for helping to mobilize
the body's defenses in combating disorder or disease.

While the way the placebo works inside the body is still not
completely understood, some placebo researchers theorize that
it activates the cerebral cortex, which in turn switches on the
endocrine system in general and the adrenal glands in particular. Whatever the precise pathways through the mind and
body, enough evidence already exists to indicate that placebos
can be as potent as—and sometimes more potent than—the
active drugs they replace.

—"The Mysterious Placebo," in *Anatomy of an
Illness* (Toronto: Bantam, 1981): 50–51.

DESCRIPTION

▼

Whenever writers need to provide more than the most general or
abstract statement, they usually add sensory details that enable readers
to experience or imagine what they have experienced or imagined. For
example, a *Time* magazine correspondent uses specific visual images
to portray the grimness of an abandoned apartment building where a
homeless Muscovite has found shelter:

> Yuri Pronin sleeps on a rough plank door liberated from a
> neighboring apartment and balances atop heavy rusting water
> pipes in the tiny Moscow abode that he has called home since
> last December. The room has no electricity and no running

water. A dented tin bread box and several empty jars serve as his kitchen, while a cardboard box doubles as chair and closet. The decor is Dickensian: bare paint-chipped walls, splintering floorboards, and windows caked with dirt. Apartments in the old Soviet Union were none too luxurious, but this is a big step down.

—Ann M. Simmons, "Brother, Can You Spare a Ruble?" *Time* (July 13, 1992): 58.

The visual details of the first four sentences let readers see at once the grimness of Pronin's shelter. The statement "The decor is Dickensian" and the last sentence are comments on the overall impression of the scene.

Descriptive writing requires keen observation and the ability to select the details that reveal not only how something, someplace, or somebody looks but also how things sound, smell, taste, and feel. While sight is often the essence of good description, John Steinbeck, one of America's Nobel Prize winners, relies primarily on details of sound to recreate the atmosphere of a night in the Gulf of California:

Nights at anchor in the Gulf are quiet and strange. The water is smooth, almost solid, and the dew is so heavy that the decks are soaked. The little waves rasp on the shell beaches with a hissing sound, and all about in the darkness the fishes jump and splash. Sometimes a great ray leaps clear and falls back on the water with a sharp report. And again, a school of tiny fishes whisper along the surface, each one, as it breaks clear, making the tiniest whisking sound. And there is no feeling, no smell, no vibration of people in the Gulf. Whatever it is that makes one aware that men are about is not here. Thus, in spite of the noises of waves and fishes, one has a feeling of deadness and of quietness. At anchor, with the motor stopped, it is not easy to sleep, and every little sound starts one awake. If a dog barks on shore or a cow bellows, we are reassured. But in many places of anchorage there were utterly no sounds associated with man.

—*The Log of the Sea of Cortez* (New York: Viking, 1951): 89-90.

The passage opens with Steinbeck's feelings about the experience, followed by sentences that recreate what he perceived through the senses, primarily the sounds. The success of the description is due largely to the care with which Steinbeck uses verbs such as *rasp, splash, whisper,* refers to auditory images such as "a hissing sound," "a sharp report," and "the tiniest whisking sound," and notes the absence of the familiar sounds associated with humanity and domesticated animals. In recreating these sounds, he evokes the eeriness of the nighttime anchorage in an isolated place and enables readers to experience vicariously the sensations, impressions, and emotions that affected him.

The following description of the old part of the Moroccan city of Fez appeals equally to our senses of sight, sound, and smell to convey the essential characteristic of a part of the city that has changed very little since the fourteenth century:

> We came out on a plaza at the center of the medina, the old city. It was a crowded with people—little girls carrying wooden trays of oven-bound bread dough on their heads, veiled women doing their family wash at an exquisitely tiled public fountain, a bearded old man selling caged birds, old Berber ladies with tattooed chins squatting on curbs with their hands held out in supplication, ragged porters lashing slow-moving donkeys loaded down with ice and sheepskin and Pepsi-Cola cases.
>
> "No cars here, not even motorcycles," Abdellatif said. "The donkey is the taxi of the medina."
>
> The night air was clangorous with the rhythmic hammerings of the ironworkers at work on their kettles, coppersmiths beating a syncopated tap-da-tap-tap-da-tap on their ornate trays, the rasping voices of the street vendors, the tinselly laughter of schoolgirls in their crisp pastel smocks, and, above all, the raucous crying of the roosters, which seem to crow all night from the rooftops as if announcing some perpetual dawn of the spirit.
>
> Adding to the sensory assault were the thousand tingling aromas of spices and newly cut cedarwood, of singed oxhorn (used for combs) and sizzling hot cooking oil, of freshly baked bread and ugly-smelling animal hides—all simmering together, as it were, in the warm night air.
>
> —Harvey Arden, "Morocco's Ancient City of
> Fez," *National Geographic* 169
> (March 1986): 341.

Such details are at the heart of good descriptive writing. They convey unfamiliar scenes and experiences by means of sight, sound, and smell (and touch and taste), and readers gain a strong sense of reality that is no longer outside their range of knowledge.

Three suggestions will help you write description.

▶ Descriptions must be ordered in some way, or readers run the risk of getting lost in the details. There are several techniques of ordering. You can provide an overview of what is being described followed by a description of its parts or describe its most prominent features first and then turn your attention to smaller details. The latter is the method used by William Least Heat-Moon in *PrairyErth* to describe buildings that the Santa Fe Railroad built in the 1920s but are now abandoned in the 1990s:

> In the narrow river vales of the county, the fields lie in squares and rectangles of row crops, fence lines darkly outlining them with small trees; from above, in autumn, the pattern is of strips of plaid cloth showing through long rents in the burlap of the prairie. Beside one of these tears, which is the South Fork Valley, and up on its western terrace high enough to give a view down on the vale road and the cropped grids, sits a low stone building, gray and grim like a barracks. It has eight rooms, ten doors, five chimneys, and is built like a double-footed L on its side, ⌐￢ , and between the two longer end rooms is a roofed porch, and in front of it, a covered well. The stone blocks are, in fact, concrete cast to look like hewn rock. . . . No one has lived here in some years, but once five Hispanic families did, and now the ceilings are shucking off their plaster down to their thin lath ribs, dropping pieces onto a miscellany of piled junk; window lights are missing, doors tied shut with twists of wire, and dirt lies so caked to the floor that the cold wind stirs no grit as it haunts through and gives the place an occasional voice—a slapped gutter, a shaken door, a rattled pane.
>
> —"En las Casitas," in *PrairyErth* (Boston: Houghton Mifflin, 1991): 230.

▶ In addition to being organized, descriptive details need to be concrete and specific. Many inexperienced writers tend to use a lot of general terms and to rely heavily on adjectives and adverbs to make their descriptions more vivid. Of course modifiers are sometimes important. But the key to achieving vividness is to use nouns and verbs that appeal directly to the senses.

General and not very descriptive	More specific but relatively vague	Specific and descriptive
thick vegetation	underbrush	kudzu and wild grape vines
journeyed with difficulty	walked slowly	slogged

The more concrete and specific the nouns and verbs, the more vivid and evocative the image. Instead of writing, "Cyril journeyed with difficulty through the thick vegetation," write, "Cyril slogged through the kudzu and wild grape vines."

▶ Much descriptive writing involves orienting readers to unfamiliar or unknown things. Familiar comparisons, especially analogies, are effective ways to assist readers in connecting the known to the unknown. In the following passage, the author uses the **analogy** of the human hand to describe the topography of the rectangular Chase County, Kansas:

ANALOGY, PAGE 413

> Let this book page, appropriate as it is in shape and proportion, be Chase County. Lay your right hand across the page from right edge to left; tuck middle finger under palm and splay your other fingers wide so that your thumb points down, your little finger nearly upward. You have a configuration of the county watercourses, a manual topography of the place. Everything here has been and continues to be shaped by those four drainages: the South Fork of the Cottonwood River (thumb), the Cottonwood (index finger), Middle Creek (ring), Diamond Creek (little finger). Many more streams and brooks are here, but these four control the county. . . .
>
> —William Least Heat-Moon, *PrairyErth*
> (Boston: Houghton Mifflin, 1992): 13.

DOCUMENTATION
▼

When you draw on sources other than your own observations and experiences for data, information, opinions, ideas, and ways of thinking, you must (1) carefully credit those sources and (2) let readers know where you got the information. Those sources may be second-ary sources such as journal and magazine articles, books, chapters from books, and technical reports, or primary sources such as letters and interviews.

There are several ways to credit sources, and all of them are fairly obvious and easy to do. Just make sure you choose a standard method of documentation that identifies precisely the source you have used, and stay consistent.

Two widely used documentation systems are covered here: MLA, which is based on *The MLA Handbook for Writers of Research Papers*, 3rd ed. (Joseph Gibaldi and Walter S. Achtert. New York: The Modern Language Association, 1988); and APA, which is based on the *Publication Manual of the American Psychological Association*, 3rd ed. (Washington, DC: American Psychological Association, 1984).

MLA (Modern Language Association) Documentation

Used mostly by researchers in languages, literature, philosophy, art, and other subjects in the humanities, the MLA documentation style consists of short source references incorporated into the body of a paper or report and linked to fuller information about the sources in a Works Cited list.

The in-text citations, often partly or wholly parenthetical, briefly identify sources—usually by the authors' last names and sometimes by specific pages. Readers can find full publication information for each cited source in the Works Cited list at the end of your text.

The Works Cited list (see Figure 1, page 466) at the end of your essay or report is arranged alphabetically by the authors' last names. If a cited source has no named author, it is alphabetized by the first word of the title (other than articles, i.e., *a, an, the*). Entries in the Works Cited list provide information that allows readers to locate any source in case they want to read it themselves.

The two-part system works this way: the reader reads a passage like the following and sees the name of the author or names of the authors cited in parentheses or mentioned in the discussion:

```
    Louisiana farmers produce about 15 percent of the
    U.S. rice crop (Johnson and Linscombe), and it is
    important that the rice be kept dry in the high humid-
```

ity of the state. About a third of Louisiana's rice
growers use in-bin drying methods. However, Vermer and
Jacobsen point out that these drying methods must be
used carefully because rice is susceptible to damage
during handling and processing if it is dried in bins
at temperatures much above 38° C (80).

These in-text citations contain enough information for a reader to
find works by Johnson and Linscombe and Vermer and Jacobsen in the
Works Cited list. The authors' names and the page numbers are
enclosed in parentheses inside the normal sentence punctuation, and
there is no punctuation between the author's name and the page number. The Works Cited list provides complete information, enabling
readers to look up the works if they choose:

Johnson, L. E., and S. Linscombe. <u>Outlook of
    Louisiana's Agriculture</u>. Baton Rouge: Louisiana
    Cooperative Extension Service, Louisiana State
    University Agriculture Center, 1988.
Vermer, L. R., and L. A. Jacobsen. "On-farm Rice Drying
    Energy Use." <u>Applied Engineering in Agriculture</u> 3
    (1987): 79-86.

In-Text Parenthetical Citations

The following examples illustrate the various ways to cite sources in
your essay or report.

Place parenthetical citations at the end of the material taken from
a particular source. If you don't mention the author's name in your discussion, give the author's last name and—if appropriate—the page number(s) in parentheses.

ONE WORK BY A SINGLE AUTHOR.   Place the author's name and, if appropriate, page number or numbers in parentheses:

One reason for the decline is clear: "There are
about six minutes of commercials on the typical network
news show, which means there are only twenty-four minutes available for reportage of national and international events" (Berger 123).

When you use the source's name as part of your sentence, cite only the page number or numbers in parentheses:

> According to Arthur Asa Berger, "There are about six minute of commercials on the typical network news show, which means there are only twenty-four minutes available for reportage of national and international events" (123).

ONE WORK BY TWO OR THREE AUTHORS. Cite all names:

> Although Hemingway had married and divorced several times, he regarded himself as deeply Catholic (Herter and Herter 106-108).

> Mark Twain calls an autobiography "the truest of all books; for while it inevitably consists mainly of extinctions of the truth, with hardly an instance of plain straight truth, the remorseless truth is there, between the lines" (Anderson, Gibson, and Smith 374).

ONE WORK BY MORE THAN THREE AUTHORS. Include the name of only the first author followed by "et al." (Latin abbreviation for "and others"—there is no period after *et*, but there is after the *al.*):

> In human beings only about 1 percent of DNA seems to be involved in coding genetic inheritance (Alberts et al.).

ONE WORK BY A CORPORATE OR ORGANIZATIONAL AUTHOR. Cite the name of the corporation or organization as the author:

> Brainstorming is becoming increasingly important in solving management problems (Florida Power and Light Company).

WORK WITH NO AUTHOR. Cite the title of the article or book:

> California had the highest number of adult/adolescent and pediatric AIDS cases (7,648) reported from August 1990 through July 1991 (HIV/AIDS Surveillance 4).

AUTHORS WITH THE SAME LAST NAME.   If you cite publications by two or more authors who have the same last name (Elizabeth Wright and Thomas Wright, for instance), include the author's initials or first name in all in-text citations to distinguish the two:

> Benjamin Franklin's printing firm won the first contract to print money for the state of Pennsylvania (Thomas Wright 148).

TWO OR MORE WORKS CITED WITHIN THE SAME PARENTHESES.   Order the works alphabetically, and separate the works by semicolons:

> Several proponents of nuclear power have pointed to France's heavy reliance on nuclear energy (Donique; Freed and Waters; Millicent).

TWO OR MORE WORKS BY THE SAME AUTHOR OR AUTHORS.   To cite the work of an author or authors who have other works cited in the text, add the title of the work to the citation:

> Bridgman has emphasized that "science is what scientists do . . . there are as many scientific methods as there are individual scientists" (Reflections of a Physicist 83).

> Francis Crick has theorized about protein molecules, which he claims have several unusual properties ("Thinking About the Brain").

MULTIVOLUME WORKS.   Cite the volume number, followed by a colon, a space, and the appropriate page number or numbers. If the volume has its own title, include it after the volume number:

> "Thought without speech is inconceivable," asserted the philosopher Hannah Arendt (The Life of the Mind 1: Thinking 32).

INTERVIEWS, LETTERS, AND OTHER PERSONAL COMMUNICATIONS.   A personal interview is listed in Works Cited by the name of the interviewee and a personal letter by the letter writer's name, so in-text citations use these names. (If the interview or letter has been published, follow guidelines for the type of publication the cited source appears in.)

> One consultant said that "focus groups can achieve
> excellent results in a very short period" (Malone).

MLA List of Works Cited

The Works Cited list at the end of your text documents every source you cite. Do not include in it sources you read but do not refer to. Be extremely careful not to use ideas from a source without citing the source.

Figure 1 (page 466) illustrates the format for the Works Cited list:

Format Guidelines

❖ Start the list of works cited on a new page, continuing the pagination of the text.

❖ Center the heading *Works Cited* at the top of the page.

❖ Double-space everything.

❖ Begin each entry flush with the left margin, and indent any subsequent line(s) in the entry five spaces from the left margin.

In addition, here are some other practices to observe:

❖ Use the author's or editor's name as it appears on the title page or in the byline of the article.

❖ List multiple authors in the order of their names on the title page or in the byline of the article.

❖ Include in each entry for a book the city of publication, the publisher's name (shortened forms), and the date of publication: Englewood Cliffs, NJ: Prentice, 1993.

— If the book is published outside the United States, add the name of the country. Also identify relatively unknown cities by state (not Detroit, MI, but certainly Bear Run, MT). Abbreviate states by their two-letter, capitalized postal abbreviations. If no place of publication is given, write "N.p." for "no place."

Works Cited

Allan, Keith. Linguistic Meaning. 2 vols. New York:
    Methuen, 1986.
Ardner, Shirley, ed. Defining Females: The Nature of
    Women in Society. New York: Wiley, 1978.
Bennett-Alexander, Dawn D. "The Supreme Court Finally
    Speaks on the Issue of Sexual Harassment--What
    Did It Say?" Women's Rights Law Reporter 10
    (1987): 65-78.
Culler, Jonathan. "Reading as a Woman." On
    Deconstruction: Theory and Criticism after
    Structuralism. Ithaca: Cornell UP, 1982. 43-64.
Edelsky, Carole. "Observation of a Second-Grade
    Classroom." Women and Language News 7 (1984): 29.
---. When She's/He's Got the Floor We've/He's Got It.
    Tenth World Congress of Sociology. Mexico City,
    August 1982.
---. "Who's Got the Floor?" Language in Society 10
    (1981): 383-421.
Gates, Henry Louis, Jr. "The Blackness of Blackness: A
    Critique of the Sign and the Signifying Monkey."
    Black Literature and Literary Theory. Ed. Gates.
    New York: Methuen, 1984. 285-321.
---. "Talkin' That Talk." Critical Inquiry 13 (1986):
    203-210.
Medin, Douglas L., and Edward E. Smith. "Concepts and
    Concept Formation." Annual Review of Psychology
    35 (1984): 113-138.
Rousmaniere, John. "Little Words That Exclude." Letter.
    New York Times 26 May 1985: A14.

Figure 1. Works Cited page (MLA documentation style)

— Use shortened forms of publisher's names (e.g., Macmillan instead of Macmillan Publishing Company). Books published by university presses have *University* and *Press* abbreviated (as in U of Texas P or Indiana UP).

— If no date of publication is given, write "n.d." for "no date."

❖ Arrange the entries alphabetically by the last name of the author or editor. A work that has a corporation or organization as its author is alphabetized by the first word of the corporation or organization (excluding *a, an, the*). A work with no identifiable author is alphabetized by its title (excluding *a, an, the*).

❖ If there is more than one work by the same author, arrange them in alphabetical order by title and put the author's name in correct alphabetical order in the Works Cited list. Instead of repeating the author's name, use three hyphens followed by a period:

Moustakas, Clark. <u>Heuristic Research: Design,</u>
     <u>Methodology, and Application</u>. Newbury Park, CA:
     SAGE, 1990.
---. <u>Loneliness and Love</u>. Englewood Cliffs, NJ:
     Prentice, 1972.
---. <u>The Tower of Loneliness</u>. Englewood Cliffs, NJ:
     Prentice, 1975.

❖ For authors who have m ore than one work on the list, list single-author entries before any multiple-author entries. You may use hyphens for the single-author entries, but repeat the author's last name for the multiple-author entries.

Mandelbrot, Benoit. <u>The Fractal Geometry of Nature</u>. San
     Francisco: Freemen, 1982.
---. "An Interview." <u>Omni</u> 5 February 1984: 721.
Mandelbrot, Benoit, Dann E. Passoja, and Alvin Paullay.
     "Fractal Character of Fracture Surfaces of
     Metals." <u>Nature</u> 308 (1984): 721.

Following are sample entries for a Works Cited List:

<u>Book by one author</u>

Anderson, Charles M. <u>Richard Selzer and the Rhetoric of</u>
     <u>Surgery</u>. Carbondale: Southern Illinois UP, 1989.

If the book has no apparent author, begin with its title:

> ASAE Standards, 35th ed. St. Joseph, MI: American
>   Society of Agricultural Engineers, 1988.

Book by two or three authors

> Naisbett, John, and Patricia Aburdene. Megatrends 2000.
>   New York: Morrow, 1990.

> McCrum, Robert, William Cran, and Robert MacNeil. *The
>   Story of English*. New York: Viking, 1986.

Book by more than three authors

> DuBois, Ellen Carol, et al. Feminist Scholarship:
>   Kindling in the Groves of Academe. Urbana: U of
>   Illinois P, 1987.

Book by corporate or organization author

> American Psychological Association. "Guidelines for
>   Nonsexist Language in APA Journals." American
>   Psychologist 32 (1977): 487-494.

> Florida Power and Light Company. FPL Quality
>   Improvement Program: QI Story and Techniques.
>   Miami: Florida Power and Light Company, 1987.

> Midwest Plan Service. Structures and Environmental Hand-
>   book, 11th ed. Ames: Midwest Plan Service, 1987.

Book with editor (anthology or compilation of essays, articles, poetry, etc.)

> Gouma-Peterson, Thalia, ed. Breaking the Rules: Audrey
>   Flack, A Retrospective 1950-1990. New York:
>   Abrams, 1992.

Multivolume book

> Arendt, Hannah. Thinking. New York: Harcourt, 1978.
>   Vol. 1 of The Life of the Mind. 2 vols.

Book in other than first edition

Law, Averill M., and W. D. Kelton. <u>Simulation Modeling
      and Analysis</u>, 2nd ed. New York: McGraw-Hill, 1991.

Part of a book

Hardison, O. B., Jr. "Let's Play Architecture."
      <u>Disappearing Through the Skylight: Culture and
      Technology in the Twentieth Century</u>. New York:
      Viking, 1989. 107-120.

(This entry describes a chapter from Hardison's book.)

Holmblad, L. P., and J. Ostergaard. "Control of a
      Cement Kiln." <u>Fuzzy Information and Decision
      Processes</u>. Ed. Madan M. Gupta and Elie Sanchez.
      New York: North-Holland, 1982. 389-399.

(This entry describes an article by Holmblad and Ostergaard in a
collection of articles edited by Gupta and Sanchez.)

Miyamato, S., S. Yasurobu, and H. Ihara. "Predictive
      Fuzzy Control and Its Application to Automatic
      Train Operation Systems." <u>Analysis of Fuzzy
      Information</u>. Ed. James C. Bezdek. Vol. 2 of
      <u>Artificial Intelligence and Decision Systems</u>.
      N.p.: CRC Press, 1987. 59-72. 2 vols.

("N.p." stands for "no place." That is, no place of publication is
given in the book.)

St. Vincent Millay, Edna. "Oh, oh, you will be sorry
      for that word!" <u>Collected Sonnets</u>, rev. and
      enlarged edition. New York: Harpers, 1988. 31.

(This work cited is a poem from St. Vincent Millay's collection of
poetry.)

Suhor, Charles. Foreword. <u>A Teacher's Introduction to Deconstruction</u>. By Sharon Crowley. Urbana: National Council of Teachers of English, 1989. vii-viii.

(The cited work is to the Foreword written by Charles Suhor in a book by Sharon Crowley. Note that a foreword, preface, introduction, or afterword is capitalized but is neither enclosed in quotation marks nor underlined.)

Unpublished thesis or dissertation

Guritno, P. "Moisture Sorption of Bagged Grain Stored Under Tropical Conditions." M.S. Thesis. Kansas State University, 1988.

Berthnal, N. "Motherhood Lost and Found: The Experience of Becoming an Adoptive Mother to a Foreign Born Child." Diss. Union Institute, Cincinnati, 1990.

Article in a journal with continuous pagination

Knight, Virginia Curtin. "Zimbabwe: The Politics of Economic Reform." <u>Current History</u> 91 (1992): 219-223.

Vergano, P. J., R. F. Testin, and W. C. Newell. "Distinguishing Among Bruises in Peaches Caused by Impact, Vibrations, and Compression." <u>Journal of Food Quality</u> 14 (1991): 285-298.

(Journals that use continuous pagination number pages consecutively for [usually] a year's issues. *National Geographic* is a widely known publication that uses continuous pagination.)

Article in a journal that numbers pages separately in each issue

Guth, A. H., and P. J. Steinhardt. "The Inflationary Universe." <u>Scientific American</u> 250.5 (1984): 90-102.

(For journals that begin each issue with page 1, add a period and the issue number after the volume number: 250.5 stands for volume 250, issue 5.)

Article in a popular magazine

McGeary, Johanna. "Voice of Her People." <u>Time</u> 25 May
       1992: 48-50.

Article in a newspaper

Barringer, Felicity. "Majority in Poll Back Ban on
       Handguns." <u>New York Times</u> 4 June 1993: A14.

Article in a reference book

"Low-temperature Acoustics." <u>McGraw-Hill Encyclopedia
       of Science and Technology</u>, 7th ed. 1992.

(When citing familiar reference books that frequently appear in new editions, give only the edition and year of publication. If the reference work arranges entries alphabetically, you may omit volume and page numbers.)

"Applications Software, Evaluation." <u>Encyclopedia of
       Microcomputers</u>. Vol. I. New York: Dekker, 1988.
       222-239.

"Kovacs, Bela A." <u>American Men and Women of Science,
       1992-1993</u>, 18th edition. Vol. 4. New Providence,
       NJ: Bowker, 1992. 483.

Unpublished paper or speech

Poovey, Mary. "Speaking of the Body. A Discursive
       Division of Labor in Mid-Victorian Britain."
       Colloquium on Women, Science, and the Body;
       Discourses and Representations. Society for the
       Humanities, Cornell University, Ithaca. May 1987.

Computer software

```
Thiesmeyer, Elaine C., and John E. Thiesmeyer. Editor:
    A System for Checking Usage, Mechanics,
    Vocabulary, and Structure. Version 4.0. Modern
    Language Association, 1990.
```

Personal communication

```
Blair, Ray. Letter to the author. 15 March 1993.

Kaline, Al. Personal interview. 21 May 1993.

Malone, Susan. Telephone interview. 25 July 1993.

Powell, Mary. Letter to Frank Meiers. 2 January 1993.
    Frank Meiers Papers. Missouri State Historical
    Society, Columbia.
```

APA (American Psychological Association) Documentation

Like the Modern Language Association documentation, American Psychological Association documentation consists of short source references incorporated into the body of a text and linked to fuller information about the sources in the References list that appears at the end. APA style is used widely by researchers in the social and natural sciences.

The two-part system works this way: the reader reads a passage like the following and sees the name of the author or authors, the year of publication, and, if appropriate, the page number or numbers cited in parentheses:

```
        Louisiana farmers produce about 15 percent of the
U. S. rice crop (Johnson & Linscombe, 1988), and it is
important that the rice be kept in the high humidity
of the state. About a third of Louisiana's rice grow-
ers use in-bin drying methods. However, Vermer and
Jacobsen point out that these drying methods must be
```

```
used carefully because rice is susceptible to damage
during handling and processing if it is dried in bins
at temperatures much above 38° C (1987, p. 80).
```

These citations contain enough information for a reader to find works by Johnson and Linscombe and Vermer and Jacobsen in the References list. The authors' names may be in parentheses; the year of publication usually in parentheses. If you are quoting or are referring to a specific part of the work, you must give the page number or numbers, always in parentheses. A parenthetical citation is inside the normal sentence punctuation. There is a comma between the author's name and the year of publication. If page numbers are given, they are separated from the year of publication by a comma.

The References list provides complete publication information, enabling readers to look up the works if they choose:

```
Johnson, L. E., & Linscombe, S. (1988). Outlook of
    Louisiana's agriculture. Baton Rouge: Louisiana
    Cooperative Extension Service, Louisiana State
    University Agriculture Center.

Vermer, L. R., & Jacobsen, L. A. (1987). On-farm rice
    drying energy use. Applied Engineering in
    Agriculture, 3, 79-86.
```

In-Text Parenthetical Citations

Place parenthetical citations at the end of the material taken from a specific source. If you do not use the source's name in your sentence, give it, the year of publication, and—if appropriate—the page number(s) in parentheses.

ONE WORK BY A SINGLE AUTHOR. Place the author's name, year of publication, and—if appropriate—the page number(s) in parentheses:

```
    Some students appear to be turned off by the
expensively produced admissions packages that they
receive from very exclusive schools (Desmond, 1991).
```

When you use the author's name as part of your sentence, cite only the year of publication and—if appropriate—the page number(s) in parentheses:

> The reaction of William Desmond, a graduate of Loyola High School in Baltimore, may be typical: "My euphoria began to fade. I began to wonder about schools that send out slick admission packages that cost $3 to mail" (1991, p. 1).

ONE WORK BY TWO AUTHORS. Spell out *and* when you use the names of authors in your sentence. When the authors' names are in parentheses, use an ampersand (&) :

> Briggs and Peat (1989) explain the new theories of physics concerning synchronized chaos.
>
> During the 1970s and 1980s, many scientists, mostly physicists, developed theories of synchronized chaos (Briggs & Peat, 1989).

ONE WORK BY MORE THAN TWO AUTHORS. When citing a work by three to five authors, cite all the names the first time you refer to the work. In subsequent references use the name of only the first author followed by "et al." (Latin abbreviation for "and others"—there is no period after "et," but there is after "al.")

first reference

> Crutchfield, Farmer, Packard, and Shaw (1985), four pioneers in chaos theory, claim that finite precision in measurements is inadequate.

second reference

> Crutchfield et al. (1985) point out that it is impossible to predict physical effects because of miniscule gravitational forces.

ONE WORK BY SIX OR MORE AUTHORS. Use the name of the first author and "et al." for all citations:

> Olstead et al. (1993) offer several examples of infinite variations to illustrate synchronous chaos.

ONE WORK BY A CORPORATION OR ORGANIZATION AUTHOR. Cite the name of the corporation or organization as the author:

> Brainstorming is becoming increasingly important in solving managerial problems (Florida Power and Light Company, 1989).

WORK WITH NO AUTHOR. Cite the title of the book or article:

> California had the highest number of adult/adolescent and pediatric AIDS cases (7,648) reported from August 1990 through July 1991 (HIV/AIDS Surveillance, 1991, p. 4).

> About 90 percent of the country's annual maize yield (approximately 140,000 metric tons) is produced by small scale farmers ("Guatemala Agriculture," 1993).

AUTHORS WITH THE SAME LAST NAME. If you cite works by two or more authors who have the same last name (Elizabeth Wright and Thomas Wright, for instance), use the author's first initial in all in-text citations to distinguish the two:

> Benjamin Franklin's printing firm won the first contract to print money for the state of Pennsylvania (T. Wright, 1991, p. 148).

TWO OR MORE AUTHORS CITED WITHIN THE SAME PARENTHESES. Order the works alphabetically by authors and separate the works by semicolons:

> Several proponents of nuclear power have pointed to France's heavy reliance on nuclear energy (Donique, 1993; Freed & Watson, 1988; Millicent, 1992).

TWO OR MORE WORKS BY THE SAME AUTHOR OR AUTHORS.   The work of an author or authors who have other works cited in the text is identified by the year. If the same author has more than one publication in a year, add *a* or *b* after the year so that sources correspond to the References list.

> Francis Crick (1960, 1964) has theorized about protein molecules, which he claims have several unusual properties.

> Bridgman (1955b) has emphasized that "science is what scientists do . . . there are as many scientific methods as there are individual scientists" (p. 83).

MULTIVOLUME WORKS.   Cite the author, year, and page number(s). For multivolume works published in the same year, add *a* or *b* after the year to correspond to the References list.

> "Thought without speech is inconceivable," asserted the philosopher Hannah Arendt (1978a, p. 32).

PERSONAL COMMUNICATIONS.   Telephone conversations, interviews, and personal correspondence are not included in the References list. Provide full information in the parenthetical citation:

> "Focus groups," according to consultant Susan Malone, "can achieve excellent results in a very short period" (personal communication, July 25, 1993).

References List

The Reference list at the end of the text includes every work cited. Each work cited in your text must appear in the References list, and each entry in the References list must be cited in your text.

Figure 2 (page 477) illustrates the format for the References list.

Format Guidelines

❖ Start the References list on a new page, continuing the pagination of the text.

References

Allan, K. (1986). <u>Linguistic meaning</u> (Vol. 1). New
    York: Methuen.
Ardner, S. (Ed.). (1978). <u>Defining females: The nature
    of women in society</u>. New York: Wiley.
Bennett-Alexander, D. D. (1987). The supreme court
    finally speaks on the issue of sexual harassment—
    What did it say? <u>Women's Rights Law Reporter</u>, <u>10</u>,
    65-78.
Culler, J. (1982). Reading as a woman. In <u>On decon-
    struction: Theory and criticism after structuralism</u>
    (pp. 43-64). Ithaca, NY: Cornell University Press.
Edelsky, C. (1981). Who's got the floor? <u>Language in
    Society</u>, <u>10</u>, 383-421.
Edelsky, C. (1982, August). <u>When she's/he's got the
    floor we've/he's got it</u>. Paper presented at the
    Tenth World Congress of Sociology, Mexico City.
Edelsky, C. (1984). Observation of a second-grade
    classroom. <u>Women and Language News</u>, <u>7</u>, 29.
Gates, H. L., Jr. (1984). The blackness of blackness: A
    critique of the sign and the signifying monkey. In
    H. L. Gates, Jr. (Ed.), <u>Black literature and liter-
    ary theory</u> (pp. 285-321). New York: Methuen.
Gates, H. L., Jr. (1986). Talkin' that talk. <u>Critical
    Inquiry</u>, <u>13</u>, 203-210.
Medin, D. L., & Smith, E. E. (1984). Concepts and con-
    cept formation. <u>Annual Review of Psychology</u>, <u>35</u>,
    113-138.
Rousmaniere, J. (1985, May 26). Little words that
    exclude [Letter to the editor]. <u>The New York Times</u>,
    p. A14.

Figure 2. References list (APA documentation style)

❖ Center the heading *References* at the top of the page.

❖ Double-space everything.

❖ Begin each entry flush with the left margin, and indent any subsequent line(s) in the entry three spaces from the left margin.

In addition, here are other practices to follow:

❖ Use the author's initials with his or her last name: *A. D. Santayana*, not *Andrew D. Santayana*.

❖ List multiple authors in the order in which they appear on the title page of the book or in the byline of the article.

❖ Invert all authors' names: *Norwood, A. D., & Sabino, R. J.*

❖ For edited books, place the editors' names in the author position and enclose the abbreviation "Ed." or "Eds." in parentheses after the last editor.

❖ Capitalize only the first word and proper nouns of titles and subtitles:

<u>**books and reports:**</u>

<u>Flashback: A brief history of film</u>

<u>**articles:**</u>

Communicating with Japan's leaders

❖ Note that unlike MLA style, APA style does not enclose titles of articles within quotation marks.

❖ Capitalize the first word and other important words of titles of conference proceedings and of journals and magazines:

<u>Japanese Journal of Experimental Social Psychology</u>

<u>Psychological Bulletin</u>

❖ For books, include the city of publication, the publisher's name, and the date of publication:

Englewood Cliffs, NJ: Prentice Hall, 1994

—If the book is published outside the United States, add the name of the country. Also identify relatively unknown cities by state (not New York, NY, but certainly Bear Run, MT). Abbreviate states by their two-letter, capitalized postal abbreviations.

—Use shortened forms of publishers' names, omitting Co., Inc., and the like, but spell out names of associations, *University*, and *Press*: Macmillan instead of Macmillan Publishing Company; University of Texas Press instead of U of Texas P.

❖ Arrange the entries alphabetically by the last name of the author or editor. A work that has a corporation or organization as its author is alphabetized by the first word of the corporation or organization (excluding *a, an, the*).

❖ If there is more than one work by the same author, arrange them as follows:

—single-author entries precede multiple-author entries:

> Mandelbrot, B. (1982). <u>The fractal geometry of nature</u>. San Francisco: Freeman.
>
> Mandelbrot, B. (1984, February 5). An interview. <u>Omni</u>, p. 721.
>
> Mandelbrot, B., Passoja, D., & Paullay, A. (1984). Fractal character of fracture surfaces of metals. <u>Nature</u>, *308*, 721.

—References with the same first author and different second or third authors are arranged alphabetically by the last name of the second author, and so on.

—References by the same author are arranged by year of publication:

> Kael, P. (1965). <u>I lost it at the movies</u>. Boston: Little, Brown.
>
> Kael, P. (1984). <u>Taking it all in</u>. New York: Holt, Rinehart and Winston.

—References by the same author with the same publication date are arranged alphabetically by title, and letters are added to the year to differentiate works for in-text citations:

Smith, J. (1974a). <u>Models in ecology</u>. Cambridge, England: Cambridge University Press.

Smith, J. (1974b). The theory of games and the evolution of animal conflicts. <u>Journal of Theoretical Biology</u>, <u>47</u>, 209.

Following are sample entries for a References list:

<u>Book by one author</u>

Anderson, C. M. (1989). <u>Richard Selzer and the rhetoric of surgery</u>. Carbondale: Southern Illinois University Press.

If the book has no apparent author, begin with its title:

<u>ASAE standards</u> (35th ed.). (1988). St. Joseph, MI: American Society of Agricultural Engineers.

<u>Book by more than two authors</u>

Naisbett, J., & Aburdene, P. (1990). <u>Megatrends 2000</u>. *New York: Morrow.*

McCrum, R., Cran, W., & MacNeil, R. *(1986).* <u>The story of English</u>. *New York: Viking Press.*

<u>Book by six or more authors</u>

DuBois, E. C. et al. (1987). <u>Feminist scholarship: Kindling in the groves of academe</u>. Urbana: University of Illinois Press.

<u>Book or article by corporate or organization author</u>

Florida Power and Light Company. (1987). <u>FPL quality improvement program: QU story and techniques</u>. Miami: Florida Power and Light Company.

American Psychological Association. (1977). Guidelines
for nonsexist language in APA journals. <u>American
Psychologist</u>, <u>32</u>, 487-494.

Midwest Plan Service. (1987). <u>Structures and environmental
handbook</u> (11th ed.). Ames, IA: Midwest Plan Service.

Book with editor (anthology or compilation of essays, articles, poetry, etc.)

Gouma-Peterson, T. (Ed.). (1992). <u>Breaking the rules:
Audrey Flack, a retrospective 1950-1990</u>. New York:
Abrams.

Multivolume book

Arendt, H. (1978a). <u>The life of the mind: Vol. 1.
Thinking</u>. New York: Harcourt.

Book in other than first edition

Law, A. M., & Kelton, W. D. (1991). <u>Simulation modeling
and analysis</u> (2nd ed.). New York: McGraw-Hill.

Part of a book

Hardison, O. B., Jr. (1989). Let's play architecture.
In <u>Disappearing through the skylight: Culture and
technology in the twentieth century</u> (pp. 107-120).
New York: Viking Press.

St. Vincent Millay, E. (1988). Oh, Oh, you will be
sorry for that word! In <u>Collected sonnets</u> (rev. and
enlarged ed., p. 31). New York: Harpers.

Holmblad, L. P. & Ostergaard, J. (1982). Control of a
cement kiln. In M. M. Gupta & E. Sanchez (Eds.),
<u>Fuzzy information and decision processes</u> (pp.
389-399). New York: North-Holland.

(*This entry describes an article by Holmblad and Ostergaard in a
collection of articles edited by Gupta and Sanchez.*)

Suhor, C. (1989). Foreword. In S. Crowley, <u>A teacher's introduction to deconstruction</u> (pp. vii-viii). Urbana, IL: National Council of Teachers of English.

(This entry describes a foreword written by Suhor in a book by Crowley.)

Unpublished thesis or dissertation

Guritino , P. (1988). <u>Moisture sorption of bagged grain stored under tropical conditions</u>. Unpublished master's thesis, Kansas State University, Manhattan.

Berthnal, N. (1990). <u>Motherhood lost and found: The experience of becoming an adoptive mother to a foreign born child</u>. Unpublished doctoral dissertation, Union Institute, Cincinnati, OH.

Article in a journal with continuous pagination

Knight, V. N. (1992). Zimbabwe: The politics of economic reform. <u>Current History</u>, <u>91</u>, 219-223.

Article in a journal that numbers pages separately in each issue

Guth, A. H., & Steinhardt, P. J. (1984). <u>The inflammatory universe. Scientific American</u>, <u>250</u>(5), 90-102.

(For journals that begin each issue with page 1, add the issue number in parentheses after the volume number: 250(5) stands for volume 250, issue 5.)

Article in a popular magazine

McGeary, J. (1992, May 25). Voice of her people. <u>Time</u>, pp. 48-50.

Article in a newspaper

Barringer, F. (1993, June 4). Majority in poll back ban on handguns. <u>The New York Times</u>, p. A14.

Article in a reference book

```
Low-temperature acoustics. (1992). McGraw-Hill encyclo-
    pedia of science and technology (7th ed.) (Vol. 10,
    pp. 201-205)
```

(When citing familiar reference books that frequently appear in new editions, give only the edition, year of publication, and page numbers.)

```
Applications software, evaluation. (1988). Encyclopedia
    of microcomputers (Vol. I, pp. 222-235). New York:
    Dekker.
```

Unpublished paper or speech

```
Poovey, M. (1987, May). Speaking of the body. A discur-
    sive division of labor in mid-Victorian Britain.
    Paper presented at the colloquium on Women, Science,
    and the Body; Discourses and Representations, spon-
    sored by the Society for the Humanities, Cornell
    University, Ithaca, NY.
```

Computer software

```
Thiesmeyer, E. C., & Thiesmeyer, J. E. (1990). Editor:
    A system for checking usage, mechanics, vocabulary,
    and structure. Version 4.0. [Computer program]. New
    York: Modern Language Association.
```

Personal communication

Sources without "recoverable data"—that is, that have not been recorded or written down and are thus unavailable to others— should not appear in a References list according to the APA *Publication Manual* (p. 110). Most personal communications and interviews are "unrecoverable" and should simply be fully described in a parenthetical text citation.

EMPHASIS

▼

There are always words and ideas that a writer wants to emphasize. Fortunately, writers have a half dozen or more ways to make important words and ideas conspicuous. Three such ways are used in the following sentence to emphasize what the writer identifies as Albert Einstein's chief personal trait:

> He was one of the greatest scientists the world has ever known, yet if I were to convey the essence of Albert Einstein in a single word, I would choose *simplicity.*

> —Banesh Hoffman, "Unforgettable Albert Einstein," *Reader's Digest* 92 (January 1968): 107.

The writer gives weight and importance to Einstein's simplicity in these ways:

1. Making a direct statement about the importance of the word ("if I were to convey the essence of Albert Einstein in a single word, I would choose *simplicity.*"). Other explicit statements that emphasize the importance of an idea are "The important point is that . . ." "The most alarming situation . . ." "More importantly . . ." "Above all . . ." etc.

2. Placing the key word at the end of the sentence. One of the most effective ways to achieve emphasis is to position an idea at the beginning or the end of a passage (a phrase, a sentence, a paragraph, or a major section of text). Ideas that are positioned in the middle are not regarded as important as ideas at the beginning or the end.

3. Italicizing the word to make it stand out from the rest of the text. Other typographical devices that are used most commonly for emphasis are underlining, **boldface type**, and ALL CAPITAL LETTERS.

These three techniques are easy to use. But they should be used infrequently. The more they are used, the less emphatic they become. Following are three other ways of achieving emphasis, and they, too, should be used sparingly, for if they are overused they lose their impact.

4. Repeating a word or an idea several times. An idea that is mentioned in the title of the text and is repeated several times throughout the text will catch most readers' attention. Another form of repetition—alliteration—the repetition of sounds, can give a statement a marked emphasis and make it memorable.

5. Deviating from normal word order (which is subject-verb-direct object for assertions) in a sentence. Putting the verb before the subject makes the subject more emphatic:

> *normal word order:*   Geraldine aced the test.
>
> *inverted word order:*   Acing the test was Geraldine.
>   It was Geraldine who aced the test.

Placing the modifier of the verb before the subject makes the modifier emphatic:

> *normal word order:*   The price of crude oil tripled in the early months of 1984.
>
> *inverted word order:*   In the early months of 1984 the price of crude oil tripled.

Setting off "In the early months of 1984" with a comma creates a pause that makes the short phrase even more emphatic:

> In the early months of 1984, the price of crude oil tripled.

Words that modify a noun are made emphatic by being placed after the noun they modify:

> *normal word order:*   The poorly lighted and cramped library carrel is a terrible place to try to study.
>
> *inverted word order:*   The library carrel, poorly lighted and cramped, is a terrible place to try to study.

Words and phrases that are out of their normal order are usually separated from the rest of the sentence by commas. Setting off "poorly lighted and cramped" by dashes instead of commas makes the phrase even more emphatic:

> The library carrel—poorly lighted and cramped—is a terrible place to try to study.

FORECASTING STATEMENTS,
PAGE 503

HEADINGS, PAGE 526

6. Using **forecasting statements**, such as displayed lists and **headings**, and numbers to enumerate several facts, ideas, or questions, give increased visibility to major ideas and the way they are organized. Here, for example, is a passage that discusses exercise programs for pregnant women as it might appear with very little attempt to emphasize the main ideas:

> As might be expected, these concerns make advice about exercising during pregnancy somewhat controversial. There is no reason to tell healthy pregnant women not to exercise. In fact they should be encouraged to do so within limits. Women who have been previously sedentary are not advised to start a strenuous exercise program after becoming pregnant. They are better advised to initiate a conservative program such as daily walking. Women who are already training strenuously and become pregnant are best advised to gradually reduce the intensity during the course of pregnancy. In either case, women should avoid training that requires heart rates in excess of 160 bpm, extends over long periods (e.g., distance running), is likely to produce dehydration or hyperthermia or both, or is likely to increase the risk of abdominal trauma. Informed caution should be the guide during this time.

The passage contains three major points about pregnant women engaging in exercise programs. But most readers will have to read very carefully, perhaps even reread, to pick them out. The reason, of course, is that the words which state the major points look like all the other words in the passage and thus are given no particular emphasis.

Two ways to give emphasis to the main points are to provide a statement that lets the reader anticipate that significant information is coming and to number the major points. Here is a version of the passage with slight emphasis added by a new sentence inserted after the third sentence to serve as a lead into the three major points to be made, by numbers to set the major points in sequence, and by lower-case letters to identify the subitems of the third major point:

> As might be expected, these concerns make advice about exercising during pregnancy somewhat controversial. There is no reason to tell healthy pregnant women not to exercise. In fact, they should be encouraged to do so within limits. The following plan represents a prudent approach that can help main-

tain a reasonable fitness level while protecting both the mother and the developing child. (1) Women who have been previously sedentary are advised not to start a strenuous exercise program after becoming pregnant. They are better advised to initiate a conservative program such as daily walking. (2) Women who are already training strenuously and become pregnant are best advised to gradually reduce the intensity during the course of pregnancy. (3) In either case, women should avoid training that (a) requires heart rates in excess of 160 bpm, (b) extends over long periods (e.g., distance running), (c) is likely to produce dehydration or hyperthermia or both, or (d) is likely to increase the risk of abdominal trauma. Informed caution should be the guide during this time.

Following is the version as it was actually written. Notice the several devices that emphasize the major ideas and the structure of the passage, especially the change in format so the three major points and the four subpoints of item 3 are shown in a vertical list. The passage is longer than the other two, primarily because the three items listed are set off on separate lines. But the important thing is that this version is quicker to read and easier to understand. Readers do not have to expend enormous amounts of energy to identify the major points and how they are organized.

As might be expected, these concerns make advice about exercising during pregnancy somewhat controversial. There is no reason to tell healthy pregnant women not to exercise. In fact, they should be encouraged to do so within limits. The following plan represents a prudent approach that can help maintain a reasonable fitness level while protecting both the mother and the developing child.

1. Women who have been previously sedentary are advised not to start a strenuous exercise program after becoming pregnant. They are better advised to initiate a conservative program such as daily walking.
2. Women who are already training strenuously and become pregnant are best advised to gradually reduce the intensity during the course of pregnancy.
3. In either case, women should avoid training that
   a. requires heart rates in excess of 160 bpm
   b. extends over long periods (e.g., distance running)

    c. is likely to produce dehydration or hyperthermia
      or both
    d. is likely to increase the risk of abdominal trauma

Informed caution should be the guide during this time.

> —David K. Miller and T. Earl Allen, *Fitness: A
> Lifetime Commitment*, 4th ed. (New York:
> Macmillan, 1990): 71.

As you compare these three passages, you can see in the second and third versions the main ideas, like pictures in a tray of developer, emerge with greater and greater clarity. Certainly not all passages would benefit from this kind of formatting. There is such a thing as overkill. But in a passage where you want to be sure that readers can easily identify the major points, this kind of strongly visual format is helpful.

EXEMPLIFICATION (ILLUSTRATION)
▼

When good writers think that readers need more information to understand a term or an idea, they usually provide examples.

An example can be as short as a word or two, as in the following statement where the term *lower vertebrates* is defined by examples:

> Few species of the lower vertebrates, that is, the fishes,
> amphibia, and reptiles, build nests of any kind. . . .

> —Karl von Frisch, *Animal Architecture*, trans.
> Lisabeth Gombrich (New York: Harcourt Brace
> Jovanovich, 1974): 152.

The specific examples ("the fishes, amphibia, and reptiles") make clear what "the lower vertebrates" refers to.

Or an example may be stated in a sentence, or a series of examples may extend through several sentences or even paragraphs. The following passage, written by the noted science essayist Lewis Thomas, consists of a general statement that is followed by a barrage of specific examples:

> Almost anything that an animal can employ to make a sound
> is put to use. Drumming, created by beating the feet, is used by
> prairie hens, rabbits, and mice; the head is banged by wood-

peckers and certain other birds; the males of deathwatch beetles make a rapid ticking sound by percussion of a protuberance on the abdomen against the ground; a faint but audible ticking is made by the tiny beetle *Lepinotus inguellinus*, which is less than two millimeters in length. Fish make sounds by clicking their teeth, blowing air, and drumming with special muscles against tuned inflated air bladders. Solid structures are set to vibrating by toothed bows in crustaceans and insects. The proboscis of the death's head hawk moth is used as a kind of reed instrument, blown through to make high-pitched, reedy notes.

Gorillas beat their chests for certain kinds of discourse. Animals with loose skeletons rattle them, or, like rattlesnakes, get sounds from externally placed structures. Turtles, alligators, crocodiles, and even snakes make various more or less vocal sounds. Leeches have been heard to tap rhythmically on leaves, engaging the attention of other leeches, which tap back, in synchrony. Even earthworms make sounds, faint staccato notes in regular clusters. Toads sing to each other, and their friends sing back in antiphony.

> —"The Music of *This* Sphere," in *The Lives of a Cell: Notes of a Biology Watcher* (New York: Viking Press, 1974): 21–22.

The passage is more interesting and credible with the examples than if Thomas had remained general and abstract. The number and variety of examples are, in themselves, interesting and informative. Most readers will recognize at least some of the noise-making methods, and all readers will have a better understanding about the great number of signals that are transmitted in nature.

The use of specific examples, typical instances, sample cases, and illustrated anecdotes to clarify a concept or support a point is called *exemplification*. Its most important effect is to link the writer's ideas to concrete and familiar experiences and things that give readers something specific to relate to. Often the link is signaled by such expressions as "for example," "to illustrate," or "for instance," as it is in the following paragraph that explains a problem in certain kinds of federal income transfer programs:

> A third problem with the categorical nature of the transfer system in the United States is that payments sometimes go to non-needy recipients. As an example, the complex agricultural subsidy programs have ballooned to total spending levels approaching $25 billion in the 1980s and primarily reward afflu-

ent corporate farm owners, ironically, in a country that values work, for work they do not perform. Created during the Great Depression, these programs have long outlived their usefulness, encourage overproduction, and have not saved the family farm (which, probably should not be saved at public expense, any more than any declining industry should be saved). If categorical aid were abandoned, and transfer payments were based strictly on poverty and income-based needs, most recipients of agricultural subsidies would not (and should not) be eligible.

—Marcia Lynn Whicker and Raymond A. Moore, *Making America Competitive: Policies for a Global Future* (New York: Praeger, 1988): 125.

Writers draw factual examples from their own experiences and those of others. They create hypothetical examples by generalizing from many experiences.

Factual examples have high credibility because they describe real instances or experiences. In the following passage, a problem is stated in the first paragraph and is followed by a brief anecdote from the writer's personal experience that illustrates the problem:

... I am willing to admit that there are some real and useful things to learn from men. Not from all men—in fact, we may have the most to learn from some of the men we like the least. This realization does not mean that my feminist principles have gone soft with age: what I think women could learn from men is how to get *tough*. After more than a decade of conscious-ness-raising, assertiveness training, and hand-to-hand combat in the battle of the sexes, we're still too ladylike. Let me try that again—we're just too damn ladylike.

Here is an example from my own experience, a story that I blush to recount. A few years ago, at an international confer-ence held in an exotic and luxurious setting, a prestigious pro-fessor invited me to his room for what he said would be an intellectual discussion on matters of theoretical importance. So far, so good. I showed up promptly. But only minutes into the conversation—held in all-too-adjacent chairs—it emerged that he was interested in something more substantial than a meeting of minds. I was disgusted, but not enough to overcome 30-odd years of programming in ladylikeness. Every time his com-ments took a lecherous turn, I chattered distractingly; every time his hand found its way to my knee, I returned it as if it were something he had misplaced. This went on for an unconscionable period (as much as 20 minutes); then there was a minor scuffle, a dash for the door, and I was out—with nothing violated but my self-esteem. I, a full-grown feminist, conversant with such matters as rape crisis counseling and sexual harassment at the workplace, had behaved like a ninny—or, as I now understand it, like a lady.

> —Barbara Ehrenreich, "What I've Learned
> from Men: Lessons for a Full-Grown Feminist,"
> *Ms.* (August 1985): 24.

Factual and hypothetical examples are often drawn from research, as illustrated in the following passage by Arlene Skolnick, a research psychologist at the Institute of Human Development, University of California at Berkeley, in which she describes the lack of privacy for families in earlier times:

> Perhaps what distinguishes the modern family most from its colonial counterpart is its newfound privacy. Throughout the 17th and 18th centuries, well over 90 percent of the American population lived in small rural communities. Unusual behavior rarely went unnoticed, and neighbors often intervened directly in a family's affairs, to help or to chastise.
>
> The most dramatic example was the rural "charivari," prevalent in both Europe and the United States until the early 19th century. The purpose of these noisy gatherings was to censure community members for familial transgressions—unusual sexual behavior, marriages between persons of grossly discrepant ages, or "household disorder," to name but a few. As historian Edward Shorter describes it in *The Making of the Modern Family*:
>> Sometimes the demonstration would consist of masked individuals circling somebody's house at night, screaming, beating on pans, and blowing cow horns . . . on other occasions, the offender would be seized and marched through the streets, seated perhaps backwards on a donkey or forced to wear a placard describing his sins.
>
> The state itself had no qualms about intruding into a family's affairs by statute, if necessary. Consider 17th-century New England's "stubborn child" laws that, though never actually enforced, sanctioned the death penalty for chronic disobedience to one's parents.

> —"The Paradox of Perfection," *Wilson
> Quarterly* (Summer 1980): 116.

Hypothetical examples refer to or describe imaginary things or experiences. They are used when a concrete example is needed to illustrate an idea and no actual example is available or a hypothetical example would be simpler for the reader to understand. In most cases, a hypothetical example is as good as a factual example. Consider the following one that explains how value-added taxation works:

> Value-added taxes are widely used abroad because they raise large amounts of money while simultaneously creating incentives to consume less and save more. Instead of being taxed upon what one puts into society (the income from work and savings) one is taxed on the consumption one takes out of society. With a 15 percent valued-added tax, a person who buys a $10,000 car must pay an extra $1,500 in value-added taxes when he buys the car but can completely avoid those taxes if he instead saves the $10,000. As a result, the incentive effects of value-added taxes work in favor of what society wants, less consumption, rather than against what society wants, more savings and work, as in the case with higher personal income taxes. As a result value-added taxes are an integral part of any program seeking to encourage more private savings and to transform government from a dissaver into a saver.
>
> —Daniel Bell, *The Deficits: How Big? How Long? How Dangerous?* (New York: New York UP, 1985): 110-111.

To be effective, examples must be chosen carefully. Factual examples, of course, must be factually correct. All examples must be relevant to and representative of the general idea or point being discussed. In addition, samples must be developed in sufficient detail when readers are not familiar with either the general idea or the example. For instance, when Skolnick uses the example of the shivaree ("charivari") to illustrate community pressure on misbehaving families during the seventeenth and eighteenth centuries, she explains its purpose and occasions and quotes a historian to cite several of its forms.

Finally, there is the question of how many examples are sufficient to support a generalization or illustrate a concept. That is a difficult question to answer. The number depends in large part on how well informed the readers are and whether the point being made conflicts with the readers' beliefs. Some concepts and arguments are supported adequately by a single extended example, but most are supported by several, for one example does not always seem to be sufficient. Two or three examples often seem just right. More than three or four seem to belabor the point, unless the writer's argument conflicts with long-held beliefs of the readers.

FIELD RESEARCH

▼

Writers often need to research a topic to gain sufficient information and a good understanding of what they plan to write about. These investigations may involve **library research** to discover what has already been written about the topic. Research may also involve gathering information first-hand, by interviews, questionnaires, and/or direct observation—the various kinds of field research.

LIBRARY RESEARCH, PAGE 534

Interviews

Interviewing involves asking somebody to give his or her thoughts about a particular topic. When you were deciding on your major area of study in college, you probably interviewed an academic advisor or a faculty member whose experience and knowledge added to your understanding of the major. If you have ever had to select a site for an organization's banquet, you probably interviewed or surveyed group members to find out their preferences.

Interviewing is an effective way to gather authoritative information that is not readily available in published sources. Here are several suggestions on how to prepare for an interview, how to conduct an interview, and what to do following an interview.

Preparing for the Interview

Preparation for the interview involves gaining a basic understanding of the topic you are researching, developing the questions you will ask, and selecting the person or persons you will interview.

▶ Read enough about your research topic so you will know the important questions to ask. Much basic information is available in encyclopedias, atlases, and almanacs, and you should do some preliminary reading so that you will be informed enough to ask intelligent questions about more technical and complex aspects of your topic. You do not want the person you are interviewing to think that you are asking him or her to do the basic homework for you.

▶ **Determine the objectives or goals of the interview.** It is important to know what kind of information you want from the interview. Your objectives will depend upon your stage of research. For example, you might be researching the occurrence of campus crime and already be knowledgeable about the basic and more general aspects of the topic but need to obtain specific information concerning the occurrence of date-rape or burglaries on your own campus. Or you might be having difficulty finding published material on the development of computerized navigational aids for long-distance travel in automobiles. Asking a librarian who is knowledgeable about reference materials or a professor whose specialization is related to transportation, automotive technology, or computer applications will probably develop some useful leads to published material. Knowing what you want to learn from an interviewee will help you focus on the types of questions you need to ask.

▶ **Prepare a thorough list of questions.** Select the points or issues you wish to explore during the interview and develop questions that will help you do that. Also consider the kinds of follow-up questions you might ask in case the interviewee provides certain kinds of information that seem worth pursuing or responds too generally or vaguely to a question. For instance, questions such as "Why do you think this happened?" or "Can you explain a bit more about what you mean by . . . ?" or "What do you believe is the most important instance or example of this?" can help you gain additional information that will enable you to understand more thoroughly the interviewee's responses and may give you useful authoritative statements to quote.

▶ **Select an interviewee who is an expert on the topic you are researching.** Because interviews can provide you with valuable material and additional authority to support your ideas, you should select the most expert persons available. Special benefits can come from using expert testimony: your readers will likely appreciate getting the expert information, and your own credibility will likely increase as a result.

▶ **Arrange a specific place and time for the interview.** Experts are usually busy people, and you will probably need to schedule your interview well in advance. When you contact a person you do not know, introduce yourself and explain the purpose of the interview, the kind of information you want, and why you want it. Even if you contact someone you have met before, be courteous and explain your purpose. Be prepared to explain the nature and purpose of your research and to estimate the amount of time you think the interview will take. Also be prepared to meet at a time and place that is convenient for the interviewee. If you want to record the interview, ask permission beforehand. Don't assume that you may tape record an interview without permission. It is unethical to conceal the taping of an interview. Most interviewees will cooperate and agree to your taping the interview. However, if the interviewee does not agree to being taped, don't push it.

Conducting the Interview

Most interviews go quite well. Someone who agrees to be interviewed is taking your request and your research seriously and will be willing to help you. Just make sure to do your part by showing up on time, having all the materials and equipment you need, and conducting the interview professionally.

▶ **Arrive on time and have everything you need.** Arriving on time for an interview is crucial in getting the cooperation of an expert who probably has a busy schedule. If you are unsure of the location of the interview, ask for directions and start early enough to allow for extra time that might be needed to find a parking space and to locate the interviewee's office or work area. Make sure that you have your list of questions and equipment for taking notes—pen, paper, tape recorder.

▶ **Conduct the interview professionally.** Your main responsibility during the interview is to keep it going by listening carefully to responses to your questions and asking the next question. Actually once the interview is underway it will probably resemble a conversation. But don't let the interview become chatty to the point that you begin stating your opinions—perhaps even arguing with the interviewee—and cannot get answers to all your questions. Talk no more than is necessary to keep the interview going. Let the interviewee do the talking. Allow the interviewee to respond freely to your questions, for what at first might appear to be a rambling response could result in a very important new perspective or statement. Remember, the purpose of the interview is to get the interviewee's opinions and ideas.

▶ **Ask follow-up questions when necessary.** Be on the lookout for possible new developments of your topic. Follow-up questions such as

"Could you explain that a bit more?" "Why do you suppose that is so?" and "Could you explain what you mean by 'integrated graphics applications'?" can elicit additional information. The additional information may help you understand an idea more fully or provide you with more details. Depending on the response to some of your later questions, you might want to ask for clarification of some earlier point that you believe might be an inconsistency or to correct some piece of information that you think you may not have remembered correctly.

▶ Take minimal notes. As you listen to the interviewee, maintain as much eye contact as you can and still take notes. (Even if you tape the interview, be prepared to take some notes.) You won't be able to take voluminous notes, but try to write down key words or phrases that will help you recall the interviewee's full responses when you write up the results of the interview later. It is helpful to double-space your notes so that you can fill in details after the interview.

▶ Be considerate of the interviewee's time and end the interview within the time allotted. When the interview closes, thank the interviewee for his or her time and information and ask if you can call if you have further questions. Also ask if the interviewee would like to see how you used the material from the interview. Offer to send the interviewee a copy of your completed paper.

Following the Interview

A good interview is likely to provide authoritative information that supports many of your own ideas and to clarify your own thinking on certain points. It might even produce information that you never had thought about. Once you have completed the interview, go through your notes, fleshing them out with examples and illustrations that you can remember from the interview. Check your notes to be certain that the statements you attribute to the interviewee accurately reflect his or her ideas. If you taped the interview, you will want to listen to several parts of it carefully. If you find that you need more information on some point or want to be sure that you are quoting the interviewee correctly, call or visit the person to ask for additional information or

DOCUMENTATION, PAGE 460

to double-check your information. Be sure that your **documentation** of the interview includes the name of the interviewee (and his or her position or title if appropriate), and the place, date, and time of the interview.

Questionnaires

A questionnaire is a formalized type of written interview that uses the same wording and sequence of questions to gain information from a large number of people in exactly the same way. It is useful when you want to compile several comparable answers from several respondents. For instance, questionnaires could help you discover how the students enrolled in a particular course prefer to schedule their lab sessions or what juveniles in a specific community think of police officers. These groups, of course, could be interviewed individually, but using a questionnaire is a quick and easy way to question uniformly and get responses from a large number of a particular group of people.

Determine the objectives of the questionnaire and select the group whose responses you want. You may give the questionnaire to respondents to fill out and return to you, or you may read the questions to each respondent and mark or record answers on the form. However you administer the questionnaire, there are several points to consider.

▶ Ask closed questions to gather factual and quantitative information. Closed questions limit possible responses to a specific answer from a list of allowable responses. The simplest kind of closed question requires the answer *yes* or *no*:

> **3.** Have you used the library's electronic catalog this term?
> Yes _____   No _____

Another type of closed question requires an answer from a list of possible responses:

> **4.** If your answer to Question 3 is "yes," about how often, on average, have you used the library's electronic catalog this term?
>
> _____ more than once a week
>
> _____ once a week
>
> _____ about once every two weeks
>
> _____ less often than every two weeks

Sometimes the closed question is in the form of a rating scale, such as the five-point Likert scale, which requires respondents to choose the appropriate degree of agreement or disagreement with a statement.

5. The library's electronic catalog is easy to use.

(1) strongly agree   (2) agree   (3) uncertain
(4) disagree   (5) strongly disagree

This type of scale is useful for measuring attitudes.

▶ Ask open-ended questions to gather opinions or attitudes. Open-ended questions allow respondents more freedom in their answers.

6. How has the library's electronic catalog affected your research strategies?

_____

_____

_____

_____

_____

Answers to open-ended questions are difficult to quantify, but they can be among the most interesting and helpful responses.

▶ Design the questionnaire so that it is easy to use. The general layout of questionnaires varies a great deal, but these three features are most helpful:

❖ Place instructions needed to fill out the questionnaire at the top of the first page of the questionnaire.

❖ Print the questionnaire in a typeface that is easy to read.

❖ Leave plenty of space for respondents to answer open-ended questions.

▶ Since you will be drawing conclusions and perhaps making recommendations based upon statistical treatment of responses, be sure that you have taken an adequate sample of the group you are surveying. Ideally you should strive to achieve universal sampling by canvassing all the members of an identifiable group, but that is not always possible or feasible. You may also do random sampling, in which every person in an identifiable group has a known chance to be selected. There are also other types of sampling methods. The important things are to be sure that you have an adequate sample before making generalizations about the results and to be prepared to explain the criteria used for selecting respondents and the procedure for administering the questionnaire.

▶ **Use the exact wording and the same sequence of questions in all questionnaires.** Personal interviews usually involve fairly free conversation between the researcher and the interviewee. Questionnaires, on the other hand, consist of carefully worded questions or statements to which all respondents are asked to respond. The primary purpose for using a questionnaire is to insure comparable answers, no matter who administers the questionnaire or who answers the questions. Variation in the wording of questions can significantly influence respondents' answers and make the information useless to the researcher. Consider, for example, these three questions about beginning salaries offered to entry-level hotel and restaurant managers:

> "What is your gross income?"

> "What is your net income?"

> "How much is your salary?"

Clearly, it would be unwise to add or average the answers to these questions. The answer to the first question would be a gross salary figure; the answer to the second question would be a net salary figure; and the answer to the third question might be either a gross or a net salary figure.

▶ **Encourage respondents to answer every question and return the questionnaire to you.** Whether the questionnaire is distributed personally or by mail, the instructions for completing it must be clear so that respondents will answer every question you want them to answer. Sometimes a questionnaire contains questions that are to be answered or not answered according to how a previous question or questions were answered (for example, the fourth question is to be answered only by respondents who answered *yes* to the third question and the fifth question would be answered only by respondents who answered *no* to the third question). To make sure that respondents can follow the instructions, you should test the questionnaire on a small group and revise questions or instructions if the test respondents have trouble.

   If the questionnaire is mailed to respondents, you should make a special effort to secure a high return rate. Use a cover letter that explains the purpose of the research and how the respondent was selected, identify the sponsor of the research, and give assurance that the responses will be confidential. Enclose a stamped, addressed return envelope in the mailing to make it easy for respondents to return the questionnaire to you.

Observation

While writers can get lots of information by library research and by interviews and questionnaires, much of what they write is based on their experience and observation. In fact, much of the success of great writers comes from their remarkable ability for accurate, detailed observation and from their exact memory and careful notes in dealing with the sensory experience of their lives. Henry David Thoreau's account of the ways of the ant, Annie Dillard's description of a mosquito sucking blood from a poisonous snake, and Paul Theroux's depiction of a train arriving in a border town in Outer Mongolia illustrate a high degree of accuracy in observation and great precision in describing what they observed.

CREDIBILITY, PAGE 443 Because first-hand reports carry so much **credibility,** part of researching your subject is to observe its tangible aspects. And because odds are overwhelmingly against your chances of writing with clarity and precision if you are not working from experience and observation, you should probably resist most temptations to write about something you have never observed—even if you have read the magazines and journals that cover your subject and have checked out every book your library has on the subject. If you are researching gender relationships among people, you must observe interactions between men and women, repeatedly and at length. Reading or hearing about the number of times that men or women make certain kinds of statements or gestures during conversations or group discussions does not replace the need to observe actual conversations and group discussions. You need to keep readers engaged with first-hand anecdotes, examples, and details.

Good writing is full of specific first-hand details. However, you cannot effectively describe what you have not seen and understood. Superficial observation usually reveals no more than the most obvious details, and inaccurate observation leads to faulty information. To become a careful and accurate observer, you need to learn the valuable lessons that Samuel Scudder, an American entomologist, learned nearly 150 years ago when he studied under the naturalist Louis Agassiz at

Harvard. In Agassiz's laboratory, Scudder learned to observe by having to look at a fish—the same fish—for days. You may want to read Scudder's fascinating account of his first days in Agassiz's laboratory, "In the Laboratory with Agassiz." It has been reprinted many times.

In addition to seeing, you also need to use your other senses—your senses of smell, taste, sound, and touch. Here are some suggestions for observing.

▶ **Observe repeatedly and at length the observable aspects of the subject.** Several obstacles can make careful observation difficult. Frequently, more than one action takes place simultaneously; sometimes things happen too quickly or are too small to be seen by the naked eye; occasionally things occur too slowly or are too large to observe in a single viewing; frequently, activities occur or parts exist that are invisible or inaudible or in other ways unobservable from a particular observation point. Quite often things do not occur or appear in the same way as they did previously or in other circumstances.

To overcome the barriers to observation, you may have to resort to repeated observations and rely on technology (fast-speed, slow-motion, time-stop, or infrared photography, or enhanced computer imagery) or on more traditional things such as observation logs and sketch pads. You may have to observe the subject from several different angles and in several different contexts. You may also have to taste, touch, or smell the subject as well as look at and listen to it.

▶ **Actively observe the subject.** You may not yet be able to observe a subject as well as a trained scientist can, but you should try to develop the observational skills learned from field studies and laboratory work. Train yourself to be an active observer, for observation requires you to be more than a passive receptor of sensory data. Observation is an active mental process. You must develop an uncompromising curiosity and learn to look deliberately at everything and ask what is happening and why things are the way they are or not the way they should be or the way you expect them to be.

You not only have to look at each detail, you have to look *for* each detail. Depending on the nature of your research, it might be appropriate for you to intervene in an event or to modify a feature to see what happens, or it might be desirable for you to remain an uninvolved, detached observer. But in either case, look and listen—and when appropriate, taste, touch, and smell the feature and record your observations about shape, size, sound, texture, aroma, spatial and chronological relationships, and the like. Certainly not every detail you observe and record will go into your final draft, but you will not know what details are significant until you have made extensive and repeated observations and kept careful notes of your observations.

▶ **Develop a hypothesis to help guide further observation.** In the early stages of your research you should try to be spontaneous, freely associative, and all-encompassing in your observations. Try not to have any preconceptions that would cause you to ignore, suppress, or exaggerate certain aspects of the subject. This kind of broad observation helps produce an enormous amount of data—so much information that you may feel as if you are in danger of sinking under its weight and of thinking that there is no way you can get a handle on all of it.

At some point in your research—usually after considerable observation—you will need to focus more narrowly on your subject and develop a hypothesis that will help you decide the kinds of information that are more interesting and significant for your purposes. The hypothesis should help explain the facts you have collected so far and also serve as a basis for further observation and analysis. For instance, in your observation of men and women in conversation, you may develop the impression that women ask more questions or nod in agreement more often and that consequently they are more supportive and accommodating than men. With this as your hypothesis, you are ready to focus on that particular aspect of your subject and are prepared to continue observing, but deliberately looking now for specific things that you have decided might be significant.

Your hypothesis will guide you in your further observations, for you are now trying to test the hypothesis. A hypothesis is an *unproven* theory, and your purpose is to determine whether it is true or false. You should be equally happy to prove it one way or the other, for your goal is to determine the truth as far as it is ascertainable. You must be careful not to become too attached to your hypothesis so that you begin ignoring or suppressing information that might refute it. You should give as much consideration to information that does not support your hypothesis as to that which supports it. Further observation may encourage you to modify or abandon your hypothesis if data do not support it. However, further observation may support your hypothesis, and you may eventually regard it as your **thesis,** a proposition that you are prepared to defend.

THESIS, PAGE 599

FORECASTING STATEMENTS
▼

All texts contain information arranged in a specific order. Readers can make their way through a text fairly easily if they can predict (1) the topics that will be discussed, (2) the order of their presentation, and (3) the places where a text will undergo significant changes in topic.

Once readers get the big picture, they can read optimally. They can anticipate the way the thesis will be developed, even during the first reading of the text. They can retrieve specific information or parts of the text efficiently when reviewing or rereading the text.

It is the writer's responsibility to orient readers to content and organization. However, because writers are so familiar with what they have written and know what will happen next in their texts, they are not always sensitive to the readers' needs. They forget or are unaware that readers do not know in advance the organization and have to figure it out as they read.

To guide readers through your text, you can provide forecasting statements that announce the topics and preview the way they are organized. There are two kinds of forecasting statements: explicit and implied. The opening paragraph of an essay by Bertrand Russell on the necessity of achieving wisdom illustrates an explicit forecasting statement in the last sentence:

> Most people would agree that, although our age far surpasses all previous ages in knowledge, there has been no correlative increase in wisdom. But agreement ceases as soon as we attempt to define "wisdom" and consider means of promoting it. I want to ask first what wisdom is, and then what can be done to teach it.
>
> —"Knowledge and Wisdom," in *Portraits from Memory* (New York: Simon & Schuster, 1956): 173.

The last sentence enables readers to anticipate what Russell will discuss and in what order. Their view of a text is continuously adjusting to cues that set up specific expectations.

Implicit forecasting statements provide an overview of text organization without referring so baldly to the writer's intentions. The opening paragraph in a passage that discusses the conflicting theories of the labor market states the subject and then identifies the four conflicting theories that the writer will discuss:

Just as archaeologists have two sources of information on ancient civilizations—artifacts and writings—so an observer of economic activity has two sources of information on the labor market: he can examine the observed distribution of wages and employment, or he can turn to the economic literature for a view of how wages and employment are determined. There are problems of a striking mismatch between observed data and theory, but within the theoretical literature is another peculiar phenomenon. At least four different theories of the labor market present themselves. Equilibrium price-auction economics, Keynesian macro-economics, monetarists' macro-economics, and labor economics all have different theories to explain what occurs. The theories are mutually inconsistent, but each has its advocates and economic practitioners.

—Lester C. Thurow, *Dangerous Currents: The State of Economics* (New York: Random House, 1983): 181.

As readers would expect, Thurow divides his discussion into explanations and comparisons of these four theories, taking them up in the order in which they are listed in the next-to-last sentence of the paragraph. Here are the topic sentences that begin the discussions of these theories:

In the standard price-auction model, the labor market is treated as if it were like any other market in which price (wage) is the short-run market-clearing mechanism. (p. 181)

In the economic models of Keynesian macro-economics, the demand for labor depends upon total output, not upon the wage rate. (p. 182)

Monetarist macro-economics similarly depends upon assumptions of rigidity in the labor market. (p. 182)

In institutional labor economics, inter-skill or inter-industry wage differentials become the focus of analysis. (p. 183)

After discussing the four theories, Thurow cues readers that the text is shifting into a more generalized discussion of the conflicting theories with this sentence:

Unfortunately, these four theoretical perspectives are often mutually inconsistent. (p. 183)

Other features you can use to increase readers' ability to predict topics and organization are informative **titles,** tables of contents (for lengthy texts), **headings,** and **transitions.**

TITLES, PAGE 604

HEADINGS, PAGE 526

TRANSITIONS, PAGE 612

FORMAT
▼

Format in writing refers to the physical appearance of the text—the typeface, the white space, the placement of text on the page, the size of the page itself. A text that is professional in appearance, easy and inviting to read, and free of format errors is more likely to be read. Although neatness and attractiveness help create respect and confidence, they are not the most important aspects of format. We assume you know that the kind of sloppy work associated with incorrect spelling, faint type due to a wornout typewriter or printer ribbon, or tattered or smeared paper is unacceptable.

We discuss format here as a way to help readers understand what we write. Many texts, like short essays and fiction, make only minimal use of conventions of format. The standard printed page is a rectangular block of text surrounded by white margins. Consistent margins, paragraph indentations, capitalization, punctuation, and spaces between words and after punctuation are the most noticeable visual features of such texts, as the following passage illustrates:

> *Roseanne* the sitcom, which was inspired by Barr the stand-up comic, is a radical departure simply for featuring blue-collar Americans—and for depicting them as something other than half-witted greasers and low-life louts. The working class does not usually get much of a role in the American entertainment spectacle. In the seventies, muscular blue-collar males (*Rocky, The Deer Hunter, Saturday Night Fever*) enjoyed a brief modishness on the screen, while Archie Bunker, the consummate blue-collar bigot, raved away on the tube . . .
>
> —Barbara Ehrenreich, "The Wretched of the Earth," *The New Republic* (April 2, 1990): 28.

The format conventions in this paragraph are so familiar, you are probably unaware of them. You probably have learned unconsciously these conventions that have become customary in our language and culture. However, anything that affects the arrangement and appearance of the text is format. Even these relatively few format conventions provide helpful clues about how to read the text. If paragraph indentation, justified left margin, uppercase and lowercase letters, spacing, and punctuation had not been invented as writing developed, our texts would look like an unbroken string of letters of the same size (or of no particularly consistent size) with no space between them and with no punctuation, much like this:

ROSEANNETHESITCOMWHICHWASINSPIREDBY
RAPEDLACIDARASICIMOCPUDNATSEHTRRAB
TURESIMPLYFORFEATURINGBLUECOLLARAM
HTEMOSSAMEHTGNITCIPEDROFDNASNACIRE
INGOTHERTHANHALFWITTEDGREASERSANDL

These few lines are enough to give you an idea of how writing without format (except for the conventions of letters such as *R, S, E,* and so on, facing a particular direction and of the lines running horizontally) looked in early manuscripts. You can see the difficulty in trying to read more than a few words of it. So even minimal format conventions, especially those that are so familiar that both writers and readers are unaware of them, are essential for reading ease.

Although easily distinguishable from prose, the format of much poetry shares the generally conservative aspects of this most elemental level of format. The opening two stanzas of "The Demon Lover" illustrate a definite format that is easily recognized because of its neat arrangement—the consistent repetition of line lengths, placement of rhyming words, indentation of alternating lines, and the unjustified right margin. These are signs of certain kinds of poetry in print format.

"O where have you been, my long, long love,
    This long seven years and more?"
"O I'm come to seek my former vows
    Ye granted me before."
"O hold your tongue of your former vows,
    For they will breed sad strife;
O hold your tongue of your former vows
    For I have become a wife."

—Anonymous, "The Demon Lover"

These elements, whether in prose or poetry, are relatively simple matters. But since they establish the basis for a good general appearance on the page, you should give them careful attention even as you begin the first draft.

Other texts, such as letters, brochures, manuals, advertisements, and formal reports, also rely on most of the format elements just mentioned. But longer and more complex texts depend more heavily on visual information. Effective use of white space, variation in typeface, graphics, numbers, bullets, and lists prominently display the structure and logical relationships in the text. At this more advanced level there are format decisions to make about headings, lists, graphics, and special displays for quotations and equations.

Headings

Headings serve two major purposes: (1) they break up the mass of text to indicate the organization and scope of the material, thus helping browsers who are curious about what information the text contains, and (2) they serve as a kind of outline of the subject matter and as guideposts to readers who seek specific information in a particular part of the text. Headings are distinguished from the regular text by their position and the surrounding white space, and sometimes they are given additional emphasis by their typeface (underlined, bold, italicized, etc.). They are most helpful when they are informative (see **headings**).

HEADINGS, PAGE 526

Lists

A list is an itemized series, often arranged in a particular order. It may be part of the running text or in outline form. The outline form makes the list more visible and more prominent. Lists in outline form should be used sparingly and only when you want to emphasize the items in a series. For example, consider the following list, which is part of the running text:

> The main criteria for selecting a computer monitor should be that the display (1) supports a full assortment of characters, numbers, and punctuation marks, (2) is easy to read, (3) is comfortable to view so as to minimize operator fatigue, (4) has operator controls for brightness and contrast, and (5) minimizes light reflection.

Compare that passage with the following outline list:

> The main criteria for selecting a computer monitor should be that the display
> 1. supports a full assortment of characters, numbers, and punctuation marks,
> 2. is easy to read,
> 3. is comfortable to view so as to minimize operator fatigue,
> 4. has operator controls for brightness and contrast,
> 5. minimizes light reflection.

Allow your eyes to linger on each version a moment, and you will discover that the outline list has spatial action. The outline form is powerful because it pulls the attention of readers and directs their eyes toward the items in the list, heightening the list by breaking it away from surrounding text which is normally seen as a solid block. Each item is seen completely and not buried within the passage, enabling readers to distinguish each item in the series. The items of information in the outline list are clearly more noticeable than the ones in the running text, which have only numbers and commas separating them. Numbering the items in a list suggests that the order is important and the list is complete. If the sequence of the list is unimportant or if the entries in the list represent only some of the possible items, then use bullets (•) or dashes (—) instead of numbers as eye guides.

Format is often an important rhetorical consideration. Because the heightening created by the outline form of lists directs immediate attention to the information it contains, you need to consider your readers' feelings when deciding which list format to use. If you are conveying bad news—perhaps explaining why you cannot grant the reader or readers their request, or perhaps detailing the reasons why you do not share their opinion—politeness and common sense demand that such information be visually embedded on the page by making it part of the running text. That way, the list is less accessible and readers will encounter the items sequentially rather than being directed to them at first glance.

Graphics

GRAPHICS, PAGE 519   **Graphics** (tables and figures) may be incorporated on the page with regular text or may be on separate pages. Unless a graphic is large, it is usually not good practice to place it on a page by itself. The advantages of placing graphics on a page with text are that it reduces the number of pages necessary for the composition, and it places the graphic close to the related text, making it less likely that the readers will have to flip pages to look at the graphic and to read the text pertaining to it. In preparing graphics, be sure that the final size of the graphic fits along with accompanying text within the margins of the page without being too crowded and the graphic is placed near its reference in the text.

Quotations

If your composition contains material quoted directly from other sources, there are three conventions of format to observe.

▶ Short direct quotations (normally of four or fewer typed lines) are usually embedded into the text and enclosed in quotation marks:

> The effect of the American Revolution on the nature of government in the society of Europe was felt and recognized from the moment it became a fact. After the American rebellion began, "an extraordinary alternation took place in the mind of a great part of the people of Holland," homeland of St. Eustatius, recalled Sir James Harris, Earl of Malmesbury, who was British Ambassador at The Hague in the years immediately following the triumph of the American Revolution. "Doubts arose," he wrote in his memoirs, "about the authority of the Stadtholder" (Sovereign of the Netherlands and Prince of Orange).
>
> —Barbara W. Tuchman, *The First Salute* (New York: Knopf, 1988): 5–6.

Embedding short quoted phrases enables you to make a point by quoting credible sources and then to move on in your own voice.

▶ Long direct quotations (normally of five or more typed lines) are typically set off from the running text by indenting the quoted material ten spaces to the right and without adding quotation marks. These kinds of quotations are called *displayed* quotations. In the following passage, both short quotations and a longer, displayed quotation are used:

> Freud, on the other hand, remained profoundly concerned throughout his career to overcome the paradox. He was still struggling to do so in the last article he wrote, which he had to leave unfinished. In this article, Freud postulated that the ego of a person in analysis must, when young, "have behaved in a

remarkable manner" under the influence of "a powerful trauma." The child must have been tormented both by the desire to satisfy a strong instinct and by fear of the dangers that might ensue through doing so. The response is a split whereby the child both satisfies the instinct symbolically and rejects any knowledge concerning the matter:

> The two contrary reactions to the conflict persist as the center-point of a split in the ego. The whole process seems so strange to us because we take for granted the synthetic nature of the workings of the ego. But we are clearly at fault in this. The synthetic function of the ego, though it is of such extraordinary importance, is subject to particular conditions and is liable to a whole series of disturbances. (p. 373)

> —Sissela Bok, "Secrecy and Self-Deception," in *Secrets: On the Ethics of Concealments and Revelation* (New York: Pantheon, 1982): 63.

▶ Short direct quotations, especially poetry, are given emphasis by being formatted the same way as long direct quotations:

> In the great chain of being, each organism forms a definite link in a single sequence leading from the lowest amoeba in a drop of water to ever more complex beings, culminating in, you guessed it, our own exalted selves.
>> Mark how it mounts to man's imperial race,
>> from the green myriads in the people grass.
> wrote Alexander Pope in his expostulations in heroic couplets from the *Essay on Man.*

> —Stephen Jay Gould, *The Flamingo's Smile* (New York: Norton, 1985): 282.

Since they stand out from the regular text, it is important that short displayed quotations be worthy of the attention given them.

Equations and Formulas

Equations and formulas represent mathematical relationships and chemical or physical processes, and they should be used only if readers can understand them or if they are thoroughly defined. When you use equations or formulas, you will need to give them special attention in making format decisions. Simple questions and formulas sometimes run in the line of text, like this:

Arithmetic and algebra are also founded on experience. The expressions 2 + 2 = 3 + 1 = 4 are psychological generalizations. Algebra is simply a more abstract extension of such generalizations.

—Morris Kline, *Mathematics and the Search for Knowledge* (New York: Oxford UP, 1985): 19.

More often, an equation or formula is *displayed,* placed on a line by itself. No punctuation follows the displayed equation or formula except when it ends a sentence, as in this example:

The cosmic rays demonstrate the existence of a physical world in which the energy of the particles is many times that of their mass when at rest. The velocities are therefore almost c because

$$p = \frac{mv}{\sqrt{(1-v^2/c^2)}} \quad , \quad E = \frac{mc^2}{\sqrt{(1-v^2/c^2)}} \; .$$

This means that the v are not suitable physical parameters; so much can happen in a minute range of v, which contains an enormous range of p and E values. I interpret this in the sense that p and E cannot be reduced to, or measured by, v, but have an independent significance. There are other indications in support of this, but we cannot go into this here. [Nuclei with v of the order $c/5$ to $c/10$ (for protons or neutrons) are an intermediate stage]. The problem is to extend classical mechanics so as to include this hypothesis. I use the fact that the canonical transformations are symmetrical in x and $p;$ e.g., if they are defined through the Poisson brackets:

$$(u, v) = \sum_k \left(\frac{\partial u}{\partial x_k} \frac{\partial v}{\partial p_k} - \frac{\partial u}{\partial p_k} \frac{\partial v}{\partial x_k} \right)$$

then the transformation $(x,p) \rightarrow (X,P)$ is canonical when

$$(X_{k3}X_l) = 0_3 \quad (P_{k3}P_l) = 0_3 \quad (X_{k3}P_l) = \delta_{kl}.$$

—Letter from Max Born to Albert Einstein, April 11, 1938, from *The Born-Einstein Letters* (New York: Walker, 1971): 132.

A sequence of important equations or formulas is set off from the text (displayed), and if they are referred to elsewhere in the text they are numbered in parentheses flush with the right margin for easy reference.

He [Galileo] discovered that if air resistance is neglected, all bodies falling to the surface of the Earth have the same constant acceleration a: that is, they gain velocity at the same rate, 32 feet per second each second. In symbols,

$$a = 32 \tag{1}$$

If the body is dropped—that is, merely allowed to fall from the hand—it will start with zero velocity. Hence, at the end of 1 second its velocity is 32 feet per second; at the end of 2 seconds its velocity is 32 times 2 or 64 feet per second; and so forth. At the end of t seconds its velocity v is $32t$ feet per second; in symbols,

$$v = 32t \tag{2}$$

This formula tells us exactly how the velocity of a falling body increases with time. It says, too, that a body that falls for a longer time will have a greater velocity. This is a familiar fact, for most people have observed that bodies dropped from high altitudes hit the ground at higher speeds than bodies dropped from low altitudes.

We cannot multiply the velocity by the time to find the distance that a dropped body falls in a given amount of time. This would give the correct distance only if the velocity were constant. Galileo proved, however, that the correct formula for the distance d the body falls in t seconds is

$$d = 16t^2 \tag{3}$$

where d is the number of feet the body falls in t seconds. For example, in 3 seconds, the body falls 16×3^2 or 144 feet.

By dividing both sides of formula (3) by 16 and then taking the square root of both sides, we find that the time required for an object to fall a given distance d is given by the formula $t = \sqrt{d/16}$. Notice that the mass of the falling body does not appear in this formula. We can thus see that all bodies take the same time to fall a given distance. This is the lesson Galileo is supposed to have learned by dropping objects from the tower of Pisa. People still find it difficult to believe, nevertheless, that a piece of lead and a feather when dropped from a height in a vacuum reach the ground in the same time.

—Morris Kline, *Mathematics and the Search for Knowledge* (New York: Oxford UP, 1985): 104–106.

For more information on specific methods of expressing equations and formulas, see a standard style guide, such as *The Chicago Manual of Style* or *Mathematics into Type.*

Unorthodox Formats

In addition to the conventional format elements just described, there is yet another style of format that is unorthodox and sometimes violates conventional format designs. This type of format is most often found in poetry and experimental prose. One of the notable writers who departs from conventional format is the poet E. E. Cummings, the author of the following sentence:

high
the &   for me is SELF ('the individual or indivisible')
low

—E. E. Cummings, quoted in Milton A. Cohen, *Poet and Painter: The Aesthetics of E. E. Cummings' Early Work* (Detroit: Wayne State UP, 1987): 79.

The unorthodox placement of *high* above the line of type and *low* beneath the line of type is more than just a stunt or joke. In conjunction with *SELF* spelled in all capital letters, they show how format is related to the idea expressed by the writer: the sanctity of self.

Many writers have manipulated format, sometimes playfully as in Lewis Carroll's *Alice in Wonderland* in which the tale the mouse tells Alice visually resembles a long tail trailing down the page and sometimes more seriously as in the emblematic poems of the seventeenth-century English poets Robert Herrick and George Herbert. Much modern poetry departs from conventional format, as does the follow-ing poem. At first the poem may appear to be formless, but the unusual typographic features add to the aesthetic value of the format:

l(a

le

af

fa

ll

s)

one

l

iness

—E.E. Cummings, *95 Poems* (New York:
Harcourt, Brace, 1958): 1.

This unusual format helps writing draw attention to itself as writing. It insists on being recognized as writing but announces clearly its radical departure from orthodox format. No longer is the white background a neutral medium on which the text is printed. It has become an expres-sive part of the text. Displaying the words and letters in such an unusual way makes it difficult for readers to see recognizable words and sentences easily or to pronounce the words in a normal manner. To understand the poem, readers are forced to look at it as a physical fact. The vertical arrangement of the poem captures the image of a falling leaf. Upon closer examination, we can rearrange the letters hor-izontally to read *L (a leaf falls) oneliness*. Then we see that if we move the *L* in front of *oneliness*, we get *loneliness*. The image of a single falling leaf is a traditional symbol of absence or loneliness or death, and the vertical arrangement of the letters down the page is an exam-ple of how format matches the action of concept or feeling described. The separation of the *L* from the rest of the word *oneliness* and the separation of letters from each other by lines that are only one to five letters long illustrate visually both the separation that is the primary cause of loneliness and the identification of *loneliness* with *oneliness*.

As E. E. Cummings's innovative uses of capitalization, punctua-tion, and space in patterns that support meaning illustrate, there are format designs that more appropriately and imaginatively communicate the subject matter than do some conventional formats. Paying attention to format does not mean you are abandoning well-chosen words or ignoring well-written sentences. Words and sentences continue to be our native media. But you must begin paying more attention to the format. It is always there. Good writers know how to control it for their own purposes.

At the most elemental level there are several format decisions to make concerning paper quality (good quality bond for important letters and papers); sheet size (8½ x 11 inches is generally preferred when another size is not specified); binding (paper clipped or stapled in the upper left corner, etc.); page design (for example, text on one side of the page only, 1 inch margins all around, double spaced with indented beginnings of paragraphs for regular text, ragged right margins, and page numbers in the upper right corner directly above the end of the type line or at the bottom of the page in the center); and typography (serif type of a size and style that is easy to read, but not too large).

Always check to see if your text should conform to particular format specifications required or preferred by your teacher, editor, co-author, publisher, or audience. If not, you will have to decide for yourself what format seems best for the situation. Even if there are changes in format later, your initial choice of format will give you a stable target to work toward. The same text formatted different ways is illustrated in Figures 3, 4, and 5.

Figure 3 shows the text single spaced with the long important quotation run in to the text and with the right margin justified. Unless your printer prints proportionally (that is, creates equal spaces between each word in a line), justified right margin creates unequal spaces between words as the printer attempts to make all lines the same length. In the first line of text in Figure 3, there are wider than normal spaces between *Temple* and *Bar* and between *which* and *attempted.* This format is crowded and looks uninviting and difficult to read. It is the poorest format of all.

The text in Figure 4 is double spaced and the long important quotation is displayed, although not very well. The right-justified margin again creates uneven spacing between words in a line.

The text in Figure 5 is double spaced and the long important quotation is displayed. The right margin is not justified (that is, the lines have a common starting point on the left margin—except for the indentation at the beginning of paragraphs and the displayed quotation—but the lines do not end at the same space on the right margin). Unjustified right margins allow your printer to create equal spaces between words in the same line. This format is the best of the three.

38

of <u>Temple Bar</u>, and which   attempted to counter
Matthew Arnold's disparagement of Loud Macaulay.
According to the anonymous author of the <u>Temple
Bar</u> article, Arnold is guilty of extreme ingratitude: To be a great civiliser is surely no small
title to gratitude, if not to fame. To leave men
and things better, if by ever so little, than one
found them--he who had done this much, if he had
done no more, may surely go down well content into
his grave. ("A Plea for an Old Friend" 86) And
this writer continued, it was Macaulay who "stimulated and prepared us to receive the higher culture which Mr. Arnold has preached so untiringly,
so elegantly." He has "revived in us the taste
for what our fathers . . . were wont to speak of
as polite learning. . . ." (86-87). This notion
that Macaulay was largely responsible for the
growth of the number of middle-class readers during the generation immediately preceding Arnold's
period of literary criticism provides the kind of
assessment of Macaulay that will allow the last
third of the twentieth century to understand his
place as a literary critic. Macaulay's practice
as a critic, although it was perhaps more energetic and declamatory than Arnold's, was also
serious and responsible. Although his voice was
at times loud and strident, it helped prepare the
way for the quieter, calmer voice of Arnold.
     If Macaulay's general goals of criticism were
similar to Arnold's, his approach was not. To
develop taste in his readers and establish critical guidelines for other literary and social critics, Macaulay believed that the literary critic
had to become occupied by what would appear to
Arnold like "practical considerations." What made
this seem so different from Arnold was not his
attitude toward literature but his practice as a
critic. E. K. Brown, in a study of Arnold's performance as a critic, distinguished between the
disposition and the strategy of Arnold as a "dis-
interested" critic: "In one meaning of the word
Arnold is recommending . . . a critical strategy,
a quality in one's mode of presenting one's ideas
which is essential if these ideas are to become
widely operative. For a Victorian critic's ideas

Figure 3. Single-spaced text with justified right margin. Notice the crowded
appearance and the uneven spaces between words in the same line. The long
important quotation is not displayed.

38

of Temple Bar, and which attempted to counter
Matthew Arnold's disparagement of Lord Macaulay.
According to the anonymous author of the Temple
Bar article, Arnold is guilty of extreme ingrati-
tude:

> To be a great civiliser is surely no small
> title to gratitude, if not to fame. To leave
> men and things better, if by ever so little,
> than one found them--he who had done this
> much, if he had done no more may surely go
> down well content into his grave. ("A Plea
> for an Old Friend" 86)

As this writer continued, it was Macaulay who
"stimulated and prepared us to receive the higher
culture which Mr. Arnold has preached so untiringly, so elegantly." He has "revived in us the
taste for what our fathers . . . were wont to
speak of as polite learning. . . ." (86-87). This
notion that Macaulay was largely responsible for
the growth of the number of middle-class readers
during the generation immediately preceding
Arnold's period of literary criticism provides the
kind of assessment of Macaulay that will allow the

Figure 4. Double-spaced text with justified right margin. Notice the uneven spaces between words in the same line. The long important quotation (lines 6 through 12) is displayed, but not displayed well.

38

of <u>Temple Bar</u>, and which attempted to counter Matthew Arnold's disparagement of Lord Macaulay. According to the anonymous author of the <u>Temple Bar</u> article, Arnold is guilty of extreme ingratitude:

> To be a great civiliser is surely
> no small title to gratitude, if not
> to fame. To leave men and things
> better, if by ever so little, than
> one found them--he who had done this
> much, if he had done no more, may
> surely go down well content into his
> grave. ("A Plea for an Old Friend" 86)

And this writer continued, it was Macaulay who "stimulated and prepared us to receive the higher culture which Mr. Arnold has preached so untiringly, so elegantly." He has "revived in us the taste for what our fathers . . . were wont to speak of as polite learning. . . ." (86-87). This notion that Macaulay was largely responsible for the growth of the number of middle-class readers during the generation immediately preceding Arnold's period of literary criticism provides the kind of assessment of Macaulay that will allow the last

Figure 5. Double-spaced text with unjustified right margin. Notice that shortening the lines of the displayed quotation (lines 5 though 12) gives the quotation more emphasis.

GRAPHICS

▼

Graphics, widely used in business, technical, and scientific writing, can help writers make certain kinds of information readily understandable in other kinds of texts. Pictures, tables, flow diagrams, and charts convey concepts and data so that objects and scenes are easy to visualize, processes are easy to follow, comparisons are easy to make, and trends and other relationships are easy to spot. Fortunately, you do not have to be an artist or commercial illustrator to create the kinds of graphics you will most likely use. If you have the opportunity, familiarize yourself with a computer graphics program; one may be available with your word-processing program. However, until you learn how to use a computer graphics program, you can create acceptable graphics with a ruler (for measuring and drawing straight lines), a drafting compass (for drawing circles and arcs), and a protractor (for laying down angles).

Photographs and drawings are particularly useful in supporting **description**. Photographs are nearly ideal for giving the actual appearance of physical things. Their high degree of reality can show vividly and explicitly the effects of a forest devastated by acid rain, the details of a floral arrangement, or the physique of Arnold Schwarzenegger. Their two major drawbacks are that they show only the external appearance of an object and they may include realistic clutter that can distract from what is being illustrated. Photographs should center on the object of interest and include as little irrelevant background material as possible. They should be black and white (unless color is important) and be focused to bring out significant details.

DESCRIPTION, PAGE 456

While less realistic than photographs, drawings are often more useful because they allow for greater selectivity of details. Figure 6 is a series of line drawings that illustrate four arrangements of nozzles on field equipment for spraying insecticides and herbicides. Unlike a photograph, it shows only the details that need to be shown.

Almost any kind of data can be presented in tables, one of the easiest forms of presenting information from the standpoint of both writers and readers. The table in Figure 7 reports information about presidential vetoes of congressional bills from 1961 to 1988 in such a way that readers can compare the data and draw conclusions quickly and accurately. The table presents the information in a concise and orderly manner in a compact space that allows for easy side-by-side **comparison/contrast** and eliminates the extraneous words that would be necessary if you presented information in traditional sentence form.

COMPARISON/CONTRAST, PAGE 437

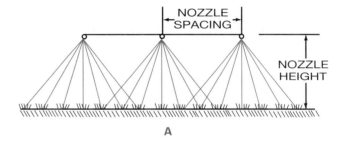

A

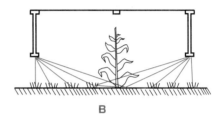

B

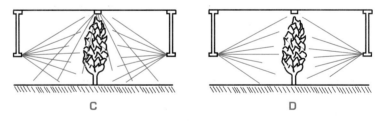

C   D

A. Complete overtop coverage for weeds or insects and between narrow rows for weed control.

B. Between rows for weed control.

C. Over and between rows for insect control.

D. Between rows for insect control.

Figure 6. Line drawing illustrating nozzle arrangements for spraying insecticides and pesticides. Line drawings allow for greater selectivity of details than photographs do, showing only the important details. (William Mayfield, *Field Sprayer Equipment and Calibration*, Circular R-11.)

No. 427. Congressional Bills Vetoed: 1961 to 1988

[See also *Historical Statistics, Colonial Times to 1970*, series Y 199–203]

PERIOD	PRESIDENT	Total vetoes	Regular vetoes	Pocket vetoes	Vetoes sustained	Bills passed over veto
1961–1963	Kennedy	21	12	9	21	—
1963–1969	Johnson	30	16	14	30	—
1969–1974	Nixon	42	24	18	36	6
1974–1977	Ford	72	53	19	60	12
1977–1981	Carter	31	13	18	29	2
1981–1988	Reagan	78	39	39	69	9

Figure 7. A table is a compact display of information in columns and rows. (U.S. Bureau of Census. *Statistical Abstract of the United States 1990.* 110th ed. Washington, DC: U.S. Government Printing Office, January 1990. 255.)

Flow diagrams are especially useful for showing processes and procedures. They trace action through a series of steps, providing good overviews of **narration**. In a block diagram, the simplest kind of flow diagram to make and to read, each step is represented by a "block" (usually a rectangle or square) with the name of the activity appearing in the box. The blocks are connected by lines with arrow heads to indicate the direction of movement in the process. Figure 8 is a block diagram that lists the major activities required to build a house. The diagram identifies the four major stages and breaks down the work involved in each stage.

NARRATION, PAGE 558

Line charts are useful for showing trends and making comparisons of data easy. They are constructed by plotting data on a grid and connecting the data by lines. Figure 9 shows data concerning marriage rates at 2-year intervals over a 16-year period. The six sets of data (for single men and women, divorced men and women, and widowed men and women) are distinguished by broken lines for men and solid lines for women and by clear labeling of each line.

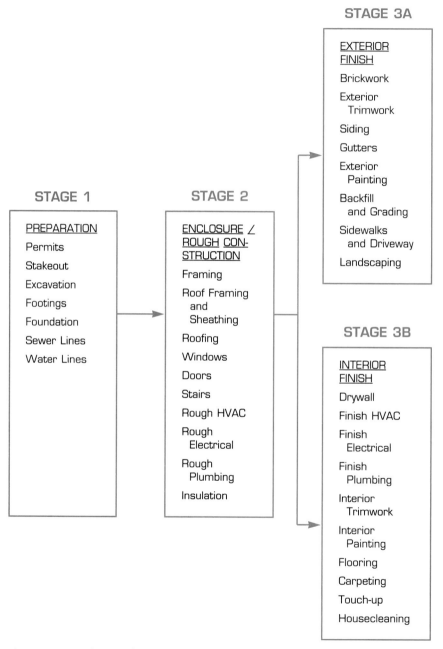

STAGE 3A

EXERIOR
FINISH

Brickwork

Exterior
 Trimwork

Siding

Gutters

Exterior
 Painting

Backfill
 and Grading

Sidewalks
 and Driveway

Landscaping

STAGE 1

PREPARATION
Permits
Stakeout
Excavation
Footings
Foundation
Sewer Lines
Water Lines

STAGE 2

ENCLOSURE /
ROUGH CON-
STRUCTION
Framing
Roof Framing
 and
 Sheathing
Roofing
Windows
Doors
Stairs
Rough HVAC
Rough
 Electrical
Rough
 Plumbing
Insulation

STAGE 3B

INTERIOR
FINISH
Drywall
Finish HVAC
Finish
 Electrical
Finish
 Plumbing
Interior
 Trimwork
Interior
 Painting
Flooring
Carpeting
Touch-up
Housecleaning

Figure 8. Box diagram listing major stages of work required to build a house.
Stage 1 must be completed before Stage 2 can begin; Stage 2 must be completed
before Stages 3A and 3B can begin; Stages 3A and 3B can occur at the same time.

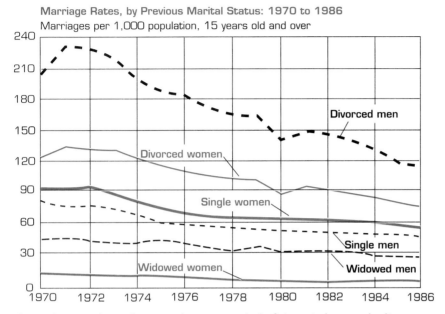

Figure 9. Line charts show trends over a period of time. As long as the lines are distinct and clearly labeled, several items can be plotted in a single chart. (U.S. Bureau of Census. *Statistical Abstract of the United States 1990.* 110th ed. Washington, DC: U.S. Government Printing Office, 1990. 61.)

Bar charts are useful for comparing different items at the same time. Figure 10 shows the number of paying passengers enplaned at the 10 busiest airports (the different items) in the United States during 1988 (the same time). A multiple bar chart is one that compares several items at different times. The multiple bar chart in Figure 11 has about the maximum number of items and times that can be compared effectively: the percentages of four groups at three different times.

Pie charts (see Figure 12) are useful for showing how parts of a whole (percentages that total 100 percent) are distributed. They compare the portions with one another and with the total at the same time. A pie chart (the analogy is made to the top of a pie) consists of a circle (representing the whole pie) divided into segments (representing the slices of the pie). Five or six segments are about the maximum that can be shown effectively. More than that and the segments become so small they may be difficult to label.

Whether you create graphics by hand or from a computerized graphics program, keep these four principles in mind when using them:

▶ **Graphics must be relevant.** It is tempting to borrow existing graphics from other sources, much as you would quote information from other sources. But graphics in other sources were created for specific purposes and specific audiences that might not be identical or even similar to your purpose and audience. A photograph of a glistening SST Concorde in flight in an azure sky may make a beautiful picture, but it is of little use to readers who need to know the location of the fuel tanks.

▶ **Graphics must be clearly legible with sharp detail and good contrast.** If a photograph or a photocopy of a photograph or other graphic is too dark or too light, the resolution of detail will be inadequate. The size of the labels and symbols should be large enough to be read easily. Poorly designed or poorly reproduced graphics test the patience of even the most gentle readers.

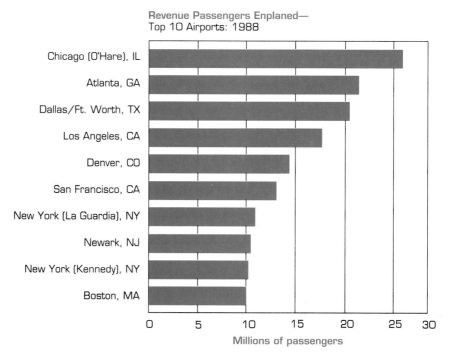

Figure 10. Bar charts compare different items at the same time. (U.S. Bureau of Census. *Statistical Abstract of the United States 1990.* 110th ed. Washington, DC: U.S. Government Printing Office, 1990. 618.)

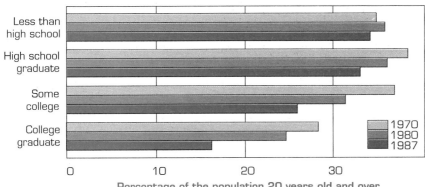

Figure 11. Bar charts with multiple bars grouped together compare different items at any given time and also trace a trend over a longer period of time. (U.S. Bureau of Census. *Statistical Abstract of the United States:1990.* 110th ed. Washington, DC: U.S. Government Printing Office, 1990. 90.)

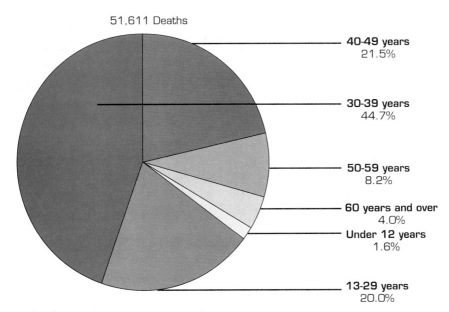

Figure 12. Pie charts, also called circle charts, show how parts of a whole are distributed. Each segment of the circle represents a percentage of the whole. (U.S. Bureau of Census. *Statistical Abstract of the United States: 1990.* 110th ed. Washington, DC: U.S. Government Printing Office, 1990. 61.)

▶ **Graphics must be easy to understand.** Do not try to pack too much data into a table, chart, or diagram. Photographs that are cluttered with lots of extraneous details obscure the main point. Line charts that resemble tangled spaghetti and diagrams that look like global weather patterns make comprehension difficult. A series of graphics is preferred to one that has too much information crammed into it.

▶ **Graphics should be conveniently placed—for the readers.** If possible, place a graphic close to the discussion of it. It is tempting to place a graphic at the end of the written text regardless of where it is discussed in the text. But a discussion on page 2 of a chart on page 6 that contains the results of a table on page 5 tests the patience of readers as much as a poorly reproduced graphic. Remember that it is the reader's convenience—not the writer's—that should determine where a graphic is placed. Do not force readers to flip back and forth between a graphic and the discussion of the graphic.

HEADINGS
▼

Headings are words or phrases that divide a text into sections and sometimes into subsections. Short texts are usually not divided into formal sections and subsections, but longer texts, especially those that serve pragmatic purposes, generally are. Such evident divisions are frequently helpful in long or complex texts because readers can absorb new information faster if the organization of the text is easily recognizable.

Headings show the organization and scope of the material, thus helping browsers who are curious about what information the text contains and assisting readers who seek specific information in a particular part of the text. Like headings, **forecasting statements**, **format**, **transitions**, and **topic sentences** also help readers use and understand texts and grasp their hierarchical structure.

FORECASTING STATEMENTS,
PAGE 503

FORMAT, PAGE 505

TRANSITIONS, PAGE 612

TOPIC SENTENCES, PAGE 609

To illustrate how well-written headings (and subheadings) tell readers what is coming in a text, look at the following excerpt from a student paper by Toni Gagnon that proposes her university's Small Business Development Center provide accounting advice to its clientele. The excerpt is from a section that discusses possible ways the Small Business Development Center can offer the service.

PROPOSED SOLUTIONS

Five possible solutions seem worthy of the Small Business Development Center's consideration: (1) requesting additional funds to hire an accounting major to perform the consulting, (2) allowing accounting majors to participate in an SBDC internship for accounting credit, (3) recruiting volunteers to provide the service, (4) taking accounting problems brought to the SBDC by its clientele to accounting classes as course projects, and (5) awarding elective accounting credit to students in exchange for their consulting work.

Accounting Majors as Consultants

The most apparent and perhaps most advantageous solution for SBDC clients is for the Center to request an increase in its budget so it can hire an accounting major to provide the support services. If such employment was offered to students, the position would likely be highly competitive and attract well-qualified students. Because there is a large pool of qualified accounting students available, I would recommend that the search be restricted to accounting students. However, according to Harriett Friedman, Administrative Assistant to the Dean of the College of Business, approval of an additional position does not appear to be available in the near future.

Internships for Accounting Course Credit

The Small Business Development Center could offer internships to senior accounting majors. These internships would allow students the opportunity to work as consultants to those local business that are clients of the Center, while receiving academic credit for an accounting course. Although this practice is common in other business disciplines, the School of Accountancy, as a matter of policy, has disallowed AC 400 Student Internship Programs for accounting majors. Therefore, this recommendation does not comply with school policy.

Student Volunteers

The Small Development Center should consider requesting accounting students to volunteer to staff the Center. Although the experience would be valuable to students, the lack of either pay or academic credit presents serious disadvantages. Other concerns include various inefficiencies often associated with volunteer programs, such as difficulties in training volunteers, problems in consistent scheduling, and lack of continuity in service to clients. . . .

The opening paragraph provides an overview of the recommendations contained in this section. The headings are derived from the overview list in the opening paragraph.

▶ **Headings are distinguished from regular text by their position and the surrounding white space, and sometimes they are given additional emphasis by their typeface** (<u>underlined</u>, **bold**, *italics*, etc.). Because of the way they are formatted, headings and subheadings provide additional white space and convenient breaks from the normal text so that readers, if they choose, can pause to reflect on what they have just read—to let the ideas sink in—before going to the next section.

▶ **Headings and subheadings should be formatted so they reflect the hierarchical structure of the text.** Centering a main heading on a line by itself and placing subheadings flush left clearly indicate the relationship between major and subordinate topics.

▶ **Headings are most helpful when they are informative.** Compare the following headings. The headings on the left are specific enough to give readers a good idea of what is contained in each section. The headings on the right are so abstract that they convey very little of the contents of each section.

<u>Informative Headings</u>	<u>Noninformative Headings</u>
Preface	Preface
I. Cycling Your Way to Better Health	Part I
II. Practical Tips for Bicycling Safety	Part II
III. Fitting Your Bicycle to You	Part III
Appendix A: Cycling Terms	Appendix A
Appendix B: Cycling Organizations	Appendix B
Appendix C: Cycling Magazines	Appendix C

Headings should be concise, but precise enough to indicate the content that follows. Single-word headings are usually too vague or weak.

▶ **There should be at least two lines of text below the last heading on a page, or else the heading should be repositioned to the top of the next page.** Do not leave a heading without text at the bottom of a page.

INVENTION (PREWRITING)
▼

Anything you do before you write that helps you when you write can be considered *invention.* Although thinking—constructing a text in your mind—may be the most powerful form of invention, it is not the only form. Invention is often thought of as prewriting, but it is not limited to the thinking you do before you write. Invention encompasses not only writing but also reading, listening, and talking. The reading and research you do, the conversations you have, the scribbling, listing, notetaking, and outlining you engage in are all methods of invention—ways of learning about a subject and preparing to write on that subject. Supposedly, a poet named Saint-Pol-Roux even considered sleep a form of invention. When he was asleep, he hung a sign outside his door that read "The poet is working" (Annie Dillard, *The Writing Life* [14], HarperPerennial, 1989).

Most experienced writers depend on an established pattern of invention—a certain routine they go through to prepare for a writing task. For example, according to a recent interview, P. D. James, a well-known British mystery writer, has established the following pattern:

> . . . she prefers to write her novels at the kitchen table, in her dressing gown, before breakfast. But the actual writing takes less time than the planning and plotting, which she does on long solitary walks beside the sea, before making meticulous notes of timetables, room layouts, and so on. Extraordinarily, she writes her big set-piece scenes first, and then wraps the bread-and-butter stuff around them, "rather like knitting."

> —Lynn Barber, "The Cautious Heart of P. D.
> James," *Vanity Fair* (March 1993): 84.

James's combination of writing and thinking, thinking and writing is typical of most writers' invention processes. Whatever else writers do to prepare to write, they nearly always devote some time to writing and thinking about their subject.

You may think of invention as prewriting and thus relegate it to the first of the writing process, assuming that it occurs and then is over once you begin to write. It is true that invention is usually the focus when writers first assume a writing task, just as revision is usually the focus as writers complete a writing task. But invention does not end once writing begins. At any point in the process, a writer may discover additional information and take new directions. In fact, once writing begins, invention and revision often become one: in revision writers discover new insights and change the direction and shape of a text.

In the real world of writing, where writers assume or acquire writing tasks for real reasons, invention is always an integral part of the task. However, in the composition classroom you may write for no real reason other than to fulfill an assignment or to improve your writing. Under these circumstances, different types of invention strategies are often needed. These strategies will help you discover a topic and what you want to say about it.

A number of different invention strategies are described as part of the writing assignments at the end of Chapters 2–6. These include primarily listing, outlining, brainstorming, freewriting, and keeping a journal, the most useful forms of invention and the ones that experienced writers use most often. Here are other strategies that might be useful to you if you are having difficulty deciding on a subject or discovering something to write about your subject.

Asking Reporter's Questions

The five questions that every journalist is taught to ask are Who? What? Where? When? Why? How? Answering these questions can generate a great deal of useful information and may even help you discover something interesting about your subject that could be developed into a thesis. Write as much as you can in answer to each question, forcing yourself to be not only complete but also specific.

Assuming Different Perspectives

Looking at a subject from more than one perspective is a good way to generate information and to ensure that your view of your subject is not one-sided. You can assume different physical perspectives, describing a subject from a variety of viewpoints—front, back, and side; above and below; left and right, close and distant. For example, if you are writing about what goes on in a certain class, you can view the class from different places (front of the room, back of the room, by the door, etc.) or from the teacher's perspective behind the desk or lectern at the front of the room. You can also try out different psychological perspectives, writing about your subject from the viewpoint of one who is objective and then biased or from first a positive and then a negative viewpoint. Finally, you can assume different people's perspectives on a subject. How does a teacher's view of a class differ from a student's? How does an administrator's view differ from both the teacher's and student's? This exercise will result not only in your generating a lot of new ideas and perspectives but will also help you view your subject more intelligently and fairly.

Mapping

Some writers are more visual than others and, therefore, need to draw a picture of what they are thinking. Such writers often benefit from mapping—drawing a visual representation of the text they plan to write. A map is essentially an informal outline. Instead of constructing a linear, sequential list of numbered items, however, you begin mapping by writing a key word or phrase in the center of a blank page.

You then branch out from that central idea, adding other ideas as they occur. The result is a kind of map of your thinking that makes explicit the connections between ideas, the relative importance of different ideas (what supports what), and the order in which these ideas should unfold. Drawing a map or picture of your text may not only help you discover what you want to say but also how you want to say it.

For example, this map began with the phrase "Communication Styles."

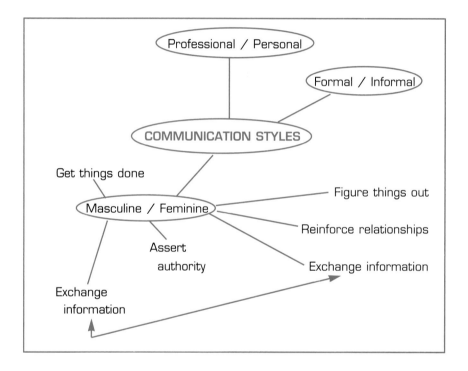

Clustering

This invention strategy is an extension of brainstorming. Once you have generated a brainstorming list, the longer the better, cluster (or connect) those items on the list that are related. For example, if your subject is health care in your community, you might have a long brainstorming list that includes names of individual doctors and health-care facilities as well as items such as "expensive," "overburdened," "tied to insurance," "lots of choice," "long waits," and "unavailable to many." Rather than working with this long list of disparate items, you can cluster, or connect, those that seem related. For example, you could cluster the doctors into different specialties, cluster the hospitals and clinics into public and private, and connect items such as "overburdened" and "long waits." Clustering related items on your list may help you discover patterns or connections that will lead you to a thesis.

Looping

Just as clustering is an extension of brainstorming, looping is an extension of freewriting. When you loop, you freewrite for a brief period, then read what you have written, select from your freewriting one sentence or idea that seems true (or important, interesting, essential, or productive), and use it to begin a new freewriting. This spiraling pattern of writing, reading, focusing, and writing again can continue as long as it is productive. The primary benefit of this type of invention strategy is that it can help you narrow a general topic to a more specific, focused subject for writing.

Using Classical Invention Strategies

The methods of development emphasized throughout this textbook—**comparison/contrast**, **cause and effect**, **classification**, **description**, **narration**, **definition**—can also be used as invention strategies. In fact, they were originally used, in Classical Greece and Rome, primarily for the purpose of invention. Rather than using just one of these approaches, you can apply several of them to your subject if your purpose is to generate new ideas and perspectives on your subject. Thus, if your subject is MTV, you could compare and contrast MTV to other types of television programming: discuss its causes (why did it come into existence) and effects (on young people, on television programming, on advertising, on music, on politics, etc.); classify it (entertainment or advertising, art or business, music or drama); analyze it (why is it successful, what are its main features, how is it structured, which types of music have been adapted to its format); describe it (irreverent, innovative, visual, etc.); or tell a story about it (how the genre was developed or how a certain song was translated into the MTV format). You can readily see what a wealth of information such an exercise might generate. This strategy will help you develop your topic as well as discover what you want to write about.

For additional information about invention, see the Writing Assignments in Chapters 2–8 and the entries on **library research**, **field research**, **narration**, **description**, **comparison/contrast**, **classification**, **cause and effect**, and **exemplification**.

COMPARISON/CONTRAST, PAGE 437

CAUSE AND EFFECT, PAGE 418

CLASSIFICATION, PAGE 422

DESCRIPTION, PAGE 456

NARRATION, PAGE 558

DEFINITION, PAGE 452

LIBRARY RESEARCH, PAGE 534

FIELD RESEARCH, PAGE 493

NARRATION, PAGE 558

DESCRIPTION, PAGE 456

COMPARISON/CONTRAST, PAGE 437

CLASSIFICATION, PAGE 422

CAUSE AND EFFECT, PAGE 418

EXEMPLIFICATION, PAGE 488

LIBRARY RESEARCH

▼

FIELD RESEARCH, PAGE 493 Writers base much of their work on personal experience and on **field research** methods such as observation, interviewing, and surveying by questionnaires to generate primary data. However, few writers know everything that needs to be known about their subjects. Writers also need to develop their thinking and their inner explorations in relation to those of others who have written on the subject. Knowing how to gather information and read for research purposes is important.

Becoming Familiar with the Library

The search for published information can be frustrating and produce disappointingly few sources unless you go about it systematically and know where to look for certain kinds of information. Unfortunately, it is almost impossible to give universally useful advice about information gathering because technology is revolutionizing the way information is stored and accessed. You may have a computer network in your dormitory that gives you access to every university library in the world, or your school's library may use a card catalog and casebound subject indexes.

If your school's information systems are technologically advanced, you need specialized instructions on how to gather information. The discussion of library research here focuses on libraries that operate conventionally.

Fortunately, whether libraries are relatively small community or college libraries or massive research libraries at national research institutes or large universities, they all have essentially the same kinds of *basic* holdings and are organized and catalogued similarly. These common characteristics of all libraries allow you to locate reference materials and track down specific items in the library's collection fairly quickly, regardless of its size.

Visit the Circulation Desk

You can start by stopping at the circulation desk (that is where items are checked out and returned) and ask about the library's regulations and hours. Many circulation desks provide free printed brochures and guides to the library. Here are some of the kinds of information about your library that are available at the circulation desk.

▶ **The hours the library is open.** Some libraries are open twenty-four hours a day; others at different hours during the week and on week-ends. Check also for special holiday and semester- or quarter-break hours.

▶ **The maximum number of items that can be checked out and how long they can be kept.** Usually you will be able to check out a limited number of items. Try to avoid fines for not returning overdue library materials.

▶ **The classification system used to organize the library's collection.** Libraries use either the Dewey Decimal Classification System or the Library of Congress Classification System. See Figure 13 for a general breakdown of the Dewey system and Figure 14 for the Library of Congress System. Each system breaks down further into numerous subclasses. You will need to know the general classification number of an item to locate the general area of the library where it is housed.

▶ **The type of catalog.** Until recently, nearly all libraries used a card catalog, consisting of rows of file cabinets with alphabetically arranged small drawers that contained cards on all the holdings. Every item in the library had at least three cards in the card catalog: one for the author, one for the title, and one or more for the subject. Figure 15 shows examples of cards for Albert Gore's *Earth in the Balance*. In

---

000	General works
100	Philosophy and related disciplines
200	Religion
300	Social sciences
400	Language
500	Pure science
600	Technology (Applied sciences)
700	The arts
800	Literature
900	General geography and history

Figure 13. Dewey Decimal Classification System

General Works	A
Philosophy & Religion	B
Auxiliary Sciences of History	C
History: General & Old World	D
History: America	E–F
Geography. Maps. Anthropology	G
Economics & Business	H–HJ
Sociology	HM–HX
Political Science	J
Law (General)	K
Education	L
Music	M
Fine Arts	N
Language & Literature	P
Science	Q
Medicine	R
Agriculture	S
Technology	T
Military Science	U
Naval Science	V
Bibliography. Library Science	Z

Figure 14. Library of Congress Classification System

recent years, libraries are increasingly using or are planning to convert to a computerized catalog that uses computer terminals to gain access to the library catalog, which is displayed on a computer screen. See Figure 16 for the kind of screen you might get on such a system. A few libraries use a COM Catalog (computer output microform) in which entries are displayed on microfilm or microfiche.

▶ **The extent of the library's collection.** All libraries have books and periodicals (newspapers, magazines, and journals), but some also have film, recordings, works of art, and maps that can be checked out.

▶ The different areas of the library where certain parts of the collection can be found. Different areas in the library house books for different disciplines, a reference section, special collections, a reserve desk where items that professors designate for use in specific courses are kept, current newspaper collection and reading room, a microform

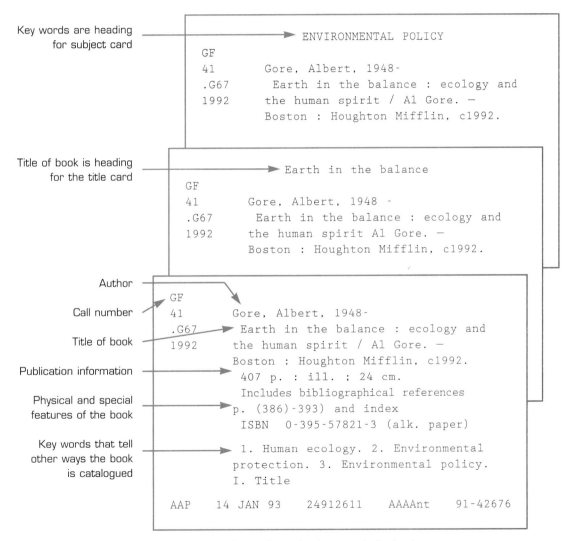

Figure 15. Author, title, and subject cards for book.

```
Search Request: A=GORE,                                              LUIS
BOOK — Record 2 of 4 Entries                                    Long View
┌──────────────────────────── + Screen 1 of 2 ────────────────────────────┐
│                                                                          │
│   Author:                  Gore, Albert, 1948–                           │
│   Title:                   Earth in the balance : ecology and the human spirit │
│   Variant Titles:          Ecology and the human spirit.                 │
│   Publication Information:  Boston : Houghton Mifflin, :1992              │
│   Description:             407 p. : ill. ; 24 cm.                         │
│   Subjects:               Human ecology.                                 │
│                           Environmental protection.                      │
│                           Environmental policy.                          │
│                                           Continued on next screen  ─────┘
```

COMMANDS: BR   Brief View   P   Previous Record
                   F   Forward   I   Index
O   Other Options N   Next Record   H   Help

NEXT COMMAND:

```
Search Request: A=GORE,                                              LUIS
BOOK – Record 2 of 4 Entries                                    Long View
┌──────────────────────────── + Screen 2 of 2 ────────────────────────────┐
│                                                                          │
│   Title:            Earth in the balance : ecology and the human spirit  │
│   Notes:            Includes bibliographical references (p. [386]-393) and index. │
│   ISBN:             0395570213                                           │
│                                                                          │
│   LOCATION:              CALL NUMBER          STATUS:                     │
│   1.Current Literature   GF 41 .G67 1992      Charged, Due: 08/31/93      │
│   Collection                                                             │
│   2.RBD Library          GF 41 .G67 1992      Charged, Due: 07/23/93      │
│                                                                          │
└──────────────────────────────────────────────────────────────────────┘
```

COMMANDS: BR   Brief View   P   Previous Record
                   B   Back   I   Index
O Other Options   N   Next Record   H   Help

NEXT COMMAND:

Figure 16. Computer screen of an on-line catalog showing entry for a book. The entry is from LUIS, the electronic library system of Auburn University. Copyright © 1993 by NOTIS Systems, Inc. All rights reserved.

collection, government documents, and so on. Walk around the library until you have a general idea of where things are located. If the library is large, it is likely to consist of several floors. Check to see if there are maps or guides for the library as well as for each floor.

▶ The location of photocopiers and change machines. Most libraries have photocopiers that enable you to make copies of library material (usually at 10 cents a page). Know where several of these machines are in case there are lines of patrons waiting to use them.

Sign Up for Library Tours and Training Sessions

Once you have a sense of how the library is organized, check back at the circulation desk to see if there are tours or training sessions offered on how to use the library's electronic catalog and other computerized systems, such as computerized databases (on-line searches using telecommunications or CD/ROM—compact disk/read-only memory—using a computerized database stored in your library). Perhaps one of your instructors will arrange to have your class attend an orientation session for the library. If not, sign up on your own for a tour and training session, if they are available and if you feel the need to.

Visit the Reference Section

There will be countless times when you will need to find such things as the winner of the Nobel Peace Prize for a particular year, the year and place of birth of a particular person, the location of some constellation in the Southern Hemisphere or the winter capital of a country located in the Tropics, the atomic weight of a specific element, the job prospects of college graduates in your discipline, and so on—answers to what librarians call "ready reference questions." These kinds of information are easily obtainable in publications that are kept in the reference section, the most used part of any library. Reference works, such as almanacs, atlases, bibliographies, dictionaries, encyclopedias, handbooks, and yearbooks, are chock-full of factual information that is considered accurate and authoritative by virtually all readers.

You should spend some time learning the location of these kinds of reference works and their contents. Introduce yourself to the reference librarians on duty and ask about the scope of the reference section and for any brochures or booklets that may be available to explain your library's reference section. The librarians are usually available most of the hours that the library is open, and they can be very helpful in answering questions about such things as reference sources and electronic databases. Check two or three atlases, encyclopedias, and handbooks, and look around in them to discover the variety of information available.

In addition to such basic ready reference works, you should also become familiar with periodical indexes and abstracting journals, which may be available in print, electronic, or microform versions.

▶ Check periodical indexes for articles appearing in magazines and journals. The most recent information on a subject is usually found in periodicals. In fact, much of that information may never appear in books. Your library subscribes to several dozen, perhaps hundreds, of periodicals, and the indexes are your guide to the articles published in them. General indexes, such as *The Readers' Guide to Periodical Literature*, cover articles appearing in such commercial magazines as *Business Week, Scientific American*, and *Sports Illustrated*. More specialized indexes, such as the *Applied Science & Technology Index, Humanities Index*, and *Index to Government Periodicals*, will lead you to articles on more technical and advanced subjects. Figure 17 illustrates typical entries in the *Humanities Index*. Figure 18 explains how to read an entry from the *Humanities Index*.

▶ Check newspaper indexes for news articles appearing in major newspapers. *The New York Times Index* lists all the articles published in *The New York Times* since 1851. *The National Newspaper Index*, available only in microform or on a computer terminal, indexes articles from *The New York Times, Wall Street Journal, Christian Science Monitor*, and *Los Angeles Times*. *NewsBank* goes beyond indexing and reproduces news articles from over 450 newspapers.

▶ Check abstracting journals not only to find articles but also abstracts (short summaries) of the articles. Abstracting journals, which are available in both print and electronic forms, cover most disciplines. They are useful because they include abstracts (short summaries) of each article as well as its bibliographical citation. Their titles indicate their coverage. *Biological Abstracts, Chemical Abstracts, Forestry Abstracts, Pollution Abstracts, Psychology Abstracts* are only a few of the many that are available. Figure 19 shows a typical entry from *Biological Abstracts*.

Reading for Research

To conduct research, especially library research, it is essential that you be able to read well, for reading gives you the opportunity to relate your thinking to that of others who have written on the subject.

Inexpert readers are likely to read all texts the same way and without any investigative method or direction. To them, reading is a

Indians in literature
See also
Indian theater
Fragments and Ojibwe stories: narrative strategies in Louise Erdrich's Love medicine. I. A. Schultz. bibl *Coll Lit* 18:80-95 O '91
Indians playing Indians. K. Lincoln *MELUS* 16-91-8 Fall '89/'90
A lament for the vanishing. L. R. Bowden, *Cross Curr* 41:107-15 Spr '91
MELUS interview: Hanay Geioganah V. Lincoln *MELUS* 16:69–81 Fall '89/'90
MELUS interview: William Yellow Robe. R. Uno. *MELUS* 16:83-90 Fall '89/'90
New warrior, new West: history and advocacy in James Welsh's The Indian lawyer [review article] R. F. Gish. *Am Indian* Q 15:369-74 Summ '91
The other within: Indianization on The Oregon trail, P. G. Terrie. *N Engl* Q 64:376-92 S '91
Postmodernism, native American literature and the real: the Silko-Erdrich controversy, S. P. Castillo. *Mass Rev* 32:285-94 Summ '91
Sleeping with a savage: deculturation in Moby-Dick. R. Martin, bibl *ATQ* ns5:195-203 S '91
Spotted cattle and deer: spirit guides and symbols of endurance and healing in Ceremony. S. Blumenthal. *Am Indian* Q 14:367-77 Fall '90
The two worlds of Durango Mendoza's Summer water and Shirley. E. Benzinger and G. R. Benzinger, Jr. *Stud Short Fict* 27:587–90 Fall '90
Vanishing Americans: gender, empire, and new historicism. L. Romero. *Am Lit* 63:385-404 S '91
Word medicine: storytelling and magic realism in James Welch's Fools Crow. R. F. Gish. *Am Indian Q* 14:349-54 Fall '90
Indians in motion pictures
Boo the right thing. B. Israel. il *Am Film* 16:64 Ag '91
Costnerama. A. L. J. James, *Christ Crisis* 51:78 Mr 18 '91 *Discussion* 51:142–3 My 13'91
Dances With Wolves. L. R. Bowden. *Cross Curr* 41:391-6 Fall '91
Indian love call. R. Grenier. *Commentary* 91:46-50 Mr '91
Oscar eaten by wolves. W. M. Sarf. Il *Film Comment* 27:62-4+ N/D '91

Figure 17. Typical entries in the *Humanities Index*. Source: *Humanities Index*, April 1991 to March 1992. New York: H. W. Wilson, 1992. 573. Copyright © 1992 by the H. W. Wilson Company and reproduced by permission of the publisher.

simple task. But reading for research purposes is not merely a matter of running your eyes over a text and through some kind of visual osmosis passively absorb its meaning. Nor is reading simply a process of extracting the fixed and identifiable meanings that reside exclusively in a text as if they were artifacts to be uncovered.

SAMPLE ENTRY

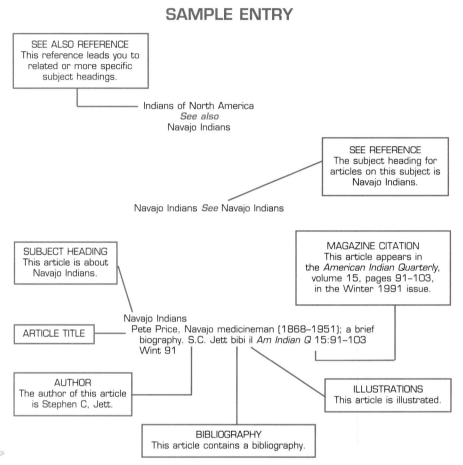

Figure 18. Explanation of index entry. Source: *Humanities Index*, April 1991 to March 1992. New York H. W. Wilson, 1992. Copyright © 1992 by the H.W. Wilson Company and reproduced by permission of the publisher.

In reading to research, you must engage intellectually with a text, seeking to grasp the ideas the writer wishes to transmit and the basis for the writer's belief in those ideas, evaluating the writer's view of reality, relating the material to your own cultural, political, and emotional experiences and beliefs and to your own purposes, and integrating new information and insights with other texts you have read and with what you already know. In short, when you read for research purposes you are an active creator of whatever meaning, pleasure, and value a text has. You are participating in a social process, carrying on a silent conversation with the writer about the text.

Reference Number — Author — Author's Address

Journal, Volume, (Issue), Pages, Year — Article Title — Abstract

90236. KAUFMANN, DAVID L. (Albert Einstein Coll. Med., Bronx, N.Y. 10461.) EINSTEIN Q J BIOL MED 9(4): 141–147. 1992. **Case study: Medical paternalism and the treatment of psychiatric patients.**—The case to be considered in this article provides a concrete example of some of the ethical dilemmas facing doctors as a result of the changing nature of the doctor–patient relationship. Specifically, it raises the issue of the place of the historical medical model of "paternalism" in modern medicine and its particular relevance to psychiatry, where questions of patient competence and autonomy can be particularly complex and confusing. In order to clarify some of these questions, the present article attempts a philosophical analysis of the basic concepts and terminology that underlie these kinds of cases and structure the ethical problems which may develop from them. The conceptual distinctions and framework derived from this analysis are then applied to the specific case under consideration with the aim of developing a prescriptive recommendation and informing the abstract principles involved with practical meaning and substance.

Figure 19. Entry from *Biological Abstracts*, Volume 94, 1992. 94(8): AB-1059. Copyright © 1992 by Biological Abstracts, Inc. and reproduced by permission of the publisher.

Although it is impossible to predict the many kinds of responses to a text, there are remarkably similar strategies and conventions writers and readers share in constructing texts. Most accomplished writers take great care in using these conventions to help readers interact with their texts, which makes reading their texts comparatively easy. But whether a text is well written or not, the application of a few basic strategies can lead to successful reading:

❖ Explore the text to discover its subject, scope, and purpose.

❖ Determine the overall organization of the text.

❖ Read the text more intensively to synthesize it with your own thinking.

Used flexibly, these strategies help you read efficiently. Used rigidly, they can impede the development of critical reading skills. Not applied at all, your reading can go rough no matter how slowly or fast you read, how carefully you look at each word, phrase, and sentence, or how diligently you try to reread a passage.

Exploring the Text

Much of your reading is to acquire additional information and to understand viewpoints that you do not have or of which you are only vaguely aware. Thus, when you read as part of your research, you usually have an interest in the subject or topic treated by the text.

Exploring a text helps you learn what to expect in it, decide whether you want to read it more thoroughly, and, if so, prepare to read it. When exploring a lengthy text, set aside at least an hour of uninterrupted time so you can really get into it. Of course, you have to read the entire text to understand everything that is going on, but during the first hour or so you can become immersed in the text.

Exploring consists of scanning the text fairly quickly to find the answers to these questions:

▶ **What is the significance of the title?** The title usually identifies the topic or basic points of the text and sometimes indicates the writer's general purpose or intentions.

▶ **Who is the writer and what do you know about him or her?** Knowing the writer's credentials sometimes helps you determine the credibility of the text. It also enables you to characterize the source's authority in case you cite him or her in your own writing. The author of a book is identified on the title page. Sometimes the author's professional affiliation and title are also given on the title page. Frequently the inside flap of a dust jacket or a paperback's back cover contains a brief note about the author's background and credentials. In magazines and collections of essays, the author's credentials are sometimes given in notes at the beginning or end of the essay or article.

▶ **What is the date of the text?** The contents may be correct but could be out of date. Does the text contain up-to-date information? The publication date is important when you write about a subject that changes quickly. The date of a book or pamphlet is usually given on the title page, on the back of the title page, or on a separate copyright page. Essays and articles appear in magazines that carry the issue date on the front cover or on the table of contents page.

▶ **What is the major thesis, theme, or idea?** The title contains key words that suggest the important concepts that are treated in the text. In books and formal reports, the abstract, preface, introduction, and closing usually state the thesis and contain statements about the writer's reasons for writing the text, his or her objectives, the rationale or justification for the research reported or the topic treated, and sometimes the importance or significance of his or her work. In essays and articles, the introduction and closing usually express these same things.

▶ What are the writer's purposes or objectives? Writers write primarily because something has motivated them to do so, and you will need to consider the text's purpose so you can better analyze and evaluate the points the writer makes. Is the writer trying to provide general enlightenment on how government regulations affect businesses? Is the writer exploring a specific issue such as the possible impact of proposed family-leave legislation on employers, employees, families of employees, or on government agencies that would be charged with implementing and administering the legislation once it is enacted? Does the writer take a position on a proposed family-leave plan and give reasons for supporting or opposing it? Is the writer showing or dramatizing in literary form the experience of a family in which one or more members are faced with choosing between caring for another family member or making arrangements for somebody else to care for the family member? Is the writer explaining how a specific family-leave proposal was developed? Is the writer providing instructions on how to apply for family leave in an organization that already has such a plan? Is the writer offering advice on how an organization can fund or implement a family-leave policy of its own? Knowing the writer's purpose helps you understand the role of the writer and the role you are invited to take while reading the text. As our students occasionally remark, "Writers usually have designs on their readers, and it's best to know what they are."

Some writers state their purpose and objectives explicitly in the title of their text. "Why We Should Adopt Plan C" indicates that the writer is going to attempt to persuade you to adopt a specific course of action. Often writers identify their purpose in the opening of the text. Other writers do not state their purpose and objectives directly, leaving you to infer the purpose from your reading of the text.

▶ How is the text organized? Virtually all writers follow some organizational pattern as they write their texts. Some texts are designed to be read linearly or serially, primarily from beginning to end. Others are designed so that readers can gain access to specific information directly by going straight to a particular block of information. Books, formal reports, and pamphlets provide a table of contents that lists the main sections, sometimes the subsections, and the page on which each section begins. The writers of books and reports usually explain in a preface or introduction the rationale for organizing their information and ideas. The writers of essays and articles may explain in their introduction the way their text is organized.

Most informative texts (for example, books, chapters of books, reports, articles, essays, and letters) are presented straightforwardly, making it fairly easy to get an overall view of the writer's purpose, thesis, and plan. Exploring literary texts (for example, poems, novels, short stories, plays) is different because their purposes and formats are different. The best way to explore a literary text is to read it once just to experience it, to get a feel for it, to enjoy it. Just as when you watch a movie or a television program, you must be willing to become part of the world created by the author.

The purpose of exploring a text is to get an overview of the material. It may seem to be delaying unnecessarily the real event of reading, but we assure you that it is not. Exploring makes you concentrate on the text, provides you with a good sense of the writer's purpose and main points, and alerts you to the possibilities for meanings that the text may have for you.

Determining the Organizational Design of the Text

All texts are organized. That is, the writer does not simply throw together a random set of statements and call them a text. Rather, the writer selects and arranges the information related to her or his thesis or main point into a pattern that can be the design of an entire text or a piece of a text. Seldom will you come across a text that is a collection of isolated bits of information. The design is there, at least in the mind of the writer, even if some readers have difficulty recognizing the parts that make up the text or perceiving the pattern by which the parts are organized.

Understanding how a text is organized prepares you for a closer, more careful reading of the text. You will be able to anticipate what is coming next and how it relates to what has gone before and to what is coming. You will have a mental road map of the text that will enable you to find your way through the text, avoiding having to read each sentence or paragraph as if it were an unfamiliar street of unknown origin, length, or destination. You will be able to use the writer's organizational pattern to organize your own memory of the text.

The organization of informative texts is almost always hierarchical. The thesis or main point is usually stated explicitly at the beginning. The following sections or paragraphs explain or support the thesis by providing specific facts and ideas. Each chapter or section contains its own thesis or central idea, which relates both to the larger thesis of the entire text and to the main ideas of its own stretch of text.

Many paragraphs will have a topic sentence that presents a specific point related to the thesis. Often the topic sentence is the first sentence of the paragraph.

In your exploration of a text, you were probably able to identify its general organization. Informative texts are commonly designed into hierarchical arrangements that include the following organizational patterns: **classification** by categories, **comparison/contrast** of a subject, **description** of a subject, explanation of a process, **narration** of an event, the relationship of **cause and effect**, statement of a problem and analysis of possible solutions, **thesis** and support, and so on. The list is not complete, and writers may use variations and combinations of these typical patterns. The table of contents, preface, and introduction are often packed with clues about what organizational patterns to expect. Sometimes the closing contains a summary of the main points, the order they were treated, and certain organizational clue words. Here are some suggestions on how to determine organization:

CLASSIFICATION, PAGE 422

COMPARISON / CONTRAST, PAGE 437

DESCRIPTION, PAGE 456

NARRATION, PAGE 558

CAUSE AND EFFECT, PAGE 418

THESIS, PAGE 599

▶ Analyze the title of the text to see if it contains clues that suggest an organizational pattern. Sometimes the title will contain words such as *classification, comparison, contrast, definition, description, process*, and similar words derived from them.

▶ Read carefully the opening (including the preface or abstract if there is one) and closing for statements concerning the way the text is organized. If the text is divided into large sections, analyze their subtitles and read their openings and closings, too.

▶ Look for headings and subheadings that signal topics, key ideas, or organizational patterns. These signals will help bring into focus the scope and the major ideas of the text.

▶ Read the first sentence of each paragraph. That is likely to be where the main idea of the paragraph and information on how it is organized can be found.

▶ Use your familiarity with conventions of genre. The organizational patterns of literary texts, such as novels, short stories, poems, songs, and plays, can be classified into two major types. The first type consists of relatively stable conventional patterns that are associated with various genres, such as the sonnet, the ballad, the picaresque novel, the revenge tragedy, the epic, reggae. Although there are many variations and much mixing of genres, knowledge of genres—which becomes quite extensive from reading more and more literature and responding to texts—guides a reader's expectations about how certain texts are organized. For example, prior knowledge about Greek tragedy enables a reader to anticipate what kinds of events are likely to occur and in what order. Familiarity with Petrarchan or Italian sonnets guides a reader's expectations about how the two major parts of the poem relate.

The second type of organizational pattern consists of those unpredictable texts in which the writer has purposefully chosen to go against some specific convention or to use a traditional technique in some new or unusual way, attempting to disrupt the normal reading processes to force readers into exploring new kinds of relationships between elements of a text. But even in these experimental texts, the content is usually arranged in some systematic—although original—way.

Regardless of the types of texts you read, being familiar with a wide variety of organizational patterns makes it easier to adjust your reading expectations to fit the expectations you have about how a specific text is organized. Once you determine the organizational design of a text, it will be easier for you to locate major ideas, follow the writer better through development of the topic, remember subordinate ideas and minor details, and understand how the sections of the text relate to one another. When you can do these things, your reading will be more purposeful and enjoyable.

Reading the Text Intensively

Once you possess an overview of the text provided by exploring it and by determining its organizational design, you are anchored in its social circumstances and writing context, which gives you a good sense of what is being said to whom and for what purpose and how it is presented. You now have a framework that enables you to work intensively with the text, reading and, if necessary, rereading passages slowly without getting lost among the details or losing the direction the text is taking.

Marking and annotating a text help you work with it—and in some ways rewrite it to make it your own. Anytime you circle an important word or underline a key phrase or statement, you change the emphasis of those elements. When you write a note in the margin in response to something you read, you add to the text. When you paraphrase a passage, you rewrite it. When you mark points with which you agree or disagree, you close the distance between the writer's text and your own developing mental text.

There are several strategies for marking and annotating text. Never use these strategies on texts from the library. Make any annotations of library texts on Post-Its or on photocopies.

▶ **Underlining or circling important words and key terms and phrases.** Often writers themselves emphasize certain words and phrases by using different typefaces, underlining, and all capital letters.

▶ **Numbering the order of ideas and supporting points.** Writers employ a variety of organizational patterns, and the awareness of these patterns helps readers understand more fully the writer's information.

▶ **Bracketing unfamiliar words and providing a synonym in the margin after you have looked the term up in a dictionary or encyclopedia.** It is essential that you understand the meaning of words as they are used in context.

▶ **Placing some kind of distinguishing check mark in the margin next to statements with which you agree or disagree.** This is a useful way to mark significant material for future reference or review. Your research invariably produces answers to questions, and these answers in turn are likely to create new questions. Your own knowledge and beliefs are often modified by this process, and you need a way to locate important points for consideration.

▶ **Drawing a vertical line in the margin next to passages that you think you might want to quote or paraphrase.**

▶ **Writing outlines or paraphrases in the margin.**

Marking and annotating a text in these ways will make reviewing it much easier, especially if you do not return to it for several days.

Integrating Sources into Your Text

Effectively integrating source material into a text requires some effort and knowledge on your part. First, you must decide how to present the source material you want to include. Will you summarize it, paraphrase it, or quote it? Here are some general guidelines.

▶ *Summarize* material that is pertinent but is too long to paraphrase or too uninteresting to quote. In a summary you include only the

main idea and major supporting points of the source material, expressing them in your own words. For example, Rachel Carson in the selection from *Silent Spring* that is on pages 332–336 of this textbook
summarizes Justice William O. Douglas's book *My Wilderness: East to
Katahdin,* providing her readers with a brief overview of the events in
Douglas's book so that they can understand how it relates to and supports her own arguments. You may want to summarize articles or
chapters from books for your readers for the same reason. You may
also choose to summarize if the material in question is not particularly
well written.

▶ *Paraphrase* brief passages that include important information but
are not stated in language that is unusually forceful, interesting, or
memorable. In a paraphrase you include all of the ideas and information in the original but put them in your own words. Thus, you do not
want to paraphrase very long passages.

▶ *Quote* material if it is (1) not too long, (2) from a source that has
a great deal of credibility, or (3) is stated in language that is unusually
forceful, interesting, or memorable. In other words, you should quote
material when it is important to retain the original language—language
that is significant either because of who said it or how it is said.

Introducing Sources

Whether they are summarizing, paraphrasing, or quoting, careful writers introduce all source material by identifying the source. This may be
done by citing the author's name (or, if the name is not known or not
significant, the title of the source) as in the examples below:

> According to Alexander Harris, whose house
> includes a solar energy system, heating with solar
> energy is not always satisfactory. (summary)

> Sarah Wyatt, an industrial engineer, agreed that
> solar energy systems require constant supervision if
> they are to function properly. (paraphrase)

> Taylor Moore, Director of the Federal Bureau of
> Energy Research, stated: "Solar energy is not the solu-
> tion to all of our energy problems, but it is a viable

```
alternative to the use of fossil fuels for heating
homes and commercial buildings in the Southwestern
regions of our country." (quotation)
```

In each of these examples a reader knows exactly where the source material begins and knows the name of the person whose words are being summarized, paraphrased, or quoted. In the case of quotations, you may include the name at the end rather than the beginning because the initial quotation marks signal the beginning of the source material:

```
"Solar energy is not the solution to all of our
energy problems, but it is a viable alternative to the
use of fossil fuels for heating homes and commercial
buildings in the Southwestern regions of our country,"
stated Taylor Moore, Director of the Federal Bureau of
Energy Research. (quotation)
```

As these examples illustrate, you can also characterize a source's authority and credibility by identifying his or her position, profession, or status.

Punctuating Quotations

Summaries and paraphrases are not difficult to integrate into a text because a writer is using his or her own words. However, quotations must not only be integrated carefully into the existing text but must also be punctuated correctly (that is, according to certain conventions of punctuation). The only general punctuation rule that applies to all quotations is to place double quotation marks around the quoted material. However, there are four types of quotations, each of which requires slightly different conventions of punctuation.

Quotations that are separated from the sentence in which they appear: Quotations may be punctuated as if they are separate sentences even though they appear as part of your own sentence. These quotations are (1) introduced, interrupted, or followed by a brief citation, (2) begin with a capital letter, and (3) are separated from the rest of the sentence by a comma or colon:

```
        According to Vice President Al Gore, "We cannot
    simply create larger and larger quantities of waste and
    dump it into the environment and pretend that it
    doesn't matter."

        Vice President Gore states: "We cannot simply create
    larger and larger quantities of waste and dump it into the
    environment and pretend that it doesn't matter."

        "We cannot simply create larger and larger quanti-
    ties of waste and dump it into the environment," says
    Gore, "and pretend that it doesn't matter."

        We cannot simply create larger and larger quanti-
    ties of waste and dump it into the environment and pre-
    tend that it doesn't matter," argues Vice President
    Gore (159).
```

Quotations that are integrated into the sentence in which they appear: Other quotations become part of your own sentence. They are usually introduced by the word *that* and do not begin with a capital letter, as in the following example:

```
        Vice President Gore argues that "we cannot simply
    create larger and larger quantities of waste and dump it
    into the environment and pretend that it doesn't matter."
```

Occasionally, a quotation will have to be modified before it can be smoothly integrated into your sentence. In the following example notice how the quotation is modified when it becomes part of the writer's own sentence:

```
        Vice President Gore stated: "I have found over-
    whelming public enthusiasm for the process."

        Vice President Gore stated that he has "found
    overwhelming public enthusiasm for the process."
```

In the second sentence, the subject of the quoted sentence, *I*, is changed to *he* so that the resulting sentence will not be confusing. Notice what happens if this change is not made:

```
Vice President Gore stated that "I have found
overwhelming public enthusiasm for the process."
```

This sentence is not only awkward but also confusing because it is not clear whether *I* refers to the writer or to Vice President Gore.

Quotations that are more than four lines long: Separate long quotations (those that are more than four lines) from your own text by indenting each line in the quotation ten spaces from the left margin. These long, indented quotations are also often introduced by a colon, as in the following example:

```
Recycling is often pointed to as the solution to
waste management. However, as Vice President Al Gore
points out, recycling is not always the answer:

    In conducting workshops in Tennessee and
    hearings in Washington in recycling, I have found
    overwhelming public enthusiasm for the process.
    But I have also found tremendous disappointment
    among individuals and groups who have dutifully
    collected and sorted those elements of their
    municipal waste that they knew could be prof-
    itably recycled, only to find that it was impos-
    sible to find buyers for the material. (159)
```

Notice that quotation marks are not used when a long quote is indented as it is in this example.

There are three other minor rules of punctuation that you need to know in working with quotations:

▶ Use ellipsis points to indicate omission. You may omit part of a quotation if you indicate the omission by the use of ellipsis (three spaced periods).

```
Gore argues that "we cannot simply create larger
and larger quantities of waste and . . . pretend it
doesn't matter."
```

▶ Use square brackets to indicate addition. You may add words to a quotation to make it clearer if you indicate the addition by the use of square brackets.

> Gore states that he has "found overwhelming public enthusiasm for the process [of recycling]."

> According to Gore, "These states [Washington and New Jersey] have achieved high rates of recycling."

▶ Use single quotation marks to indicate a quotation within a quotation. If the person you are quoting is quoting someone else or has used double quotation marks for any other reason, you indicate this double quotation by using single quotation marks to enclose the inside quotation.

> According to Rachel Carson, "When Justice Douglas visited the area in 1959, the year of the spraying, he was shocked to see the shriveled and dying willows--the 'vast, incredible damage.'"

> Gore points out that "we have come to think of almost any natural resource as 'going to waste' if we have failed to develop it."

Acknowledging Sources

Sources must not only be located, evaluated, integrated, and punctuated but also acknowledged. You must acknowledge any source that you use unless the information you obtained from the source is general knowledge that is available from multiple sources. For example, Michio Kaku includes in his article "War and the Environment" (see pages 337–340 of this textbook) information about the dropping of the atomic bomb on Hiroshima that is generally known and could be found in a number of sources including encyclopedias. It is, therefore, not necessary to acknowledge him if you include that information in an essay or report of your own. However, if you summarize his own arguments in which he compares Hiroshima to the Gulf War or if you quote him directly, you must, of course, acknowledge him as the source.

The conventions by which we acknowledge sources in writing are known as **documentation**. There are a number of different docu-

DOCUMENTATION, PAGE 460

mentation styles, each of which involves slightly different conventions. Writers use the style that is appropriate for their own profession or discipline. However, familiarity with one style usually makes it easy to adapt to a different style because all of them operate on the same general principles. It is only in specifics that they differ. The style we use in this book is based on the *MLA Handbook for Writers of Research Papers*, 3rd ed. MLA documentation, like most styles used today, includes two forms of documentation for each source: in-text parenthetical citations and the list of works cited. The two citations work together to provide readers with the information they need to identify, verify, or locate sources.

Parenthetical Documentation

The first citation occurs in the form of a brief parenthetical note found in the text of the paper immediately after the source material. Included in the parentheses are the name of the author, if you did not use it to introduce the source material (as we suggest), and the page number of the original source from which you took the quoted, summarized, or paraphrased material. If you are including references to several works by the same writer, you will also need to include within the parentheses a shortened version of the title, as these examples illustrate:

> According to Rachel Carson, "Our attitude toward plants is a singularly narrow one" (63).

> "Our attitude toward plants is a singularly narrow one" (Carson 63).

> Carson argues that "our attitude toward plants is a singularly narrow one" (Silent Spring 63).

Note that the parenthetical citation follows the quotation marks but precedes the period that ends the sentence. If, however, the sentence being quoted is a question or exclamation, the question mark or exclamation point occurs before the final quotation marks, but the sentence still ends with a period.

> Patricia Parker asks, "Will more corporate officers go to jail in the next decade?" (39).

Long indented quotations do not require quotation marks because being indented sets them off from the surrounding text. Thus, readers know where they begin and end. An indented quotation is followed by the usual parenthetical citation, but it comes after the terminal punctuation (even if it is just a period).

> In spite of the massive environmental destruction caused by the Gulf War, Michio Kaku is hopeful about the future:
>
>> Throughout recorded history, nations have engaged in predatory wars in the quest to secure power, resources, and wealth. But we may now be seeing the dawning of a New Environmental Order, where the overarching necessity of controlling worldwide pollution and environmental desecration will force unwilling nations to cooperate on an unprecedented basis. (93)

Summarized and paraphrased material is also followed by a parenthetical citation. As in documenting quotations, you include in the parentheses the name of the author, if it is not used to introduce the source material, and the page number. It is, however, much better to use the author's name at the beginning of the summary or paraphrase. Otherwise, your readers will have no way of knowing where the source material begins since you will not be using quotation marks.

> Patricia Parker points out that prosecution of environmental criminals is increasing and argues that sentencing is an effective deterrent (35-39).

List of Works Cited

The second part of the documentation system consists of compiling a list of works cited to place at the end of your paper. The list of works cited differs from a bibliography primarily in that it is limited to those sources that you actually cite in your paper. It works with the parenthetical citations to provide your reader with complete publication data on each source you cite. A reader will know the author's name and the page number from your introduction of your source and the parenthetical citation you have included. The list of works cited will supply the following basic information:

Author's name.

Title of source.

Publication history (place of publication, publisher, and date of publication).

The list of works cited is arranged alphabetically, according to author's last name, which is written first. The first line of each entry is *not* indented, but succeeding lines are (this is known as hanging indention). Thus, readers can use the name of the author that is given in the text of your paper to look up the source in the list of works cited if they want additional information.

The format of an entry differs, depending on the source. In general, books follow one format, and articles from magazines and journals follow another. Below you will find examples of these two general types of entries.

```
Carson, Rachel. Silent Spring. Boston: Houghton
     Mifflin, 1962.
Kaku, Michio. "War and the Environment." Audubon
     Sept.-Oct. 1991: 91-93.
Webster, Martin. Personal interview. 21 May 1992.
```

In general, each major part of an entry is followed by a period. Thus, you put a period after the author's name, after the title, and at the end of the entry, after the publication history. For specific examples of different types of entries, see **documentation**.

DOCUMENTATION, PAGE 460

Brief Summary

1. Introduce all source material by using the author's name or the title of the source.

2. Place immediately after the source material a parenthetical citation that includes the page number(s) of the original in which the source material can be found.

3. Include in the list of Works Cited an entry that includes the name of the author(s), the title of the source, and the publication data.

NARRATION

▼

People are surrounded by narration, the relating of a sequence of events or actions, the telling of stories. There is a great deal of narration—arranged largely in chronological order so that readers see events as they happened—in newspaper and magazine articles, short stories, novels, biographies and autobiographies, and histories and case studies.

Although narration is probably the simplest method of organizing information, it has a wide range of functions. A frequent use of narration is to report an event or to set the record straight about exactly what happened in the past. The following account describes one of several incidents in which the United States military failed to recognize the imminent Japanese attack on Pearl Harbor.

> At almost this same moment another warning was being reported to the Army—and also discounted—from the Opana outpost at Kahuku Point on the northern tip of Oahu. Private George Elliott, Jr., of the 515th Signal Aircraft Warning Service, a recent transfer from the Air Corps, had seen a large blip on his radar unit at 7:06 A.M. He called over Private Joseph Lockhart, who had much more experience. It was the largest group Lockhart had ever seen on the oscilloscope and looked like two main pulses. He figured something had gone wrong with the machine, but after a check agreed with Elliott that it was really a large flight of planes.
>
> By now Elliott had located the blip on the plotting board: 137 miles to the north, 3 degrees east. He was so excited that he suggested they call the Information Center at Fort Shafter. At first Lockhart was reluctant but finally let his assistant make the call. The switchboard operator at the Information Center could find no one on duty except a pilot named Kermit Tyler. When told that the blips were getting bigger and that the planes were now only ninety miles from Oahu, Tyler said, "Don't worry about it," and hung up—the blips must represent the flight of Flying Fortresses coming in from the mainland or planes from a carrier.
>
> —John Toland, *The Rising Sun: The Decline and Fall of the Japanese Empire 1936-1945*, Vol. 1 (New York: Random House, 1970): 261.

This brief passage is a good example of narration.

▶ The passage presents the sequence of events in the order in which they occurred. The order is made clear by the use of expressions that show time relationships: "At almost the same moment," "at 7:06 a.m.," "but after a check," "By now," "At first," "but finally when told that," and "the planes were now only ninety miles from Oahu."

▶ The passage is packed with specific details. The details show the action in terms of specific locations and of specific persons and their relationships with others, making the narration vivid and believable and helping readers get involved in the story: what is happening? where and when are things happening? to whom are these things happening?

▶ The narration has a purpose. It supports the thesis that the U. S. military ignored several warnings that a Japanese aerial attack might be imminent.

Another major use of narration is to describe action, especially how equipment works or how natural or synthetic processes occur. In this example, the writer's purpose is to explain how laser printers work:

> The laser printer is the most significant development in output technology of the past 20 years. Unlike line, daisy-wheel, and dot-matrix printers, which print a line at a time, laser printers store a full page of characters (or dots in an image) before the printing begins. To create a page, the computer sends signals to the printer, which shines a laser at a mirror system that scans across a charged drum. Whenever the beam strikes the drum, it removes the charge. The drum then rotates through a toner chamber filled with thermoplastic particles. The toner particles stick to the negatively charged areas of the drum in the pattern of characters, lines, or other elements the computer has transmitted and the laser beam mapped.
> Once the drum is coated with toner in the appropriate locations, a piece of paper is pulled across a so-called transfer corona wire, which imports a positive electrical charge. The paper then passes across the toner-coated drum. The positive charge on the paper attracts the toner in the same position it occupied on the drum. The final phase of the process involves fusing the toner to the paper with a set of high-temperature rollers.
>
> —Richard Golub and Eric Brus, eds. *The Almanac of Science and Technology* (Boston: Harcourt Brace Jovanovich, 1990): 226.

The difference between this passage and the earlier one is not in the order of the details, but in purpose. Here, the purpose is to explain what something does or how it works. Describing a process well makes it seem as if readers had witnessed a demonstration of the process.

Here are a few things to keep in mind when writing narration:

▶ Break the actions or series of events into major steps or phases. Use paragraphing to reflect the major divisions.

FORECASTING STATEMENTS, PAGE 503

TRANSITIONS, PAGE 612

HEADINGS, PAGE 526

GRAPHICS, PAGE 519

▶ If the narration is lengthy or complicated, use **forecasting statements**, **transitions**, and **headings** and other format features to help readers follow the narration.

▶ Use **graphics** (pictures and flowcharts) when possible.

PACE
▼

Pace refers to the speed or tempo at which information is presented to the reader. A well-paced text feeds information slowly enough that the reader is able to understand it easily but fast enough that the reader does not feel bored, and it presents important ideas when the reader is ready for them.

A page is filled with words—one after another—arranged left to right in lines across the page and with lines arranged from top to bottom down the page. The fact that the words and lines seem fixed on the page might suggest that writing is static and cannot be paced. However, an experienced writer controls the speed at which the readers' eyes and minds travel into, through, and around the writing.

Reading is a relatively unconscious activity, and readers are usually unaware of pace unless it is faulty. The normal silent reading speed for most readers of conventional nonfiction prose is about four words per second or an 8½ × 11-inch page of double-spaced typewritten text in little over a minute (G. W. McConkie, *Eye Movements and Perception During Reading* [Technical Report No. 229], Champaign, IL: University of Illinois Center for the Study of Reading, 1982). Several factors influence how much faster or slower a reader moves through a particular text. Obviously, inept writing can pose problems for readers. Unfamiliar or vague words, unclear pronoun references, and poor sentence structure can unintentionally slow the reading to a crawl or bring it to a standstill. The reader who is forced to slow the pace for such reasons is likely to lose interest and become less receptive. Densely packed passages can present too much information too fast for the reader to assimilate easily. The reader is likely to miss something important or to become exasperated with having to reread a passage in an attempt to pick out the main and supporting ideas. But the writer also can purposely slow the pace when important and complex concepts are being presented or can intentionally quicken the pace when it seems appropriate to do so, as when familiar information is being given straightforwardly or when description or narrative should move rapidly. The proper pace is one that enables readers to grasp new information quickly and work it into their minds, efficiently relating it to what they already know or have already read.

The pace becomes tortuously slow if the passage inches along in a series of short sentences that present information in bits and pieces:

> Alice is my aunt. She is retired. But her day is full. She goes to exercise class every morning. She also is a volunteer in a hospital gift shop for two hours every morning. She walks two miles outdoors every afternoon. She walks outdoors whether it is rainy or sunny.

Choppy, choppy, choppy. This passage has too many stop-and-go points and too many little unnecessary words between significant information. If this snail's pace were to continue much longer, the reader would soon tire. Consolidating the seven sentences into three links the significant information more closely, and getting rid of several unnecessary words shortens and streamlines the passage, as does this version that says the same thing in ten fewer words (a 20 percent reduction):

> Although my aunt Alice is retired, her day is full. Every morning she goes to an exercise class and works as a volunteer for two hours in a hospital gift shop. Every afternoon in rain or sun she walks two miles outdoors.

The significant information and details are necessary, and they are still there. It is all those little unnecessary words and periods which drag the pace to a crawl that have been removed.

A series of very short sentences is not always bad. But the series must be kept short, must play off an established sequence of longer sentences, and must be used sparingly. Such sentences can be used effectively to change the pace from the established normal reading or speaking speed for a rhetorical effect, such as asserting emphatic statements. Note how Lewis Thomas, a noted physician, medical researcher, and bestselling author, alters the pace of the following passage with three very short sentences near the end. The effect may be subtle, but it is definitely there. It is not elusive; it can be sensed and felt. To get the full effect of the change of pace, read the paragraph aloud.

> The argument rests, of course, on certain assumptions about the core of human beings, and is necessarily speculative. You have to agree in advance that man is fundamentally a bad lot, out for himself alone, displaying such graces as affection and compassion only as learned habits. If you take this view, the story of the Iks can be used to confirm it. These people seem to be living together, clustered in small, dense villages, but they are really solitary, unrelated individuals with no evident use for each other. They talk, but only to make ill-tempered demands and cold refusals. They share nothing. They never sing. They turn the children out to forage as soon as they can walk, and desert the elders to starve whenever they can, and the foraging children snatch food from the mouths of the helpless elders. It is a mean society.
>
> —"The Iks," in *The Lives of a Cell: Notes of a Biology Watcher* (New York: Viking Press, 1974): 107–108.

The change of pace is especially noticeable when we examine the length of the sentences in the paragraph. The paragraph has nine sentences totaling 148 words—an average of 16.5 words per sentence. The average, by the way, means little, as you will see, for only two sentences (the first sentence with 18 words, and third sentence with 16 words) are close to the average. The other sentences range from 3 words to 35. The number of words per sentence is 18, 28, 16, 26, 11, 3, 3, 35, and 5, and it is in the three short sentences at the end of the paragraph where Thomas slows the pace to drive home those major points about the nature of the Iks: "They share nothing. They never sing." "It is a mean society." Such simple sentences are powerful in summing up major points.

Your writing should move along fairly fast. But that does not mean you have to cram everything into one sentence. A pace that is too rapid can be as bad as a pace that is too slow. The pace is too rapid if the reader is presented with too much information within a short passage on a first reading:

> The candidate, although she does not represent the majority party, is not without a strong opponent, and is not unconcerned that popular opinion might turn against her and cause her to lose votes in Cedar Township, opposes the new school bill.

This information is presented in a form that is grammatically correct but hard to understand, mainly because the density of information is too high for many readers. To sort out and digest the meaningful information, the reader must understand five ideas and their relationships, must hold in mind the subject of the sentence while reading or hearing thirty-four subsequent words until the verb is reached, and must transform two double negatives ("is not without" and "is not unconcerned") into positives. When you think about it, this effort is more than a minor nuisance or strain. It involves lots of bridging and translation work and is usually too much for easy reading.

Of course, if your readers *have* to read something and take self-interested action, they will likely make a significant effort to decode even difficult texts. If you need to encourage your readers to read, you must make the text easily assimilable.

Perhaps the simplest and most effective adjustment in overcrowded sentences is to use what linguists call *right-branching sentences*, that is, sentences that branch into modifiers or completing elements *after* the subject and verb:

> The candidate opposes the new school bill, although she does not represent the majority party, has a strong opponent, and is concerned that popular opinion might turn against her and cause her to lose votes in Cedar Township.

Beginning the sentence with the subject, followed by the verb, followed by the modifiers keeps the subject and verb close together and allows the elaboration to follow the main idea. Such sentence structure seems natural and is easy to read. In addition, although most readers tolerate an occasional double negative ("is not without," "is not unconcerned,"), it takes them less time to grasp positive statements ("is with," "is concerned"). So use positive statements unless there is some rhetorical gain in using a harder-to-understand double negative.

Left-branching sentences (those that place modifiers and complements *before* the subject and verb) can be effective if used occasionally to delay the main idea until the end of the sentence:

> Although she does not represent the majority party, has a strong opponent, and is concerned that popular opinion might turn against her and cause her to lose votes in Cedar Township, the candidate opposes the new school bill.

This structure forces the reader to hold in suspension the first part of the sentence—approximately 80 percent—before reaching the subject and the verb. This suspension organizes the sentence into a distinctly climactic order, drawing the audience along through the words, withholding an essential piece of information, building toward a sense of revelation or completion, and finally delivering the main idea. Such a sentence can break up the monotony of many standard right-branching sentences and can thus add variety to the text. But because these structures deviate from the right-branching pattern of most sentences, they may appear artificial and slightly stilted. When a lot of modifiers and complements precede the subject and verb, they can overload the audience's ability to retain them until the end of the sentence is reached. Thus you should use left-branching sentences sparingly, cautiously, and deliberately.

Pace can also be an important factor in stretches of text longer than a sentence. For example, a series of brief paragraphs, each enumerating a separate point, are sometimes used to keep the text moving rapidly. In the passage that follows, Richard Shenkman, after introducing his thesis that much of the violence associated with the American frontier is myth, uses five short paragraphs to present five different examples to back up his position before going on to a more sustained and extended treatment of his thesis. The effect is similar to that of a quick list of facts.

> The popular image of the frontier as a place of violence is only partly due to the fact that the place often was violent. Most of it is due to hype, particularly Hollywood hype. The truth is many more people have died in Hollywood westerns than ever died on the real frontier (Indian wars considered apart). In the real Dodge City, for instance, there were just five killings in

1878, the most homicidal year in the little town's frontier history—scarcely enough to sustain a typical two-hour movie. In the most violent year in Deadwood, South Dakota, only four people were killed. The only reason the OK Corral shoot-out even became famous was that town boosters deliberately overplayed the drama to attract new settlers. "They eventually cashed in on the tourist boom," historian W. Eugene Hollon says, "by inventing a myth about a town too tough to die."

The most notorious cow towns in Kansas—Abilene, Dodge City, Ellsworth, Wichita, and Caldwell—did see comparatively more violence than similar size small towns elsewhere but probably not as much violence as is believed. Records indicate that between 1870 and 1885 just forty-five murders occurred in the towns.

Most surprisingly, there is no evidence anyone was ever killed in a frontier shoot-out at high noon.

In fact, few of those who are famous for shooting people shot as many people as commonly thought. Billy the Kid was a "psychopathic murderer," but he hadn't killed twenty-one people by the time he was twenty-one. Hollon says authorities "can only account for three men he killed for sure, and there were probably no more than three or four more."

Bat Masterson is another overrated killer. He's been credited, says Hollon, with killing between twenty and thirty men; "the actual number was only three."

Wild Bill Hickok, the Abilene marshal, claimed to have killed six Kansas outlaws and secessionists in the incident that first made him famous. He lied. He killed just three—all unarmed. And he never killed anybody for violating the ordinance against firing guns within the town limits.

—"The Frontier," in *Legends, Lies, and
Cherished Myths of American History* (New York:
Morrow, 1988): 112–113.

The opening paragraph—which has seven sentences—is followed by paragraphs that are 2, 1, 3, 2, and 4 sentences long. The paragraphs that immediately follow this passage are 7, 8, 6, and 8 sentences long.

No absolute rules dictate how many short staccato paragraphs can be run in succession, but here are some guidelines to help decide when a series of short paragraphs might be effective:

❖ When a short paragraph has not been used for several paragraphs and the pages are filling up with long paragraphs.

❖ When it is desirable to establish a series or a pattern or trend by accumulating specific events, facts, and examples—almost as in a quick list—before moving on to more extended accounts.

❖ When a point can be supported by reference to several familiar examples that do not require thorough explanation.

Five or six very short paragraphs in succession are probably enough. More than that may belabor the point being made or may arouse suspicion that the writer has not thought sufficiently about the subjects of the paragraphs to organize them into a single coherent paragraph. It is best to end a string of very short paragraphs before readers quit reading.

Pace is closely related to the readers' attention span and memory capacity. Because of individual differences in experience and interest among readers, no set rules can determine whether a particular passage is so densely packed with information that it is difficult to understand: the pace for one reader may not always be the proper pace for others. In addition, a writer's sense of pace is likely to be much different from the reader's. A writer's response to his or her own writing is immediate, subjective, and almost instinctive. Having already thought and rethought the contents through perhaps several revisions, a writer's mind will understand what is stated regardless of the pace.

However, pace is not an elusive aspect of writing. No specialized knowledge is necessary to develop a sense of pace for most situations. In checking for pace, watch for the kinds of problems just discussed—a series of short, choppy sentences that seem to jolt along a cobblestone road and densely packed passages that overload the reader's attention span and memory. As you read over your text, allow your eyes to catch the length of phrases, clauses, sentences, and paragraphs. If you do not have at least one paragraph break on each 8½ × 11 sheet of paper, your paragraphs are probably too long. Avoid writing sentences or paragraphs that are all the same length. Such monotony distracts readers and makes them less receptive. See if the information is coming at an acceptable pace to someone who is not as familiar with the topic as you are.

Here are seven important tactics to help create the normal reading pace of four words per second:

▶ **Read your text aloud to check its pace.** The pace of reading aloud is slightly slower than reading silently. But when you speak your words and sentences at a normal speaking pace, you *hear* the pace of your reading, which may help you detect problems with pace that you might otherwise overlook if you only see your words and sentences.

▶ Without cutting details (and hence substance) from sentences, combine short sentences. The rewording and restructuring will (1) avoid choppiness, (2) help create the necessary coordination and subordination of ideas, and (3) result in frequent modification that will bring modifiers and what is modified closer together.

▶ Generally, use right-branching sentences that present the focal point of the sentence—the subject and the verb—before elaborating. Subject-verb-object/complement is the easiest structure to follow.

▶ For the same reason, place **topic sentences** at or near the beginning of paragraphs. The repetition of opinion or assertion followed by factual support establishes an easily recognized and easily followed pattern, moving from the abstract or general to the concrete and specific.

TOPIC SENTENCE, PAGE 609

▶ Vary the length of sentences and paragraphs to avoid monotony. Monotony will induce boredom and, perhaps, heavy eyelids.

▶ Occasionally relieve long stretches of verbal text by using **graphics** (photographs, line drawings, tables, or charts of various kinds). These visual changes will break up the heavy look of the page as well as break up the density of information.

GRAPHICS, PAGE 519

▶ Use informative **headings** to reveal the topic or main idea of major sections of the text. The headings (1) forecast the focal point of the section, much as topic sentences do for paragraphs, (2) display how information is organized, and (3) help break up long stretches of text similar to the way graphics do.

HEADINGS, PAGE 526

PARAGRAPHS
▼

In Stephen Jay Gould's 1983 book *Hen's Teeth and Horse's Toes*, a chapter is titled "What, If Anything, Is a Zebra?" We might ask a similar question. What, if anything, is a paragraph?

The concept of a paragraph has changed over time, and no consensus exists about how to define a paragraph today. Centuries ago, in Greek manuscripts, a paragraph was a line drawn in the margin to call attention to a particular part of a text (the root word for *paragraph* is the Greek word *paragraphos*, *para* = "beside," *graph* = "to write").

Later, the paragraph mark became the familiar symbol ¶ to designate a change in the subject being discussed in the text. By the seventeenth and eighteenth centuries, the symbol ¶ had fallen into disuse (retained today only as a editing mark, except in certain specialized reference works), and the paragraph had evolved into a section of text set off at the beginning by indentation of the first line and at the end simply by the last line ending with the final word of the last sentence, even when it fell short of the right margin. By the twentieth century, the paragraph was no longer thought of so much as a format device that set off parts of text but rather was broadly conceived as the text that lay between the indentations.

Because the characteristics and boundaries of paragraphs shift from time to time and the concept of a paragraph has moved away from a format mark toward a rhetorical unit of text, we might receive several answers to our question about what, if anything, is a paragraph:

TOPIC SENTENCE, PAGE 609

1. A paragraph is like an expanded sentence. It contains a **topic sentence** that is developed and modified by other sentences much the same way that the base clause of a sentence is developed and modified by other phrases and clauses.

2. A paragraph is a miniature essay. It is a self-contained unit that develops a limited idea similar to the way a larger text develops a more comprehensive subject.

3. A paragraph is a subdivision of a longer stretch of text. Instead of being isolated and self-contained, several paragraphs may be connected closely in thought, with each paragraph focusing on a specific aspect yet contributing to the progress of thought from one paragraph to the next.

4. A paragraph is any text that is placed between two indented lines. (In a similar manner, word processors define a paragraph as any text set between two "return" commands.)

Another answer might be that a paragraph is all of the above. Certainly none of the answers just listed are incorrect. Although the definitions overlap, they indicate both the breadth and specificity of perspectives on paragraphs.

The concept of a paragraph undergoes a significant change of emphasis depending on which definition we consider. In this section we categorize paragraphs as (1) topic paragraphs (related directly to definitions 1 and 2 and partly to definitions 3 and 4); (2) paragraphs in

a series (related directly to definition 3 and partly to the other definitions); and (3) short functional paragraphs (directly related to definition 4 and partly to the other definitions).

Topic Paragraphs

Any text longer than a page is usually divided into several paragraphs.
While there may be short introductory, transitional, and concluding
paragraphs, most of the paragraphs will be topic paragraphs. A topic
paragraph is a block of sentences that presents a statement about a
fact, an opinion, or an experience, or in some other way treats a topic
that is an important part of the subject of the entire text. It is the primary means by which writers organize information into meaningful
blocks of text and focus and develop major ideas.

The meaning of each topic paragraph is usually tied to a topic
sentence supported by detailed data and examples that furnish clarification, proof, and evidence. Ordinarily, a bare statement unsupported
by details is not convincing. Thus if an idea is important enough to be
set off as a separate paragraph, it probably requires several sentences
to develop it. For instance, if the statement is "The institution of the
Church stood an extraordinarily physical presence in my world," a natural way of supporting this statement is to cite specific examples of the
physical presence of the church:

> The institution of the Church stood an extraordinarily physi-
> cal presence in my world. One block from the house was
> Sacred Heart Church. In the opposite direction, another block
> away, was Sacred Heart Grammar School, run by the Sisters of
> Mercy. And from our backyard, I could see Mercy Hospital,
> Sacramento's only Catholic hospital. All day I would hear the
> sirens of death. Well before I was a student myself, I would
> watch the Catholic school kids walk by the front of the house,
> dressed in gray and red uniforms. From the front lawn I could
> see people on the steps of the church, coming out, dressed in
> black after funerals, or standing, the ladies in bright-colored
> dresses in front of the church after a wedding. When I first
> went to stores on errands for my mother, I could be seen by
> the golden-red statue of Christ, where it hovered over the main
> door of the church.
>
> —Richard Rodriguez, *Hunger of Memory*
> (Boston: Godine, 1982): 81.

Since a topic paragraph can develop one topic or a subtopic of a larger subject, it may be nearly complete in itself or it may be only one of a group of closely related topic paragraphs. Here we discuss the topic paragraph that is nearly complete in itself. In the "Paragraphs in a Series" section, we discuss it as part of a larger passage.

Few concepts of writing have enjoyed more widespread acceptance in the past century than the topic paragraph. While having multiple purposes, diverse organizational patterns, and varying lengths, it possesses two central features: (1) a main idea usually expressed in a **topic sentence** and (2) a coherent sequence of information that supports, clarifies, or amplifies the topic sentence (see **amplification**).

TOPIC SENTENCE, PAGE 609

AMPLIFICATION, PAGE 404

The topic sentence expresses the main idea or in some way summarizes the contents of a paragraph. It is frequently the first sentence, but it can appear any place in the paragraph. Since its primary function is to bring into focus the main point of the paragraph, it is placed where the writer wants the reader to encounter it. One advantage of placing it at the beginning is that it helps establish the important given information that is crucial to understanding new information. Occasionally, for special effects, the topic sentence is placed at the beginning and restated at the end. What follows here are illustrations of the placement of topic sentences and examples of a few typical organizational patterns in topic paragraphs.

First, a topic sentence at or near the beginning of the paragraph—such as the one in the paragraph from Richard Rodriguez's *Hunger of Memory*—makes it more likely that the writer will stick to the subject and that the reader will discover instantly the central idea and will know what to expect in the paragraph.

Second, a topic sentence at the end of the paragraph, such as the following one from James Gleick's *Chaos: Making a New Science* (1987), allows the writer to provide several examples and then comment on their significance or meaning:

> Ravenous fish and tasty plankton. Rain forests dripping with nameless reptiles, birds gliding under canopies of leaves, insects buzzing like electrons in an accelerator. Frost belts where voles and lemmings flourish and diminish with tidy four-year periodicity in the face of nature's bloody combat. The world makes a messy laboratory for ecologists, a cauldron of five million interesting species. Or is it fifty million? Ecologists do not actually know.
>
> —(New York: Penguin, 1987): 59.

The topic sentence placed at the end can create a climax or vary the structure of paragraphs by holding off the principal idea that unifies the paragraph until the end.

Third, occasionally as a transition from one paragraph to another, the topic sentence of a paragraph is the last sentence of the preceding paragraph, as in this passage (topic sentence is italicized):

> Under the Kennedy and Johnson administration, federal efforts to reduce unemployment through employment and training programs were greatly increased. The 1961 Area Redevelopment Act that introduced federally financed skill training for unemployed workers in distressed areas was short-lived. The 1962 Manpower Development and Training Act and the 1964 Economic Opportunity Act expanded the concepts of direct federal employment and training for the unemployed. A major operating division of the Office of Economic Opportunity was the Job Corps, conceived by OEO director Sargent Shriver, to be not merely a vocational training program, but an educational venture. Up to 100,000 trainees between the ages of 16 and 21 entered the program, and many disadvantaged young men and women graduated to secure steady jobs. Problems of mismanagement plagued the program, which soon fell into disfavor with Congress and then faded away under the Nixon administration. *However, the largest federal employment programs occurred during the 1970's.*
>
> In 1971, the Emergency Employment Act authorized the first large-scale direct federal employment initiative since the 1930s and cost $2.25 billion over two years. In 1973, the Comprehensive Employment and Training Act (CETA) was passed with bipartisan support. Its purpose was to consolidate more than the dozen separate employment and training programs that had developed in the 1960s into one, and to turn administrative control over to elected state and local officials.
>
> —Marcia Lynn Whicker and Raymond A. Moore, *Making America Competitive: Policies for a Global Future* (New York: Praeger, 1988): 153.

Fourth, a topic sentence placed at the beginning and restated or paraphrased at the end gives special emphasis to the main idea of the paragraph, rounds out the discussion, and achieves a sense of completeness (topic sentences italicized):

> *Between 1890 and 1925, dating—in practice and in name—had gradually, almost imperceptibly, become a universal custom in America.* By the 1930s it had transcended its origins: Middle America associated dating with neither upper-class rebellion nor the urban lower classes. The rise of dating was usually explained, quite simply, by the invention of the automobile. Cars had given youth mobility and privacy, and so had brought about the system. This explanation—perhaps not consciously but definitely not coincidentally—revised history. The automobile certainly contributed to the rise of dating as a *national* practice, especially in rural and suburban areas, but it was simply accelerating and extending a process already well under way. *Once its origins were located firmly in Middle America, however, and not in the extremes of urban upper- and lower-middle class life, dating had become an American institution.*
>
> —Beth L. Bailey, *From Front Porch to Back Seat: Courtship in Twentieth-Century America* (Baltimore: Johns Hopkins UP, 1988): 19.

NARRATION, PAGE 558

DESCRIPTION, PAGE 456

EXEMPLIFICATION, PAGE 488

COMPARISON/CONTRAST, PAGE 437

COHERENCE, PAGE 426

The placement of the topic sentence influences the organization and coherence of the paragraph to some extent. But more important are various organizational patterns—such as **narration**, **description**, **exemplification**, and **comparison/contrast**—that establish the sequence of information. The number of patterns are almost endless. Writers employ whatever patterns enable them to unfold successive ideas intelligibly. Following are only a few examples of the many patterns. For more detailed information on achieving coherence, see **coherence**, especially pages 431–437.

Narration

Narration can be used several ways in paragraphs. For example, Richard Rodriguez describes the physical pleasure of working at a summer construction job while he was an undergraduate at Stanford University by summarizing a typical workday:

> I labored with excitement that first morning—and all the days after. The work was harder than I could have expected. But it was never as tedious as my friends had warned me it would be. There was too much physical pleasure in the labor. Especially early in the day, I would be most alert to the sensations of movement and straining. Beginning around seven each morning (when the air was still damp but the scent of weeds

and dry earth anticipated the heat of the sun), I would feel my body resist the first thrusts of the shovel. My arms, tightened by sleep, would gradually loosen; after only several minutes, sweat would gather in beads on my forehead and then—a short while later—I would feel my chest silky with sweat in the breeze. I would return to my work. A nervous spark of pain would fly up my arm and settle to burn like an ember in the thick of my shoulder. An hour, two passed. Three. My whole body would assume regular, even movements. Even later in the day, my enthusiasm for primitive sensation would survive the heat and the dust and the insects pricking my back. I would strain wildly for sensation as the day came to a close. At three-thirty, quitting time, I would stand upright and slowly let my head fall back, luxuriating in the feeling of tightness relieved.

—*Hunger of Memory* (Boston: Godine, 1982):
131–132.

Another type of narration is the anecdote, a brief account of an incident to support or clarify a major point or to illustrate a striking characteristic of a person or group. For instance, Tom Wolfe, a notable writer of so-called literary nonfiction, reports the following anecdote to illustrate the snobbish influence of New York City nannies on the upper-middle-class children in their care. The anecdote comprises the first paragraph.

Lord, the nannies are absolutely dictatorial about what you have to buy. Charlotte remembers that first day, when she went into the playground by herself, there was this poor little girl, about six, who came in with her nurse. The nurse was a col-ored girl. Neither of them knew a thing, poor dears. The little girl saw these other little girls her age, and, oh, she wanted to play with them. Her little eyes lit up like birthday candles in her little buttery face and her little legs started churning, and there she was, the original *tabula rasa* of joy and friendship. Did they let *her* have it! Rather! The first girl she came up to, Carey K-----'s little girl, a real budding little bitch named Jennifer, if you wanted Charlotte's frank opinion, just stared at her, no smile at all, and said, "My shoes are Indian Walk T-strap." Then another little girl came up and said the same thing, "My shoes are Indian Walk T-strap." Then Jennifer says it again, "My shoes are Indian Walk T-strap," and then they both start whining this at the poor little thing, "My-shoes-are-Indian-Walk-T-Strap!" And the little girl—all she had done was come into the playground, to try to make friends, with the wrong shoes on—she's about to cry, and she says, "Mine are, too," and little Jennifer starts saying in that awful sarcastic sing-song kids pick up as one of their early instruments of torture: "Oh-no-they're-not—your shoes are *gar*bage!" So the other little girl starts saying it, and they start chanting again, and the little girl is bawling, and the colored girl can't figure out what's going on—and the other nannies, Jennifer's nanny, all of them, they're just *beau*tiful, as Charlotte remembers.

"They just sat there through the whole performance with these masks on, until their little terrors had absolutely annihilated this poor kid, and *then* they were so concerned.

"'Now, Jennifer, you mustn't tease, you know. Mustn't tease.'" The whole time, of course, she was just delighted over how well Jennifer had learned her lessons."

—"The Nanny Mafia," in *The Kandy-Kolored Tangerine-Flake Streamline Baby* (New York: Farrar, Straus & Giroux, 1965): 269–270.

A third use of narration is to describe a process, as Lewis Thomas, a physician, medical researcher, and gifted essayist, does in the following paragraph that speculates on the collaborative work of termites:

Termites are even more extraordinary in the way they seem to accumulate intelligence as they gather together. Two or three termites in a chamber will begin to pick up pellets and move them from place to place, but nothing comes of it; nothing is built. As more join in, they seem to reach a critical mass, a quorum, and the thinking begins. They place pellets atop pellets, then throw up columns and beautiful, curving, symmetrical arches, and the crystalline architecture of vaulted chambers is created. It is not known how they communicate with each other, how the chains of termites building one column know when to turn toward the crew on the adjacent column, or how, when the time comes, they manage the flawless joining of the arches. The stimuli that set them off at the outset, building collectively instead of shifting things about, may be pheromones released when they reach committee size. They react as if alarmed. They become agitated, excited, and then they begin working, like artists.

—"Societies as Organisms," in *The Lives of a Cell: Notes of a Biology Watcher* (New York: Viking Press, 1974): 13.

Description

The aim of description is to create sensory details—of sight, sound, touch, taste, and smell—that vividly create images and understanding. Descriptive paragraphs present verbal pictures, as illustrated in the following paragraph by Alfred Kazin, which describes the kitchen of his childhood home in a tenement section of New York City:

> The kitchen held our lives together. My mother worked in it all day long, we ate in it almost all meals except the Passover *seder*, I did my homework and first writing at the kitchen table, and in winter I often had a bed made up for me on three kitchen chairs near the stove. On the wall just over the table hung a long horizontal mirror that sloped to a ship's prow at each end and was lined with cherry wood. It took up the whole wall, and drew every object in the kitchen to itself. The walls were a fiercely stippled whitewash, so often rewhitened by my father in slack seasons that the paint looked as if it had been squeezed and cracked into the walls. A large electric bulb hung down the center of the kitchen at the end of a chain that had been hooked into the ceiling; the old gas ring and key still jutted out of the wall like antlers. In the corner next to the toilet was the sink at which we washed, and the square tub in which my mother did our clothes. Above it, tacked to the shelf on which was pleasantly ranged square, blue bordered white sugar and spice jars, hung calendars from the Public National Bank on Pitkin Avenue and the Minsker Progressive Branch of the Workmen's Circle; receipts for the payment of insurance premiums, and household bills on a spindle; two little boxes engraved with Hebrew letters. . . .
>
> —*A Walker in the City* (New York: Harcourt, Brace, 1951): 65–66.

Exemplification

One of the most frequently used methods of developing a topic sentence is exemplification—giving a specific example or several examples that show how an idea or concept applies to actual things or in specific instances.

> Good families prize their rituals. Nothing welds a family more than these. Rituals are vital especially for clans without histories,

because they evoke a past, imply a future, and hint at continuity. No line in the Seder service at Passover reassures more than the last: "Next year in Jerusalem!" A clan becomes more of a clan each time it gathers to observe a fixed ritual (Christmas, birthdays, Thanksgiving, and so on), grieves at a funeral (anyone may come to most funerals, those who do declare their tribalness), and devises a new rite of its own. Equinox breakfasts and all-white dinners can be at least as welding as Memorial Day parades. Several of us in the old *Life* magazine years used to meet for lunch every Pearl Harbor Day, preferably to eat some politically neutral fare like smorgasbord, to "forgive" our only ancestrally Japanese colleague Irene Kubota Neves. For that and other reasons we became, and remain, a sort of family.

> —Jane Howard, *Families* (New York: Simon & Schuster, 1978): 242–243.

Comparison/Contrast

Comparison/contrast shows similarities and differences between two or more things. The contrast between Monte Carlo and Las Vegas in the following paragraph makes a point about the values and atmosphere of Las Vegas:

> Las Vegas has become, just as Bugsy Siegel dreamed, the American Monte Carlo—without any of the inevitable upper-class baggage of the Riviera casinos. At Monte Carlo there is still the plush mustiness of the 19th century noble lions—of Baron Bleichroden, a big winner at roulette who always said, "My dear friends, it is so easy on Black." Of Lord Jersey, who won seventeen maximum bets in a row—on black, as a matter of fact—nodded to the croupier, and said, "Much obliged, old sport, old sport," took his winnings to England, retired to the country and never gambled again in his life. Or of the old Duc de Dinc who said he could win only in the high-toned Club Privé, and who won very heavily one night, saw two Englishmen gaping at his good fortune, threw them every mille-franc note he had in his hands and said, "Here, Englishmen without money are altogether odious." Thousands of Europeans from the lower orders now have the money to go to the Riviera, but they remain under the century-old status pall of the aristocracy. At Monte Carlo there are still Wrong Forks, Deficient Accents, Poor Tailoring, Gauche Displays, Nouveau Richness, Cultural Aridity—concepts unknown in Las Vegas. For the grand debut

of Monte Carlo as a resort in 1879 the architect Charles Garnier designed an opera house for the Place du Casino; and Sarah Bernhardt read a symbolic poem. For the debut of Las Vegas as a resort in 1946 Bugsy Siegel hired Abbott and Costello, and there, in a way, you have it all.

> —Tom Wolfe, "Las Vegas," in *The Kandy-Kolored Tangerine-Flake Streamline Baby* (New York: Farrar, Straus & Giroux, 1965): 16.

Paragraphs in a Series

Many times a topic paragraph is only one of several paragraphs that form a longer stretch of closely related text. Usually the series opens with a statement that defines the subject for the entire stretch of text, and the individual paragraphs connect by means of their own opening statements, which are both transitional and topic sentences.

The following passage is an excerpt from Phyllis Rose's *Parallel Lives*, a study of the marriages of five major British literary figures and their spouses during the nineteenth century. The three paragraphs are part of Rose's discussion of the disintegrating marriage of John Ruskin, a late nineteenth-century art, literary, and social critic, and Effie Gray. Rose contrasts the opinions of the parents of the couple in the first two paragraphs (presenting the Ruskins' viewpoint in the first and the Grays' in the second). The final paragraph offers Rose's interpretation of the two positions and makes clear her own feelings about the matter.

> Something had clearly gone wrong with the marriage, and both "sides"—the elder Grays and Ruskins as well as the married pair—attempted to fix the blame. Neither set of parents knew the marriage was unconsummated, but they found plenty of other problems to discuss. From Mr. Ruskin's point of view, Effie was an undutiful wife, unsupportive of her husband's work. She had unaccountably withdrawn from them and gone to Perth, where she knew John would not follow. She seemed unsympathetic to his stay in Europe, perversely wanting him home. Didn't she realize that going home would mean giving up the "Haunts where his Genius finds food and occupation"? Ordinary people might find John's business in the Alps incomprehensible, but didn't Effie realize that only by such labor could he do the work he'd been put on earth to do? Mr. Ruskin recommended (to her father) that she sacrifice all other feelings to duty and attempt to find pleasure in causing her husband no anxiety.

But Mr. Gray saw it differently. He knew that his daughter was not jealous of her husband's work. That was a false issue. There was only one problem in the young people's marriage: the elder Ruskins. If he might offer a word of advice, it was that Mr. and Mrs. Ruskin should leave John and Effie to themselves as much as possible. "Married people," he ventured to say, "are rather restive under the control and supervision of Parents tho' proceeding from the kindest and most affectionate motives."

How one warms to Mr. Gray! How right he seems! While Mr. Ruskin with his notions of duty and submissiveness sounds archaic, Mr. Gray expresses the wisdom a contemporary upper-middle-class American would offer in response to the same situation. Freedom. Independence. Not for nothing did we cut the ties with the Mother Country. But Ruskin, in the opening paragraph of his autobiography, proclaims that he was, like his father before him, a Tory of the old school, of the school of Homer and Sir Walter Scott, men who believed in kings, in some people being better fit to rule than others, in such people exercising power for the good of their followers without the right to expect anything in return except deference. But deference they could expect. This political model applies to the family as well as the state, and one should see that the battle between John and Effie, between the Ruskins and the Grays, was to some extent an ideological battle, a clash of two sets of assumptions about power and authority.

—*Parallel Lives: Five Victorian Marriages*
(New York: Vintage, 1984): 67–68.

A fairly broad lesson about paragraphing can be learned from this passage. It is not always possible to predict where paragraph breaks will occur, although it is fairly easy to identify the points of potential paragraph breaks. A century ago, these three paragraphs might have been written as one paragraph. But today, writers make paragraph breaks more often to avoid the formidable appearance of large blocks of text that have no place to rest the eye. Once a paragraph becomes longer than it is wide, writers tend to look for places to indent and start a new paragraph. In a series of closely related paragraphs, such as this one, there are certain points where the writer changes the line of thought or shifts to another aspect of the subject. It is at those junctures that writers often make paragraph breaks. Usually the new paragraph begins with a transition and a topic sentence that cue readers to the change.

Short Functional Paragraphs

Defining a paragraph as the text between indented lines raises the question of how long a paragraph can be. The length is sometimes determined by the size of the topic, but not always. It might be that a fairly large and complex topic may require a long paragraph, a relatively minor point a short one. But unity of thought is not always a clear reason for paragraphing. A paragraph break might be related to eye ease, attention span, or emphasis. Although some paragraphs are extremely long, most paragraphs today seldom exceed 200 to 250 words. But it was different a century ago. Paragraphs in William Henry Herndon's biography of Abraham Lincoln, *Herndon's Lincoln* (1884), for example, average several hundred words each. Some are as long as whole essays are these days. Many of the paragraphs in the essays of John Henry Cardinal Newman, Matthew Arnold, Ralph Waldo Emerson, and Henry David Thoreau run over 300 and 400 words.

But paragraphs can also be short.

Many people believe a paragraph develops a thought thoroughly and thus must have a certain heft. While these attributes may be generally appropriate for what we call topic paragraphs, paragraphs today do not always develop a single idea—if they ever did—and seldom reach the marathon lengths of those of a century ago. In fact, sometimes very short paragraphs are desirable.

A short paragraph—especially a one- or two-sentence one—can make an emphatic and vigorous statement that gets the text (and the readers) off to a quick start. It can provide a brief but strong transition between longer paragraphs or sections of text, place significance on a particularly important example or concept, or end the text or a section of text with a brief but emphatic conclusion.

Set off from subsequent paragraphs or surrounding paragraphs, a short paragraph encourages readers to notice it. The shorter the paragraph is in relation to its neighbors, the more emphatic it is. Short paragraphs should be used sparingly for emphasis, for they quickly stop having the desired effect.

Introductions orient readers about what to expect by announcing the subject, supplying necessary background information, stating the problem or purpose related to the occasion for writing, and providing an overview of how content is organized. The danger of a routine introduction is that readers who are not part of a captive audience will lose interest and stop reading. It is a mistake to assume that readers are going to be very interested in what you have to say, for most of them will read only about two or three paragraphs of the text before deciding to stay with it or not.

One way to motivate readers to keep reading is to start with a lead that catches their interest and plunges them right into the text. Even when it is necessary to provide background information or do a little stage setting, a short introductory paragraph that captures the reader's interest can be effective.

David Quammen, a columnist for *Outdoor* magazine and a novelist, is exceptionally good at writing short, admirably vigorous paragraph leads. Here are a few opening paragraphs from some of his articles that have been reprinted in a collection titled *Natural Acts: A Sidelong View of Science and Nature*, which was published in 1985.

> What the world needs is a good vicious sixty-foot-long Amazon snake. ("Rumors of a Snake")

> There are extinctions, and then again there are Extinctions. ("The Big Goodbye")

> In the fifth chapter of Matthew's Gospel, Christ is quoted as saying that the meek shall inherit the earth, but other opinion lately suggests that, no, more likely it will go to the cockroaches. ("A Republic of Cockroaches")

> Here's a cheerful thought. Some knowledgeable people believe that black widow spiders, like locusts and jack rabbits, come in plagues. ("The Widow Knows")

Quammen gets at once into his articles—focusing on a specific detail or sometimes flooding the reader with several details and building an article around them, or providing a hypotheses to be explored, or making a general observation and tying it to his subject.

Here are other short opening paragraphs by other writers. Like Quammen's introductory paragraphs, each of these creates a certain expectation about what will follow and introduces the voice of the writer.

> Growing up in America has been an assault upon my sense of worthiness. It has also been a kind of liberation and delight.
>
> —Michael Novak, "I. Neither WASP nor Jew nor Black," in *The Rise of the Unmeltable Ethnics* (New York: Macmillan, 1973): 63.

A revolution in chemistry is taking place in a small room in a converted mining building in Tuscon, Ariz., where a woman wearing a solid smock and a face mask is painstakingly scraping soot off a metal container.

—Edward Edelson, "Buckyball: The Magic Molecule," *Popular Science* (August 1991): 52.

Suppose an operator asked a machine whether it was intelligent and the machine answered "yes." How would the operator prove it was lying?

—O. B. Hardison, Jr., "Syntax and Semantics," in *Disappearing Through the Skylight: Culture and Technology in the Twentieth Century* (New York: Viking Press, 1989): 317.

Human beings are the only animals that experience the same sex drive at times when we can—and cannot—conceive.

—Gloria Steinem, "Erotica and Pornography: A Clear and Present Difference," *Ms.* (November 1978): 53.

With one exception, each introduction plunges readers into the text and involves them in the subject in less than twenty-five words. However, it is not just the shortness that makes these opening statements effective. It is also the element of surprise, the directness, the tone, and the focus on something specific that indicates the substance of the information that follows. When well done, introductions focus readers' attention and draw them into the text.

After getting the text off to a striking start, single brief paragraphs are also sometimes needed to carry readers from one long paragraph to another or from one section of the text to another. Readers must feel as if they are moving along; if they bog down, the writer is in trouble (see **pace**). Short transitional paragraphs in the right places keep readers moving through the text. Following is a seven-paragraph passage in which Gloria Steinem, co-founder of *Ms.* magazine and author of several articles and books, distinguishes between erotica and pornography. She begins by defining the terms and then illustrates them by examples and analysis. The emphatic two-sentence transition

PACE PAGE, 560

in the second paragraph guides the reader from the long paragraph that discusses the origins of the two words to the paragraphs that provide examples and analysis. It does so by summarizing the preceding paragraph in the first short sentence and by anticipating the contents of the succeeding paragraph in the second short sentence. Finally, the one-sentence paragraph at the end of the passage restates strongly the contrast between erotica and pornography.

> . . . Sex as communication can send messages as different as life and death; even the origins of "erotica" and "pornography" reflect that fact. After all, "erotica" is rooted in *eros* or passionate love, and thus in the idea of positive choice, free will, the yearning for a particular person. (Interestingly, the definition of erotica leaves open the question of gender.) "Pornography" begins with a root meaning "prostitution" or "female captives," thus letting us know that the subject is not mutual love, or love at all, but domination and violence against women. (Though, of course, homosexual pornography may imitate this violence by putting a man in the "feminine" role of victim.) It ends with a root meaning "writing about" or "description of" which puts still more distance between subject and object, and replaces a spontaneous yearning for closeness with objectification and a voyeur.
>
> The difference is clear in words. It becomes even more so by example.
>
> Look at any photo or film of people making love; really making love. The images may be diverse, but there is usually a sensuality and touch and warmth, an acceptance of bodies and nerve endings. There is always a spontaneous sense of people who are there because they *want* to be, out of shared pleasure.
>
> Now look at any depiction of sex in which there is clear force, or an unequal power that spells coercion. It may be very blatant, with weapons or torture or bondage, wounds and bruises, some clear humiliation, or an adult's sexual power being used over a child. It may be much more subtle: a physical attitude of conqueror and victim, the use of race or class difference to imply the same thing, perhaps a very unequal nudity, with one person exposed and vulnerable while the other is clothed. In either case, there is no sense of equal choice or equal power.
>
> The first is erotic: a mutually pleasurable, sexual expression between people who have enough power to be there by

positive choice. It may or may not strike a sense-memory in the viewer, or be creative enough to make the unknown seem real; but it doesn't require us to identify with a conqueror or a victim. It is truly sensuous, and may give us a contagion of pleasure.

The second is pornographic: its message is violence, dominance, and conquest. It is sex being used to reinforce some inequality, or to create one, or to tell us the lie that pain and humiliation (ours or someone else's) are really the same as pleasure. If we are to feel anything, we must identify with conqueror or victim. That means we can only experience pleasure through the adoption of some degree of sadism or masochism. It also means that we may feel diminished by the role of conqueror, or enraged, humiliated, and vengeful by sharing identity with the victim.

Perhaps one could simply say that erotica is about sexuality, but pornography is about power and sex-as-weapon—in the same way we have come to understand that rape is about violence, and not really about sexuality at all.

—"Erotica and Pornography: A Clear and
Present Difference," *Ms.* (November 1978): 53.

One of the axioms of writing is that the most important idea, image, or concept should go either at the beginning or the end. Placed in the middle, it gets buried. We've already seen how David Quammen and others use brief paragraphs to begin a text. We've also seen how Gloria Steinem concludes a series of paragraphs emphatically with a brief paragraph. The end of a text often requires paragraphs longer than a sentence or two. Sometimes an entire section of related paragraphs is needed to recapitulate the main line of reason, summarize the main ideas, or restate a position or problem and call for action.

However, a short paragraph can bring a text or section of text to an effective end as illustrated in the following passage that comes from Robert Pirsig's bestselling *Zen and the Art of Motorcycle Maintenance.* Set off by itself, the concluding statement produces in readers the appropriate final feeling, image, or idea in a bold, memorable, and emphatic manner.

The real University . . . has no specific location. It owns no property, pays no salaries and receives no material dues. The real University is a state of mind. It is that great heritage of rational thought that has been brought down to us through the centuries and which does not exist at any specific location. It's a state of mind which is regenerated throughout the centuries by a body of people who traditionally carry the title of professor, but even that title is not part of the real University. The real University is nothing less than the continuing body of reason itself.

In addition to this state of mind, "reason," there's a legal entity which is unfortunately called by the same name but which is quite another thing. This is a nonprofit corporation, a branch of the state with a specific address. It owns property, is capable of paying salaries, of receiving money and of responding to legislative pressures in the process.

But this second University, the legal corporation, cannot teach, does not generate new knowledge or evaluate ideas. It is not the real University at all. It is just a church building, the setting, the location at which conditions have been made favorable for the real church to exist.

Confusion continually occurs in people who fail to see this difference . . . and think that control of the church buildings implies control of the church. They see professors as employees of the second University who should abandon reason when told to and take orders with no backtalk, the same way employees do in other corporations.

They see the second University, but fail to see the first.

—(New York: Bantam, 1974): 143–144.

In eleven words, Pirsig summarizes the principal point of the passage. Here are four additional short paragraph endings that close a text or section of text with a bang. Out of context, these paragraphs do not have their original impact and strength. To experience the full effect, you should read the entire text.

For better or worse, there is no subjunctive mood in politics. History is made without rehearsals. It cannot be replayed. That makes it all the more important to perceive its course and its lessons.

—Mikhail Gorbachev, "What Do We Expect from the United States," in *Perestroika: New Thinking for Our Country and the World* (New York: HarperCollins, 1987): 214.

The trouble was, I no longer believed him. It was beginning to strike me that Father, who knew the real world so well, got some of it wrong. Not much; but some.

> —Annie Dillard, *An American Childhood*
> (New York: Harper & Row, 1987): 204.

Europe is "the old continent." Its qualities, then, should be the qualities of many, though not all, older people: wisdom, tolerance, and understanding.

> —Václav Havel, "The Chance That Will not
> Return," *U.S. News & World Report* (February 26,
> 1990): 31.

Women need to clearly get more convincing, and men need to believe them more. But until that ideal time, Montana State's Jan Stout warns, "Because men have been socialized to hear yes when women say no, we have to scream it."

> —Ellen Sweet, "Date Rape: The Story of
> an Epidemic and Those Who Deny It." *Ms.*
> (October 1985): 85.

PROOFREADING
▼

Writers are responsible for getting the final version of their text in as perfect shape as possible before turning it over to their readers. Even if somebody else has helped them type it or key it into a computer, they must make sure their text conforms to standard English, acceptable format, and accuracy in everything from spelling to the most minute fact. When their text is in its final form, writers proofread it. That is, they check it closely word by word—sometimes character by character—to ensure that all editing changes have been made and that there are no remaining typographic, spelling, punctuation, or usage errors. Only after the text has been "proofed" is it distributed to readers.

However, many writers do this task inadequately. For one thing, they probably work on a text so much—revising it several times, looking at essentially the same ideas again and again—and become so familiar with it that they are unable to see the errors. Their minds, not their eyes, tell them what they think is on the page. For another, all writers occasionally suffer the myopia of assuming that all is finally well and the text does not require a final check. Third, they tire mentally, perhaps even physically, from working on the text for long periods of time and are unable to absorb themselves in what they consider a tedious and boring last step. Fourth, they assume that running their text through a computer spell- or style-checking program has caught the typographical errors, misspelled words, and major grammatical problems. Finally, they sometimes are confronted by a fast-approaching deadline and don't have sufficient time to do more than give the text a quick glance before turning it in.

Here are a few suggestions to overcome some of the more common rationalizations for not doing a thorough job of proofreading.

If you believe . . .	then . . .
that you are so familiar with the text you can no longer see the errors . . .	allow enough time to pass so you can gain some distance from your own work.
that you have revised the text and all is well . . .	never assume all is well. Don't be too satisfied too soon with the condition of your text.
that you are up against a deadline that allows no time for proofreading . . .	ask for a brief extension of the deadline *once*. After that, schedule your work so you will have sufficient time to let the text sit for a couple of days before you proofread it and make the final necessary changes.
that your spell- or style-checking program has caught the typos, misspellings, and usage errors . . .	assume that these computer programs are helpful but that they cannot substitute for your own proofreading, since no computer program will catch typos or misspellings that are themselves words (for instance, *saw* for *was*, *pursue* for *peruse*, *bead* for *bread*, and *argue* for *agree*).

It is essential that you proofread the completed text to make sure everything is as you want it. Usually you proofread what you believe is the final printed text. You may be allowed to make a correction or two per page on the final draft. Or you may be required to correct the errors and print a new copy of your text, which in turn should be proofread to make sure the errors were corrected and that no new errors were introduced in the process. In any event, the corrections must be neat and legible.

Here are some practices we recommend to help you proofread your text:

▶ Use standard proofreading marks. Standard proofreading marks give you a widely recognized system to indicate corrections or changes.

Marks for Insertions

❖ To insert material in your text, place a caret (∧) just below the line where the material should go and write the material above it:

```
                        any
There does not seem to be ∧doubt about the danger of
                          e
storing nuclar waste.
              ∧
```

If you have omitted an entire line of text or a couple of sentences, it is best to retype that part of the text and print a new page.

❖ To insert a space, place a # just above the line where the space should go:

```
                                   #
The conversation quickly changed into an/argument.
```

❖ To insert punctuation, use the following proofreading marks:

—To add a comma, insert a comma where you want it and make a caret (∧) over it:

```
However⌃ it was already six o'clock when we arrived.
```

—To add quotation marks or an apostrophe, use an inverted caret (v) and place the punctuation above it:

```
We arrived at six oclock.

In "Beauty and Pain: Notes on the Art of Richard
Selzer, David Morris investigates Selzer's sense of
aesthetics.
```

—To add a period or colon, insert it where you want it and draw a circle around it so it will not be mistaken for a stray pen or pencil mark:

```
Home insurance usually costs less from companies
that sell directly through their own company-
employed agents These include companies like Kemper,
State Farm Mutual, and National Mutual.

At the end of the last Ice Age, a puzzling mass
extinction occurred and several large mammals van-
ished forever mammoths, mastodons, saber-tooth
tigers, ground sloths, and giant beavers.
```

—To add a semicolon, question mark, or exclamation mark, insert it where you want it without any additional markings:

```
Whether Young Goodman Brown's night in the forest is
dream or reality makes no difference he is convinced
beyond redemption that the Devil is correct.

The nurse in the emergency room began asking ques-
tions: Contact lenses Dentures or partials Allergies
```

Marks for Deletions

❖ To delete a letter in the middle of a word, draw a vertical line through it and make close-up marks to delete the space:

```
The pancreas in an adult is about the size and shape
of a fillet of sole.
```

❖ To delete a mark of punctuation, make sure that the deletion mark (⋎) goes through the punctuation to be deleted:

```
Neptune's symbol of power ⋎ was the trident, or spear
with three points.
```

❖ To delete a blank space, use close-up marks:

```
Acid rain is a wide ⌢ spread problem with well-documented
adverse effects on the environment.
```

❖ To delete an unintended line break, use this mark:

```
Booth has noted how the Romantic playwrights fell into
"the fatal error of trying to write like the
Elizabethans," (8) and Wilde falls into the equally
fatal one of trying to write like the Romantics trying
to write like the Elizabethans.
⌐Elizabeth Worth, in her chapter on The Duchess of
Padua, states that the play "was clearly influenced by
Shelley's The Cenci" (40).
```

Marks for Replacement

❖ To replace a wrong word or a badly misspelled word, draw a line through it and write the correction immediately above it:

```
     electroweak
The  eltoweak  theory, which was developed by Steven
Weinberg who at the time was at the Massachusetts
Institute of Technology, unites both the electromag-
netic and weak forces in a single framework.
```

Do not cross out completely or erase original words so they can no longer be read. You may have second thoughts about your substitution and wish to use the original wording.

❖ Transpose letters or words this way:

Monoclonal antibodies have potential for also treating multiple sclerosis, diabetes, and rheumatiod
arthritis.

❖ To change a capital letter to a lowercase letter, draw a diagonal line through the capital letter:

The normal development of organisms can be disturbed
by exposing Embryos to toxic chemicals, X Rays, and
heat.

❖ To change a lowercase letter to a capital letter, draw three horizontal lines directly below the letters you wish to capitalize.

Picasso's Guernica depicts german planes bombing a
basque town during the spanish civil war.

❖ To spell out a numeral, circle it and use the abbreviation *sp* above it:

New principals were assigned to 2 of the 5 middle
schools.

❖ To substitute a numeral for a spelled-out number, cross out the word and place the numeral above it:

Along its ~~fourteen~~ 14 -mile path, the tornado picked up oil
storage tanks, trucks, farm machinery, and barns.

❖ To change a character or word from regular (or Roman type) to italics, underline the text to be italicized and write *ital* in the margin at the beginning or end of the line. If italic type is not possible, underlining can be substituted.

Norman Cousins, former editor of <u>Saturday Review,</u>
 wrote in the <u>New York Journal of Medicine</u> that he had
cured himself of spinal arthritis by adopting a
healthy mental attitude and taking lots of vitamin C.

Two distinctly different approaches to problem solving
are represented by the words <u>algorithm</u> and <u>heuristic.</u> *ital*

▶ **Read slowly, word by word, and sometimes character by character.**
Do whatever you need to slow down when you are proofreading your
text. You need to read one word at a time, so look at each word carefully. If you are alone, read aloud. If necessary, use a ruler or pen to
guide your eyes along each line. If you are proofreading on a word
processor, scroll the text up one line at a time, reading the line carefully before bringing the next line into view. Look at the text upside
down or sideways for spacing or alignment errors. If you do not slow
down and look at each word, punctuation mark, capital letter, or number, you will not be able to see typographical errors, missing words,
and the like.

▶ **If possible, do several proofreading passes.** Proofreading should be
done carefully and precisely. Especially if you have difficulty spotting
certain kinds of errors, do several proofreading passes in which you
concentrate on a specific, limited problem each time. You can combine
some of the passes as you become more confident in your proofreading skills. Here is a possible order for proofreading:

1. Begin by checking for typographical errors and misspellings.

2. Check punctuation. In addition to making sure sentences are correctly punctuated, be alert for an opening parenthesis that needs
a closing parenthesis. Brackets, quotation marks, and—sometimes—dashes also come in pairs. Be sure both the opening and
closing marks are there.

3. Check grammar and usage, especially subject-verb agreement,
noun-pronoun agreement, pronoun case, dangling and misplaced
modifiers, and malaprops.

4. Check numbering and anything else that is overtly sequential,
such as alphabetizing. Look for omissions or duplications or both

as well as proper sequence in glossaries and the Works Cited list. Use a calculator to check the totals in tables.

5. Check for consistency in facts, dates, spellings, and names of places and persons.

6. Check the title, headings and subheadings, and documentation for accuracy and consistency.

7. Check format for appearance and consistency, especially spacing, indentions, margins, and the position and sequence of page numbers, lists, titles or graphics and tables, and formulas and equations.

8. Check unusual elements such as formulas, equations, symbols, and abbreviations—*character by character*—for accuracy, completeness, and consistency.

Two rounds of these passes should catch most errors, especially if you allow time between each round to gain a bit of distance or objectivity.

Here is what a text that has been proofread might look like:

The missfortunes of the north in the first months of the Civil War, affected Thoreau so profoundly that he is known to have said t hat he could never recover while the war lasted and he told his friends that he was "sick for his Country, But he was also disastified with his country, and the base of his dissatisfaction was his conviction that humans, and hence their countries, are perfectible.

After you have incorporated the changes in your text, print out a hard copy and try yet a third round to see if there is still that proverbial error somewhere that everybody can see but you:

The misfortunes of the North in the first months of the Civil War affected Thoreau so profoundly that he is known to have said that he could never recover while

```
the war lasted, and he told his friends that he was
"sick for his country" (Whicher 74). But he was also
dissatisfied with his country, and the base of his dis-
satisfaction was his conviction that humans, and hence
their countries, are perfectible.
```

REVISING AND EDITING
▼

Writers often revise their thoughts as they put them on paper or on a computer screen. Even when they are writing briskly, they sometimes revise their thinking even before they formulate an idea completely enough to write it down. The early stages of creating a text consist of false starts, blind alleys, wrong turns, changes of direction, and starting overs.

Don't be too frustrated or discouraged by what seems like a messy and stumbling process that might even appear to be directionless. Things are not necessarily going badly. Initial drafting seldom goes smoothly but is never a waste of time. These tentative draftings are part of the normal writing process by which writers capture enough of a newborn idea to get a glimpse of what they think or know or believe and what they want to say about something. There is no clear line of demarcation dividing initial drafting from revising. Just keep writing until you have created a text that is substantial enough to revise—a draft that is variously called an initial draft, a "zero" draft, or a discovery draft. Write as many paragraphs or pages as you can. In general, a text should consist of at least several paragraphs before you attempt to revise it. You must have something to revise.

Revising

After you have created a text, even if it is fragmentary and messy (and it undoubtedly will be), you have something you can read and work on. You can then begin to revise extensively and repeatedly—adding, deleting, compressing, restructuring, and rewording sentences, paragraphs, and longer stretches of text. You can rewrite, re-view, and rethink again and again, perhaps occasionally mumbling to yourself as you try to get an idea fixed in your mind or as you try to make one item consistent with another. With this kind of extensive revision, content is likely to be changed substantially as you condense a passage that is too wordy or too detailed or expand a passage that needs **amplification** or come up with better examples to shore up an argument that is on shaky ground or discover a better way of expressing an idea. Organization and structure are likely to be altered significantly as you attempt a new way to develop an idea or a different arrangement to strengthen a line of argument or emphasize the transition from one topic to another to improve the coherence of a passage.

AMPLIFICATION, PAGE 404

As you work over a part of your text, you make changes that will probably require modifications elsewhere in the text. This kind of extensive revision should not include the cosmetic changes you will make later when you proofread the final drafts of your text, although it will be difficult to ignore an obvious misspelling, punctuation error, or usage error. Go ahead and correct such errors if you must, especially if it can be done as you revise. However, it is better to delay looking for these kinds of errors until you have finished revising because you might spend time tinkering with a statement or polishing a sentence that will be deleted or changed drastically later.

When you revise, you are not correcting surface errors. You are exploring your subject and shaping your thoughts. You are bringing discipline to your thinking, which in turn helps bring discipline to your writing. Writing helps you discover what you think, even—actually, especially—when you write something that seems to be different from what you intended to write. Reading what you have written helps clarify your thinking, which in turn gets fed back into your writing. This reading, writing, reflecting, and writing again moves you along. Do not regard your text as final until you are satisfied with your revision or you run out of time and must begin editing and **proofreading**.

PROOFREADING, PAGE 585

It is a myth that good writers can create clean, graceful, and correct texts in an initial draft. You are not a poor writer because you have to revise. Good writers revise, just as good actors rehearse and rehearse, good fishermen practice casting over and over again, and good cross-country runners run and run and run. Revising is essential to discovering what you want to say and to deciding how to say it.

Since the initial draft is sure to be rough, it is sure to need major revisions. But at least at this stage you have text that can be worked on. It is probably a good idea, if time permits, to set the text aside for a while—at least overnight—so that when you return to it you can see it with fresh eyes. It is now time to begin seriously to revise. Following are several suggestions to keep in mind as you revise.

▶ In the early stages of revision you should concern yourself with content, purpose, and the organization of the entire text. Start by reading it from beginning to end. Check to see you have covered the topics you wanted to cover. Look at the organization. Is there some kind of logical structure that can be followed easily? Is there a clear **thesis statement**? Are **paragraphs** arranged in a perceivable order? Are there **topic sentences** that state the main ideas of paragraphs or blocks of paragraphs? Does the text hold together? Do **forecasting statements** and **transitions** help establish **coherence**? Are the lines of development easy to follow?

THESIS STATEMENT, PAGE 599

PARAGRAPHS, PAGE 567

TOPIC SENTENCES, PAGE 609

FORECASTING STATEMENTS, PAGE 503

TRANSITIONS, PAGE 612

COHERENCE, PAGE 426

AMPLIFICATION, PAGE 404

As you read and reread parts of the text, look at the **amplification** of major ideas. Find what you regard as the strongest part of the text and see if you can develop its main point further. Are there additional examples or details that could strengthen the main point? Can you substitute another example or detail that would be better than what you already have? Are there passages that can be deleted? Are there other passages that need further development? How is the **pace**? Are ideas presented at a rate that is easy to grasp?

PACE, PAGE 560

▶ When you are satisfied with the amplification, check the accuracy and consistency of the content, especially references to numbers, dates, places, and names. Recheck your sources to make sure there are no misstatements in quoted material. Review for accuracy any data and statistics that are presented in tables and graphs. Scrutinize formulas and equations. Double-check any math.

▶ If you are working with a word processor, try to make revisions directly on screen. If you are working with printed text, you must make the revisions by hand, so the text will start getting messy. In any event, you will probably need to print a revised text so you can continue working on it without the interference of your previous revisions. Once you have a clean revised text, look at the organization again to see if any condensing, deleting, adding, or moving of text has created gaps or inconsistencies between forecasting statements and transitions and the current text. One of the most necessary tasks in revising—especially on a computer—is to check to make sure that the revised text reads logically and smoothly, that the order and logic have not become confused as a result of the changes that have been made. It is important that the text contain no gaps, redundancies, or inconsistencies brought about by revisions.

FORMAT, PAGE 505

▶ Now that you have a clean text, examine its format. Is each paragraph properly indented? Should some paragraphs be combined? Should others be divided? Are headings and subheadings properly formatted? Are there places where a series should be numbered and broken out into a list? Are equations and long quotations displayed

DOCUMENTATION, PAGE 460

properly? Have you used the appropriate **documentation** system?

Editing

CONCISENESS, PAGE 440

Now, finally, you are ready to edit—to make changes at the most local level, the phrase and word level. Work at achieving **conciseness**. Are there words that can be cut or phrases that can be replaced with single words? Make sure your diction is appropriate, avoiding unnecessary slang and abstract language, and that there are no gross errors such as wrong words or gender-biased language.

When you have finished editing at the word or phrase level, you have completed a substantive revision. However, your text is not ready for proofreading. Not yet. For now, you should have a revised and edited text that is much stronger than the initial one: the focus should be sharper, the meaning clearer, the organization tighter and more obvious, and the evidence stronger. You should be getting a better sense of where your ideas are headed and how well you are doing at getting there. It is now time to cool off from the intensive revision. Allow time for a gestation period so you can reread and revise and edit again with fresh eyes and an alert mind.

STYLE AND VOICE

▼

Teachers of writing love to talk about style and voice, but in truth, these abstract terms probably don't have a very clear meaning for most students of writing. Even when teachers of writing or experienced writers discuss style or voice, they may not be talking about the same things. Although precise definitions are not possible, you can understand these terms generally and learn to distinguish between them.

Style

Style is most often thought of as a conscious variation in the way a person writes. A writer's decision to adopt a certain style is usually determined by his or her purpose and audience. The most simple variation in style, for example, is level of formality. If the intended reader is someone the writer does not know well or who holds a position of authority, the writer will probably use a rather formal style. If, in contrast, the reader is a close friend, the writer will usually adopt an informal style. Some additional stylistic options include the following:

* terse versus verbose

* businesslike versus chatty

* direct versus indirect

* plain versus ornate

* outspoken versus diplomatic and polite

Such options are available to you as a writer each time you construct a text. Depending on your purpose and audience, you can choose one or the other or anywhere in between. Rather than absolute choices, these options should be viewed as opposite ends of a continuum. You can opt to be mildly formal in one document and somewhat informal in another, totally outspoken in one document and less so in another. These are qualities over which you have considerable control. As you become a more experienced writer, you will be aware of even more options, and your control over them will increase.

Voice

Whereas variations in style result from deliberate choices, your writing voice is personal and unique. Like your speaking voice, it is characteristic of you—a personal quality that reflects you as a person. Although experienced writers of poetry, fiction, and drama can usually vary their voice, or tone, to represent different characters, most of us have just one writing voice that is reflected in everything we write. In other words, most writers have a variety of styles at their disposal but only one writing voice.

Although you may not be able to change your writing voice as freely and consciously as you do your writing style, it may very well change over the years (or even a quarter or semester) as you become more comfortable and experienced as a writer. Your reading experiences also affect your writing voice. As you read different authors and different types of texts, your own voice will develop and change. But, in general, your writing voice is not something you can change at will.

What Determines Style and Voice

What makes one style or one voice different from another? It is easier to explain what determines style and voice than to define the concepts. Writers work with words. With the exception of a few kinds of graphics, words are all they have to construct their texts, and all they have to vary their writing styles and develop their writing voice. As a writer, you work with words in two ways:

1. You choose which words to use.

2. You arrange these words in different ways.

Word choice (diction) and the arrangement of words into sentences (syntax) determine both style and voice. For example, read the following pair of sentences:

❖ The little boy looked through the window at the cows.

❖ The lad peered through the pane at the cattle.

Both of these sentences say the same thing. But the word choice in the two sentences varies. The second sentence uses less common words and thus has a different style and voice. Your choice of words determines more than the sense of what you say; it determines your style and voice.

Now compare the following sentences:

❖ The girl mounted the high-strung, impatient horse with speed and grace.

❖ With speed and grace, the girl mounted the high-strung impatient horse.

The words are exactly the same in these two sentences, but the arrangement of the words is different. As a result, the style and voice of the sentences differ. The second sentence emphasizes the "speed and grace" rather than the woman or the act of mounting. Notice what happens if we change the syntax in other ways:

❖ Speedily and gracefully, the girl mounted the high-strung, impatient horse.

❖ The girl mounted the horse, which was impatient and high strung, speedily and gracefully.

❖ The impatient, high-strung horse was mounted by the girl with speed and grace.

❖ With speed and grace, the girl mounted the high-strung, impatient horse.

❖ The girl mounted the horse, which was impatient and high strung, with speed and grace.

❖ The horse, high strung and impatient, was mounted by the girl with speed and grace.

Each of these different ways of arranging the same words results in a slightly different sentence. Although the meaning is the same, the style and tone change subtly but clearly in each.

Now look at still another variation on this same sentence. This time we are changing the word choices:

❖ The gal hopped on the jittery, nervous bronco quickly and lightly.

You can see how the style and voice of the sentence changes with each manipulation of diction and syntax. As a writer, you have these same options in determining your own style and voice.

THESIS AND THESIS STATEMENT
▼

The thesis is the central or dominant idea that controls and unifies the text. Whether it is stated explicitly (hence the "thesis statement") or is implied, the thesis is the center of interest in a text—it is the point you want to make and the idea, attitude, or opinion you hope your readers will accept as true and carry away with them after they finish reading. All texts have a thesis, but not all texts contain a thesis statement.

However, when you take a stand on a debatable issue, you don't want to fool around. Most of the time you will want to express your thesis explicitly in a thesis statement to minimize ambiguity. Any text is open to different interpretations—whether the reader is carelessly inattentive or is attentive but influenced by beliefs, knowledge, or expectations that would allow for an interpretation different from what you intend. Thus it is important that you state your thesis as clearly as you can make words express it and in language that your readers understand easily. You express your opinion early—usually in the first or second paragraph—and clearly—either as a declarative sentence or a question—and then support the thesis statement with evidence or answer the question. Such is the nature of most of your texts that have an argumentative edge: they indicate to readers that you are going to argue for a certain proposition, get them involved early, and entice them to want to read the whole text. Here are four thesis statements that do just that.

The first one is the first sentence of an article by a natural science columnist for *Outsider* magazine:

> In the fifth chapter of Matthew's gospel, Christ is quoted as saying that the meek shall inherit the earth, but other opinion lately suggests that, no, more likely it will go to the cockroaches.
>
> —David Quammen, "A Republic of Cockroaches," in *Natural Acts: A Sidelong View of Science and Nature* (New York: Nick Lyon's Books, 1985): 53.

The second example is the very first sentence in E. D. Hirsh, Jr.'s 1987 national bestselling book. It states the essence of his argument that cultural literacy (the background information that an audience needs to understand what is said in books, newspapers, magazines, television programs, etc.) is essential to being a successful citizen or worker in our society:

> To be culturally literate is to possess the basic information needed to thrive in the modern world.
>
> —*Cultural Literacy: What Every American Needs to Know* (Boston: Houghton Mifflin, 1987): xiii.

At times, you may want to lead into your thesis statement by providing brief background or context, as in the third and fourth examples.

The third is a strong assertion at the end of the opening paragraph that will be defended by information that follows:

> Each child has a dream. I had two. One was to be a marine and the other was to be a policeman. I tried other endeavors but I was just not cut out for it. I am a policeman. It is one of the most gratifying jobs in the world.
>
> —Studs Terkel, "Vincent Maher," in *Working*
> (New York: Avon, 1974): 183.

The fourth example comes at the end of the second paragraph of one of the most famous articles published in *Ms.* magazine. It states the main idea of the piece, followed by a question that helps focus the issue and propel the reader to read on to find the answers:

> I belong to that classification of people known as wives. I am a wife. And, not altogether incidentally, I am a mother.
> Not long ago a male friend of mine appeared on the scene fresh from a recent divorce. He had one child, who is, of course, with his ex-wife. He is looking for another wife. As I thought about him while I was ironing one evening, it suddenly occurred to me that I, too, would like to have a wife. Why do I want a wife?
>
> —Judy Syfers, "I Want a Wife," *Ms.*
> (April 1972): 56.

In addition to stating the main idea, a thesis statement can also be constructed so it has predictive power. For instance, it can be stated so it signals a particular method of development for a piece of writing. Here is a statement that suggests a cause-and-effect method of development: "The 18 percent reduction in employee absenteeism at the Fillmore Plant appears to be the direct result of the new employee incentives programs introduced last year." A thesis statement can also be designed so it both suggests the method of development and indicates the organization of the content in a piece of writing. Here is a statement that suggests a comparison method of development and forecasts that three criteria (cost, ease of use, and availability of software) will be discussed in the order listed: "The Azcar 1588b is the best buy because it is the least expensive system in its class, it appears to be the easiest to learn to use, and it has the most available software." Once such an anticipatory summary has been made, it must be fulfilled in the ensuing text (also see **forecasting statements**).

FORECASTING STATEMENTS, PAGE 503

Most of the time, as these sample thesis statements illustrate, the traditional strategy in persuasive writing is to state the thesis first (sometimes also predicting the plan of organization) and then present the reasons, facts, and evidence that will lead the reader to accept your opinion. In its most basic form, such tightly organized arguments look like the one that follows, in an interpretation of Ernest Hemingway's "The Snows of Kilimanjaro."

The opening paragraph ends with this statement of the issue and the author's proposition.	. . .Ernest Hemingway's use of death symbols in "The Snows of Kilimanjaro" has been pointed out many times. Nevertheless, Caroline Gordon and Allen Tate object to Hemingway's use of snow-covered Kilimanjaro as a symbol of death (*The House of Fiction*). They claim that the symbol "does not operate as a controlling image" of the story and that it "seems something the writer has tacked on, rather than an integral part of the story" (421). Yet the snow-covered western summit does serve as symbol; it is the whiteness of Kilimanjaro's snow, the unusual whiteness attending Harry's fatal infection, and the weird aura of whiteness in Harry's reveries which officiate over his death.
The second paragraph begins with this statement that supports the thesis. The rest of the paragraph consists of factual support for this opinion.	Hemingway uses whiteness in connection with the death of his central characters. . . .
The third paragraph begins with this statement of support for the thesis. The rest of the paragraph consists of factual support of this opinion.	In "The Snows of Kilimanjaro" whiteness again attends death. . . .

The third paragraph begins with these statements that support the thesis. The rest of the paragraph consists of factual support for this opinion.

As Harry passes through a series of feverish reveries toward death, whiteness appears with increasing recurrence and persistence. The more vacuous Harry becomes, the more obvious the aura of whiteness. . . .

After the three areas of support are each presented in a paragraph, the last paragraph states what the author hopes is the inevitable conclusion.

The many instances in which Hemingway associates whiteness with the death of his central characters, and particularly the frequent and persistent appearance of whiteness that accompanies Harry's trip to death, makes it clear that Hemingway was fully conscious and in control of his symbolic use of the white snows of Kilimanjaro.

This extract shows the essence of the argument. The most important conclusion and the biggest idea is the thesis: the snow-covered western summit of Mount Kilimanjaro is an integral symbol in the story. The tight organization of the argument conveys a strong sense of a beginning, middle, and end. The five paragraphs contain the thesis statement, three main statements of support to affirm the thesis, and then the conclusion. This form, easy to master, is one of the most common of all forms in writing, and keeps the argument focused by clearly stating the point under dispute and displaying the line of reasoning briskly and efficiently. It satisfies readers' desire to know what the writer wants to tell them and also what to expect in the rest of the text. It is equally well suited to analyzing relatively minor questions and to arguing the complexities of large and difficult subjects.

However, not all texts must have such tightly structured arguments. There are other options. For instance, in more informal, relaxed personal writing, the thesis may appear anywhere, including in the middle of the piece. Russell Baker's chapter about his Uncle Harold in his autobiography *Growing Up* illustrates the variation. The chapter begins, "Uncle Harold was famous for lying." But that sentence, while it starts the chapter with a bang, does not state the main idea. Baker comes to recognize that Uncle Harold was not really a liar but was a romantic who wanted life to be more interesting than it was. Here's the way Baker writes it (in the fifty-sixth paragraph!).

My first awe of him had softened as I gradually realized his information was not really intended to be information. Gradually I came to see that Uncle Harold was not a liar but a teller of stories and a romantic, and it was Uncle Harold the teller of tales who fascinated me.

—Growing Up
(New York: Congdon & Weed,
1982): 143.

Baker's decision to hold back the thesis statement until nearly two-thirds through the chapter is effective in helping us decide whether Baker's opinion of Uncle Harold is accurate. To have begun the chapter with this main point would have robbed Baker (and us) of the opportunity to share the experiences that eventually led him to understand Uncle Harold's true nature. Baker's delaying the main point until late in the chapter reflects his gradual discovery of the truth about Uncle Harold.

TITLES
▼

Positioned as it is at the beginning, the title influences how a reader responds to the text because it is generally the first clue as to what is at the heart of the text—the writer's intention and the topic, subject matter, or theme.

A good title performs several functions, one of the the most important of which is to indicate the topic of the text. The following untitled passage illustrates how important a title or the lack of a title is in giving an indication of topic:

Rocky slowly got up from the mat, planning his escape. He hesitated a moment and thought. Things were not going well. What bothered him most was being held, especially since the charge against him had been weak. He considered his present situation. The lock that held him was strong but he thought he could break it. He knew, however, that his timing would have to be perfect. Rocky was aware that it was because of his early roughness that he had been penalized so severely—much too severely from his point of view. The situation was becoming frustrating; the pressure had been grinding on him too long. He was being ridden unmercifully. Rocky was getting angry now. He felt he was ready to make his move. He knew that his success or failure would depend on what he did in the next few seconds.

> —Quoted in Lester Faigley, "The Problem of Topic in Texts," in *The Territory of Language: Linguistics, Stylistics, and the Teaching of Composition*, ed. Donald A. McQuade (Carbondale: Southern Illinois UP, 1986): 134.

Do you know what this passage is about? Your answer depends on the assumptions you make about the topic. Without a title to inform readers about the topic, the passage is ambiguous, as was demonstrated when researchers read the passage to selected college students. Physical education majors believed the passage was about wrestling; other students thought it was about a prison escape (Richard C. Anderson, Ralph E. Reynolds, Dianne L. Schallert, and Ernest T. Goetz, *Framework for Comprehending Discourse*, Technical Report No. 12 [Urbana, IL: Center for the Study of Reading, 1976], ERIC Document Reproduction Service No. ED 134 935). The reader's reactions will inevitably be in terms of his or her own temperament, interests, and background. Thus physical education majors, wrestlers, former wrestlers, and fans of wrestling are likely to share the same assumptions and thus come to similar interpretations about the topic.

Because readers' responses are shaped by what they know, are interested in, and think important, the possible meanings in a text are provisional and can shift from one reader to the next and can vary from one moment to the next. Key words in a title can help stabilize meaning by establishing a general framework of meaning and a strong clue of what the topic is by providing information that is not given in the text itself. Lacking such information about an untitled text, readers—like the students in the experiment just cited—must concentrate on building a hypothesis about the topic as they read. This effort to deduce or recognize the topic can be profoundly influenced by these three factors: (1) the readers' familiarity with what they assume is the unstated topic (prior knowledge can make a dramatic difference, as illustrated in the preceding passage); (2) the readers' sophistication in reading (the awareness that other interpretations of the topic are possible); and (3) the readers' needs for certain kinds of information (the readers are likely to see what they are interested in).

The meaning of a text is created by these variable subjective perceptions, which leave a text open to a range of different understandings and interpretations. But guided by a title such as "Wrestling" or "The Prisoner," the reader is able to limit possible interpretations of the topic and without much effort will have particular expectations about the topic and can focus and shape meaning that is more in line with the author's intention. With such an informative title, the readers of the passage would have been able to identify the topic not so much from what the text said as from what the title said. A specific title almost guarantees that the topic will be recognized.

A more ambiguous title, such as "The Escape," would have kept the text open to various interpretations, which is often a desirable feature of literary writing. Thus a title can destabilize the meaning of a text as well as stabilize it. In choosing a title for your text, you must consider whether you want the title to indicate the topic directly and clearly. If your purpose is primarily informative, a title that clearly states the topic is probably best. If your purpose is primarily literary, a title that is not immediately clear and perhaps even playfully ironic, but which nevertheless becomes clear and appropriate as the reader reads, can be very effective. Titles such as "A Rose for Emily," *To Kill a Mockingbird, Catcher in the Rye, The Color Purple, The Joy Luck Club,* "The Short Happy Life of Francis Macomber," and *Love in the Time of Cholera* are titles of literary works that are symbolic, evocative, ironic, or in some other fashion suggestively rich.

A second function of an effective title, especially for pragmatic texts, is to define the writer's purpose and the scope of the text. Titles such as "How to Reduce Stress During Final Examinations," "A Guide to the Ready-Reference Section of the University Library," and "Proposal for an Analysis of Water Imagery in Hemingway's Fiction" are fairly long but allow the reader to identify the writer's purpose in precise terms. Exact and specific titles work well for professional audiences and others who are engaged in the serious reading of informative texts. An example is "Coherent Vortical Features in a Turbulent Two-Dimensional Flow and the Great Red Spot of Jupiter" (Phillip S. Marcus, paper presented at the 110th Meeting of the Acoustical Society of America, Nashville, TN, November 5, 1985).

While most readers no longer expect the title to cover the entire subject, they do expect a title to indicate the main focus. A title such as *Resisting Earthquakes* is too broad if the topic is the design of earthquake-resistant features in tall buildings in Los Angeles. However, a long title does not guarantee a precise title. Here is some deadwood that shows up more often than is desirable in academic and professional writing: *An Analysis of . . . , An Investigation of . . . , A Report on . . . , A Study of. . . .* These words state the obvious and therefore contribute nothing to the meaning of the title. Since they are the first words in titles, they occupy a strong position that should be given to words which contribute more substantively to the title. *An Investigation of the Use of Phase Transitions in Artificial Intelligence Systems* is twice as long as need be: *Phase Transitions in Artificial Intelligence Systems.*

A third function of a title is to capture attention and entice the reader to begin reading the text. The amount of luring required depends largely on the audience. For readers of scientific, professional, and academic writing, titles should usually announce the topic, purpose, and scope. The readers' needs for specific kinds of information and the reputation of the publication or publisher are generally sufficient for motivated readers. For readers who are reading primarily for entertainment or to satisfy personal interests, titles need to be more intriguing. There are several ways to do this. Titles such as "Shipwrecked on the Shores of Switzerland," "What You Don't Know About the Selection of the Homecoming Queen," and "What They Don't Teach You at the Harvard Business School" arouse interest and curiosity. Titles that ask questions carry the implied promise that the reader will learn the answer if he or she reads the text. Inquisitive titles such as "Can South Africa Be Saved?" or "Should You Fight a Library Fine?" or "How Long Is the Coast of Britain?" not only express the topic of the text but serve well as hooks if the question interests the reader.

Coming up with a good title takes some time, and it is worth thinking about early in your writing. It's probably not quite as important as naming your firstborn child, but the effort can help guide you in focusing on your central idea. Here are three suggestions about creating titles.

▶ Choose a title that in some way fits the text. Do not try to fool a reader or yourself with a catchy, humorous, or bizarre title that is not appropriate. Ellen Coughlin, the book review editor for the *Chronicle of Higher Education*, observed that the subtitle of W. V. Quine's book

Quiddities: An Intermittently Philosophical Dictionary was inappropriate: "This is not a dictionary and it is not terribly philosophical" (October 21, 1987: A9).

▶ **Do not accept uncritically the first title that pops into your mind.** Many well-known books would not be recognized by their original titles: Leo Tolstoy's *All's Well That Ends Well* became *War and Peace* and Thomas Wolfe's *O Lost* was published as *Look Homeward, Angel.* One of the all-time bestsellers in America, Margaret Mitchell's *Gone with the Wind,* at first had the working title *Another Day,* and Mitchell also considered *Milestones, Jettison, Ba! Ba! Blacksheep, Not in Our Day,* and *Bugles Sang True.* It is not necessarily true that a rose by any other name would smell as sweet. Keep plugging away at the title until you have one that can stand for the central idea or symbolize the meaning of your text.

▶ **If a good title eludes you early on, keep on writing.** It is really not necessary to think up a title before you can write. But sometimes during writing and revising, study closely the beginning and ending of your text, looking specifically for cues that might lead to a title. You will probably find a phrase or sentence containing key words that state your purpose and intent or that capture the idea of the thesis. If you are indecisive about a title, draft two or three possible titles and ask the opinion of a classmate who is providing a critique of your writing. One of the alternative titles might be stronger than the others, or portions of two or more of the alternative titles might be selected in reconstructing a new title. Perhaps even a totally new title will emerge. There will, of course, be some blind alleys, but there will also be a few promising avenues to explore. Sooner or later, you will come up with a title that attracts readers and predisposes them to focus on your topic as they begin reading your text.

There are two basic positions for a title. The title can be put on a separate sheet of paper, appropriately called a title page, at the front of the text, or the title can be centered at the top of the first page of the text. Punctuation and capitalization of titles vary. Do not place the titles of your own text in quotation marks. Do not place a period at the end, although a question mark or exclamation mark may be used when one is appropriate. Generally the first word and every important word in the title are capitalized, and articles, conjunctions, and prepositions (*a, the, and, yet, of, with,* etc.) are left in lowercase unless they are the first word of the title: The Formation of Professions. Since most titles are short, the title may also be typed in all capitals or underlined for emphasis:

The Formation of Professions,

THE FORMATION OF PROFESSIONS,

THE FORMATION OF PROFESSIONS.

TOPIC SENTENCE
▼

Just as a **thesis statement** is the controlling idea of an essay, a topic sentence is the controlling idea of a paragraph or section of an essay. A topic sentence is like a mini-thesis: it expresses the main idea of one segment or distinct subdivision of a text, instead of the main idea of an entire text. Sometimes the segment or subdivision is a series of paragraphs. More often it is a **paragraph**.

THESIS STATEMENT, PAGE 599

PARAGRAPHS, PAGE 567

    A number of important parallels can be drawn between a thesis statement and a topic sentence. Both, of course, embody a major idea that may be stated or implied. The first sentence of the following paragraph explicitly states the main idea that the ensuing sentences develop:

> One of the cruel aspects of the bombing campaigns of the Second World War was the far worse suffering of the poorer-paid manual worker, whether of Dortmund and Essen, London or Coventry. The poorer people lived close together and close to their places of work, which in turn were prime targets of the bombers. The rich got out, the middle class were more scattered and often distant from targets. London exemplified this injustice. The Germans were not bombing indiscriminately in 1940, either in London or Coventry. In London the first target in the early days was dockland, where the dockers and their families of the East End lived next door to their work—the people of Bermondsey, Whitechapel, and Isle of Dogs and Stepney. Their agony during the autumn and winter of 1940–1941 was appalling and on a different scale from any-

thing experienced in west, north and south London, where life at first was uncomfortable and noisy but nothing like as dangerous as the east of the city.

—Richard Hough, *Edwina: Countess Mountbatten of Burma* (New York: Morrow, 1983): 150.

Sometimes the controlling idea of a section of text is not explicitly stated but only implied. In such instances, if the segment is well written, all the sentences and paragraphs imply an idea about which a topic sentence *could* be written. However, in most informative and persuasive writing, it is usually desirable to make topic sentences explicit. The value of an explicit topic sentence is that it identifies the topic of the paragraph and focuses the reader's attention on the main point of the passage, to which he or she can relate the more specific details of the passage. Everything falls more easily into place for the reader who at the beginning knows what the passage is about.

In addition to expressing the central idea, a topic sentence shares three other characteristics with a thesis statement: its form, its position, and its need to be substantiated.

Both a thesis statement and a topic sentence are usually expressed as a single declarative statement or question. It may appear anywhere in a passage, but as a matter of emphasis it usually—though not always—appears at the beginning of the segment that it controls. In the following passage, which is taken from a letter written by Albert Einstein, we can see that the topic sentence (italicized) is valuable even in texts that are not essays:

Scientific life has almost ceased to exist here. No journals are being published, neither are there opportunities to have anything printed. A minimum of scientific work is being done; anyone wanting to do it would soon starve. Furthermore, for the last three years we have not received any foreign journals. Therefore, I have very little idea of what is currently being thought about in scientific circles.

—Letter to Max Born, August 18, 1920, *The Born-Einstein Letters* (New York: Walker, 1971): 47.

This topic sentence works just like a topic sentence in an essay: it states a generalization that is developed or substantiated by particular data, concrete examples, and specific facts. Beginning a passage with a topic sentence has the effect of summarizing what is to come and thus offers several advantages to both the writer and to readers: it helps the writer stay on the topic; it enables readers to know at once what the passage is about so they can adjust their thinking to the main focus of the passage; and it provides a framework for the many details in the ensuing sentences. Thus it does not hurt to make the topic sentence—wherever it appears—as obvious and as strong as the thesis sentence statement. That way, especially in longer segments or subdivisions, readers will be sufficiently aware of the main point.

The topic sentence has another equally important function. While it expresses an idea that controls a segment or subdivision of the text, it is subordinate to a larger idea—the thesis statement. A text generally has several topic sentences that relate to the thesis. Each topic sentence in turn is at the center of a series of sentences or paragraphs that relate to the topic sentence. Indeed, a text can be regarded as a series of topic sentences each with its own lesser series of sentences or paragraphs. Everything is related in a well-structured piece of writing, and topic sentences are a major contributor to the organization and coherence.

Because of its intermediate position between the thesis and the more specific details, examples, and facts that support the thesis, the topic sentence is a key element in the most basic pattern of composition: introduction containing the thesis statement followed by several paragraphs that support the thesis statement.

Here are four paragraphs that develop the idea that westerners are succinct in their speech. Note how the topic sentences (which are italicized) start the paragraphs with a little bump and give unmistakable direction to their content.

The solitude in which westerners live make them quiet. They telegraph thoughts and feelings by the way they tilt their head and listen; pulling their Stetsons into a steep dive over their eyes, or pigeon-toeing one boot over the other, they lean against a fence with a fat wedge of snoose beneath their lower lips and take the whole scene in. These detached looks of quiet amusement are sometimes cynical, but they can also come from a dry-eyed humility as lucid as the air is clear.

Conversation goes on in what sounds like a private code: a few phrases imply a complex of meanings. Asking directions, you get a curious list of details. While trailing sheep, I was told to "ride up to the kinda upturned rock, follow the pink wash, turn left at the dump, and you'll see the waterhole." One friend told his wife on roundup to "turn at the salt lick and the dead cow," which turned out to be a scattering of bones and no salt lick at all.

Sentence structure is shortened to the skin and bones of a thought. Descriptive words are dropped, even verbs; a cowboy looking over a corral full of horses will say to a wrangler, "Which one needs rode?" People hold back their thoughts in what seems to be a dumbfounded silence, then erupt with an excoriating perceptive remark. Language, so compressed, becomes metaphorical. A rancher ended a relationship with one remark: "You're a bad check," meaning bouncing in and out was intolerable, and even coming back would be no good.

What's behind this laconic style is shyness. There is no vocabulary for the subject of feelings. Its not a hangdog shyness, or anything coy—always there's a robust spirit in evidence behind the restraint, as if the earthdredging wind that pulls across Wyoming had carried its people's voices away but everything else in them had shouldered confidently into the breeze.

—Gretel Ehrlich, "Wyoming," in *The Solace of Open Spaces* (New York: Viking Penguin, 1985): 6–7.

THESIS STATEMENT, PAGE 599

PARAGRAPHS, PAGE 567

TRANSITIONS, PAGE 612

It should be clear from this passage how a topic sentence and the accumulated past topic sentences make the focus of the text apparent, giving it more solidity and strength. Each topic sentence expresses an idea that relates to an aspect of the thesis. In turn, each embodies the core of meaning and controls the development of its segment of the text. Like **thesis statements, paragraphs,** and **transitions**, the topic sentence is an invaluable tool for thinking, writing, and reading.

TRANSITIONS

▼

A transition is both a *process* of moving from one place to another and a *device* that enables the movement to go smoothly.

As readers move from one idea to the next in a piece of writing, they try to understand the relationships among those ideas. In texts in which order, continuity,and logical development are important, writers help readers get from place to place by designing a sequence that reveals and reinforces the relationships among ideas and information. Writers can also help readers become aware of those relationships by using transitional words, phrases, or passages and by using certain format devices, such as headings and the placement of text on the page.

To illustrate how simple transitional words can strengthen logic and can smooth style, compare the following passages. In the first, three successive thoughts are not joined by transitions:

> The price of crude oil rose rapidly from 1973 to 1981. It fell in 1982. Petroleum producers did not pump as much crude oil in 1983 as they had done before.

Note how insecurely these thoughts stand together and how bumpily the passage reads. Even though the sentences are successive and closely related in thought, their relationship is not evident. By providing only two transitional words, *but* and *therefore*, we join the thoughts and sentences solidly together and make clear their relationship:

> The price of crude oil rose rapidly from 1973 to 1981. *But* it fell in 1982. Petroleum producers, *therefore*, did not pump as much crude oil in 1983 as they had done before.

Two transitional words in a passage of thirty-one words. That is probably the right ratio in ordinary passages. Transitions comprise a very small percentage of writing, but they serve the crucial task of relating ideas, displaying organization, underscoring logic, predicting the direction of ensuing sentences, and generally smoothing out style.

Whenever you are writing a draft, don't worry too much too early about providing a transition from one topic or paragraph to the next. If a transition presents itself naturally while you are writing, fine. Take it. It will probably help you clarify your thinking and strengthen your logic. But sometime during revision look specifically for those places where you need to show the relationship of your successive thoughts, for if you do not take care to show it, your writing may not appear connected even though you have arranged your ideas in an orderly

manner. If transitions are not used well, the text will have a disconnected feel to it, appearing to be a random or accidental sequence of
statements, rather than a connected entity.

Several kinds of transitions and connective devices can be helpful.
Some occur rather naturally as you write sentences and paragraphs.
Others do not. But all require your careful attention when revising.

Among the most natural transitional and connective devices are
variations or substitutions of earlier key words in the form of personal
pronouns (*he, she, it, they, I,* etc.) and demonstrative pronouns and
adjectives (*this, that, these, those,* etc.). When the word to which the
pronoun or adjective refers (its antecedent) is in the preceding sentence, the pronoun or adjective links the thought of the two sentences.
Here is an example of an antecedent-pronoun link:

> *Over one hundred fans* were outside the stadium two hours
> before game time. *They* wanted to be there to greet the team
> when it arrived by bus.

The phrase *over one hundred fans* and the word *they* refer to the
same entities, thus providing continuity.

Here is a passage that contains an antecedent-demonstrative
adjective link:

> In Britain *James Watt* and *Richard Arkwright* embodied the
> spirit of the industrial revolution. *These two men* were associ-
> ated with the development of the steam engine and the burst
> of inventions in the textiles industry.

These two men points back to the previously mentioned men.

Here is a passage that contains antecedent-prounoun-demonstra-
tive adjective links:

> *Tubular tires* are the kind used by track- and road-racing
> cyclists. *They* come standard on most expensive European bicy-
> cles and on a few high-grade American racing bicycles. *These
> tires* come in a variety of weights. . . .

They and *these tires* refer back to *tubular tires.*

Although each of the sentences in the preceding examples begins
with a connective device, not every sentence has to start with a transi-

tion of some kind. But when you need a transition to give your text coherence and logic, you need to know where to place it. Because a transition works as a kind of signal or bridge, it should be placed early enough to be effective.

Transitions to indicate logical relationships can usually be achieved by merely adding a word or two where the relationship needs to be made explicit. Such transitions are slightly more formal than the repetition of nouns, pronouns, and demonstrative adjectives. Here is a list of the most important ones that you will likely use.

To add, coordinate, or show sequence	*first, second, the third . . . moreover, also, and, in addition, next, then, last*
To indicate simultaneity	*meanwhile, at the same time*
To introduce an example	*for example, for instance, in particular, namely*
To show result, cause, or consequence	*consequently, as a result, thus, therefore, for, because, since*
To restate	*in other words, that is*
To conclude or summarize	*in conclusion, to sum up, on the whole*
To contrast, oppose, or show alternatives	*but, yet, on the other hand, nevertheless, on the contrary, in contrast, however, or*
To compare	*similarly, likewise, in like manner*

The following paragraph illustrates how two or three formal transitions like these, wisely placed, reveal logical relationships:

Since the study of extraterrestrial life lacks any proven subject, opinions about the form and frequency of nonearthly beings record the hopes and fears of speculating scientists more than the constraints of evidence. Alfred Russel Wallace, *for example,* Darwin's partner in the discovery of natural selection, and the first great scientist to consider exobiology in any detail, held firmly that man must be alone in the entire cosmos—*for* he could not bear the thought that human intelligence had not been the uniquely special gift of God, conferred upon an ideally suited planet. He wrote in 1903 that the existence of abundant and brainy extraterrestrials "would imply that man is an animal and nothing more, is of no importance in the universe, needed no great preparations for his advent, only, perhaps, a second-rate demon, and a third- or fourth-rate earth."

> —Stephen Jay Gould, "The Wisdom of Casey
> Stengel," *Discovery* 4 (March 1974): 62.

When the text is fairly long or difficult, "mega-transitions" (transitional clauses or sentences) help the reader get from one major idea to another, as in the following two examples:

We have attempted to explain the spirit which moderated and the strength which supported the power of Hadrian and the Antonines. *We shall now endeavor, with clearness and preciseness, to describe* the provinces, once unified under their sway, but at present, divided into so many independent and hostile states.

> —Edward Gibbon, *The History of the Decline
> and Fall of the Roman Empire.*

The second example is from an even earlier writer, the poet Geoffrey Chaucer, writing in the latter part of the fourteenth century:

Now that I've told you shortly, in a clause, The rank, the dress, the number, and the cause Why these were all assembled at the inn Called Tabard—near the Bell—*I must begin And tell you whast we did that selfsame night, And later of the pilgrimage I'll write.* . . .

> —"Prologue," *Canterbury Tales*, trans. R. M.
> Stauffer, in *The Canterbury Tales* (Baltimore:
> Penguin, 1958).

Writers can use explicit forecasting statements to anticipate what follows without referring so baldly to themselves, as Gibbon and Chaucer did, as in the following example:

The flavor of this book can best be conveyed by showing the motifs which recur most frequently throughout the book: namely, W-Hollow as "place," the cycle of the seasons, home town as joy and agony, death, and the centrality of his father to Stuart's life.

> —Ruel Foster, "Introduction" in *The Year of My Rebirth* (Ashland, KY: The Jesse Stuart Foundation, 1991): xiii.

The sentence forecasts for the reader that the five major motifs are discussed in the rest of the introduction. By noting the sentences that open the discussion of each of these motifs, we can see how explicitly they cue readers to the organization:

At first he can only walk to the window and look out on the hills and hollows of W-Hollow and watch the ever changing weather. But he feels the importance of this as "place" to him. (p. xiii)

Interwoven with the W-Hollow motif is Stuart's fascination with the seasons. (p. xv)

Stuart often thought during this year of his recuperation of his strange mixed-up relations with Greenup, his home town. (p. xvi)

One of the major motifs in the journal is death. Conscious as he is of how close he has come to dying, Stuart's mind broods over all his other escapes with death. (p. xviii)

Aside from Stuart himself, the man who dominates *The Year of My Rebirth* is Stuart's father. (p. xix)

Forecasting statements and transitions are also important within a paragraph, as in the following one in which the anticipating and connecting devices are italicized. The italicized sentence forecasts the two subtopics to be developed in the paragraph: ordering from mail-order houses and buying from garden centers.

FORECASTING STATEMENTS, PAGE 503

One never runs out of dahlia stock but does get bored with the endless multiplication of the same cultivars. *There are two ways to buy new ones: mail order or off the shelf at a garden center, and oddly enough I have done better with the latter. Many mail order houses* send out a single tuber coated with wax and charge $2.50 and up for it. At best, these produce a skimpy plant and often they come to nothing. *At garden centers* you can often find unwaxed clumps from Holland, packed in peat moss and costing a modest $1.98. A color photograph is clipped to the packet, and it is accurate. What you see is what you get, complete with instructions for planting. These, to my mind, are the best dahlias on the market and an amazing bargain.

—Eleanor Perenyi, *Green Thoughts: A Writer in the Garden* (New York: Vintage, 1983): 52–53.

Sometime during the second sentence, both the writer as he or she writes and the reader as he or she reads begin to gain a sense of the direction of the paragraph. By the third sentence, the reader knows that "mail-order houses" and "garden centers" are at the heart of the paragraph.

As we describe these simple and mega-transitions, you may be struck by their sheer number. You may wonder at this point whether you believe such overt statements about organization and logical relationships are really necessary in writing that is well organized. After all, you might think, isn't good writing brief and to the point? Doesn't inserting these expressions take up a lot of space? Would the use of such direct statements insult the intelligence of readers by pointing out the obvious?

These are fair questions to ask.

We agree that good writing is not *overloaded* with such expressions. We also agree that good writing saves space. But we know that good writing, in which order, unity, and logical development is important, saves time—the reader's time. There is, of course, another possibility. There is the option to produce other kinds of writing—extremely informal but energetic, pronouncedly elliptical, and disjointed writing—in which logical relationships are not clarified and connections, if any, are unmarked. Such ambiguous, disconnected writing is sometimes appropriate in mirroring a confusing, discontinuous, and fragmented world, especially in fiction and poetry.

But we believe that explicit transitions and connectors such as we have been describing are necessary in most writing when you are trying to convey information efficiently, for they foster clear thinking in both the writer and the reader. Simple and mega-transitions point back to what has just been said and point forward to what is gong to be said, thus making the passage hang together. Not providing adequate signals to the logic and organization of the text causes a major problem. The problem lies not in whether the writer has organized his or her material well, but in whether the reader can perceive the logic and organization easily. The writer's view of a text is different from that of the reader. Even when transitional and connective devices are not in a passage, the writer knows the relationships—after all, he or she has internalized them after thinking about them so much. And because he or she sees the unity and logic, the writer assumes that readers also see them.

Unfortunately, such an assumption encourages many writers to omit explicit statements that help guide readers as they move through sentences, between sentences within a paragraph, and between larger units of text. These omissions will inevitably slow readers down and make them work harder to follow the discussion—if they have the interest or patience to do so. Just because writing can be reread and studied does not mean that readers will be willing to do it. Used well, a transition can signal that an example is an example. It can show that an upcoming idea is or is not a change in the subject. It can tell readers that point 4 is point 4. There is no better way to get readers from beginning to end than by marking the route clearly.

Douglas Olson, *Cowhand Putting on Chaps*

PART FOUR

▼

HANDBOOK

▶ INTRODUCTION

Correctness in diction, usage, punctuation, and mechanics—like most principles of writing—is ultimately a matter of audience. You want to follow those rules that readers will expect you to know and observe. If you do not, your credibility will be lessened. Your readers will remember only that you used the wrong word or that your subjects and verbs did not agree rather than being convinced that your arguments were sound or your solution plausible.

In addition, errors may confuse your readers or even cause them a great deal of trouble or expense. At the least, the omission of a comma, the misplacement of a modifier, or an ambiguous word may result in readers' having a significantly different understanding than the one you intended.

Part Four focuses on those rules and conventions that will make you a more credible writer. Rather than attempting to be comprehensive, we include only what we think college students need to know.

The Handbook consists of four main sections: diction, usage, punctuation, and mechanics. Each of these is subdivided into different entries, which are arranged alphabetically. Some entries include references to related entries in the Handbook or in Part Three (Strategies).

D. DICTION ◀

D.1 CLICHÉS

During the Persian Gulf War, Saddam Hussein's belligerent statement that the United States and its allies would experience "the mother of all battles" struck most Americans as unusual, perhaps even original. Partly in mockery but also partly in imitation of an original saying, Americans within weeks were using phrases like "the mother of all defeats" and "the mother of all parades." Home owners were referring to "the mother of all telephone bills," and students were fretting over "the mother of all final exams." Quickly, "the mother of all" became a cliché. It will be interesting to see how long the expression stays around.

Clichés are tired, trite expressions that when first coined seem a clever and original way of saying something. The first poet to compare his love to a red rose or old age to autumn made the reader or listener think about the improbable comparison. But because the newly coined expressions were so effective, they became familiar, then overused, and through overuse quickly lost their sharpness, vividness, and impact and became dull old sayings.

Thus expressions such as "green with envy," "law of the jungle," and "a sea of faces" were once vivid but have long since lost their brightness. Once famous literary quotations such as "ignorance is bliss," "eat, drink, and be merry," and "better late than never" have become threadbare. Once sparkling alliterative analogies such as "good as gold," "clear as crystal," and "busy as a bee (or beaver)" are now as flat as a three-day-old cola. How zippy does Bart Simpson's "Man, don't have a cow" sound these days?

The freshness of an original expression usually lasts only a few weeks or months. But while it may no longer ring with compact energy, its half-life may continue for years, tempting us to use it because it is ready-made and familiar. However, by the time you have heard or seen a vogue expression a few times, it is no longer fresh and lively because your readers also have probably heard or seen it several times, too. Its fading freshness will make your ideas and thinking seem stale. In the minds of many readers clichés of expression indicate clichés of thought—that nothing new is being said.

Clichés are in everybody's vocabulary. For almost all of us, "implications" are "far-reaching," "glances" are "furtive," and "truth" is "somewhere between the two extremes." But even if you believe that expressions like "ignorance is bliss," "better late than never," "don't count your chickens before they are hatched," and "the grass is always greener on the other side of the fence" convey the wisdom of the ages, it is best not to use them. They actually convey little information and take up plenty of space.

D.2   CONNOTATION

Accuracy in diction is achieved by choosing words that say exactly what is intended. Connotation is one more aspect of diction to be considered.

Several words may refer to the same thing in general, but each has shades of meaning and associations that the others do not. The reason is that in addition to their denotative meanings (meanings found in dictionaries), most words also have connotations—the thoughts and emotions aroused in the reader by the word. For instance, the terms *lactating female* and *nursing mother* denote the same thing, but *nursing mother* is much richer in connotation and will probably evoke an emotional response from a reader or listener. And because such psychological associations as these abound, it is important that writers make sure their words carry the intended connotations.

Some connotations are fairly easy to predict. Words like *home, mother,* and *honor* are supercharged with favorable connotations. Other words are equally supercharged with unfavorable connotations. But the connotations of some words are difficult to predict, because what a person associates with a word depends largely on the person's personality and background. The word *Texas,* for example, connotes something very different to a native Texan than it does to somebody who has never visited the state and whose knowledge of the state has been gained only by reading about it. To a career public official, a bureaucrat is an unelected public official who administers government policy. To others, a bureaucrat is a person who insists on rigid adherence to arbitrary rules, regulations, forms, and procedures. Alben Barkley, vice president of the United States under Harry S. Truman (1949–1952), once defined a bureaucrat as "a Democrat who holds a public office that some Republican wants."

Some words have fewer connotations and are regarded as "neutral." Other words have negative or unfavorable connotations, and still others have positive or favorable connotations. Of the three words *horse, nag,* and *steed,* for example, the first is the most neutral, the second negative, and the third positive. (Notice how each word creates a different image in your mind.) Oliver Cromwell, the Puritan religious, military, and political leader who served as dictator of England from 1653 to 1658, had more power than most English kings. But since his followers detested the word *king,* he called himself "Lord Protector of the Commonwealth." At the time, *Protector* had no political association and had generally positive connotations.

D.3   EUPHEMISMS

A euphemism is a mild word or pleasant-sounding expression that is used in the place of a supposedly harsh or objectional word or disagreeable expression. Its major function is to cushion or disguise an unpleasant or disagreeable fact or idea. H. L. Mencken, an American journalist, editor, and critic during the first half of the twentieth century, called euphemisms "scented words." We use euphemisms when we refer to "perspiration" instead of "sweat" or call "sexual intercourse" (itself a euphemism) "conjugal relations" or "intimate relations" or say "gosh darn" instead of "goddamn." The point in using euphemisms is to substitute a socially or politically acceptable expression for one that is considered unacceptable in a particular situation.

Probably more euphemisms are employed in softening the harsh reality of death than with almost any other concept. We can all imagine occasions when it would be inappropriate or bad manners, perhaps even thoughtless or cruel, to refer to death in a bald, direct way. The most commonly used euphemisms for the verb *to die* are "to pass away" or "to pass on." Flyers in the U.S. Air Force refer to their comrades who are killed as having "bought the farm." Humorous (and clichéd) euphemisms exist: "launched into eternity," "cashed in his (or her) chips," "kicked the bucket," or "stoking Lucifer's fires (or furnaces)"—referring to someone, we assume, who apparently led a sinful life. Other, more reverent euphemisms include "was claimed," "went to a better world," "glory bound," or "went to meet his (or her) maker." Less known euphemisms for dying are "returned to dust," "going West," and "his (or her) clock stopped." Some abstract, pseudo-scientific euphemisms disguise death in accounts of scientific experiments. The statement "The biota experienced 100% mortality" apparently means that all the specimens died.

Euphemistic terms abound in our vocabulary. Just as a stairway and an elevator shaft in a new addition of a library can be transformed verbally into an impressive-sounding "vertical access area," so can a room furnished with a photocopy machine, a large wastebasket, and a cabinet for storing paper become a "copy center." "Vertical access area" and "copy center" sound more impressive than stairs and elevators and a room with a photocopy machine in it. It's conceivable that a vertical access area might cost considerably more than stairs and an elevator, and it is probably true that it is more fun to work in a copy center than in a room with a photocopier. Such verbal metamorphoses are numerous: salespersons are now account executives, night watchmen are now private security officers, janitors and custodians (originally euphemisms themselves) now are labeled facility or building services specialists. Unemployment offices are now job centers, economically depressed areas are now known as economic development districts, and underdeveloped countries progress into developing countries and then become Third World nations. *MahiMahi* is now the preferred name of dolphinfish when it appears on menus, primarily because the general public has confused dolphinfish with dolphins and cannot tolerate the thought of eating Flipper or one of his friends.

Certainly not all euphemisms are bad, because many are necessary for polite behavior and are useful for softening harsh reality. But once we start using euphemisms, some problems occur. One problem is that a euphemism usually loses its pleasant sound or scent and becomes as identified with the supposedly distasteful or unpleasant thing as the words it replaced. When this happens, new euphemisms have to be coined. In an attempt to avoid terms that refer to some noticeable physical incapacity, the handicapped (originally a euphemism) became the disabled, and are now sometimes referred to as the "physically challenged" or the "differently abled." The status and dignity of Indians have been enhanced anew by the terms "Amerindian" and "Native American." The number of euphemisms that have been used to soften the reality of death indicates how quickly the euphemism loses its dignity and must be replaced.

Another problem with euphemisms is that many are sort of silly, because they exaggerate or aggrandize the normal and the routine (referring to stairwells and elevators as "vertical access areas"). And some euphemisms—the really dangerous ones—are insidious and destructive because they obfuscate certain truths that discomfort the prudish, genteel, or hypocritical and mask undesirable and possibly heinous acts of politicians and dictators who must retain the loyalty of their followers or subjects. Remember the Nazi's "final solution" (*endgültige Lösung*) for European Jews? The "New-Life Hamlets" of South Vietnam? The "United Nations Police Action" in Korea from 1950 to 1953? These examples of euphemisms—commonly referred to as doubletalk—are used to mask a truth that some faction, usually political, wants covered up. Among the more memorable examples of doubletalk in 1991 were the Department of Defense's use of "armed situation" to refer to what news networks called the war in the Persian Gulf and "force packages" to denote bombing attacks against Iraq by warplanes. In a similar manner, Iraqi buildings were called "hard targets"; Iraqi personnel were called "soft targets."

You need to be able to identify euphemisms and to use them responsibly.

D.4   FOREIGN WORDS

D.4

Most native speakers of English are not aware that English has borrowed extensively from other languages and are not informed about the multiplicity of roots from which our language has sprung. Hardly anybody—from Hoboken to Hattiesburg to Hilo—thinks of the Italian word *piano*, the Spanish word *machismo* (from which *macho* is derived), or the Swedish word *sauna* as foreign words. Even fewer regard the German words *pretzel* and *stone* or the Amerindian word *skunk* as foreign. Still fewer think of originally Latin and Greek terms such as *democracy, oral, senate*, or *stellar* as foreign words. These and countless other words like them have been used so long that they have become part of the language, no longer needing to be italicized to indicate their foreign status. They have become established as good English, and we use them freely without thought to their foreign origins. Similarly, American English words like *baseball, hotdog,* and *weekend* and many native English words of Britain, Canada, Australia, and New Zealand have become part of other languages.

As a living language, English changes and evolves. Current words will change meaning, and some will become obsolete. New words will be coined or be borrowed from other languages. The concern about using foreign words pertains to those words that have not yet become part of the general English vocabulary. If you use an obviously foreign word or phrase, it should be italicized or underlined to indicate that it has not yet been adopted into English.

Whether to use foreign words and phrases depends on purpose and audience. Most of us are acquainted with somebody who sprinkles his or her writing with foreign expressions such as *c'est la vie, moi, touché, gonif, ciao,* and so forth. Since the vast majority of us don't consciously use foreign expression, we tend to believe those who do are perhaps overcompensating for doubts about their intellectual attainments. Unless we sense the words are being used humorously, we tend to suspect the person of parading his or her scant knowledge of foreign languages.

There are, of course, special contexts in which foreign words and expressions are used extensively and acceptably: in law (*bona fide* and many other Latin terms), in politics (*coup d'état* and especially other French expressions), in logic (*a priori* and other Latin phrases), in music (*fortissimo* and other Italian words), and in literary and philosophical studies (*denouement, Zeitgeist, ethos,* and other French, German, and Greek terms). These words and expressions are clear and convenient for readers and listeners who are familiar with legal, political, musical, and literary and philosophical language. But to others, such expressions are not clear without explanation and may appear to be bookish, if not downright pretentious.

With the exception of the special contexts just mentioned, it is probably best not to use foreign expressions when there is a perfectly good equivalent expression in English. We should always consider whether to substitute an easier and much more frequently occurring word. However, we should not remain rigidly ethnocentric. Braj Koichru, a linguist on the faculty of the University of Illinois, estimated the number of English speakers in 1991 from 800 million to 2 billion (Deane Allen, "Seeing English in a New Light: As World Language," *The Council Chronicle* [National Council of Teachers of English] [September 1991]: 1). As English becomes the dominant language in the world, extending beyond the original native-speaking English cultures, it will in turn continue to borrow words and expressions from native languages of Africa, Asia, Europe, and South American cultures. There is nothing inherently wrong with using foreign words and expressions if they are the best words to use in a given situation.

D.5   GENDER-NEUTRAL LANGUAGE

Many students of English have noted a gender bias in some words and usages of the language that helps perpetuate social and cultural inequality between males and females. Three common signs of this bias are these conventions:

1. Using the masculine third-person singular pronoun (*he, him, his*) as the generic pronoun, when a male or a female may be the referent, in a statement like "Each student is to provide his own disk."

2. Using the word *man* or the suffix *-man* to refer to both males and females (*mankind, chairman, policeman, freshman, mailman*).

3. Assuming that a base word is primarily masculine and that a female form is required (*poet/poetess, prince/princess, aviator/aviatrix*). Where pairs of masculine and feminine terms exist, the feminine often suggests a less important status, as in *governor, governess* and *major, majorette*; or the female version has become pejorative but the male term has not (*master, mistress*).

Some writers are surprised that the use of words like *man, foreman,* and *manhours* instead of gender-neutral words like *humans, supervisor,* and *employee hours* offend large groups of readers. However, most people are beginning to understand that how the writer feels is not so important as how readers feel. Readers who object to gender-biased words and expressions point out that the use of such words as *he* and *foreman* create images of males in the minds of most people and as a result exclude women from the general frame of reference.

The solution to this problem is to use language that treats both sexes in the same way. The following guidelines for avoiding prejudicial gender language are from the *Prentice Hall Author's Guide*, 5th ed. (Englewood Cliffs, NJ: Prentice Hall, 1978): 19-20:

In your writing, be certain to treat men and women impersonally in regard to occupation, marital status, physical abilities, attitudes, interests, and so on. Depending on the requirements of your subject, avoid attributing particular characteristics to either sex; instead let your writing convey that one's abilities and achievements are not limited by gender. Your text should support the fact that both sexes play equally important roles in all facets of life and that activities on all levels are open to both women and men alike.

Men and women should be portrayed as people rather than as male or female. Be careful to avoid sexist language that excludes men or women from any activity or that implies that either sex is superior or dominant in a particular role. Where possible, in referring to people use words that have no sexual connotations—for example, human being, salesperson, supervisor, student, and the like. Try to avoid the use of *he* or *man* in the generic sense.

Here are five ways to achieve gender-neutral language:

▶ If you refer to a man by his last name, refer to a woman by her last name, too. Keep references to peoples' sex and marital status as equal as possible. No longer is it acceptable to refer to William Jones and Miss Perkins or to Jones and Betty.

▶ Use true generic nouns in the place of *man* or *mankind*. *Humans, human beings, humanity, women and men, people,* and *society* are possible alternatives, depending upon the context.

▶ Use professional and occupational titles that include both men and women. A helpful authoritative guide is the *U.S. Government Dictionary of Occupational Titles*, which suggests these kinds of substitutes for gender-biased titles: instead of *manpower* use *work force;* instead of *policeman* use *police* or *police officer.* If you refer to a man who is a high-ranking diplomatic official as an *ambassador,* refer to a woman who holds the same rank exactly the same way: *ambassador.* If gender needs to be distinguished, and more often than not, it does not, using a first name (Ambassador Anne Martin, Ambassador Alan Martin) works.

▶ Avoid unnecessarily using third-person singular pronouns. For example, when referring to a hypothetical person or people in general do not write

Ideally, a full-time student should spend approximately thirty hours a week studying for *his* classes.

Instead, write it one of these ways:

❖ Omit the unnecessary pronoun *his*:

Ideally, a full-time student should spend approximately thirty hours a week studying for classes.

❖ Recast into plural noun and omit the pronoun or use the plural pronoun *their*:

Ideally, full-time *students* should spend approximately thirty hours a week studying for classes [or for *their* classes].

❖ Include the third-person feminine pronoun:

Ideally, a full-time student should spend approximately thirty hours a week studying for *his or her* classes.

❖ Shift person, if appropriate:

Ideally, you should spend approximately thirty hours a week studying for classes [or *your classes*].

▶ Avoid using stereotypical expressions such as *housewife, employees and their wives, girls*, (or any diminutive to refer to adult women), and *man-sized jobs*. Instead use expressions such as *homemaker, employees and their spouses, women* (not *ladies*), and *huge job*, or *challenging job*.

D.6   GENERAL AND SPECIFIC WORDS

D.6

There are degrees of precision, and it is the writer's responsibility to use the appropriate level. If we state "She entered the room," we have indicated the fact in a very general way. The word *entered* does not tell whether she came into the room on a pair of roller blades, the shoulders of her brother, or a pair of 3-inch heels. If we wish others to visualize precisely how she came into the room, we should be more definite and use a word like *glide, burst, slip, totter, strut, stumble, saunter, slink*, or *bustle* or some expression that describes the specific manner of entry. There are times, though, when a general word like *enter* is appropriate, as in this statement:

> If you enter the building through the walkway from the parking garage, take the left corridor to the elevators and ride the elevator to the fifth floor.

Enter, take, and *ride* are appropriately general words because it is not necessary in these instructions to specify the manner in which one enters the building or takes the corridor or rides the elevator. In choosing words, use the most specific word required for the idea to be expressed.

The problem is not so much with using general and abstract words themselves, but in using highly general words when the idea is really specific. For instance, the statement "Above a piece of furniture is a picture of a building" conveys only a vague meaning at best, because the words are far removed from the objects themselves. "Above my desk is a watercolor of Cincinnati's old Union Station" is much clearer and more vivid, because the words create a much clearer idea of the objects themselves. A statement such as "Something that the person told us made us feel uneasy" places most of the work on the reader or listener to interpret how we felt, what was told, and who told it. A more specific statement like "The police officer's description of the accident scene sickened us" is much clearer. The more we use concrete words, the closer we move toward reality.

The closer we move toward reality, the clearer our meanings become. *Something, told,* and *made us feel uneasy* are general and relatively vague words and expressions, and readers tend to believe that vague words reflect vague thinking, evasive intentions, or the inability to express clearly what is meant. Try to remember that intead of writing something like "The length of the lines during registration was *affected*," write "The length of the lines during registration was *reduced*" or "The lines became *shorter* during registration" (or however the lines were affected). Instead of remaining on an abstract level, mention the specifics that you are really referring to or the specifics that led you to use the abstract word.

Abstract words can sound pretentious. Unnecessarily abstract language can become an obstacle not only to easy understanding but also to clear thinking. Creating a text, at least for most persons, is an act of discovery. Details present themselves, sometimes almost mysteriously, and in the course of writing or speaking these details often lead to further details, concepts, and generalizations. Often it is a cluster or pattern of specific details that leads to insights and new knowledge. But if the level of language remains abstract, the meaning implicit in the text is only dimly discerned by the writer, if at all. Too much general or abstract language presents the same difficulty for readers. Inevitably, if they stay with the text for any length, they will be forced to overinterpret the meager details they are given.

D.7   SLANG

Slang is that special part of the American English vocabulary that names the ocean *the big pond,* a dog a *mutt* or *pooch,* or refers to a class period that is canceled because of the teacher's absence as *a walk.* When sailors call candy *geedunk* and a torpedo a *tinfish,* they are using slang. Referring to money as *bread, dough, do-re-mi, lettuce, bucks, sawbucks, George, shekels, simoleons, wad,* or *paper* is using slang.

Slang is related to jargon, **technical terms**, and dialect in that it helps foster a sense of community among its users. And it appears in similar ways. Many slang words are formed from other words (*bigwig, egghead,* or *snafu*) or extend the meanings of existing words (*bad, chill out, fierce, weird*). Others are coined or invented (*teenybopper, rookydoo, payola, snarf, tizzy, jazz*). But the fact that this kind of language has its own label—*slang*—indicates that it is different from the larger vocabulary shared among most users of American English.

TECHNICAL TERMS, PAGE 636

Slang is a mixture of the colorful, trendy, and often humorous on the one hand and of the undignified, flippant, and irreverent on the other. Which it is, of course, is determined by the perceiver.

Many people categorically oppose the use of slang, claiming it is too restricted in a social and geographical sense, is closely associated with the rejection of prevailing social values, is part of the general debasing of the language, or worse. Opposition to slang has almost always been there. In the eighteenth century Jonathan Swift and Richard Steele, who spent much of their considerable literary energy trying to stabilize and purify the English language, railed against the slang word *mob,* which at the time was considered a vulgar abbreviation of the Latin phrase *mobile vulgus.* Of course, today no one questions the use of *mob* as acceptable English.

Many slang expressions do not wear well and are short lived. *Bought the farm,* which originated as a slang term among military fighter pilots for dying in a plane crash and was popularized by Tom

Wolfe in *The Right Stuff*, is now a cliché; *hepcat*, a term used during the 1940s to refer to a performer or devotee of swing or jazz music, has become a verbal fossil. Sometimes, though, slang expressions satisfy a real need and become established in the language. Often they remain unsanctioned as standard English or good usage in serious or formal writing, but they persist just outside the realm of formal acceptability for decades. Sometimes a slang word or expression becomes part of the language and is accepted as standard usage.

Writers may find slang an appropriate language resource at times. However, slang can trigger several negative reactions for the unwary writer, and there are at least these four reasons for using it carefully and sparingly.

▶ Slang is not always understandable to audiences, as you can see from a quick look at some recent slang used by college students. Here are ten slang words used on college campuses during the mid-1980s. If you do not recognize every one of them, you will understand why slang should not be overused—it changes from one place and time to another:

dweeb	Kraeusened
dork	lurking
generic	nosh
grimbo	'rents
hardcore	'shmen

For an interesting discussion of these terms and other college slang, see William Safire, "Back to Tool," *New York Times Magazine* (September 22, 1985): 14.

▶ Slang, like overly abstract words, may not convey precisely the meaning intended. Beginning writers are too often satisfied with general or abstract terms, slogans, and catchwords rather than searching for precise words to express ideas precisely. For example, stating that an idea was *shot down* or *ixnayed* does not convey whether the idea was rejected completely, only discouraged, or delayed for reconsideration. Slang often impedes the precision and exactness that are necessary for clear thought and communication.

▶ Much slang is generated in the spirit of innocent fun. But some slang comprises a vocabulary of insult and prejudice that is based on fear, distrust, and dislike of one group of people for another. The many words used to deliver ethnic and gender slurs, like *greaser, camel jockey, stud, bitch,* and endless others, are intended to dehumanize and demean persons different from the writer. If you realize you are using slang to cover discriminatory or derogatory feelings, you need to rethink the entire matter and start revising your thinking as well as your diction.

▶ **Most slang is generated to enliven language.** Ironically, a lot of slang quickly loses its linguistic vitality and becomes trite within weeks or months. Few things are more noticeable than last year's fads in clothing, hairstyle, and language. Readers may understand words like *jerk* or *flick* and expressions like *This is where it's at* and *I can work with that,* but they will not reward such language for freshness, vividness, or originality.

D.8   STANDARD AND NONSTANDARD WORDS AND EXPRESSIONS

Standard usage is partly in the eye or ear of the message receiver, but most teachers (and many other audiences) expect writers to use language that can be found in a college dictionary and that carries no usage labels (**slang**, archaic, or nonstandard).

SLANG, PAGE 633

Although clarity is of the utmost importance, social approval (especially in terms of the relationship of writers to readers and speakers to listeners) is usually why standard words and expressions should be used. For instance, in the statement "The group is enthused about the new schedule" the word *enthused* is not well established as good usage. Too many persons still prefer *enthusiastic* as the preferred word. Whether *enthused* or *enthusiastic* is used does not affect the meaning of the statement or others' understanding of the statement. But which word is used can affect significantly the reader's or listener's reaction to the one who uses it, for the pressure toward conformity is strong. If one writes "The meeting produced more heat than light as the lawyers argufied over technicalities of procedure" (as opposed to "argued over technicalities of procedure"), it had better be for humorous purposes or to recreate the language of a character or person being quoted. Otherwise, the writer is likely to lose some authority, because the reader will infer that the writer has little acquaintance with the words *argue, argued, argument,* and *arguing* from reading or listening and is relatively uneducated and unsophisticated. In short, the writer should have known better than to use *argufied*.

It is the users of a language—English, German, Chinese, Swahili, or Hopi—that decide whether a word or expression changes, lives or dies, or is deemed standard or nonstandard. And the conventions of usage allow many ways to state things differently—but competently—for different audiences, regardless of the efforts of those who attempt to take an authoritative approach and would presume to regulate the language.

D.9

D.9   TECHNICAL TERMS

Every occupational, professional, or interest group has its own specialized vocabulary, sometimes referred to as jargon. Actors, airplane pilots, archeologists, cattle breeders, dental hygienists, dog trainers, financial consultants, lawyers, literary critics, parachutists, physicians, sailors, soldiers, violinists, wine drinkers, baseball players, bullfight aficionados, golfers, stamp collectors, scuba divers, and tobogganists all have their own jargon that is not shared commonly by all users of a language. The most obvious difference between the technical terms that make up these specialized vocabularies and the words that are in our general vocabulary is that the technical terms are difficult, if not incomprehensible, for persons who do not have the special knowledge needed to understand them.

Many technical terms are unfamiliar words, such as nautical terminology like *halyard, capstan, gunnel, bilge, marlin spike*, and *flukes*. Other technical terms are familiar words that have acquired special meanings, such as nautical terminology like *boom, watch, fantail, running lights, poop deck*, and *yardarm*. These unfamiliar words and familiar words with unfamiliar meanings are the private languages for those who belong to the group. Some nautical terms, such as *deck, port*, and *starboard*, have become so familiar to persons outside the group that they are now regarded as ordinary language. Other nautical terms, such as *aft, bulkhead, quarterdeck*, and *granny knot*, are on their way to becoming more widely known.

As with other choices of words, the use of technical terms is appropriate or inappropriate depending on the circumstances, audience, and purpose. One specialist might appropriately use technical terms with another specialist that would be out of place with nonspecialists. Anyone who has had a lawyer draw up a will or contract knows that while the legal language may be strictly accurate and legally enforceable, it is not very clear to the general reader. But laws and regulations pertaining to clear language aside, most contracts are not written for general readers but for other lawyers and judges to interpret.

Technical terminology has three important uses: (1) it conveys precise facts and ideas (the word *ampere* means the same thing to all electricians, electronic technicians, and electrical engineers); (2) it presents information economically (the word *bargeboard* is much more concise for carpenters and architects than "the finished board or strip of material covering the exposed edge of a gable roof"), and (3) it serves as a not-so-subtle demonstration of special capability (the ability to state knowingly that "the landing gear seems to be off a Cessna 6061 because it has a lug welded on it, and those off the 2024 don't weld well" displays knowledge and language that indicate the speaker is worthy of belonging to the group sharing that knowledge).

Here are four guidelines for using technical terminology:

▶ Make sure you use technical terms accurately. A malaprop in this instance is an especially serious error.

▶ Be sure your readers know the meaning of a technical term or else define it clearly for them. If your readers do not understand the technical terms, you might as well be writing in a foreign language. They are likely to dismiss you as an egghead, propeller head, or some other kind of head.

▶ Be sure the occasion calls for the precision and brevity of technical terminology or for the demonstration of specialized knowledge. Otherwise, your readers are likely to suspect you are using gobbledygook or bafflegab to impress or obfuscate rather than to inform.

▶ Do not hesitate to use technical terms, however, if they are appropriate for the occasion.

D.10 WRONG WORDS

Language experts have a technical term for the use of a wrong word for a context: *catachresis* (pronounced "kat-a-KREE-sis"). One kind of wrong word use, called *malapropism*, can have great comedic effect. *Malapropisms* are named after Mrs. Malaprop, a character in Richard Sheridan's eighteenth-century British comedy *The Rivals*, who was absurdly inaccurate in the use of words. Her name has come to be used to describe a ridiculous and comical confusion of words, as in her comment, "She's as obstinate as an allegory on the banks of the Nile." You may have seen performer Norm Crosby, whose comedy routines rely on malapropisms. Usually, however, wrong word choices are not funny. For example, it is a major error to confuse words such as *cellulose* and *celluloid* in informative writing. Writers who confuse the denotative meanings of words (the common definitions as recorded in a dictionary) lose **credibility** with many readers and listeners, who regard such mistakes as signs of ignorance or stupidity.

CREDIBILITY, PAGE 443

A common error is to confuse *homonyms*, words that sound alike but differ in meaning: *profit, prophet; rain, rein, reign; chord, cord; gorilla, guerrilla*. Almost as frequent an error is to confuse near homonyms: *lose, loose; liable, libel; absorb, adsorb; fraction, faction*). Familiarity with the written form of the word is the only prevention for this kind of confusion.

Other words used erroneously are logically related to the right word (words with opposite meanings, called *antonyms*, such as *ascend* and *descend* or *infer* and *imply;* or words that have distantly related meanings, such as *curtail* and *cease* or *capacity* and *capability*).

Writers also confuse words because they do not have a sufficient grasp of the denotative meanings. Language is rich in synonyms— words that have the same general meaning: *bait, enticement; big, gigantic; positive, affirmative; soldier, warrior; student, scholar*. But these words are only generally interchangeable, for no two words mean exactly the same thing. The terms *farmer, rancher, sharecropper*, and *agriculturalist* all denote a person who makes a living from the soil. But while these terms convey the same general idea, they have different particular meanings.

The words *elderly* and *senior* are appropriate adjectives to describe humans. *Antique* might appropriately describe an object such as a chair or a trunk. *Archaic* or *obsolete* might appropriately describe an outdated word or process. *Old, aged*, and *ancient* might appropriately describe animate or inanimate objects. Careful writers can read, use dictionaries, and ask questions to make sure their word choices have the right denotation.

▶ **U. U S A G E**

U.1 **FRAGMENTS**

A complete sentence makes an assertion or asks a question. An incomplete sentence, one that does not make an assertion or ask a question, is known as a fragment. A fragment may or may not have a subject and verb but is often lacking one or the other.

<u>Examples</u>

Fragment: The student being unfamiliar with the library's new computerized retrieval system.   [This fragment has no verb because *being* describes the student rather than making a statement about the student.]

Correction: The student *was* unfamiliar with the library's new computerized retrieval system.

Fragment: Because the student had always used the card catalog in the past.   [This fragment has both a subject and verb (student/had used) but does not make an assertion or ask a question. It is a dependent, or subordinate, clause and should be attached to another sentence.]

Correction: Because the student had always used the card catalog, she didn't like the new computerized system at first.

Fragment: A marvelous example of how computer technology can make our lives easier.   [This fragment includes a subject and verb (technology/can make), but does not make an assertion or ask a question.]

Correction: The new system, a marvelous example of how computer technology can make our lives easier, was not difficult to use.

The following suggestions should help you avoid fragments:

1. Be sure each sentence you write has a subject and verb.

2. If a group of words includes a subject and verb, remember that it may still not be a sentence if it is a dependent clause (i.e., it begins with a subordinating conjunction such as *because, when, if, as, unless,* etc.).

3. Remember that if a verb ends in *ing,* it cannot serve as the main verb of a sentence unless it is part of a verb phrase (e.g., *was going, is singing, will be leaving*).

4. Test a sentence you suspect of being a fragment by adding a "tag question" to it. For example, to the sentence "The driver was signaling when he turned," you can logically add the tag question "Wasn't he?" But to the fragments "The driver signaling when he turned" and "If the driver signals when he turns," you cannot logically add a tag question. If a sentence is complete, you can always add a tag question to the end of it.

U.2 MISPLACED AND DANGLING MODIFIERS

Modifiers should be placed as close as possible to the words they modify. Confusion often occurs when a modifier seems to modify something other than what it was intended to modify. In an attempt to interpret such statements, the reader is forced to rethink and rearrange the words to untangle the meaning.

Examples

Misplaced: Aunt Georgina stood beside the horse wearing a new green riding outfit.

In this example, the confusion is due to the placement of the phrase *wearing a new green riding outfit* at the end of the sentence where it seems to modify the horse when it actually modifies *Aunt Georgina.* Readers almost automatically assume that modifiers relate to the nearest unit. Placing the phrase next to the word it modifies improves coherence and avoids the ludicrous image of the horse attired in the new green riding outfit:

Correct: Aunt Georgina, wearing a new green riding outfit, stood beside the horse.

or: Wearing a new green riding outfit, Aunt Georgina stood beside the horse.

Misplaced: At age fourteen, my family moved to Denver.

In this sentence, the confusion is caused by the fact that the phrase *At age fourteen* is placed next to *my family,* words that it cannot logically modify. The word modified by the phrase (the person who was fourteen) is not expressed in the sentence. Rephrasing the statement so there is an element that the phrase logically modifies improves coherence.

> Correct: When I was fourteen, my family moved to Denver.
>
> or: My family moved to Denver when I was fourteen.
>
> or: At age fourteen I moved to Denver with my family.

No writer intentionally creates a confusing sentence. But because the connections between your thoughts are so clear to you, you may forget that your readers don't know your thinking as well as you do, and you may fail to realize how ambiguous a misplaced or dangling modifier can be. There is a difference between understanding something in your own head and explaining it to someone else. *You* know what you mean when you write or say something like this:

> First draft: She discovered what a good role model her mother was later in life.

The possible confusion in this sentence is due to the placement of the phrase "later in life," which seems to indicate when her mother became a good role model. If that is the intended meaning, then the statement can be improved by restating as follows: "She discovered what a good role model her mother became later in life." However, if the writer meant to state it was not until later in life that she became aware her mother had been such a good role model, then she should place the phrase "later in life" next to "she discovered."

> Revision: She discovered later in life what a good role model her mother had been.
>
> or: Later in life, she discovered what a good role model her mother had been.

> Misplaced: As the truck sped along, we noticed the break in the pavement, just as it rounded the curve.

When first reading or hearing this statement, most persons will hesitate between possible meanings—including the possibilities that the break in the pavement rather than the truck came speeding around the curve or that the writer was not in the truck at all but was observing from a distance. You do not want your readers confused, even momentarily. To eliminate confusion, you could write the sentence as follows:

Correct: Just as we sped around the curve in the truck, we noticed the break in the pavement.

Probably the most misplaced words in the English language are one-word modifiers such as *only, even,* and *almost.* You should take special care where you place them in a sentence because their position can drastically change the meaning. To realize the changes in meaning that the position of the word *only* causes, place it in the blanks in this sentence:

_____ Professor Werner _____ teaches _____ Intermediate German.

Only Professor Werner teaches Intermediate German.   [Professor Werner is the only one who teaches Intermediate German.]

Professor Werner *only* teaches Intermediate German.   [Professor Werner has only one responsibility: to teach Intermediate German. She does not do research or serve on committees.]

Professor Werner teaches *only* Intermediate German   [Intermediate German is the only course that Professor Werner teaches.]

The following suggestions should help you avoid misplaced and dangling modifiers:

1. Be sure each modifying word or phrase modifies a word or group of words that is stated in the sentence.

2. Place modifying words and phrases as close as possible to the word or group of words they modify.

3. Be especially careful to place modifiers like *only, even,* and *almost* directly before the word or phrase they modify.

U.3   PRONOUN-ANTECEDENT AGREEMENT

A pronoun should agree with its antecedent (the noun or pronoun to which it refers) in number, person, and gender. Thus you should use a singular pronoun if the word to which it refers is singular and a plural pronoun if the word to which it refers is plural.

<u>Example</u>

Maria wore a red hat on her birthday because she wanted to be noticed.

Of course, you should also use pronouns that agree with their antecedents in gender. For example, you would not write that "Maria wore a red hat on *her* birthday because *he* wanted to be noticed." Native speakers of English practically never have problems with gender, and even non-native speakers find gender one of the more sensible aspects of the English language. In some languages gender is rather arbitrarily assigned to nouns, but in English gender is determined naturally; that is, all nouns are considered neuter if they do not refer to people or animals that are actually male or female.

Similarly, using a pronoun that agrees in person with its antecedent is seldom a problem. You would logically and naturally say "I like myself" or "You should wear your coat" not "I like himself" or "You should wear my coat" (unless you really intend to give your coat to the person to whom you are speaking). The problem that most often occurs in pronoun-antecedent agreement is with number—using a singular pronoun to refer to a plural antecedent or vice versa. The following are some examples of typical errors that occur when subjects and verbs do not agree in number:

I want *each* of my guests to enjoy *themselves.*

Stress affects *everyone* at some time in *their* lives.

A good *dog* is obedient and behaves *themselves.*

Once a *student* has left home, *they* have to make *their* own way in the world.

These errors can be corrected as follows:

I want *all* of my guests to enjoy *themselves.*

Stress affects *everyone* at some time in *his or her* life.

A good *dog* is obedient and behaves *itself.*

Once *students* have left home, *they* have to make *their* own way in the world.

As you can see, most pronoun-antecedent agreement errors involve pronouns that refer to antecedents that are indefinite pronouns. Because indefinite pronouns are responsible for many subject-verb and pronoun-antecedent agreement errors, we include a chart that indicates which indefinite pronouns are singular and which are plural. Note that, unlike personal pronouns, indefinite pronouns are always third person and have only one form.

<u>**Singular Indefinite Pronouns**</u>

everybody	one
everyone	someone
each	somebody
anyone	nobody
anybody	everything
neither	nothing
none (may also be plural)	

<u>**Plural Indefinite Pronouns**</u>

all	any
some	few
both	several
none (may also be singular)	

GENDER-NEUTRAL LANGUAGE,
PAGE 629

Note: See the entry on **gender-neutral language** for a discussion of nonsexist use of indefinite and personal pronouns.

The following suggestions should help you avoid errors in pronoun-antecedent agreement:

1. If a sentence includes an indefinite pronoun, be sure any other pronoun in the sentence that refers to it agrees with it in number.
2. If possible, use plural rather than singular indefinite pronouns when referring to more than one person or thing. For example, write "All of the students will need their books" instead of "Everyone will need their books."

U.4   PRONOUN REFERENCE

Ambiguous references to personal pronouns often cause confusion for readers. The antecedent of every pronoun should be unmistakable, for if readers have to guess at an antecedent, they are likely to guess incorrectly. Examine the following sentences, which are unclear because of problems with pronoun reference.

Unclear: Mario asked his father if he could help him.

The writer knows what the words *he* and *him* refer to and assumes that a reader would too. But readers cannot create a coherent interpretation of this sentence because they are unable to decide which of the two possible antecedents (*Mario* or *father*) is correct. The general rule is that a pronoun refers to the nearest preceding noun that agrees with it in number and gender. But here it is impossible to tell whether Mario asked his father to help him or whether he volunteered to help his father. Depending on the intended meaning, the sentence could be stated in several ways. Substituting nouns for the pronouns would resolve the ambiguity of the references but would result in clumsy, unnecessary repetition:

Awkward revisions: Mario asked his father if he (his father) could help him.

Mario asked his father if he could help Mario.

Other revisions would be equally clear and would get rid of the clumsy repetition:

Better revisions: Mario asked his father, "Could you help me?"

Mario asked his father to help him.

Mario asked his father, "Can I help you?"

Mario volunteered to help his father.

However, there are constructions where repeating the noun is probably the best solution:

Unclear: Learning that Barnes maintained close ties with Garcia, who used to live in Cuba, the Illinois Bureau of Investigation has begun an exhaustive investigation into his background.

The ambiguity in this sentence is caused by two or more possible antecedents. Does *his* refer to Barnes or to Garcia? Readers may automatically assume that *his* refers to the nearest agreeing noun, which in this case is *Garcia*. But there is no way to decide for certain whether Barnes or Garcia is the antecedent. Depending on the intended meaning, the sentence should end either "into Barnes's background" or "into Garcia's background."

The following suggestions should help you avoid pronoun reference errors:

1. Be sure each pronoun you use refers clearly to a stated, unambiguous antecedent.

2. If necessary, repeat a noun rather than using a pronoun that does not have a clear, unambiguous antecedent.

U.5   RUN-ON SENTENCES AND COMMA SPLICES

A run-on sentence or comma splice error results when a writer combines two or more sentences incorrectly. In a run-on sentence, the two sentences (or independent clauses) are simply run together. A comma splice error occurs when a comma is placed between the two incorrectly joined sentences (or independent clauses).

Examples

Comma splice: Amy loved comic books, she had a whole room full of old copies of *Superman, Wonder Woman,* and *Archie.*

Comma splice: She loved them all, however *Batman* was her favorite.

Run-on: She would spend hours sorting the comics then she would spend even more hours arranging them in neat stacks.

Such errors can usually be eliminated by merely correcting the punctuation. Two sentences, or independent clauses, can be correctly joined or separated in the following ways:

1. By using a period

Example: Amy loved comic books. She had a whole room full of old copies of *Superman, Wonder Woman*, and *Archie*.

2. By using a semicolon and a conjunctive adverb

Example: She loved them all; however, *Batman* was her favorite.

Example: She would spend hours sorting the comics; then she would spend even more hours arranging them in neat stacks.

3. By using just a semicolon

Example: Amy loved comic books; she had a whole room full of them.

4. By using a comma and a coordinating conjunction (*and, or, but, for, yet,* and *so*)

Example: She loved them all, but *Batman* was her favorite.

The following suggestions should help you avoid run-on sentences and comma splice errors:

1. If you have difficulty identifying run-on sentences, check carefully when you use a personal pronoun (such as *I, he, we, they,* etc.) because personal pronouns often function as the subject of a sentence. (Example: It was my turn next. I stepped up to the plate.)

2. Beware the little word *then*, which is often used to begin another sentence. (Example: She turned to go. Then she paused.)

3. Remember that length is not a factor. Run-on sentences may be very short or very long.

U.6   SHIFTS IN POINT OF VIEW

U.6

Because readers expect consistency in point of view, take care not to shift needlessly and unintentionally from first person (*I* or *we*) to second person (*you*) or third person (*he, she,* or *it*).

Knowing which point of view to use can be confusing if you have been instructed to avoid first- and second-person point of view—that is, not to use *I* or *you*. However, it is perfectly all right to use *I* or *you* in many instances. If you are writing about yourself, you should, of course, use *I*. If you want to address your reader directly (for example, when you are writing instructions or advice), you should use *you*.

In fact, avoiding the use of first and second person often results in awkward, hard-to-read prose. For example, the indefinite pronoun *one* can be substituted for *I* or *you*, but the result is stiff and awkward.

> Example: *You* can find the answer in a dictionary.
>
>   *One* can find the answer in a dictionary.

You should feel free to use *I* or *you* when you are referring to yourself or your reader. However, you should avoid shifting from one point of view to another for no good reason.

> Example: *I* like walking as a form of exercise because *you* can set *your* own pace.

In the preceding example there is no reason to shift from first-person *I* to second-person *you*. To avoid this shift, you can simply use first person.

> Example: *I* like walking as a form of exercise because *I* can set *my* own pace.

Passive Voice

Even more detrimental to effective, clear writing is the use of passive voice to avoid using *I* or *you*.

> Example: I *found* the answer in a dictionary.
>   (active)
>
>   The answer *was found* in a dictionary.
>   (passive)

Passive voice is often less direct, less clear, and less responsible than active voice. In passive voice, the subject of the sentence (*answer*) does not perform the action/being implicit in the verb (*was found*). Rather, the subject is being acted upon (i.e., the answer is not doing the finding but is the object of the finding). It is nearly always better to use a subject that functions as the agent (the doer) in the sentence. Although in the past certain disciplines and professions (especially science, government, and law) seemed to prefer passive voice, this is no longer the case. Most people now agree that writers should avoid passive voice when it is possible to do so.

The following suggestions should help you avoid shifts in point of view:

1. Use *I* or *you* if you are referring to yourself or your audience, but be consistent (i.e, don't shift needlessly from one to another).

2. Do not use passive voice as a way of avoiding *I* or *you*.

U.7   SHIFTS IN VERB TENSE

U.7

Careful writers do not shift needlessly from one tense to another. If you begin a text using one tense, your reader expects you to continue in that tense unless there is a logical reason for you to change to another. Illogical, careless shifts in tense are confusing to a reader.

> **Example:**   The concert *began* at 8 P.M., *lasts* for four hours, and *will be* over by midnight.

This sentence begins with a past tense verb (*began*), shifts to present tense (*lasts*), and then shifts again to future (*will be*). Notice how much clearer the sentence is with a consistent use of present tense verbs:

> **Example:**   The concert *begins* at 8 P.M., *lasts* for four hours, and *is* over by midnight.

Most shifts in tense occur not within single sentences but within longer texts. It is easy to shift unintentionally from one tense to another several times in writing a text of several pages. Especially common is a shift to conditional verbs (*would go, would think*, etc.).

> **Example:**   The man *drove* like a maniac. He *sped* out of his driveway in reverse, barely pausing to see if cars were coming. Then he *shifted* into forward and accelerated rapidly down the quiet tree-lined street on which he lived. He *would sail* through intersections without glancing to the left or right and *would stop* at red lights only if other cars were stopped in front of him.

Unintentional shifts in tense such as these should be eliminated when you edit your text. Remember, however, that some shifts in tense are logical and necessary.

Example: When I *entered* high school, I *weighed* only 102 pounds; today I *weigh* 167 pounds.

It is just the unintentional, illogical shifts that you want to eliminate.

The following suggestions should help you avoid shifts in verb tense:

1. Shift from one tense to another only when a shift is appropriate to your meaning.

2. Avoid using the conditional (*would* or *will*) unless you are indicating condition or probability. (Example: I would go with you if I could/I will be there if I can.)

U.8 SUBJECT-VERB AGREEMENT

Subjects and verbs should agree in number (singular or plural) and person. If a subject is singular, then its verb must be singular; if a subject is first person, then the verb must be first person.

The concept of person is best explained by focusing on pronouns, since it is only pronouns that clearly distinguish person. The following chart outlines what is meant grammatically by person:

	Singular	*Plural*
First person	I	we
Second person	you	you
Third person	he, she, it	they

First person is used when the writer or speaker refers to herself or himself.

Example: *I* ate my lunch.

Second person is used when the writer or speaker refers to the person being addressed.

Example: *You* ate my lunch.

And third person is used when the writer or speaker refers to someone or something other than himself or herself or the person being addressed.

Example: The dog (or *it*) ate my lunch.

Notice in the preceding examples that the verb (*ate*) remains the same because it is a past tense verb. Fortunately, future tense verbs and past tense verbs (except for the verb *to be*) do not change in form to indicate person, so you can all but forget about agreement problems if you are writing or speaking in either of these tenses. Unfortunately, present tense verbs do change to indicate tense, at least in one instance—third-person singular. Notice what happens to our series of examples if we change to present tense.

I eat my lunch.   [first-person singular]

You eat my lunch.   [second-person singular]

The dog *eats* my lunch.   [third-person singular]

In the present tense, all third-person singular verbs end in *s*. Thus you simply add *s* (or *es*) to the first-person present tense form of regular verbs (those that add *ed* to form the past tense) to form verbs such as *jumps, walks*, and *reaches*. Some irregular verbs also require only an *s* or *es* (e.g., *eats, teaches*, and *does*). However, two irregular verbs (*to be* and *to have*) change more drastically. The verb *to have* changes to *has* in the third-person singular (note it still ends in *s*) but otherwise is like other irregular verbs. However, the verb *to be* is highly irregular, as the following chart illustrates:

Present Tense

	Singular	*Plural*
First person	I *am*	we *are*
Second person	you *are*	you *are*
Third person	he, she, it *is*	they *are*

Past Tense

	Singular	*Plural*
First person	I *was*	we *were*
Second person	you *were*	you *were*
Third person	he, she, it *was*	they *were*

Even though the verb *to be* presents some special problems, subject-verb agreement is seldom a problem if the subject is a noun or personal pronoun and/or is located close to the verb.

Example: She *was* an excellent student.

However, if the subject is an indefinite pronoun (such as *each, everyone*, or *anybody*) and is not adjacent to the verb, the agreement between the two is not as obvious.

Example: Everyone in my math and history classes *was* an excellent student.

Example: Each of us *was* an excellent student.

Example: Anybody who takes calculus and economics *is* an excellent student.

The following suggestions should help you avoid errors in subject-verb agreement:

1. Anytime you are in doubt about subject-verb agreement, identify the subject and verb and be sure they are both singular or both plural.

2. When you are using third-person singular present tense verbs, be sure your verb ends in *s*.

3. When your subject is a singular indefinite pronoun such as *everyone, anybody*, or *each*, check to see if your verb is also singular.

P. PUNCTUATION

P.1 APOSTROPHE

The apostrophe has five main uses:

a. Forming the Possessive of Nouns

To form the possessive of singular nouns and plural nouns not ending in *s*, add *'s*:

Allen Ross's car	the family's trip
the boy's shoes	women's rights
the children's playground	

To form the possessive of plural nouns already ending in *s*, add only the apostrophe:

the Rosses' car	the actors' rehearsal
the boys' shoes	the teachers' salaries
the farmers' trucks	

b. Forming the Possessive of Indefinite Pronouns

Possessive personal pronouns, such as *its, ours, his, hers, yours, theirs,* and *whose*, are written without apostrophes. However, possessive indefinite pronouns such as *everybody, everyone, nobody, anybody, anyone,* and *someone* require an apostrophe and *s*.

    everybody's shoes

c. Replacing Letters and Numerals

To form a contraction, place an apostrophe where the omitted letter(s) or numeral(s) would be:

    I'm sure you're early.

The flight doesn't leave until four o'clock.

Many social critics refer to the '80s as the decade of greed.

d. Forming Plurals of Letters, Symbols, and Numerals

Use the apostrophe and *s* to form the plural of letters and symbols:

Accommodate is spelled with two *c*'s and two *m*'s.

How many +'s are in that equation?

You may also use the apostrophe plus *s* to form the plural of numerals, but frequently the *s* is used alone:

In the 1990's (*or* 1990s) biologists began to notice a sharp decrease in frog populations.

e. Indicating a Quotation Within a Quotation

Use single quotation marks around a quotation within a quotation (except in a displayed quotation). Since most typewriters and computer keyboards do not have a character for the single quotation mark, use the apostrophe:

John Clive discusses what he calls Macaulay's "propulsive imagination," which Clive describes as the "instinctive ability to propel inert facts into motion." Clive, using the analogy of photographic film development, writes: "Macaulay's travels to the scenes of events he was describing helped him collect, as he wrote after his trip to Ireland in 1849, 'a large store of images and thoughts,'—images which his photographic memory retained, so to speak, as negative film to be developed into positives when he came to write" ("Macaulay's Historical Imagination," 22).

P.2   BRACKETS

Like parentheses, brackets always come in pairs, one at the beginning and one at the end of the enclosed materials. So check to see that both are there. In handwriting, make sure that your brackets look like brackets [ ] not parentheses ( ). Brackets are used as substitutes for parentheses in two situations:

a. Enclosing Text Already Enclosed in Parentheses

Parentheses should not be used to enclose text that is part of a statement already enclosed in parentheses. Either rephrase the statement or use brackets for the second enclosure:

> incorrect: In all animals certain patterns of motor activities are innate (for example, the way in which mammals and birds scratch themselves (Figure 3)).

> correct: In all animals certain patterns of motor activities are innate (for example, the way in which mammals and birds scratch themselves [Figure 3]).

> correct: In all animals certain patterns of motor activities are innate: for example, the way in which mammals and birds scratch themselves (Figure 3).

b. Inserting Text in Another's Writing

Use brackets to enclose text that you wish to insert in quoted material to make the author's meaning clear:

> One recent critic has declared that "Bunyan's masterpiece [*Pilgrim's Progress*] is out of harmony with the spirit of the age [the Restoration]."

P.3   COLON

The colon, which focuses attention on the information that follows it, has three main uses:

a. Introducing Lists

> Microcomputers use three types of secondary memory: cassette tapes, floppy disks, or hard disks.

> Isaac Asimov formulated three laws for robots:

> **1.** A robot may not injure a human being or through inaction allow a human being to come to harm.

2. A robot must obey the orders given it by human beings except when such orders would conflict with the First Law.

3. A robot must protect its own existence as long as such protection does not conflict with the First or Second Law.

Do not place a colon between a verb or a preposition and its object(s).

incorrect:	For dinner we had: tossed salad, baked ham, mashed potatoes and gravy, and iced tea.
correct:	For dinner we had tossed salad, baked ham, mashed potatoes and gravy, and iced tea.
incorrect	The candidates will speak in the southern district at: Berryville, McLeansboro, Jackson's Gap, and Mount Tremaine.
correct	The candidates will speak in the southern district at Berryville, McLeansboro, Jackson's Gap, and Mount Tremaine.

b. Introducing Quotations

W. E. B. DuBois was determined to be a social scientist: "I was going to study the facts, any and all facts, concerning the American Negro and his plight" (*Dusk at Dawn* 591).

Churchill challenged Chamberlain, the prime minister, to stop the transfer of huge sums of money from Czechoslovakia to Nazi Germany:

> Here we are going about urging our people to enlist, urging them to accept new forms of military compulsion; here we are paying taxes on a gigantic scale to protect ourselves. . . . (Hansard's *Parliamentary Debates* 5/26/39)

Notice that indented (displayed) quotations are not enclosed in quotation marks.

c. Introducing Important Words or Expressions

The newspaper headlined the team's pledge: "We will leave Seattle champions."

Other Uses of the Colon

To follow the formal salutation in a letter:

Dear Mr. McHenry:

To separate the subtitle from the title of a book or article or to separate the verse from the chapter in biblical references:

Disappearing Through the Skylight: Culture and Technology in the Twentieth Century

Hebrews 13:8

To separate hours from minutes in stating a specific time:

3:15 P.M.

To express a ratio:

10:5:1

Capitalization After the Colon

Usual practice is to start an independent clause (a grammatically complete sentence) following a colon with a capital letter and a dependent clause, phrase, or list with a lowercase letter:

The sign provided a clear warning: "Trespassers will be Prosecuted."

We purchased the following items for the camping trip: mosquito netting, dehydrated meals, extra pairs of socks, and a first aid kit.

P.4 COMMA

The comma is the most frequently used mark of punctuation. Because it has so many uses, most of us tend to be unsure of when to use it. But the comma is not all that difficult to use correctly. Here are its eight most important uses:

a. Separating Items in a Series

The long, hot, dusty ride lasted nearly three hours.

The portfolio must contain an essay, a report, a short story, and a poem.

It is remarkable how well we remember people, places, tunes, words, ideas, stories, events, and a host of other things without much conscious effort.

In separating items in a series, the comma may be used these ways: *first, second, and third* or *first, second and third. First, second, and third* is preferred because it is never ambiguous. Be consistent in your practice, whichever you choose.

b. Separating Clauses of a Compound Sentence

Use a comma between the independent clauses of a compound sentence joined by a coordinating conjunction (*and, but, or, nor, yet, for*):

Yesterday was hot, but today is cooler, and tomorrow is supposed to be downright chilly.

The work is not yet completed, for we were interrupted several times.

Professor Frobish spoke twenty minutes over her allotted time, and when she finished we all sighed with relief.

c. Setting Off Introductory Words, Phrases, or Clauses

However, this practice is open to debate.

Ultimately, David Bleich places primary emphasis on the reader's response.

Many years earlier, they had been converted to Mormonism.

In the midst of writing the paper, Anita realized she needed to rethink the thesis.

As you know, a person's appetite diminishes after strenuous exercise.

d. Setting Off Appositives

Carlos, the project engineer, will be flying to the site Thursday.

Her aunt, a Zeta, is hoping that Cindy pledges the sorority.

I saw Grethel, who is my brother's former wife, driving the tractor.

e. Setting Off Nouns of Address

Sit over there, Frank, next to the window.

Trish, where are you going?

f. Setting Off Interrupting Matter

Anita, realizing she needed to rethink the thesis, started over again.

This practice, however, is open to debate.

Susan, who is taking freshman composition this semester, spends a lot of time in the library.

g. Separating a Quotation from Other Parts of a Sentence

"Vote early," she said, "and often."

"Everybody writes books here," McLuhan told her mother, "not many of them worth reading either."

h. Preventing Possible Ambiguity

<u>ambiguous</u>	<u>clear</u>
Above the limbs swayed gently in the breeze.	Above, the limbs swayed gently in the breeze.
The question is is it worth the investment?	The question is, is it worth the investment?
A few days after I saw Kelly driving her new convertible.	A few days after, I saw Kelly driving her new convertible.

Other Uses of the Comma

❖ To end the informal salutation in a letter—

Dear Jonathan,

❖ To end the complimentary close in a letter—

Sincerely,

❖ To separate names from titles or degrees—

Elaine Grissom, DVM, has been named an interim board member.

❖ To separate a city from a state and the state from the word that follows it—

This year's convention in Lincoln, Nebraska, attracted 204 delegates.

❖ To separate elements in a date—

July 25, 1953, is my birthdate.   [Note that *I was born on 25 July 1953* is also acceptable, as is *I was born in July 1953*.]

❖ To indicate thousands in figures of five or more digits—*5200* or *5,200*, but *43,276* and *16,527,089*.   [Certain numbers, however, omit commas: *Engine No. 843D629115A*; *pages 2360-2362*; 12970 Boulevard East.]

Using the Comma with Other Marks of Punctuation

When a sentence element that is normally set off by a comma is followed by a parenthetical expression, place the comma *after* the closing parenthesis:

Dr. McKelly, tweedy, bearded, and young (like so many male assistant professors of philosophy), likes to expound on Jacques Derrida's influential books.

When a sentence element that is normally set off by a comma ends with a quotation mark, place the comma *inside* the closing quotation mark:

"Now *that's* a dog," Sara said, patting the big mongrel on the head.

One form of the "peg-word," which is a method taught by many memory experts, relies on memorizing words that rhyme with the concept you want to learn.

P.5   DASH

The dash, employed intelligently and sparingly, does the same things that commas and colons do. But the dash does them with pronounced emphasis.

To form a handwritten dash, make a line about twice as long as a hyphen. If your typewriter or computer keyboard does not have a dash key, strike the hyphen key twice, with no space between strikes or on either side of the dash. It should look like this:

This new concept--that space is a continuum--is difficult to grasp.

Here are the dash's most important uses:

a. Setting Off Interpolated Material

Mount Saint Helens is a typical volcano along the "Ring of Fire"--the Pacific coasts of North and South America, Japan, the Philippines, Indonesia, and New Zealand--the site of over 60 percent of the world's active volcanoes.

The plan--unprecedented in principle and vast in scope--is being studied by a committee.

As these examples illustrate, interrupting material must be set off by *paired* dashes, one at the opening and one at the closing.

b. Introducing a List
or Emphasizing Items in a List

In the first generation of American leaders, five men stood out-- George Washington, Benjamin Franklin, Thomas Jefferson, Alexander Hamilton, and John Marshall.

Little more than a drop, a cubic millimeter of blood contains

--5,000,000 erythrocytes (white blood cells)

--5,000 to 10,000 leukocytes (red blood cells)

--200,000 to 300,000 platelets (cell fragments that initiate coagulation or clotting).

c. Indicating an Interruption
or Change in Thought

He was ambitious and aggressive--but not at the expense of others.

I'm not so sure that we should--oh, what the hell, let's do it.

**d. Introducing the Author
and/or Source Line
of a Direct Quotation**

> All truths wait in all things.
> > --Walt Whitman, *Leaves of Grass*

> I am captivated more by dreams of the future than by the history of
> the past.
> > --Thomas Jefferson

P.6   ELLIPSIS POINTS

Ellipsis points are spaced periods that indicate the omission of part of
a quoted passage. When deleting material from a direct quotation, take
care not to change the meaning of the original passage.

A three-period ellipsis (. . .) indicates that what is omitted occurs
within a sentence:

original passage:	To write the Life of him who excelled all man-kind in writing the lives of others, and who, whether we consider his extraordinary endow-ments, or his various works, has been equalled by few in any age, is an arduous, and may be reckoned in me a presumptuous task.
	—James Boswell, *Life of Johnson*
passage as quoted:	Boswell states at the beginning of his *Life of Johnson* that "to write the Life of him who ex-celled all mankind in writing the lives of others . . . may be reckoned . . . a presumptuous task."

A four-period ellipsis (. . . .) shows that what is omitted contained end punctuation. The extra period is usually either the period of
the preceding sentence or of the one from which the omission is taken.

original passage:	For a structure to him meant a habit, and a habit implied not only an internal need but outer forces to which, for good or evil, the

organism had to become habituated. The orchid's flower was a device by which the plant took advantage of the habits of insects, and it was only by inquiring into this use of its various parts—which he called adaptation—that he was able to put time into natural history, and order in taxonomy. In one sense, therefore, he might well have called his book *The Origin of Habits* rather than *The Origin of Species.* Like many others, he was never quite certain just what a species was.

—F. Huxley, "Charles Darwin: Life and Habit," *American Scholar* 28 (1959): 496.

passage as quoted: Francis Huxley has summarized Darwin's attitude as follows:

A structure to him meant a habit, and a habit implied not only an internal need but outer forces to which, for good or evil, the organism had to become habituated. . . . In one sense, therefore, he might well have called his book *The Origin of Habits* rather than *The Origin of Species.* Like many others, he was never quite certain just what a species was.

P.7   EXCLAMATION POINT

Because the effect of the exclamation point relies on its infrequent use, it should be used sparingly and only after an expression of strong feeling—surprise, pleasure, anger, determination. It is used after an exclamatory expression or a short exclamatory sentence.

Wow! That lightning strike was close!

Fire!

"Let's stop it!" yelled Janis from the other boat.

When an exclamation point and a quotation mark fall together (as in the last example), place the exclamation point according to the sense of the statement. If the exclamation is part of the quotation, the exclamation point goes inside the quotation mark:

> One of the archeologists shouted, "The riddle is solved!"

If the entire sentence is an exclamation, the exclamation point goes outside the quotation mark:

> One of the archeologists just announced, "The riddle is solved"!

P.8 HYPHEN

Generally the hyphen has two basic uses:

a. Forming Compound Words

Compound words consist of two or more words that function as one word. Some are written as separate words, some are written as one word with no space between, and some are hyphenated. Since there is little logic to guide writers about how to write compounds, you should check a college-level dictionary for words you are not sure of. However, certain practices have been established through usage, and we present them here.

Compound Nouns

Use a hyphen to form the following types of compound nouns.

❖ Spelled-out cardinal and ordinal numbers from twenty-one to ninety-nine:

forty-eight	fifty-fifth
twenty-five	eighty-eighth

Numbers lower than twenty-one are single words and are not hyphenated: *thirteen, sixteenth*.

❖ Words that indicate certain family relationships:

great-grandfather	mother-in-law	great-great-aunt

But many such words are single words with no hyphen: *grandson, grandmother, stepdaughter.*

❖ Words that indicate dual roles or joint functions:

player-manager   Mercedes-Benz   radio-cassette player

❖ Compound words formed by capital letters and numerals or compounds of capital letters followed by a noun:

DC-10   A-frame   H-bomb

❖ Compounds that begin with the prefix *ex-, self-,* or *all-:*

ex-husband   self-starter   all-important

❖ Compounds that consist of a prefix and a proper noun:

anti-Semitism   all-American   pre-Columbian

❖ Compounds that end with *-elect* or *-designate:*

senator-elect   ambassador-designate

❖ Compounds in which the absence of a hyphen forms a word of a different meaning:

re-form, reform   re-cover, recover   re-create, recreate

❖ Most compounds in which the prefix ends with the same vowel that the base word begins with:

semi-independent   co-owner   non-native

Compound Adjectives

Use a hyphen when two or more adjectives function as a unit to modify the noun that follows:

English-speaking people   foreign-born professionals

When a compound adjective follows the word or words it modifies, the elements are written as separate words with no hyphens:

before the word	*after the word*
the door-to-door canvass	the canvass was door to door
a full-time job	the position is full time
paper-thin coating	the coating was paper thin

Two or more compound adjectives that modify the same element are hyphenated as follows:

a two- or four-door car   [not *two or four-door car*]

sixth-, seventh-, and eighth-grade students   [not *sixth, seventh, and eighth-grade students*]

b. Dividing Words

Thanks to the word-wrap feature of most word-processing programs, the practice of dividing a word at the end of a line and carrying the last part of the word to the next line is fast disappearing. However, if you must divide a word at the end of a line in handwriting or type-writing, observe these four practices:

- Divide the word at a syllable break, as in *feu·dal·ism*. If you are unsure of where the syllable breaks occur in a word, look them up in a college-level dictionary.

- Divide hyphenated compounds at the hyphen (or one of the hyphens if there are two or more).

- Do not divide a word that consists of one syllable or is pronounced as one syllable: *seer, proved, clutched*.

- Do not divide a word if the division will result in one letter standing alone: *a-while, cit-y*.

Additional Uses of the Hyphen

- To indicate spelling—*Can "gauge" be spelled g-a-g-e?*

- To separate segments of numbers:

(608) 491-3826	(telephone numbers)
000-00-0000	(social security numbers)

❖ To indicate a range of values or span of time, etc.:

$100-150   106-100 B.C.   1:00-2:30 P.M.

❖ To represent dialect: *I'm a-coming. . . .*

P.9   PARENTHESES

Parentheses are used for two purposes:

a. Enclosing Additional Information

Snowflake crystals generally have a sixfold symmetry, but each is unique (Figure 4).

For me, the experience meant that in a crisis (despite comfort and sympathy from others), I can feel completely alone.

Henry James (writing of old English country houses) refers to "accumulation of expressions" as the historical associations that convey meaning to the sensitive observer (*The Complete Notebooks of Henry James* 224).

When the parenthetical matter is a short sentence inserted within another sentence, omit a period that ends the enclosed sentence, but include a question mark or an exclamation point.

Although the U.S. Army Corps of Engineers has always had its critics (Justice William O. Douglas labeled it "public enemy number one"), the corps faced increasing public hostility during the 1970s.

Leaving her mother and sisters behind (how painful!), she escaped to Vienna and eventually made her way to the United States.

When a parenthetical sentence stands alone (is not enclosed in another sentence), place the end punctuation *inside* the closing parenthesis:

In recent years, the direction of most Artificial Intelligence research has been to make computers capable of dealing with real-world objects. (But many of the processes involved, though easy for a human being, turn out to be extremely difficult to simulate on a computer.)

b. Enclosing Letters or Numbers in a List

Parentheses may be used to enclose the letters or numbers of items in a list:

> The engine consists of four functional systems: (1) the fuel system, (2) the ignition system, (3) the lubrication system, and (4) the cooling system.

> *Note*: Parentheses should not be used to enclose text that is part of a statement already enclosed in parentheses (see Brackets).

P.10   PERIOD

The period has five main uses:

a. Providing an End Stop for Declarative and Imperative Sentences

> She is working on a book about Truman Capote.

> Select the color you want from the charts on the next few pages.

If a declarative or imperative sentence ends with an abbreviation that ends in a period itself, a second period is not used:

> The Beaux Arts Trio will perform Friday night in the Clapham Ballroom at 8 P.M.

b. Indicating Abbreviations

> Mr. James Ryder

> Louise Caudill, M.D.

> Gen. Norman Schwarzkopf

> etc.

> 8-in. drain pipe

Certain abbreviations are written without periods: HMO (Health Maintenance Organization). For more information about particular abbreviations, consult a college-level dictionary.

c. Indicating Initials

> Maria C. Tomas
>
> Kenneth R. Crockmeier

d. Serving as Leaders

Leaders are a series of periods that lead the eye. They are often used in tables and tables of contents:

Table of Contents

e. Setting Off Run-in Side Headings

Headings that are followed by text on the same line are usually set off by a period:

> *Fruit Limb Support.* Fruit trees occasionally have more fruit than they can hold. As a result, limbs drop under the increasing weight until they snap. The entire tree may split down the middle if major branches on opposite sides of the trunk are heavy. . . .

Using the Period with Other Marks of Punctuation

❖ If a question ends with an abbreviation that requires a period, include both the period and the question mark:

What is the meaning of *etc.?*

❖ Use a period *within* parenthetical expressions only if the expression forms a complete sentence and is not enclosed in another sentence, as in the second example:

Gloria Anzaldua writes in *Borderlands/LaFronteria*: "I grew up in two cultures, the Mexican (with a heavy Indian influence) and the Anglo (as a member of a colonized people in our own territory).

Almost every three or four years, the normal pattern of ocean temperatures in the tropical Pacific Ocean is disrupted by a phenomenon known as El Nino. (The event is called El Nino, which is Spanish for "the Christ Child," because the appearance of warm ocean waters off the western South American coast often occurs around Christmas.) During El Nino, the surface waters become unusually warm in the region and extend from the South American coast westward to the International Date Line.

❖ Always put the period inside the closing quotation mark:

In Hemingway's "The Lack of Passion," the young matador's performance in the bullring is the result not of cowardice, but of an overwhelming apathy: "I'd have killed him. Or let them take him away alive. I don't care. Let them take them all out alive."

An athlete who performs far above his normal level is referred to as being in a "zone."

ELIPSIS POINTS, PAGE 662   See also the entry for **ellipsis points**.

P.11   QUESTION MARK

The question mark has five main uses:

a. Using Question Marks for Direct Questions

The question mark indicates the end of a direct question:

When will James and Doris arrive?

Have you ever been to Wall, South Dakota?

b. Not Using Question Marks for Indirect Questions

Do not use a question mark after an indirect question. *Why are you late?* is a direct question, and it properly ends with a question mark. But look at the following example:

> She asked why you were late.

This sentence is not a direct question. It is a statement that contains an indirect question, and it should not end with a question mark.

c. Punctuating Polite Requests

Polite requests may be punctuated with a question mark or a period:

> May I see you at one o'clock.
>
> May I see you at one o'clock?

d. Using Question Marks for Series of Questions

When asking a series of questions in the same sentence, you may place a question mark at the end of the sentence or after each question, depending on how you want to emphasize the questions:

> How many people are in the car? Six or seven?
>
> How many people are in the car? Six? Seven?

e. Using Question Marks with Other Marks of Punctuation

❖ Place the question mark inside a closing quotation mark only when it is part of the quoted word(s). Place it outside if the sentence containing the quoted word(s) is a question:

> The captain asked, "Why was that ship mothballed?"
>
> What does it mean for a ship to be "mothballed"?

❖ Place the question mark inside a closing parenthesis only if it is part of the parenthetical matter:

Hemingway was probably exaggerating the severity of his war wounds (with the new biographical data available, who can think otherwise?).

❖ Place the question mark outside the parenthesis if the entire sentence is a question:

Did Hemingway exaggerate his war wounds (as the new biographical data available suggests)?

P.12 QUOTATION MARKS

Quotation marks are used in pairs in the following three ways:

a. Enclosing Direct Quotations

When you include another person's exact words in your writing, enclose them in quotation marks:

"Since about 1930," wrote George Orwell in 1945, "the world has given no reason for optimism whatever" (82).

By 1870 "over one-half of Idaho's miners and nearly one-third of the territory's population were Chinese" (Peterson 60).

Polyani (1969) has stated that "it is customary today to represent the process of scientific inquiry as the setting up of a hypothesis followed by its subsequent testing. I cannot accept these terms. All true scientific research starts with hitting on a deep and promising problem. . . ." (118)

An exception is the displayed direct quotation—one that is set off from the words that introduce and follow it and is indented. Because the setting-off serves to signal that the words are being quoted, a displayed quotation uses no quotation marks unless there are quotation marks in the original source:

Of course, constant vigilance by adults was impossible, and the romance of Mary Todd's friends Cassius Clay and Mary Jane

Warfield was an example. Unable to meet Mary Jane privately in her own house because her parents and brothers always took up stations in the parlor, Cassius was delighted when "graceful" Mary Jane

> said quietly she was going on a certain day hickory picking with a few girls—In the woods Mary Jane came to me when the others were farthest off, and picking up the nuts, empties her handkerchief on a pile. I said "Come and help me." She replied, with some tremor in her voice, "I have no seat." Putting my feet closer together as they were stretched out on the ground, I said, "You may sit down here, if you will be mine." She hesitated a moment and then down she came. . . . She just touched me with the skirts of her dress, and said "I am yours." Then she hurried off to mingle with her companions again.

But not for long, for these two married in 1832, with Elizabeth Todd Edwards as one of their attendants.

> —Jean H. Baker, *Mary Todd Lincoln: A Biography* (New York: Norton, 1987): 50.

MLA documentation style calls for setting off prose quotations more than four lines long, and poetry quotations of more than three lines. APA documentation style calls for setting off quotations of forty or more words.

Paraphrases should not be set off in quotation marks:

> In 1945 George Orwell observed that nothing had occurred during the previous fifteen years to give much reason for optimism (82).

Since these words are not Orwell's exact words, quotation marks would be misleading.

b. Enclosing Words Referred to as Words

You may use either quotation marks or italics (or underlining to indicate italics) to set off words referred to as words. Whichever format you use, use it consistently in a given piece of writing.

> "Bleed" means the printing of an image so that it extends completely across the page, leaving no margin.

> *Bleed* means the printing of an image so that it extends completely across the page, leaving no margin.

c. Enclosing Titles of Published Works

Place in quotation marks the titles of articles, essays, short stories, poems, songs, and subordinate parts of long words. (Titles of magazines, books, plays, and motion pictures should be underlined.)

> My favorite song from K. T. Oslin's <u>'80s Ladies</u> is "Do Ya."

> "Big Two-Hearted River" is the longest short story in <u>In Our Time</u>.

> A young girl's eavesdropping teaches her a lot about life in the short story "Fulfillment," which is the first story in the "Earth" section of Ferrol Sams's <u>The Widow's Mite and Other Stories</u>.

> The best writing of Oscar Wilde, outside his plays, is to be found in such essays as "The Truth of Masks," "The Critic as Artist," and "The Decay of Lying."

However, do *not* place the title of your own paper in quotation marks.

Using the Quotation Mark with Other Marks of Punctuation

❖ When a comma or a period and a closing quotation mark occur together, place the comma or period *inside* the quotation mark, even when it does not seem logical.

> Bennett did not regard his next novel, *A Great Man*, as having a serious theme. In a letter to J. B. Pinker, he called it "purely humorous," and he remarked, "Personally I don't see how anyone can read the book without laughing."

❖ Since ellipsis points indicate an omission in quoted text, place them *inside* the quotation marks.

> Jung (1959) used the term *archetype* for habitual patterns and thought they were built up by collective repetition: "There are as many archetypes as there are typical situations in life. Endless repetition has engraved these experiences into our psychic constitutions. . . ."

> Although Bennett complained that writing *Clayhanger* drove him "nearly . . . mad," he enjoyed the composition of *A Great Man* (Hepburn 185).

❖ When a question mark or an exclamation point is part of the quotation, place it *inside* the quotation mark.

Looking up from the flowchart, she asked, "Is that the way coal is processed?"

Judy Carne used to get big laughs by yelling "Sock it to me!"

❖ When a question mark or an exclamation point is part of the entire sentence, place it *outside* the quotation mark.

"Deadline" is such an awful term. Why not use "delivery date"?

Did you see that sign? It read "Falling Rock Zone"!

❖ Place a semicolon or colon *outside* the quotation marks.

The professor keeps referring to "atavism"; I'm not sure what it means.

Professor Willoughby provides this definition of "atavism": "It is the reappearance of characteristics of more or less remote ancestors." He also calls it "reversion" and "a throw-back characteristic."

P.13   SEMICOLON

P. 13

The semicolon has two main uses:

a. Separating Independent Clauses in a Compound Sentence

❖ Use a semicolon between independent clauses of a compound sentence when they are not connected by a coordinating conjunction *(and, but, or, nor, yet, for, so)*.

We might as well decide now; we will have to soon.

Of course, this sentence can be punctuated two other ways as well.

We might as well decide now. We will have to soon.

We might as well decide now, for we will have to soon.

The period creates a more pronounced break between the two statements by dividing them into two separate sentences. The comma and conjunction *for* create a much closer tie. The semicolon creates a connection somewhere between the period and the comma and conjunction.

❖ Use a semicolon between independent clauses when they are joined by conjunctive adverbs, such as *however, therefore, moreover, consequently, nevertheless.*

good: A company's image gets a definite boost when it advertises in what the average reader considers to be a prestigious national magazine; little does the reader know that the company has only purchased a limited geographical circulation of the magazine.

good A company's image gets a definite boost when it advertises in what the average reader considers to be a prestigious national magazine; however, little does the reader know that the company has only purchased a limited geographical circulation of the magazine.

poor A company's image gets a definite boost when it advertises in what the average reader considers to be a prestigious national magazine, however, little does the reader know that the company has only purchased a limited geographical circulation of the magazine.

The lack of a semicolon before *however* in the last example causes confusion because the readers cannot tell for sure which clause the *however* belongs to.

b. Separating Items in a Series When Items Already Contain Commas

An uncomplicated series of items needs nothing more than commas: *The steering committee consists of Debra Johnston, Yoshiaki Shinoda, and Ben Alexander.* But if the statement is *The steering committee consists of Debra Johnson, the senior engineer, Yoshiaki Shinoda, the contract accountant, and Ben Alexander, the security supervisor*, it needs semicolons to separate the items. Otherwise, the series could be understood to list up to five or six people, three of whom are named.

The steering committee consists of Debra Johnson, the senior engineer; Yoshiaki Shinoda, the contract accountant; and Ben Alexander, the security supervisor.

Another example:

Three kinds of engines are produced in the plant: military jet engines, in the government products division; nonmilitary jet engines, in the commercial products division; and nonmilitary gasoline engines, in the special products division.

Using the Semicolon
with Other Marks of Punctuation

Place the semicolon *outside* quotation marks and parentheses.

Those who contend that the extinction of dinosaurs occurred over a period of thousands of years are called "gradualists"; those who believe that a sudden event was responsible are called "catastrophists."

If the climate of North America warms, a great change will occur in the boreal forests in the upper Midwest (which consists primarily of fir, pine, and spruce); they will retreat slowly into Canada and gradually be replaced by northern hardwood forests (consisting primarily of beech, maple, and yellow birch).

P.14   SLASH

P. 14

The slash, sometimes called a slant sign, a diagonal, a solidus, or a virgule, is used to separate elements. With the exception of its use with poetry, there is no space between it and the text on either side of it.

Here are three main uses of the slash:

a. Separating the Numerator
from the Denominator in Mathematical
Equations and in Fractions

$PV/T = P_1V_1/T_1$

1/2, 3/5

b. Separating Elements in an Address

The address is Major Elizabeth Chai / APO 8425 / New York, NY 10009.

c. Separating Lines in Short Passages of Quoted Poetry

Use this format only to quote directly a short passage of poetry that is run into your own sentence. When quoting longer excerpts, separate the poetry completely from your own sentences and present the lines as the poet expressed them.

> Labor unrest in Ireland and England was a theme in some Victorian poetry. For example, Sybil Baker's "Belfast is a famous Northern town / Ships and linen its occupation / And the workers have a riot on / The slightest provocation" is only one of many references to labor strikes in Belfast, Londonderry, Birmingham, Manchester, Liverpool, and London.

M. Mechanics

M.1 ABBREVIATIONS

Abbreviations are shortened forms of words or a group of words. They are used primarily to save space (*mpg* as opposed to *miles per gallon*), although some abbreviations are also used because they are more familiar and pronounceable than the spelled-out words (*DNA* instead of *deoxyribonucleic acid; TNT* instead of *trinitrotoluene*).

Abbreviations are usually formed two ways: using the first letter or first few letters of a word (*m=meter, IBM=International Business Machines, Wed.=Wednesday*) or dropping the middle of the word and using only the first and last letters (*Dr.=Doctor, Mr.=Mister, St.=Saint*).

Some abbreviations are followed by a period; others are not. It is a more conservative style to use a period after an abbreviation, although sometimes a period clarifies that an abbreviation is not another word, as in *in.* for *inch* or *inches*. Consult a college-level dictionary or style guide to determine whether a period is appropriate.

Here are guidelines to help you use abbreviations effectively:

▶ Do not begin a sentence with an abbreviation.

▶ Use abbreviations sparingly in your text, although they may be used with discretion in lists, tables, and charts where space may be limited. Abbreviations should be used primarily to enhance the readability of the text for both writer and reader.

▶ Use standard abbreviations that are sanctioned by professional organizations or college-level dictionaries. Usually a list of standard abbreviations is included in style manuals.

▶ Do not capitalize abbreviations unless the word abbreviated is a proper noun:

Btu	British thermal unit
F	Fahrenheit
CST	Central Standard Time

▶ If you are uncertain that your reader will understand the abbreviation, spell out the full expression the first time you use it, and follow with the abbreviation in parentheses or vice versa. The abbreviation may be used alone in subsequent references:

> During the 1960s huge corporations bought smaller companies, leading to the need to develop large centralized computer systems known as Management Information Systems (MIS) networks. However, few of these conglomerates made significant gains in centralization using MIS.

> The standard reference source for finding out the history of meanings for a word is the OED (*Oxford English Dictionary*). In addition to the typical information about a word's pronunciation, etymology, and current meanings, the *OED* provides a history of the changing meaning of the word throughout the period in which it has been used, with examples of these uses.

▶ Be consistent. Once you abbreviate, use the same abbreviation throughout the text.

▶ Use the same abbreviation for both singular and plural: *in.* for *inch* or *inches, ft.* for *foot* or *feet.* However, an exception is *lb.* for *pound* and *lbs.* for *pounds.*

▶ Use customary abbreviations:

  ❖ Titles before names

    Dr. Peggy Porter

    Mr. Pierre Donique

    Sgt. Sharon Little

  ❖ Designations after names

    Hadley K. Franklin, Jr.

    Sen. Robert Dole (R-Kansas)

    Sir William Sloyd, M.P.

  ❖ Academic degrees

A.A.	Ph.D.
A.B.	Ed.D
M.S.	LL.D.
M.D.	

❖ Common units of measure

mph	cm
rpm	sq. ft.
C	

❖ Long names of organizations and countries

NAACP	National Association for the Advancement of Colored People (either NAACP or N.A.A.C.P. is acceptable.)
NCAA	National Collegiate Athletic Association
USDA	United States Department of Agriculture
USA	United States of America

❖ Abbreviations in bibliographic notations

ch.	chapter
sec.	section
n.d.	not dated

❖ Common Latin terms used instead of their English equivalents:

etc.	(and so forth)
e.g.	(for example)
i.e.	(that is)

❖ U.S. Postal Service two-letter abbreviations for states and outlying regions:

Alabama	AL	Georgia	GA
Alaska	AK	Guam	GU
Arizona	AZ	Hawaii	HI
Arkansas	AR	Idaho	ID
California	CA	Illinois	IL
Colorado	CO	Indiana	IN
Connecticut	CT	Iowa	IA
Delaware	DE	Kansas	KS
District of Columbia	DC	Kentucky	KY
Florida	FL	Louisiana	LA

Maine	ME	Oklahoma	OK
Maryland	MD	Oregon	OR
Massachusetts	MA	Pennsylvania	PA
Michigan	MI	Puerto Rico	PR
Minnesota	MN	Rhode Island	RI
Mississippi	MS	South Carolina	SC
Missouri	MO	South Dakota	SD
Montana	MT	Tennessee	TN
Nebraska	NE	Texas	TX
Nevada	NV	Utah	UT
New Hampshire	NH	Vermont	VT
New Jersey	NJ	Virgin Islands	VI
New Mexico	NM	Virginia	VA
New York	NY	Washington	WA
North Carolina	NC	West Virginia	WV
North Dakota	ND	Wisconsin	WI
Ohio	OH	Wyoming	WY

M.2

M.2   CAPITAL LETTERS

All letters were once written only as capitals. By the fourteenth century, both capital letters (uppercase letters) and lowercase letters were being used. Printers used a capital letter only for the first letters of a word that they felt was particularly important. That practice is still in use today. In general, the following rules govern the use of capitals:

▶ Capitalize the first word of a sentence and of a formally introduced quotation.

A long rainy season in the fall makes deciduous trees look drab.

What does this mean?

My mother looked at the stranger and asked, "Are you looking for work?"

▶ Capitalize proper nouns.

Julian Bond, a civil rights activist and politician, was born January 14, 1940, in Nashville, Tennessee.

Julian Bond, January, and *Nashville, Tennessee* are proper nouns because they are particular names of an individual person and a specific month, city, and state. The words *civil rights activist* and *politician* are common nouns because they are words that refer to general classes consisting of hundreds, perhaps thousands, of people.

Proper nouns and their derivatives include the following:

❖ Names of people

John Calvin, Calvinism

William Shakespeare, Shakespearean sonnet

Charles Darwin, Darwinism

Woodrow Wilson, Wilsonian diplomacy

❖ Days of the week, months of the year, holidays, holy days, and days and weeks of special significance

Monday	Mother's Day
April	Yom Kippur
Ramadan	National Secretary's Week
Thanksgiving Day	National Dairy Month

However, do not capitalize the names of the seasons: *winter, spring, summer,* and *fall* or *autumn.*

❖ Geographic names and names of buildings and structures

Columbia River	St. Louis County
Rocky Mountains	Greece
Cape Fear	the Taj Mahal
the Everglades	the Eiffel Tower
the Orient	the Golden Gate Bridge
Pacific Ocean	the John Hancock Building
North Pole	

Do not capitalize points of the compass—north, south, east, west—unless they designate a specific geographic region:

The railroads played a crucial role in opening the American West.

Weatherford is a little over an hour's drive west of Oklahoma City.

❖ Historical events, eras, and documents

the War of the Roses	the Holocaust
the Renaissance	the Johnstown Flood
the Chia-Ching Period	the Declaration of Independence
the Great Depression	the Versailles Treaty

❖ Political parties and religious sects

Republican	Judaism
Whig	Muslim
Baptist	Hindu
Catholic	Quaker

❖ Organizations, institutions, and complexes

Better Business Bureau	Rockbridge High School
Pemex Corporation	St. Clair Medical Center
First Christian Church	the Mid-South Coliseum
University of Pennsylvania	Rupp Arena

❖ Government bodies and organizations

Fifty-third Congress

President's Council of Economic Advisors

U.S. Government Printing Office

Department of Justice

the Supreme Court

California National Guard

Maricopa County Sheriff's Office

House of Lords

the Diet

❖ Titles, degrees, decorations, and honors

Vice President Gore

Governor Cuomo

General Patton

Betty Boothroyd, Speaker of the British Commons

Ambassador Lumb

Elroy Crenshaw, recipient of the Congressional Medal of Honor and the Order of the Purple Heart

Nobel Peace Prize

Pulitzer Prize

❖ Trade names

Fieldcrest	Polaroid
Kleenex	Pyrex
Sanka	

❖ Languages and ethnic groups

Chicano	Indian
Russian	Korean-American
Yiddish	Anglo-American

❖ Special events

the Final Four	the Kentucky Derby
the World Series	the Olympic Games
the Rose Bowl Parade	the Super Bowl
the World Cup	

▶ Capitalize letters describing **the shape of objects.**

A-frame	O-ring
C clamp	T square

▶ Capitalize the first word in a line of **conventional poetry.**

On either side the river lie

Long fields of barley and of rye,

That clothe the wold and meet the sky;

And thro' the field the road runs by

To many towered Camelot;

—Alfred, Lord Tennyson, "The Lady of Shallot"

M.3

M.3 ITALICS

Roman type is the standard typeface used today, probably because it is the most readable. These words, like most of the words in this book, are set in Roman type. Italics is another of the principal classifications of typeface, but it is used very sparingly for emphasis. It slants to the right and looks like this: *Atlantic Monthly*. When you type or hand-write, you indicate *italics* by underlining, like this:

Atlantic Monthly

Italics are used in five principal ways:

a. Indicating Titles

James Gleick's *Chaos: Making a New Science* was published in 1987.

The *Wall Street Journal* is the nation's leading financial newspaper.

The 1855 edition of Walt Whitman's *Leaves of Grass* sold only a few hundred copies.

The editors of *Time* magazine received considerable criticism for using the negative impression of Bill Clinton on the cover.

b. Indicating Foreign Words and Phrases

Cognito, ergo sum is attributed to René Descartes, but several philosophers had used the phrase before Descartes was born.

The Spanish name for Texas is *Tejas*.

1819 was an *annus mirablis*, being the birth year of James Russell Lowell, Herman Melville, and Walt Whitman.

Do not italicize foreign words and expressions that have become so common in English they are considered part of the language: milieu, samurai, alma mater, bombardier, and so on.

c. Indicating Names of Ships, Aircraft, and Spacecraft

The sinking of the Cunard liner *Lusitania* on May 7, 1915, off the coast of Ireland contributed to the U.S. entry into World War I.

The atomic bomb was dropped from a B-29 named *Enola Gay*, named after the pilot's mother.

The *Voyager* satellite gave us our first good look at the Great Red Spot on Jupiter.

d. Designating Words, Letters, and Numbers as Words

The overuse of *very* and *great* lessen their impact as intensifiers.

Writers who misspell *similar* usually add a third *i*, ending the word with *-iar (similiar)*, apparently modeling the spelling on the word *familiar*.

Bookkeeping is one of the few words in English that has three double letters in a row: *oo-kk-ee*.

My basketball jersey was *14*, which was also more points than I ever scored in a game.

Europeans use *7̶* to distinguish *7* clearly from *1*.

e. Placing Extra Emphasis on a Word or Phrase

Studies show that almost 50 percent of *fatal* automobile accidents involve a driver who was driving under the influence of alcohol or drugs or both.

George Orwell claims that it is the *privateness* of the British that cause their addiction to hobbies.

Applicants are required to have their packets postmarked *no later than April 15*.

M.4 NUMBERS

M.4

Numbers can be expressed as words (*seventeen*) or figures (*17*). The following general and specific guidelines will help you decide which form to use.

General Guidelines

❖ Use Arabic numerals (5) instead of Roman numerals (*V*), except when you want to use Roman numerals in section or chapter headings and in numbering tables.

❖ Do not state numbers twice, once in words and again as figures. The restatement adds nothing to accuracy or clarity.

not: The ledger contained entries on thirty (30) transactions.

but: The ledger contained entries on 30 transactions.

Specific Guidelines

Many style and usage books suggest spelling out numbers under ten and using figures for everything else except numbers that are more than two or three words long.

not: Sixteen hundred and fifty-two

but: 1652 or 1,652

However, there are so many exceptions to this rule that it is not always reliable. Here are some guidelines you can depend on when deciding whether to express a number as a word or a figure.

Numbers in Figure Form

Writing a number as a figure is almost always done in the following instances.

❖ Addresses:

1603 Vandiver Drive, Apartment 812, St. Paul, MN 55111

❖ Dates:

July 25, 1992 or 25 July 1992   [But not *July 25th, 1992*]

❖ Decimals:

5.2 liter engine

0.025 grams

16.5 kilometers

❖ Exact sums of money with $ or ¢:

$4.88

47¢

❖ Identifying numbers:

Station No. 7

Engine Number HD-27598-32-G

Account #394

❖ Percentages:

30 percent

4.5%

❖ References to pages, figures, etc.:

page 6

Figure 2-10

Note 25

❖ Time:

4:55 A.M.   [But also *12 noon*; otherwise, *eight o'clock*]

❖ Units of measure:

180 miles

66 kilometers

500 cc

200 lbs.

Numbers in Word Form

The general trend is to use figures more often than words. Most style and usage manuals state that numbers smaller than ten should be spelled out and those above ten should be represented as figures: *six whales, 30 whales; nine entries, 100 entries*. However, there are at least four important exceptions to this rule:

❖ When a series of numbers includes a number greater than 10, each number is expressed as a figure:

The class enrolled 3 sophomores, 14 juniors, 1 senior, and 1 graduate student.

❖ Large numbers that are rounded off are usually formed by a figure and a word:

The estate is expected to exceed $65 million.

The estate is expected to exceed 65 million dollars.   [But usually not *The estate is expected to exceed sixty-five million dollars* or *The estate is expected to exceed 65,000,000 dollars*, or *The estate is expected to exceed $65,000,000.*]

❖ Normally spell out numbers at the beginning of a sentence (or rewrite so number appears later in the sentence).

    not: 10,000 bags of peanuts were shipped by mistake.

    but: Ten thousand bags of peanuts were shipped by mistake.

    or: They shipped 10,000 bags of peanuts by mistake.

❖ Small fractions are usually spelled out:

A third of the workers were transferred.

Two-thirds of the workers remained at the old facility.

❖ When there are adjoining numbers, spell out one of them:

ten 5-minute laps

10 five-minute laps

8 twelve-volt batteries

eight 12-volt batteries

M.5   SYMBOLS

A symbol is a letter (or letters) or other mark that stands for a word or words. When you read *Fe*, the chemical symbol for iron, or *Ω*, the Greek letter symbol for *ohm* or *omega* (ending), for example, the symbol is pronounced as if it were a spelled-out word. A chemical formula, such as $2Na + Cl^2 \rightarrow 2NaCl$ (which is the formula for common table salt), is read like this: "When two atoms of sodium are reacted with one molecule of chlorine, two molecules of sodium chloride are formed."

Symbols are used widely in tables and technical material to save space. They are used less often in regular text. Symbols are one of the most abstract forms of language, and most readers are familiar with only a few standard symbols. Be sure that your reader will understand the meaning of a symbol you use, or explain it in parentheses or an explanatory note the first time it appears (as you would explain an unfamiliar abbreviation).

The first letter of a chemical symbol is always capitalized (*H, hydrogen; O, oxygen;* H_2O, *water*). When the symbol for a chemical consists of two letters, the second letter is always lowercase: *Au, gold.*

CREDITS

INDEX

697

S